BARBARIANS AT THE GATE

The Fall of RJR Nabisco

© Elena Seibert

"A superlative book, a reconstruction of awesome proportions. . . . The writing is unflawed . . . steadily builds until the very end."
—Scot J. Paltrow, *Los Angeles Times Book Review*

"*Barbarians* is a phenomenal read, an extraordinary feat of reportage, and one that has a greater grasp of novelistic pacing than do most works of fiction . . . [it] may well be the epitome of the Wall Street business book."

—Michael Hirschorn, *7 Days*

"Impressive qualities . . . delicious scenes . . . a cinematic yet extraordinarily careful book."

—Ken Auletta, *New York Daily News*

"Richly detailed."

—Melissa Turner, *The Atlanta Journal and Constitution*

"It's hard to imagine a better story to capture the essence of the 1980's business scene . . . and it's hard to imagine a better account than the one by Burrough and Helyar."

—Bill Barnhart, *Chicago Tribune*

"The stage is always set, there is dialogue and drama aplenty, and the characters are larger than life . . . brilliantly effective."

—Bill Saporito, *Fortune*

"The fascinating inside story of the largest corporate takeover in American history. . . . It reads like a novel."

—Tom Brokaw, "Today"

"Compelling, novel-like and entertaining account of an important business story."

—Keith Naughton, *The Detroit News*

"A reportorial tour de force that provides a stunningly detailed recap of the events leading up to the megabuck takeover of RJR Nabisco . . . a comprehensive and coherent account of a multilateral struggle that in many respects apotheosized a decade of wretched excess in the so-called financial community."

—*Kirkus*

"A masterful account of the battle and a window on the sometimes startling ways of Wall Street . . . a page-turner."

—Judith H. Dobrzynski, *Business Week*

BARBARIANS
AT THE GATE

The Fall of RJR Nabisco

Bryan Burrough AND John Helyar

COLLINS BUSINESS ESSENTIALS

Photos in inserts that follow pages 208 and 400 are from the authors' collection unless noted as follows: 1-6. RJR Nabisco; 7–10. Ross Johnson; 11–18. RJR Nabisco; 20–26. RJR Nabisco; 29. Jodi Buren; 32. *Women's Wear Daily*; 37. Reprinted from November 14, 1988, issue of *Business Week* by special permission © 1988 by McGraw-Hill Inc.; 38. Jacques Lowe; 39. Michael Fairchild; 41. Katherine Androiotis; 43. Shelly Katz/Black Star; 47. John Chiarson/Gamma-Liaison; 48. Bob Wagner/Onyx; 49. Stuart Smith; 51. Drawing by M. Stevens. From *The New Yorker.* © 1988 Reprinted by special permission. All rights reserved. 55, 56. RJR Nabisco; 57. *Women's Wear Daily*; 58. *Time* cover © 1988 Time, Inc. Reprinted by permission; 60-65. Michael Fairchild.

First Collins Business Essentials edition published 2005.

Designed by Barbara DuPree Knowles

Photo inserts researched, edited, and designed by Vincent Virga.

The Library of Congress has catalogued the hardcover edition as follows:
Burrough, Bryan, 1961–
    Barbarians at the gate: the fall of RJR Nabisco/by Bryan
Burrough and John Helyar.
      p. cm.
     ISBN 0-06-016172-8
     1. RJR Nabisco (Firm) 2. Leveraged buyouts—United States—Case
studies. 3. Consolidation and merger of corporations—United
States—Case studies. 4. Conglomerate corporations—United States—
Case studies. I. Helyar, John, 1951– . II. Title.
HD2796.R57B87 1990
338.8'3664'00913—dc20   89-45635
ISBN-10: 0-06-053635-7 (pbk.)
ISBN-13: 978-0-06-053635-0 (pbk.)

06 07 08 09 OS/RRD H 13 12 11 10

The officer of every corporation should feel in his heart—in his very soul—that he is responsible, not merely to make dividends for the stockholders of his company, but to enhance the general prosperity and the moral sentiment of the United States.
—ADOLPHUS GREEN, *founder, Nabisco*

Some genius invented the Oreo. We're just living off the inheritance.
—F. ROSS JOHNSON, *president, RJR Nabisco*

This business, on a legitimate basis, is a fraud.

Not that it's a fraud. You need money to be in this business. But not a lot. You need more money to open a shoe-shine shop than you do to buy a $2 billion company, let's be honest about it. But to buy a shoe-shine store, if it costs $3,000, you need $3,000. If you don't got it in cash, you need to bring it by Thursday.

But if it's an LBO, not only do you not have to bring it, you don't have to see it, you don't know where you're going to get it, nobody knows where they got it from. The whole situation comes from absolutely nothing.

But the more you need, of course, the less money you need. In other words, if there's money involved, you don't get involved in this business. This is a business for people who don't have money, but who know somebody who has money, but who doesn't put it up either . . .
—JACKIE MASON, *"What the Hell is an LBO?"*

AUTHORS' NOTE

When we wrote *Barbarians at the Gate* in 1989, it was a book about current events; now it's history. Some books age better than others. We'd like to think *Barbarians* has aged well. The book is still used in major business schools to teach any number of topics, from ethics to investment banking. In 1993 it was made into a movie on HBO. In 2002, fourteen years after its heyday, the RJR fight was dramatized once again in a documentary film on the History Channel.

This kind of reception was the furthest thing from our minds when we set out to write a book in 1989. Our primary goal, in fact, was simply to see whether we could actually *write a book*; neither of us had ever tried it before. Nor was *Barbarians* exactly a prize publishing executives were fighting to handle. Of the half dozen publishers we approached, in fact, precisely one, Harper & Row (now HarperCollins), had the slightest bit of interest. The newspapers had been saturated with the RJR story for weeks. Who wanted to read more?

As reporters for the *Wall Street Journal*, we strived to imbue *Barbarians* with the standards of excellence and accuracy we learned at the paper. Indeed, *Barbarians* would not have been possible without the encouragement—and the eight months of unpaid leave—that its editors, Norman Pearlstine and Paul Steiger, gave us.

That October, when the RJR story broke, Bryan was the *Journal's* reporter on the Wall Street mergers and acquisitions beat; based in

Atlanta, John covered the company itself. Together we covered the twists and turns of the RJR fight for six long weeks. It was only when the struggle was over, and we agreed to write a book, that we actually met each other. John held up the infamous *Time* magazine cover of Ross Johnson so that Bryan could identify him at the Atlanta airport.

We're often embarrassed to admit the research and writing of *Barbarians* occurred in eight short months, from January to August 1989. It was a manic period. From an un-air-conditioned apartment in the Park Slope section of Brooklyn, Bryan rode the subway into Manhattan to hold as many as six interviews a day; we believed strongly that all interviews should be done in person. At night he would return to collate and "write up" his interview notes, sometimes donning swim trunks and a T-shirt in the summer heat. John had more traveling to do, shuttling between Atlanta, North Carolina, and New York to assemble the story of Ross Johnson's ascent. We worked separately except for the crucial interviews with Johnson himself, informal marathon sessions held in Atlanta and Manhattan over pizza and soft drinks.

As we worked on the book, we worried that RJR would be eclipsed by some even bigger and wilder deal. Between corporate raiders, LBO artists, and junk-bond financiers, the whole 1980s business world had gone mad. The barbarians' next assault could reduce RJR from epic to footnote. (That's why Harper wanted the book so fast.) We braced for that black day, which never came.

The battle for RJR, it turned out, both defined and ended an era. KKR's winning bid of $25 billion stood for nearly a decade as the biggest business deal of all time. Several factors combined to tamp down the size of deals for several years. The great money machine behind LBOs—junk bonds—sputtered and for a time virtually stopped. Mike Milken went to jail; Drexel Burnham went bankrupt, and, in the early-'90s recession, battered overleveraged companies gave leverage a bad name. Henry Kravis ceased stalking big game, preoccupied with the care and feeding—and debt service—of RJR. Other stars of 1980s Wall Street—and combatants for RJR—also overdosed on hubris and faded. John Gutfreund was ousted as chairman of Solomon Brothers in 1991, after a treasuries trading scandal. His president, Tom Strauss, also resigned and joined Peter Cohen in obscurity at a hedge fund. Others became boutique bit players, too, including Tom Hill, at Blackstone

Group, and Steve Waters at a European private equity fund called Compass Partners.

About the only *Barbarians* figure whose star rose was Steve Goldstone. The onetime attorney to Ross Johnson eventually became CEO of RJR Nabisco. But even Goldstone's job amounted to presiding mainly over the demise of the once-mighty company. In 1999, he sold Nabisco to Phillip Morris, divested RJR's international tobacco business, and brought the company right back where it started from: a U.S. tobacco company based in Winston-Salem, North Carolina. Kohlberg Kravis exited RJR soon thereafter, with humble returns.

But even as Wall Street's gunslingers of the 1980s drifted off into the sunset, they ushered in the dawn of the even wilder decade of the '90s. The CEOs of America, at first shocked and horrified by the barbarians at their gates, ultimately emulated them. They'd learned from RJR what fabulous riches were there for the taking. They began to press for *their* piece of the action.

"CEOs learned two things from LBOs," says Dick Beattie, who remained in the midst of major deals through the '90s. "First, the way to build significant wealth was through equity ownership, not salary and bonuses, and second, you didn't need to do any LBO to build equity. You could give yourself stock options."

With that currency, the CEOs of the '90s reaped sums to make even Ross Johnson blush—and make greed as commonplace on Main Street as Wall Street. That grasping spirit extended even to once-staid accounting firms, which became more like croupiers than auditors. "It was the investment bankers," growls Paul Volcker, the former Fed chairman who made a failed effort to rescue scandal-plagued Arthur Andersen. By the time he arrived in early 2002, the big swinging dicks of Wall Street had thoroughly infected the green-eyeshade crowd. Recounts Volcker: "The accountants felt like, 'We're as good as they are and we're doing all the work.' The general atmosphere was, 'Money is out there for the taking.'"

Call it "the triumph of the barbarians," and chalk it up as one good reason this book remains relevant. The infamous CEOs of today like Dennis Kozlowski and Bernie Ebbers are really Ross Johnson's modern equivalents. They evolved what he pioneered: the CEO as self-interested no-company man; the CEO as daring swashbuckler and bold expropriator of corporate assets. They merely operated on a far grander scale, for, in the bull market and tech bubble of the '90s, the stakes and bucks were so much greater. Even nobodies like Henry Samueli and Henry Nicholas, cochairmen of a company called Broadcom, reaped $800 million apiece, cashing out stock in their company while telecom was still hot. Compared to that, Ross Johnson's once-outrageous $53 million golden parachute is parsimonious.

But even if the events in *Barbarians* have now been surpassed in terms of dollars, it remains unmatched for dramatics. And not because of the skills of the authors, Lord knows. It's because for those six weeks in 1988, when a new set of business barons vied to own a huge company and to be top dog on Wall Street, the planets were so perfectly aligned. The zeitgeist of an age was on full display in the war for RJR: raw emotions and colliding egos; improbable plot twists and even more improbable characters. Other authors have done masterful jobs with business sagas—David McClintick's *Indecent Exposure* is the template for us all—but none have been so blessed with raw materials. We had investment bankers wolfing down Milk Bones and sprinting through Midtown Manhattan, bearing last-minute bids. We had a CEO whose dog rated a corporate jet and whose life motto was: "A few million dollars are lost in the sands of time." We are forever grateful to them all. You couldn't make this stuff up.

INTRODUCTION

This book arose from the authors' coverage in *The Wall Street Journal* of the fight to control RJR Nabisco in October and November 1988. Our goal in pursuing the story behind those public events has been to meet the standard of accuracy and general excellence that the *Journal* sets for journalists everywhere.

Ninety-five percent of the material in these pages was taken from more than 100 interviews conducted between January and October 1989 in New York, Atlanta, Washington, Winston-Salem, Connecticut, and Florida. In large part due to contacts we made while working at the *Journal*, we were able to interview at length every major figure involved in the story as well as scores of minor ones. No more than a handful of people mentioned in this book declined to grant interviews.

Among the first we spoke with were the long-shot suitors, Jim Maher of First Boston and Ted Forstmann of Forstmann Little & Co., who made himself available in his New York office as well as on his private jet. At Kohlberg Kravis, Henry Kravis, George Roberts, and Paul Raether were interviewed together and separately for more than twenty hours; much of the interviewing was done in RJR Nabisco's former New York offices, where Kohlberg Kravis briefly relocated after a fire. Kravis himself sat for a half-dozen tape-recorded sessions, all but one in Johnson's former anteroom.

The last to consent to be interviewed was Ross Johnson. He was understandably gun-shy; he had taken a beating in the press and wasn't eager for further pummeling. Eventually he spent thirty-six hours in one-to-one talks with the authors. Several all-day sessions were held in his Atlanta office, where Johnson smoked cigarillos and wore sports jackets with no tie; a marathon evening session was held in his New York apartment, where Johnson donned a pair of gray RJR Nabisco sweatpants and shared pepperoni pizza and beer with the authors.

Due to the cooperation of the participants, we have managed to reconstruct dialogue extensively. By necessity this involves calling on sometimes selective memories. It is important to remember that, as Ken Auletta wrote in his definitive *Greed and Glory on Wall Street*, "no reporter can with 100 percent accuracy re-create events that occurred some time before. Memories play tricks on participants, the more so when the outcome has become clear. A reporter tries to guard against inaccuracies by checking with a variety of sources, but it is useful for a reader—and an author—to be humbled by this journalistic limitation."

We couldn't agree more. However, it should be noted that, in reconstructing critical meetings, we often were able to interview every person in the room at the time. In many cases, that amounted to as many as eight or nine people. Where their memories have differed significantly, it is noted in the text or a footnote. Where a thought or impression is conveyed in italics, it was supplied by the person in question.

A word about significance: Those looking in these pages for a definitive judgment on the impact of leveraged buyouts on the American economy will no doubt be disappointed. It is the authors' contention that some companies are well suited for the rigors of an LBO, while others are not. As for RJR Nabisco, it is important to remember that an LBO is a creature of time. In most cases its success or failure can't be determined for three, four, five, even seven years. The events in this book constitute the birth of an LBO; at this writing, the reborn RJR Nabisco is barely a year old. The baby looks healthy, but it's too soon to predict its ultimate fate.

We would like to thank Norman Pearlstine, *The Wall Street Journal*'s managing editor, who gave his blessings for a leave to do this book. We are immensely grateful to our editor, Richard Kot of Harper & Row, for his keen eye and unflagging encouragement in helping us negotiate our first journey into publishing; his assistant, Scott Terranella; Lorraine Shanley, who brought our project to Harper & Row's attention; our agent,

Andrew Wylie, who isn't nearly as nasty as people think; his colleague, Deborah Karl, for plenty of on-call hand-holding; and Steve Swartz of *The Wall Street Journal*, who provided invaluable advice on shaping the narrative. RJR Nabisco and numerous players in the RJR drama were helpful in supplying photos. Thanks are also due John Huey who, as *The Wall Street Journal*'s Atlanta bureau chief in 1988, gave John Helyar rein to delve into RJR. As editor of *Southpoint* magazine in 1989, he allowed him to finish this book before reporting for duty.

The unsung heroes of a project like this are our wives. Betsy Morris served double duty. As a *Wall Street Journal* colleague, she was among the first to "discover" Ross Johnson and chronicle the emerging RJR Nabisco story. As John Helyar's wife, she put up with long weeks' absences and long days' writing. Likewise, Marla Burrough was the manuscript's first reader, copy editor, and a source of unlimited support and patience. Their advice and guidance are marked on every page of this book.

Bryan Burrough
John Helyar
October 1989

THE PLAYERS

THE MANAGEMENT GROUP

At RJR Nabisco

F. Ross Johnson, president and chief executive
Edward A. Horrigan, Jr., chairman, RJR Tobacco
Edward J. Robinson, chief financial officer
Harold Henderson, general counsel
James Welch, chairman, Nabisco Brands
John Martin, executive vice president
Andrew G. C. Sage II, consultant and board member
Frank A. Benevento II, consultant
Steven Goldstone, of counsel
George R. ("Gar") Bason, Jr., of counsel

Clifton S. Robbins, associate
Scott Stuart, associate
Richard I. Beattie, of counsel
Charles ("Casey") Cogut, of counsel

At Drexel Burnham Lambert

Jeffrey Beck, "The Mad Dog"

At Morgan Stanley & Co.

Eric Gleacher, merger chief
Steven Waters

At Wasserstein Perella & Co.

Bruce Wasserstein

THE THIRD PARTIES

At Forstmann Little & Co.

Theodore J. Forstmann, senior partner
Brian D. Little, general partner
Nick Forstmann, general partner
Stephen Fraidin, of counsel

At Goldman Sachs & Co., Forstmann's investment banker

Geoff Boisi, investment banking chief

The First Boston Group

James Maher, merger chief
Kim Fennebresque, investment banker
Brian Finn, investment banker
Jerry Seslowe, Resource Holdings
Jay Pritzker, investor
Thomas Pritzker, investor
Harold Handelsman, of counsel
Melvyn N. Klein, investor

THE SPECIAL COMMITTEE

The Directors

Charles E. Hugel, chairman of Combustion Engineering
Martin S. Davis, CEO of Gulf + Western
Albert L. Butler, Jr., Winston-Salem businessman
William S. Anderson, former chairman, NCR Corp.
John Macomber, former chairman, Celanese

The Advisers

Peter A. Atkins, Skadden, Arps, Slate, Meagher & Flom
Michael Mitchell, Skadden, Arps, Slate, Meagher & Flom
Matthew Rosen, Skadden, Arps, Slate, Meagher & Flom
John Mullin, Dillon Read & Co.
Franklin W. ("Fritz") Hobbs IV, Dillon Read & Co.
Felix Rohatyn, Lazard Freres & Co.
J. Ira Harris, Lazard Freres & Co.
Robert Lovejoy, Lazard Freres & Co.
Luis Rinaldini, Lazard Freres & Co.
Joshua Gotbaum, Lazard Freres & Co.

Others

Smith Bagley, RJ Reynolds heir
J. Paul Sticht, former RJ Reynolds chairman
J. Tylee Wilson, former RJ Reynolds chairman
H. John Greeniaus, president, Nabisco Brands

PROLOGUE

For hours the two men sat on the back porch talking.

It was as peaceful an afternoon as the younger man, a lawyer just down from New York, had ever seen. On the horizon, the sun was a sinking red ball. Below, delicate snowy egrets poked through the reeds of the Intracoastal Waterway.

It seemed a shame, Steve Goldstone thought, as a warm Florida breeze tousled his thinning brown hair, to introduce black clouds into such a postcard landscape. He took no pleasure in the dire predictions he was about to spin. But it was his job to play devil's advocate. No one else seemed willing to do it.

Someone has to tell him.

They sat for a few moments in silence. Goldstone took another sip from his gin and tonic and glanced at the older man sitting in the patio chair beside him. Sometimes he wished he knew Ross Johnson better. They had met barely three months before. Johnson seemed so open, so trusting, so—how to describe it?—yes, naive. Did he realize the forces he was on the verge of unleashing?

Johnson was clad casually in slacks and a light blue golf shirt adorned with RJR Nabisco's corporate logo. His silvery hair was worn unstylishly long. A gold bracelet dangled from his left wrist. Goldstone knew Johnson was pondering a move that would change his life—maybe all their lives—forever.

Why are you doing this? Goldstone had asked. You're chief executive officer of one of America's great companies, you don't need any more money. Yet you're about to start a transaction in which you could lose it all. Don't you realize all the pain and suffering you'll cause?

So far his arguments hadn't swayed his client. Goldstone knew he had to press harder. "You could lose everything," he repeated. The planes. The Manhattan apartment. The Palm Beach compound. The villa in Castle Pines. The lawyer paused to let it sink in.

Don't you understand? You could lose everything.

That doesn't change the merits of the transaction, Johnson answered simply. It doesn't change the basic situation. "I really have no choice," he said.

Goldstone bore in once more. The minute you do this, he argued, you'll lose control of your company. Once you start this process, you are no longer CEO. You turn over the reins to the board of directors. I know you think these directors are your friends, he said.

Johnson nodded at that. After all, hadn't he chauffeured them around the world in his corporate jets? Hadn't he given them lush consulting contracts?

As soon as you start this, Goldstone went on, they're not your friends anymore. They can't be. Don't expect favors from them; they won't come. They'll be under the control of Wall Street advisers, people you don't even know. They'll be sued by thirty different people for millions of dollars. The pressure will be intense, the lawyer insisted, and they will resent you for it.

Goldstone stopped then, and looked out at the vivid streaks of blue and red searing the western sky. No matter how dark he painted the picture, Johnson seemed unmoved. He wasn't sure how much of this was penetrating. In five nights, he knew, they would all find out.

Later, as the two men boarded the Gulfstream jet north to Atlanta, Goldstone sensed Johnson had made up his mind. He looked hard at the president of RJR Nabisco, America's nineteenth largest industrial company, a man who held in his hands the fates of 140,000 employees, a man whose products—Oreos, Ritz crackers, Life Savers, Winston and Salem cigarettes—filled every pantry in the country.

He's so willing to look on the bright side, Goldstone worried, so trusting. God, he believes everyone is his best friend.

And he's going to do it, the lawyer thought. *He's really going to do it.*

The Atlanta air was cool and clear that October evening as the black Lincoln Town Cars began pulling up outside the Waverly Hotel. The Waverly anchored a green, suburban office park of the type common in Sun Belt cities: nearby was a multiscreen movie theater; an upscale shopping mall, The Galleria, with its array of fountains, and wide, inviting walkways; and a cluster of tall, gleaming office buildings.

Stepping from the limousines were the directors of RJR Nabisco, whose headquarters took up eleven floors in a glass tower several hundred yards away. Each had been spirited to Atlanta in a familiar RJR Nabisco jet. Through the hotel's atrium lobby, up a glass elevator and into an upstairs meeting room they went; inside, they stood in circles, drinks in hand, waiting anxiously for the evening's meeting to begin. The small talk was of their trips down, the World Series, and the presidential election, less than a month away.

It was the night before the company's regular October board meeting, normally an occasion for the directors to dine informally with their chief executive, Ross Johnson, and get an update on corporate affairs delivered in Johnson's unique, freewheeling style. But tonight the atmosphere was markedly different. Johnson had called every director and urged him or her to attend the dinner, which wasn't usually mandatory. Only a few knew what loomed before them; the others could only guess.

Some directors were introduced to Steve Goldstone and walked off with puzzled looks. What was an outsider doing here? wondered Albert Butler, a balding North Carolina patrician. Juanita Kreps, the former secretary of commerce, pulled aside Charles Hugel, the chairman of Combustion Engineering, who served as RJR Nabisco's titular chairman. "What's Ross doing?" she asked. "What's going to happen?" Hugel knew, but wouldn't say. Instead he ducked out to tell the catering people to hurry along with dinner. They had a crowded agenda tonight.

Through the milling directors Johnson circulated, vodka-and-soda in hand, a broad smile and deep-throated laugh never far from his lips. A man who had survived his share of boardroom coups, Johnson prided himself on his ability to sway corporate directors. He was a master of disarming tense situations with the strategic joke, the well-thrown wisecrack, a veritable pied piper of the boardroom. He was always the same old breezy Ross, never taking himself or his business too seriously. Tonight, against the wishes of his new Wall Street partners, he was flying by the seat of his pants.

Ed Horrigan hoped Johnson would be at the top of his form. Horrigan, head of RJR Nabisco's largest unit, Reynolds Tobacco, had enthusiastically signed on with the plan Johnson would announce tonight. He was a squat, combative Irishman who brought to business the same hell-for-leather approach that led him to single-handedly storm a machine-gun nest during the Korean War. Unlike Johnson, who never seemed to have a care in the world, Horrigan was tense. He had known and distrusted these directors for years before Johnson came on the scene; he had seen firsthand their little putsches. He knew Johnson thought he had won them over with fat consulting contracts and other favors. But Horrigan wasn't so sure. They might yet fire Johnson on the spot for his grand scheme.

In the midst of Horrigan's reverie, a man walked into the room whom he didn't know. He was dressed in a suit straight out of *Gentleman's Quarterly*, every salt-and-pepper hair in place, gazing about icily. Horrigan was reminded of the old westerns where a stranger strides through the saloon doors. A few minutes later, he was introduced to the man, a Wall Street lawyer named Peter Atkins. Atkins, Horrigan was told, was there to advise the board of its rights and duties.

"Hello, Mr. Horrigan," Atkins said coolly as the two shook hands.

Oh God . . . , Horrigan thought.

———

Dinner was being cleared away from the long, T-shaped table when, at eight-thirty, Johnson rose to speak. He discussed some minor housekeeping matters, reminded members of the compensation committee that they would meet first thing tomorrow, and went over the agenda for the regular board session. "As you all know, we've got another item on the agenda tonight," Johnson said. "I think we'll turn to that now, and that's the future direction of the company."

Taking puffs from one of the tiny cigarillos he loved, Johnson reviewed his two-year tenure at RJR Nabisco's helm: profits up 50 percent, sales up as well. The problem, as they all knew, was the stock, which had been sinking since a year before, when it had peaked in the low seventies. Nothing they had tried since the stock-market crash a year ago had gotten it back up. Even after the buy back that spring—here Johnson emitted a sharp, descending whistle, a bomb falling—the stock had sagged back

———

down into the forties. Even after the tobacco industry escaped unscathed from its toughest legal challenge in years, it hadn't budged. Everyone in the room knew the story well, although none had ever seemed as concerned about it as Johnson.

"It's plain as the nose on your face that this company is wildly undervalued," Johnson said. "We tried to put food and tobacco businesses together, and it hasn't worked. Diversification is not working. We are sitting on food assets that are worth twenty-two, twenty-five times earnings and we trade at nine times earnings, because we're still seen as a tobacco company. As a result, we have studied alternative ways of increasing shareholder values." Here, he paused. "The only way to recognize these values, I believe, is through a leveraged buyout."

There was a crashing silence.

Everyone in the room knew about leveraged buyouts, often called LBOs. In an LBO, a small group of senior executives, usually working with a Wall Street partner, proposes to buy its company from public shareholders, using massive amounts of borrowed money. Critics of this procedure called it stealing the company from its owners and fretted that the growing mountain of corporate debt was hindering America's ability to compete abroad. Everyone knew LBOs meant deep cuts in research and every other imaginable budget, all sacrificed to pay off debt. Proponents insisted that companies forced to meet steep debt payments grew lean and mean. On one thing they all agreed: The executives who launched LBOs got filthy rich.

"The wolf is not at the door," Johnson said. No corporate raider was forcing him to do this. "This is simply the option that I think is best for our shareholders. I believe it is a doable transaction, and it can be done at prices much higher than the present stock price. We're not far enough along this road to make firm conclusions or make a proposal at this point, though."

Johnson stopped a moment and looked at each of the directors: mostly current and retired chief executives, their median age was sixty-five. They had given him a free hand running RJR Nabisco, and hadn't objected when he wrenched it from its century-old North Carolina home and transformed it into a monument to nouveau-riche excess. But they had struck down his predecessor for lesser transgressions than the one he was now committing.

"I want you to understand one thing," Johnson continued. "You people will have to decide. If you think this isn't the answer or there's a better idea, there will be no hard feelings. I just won't do it. There are other things I can do, and I'll do them. We'll sell food assets. We'll buy back some more of our stock. I have no problem walking right back upstairs, going to work on plan B, and no hard feelings."

Silence.

Vernon Jordan, the civil rights leader cum Washington lawyer, was the first to speak. "Look, Ross, if you go ahead with this thing, there's a real likelihood this company is going to be put in play. Somebody might come along and buy this company for more than you can pay. You might not win. I mean, who knows what could happen?"

"That's my point, Vernon," Johnson said. "This company *should* be in play. It should be sold to the highest bidder. If somebody wants to offer eighty-five dollars [a share] or more than we can pay, then we've all done an even better job for our shareholders. The management of this company is not dedicated to retaining its jobs at the expense of the shareholders."

"What stage are you at?" asked John Macomber, the former chairman of Celanese. Macomber had been a thorn in Johnson's side for years.

"In order to preserve the confidentiality here," Johnson said, "we really haven't gone very far with the banks. We haven't got a nickel. But if the board agrees with us on this proposal, we will move forward quickly."

After a few moments, Juanita Kreps spoke. "You know, it seems a shame [that] we're forced to take steps like these, breaking up companies like this," she said. "On other boards I've been on there have been the same complaints about the stock languishing. The scenario elsewhere has been different. Managements look more to the future and beyond the immediate discounting of the stock. Why is it different here? Is it an issue of tobacco, with the decline in sales and the problems with the industry?"

"Juanita, I hear a lot of CEOs complaining about their undervalued stock, but I don't see them doing anything about it," Johnson said. "This is something you *can* do about it. The other guys are afraid to do anything about it."

It all sounded so sensible, so reasonable: No one could spin an explanation like Ross Johnson. But the directors might have asked a few more questions had they known of Johnson's plans for the company, of the favors he had doled out behind their backs, or of the unprecedented cut of the LBO's expected profits he had wrung from his hungry Wall Street partners at Shearson Lehman Hutton. But those and other matters would only come to light at the most inopportune moments for them all.

Charlie Hugel scanned the room: No more questions seemed forthcoming. He suggested Johnson and Goldstone leave so the board could caucus. "Who else here would be involved in the management group?" he asked.

Johnson ticked them off: Horrigan; Jim Welch, the Nabisco chairman; Harold Henderson, the general counsel; and an outside director and consultant, Andrew G. C. Sage II. Hugel suggested they leave, too.

When Johnson left, the directors took a quick break. Albert Butler came over to Hugel. "Did you see that?" he asked. "Andy Sage is part of it."

Hugel nodded.

"Ross wants us to double his consulting contract to five hundred thousand dollars," Butler said. "It's on the agenda for the comp committee meeting, but I don't think we can do that now."

No, said Hugel, they couldn't. He was uneasy. Johnson was his friend, but several events in the past three days had given him pause to reconsider the man he thought he knew so well. There was something here that just didn't feel right.

Other directors headed for the men's room in silence. Each knew the enormity of the decision they confronted. As each of the titans of industry sidled up to the urinals, a voice echoed over a stall: "We've got to find out if this is frivolous." Men nodded as they washed their hands and returned to the boardroom.

Inside, Hugel turned the floor over to Atkins, who walked the directors through their obligations under the law of Delaware, where RJR Nabisco and so many large public corporations were chartered. When he finished, Hugel told the others how Johnson had phoned him in South Korea the week before and mentioned the LBO idea. Hugel didn't voice his private concerns or the curious offer Johnson had made him just two days earlier.

As the directors caucused, Johnson paced an upstairs suite, passing the time with Horrigan and the others, including a Shearson team. He hadn't been waiting long before a message came that the board wanted to see him. Taking Goldstone with him, Johnson nervously returned to the boardroom.

"Ross," Hugel said, "it's the strong sense of the board that we're prepared to let you go forward." The board's debate had, in fact, been anticlimactic: If Johnson had gone this far, they had no choice but to let him continue. If he was planning a serious bid for the company, under

Delaware law it was their fiduciary duty to allow shareholders to entertain it. "But," Hugel continued, "we want to make sure that the number you were thinking about is not frivolous."

"Well, you'll have to define frivolous for me," Johnson said.

"The number has to be north of the highest price the company's stock has ever traded."

"Fine, I can do that."

"In that event, the board is prepared to have you proceed. If you wish to proceed, the board will have to issue a press release tomorrow morning."

"Peter, do you have a draft?" Goldstone asked Atkins. "Would you read it?"

Atkins did, and agreed to Goldstone's request that he and Johnson be allowed to take it upstairs to review it.

The press release was a worrisome development, although one Goldstone had anticipated on learning Atkins had been brought along by Hugel. Lifting the veil of secrecy was ordinarily enough to kill a developing buyout in its cradle: Once disclosed, corporate raiders or other unwanted suitors were free to make a run at the company before management had a chance to prepare its own bid. Still, Johnson and his partners hadn't panicked when the prospect of an announcement was raised. RJR Nabisco was so big that no one in the world seemed likely to top their bid—and certainly not without a friendly management team to lead the way.

Upstairs, Goldstone and Johnson searched for the team from Shearson Lehman. Tom Hill, the cool chief strategist, and Jack Nusbaum, his lawyer, had vanished from the suite. Goldstone raced downstairs and spotted the pair in the lobby, where they had returned from a short trip to RJR headquarters with their aides. "Jack," Goldstone cried, "where the fuck have you been?"

A press release was being prepared, Goldstone explained, and Johnson badly wanted to insert the price they were considering. Without a number, Johnson feared the stock would rise out of control, perhaps forcing his group to bid more than it wanted to. They returned to the suite, where Hill repeated his earlier suggestion: $72 a share in cash and $3 a share in preferred stock. Johnson shook his head.

"None of that," he said. "Fellows, it's got to be seventy-five cash. You can't put paper on the table. It looks low class."

Johnson didn't need to do the arithmetic to get nervous. *Seventeen billion dollars.* The largest corporate takeover in history, three times greater than the largest LBO ever attempted. They hadn't seriously considered bidding much higher; with no competition in sight, there seemed no need.

Johnson, as usual, won the argument. As the clock was about to strike midnight, Goldstone was sent down to the boardroom with the revised press release.

Suddenly, after all the weeks of planning, after all the behind-the-scenes negotiations, it was all real. They were actually going to do it. "Holy shit," Johnson told the group milling about the suite. "Now we've got to find seventeen billion dollars."

Again Johnson thought of the press release. They had so hoped this could remain their little secret with the board. A public announcement would mean publicity, lots of it, and the specter of competing bids—and all the very next morning. Johnson thought he had braced himself for this, but now the full impact hit him. "Things," he warned an aide in a postmidnight phone call, "are moving faster than we thought."

CHAPTER

1

Ross's philosophy is, "We're going to have a party, a very sophisticated, complicated party." —O. C. ADAMS, *consulting psychologist to RJR Nabisco**

Ross Johnson was being followed. A detective, he guessed, no doubt hired by that old skinflint Henry Weigl. Every day, through the streets of Manhattan, no matter where Johnson went, his shadow stayed with him. Finally he had had enough. Johnson had friends, lots of them, and one in particular who must have had contacts in the goon business. He had this annoying problem, Johnson explained to his friend. He'd like to get rid of a tail. No problem, said the friend. Sure enough, within days the detective vanished. Whatever the fellow was doing now, Johnson's friend assured him, he was probably walking a little funny.

It was the spring of 1976, and at a second-tier food company named Standard Brands, things were getting ugly. Weigl, its crusty old chairman, was out to purge his number two, Johnson, the shaggy-haired young Canadian who pranced about Manhattan with glamorous friends such as Frank Gifford and "Dandy" Don Meredith. Weigl sicced a team of auditors on Johnson's notoriously bloated expense accounts and collected tales of his former protégé's extramarital affairs.

Johnson's hard-drinking band of young renegades began plotting a counterattack, lobbying directors and documenting all the underlying rot in the company's businesses. Rumors of an imminent coup began sweep-

---

* Dr. O. C. Adams did not agree to speak to the authors about Ross Johnson, his client's chief executive, until Johnson had consented.

ing the company's Madison Avenue headquarters.

Then tensions exploded into the open: A shouting match erupted between Johnson and Weigl, a popular executive dropped dead, a board of directors was rent asunder. Everything came to a head at a mid-May board meeting. Weigl went in first, ready to bare his case against Johnson. Johnson followed, his own trap ready to spring.

As the hours wore on, Johnson's aides, "the Merry Men," wandered through Central Park, waiting for the victor to emerge. Things were bound to get bloody in there. But when it came to corporate politics, no one was ready to count out Ross Johnson. He seemed to have a knack for survival.

———

Until the fall of 1988 Ross Johnson's life was a series of corporate adventures, in which he would not only gain power for himself but wage war on an old business order.

Under that old order, big business was a slow and steady entity. The *Fortune* 500 was managed by "company men": junior executives who worked their way up the ladder and gave one company their all and senior executives who were corporate stewards, preserving and cautiously enhancing the company.

Johnson was to become the consummate "noncompany man." He shredded traditions, jettisoned divisions, and roiled management. He was one of a whole breed of noncompany men who came to maturity in the 1970s and 1980s: a deal-driven, yield-driven nomadic lot. They said their mission was to serve company investors, not company tradition. They also tended to handsomely serve themselves.

But of all the noncompany men, Johnson cut the highest profile. He did the biggest deals, had the biggest mouth, and enjoyed the biggest perks. He would come to be the very symbol of the business world's "Roaring Eighties." And he would climax the decade by launching the deal of the century—scattering one of America's largest, most venerable companies to the winds.

The man who would come to represent the new age of business was born in 1931 at the depth of an old one. Frederick Ross Johnson was raised in Depression-era Winnipeg, the only child of a lower-middle-class home. He was always "Ross," never Fred—Fred was his father's name. The senior Johnson was a hardware salesman by vocation, a woodworker by avocation, and a man of few words. Johnson's petite mother, Caroline, was the pepper pot of the household—a bookkeeper at a time when few married women worked, a crack bridge player in her free time. Young Ross owed an early knack for numbers and the gift of gab to her; an early entrepreneurial bent he owed to the times. The Johnsons weren't poverty-stricken, but neither did they own their own bungalow until Johnson was eight years old.

Around that period young Ross began working at a variety of after-school jobs. He used the money he earned for serious things, like buying clothes. He started with standard kid tasks, such as delivering magazines around the neighborhood and selling candy at the circus, then branched into more innovative ventures, such as renting out comic books from his collection. When he grew older, he sold certificates for baby pictures door-to-door. It was an enterprise he would turn to whenever he needed a buck during his years in college.

Johnson wasn't the best student in his high school, ceding that honor to his friend Neil Wood, who would go on to head the huge Cadillac Fairview real estate firm. Johnson was the kind of teenager who could rank in the upper quarter of his class, as he did, without appearing to try very hard, which he didn't. Nor was he the best athlete in school, although he was a rangy six feet three inches by the time he graduated. He was far better at memorizing baseball statistics in *The Sporting News* than hitting a fastball.

Unlike his father, who hadn't completed high school, Ross Johnson wanted to be a college man, and he took the crosstown bus each day to Winnipeg's University of Manitoba. He was average inside the classroom but excellent out of it: president of his fraternity, varsity basketball, and honors as outstanding cadet in the Canadian version of ROTC. (This despite a propensity for pranks: One night Johnson and some chums ambushed a superior officer, whom they considered a superior jerk, tied him to a diving board, and left him to contemplate his sins as the sun rose.) If there was anything that marked the playful young Ross Johnson, it was an ability to hold sway over his fellow students, even those who were far older. His college class was largely made up of returning World War II veterans, but it was Johnson, a teenager, who did the organizing and leading.

Upon graduation, Johnson plunged into the middle levels of a string of Canadian companies, where he would muddle along for nearly twenty years with little distinction. His first job, as an accountant at Canadian General Electric in Montreal, lasted six years. Bored, he moved to the marketing side in Toronto to try his hand as a salesman. "It's where the good parties are," Johnson explained to friends. There, as a low-level manager given the pedestrian task of marketing light bulbs, Johnson first displayed a zest for salesmanship. He dreamed up an idea for a premium-priced bulb, painted on the inside, and researched a name: Shadow Ban. The product did well. Johnson also did wonders for the division's Christmas-tree bulb sales.

As good as he was with light bulbs, it was in his expense accounts that Johnson's real creativity shone. He cut back the expense budgets of his salesmen, marshaling much of the money for himself. He used the additional funds to entertain customers royally, taking particular delight in plotting and executing what he called "the hundred dollar golf game," which involved a day on one of the city's finer courses, followed by drinks and dinner at one of the city's finer restaurants. It took a prodigious effort to drop $100 in the early 1960s, but Johnson was up to it. By combining his flair for spending with his gift for flattering older men, Johnson moved steadily up the corporate ladder. "Spending money was always a joyful, joyous thing to Ross," recalled William Blundell, a Canadian friend. "He was convinced that all of the decisions got made by the senior people in the accounts. He thought he could leverage that money pretty well."

From the start Johnson was a party animal. He loved nothing better than sipping Scotch and schmoozing into the wee hours. The next morning he could walk into work without missing a beat. At GE he perfected a flip, wisecracking approach to business. If there was a choice between saying something straightforwardly and saying it humorously, Johnson always chose the latter. If it was self-deprecating, so much the better. "An accountant," Johnson would say during his bookkeeping days, "is a man who puts his head in the past and backs his ass into the future." He attracted a group of young protégés who felt the same. Johnson held sway over them with an hypnotic, singsong voice, both deep and nasal, and he alternately spoke *sotto voce* and *fortissimo.* "Come along with me," his manner and mien beckoned young acolytes. "We're going to have fun." When he got married, his groomsmen capped an all-night bash by going water-skiing in their tuxedos.

Yet after thirteen years, at age thirty-two Ross Johnson was still a nobody. He was making only $14,000 a year, teaching nights at the

University of Toronto to augment his income. His first child was on the way. Except for a patina of charisma, he was like a thousand other bright young men in Toronto, struggling to get ahead. He was impatient. When his bid to be transferred to GE's U.S. operations—the big time—was turned down, he jumped ship.

Landing as a midlevel bureaucrat at T. Eaton, the big Canadian department-store chain, Johnson found a mentor, a man named Tony Peskett. Eaton was fat, sleepy, and slow, but Peskett, as head of personnel, was committed to bringing the company into the twentieth century. Johnson had come from the gray flannel of General Electric in the 1950s. Now, as a member of a guerrilla band of managers known as the "Pesketteers," he entered the 1960s. Peskett encouraged him to indulge his natural proclivity for thumbing his nose at authority. The Pesketteers believed in change for change's sake, and set out reshaping their dowdy old employer. They believed in constantly shaking things up, monitoring and reacting to the competition down the street at Sears Canada. The Pesketteers subscribed to a Bob Dylan line of the time: "He who's not busy being born is busy dying." Tony Peskett, who imbued Johnson with a lifelong belief in the creative uses of chaos, put it another way: "The minute you establish an organization, it starts to decay." Johnson, who carried that idea to every business he ever ran, boiled it down into a personal philosophy called "shit stirring": a love for constant restructuring and reorganizing.

When Peskett fell out of favor, Johnson once more jumped ship, this time landing at a Toronto company named General Steel Works, Ltd. GSW, as it was called, offered the prospect of authority (Johnson would be the number-two executive), money (a $50,000 salary), and social contacts galore. Through the company's rich owner, Johnson joined Toronto's upscale Lambton Country Club and came to know many of the city's elite, men such as hockey great Bobby Orr and Alan Eagleson, a lawyer who headed the National Hockey League players' union. Johnson loved rubbing elbows with them and found he was good at it.

Despite his social ascension, Johnson started off miserably at GSW, a tiny maker of appliances, garbage cans, and manure spreaders. When an economic downturn slowed its appliance business, Johnson's impulse was to throw money at the problem, and he fell back on the expensive marketing schemes he'd developed at Eaton and GE. His new boss, a tightfisted hard case named Ralph Barford, rejected each one in turn. "Ralph's philosophy was buy low, sell high, and argue over the bills," recalled Jim Westcott, a Johnson friend who would frequently commiserate with him over lunch. "Boy, did Ralph rip the skin off my back today," Johnson would moan.

Johnson chafed at life in a smaller company. GSW was operating on the edge, with lots of debt, and Johnson suffered through weekly grillings by its bankers. "It was a shock," he recalled. "You learned that the guy who writes the ads for the bank isn't the guy who loans the money. They break your balls." It was Johnson's introduction to the harsh realities of corporate debt, for which he developed a lifelong aversion.

Eventually, Johnson and his boss reached an accommodation of sorts and worked together for another five years. Johnson came to appreciate Barford's ability to change directions at a minute's notice. "If you could convince him you were right, he'd do a one hundred and eighty degree turn," Johnson would recall. "It was just that getting him to do that could take a panzer division." Johnson became an accomplished quick-change artist himself, an attribute that would bewilder subordinates for the next twenty years.

By the early 1970s Ross Johnson was forty years old and still hadn't run his own show. When a headhunter offered him that chance, he leapt at it, jumping this time to become president of the Montreal-based Canadian arm of an American food company, Standard Brands. Standard Brands had been created in 1928 by the House of Morgan, which had merged Fleischmann Distilling & Yeast Company, Royal Baking Powder, and Chase & Sanborn Company into one entity. That alone told Johnson something about the company's problems. Chase & Sanborn coffee was a tired old brand, and yeast and baking powder seemed like pioneer-era remnants. A ponderous, second-tier organization, Standard Brands over the years had evolved into an employer of quiet tinkerers, who came up with a sugar substitute called high-fructose syrup and developed Fleischmann's Margarine, a low-cholesterol spread. Year in, year out, the company's timeworn credo fronted its annual report, affirming Standard Brands's "commitment to use the fruits of the earth to provide a good quality of life for those we serve."

Johnson found Standard Brands hopelessly outdated. This was the age of marketing, of *movement,* and these people were trafficking in fats and oils. The Canadian subsidiary was a mess. Johnson, the ex-Pesketteer, hit Standard Brands Canada like a hurricane. In his first year, he bounced twenty-one of the top twenty-three executives, and to replace them he looked for the kind of free-spirited young men he had attracted throughout his career. Peter Rogers, an Englishman working for a Canadian candy company, had a reputation as a brilliant, profane loose cannon. "No fucking way," Rogers said when first approached by Johnson. "Your company treats people terribly, and it's messed up every acquisition it's ever made." But Rogers came; he would stay with Johnson for fifteen years. Johnson also snagged Martin Emmett, an aristocratic South African, who canceled a transfer to Australia to join Johnson's growing band of Merry Men. In later years the two became so close they were dubbed "Martini and Rossi."

The pair became the core of Johnson's rogue managers, dedicated to shaking up Standard Brands Canada by day and draining bottles of spirits by night. Johnson assigned them nicknames: Rogers was "The Rook," for Canadian Olympic Drinking Team rookie; Emmett was "The Big E," for his lanky frame. Jim Westcott, a personnel consultant, was "Buddha," for his girth and wisdom. Johnson himself was "The Pope."

As in Toronto, Johnson proved himself adept at working his way into Montreal society. Paul Desmarais, the influential chairman of a big manufacturer, Power Corporation, sponsored Johnson's membership in the exclusive Mount Royal Club and introduced him to the tight-knit Montreal business community. Among Johnson's new friends was a young lawyer named Brian Mulroney, who would go on to become Canada's prime minister. His confidence building, Johnson settled into a routine that would endure for fifteen years—staying up until all hours with his pals, talking business, sipping Scotch, and smoking cigars. Unorthodox, yes, but his guerrilla band produced results, and it got Johnson noticed. In 1973, he was promoted to head Standard Brands's international operations.

He moved to New York. Cocksure, buoyant, bubbly, Johnson was utterly unintimidated by the city. He felt he had been born to the moment. To his peers at Standard Brands's headquarters, Johnson was a brash upstart, an overnight success. They knew nothing of the hardscrabble childhood in the provinces, the twenty-one years of anonymity. In fact, Johnson was the consummate late bloomer, a man who at age forty-two was only now starting to find his stride in life.

He bought a house in the tony Connecticut suburb of New Canaan, and secured a sought-after seat on the New Canaan Club Car, a hangout for executives that was attached to the end of the 7:30 New Haven Railroad run. There, amid comforts not available to the average commuter, Johnson was introduced to a high-powered group, men such as Rawleigh Warner, the chairman of Mobil Oil. Every morning they played bridge, read the morning newspapers, talked business. Johnson's long brown hair, wide ties, and pigskin coats stood out, and the other executives—every hair in place, every other suit pin-striped—rode him unmercifully. The mod young Canadian would jovially give it right back. "You old stiffs, you old farts," he would say, "The world has gone right by you."

Johnson's new boss, Henry Weigl, though, was no joking matter. Weigl was a tyrant who ran a tight, spartan company. His proudest accomplishment was a twenty-year string of annual profit increases since becoming president in the 1950s. He did it in part by making certain results went up each year just so much and no more. That way the company wouldn't be hard-pressed to top its performance the following year. It also helped that Weigl could pinch a penny until it screamed.

Unlike the posh corporate headquarters that dotted midtown Manhattan, Standard Brands's offices were stark: linoleum floors and steel desks. Only the highest echelon qualified for carpeting and wooden desks. The rotary phone dials were locked at five each afternoon to prevent after-hours personal calls. When Standard Brands managers traveled, they were required not only to fly coach, but also to take the cheapest form of transit to the airport—a bus. On the road they stayed at Howard Johnson motels, because that chain's restaurants were major customers for Chase & Sanborn. Weigl's tightfistedness extended to big-ticket items as well. When a Standard Brands director and investment banker named Andrew G. C. Sage II put together an acquisition for the company, he was stunned to receive a letter from Weigl saying, in essence, "Thank you for the donation of your time." Sage tore up the bill he had been preparing.

Unlike the garrulous Johnson, Weigl spent so much time holed up in his office he was known as "Henry the Hermit." Subordinates lived in fear of being summoned inside. Johnson once sat in on the tongue-lashing of a junior executive. The victim was excused, and Johnson remained to talk with Weigl for a moment. When he came out, the poor fellow was lying spent in the hall, hyperventilating. Weigl once thought he saw the head of the tax department sneaking out of work early. He told an aide to investigate and fire the man. The aide came back to him and said he must be mistaken; the man had been working late. "Look," Weigl snapped, "you can either fire him or fire yourself." (No one was ultimately fired, but people on Weigl's floor began tiptoeing downstairs to catch the elevator at the next floor at day's end.) At a Christmas party, Weigl observed an executive who he thought rather too jolly. He ordered Johnson to fire him—before Christmas. Johnson did the deed but softened the blow by giving the executive and his family a vacation trip to Canada. "Fogged it," as he described the tactic.

Soon Johnson was getting pretty good at fogging it. When senior vice president Lester Applegate was forced out by Weigl, Johnson hid him on the Canadian payroll. At first Johnson managed to avoid Weigl's wrath. He delivered results and was out of the country half the time visiting the company's far-flung international operations. But Johnson's flamboyant style guaranteed an eventual collision with his indomitable boss.

As phone locks clicked on, ending each Standard Brands day, Johnson's second shift was just beginning. Always drawn to celebrities, he soon befriended the former football star Frank Gifford, then announcing "Monday Night Football" and pitching ads for Standard Brands's Dry Sack sherry. The two men took to hanging out at Manuche's, the successor to Toots Shor's as the prime watering hole for New York's sporting elite. Johnson was a hopeless sports nut, and through Gifford he met an array of big names: football commissioner Pete Rozelle; race-car mogul Roger Penske; broadcast buddy Don Meredith; Roone Arledge, who headed ABC Sports; Don Ohlmeyer, his crack producer; and a young man Arledge and Ohlmeyer shared as protégé, John Martin. Johnson and Gifford grew so close they began working together on an annual charity banquet called Dinner of Champions, where people paid a lot of money to mingle with Gifford's starry friends. The Giffer, the glitz, the contacts: Johnson thrived.

Beaten-down Standard Brands executives rallied around this buoyant newcomer. Senior managers had to endure an all-day meeting with Weigl once a month. Johnson repaired their spirits afterward by leading all-night drinking sessions he called "The Monday Evening Wrecking Club."

So, too, did he become a favorite of the Standard Brands board. In contrast to the prickly Weigl, Johnson talked with board members casually and comfortably. They rewarded him by naming him a director in 1974 and promoting him to president a year later. Weigl, sniffing a challenge to his power, did a slow burn. He forbade contacts between directors and executives outside his presence. When one of the directors, a New York lawyer named Watt Dunnington, gave a cocktail party and invited Johnson and the company's general counsel, Weigl was furious at all of them.

Johnson thought Weigl was looking for ways to trip him up. He was given a Mission Impossible: sell the company's hapless chemicals division. Miraculously, he drew an offer of $23 million. Stubbornly, Weigl wouldn't sell it for less than $24 million. Deftly, Johnson struck a side deal. The buyer would pay $24 million, but get $1 million of it right back under the table from a Standard Brands subsidiary. Weigl, not knowing about part two of the deal, approved it. "My greatest sale," Johnson would recall.

In January 1976, the board named Johnson chief operating officer, making him Weigl's heir apparent. Many employees cheered the coming emancipation—but not all. Weigl received two anonymous letters from Canadian staffers complaining of lavish spending—Martin Emmett's three company cars and chauffeur, say—and expense-account abuses. Weigl, who had torpedoed successors before, jumped on it. He dispatched a team of auditors to Canada. The going was slow. But eventually Weigl learned of Johnson's huge New York limo tab, which the company was picking up. He began gathering information on Johnson's extramarital affairs—fertile territory, with Johnson's first marriage on the rocks.

Johnson, meanwhile, prepared for war. A headhunter who gathered employee intelligence for Weigl became a double agent, also reporting to Johnson. A gathering of conspirators descended upon Johnson's New Canaan home over several weekends: Peter Rogers from Chicago, where he now ran the Planters Nut and Curtiss Candy businesses; Martin Emmett from Toronto, where he headed Standard Brands Canada; and Ruben Gutoff, a senior vice president, from New York. Together they assembled a report that would show how Weigl's tightfisted ways were slowly strangling Standard Brands. As for the tail on Johnson, two could play that game. Soon, Weigl was pretty sure *he* was being followed.

Then, a spark. Johnson had allowed an executive fired by Weigl to exercise his stock options after leaving the company. When Weigl found out, he was furious. He hadn't fired the man to see him profit on stock options. He called up Johnson, who was out of town, and gave him ten kinds of hell. Johnson should have canceled those options, Weigl stormed . . . and stormed . . . and stormed. Exercising those options had been totally legitimate, Johnson protested, and blocking it would have been against the law. "We'll write our own law," Weigl declared.

Finally Johnson could take it no longer. "Henry, you can take it and shove it," he said, and hung up.

The breech was now total, and that afternoon Johnson phoned two of the board's most powerful members to tell them so. "Look, I'm gone," he told Ellmore ("Pat") Patterson, chairman of Morgan Guaranty Trust. "This guy is completely mad. I figured I could hold it and hold it, but I can't anymore." He made the same speech to Earle McLaughlin, chairman of the Royal Bank of Canada, who had championed Johnson's rise at Standard Brands. "Well, we figured it would happen," McLaughlin said, but urged him not to move precipitously. When a special board meeting was set to discuss the matter, Johnson agreed not to resign and circulated the same message to his coconspirators. "Keep your powder dry," he said.

Then, less than two weeks before the board meeting, a popular Standard Brands executive named Bill Shaw dropped dead of a heart attack. The cause, everybody believed, was extended overexposure to Henry Weigl, and while that postmortem was medically dubious, Shaw's death did manage to crystallize the rebellion. "Ross, you've got to do something," said Bob Carbonell, who ran research and development. "If you don't do something," sputtered Emmett, "we're all gone."

It all came to a head on a Friday morning in mid-May, when the directors convened. As Johnson waited outside, Weigl recited the litany of abuses his auditors had found. Weigl concluded by proposing a two-year extension of his contract.

As his cronies wandered Central Park, Johnson was ushered in to address the board. He admitted to minor expense-account violations, but said he wasn't going to fight Weigl any longer; the man was impossible to work for. "Gentlemen," he said, "all I can tell you is I'm resigning." What other executives would do, only they could say. Then he offered up the bleak analysis of Standard Brands that he and his pals had prepared. "The shit is going to hit the fan within twenty-four months," he predicted.

Johnson left the room while the board caucused, and when he returned, Weigl was no longer in the chairman's spot at the head of the table. Instead he was sitting partway down it, white as a ghost. "Ross, here's what we're planning to do," a board member said. "Henry will continue as chairman and chief executive officer, and you will be made the president and chief executive in another year, when he retires."

Johnson should have been thrilled. Instead, he said, "That won't fly." He stepped out, then returned to a new offer: Weigl would remain chairman until his retirement, and Johnson would become chief executive immediately. Johnson approved, "with one provision: that Henry's office won't be in the headquarters building."

That bit of hardball brought Johnson command of a New York Stock Exchange company. Afterward he and the Merry Men toasted their victory with martinis late into the night. It had, they agreed, been a splendid coup. It wouldn't be their last.

Henry Weigl ultimately exacted a small measure of revenge. Some time later Johnson, looking for a Florida vacation home, bought a splashy yellow villa in the exclusive Lost Tree community in Palm Beach. Life at Lost Tree revolved around its country club, but by the time Johnson applied for admission, Weigl, also a Lost Tree resident, had begun a campaign to blackball him. Embarrassed, Johnson withdrew his application and ultimately moved up the coast to a town named Jupiter, where he bought and combined a pair of oceanside condominiums. A Johnson supporter in the coup, the director Andrew Sage, bought his Lost Tree home. "When Henry is dead and buried thirty years I'm still not going near his grave," Johnson said years later, "because I just know a hand is going to reach up through the ground and grab me by the throat."

———

After Weigl's ouster staid old Standard Brands became Phi Delta Johnson. Out the door went the linoleum and steel decor. Gone, too, was the prohibition on first-class travel. In no time, Johnson leased a corporate jet and acquired a company-owned Jaguar. Overnight the corporate culture was transformed into a facsimile of Johnson's flip, breezy manner. Now when Standard Brands managers met, the sessions were laced with outrageous profanity and raucous challenges. "All right," Johnson liked to convene problem-solving meetings, "whose cock is on the anvil on this one?" The fraternity house mien extended to all levels. Standard Brands executives didn't say, "I beg to differ," they said, "You have no fucking idea what you're talking about." Standard Brands executives had no use for reports and slide shows; they were expected to cut to the heart of the matter. To do otherwise invited Johnson's favorite withering line: "That was a blinding glimpse of the obvious" (sometimes shortened to simply "a BGO").

Often, it took only a short colloquy with Johnson to dispatch a bad idea. Once, a Planters executive came in with a proposal for a regional advertising test. "Could you afford to do this sort of thing nationally?" asked Johnson. "No," the fellow replied. "Then what the fuck are you doing it for?" asked Johnson. End of story. In a company filled with creatively profane people, no one was more profane than Johnson. Even when he gave interviews for publication, they came tumbling out. A woman who transcribed one of them handed the completed Q & A back to the interviewer, saying, "Here's the fucking transcript."

Johnson had no use for long meetings when short ones would do, or when he was due on a golf course. For that matter, he had no use for traditional business hours. "He would call you at five o'clock and say he wanted to meet you at midnight," recalled John Murray, who headed the Standard Brands sales force. "Or he would get together with you for dinner at seven P.M. and you'd wind up rambling until five A.M." Johnson firmly believed that true inspiration and insight happened only after hours. "Babies," he said, "are only born at night."

On a typical evening, Johnson and his Merry Men would knock off around seven-thirty and head out en masse for the night shift. They would stake out a table at Manuche's and drink until it closed, convening afterward at Johnson's new company-owned apartment, where they would order out for pizza or Chinese. When most other *Fortune* 500 executives were long asleep, Johnson's band would change into rumpled sweatsuits and settle back for a long night of drinking, talking business, and kicking around ideas. By the wee hours, those still conscious would collapse into the twin beds in the two bedrooms or onto the living room couch. In the morning Peter Rogers would fix breakfast, and they would be off to the races again. "It was," recalled Johnson, "like Boys Town."

Johnson's life began to resemble nothing so much as an endless buddy movie. The nicknames just kept coming: Carbonell, the Salvadoran R&D chief, was "El Supremo"; Ferdie Falk, who headed the liquor business, was "The Fonz"; Mike Masterpool, a public relations officer brought in from General Electric, was "M3"; and Ward Miller, the finicky corporate secretary, was "Vice President of Worry." If Johnson didn't have a nickname for someone, he addressed them with the generic "pards," as in "pardner." His closest partner became Emmett, who now replaced Johnson as head of international. Martini and Rossi were constant companions, conferring in their own personal shorthand. Johnson lavished gifts on Emmett, including a luxurious corporate apartment and an unlimited expense account. Other members of Johnson's fraternity wondered, in their crude way, how The Big E managed to get so close to The Pope. "Martin," one quipped, "must have a picture of Ross fucking a pig."

Yet Johnson could be fickle. He tended to get high on people, only to drop them. Sometimes he simply tired of a person's company, like an eight-year-old who moves on to a new playmate. Ruben Gutoff lasted only seventeen months as president of Standard Brands. His crime, it seemed, was that he moved too slowly: He wanted to hold monthly meetings of a commodities committee when commodities decisions had to be made hourly. He wanted to see tear sheets of every Standard Brands ad, when there were thousands of them a month. Johnson fired Gutoff with no remorse, as he did a number of other young executives who fell from his favor.

"Ross, you're a rotten fuck," a member of his entourage told Johnson after a particularly tough firing.

Johnson smiled. "You're one of the few people who know me," he replied.

Andy Sage, the board member who rescued Johnson's Florida real estate, proved equally helpful as chairman of Standard Brands's compensation committee. When Johnson took power, Weigl had been making $200,000, Johnson $130,000. With Sage's help, Johnson pushed his own salary to $480,000. Many executives saw their salaries doubled. Pay at Standard Brands went from the bottom of the industry barrel to the top of the heap.

Johnson didn't stop there. Top executives were also ensconced in company apartments, enjoyed a private box at Madison Square Garden, and got country-club memberships. At one new country club in Connecticut—whose founders were lucky enough to be friends of Johnson—twenty-four Standard Brands managers had memberships. Johnson also kept himself stocked with "whip money"—large bills to be whipped out of his suit pocket. Shortly before Christmas—peak tipping season—he was heard telling his secretary, "Get me an inch of fifties, will you?"

The hallmark of Johnson's reign was the personal touch. He had an overriding rule he felt free to invoke at any time: The chief executive can do whatever he wants. When a friend, Manhattan restaurateur Michael

Manuche, went out of business, Johnson took him on in public relations; later he put him in charge of the Dinah Shore LPGA golf tournament. Johnson gave Frank Gifford an expanded contract and an office at Standard Brands. Johnson liked having Gifford around so much he decided to bring on a whole stable of athletes, including Bobby Orr and tennis star Rod Laver, to help with promotions.

The jocks were also called on to play an occasional round of golf with the supermarket executives so important to the Standard Brands sales force. Many seemed to really be Johnson's courtiers, primarily, a fact that puzzled some of the stars themselves. Alex Webster, the former New York Giants fullback, recalled bumping into Johnson in an elevator in 1978 and being introduced by their mutual friend Gifford. The next day, Gifford called Webster to say that Johnson wanted him to go to Montreal to address a grocers' group. "But I don't know anything about Standard Brands," Webster protested. "Just tell them some stories and thank them for their business," Gifford advised. Webster would keep doing it for Johnson for more than a decade.

Jocks were just the beginning. As head of Standard Brands, Johnson became the King of Schmooze, cultivating friendships with corporate chieftains such as Martin Davis of Gulf + Western and James Robinson of American Express as well as other big names, such as the fashion designer Oleg Cassini. Johnson did it with generosity. "You had to be careful never to say you liked his sweater, because he'd take it off his back and give it to you," recalled one Standard Brands executive. He did it with a carefully cultivated sense of style, including the grand entrance. Johnson arrived twenty minutes late, punctually, to everything. "If you're on time, no one notices you," he would say. "If you're late, they pay attention." And he did it with his usual good humor, telling the best dirty jokes in the club car each morning and being the most convivial partner on the golf course.

Johnson's immediate business challenge was to keep Standard Brands from collapsing. No sooner had he taken the helm in 1976 than sugar prices fell, hammering Standard Brands's key corn sweetener market and leaving the company with operating profit declines for two straight years. Johnson had his young controller, Ed Robinson, put together what he called a "bad things" report, highlighting all the company's rotten corners. One was the liquor division, which held huge inventories of wine. Johnson met with the "bottle kissers," as he called the vintner–managers there. "Oh, Meester Johnson, this eez too good to sell," they said of the wine, as Johnson later related the story. His response: "Cut the price in half and *move* it."

A former accountant, Johnson camouflaged the company's poor results with an occasional bit of financial sleight of hand, sometimes stretching generally accepted accounting principles to their generally accepted limits. Even when Standard Brands was posting profit declines, however, Johnson couldn't muster any interest in cutting costs. "Give me the guy who can spend creatively," Johnson would say, "not the one who's trying to squeeze the last nickel out of the budget." (The public relations department, which took care of entertainment and extravaganzas, was headed by a man Johnson liked to call, among other things, "Numero Uno." Mike Masterpool, he said admiringly, is "the only man who can take an unlimited budget and exceed it.") But line managers had to scramble from quarter to quarter to make their numbers. The unofficial motto of the day was "Get through the night."

Johnson tried to compensate for the company's poor showing by devising jazzy new products, an effort that led to what one analyst called "some of the most celebrated failures in the food industry." The first was Smooth 'N Easy, an instant gravy mix sold in the form of a margarine bar, which could be melted in a skillet and whipped into chicken gravy, white sauce, and brown gravy flavors. The result of Johnson's all-night brainstorming sessions, it bombed in the supermarket. Johnson's move into Mexican foods flopped, too, crushed by the marketing muscle of a competitor, Frito-Lay.

In 1978 Johnson's love for sports and knack for marketing disasters combined in the ill-fated Reggie! bar. Named for one of Johnson's new friends, baseball star Reggie Jackson, the candy was handed to each fan entering Yankee Stadium on opening day that year, and when Jackson swatted a home run, Reggie! bars came raining onto the field. The Reggie! itself was a chocolate-and-peanut–cluster concoction made for years in Fort Wayne, Indiana, and called the Wayne Bun; Johnson had simply renamed it and taken it national. (Its namesake didn't help any. In promotional appearances Jackson seemed less interested in talking baseball than talking up pretty women.) Sales flagged, and by 1980, Reggie! was sent to the showers. (Jackson, however, was not: For years Johnson kept him ensconced in a company apartment, complete with a company car and a personal-services fee of $400,000 a year.)

If this all seemed a tad chaotic, Johnson didn't mind. In fact, he encouraged it. Ever the Pesketteer, he reorganized Standard Brands twice a year, like clockwork, changing people's jobs, creating and dissolving divisions, reversing strategic fields. To outsiders it seemed like movement for movement's sake. Johnson framed it as a personal crusade against specialization. "You don't have a job," he told the Merry Men, "you have an assignment."

"To Ross," said Paul Kolton, a former Standard Brands director, "the nature of any organization was that it got fat, dumb, and happy. He never took the line, 'If it ain't broke, don't fix it.' To him, something's always broke."

Through the rough times, the Standard Brands board never rapped its young chief's knuckles. Johnson, mindful of Weigl's fate, treated the directors like kings, making certain to throw some of the stardust from his jock stable their way. ("Hey, meet my friend Frank Gifford!") "One of the most important jobs a CEO has is the care and feeding of the directors," Johnson said. He had always been good at flattering older men, and he was a genius for putting the best spin on bad news or dissolving a tense situation with a bon mot. When Standard Brands auditors complained to the board for two years running about questionable accounting procedures at their Mexican joint ventures, the board demanded an answer from Johnson. The real answer was that jawboning his Mexican partners into following U.S. accounting rules had been impossible, and Johnson had given up trying. What he told directors was, "Did you ever try steering a motor boat from water skis?" The board dissolved in laughter and pursued it no further.

Only occasionally would his loud wardrobe or blue language push the board's limits. Johnson once brought the board word of a new wine he thought would be terrific. It was called French Kiss, Johnson announced. The directors recoiled. Couldn't we try something a little less explicit? they wondered. Johnson had his way, and when the wine was brought to market, French Kiss lasted about as long as Reggie! .

The party at Standard Brands went on like that for four years: constant upheaval, a string of marketing disasters, ho-hum profits, but lots of fun, money, and perks for Johnson and his friends. Finally, in 1980, the free-spending environment he fostered got Johnson into serious trouble. One of his senior officers, Bob Schaedler, discovered a stream of unexplained payments flowing from the company's international operations to what appeared to be a dummy corporation. The shell company, Schaedler learned, was headed by Martin Emmett's chauffeur and seemed to be billing Standard Brands for thousands of dollars of Emmett's personal expenses: food, clothes, furniture, carpets, and televisions.

Schaedler, a rival of Emmett's, quietly took the matter to Howard Pines, the company's personnel chief, and Les Applegate. Applegate, who had fallen from Johnson's favor, was about to step down from the presidency to make way for none other than Emmett himself. The trio agreed the matter couldn't be taken to Johnson, who would probably bury it— and maybe them as well—to protect his best friend. They decided to go directly to the board.

Johnson was in fine spirits as the board's audit committee convened a day before the July directors meeting. Emmett's promotion to president was to be approved the next day, and Mike Masterpool had already leaked it to *Business Week* to make the magazine's early deadline. A pair of directors, Pat Patterson of Morgan Guaranty and Paul Kolton, came in late, grim faced. They had just met with Schaedler, who had shown them a suitcase full of the Emmett receipts. They turned to Johnson. Could he explain it?

Johnson appeared shocked. He didn't know what had happened, he told the directors, but he damn sure intended to find out. The next day he reported the beginnings of an answer. For one thing, Emmett's chauffeur wasn't a typical chauffeur, but a former Central Intelligence Agency operative who had set himself up in business, with Standard Brands International as his only customer. He bought things at Emmett's behest, Johnson explained, but Emmett, when confronted, insisted everything was aboveboard. Johnson went to bat for his buddy: Investigate it thoroughly, he said, but allow Emmett to become president now.

Emmett's elevation to the presidency was announced, but not a subsequent internal probe by the company's longtime law firm. As the months wore on and the investigation continued, there was rampant speculation inside the company that both Johnson and Emmett would lose their jobs. In September, the final verdict was reached: bad judgment, perhaps, but no bad deed. Emmett got off with a slap on the wrist. Instead it was his three accusers—Schaedler, Pines, and an executive named Ed Downs— that Johnson fired. Applegate was banished to being a consultant.

"I'm sending you people out on the boat," Johnson told the trio, "and you're not coming back." The episode was to be forever known among

Johnson's entourage as the "boat people incident." For Johnson, it provided one of the few moments of jeopardy and strain he would ever know with a board.

Afterward, he seemed restless. After four years Standard Brands was still an erratic performer. Its profits were growing again, but no faster than the rate of inflation. Its rate of return was well below the industry norm. Carbonell was working on all sorts of projects out at the R&D center—a fat-free peanut and improved fermentation for corn syrup, yeast, and vinegar. But new products took time, and Johnson was growing fidgety. For a while he kept busy by selling the yeast business and buying some liquor companies. But it was as if Standard Brands was a toy he had gotten for Christmas, and Johnson, having played with it for five years, was getting bored.

Part of his disaffection was due to the fact that Johnson, now moving into his late forties, was no longer the boy wonder of the mid-seventies. The idea of becoming a sedate corporate elder made him shiver. He wasn't interested in growing older; he longed to be the enfant terrible, the eternal shit-stirring youth. Everything about him, from the still-shaggy hair to his twenty-six-year-old second wife, suggested a corporate Peter Pan. What was needed, it was clear, was a new adventure.

The opportunity came in a curious phone call from a fellow chief executive in March 1981. Bob Schaeberle, chairman of the food giant Nabisco, told Johnson his people had gotten a call from that fellow in Connecticut working for Standard Brands. Johnson didn't know what Schaeberle was talking about. You know, the Nabisco chief said, the fellow who had the idea of merging Standard Brands and Nabisco. Johnson didn't know. "Maybe there's something there, and maybe there isn't," Schaeberle said, "but I think we should talk about it," Um, sure, Johnson replied.

But first Johnson wanted to discover the identity of the agent provocateur putting his company in play. "Who the fuck is this guy?" he exploded at a Monday morning meeting of his top lieutenants. Jake Powell, the chief financial officer, and Dean Posvar, the top planner, fessed up. The man was a Greenwich-based business broker they sometimes used to come up with minor acquisition ideas. Apparently he had gone overboard. "Well, if there is anything to this idea, Bob will sure as shit never want to do it now," Johnson said. "Shit, he'll think I don't know what the hell is going on in my own company. And you know what? He's right. I don't know what the hell is going on."

Nevertheless, Johnson was intrigued. He got together with Schaeberle and liked the man. In a matter of weeks the two executives agreed to merge their companies. Nabisco Brands, as the new company would be called, was formed in a $1.9 billion stock swap in 1981, at the time one of the larger mergers of consumer-product companies. Technically, it was a marriage of equals. But that was considered so much chin music. Everyone knew Nabisco, with dominant brands such as Ritz and Oreo, was the more powerful company. Everyone knew who would be in charge.

Nabisco had been born a juggernaut. The National Biscuit Co., as it was originally called, was formed in 1898, the result of a transaction that merged one company that owned most of the nation's major eastern bakers with another that owned most of the major western ones—and ended the cutthroat competition between the two. A product of the turn-of-the-century trust era, Nabisco was often called "the biscuit trust." Yet it was also the biscuit pioneer, taking the cracker out of the cracker barrel and for the first time making it a packaged, standardized commodity. It was the first company to bring national marketing and distribution to a hitherto regional product.

The man who created Nabisco was a Chicago lawyer, Adolphus Green. Green, the company's first chairman, took a personal hand in inventing the octagonal soda cracker that was the company's first national product. Uneeda Biscuit, he called it. He selected a company trademark still used today, a medieval Italian printers' symbol consisting of a cross with two bars and an oval, representing the triumph of the moral and spiritual over the evil and the material. He designed the packaging and drafted the wording on the box: "Uneeda Biscuit. Served with every meal; take a box with you on your travels; splendid for sandwiches; perfect for picnics; unequalled for general use; do not contain sugar. This is a perfect food for everybody, and the price places them within the reach of all."

N. W. Ayer, Nabisco's advertising agency, took it from there. In early 1899, it placed a one-word ad in newspapers and on billboards: "Uneeda." Then the next step: "Uneeda Biscuit." Then, "Do you know Uneeda Biscuit?" After that: "Of course Uneeda Biscuit!" Ayer went on to present an ad campaign that showed a little boy in a slicker with a box of

Uneeda Biscuits, a simple, powerful image in an age before Madison Avenue had come to full flower. At the time it was the biggest ad campaign ever, and the first to feature a packaged ready-to-eat food.

Uneeda Biscuit was a smashing success, and set the stage for a torrent of new Nabisco products: the Fig Newton, made by a Boston baker, named in honor of that city's suburb of Newton; the Saltine cracker, from a St. Joseph, Missouri, baker; Animal Crackers, by two of the company's New York City bakers. Nabisco was the first company to figure a way to mass-produce shortbread, and the result was Lorna Doone, an immediate hit. It concocted a combination of marshmallow and jelly, covered with chocolate icing, and named it Mallomar. Even its flops had a silver lining. In 1913, Green came out with a package of three new products known collectively as "Trio." He had high hopes for two of them in particular: the Mother Goose Biscuit, which would depict scenes from nursery rhymes, and the Veronese Biscuit, an upscale hard cookie. But it was the third cookie in the trio, which featured vanilla frosting between two round chocolate wafers, that caught on. It would become the bestselling cookie in the world: the Oreo.

Green pioneered the idea of using a direct sales force in the food business rather than a middleman, dispatching salesmen to push Nabisco products across the country. Beginning with the Uneeda Cadets, Nabisco mustered a huge, hardworking army of salesmen who made their appointed rounds in horse-drawn wagons with freshly painted Nabisco logos six days a week, twelve hours a day.

A man who referred to his workers as "a great family," Green made Nabisco a benevolent employer. Within three years of its founding, he installed a system for the company's employees to buy stock on cut-rate terms, making them what he called "associate proprietors." He refused to employ child labor in an era when it was common. And although he expected his workers to churn out America's snacks from dawn to dusk, in brutally hot and often hazardous bakeries, he also felt responsible for providing them nutritious meals. "In our New York plant," he wrote in a report to shareholders, "an employee can obtain a dinner consisting of hot meat, potatoes, bread and butter, and coffee or tea for 11 cents."

Green died in 1917, and with him went much of Nabisco's innovative spirit. His successor, a lawyer named Roy Tomlinson, was less interested in biscuits than the bottom line. Profits quadrupled through the 1920s, but Nabisco was coasting on the enormous success of its early products and on its sales force. When it needed new products, it bought them, including Shredded Wheat in 1928 and Milk Bone dog biscuits in 1931.

Then, in the midst of the Depression, Nabisco's bakers came up with something novel. For years they had been trying to develop buttery crackers like those of some of their competitors. The result, covered with a thin coating of coconut oil and sprinkled with salt, was a completely new kind of cracker. They called it Ritz, and it became America's most popular cracker almost overnight. Within a year, Nabisco had baked 5 million of them. Within three years, it was baking 29 million of them a *day*, and Ritz became the bestselling cracker in the world.

But again the company rested on its laurels. For the next decade Nabisco drifted, paying its dividends, keeping out of debt, and baking the same cookies and crackers it had for years. Eventually profits dropped, its bakeries aged, and so did its management. By the mid-1940s, the average age of Nabisco's top executives was sixty-three; they were known as "the nine old men." Only when Tomlinson retired, after twenty-eight years, did the company stir again.

Yet another lawyer, general counsel George Coppers, was installed by the board as chief executive in 1945. Coppers had taken weekend management courses at the Harvard Business School and set about reshaping Nabisco with what he had learned. He cleared out the nine old men and brought in a wave of new young ones. Over a twelve-year period he spent $200 million to modernize the bakeries, real money in those days. All the funds came from profits: Perish the thought of debt at good, conservative Nabisco. Coppers allotted huge budgets to research and advertising, dragging down profits but creating a foundation for the future. By the time it built its last new cookie and cracker plant, in Fair Lawn, New Jersey, in 1958, Nabisco had cut its costs, improved its quality, and heaved its way into the latter part of the twentieth century. By 1960, the year Coppers died, *Dun's Review* recognized Nabisco as one of the twenty best-managed companies in the country.

One of Coppers's bright young men, an Idaho Mormon named Lee Bickmore, now took the helm. Bickmore began his Nabisco career as a shipping clerk in Pocatello and went on to become a salesman, pushing Ritz and Oreos in obscure corners of Utah, Wyoming, and Idaho. It was only when he wrote an earnest letter to New York headquarters, full of suggestions about training and techniques for salesmen, that he gained notice.

As president, Bickmore expanded Nabisco into foreign markets: Australia in 1960, England and New Zealand in 1962, Germany in 1964, and Italy, Spain, and Central America in 1965. He spent so much time on overseas travel he became known as "The Flying President." Bickmore also diversified, moving into frozen foods and making Nabisco the largest shower-curtain maker in the world. He took on a carpeting business and a toy business. He bought a company called J. B. Williams, which made personal-care products such as Aqua Velva shaving lotion and Geritol.

It all bombed—the foreign operations, the shower curtains, the toys, everything. To make up for the losses, Bickmore squeezed Nabisco's cookie and cracker divisions for every penny of profit. He squeezed so hard, in fact, that they began to crumble. The Coppers-era bakeries were deteriorating, and Nabisco no longer had the profits to modernize or replace them. Even after Bickmore retired in 1973, little changed. In the seventies Nabisco was run by decent, slow-moving executives who fostered a culture that venerated past glories. Good men all, but change agents they weren't. As one of its ad agency executives put it, "How could somebody who makes Oreos be mean?"

Nabisco stagnated. No one was fired. No one worked past five. No one raised a voice. No one, not even the new chief executive, Bob Schaeberle, had doors on his office. No one, not even Schaeberle, had a company car or a corporate country club membership.

Then along came Ross Johnson. It was, one wag noted, as if Hell's Angels had merged with the Rotary Club.

Bob Schaeberle became chairman and chief executive of Nabisco Brands, Ross Johnson president and chief operating officer. Below him, as the two companies combined their managements, Johnson's Merry Men were positively grouchy.

For one thing, Nabisco's morning meetings began around eight-thirty, in the midst of their hangovers. In contrast to Standard Brands's free-for-all bull sessions, Nabisco's deliberations were carefully choreographed. Executives sat around a table, each making a fifteen-minute presentation on a particular cookie or cracker. At the end of each, questions were invited. Rarely were there any; it seemed bad form. It would drone on like this into midafternoon, with a break for lunch. Johnson often arranged to be summoned from the room by a phone call, never to return, leaving

Rogers and Carbonell and the others to silently squirm.

Then one day, John Murray, the Standard Brands vice president for sales, could stand no more. It came during an especially tiresome discourse on procedures for closing company offices during snowstorms. In the event of a bad storm, a Nabisco executive said, workers would be given notice that offices would close in a matter of hours. That enabled those who needed rides a chance to line them up, and gave the company a chance to organize van pools and bring the day to an orderly conclusion. Obviously pleased with himself, the executive invited questions.

"I can't fucking believe this!" Murray exploded. "If it's dangerous out there, don't wait two hours; close the place down. Nobody's going to do shit for those two hours, anyway. That's fucking ridiculous." A stunned silence ensued. Finally Jim Welch, a senior Nabisco executive chairing the meeting, broke it. "I agree with John one hundred percent," he said.

It was one of the first shots of the cultural revolution that would transform Nabisco. Meetings began to loosen up. Murray would be detailing the performance of Fleischmann's Margarine, only to be interrupted by a shout from Peter Rogers: "Tell 'em about Blue Bonnet Baking Margarine." That brand, of course, was faring poorly. Nabisco executives prided themselves on the company's elaborate planning procedures, compiled in thick, multiyear projections and operations outlooks. Johnson chucked them all. "Planning, gentlemen, is 'What are you going to do next year that's different from what you did this year?' " he told them. "All I want is five items."

On paper Schaeberle remained the top executive of Nabisco Brands, but Johnson found it easy to get his way. Their offices were adjacent, and Johnson wasted no time ingratiating himself with the boss. He deferred to Schaeberle in every regard, obsequiously addressing him in meetings as "Mr. Chairman." Johnson's many country club memberships were paid for by the company; he insisted that Schaeberle's dues be picked up, too. They were. Johnson and his executives drove flashy company cars; he insisted Schaeberle and his aides do so, too. They did. Johnson donated $250,000 to Pace University to endow a Robert M. Schaeberle Chair in accounting. Surprised by the announcement at a Pace dinner, an honored but stunned Schaeberle said, "Who's going to pay for this?"

The company was, of course. The company also had to vastly upgrade its pay scale, since thirty-six Standard Brands executives made more than $100,000 compared to fifteen Nabisco ones. Johnson's base pay was more than double Schaeberle's, requiring a vast raise for the chairman. He accepted it reluctantly, but later balked when told his 1983 salary and bonus would total more than $1 million. What would the shareholders say? Schaeberle ordered that his bonus be cut enough to get him back into six figures. Johnson talked him out of it, saying he had it coming to him. If Schaeberle made a million, Johnson had it coming to him as well, of course.

Johnson continued to upgrade his own life-style, buying a huge French chateau-style house with a forty-acre estate in Sparta, New Jersey. He attempted to commute via helicopter to Nabisco's headquarters in East Hanover, New Jersey, but was thwarted when town fathers repeatedly refused to allow helicopters to land there.

Slowly but surely, Johnson closed his grip around Schaeberle's company. One by one, veteran Nabisco executives began to vanish, replaced by Johnson men. The fall of Nabisco's powerful chief financial officer, Dick Owens, was a prime example of the way Johnson worked. At the time of the merger, Owens appeared to be at the height of his powers. He was made an executive vice president and sat on the combined companies' board. Whatever Owens wanted, Johnson got him. He approved a steady stream of Owens's requests for new aides: a senior vice president here, a vice president there, a veritable raft of assistant vice presidents. In Johnson's warm embrace, Owens's financial fiefdom grew steadily.

Then one day Johnson walked into Schaeberle's office with his brow furrowed. "Dick is building up a huge financial organization," Johnson fretted. With unassailable logic, he laid out the dangers of substituting the analysis and judgments of people at headquarters for those of line managers. "We shouldn't be doing the numbers for the business managers," Johnson suggested.

"Well," Schaeberle asked, "what should we do?"

"I think Dick is congenitally incapable of decentralizing," replied Johnson. "I think we need to make a change."

And so Owens was shunted aside, replaced, for a time, by Johnson himself. Johnson immediately installed Standard Brands people beneath him, and replaced Nabisco's financial controls with a system devised at Standard Brands. Only Standard Brands people seemed to understand the new system, which suited Johnson fine. Having changed the playbook, Johnson's troops now emerged victorious in a string of minor bureaucratic battles. "At any meeting," recalled a former Johnson lieutenant, "you could embarrass the Nabisco guys."

Johnson had Standard Brands's Dean Posvar named planning director, a job that put Posvar—and thus Johnson—in charge of board presentations and enabled the Johnson troops to define and thus control board discussion. Johnson's crony Mike Masterpool took over public relations, giving him control of the outward dissemination of information as surely as Posvar's planning group and the financial apparatus regulated the inner flow.

It was the same story all the way down the line, thanks to another Johnson move. Schaeberle had originally planned to keep Nabisco and Standard Brands operations separate within the combined company. But on Johnson's suggestion, they were integrated. As departments were combined, the timid Nabisco executives were forced to swim with the Standard Brands sharks. When choices for a top position had to be made, Johnson walked into Schaeberle's office and, while insisting he wasn't playing favorites, laid out a compelling case for the Standard Brands man. "You're right," Schaeberle would say. "This guy is better."

To some who caught Johnson's act during this period, he was less a business dynamo than a corporate Eddie Haskell, sucking up to Schaeberle while kicking the Beaver in the teeth. Whatever the case, it worked: Within three years, twenty-one of the company's top twenty-four officers were Standard Brands men. The Nabisco officers had been killed so softly that Schaeberle never realized what had happened. At meetings, he would say, "It's so great to see all these young people around the table."

As Johnson's power grew, much of Nabisco's future began to be planned at all-night drinking sessions at his apartment. The roster hadn't changed much in ten years. There was Peter Rogers, still The Rook; Martin Emmett, The Big E; and Bob Carbonell, El Supremo, among others. Johnson, The Pope, used the sessions to throw out all manner of ideas—for restructuring the company, for hastening the Old Guard's exit, for new products. Many were profanely hooted down, and Johnson, sipping Scotch, would cheerfully withdraw and move to the next.

Even as he reshaped its executive suite, Johnson moved to mold Nabisco's business mix to his own tastes. On its face it was an impossible task—Nabisco's vast, entrenched bureaucracy seemed impervious to change—but with his newfound sway over Schaeberle, Johnson made steady progress. It was always Johnson initiating, Schaeberle assenting; Johnson spinning out sweet reason, Schaeberle accepting it. "You know, it just doesn't make sense to have anything that's not number one or number two in its industry," Johnson would say. "That's right, Ross," Schaeberle would reply.

In the last quarter of 1982 alone, Johnson sold J. B. Williams, Freezer Queen frozen foods, Julius Wile wine and spirits, Hygiene Industries shower curtains, and Everlon Fabrics draperies. At the same time, he cut loose some of Standard Brands's old businesses: Chase & Sanborn and high-fructose syrup. Johnson discovered he was an excellent auctioneer. Nobody thought that J. B. Williams, home of over-the-hill brands such as Geritol and Aqua Velva, would fetch more than $50 million. But Johnson unloaded it for twice that, applying his usual charm and telling potential buyers how badly Nabisco had been running the business. He convinced them that Williams had worlds of unexploited potential. "I learned," he said, "you always tell people how badly you've been running the goddamned company, so they've got some upside."

As successful as his manipulations were, Johnson could see it would take something like wartime conditions to attain a complete overhaul of Nabisco Brands. To his surprise, he soon reached that juncture in a period that came to be known as "the cookie wars."

Nabisco had fairly invited attack on its position atop the multibillion-dollar cookie business. It had grown soft: Its bakeries were old, its profit margins were big, and it dominated its few competitors. The company's Pearl Harbor came in Kansas City. The attacker was Frito-Lay, the nation's premier salty-snack maker, home of brands such as Ruffles, Doritos, and Tostitos. Frito-Lay hit the Kansas City shelves in mid-1982 with a new line of soft cookies called Grandma's. Cocky Frito executives boasted publicly how quickly Grandma's would thrash Nabisco, which didn't make a soft cookie. Nabisco's lock on the cookie business, they predicted, would break, and the $2.5 billion market would become "a Coke–Pepsi kind of thing." The Frito generals looked as good as their word in the early days, capturing 20 percent of the Kansas City market.

Even as Johnson scrambled to meet that onslaught, another attacker struck. Procter & Gamble, the Cincinnati consumer goods giant, unveiled its own Duncan Hines line of soft cookies. P&G began construction on a massive bakery, applied for a patent on its cookies, and started its own assault on Kansas City. Within days the city became a cookie-crazed battleground. Spurred on by coupons, special displays, and advertising, Kansas City consumers were buying 20 percent more cookies.

Nabisco was getting clobbered. But Johnson, as always, remained upbeat and confident. There were problems with soft cookies nobody had yet focused on, he assured Nabisco's worried directors. He told them how he had eaten some of the competitors' cookies late one morning, then gone off to lunch depressed because they tasted so good. When he returned later, he found the remaining cookies stale.

"Well, how stale were they?" a director asked.

"Ever try biting into a hockey puck?" Johnson replied. Everyone roared. The Pope was already a board favorite.

At first all Johnson could do to retaliate was to cram more chips into Nabisco's Chips Ahoy chocolate chip cookies. In the meantime, he used the wartime footing as an excuse to rid the company's top echelons of its remaining Nabisco veterans. "Look," he told Schaeberle, "the guys that got you in trouble aren't going to get you out of it." Schaeberle, as always, agreed. Peter Rogers was brought in to head the war effort, while Carbonell flogged the R&D people to develop Nabisco's own soft cookie.

By mid-1983, Nabisco was ready to counterattack. With the introduction of its own soft cookie entry, Almost Home, it joined the battle for Kansas City. "It was a holocaust," Johnson would later recall. "P&G would coupon one dollar, we'd coupon a dollar fifty. Bodies flying all over the place." Johnson didn't care what the coupons cost. He didn't care what overtime his salesman put in for. Nabisco was going to take back those shelves.

In the end Johnson and Nabisco lost the struggle for Kansas City. But they won the war. The two newcomers didn't have the mass production and distribution systems in place to quickly go national. Once Nabisco had a product, it established impenetrable beachheads in city after city before the competition could arrive. By 1984, the cookie wars were all but over.

As the smoke cleared, Johnson emerged triumphant, both inside and outside Nabisco. As far as Schaeberle and the board were concerned, he could do no wrong. That year Schaeberle rewarded Johnson by ceding him the title of chief executive. Nabisco's huge new research center was about to be unveiled, and Johnson, in a spasm of flattery, repaid the favor by naming it the Robert M. Schaeberle Technology Center. Schaeberle was moved. The Merry Men thought it was a brilliant way to put Schaeberle out to pasture. A man who had his name on a building, they reasoned, might as well be dead.

After only a decade in New York, Johnson had achieved the pinnacle of success: CEO of one of America's great food companies. He was a new breed of chief executive for a new age of American business. The old-timers at Standard Brands had seen themselves as corporate stewards. "Your company is the ship," they would say, "the chief executive is only the captain." That steady-as-she-goes ethos was fine for men scarred by the 1930s and scared to make waves. But Johnson, like many of his peers, hadn't lived through a Depression, hadn't fought a world war, and wasn't about to acknowledge limits. He was no old-style team player but a Broadway Joe or Reggie Jax, an iconoclastic superstar, a cool, television-age man loyal to little but his own whims.

To outsiders, he was the same old backslapping Ross. In his early fifties, he was tall and slim and wore his silvery hair boyishly long. The only hint of Canada was in his voice: he said "bean" instead of "been," sprinkled his jokes with the British "bloody," and occasionally ended a sentence with "eh?"

But even as he assumed Nabisco's throne, Johnson seemed to lose interest in running it. Glitz now fascinated him far more than Ritz. If they weren't off with Gifford and a girlfriend, the Johnsons were on a Mediterranean vacation with Jim Robinson of American Express and his wife Linda, then an up-and-coming Wall Street public relations expert. Among the Johnsons' closest friends were Canadian Prime Minister Brian Mulroney and his wife, Mila. Mila and Laurie Johnson would prowl Manhattan, power shopping for the prime minister's residence. Nabisco began sponsoring the Dinah Shore women's golf tournament, and Johnson transformed it into a star-studded affair. His growing stable of celebrity athletes, now called Team Nabisco, was paraded about at the tournament. Gerald Ford and Bob Hope graced the Pro-Am. Johnson's friend Oleg Cassini put him on a billboard.

Johnson had always loved rubbing shoulders with celebrities, of course. But in the past there had been a sense that it stemmed from his recognizing the foibles of the upper class. He would return from an elite social occasion in Britain giggling about how the royal family was "all fucked up," or telling tales of that crazy Maggie Thatcher: "A pisser," he would chortle. The Merry Men, mired in cookies and crackers, loved it, even while some of them began to worry their man was becoming more an insider of the circles he ridiculed than an outsider.

If Johnson grew indifferent toward Nabisco, it was because he could no longer see much of a future in it. The cookie wars had changed his thinking; he regarded the battle with Frito-Lay and P&G not as a final victory, but as the successful deflection of a shot fired across his bow. There would be another giant like Procter & Gamble—maybe even P&G itself—that would come after him again. Nabisco, after all, had fatal weaknesses. No amount of work was going to revitalize its aging bakeries anytime soon. Johnson, in fact, never bothered to formulate any kind of master plan for reshaping Nabisco. Years of scrambling had soured him on long-range planning. Instead he spent his time enjoying the high life, putting out corporate fires as they flared, and waiting.

Someone had once codified the Standard Brands culture into twenty Johnsonisms. Number thirteen was "Recognize that ultimate success comes from opportunistic, bold moves which, by definition, cannot be planned."

On a spring day in 1985, less than a year after being tapped Nabisco's chief, Johnson took a call from J. Tylee Wilson, chairman and chief executive officer of RJ Reynolds Industries, the North Carolina–based tobacco giant. Would Johnson be interested in getting together for lunch? Maybe, Wilson said, they could do some business.

CHAPTER

2

Imagine you lived in this great old house. You grew up in it, and all your happy
memories are in it, and you take special care of it for the next generation. Then
one day, you come home to discover it's been turned into a brothel. That's how
I feel about RJR.   —*A former RJR Nabisco employee in Winston-Salem*

If not for the RJ Reynolds Tobacco Company, the modest skyline of
downtown Winston-Salem, North Carolina, would not exist at all. For
years the business was headquartered in a twenty-two-story stone building
that, when completed in 1929, was considered such an architectural gem
it was decided to take the design to New York and execute it on a grander
scale: the Empire State Building.

On one side of the miniature Empire State is the stolid headquarters
of Wachovia Bank & Trust. Its vaults stuffed with Reynolds stock and
deposits, Wachovia grew to be one of the South's preeminent banks.
On the far side of the Reynolds building is a taller, more modern structure that houses the overflow of employees from headquarters. Two
blocks away rises a glass-sheathed skyscraper that is the tallest in town.
Its anchor tenant is Womble, Carlyle, Sandridge & Rice, North Carolina's biggest law firm, whose practice is firmly anchored in Reynolds
Tobacco.

If not for Reynolds, Winston-Salem would be like a lot of other little
southern cities of 140,000 souls. Except for the demiskyscrapers, the
downtown is largely scruffy—a place of tired old stores and tired old

40

people. Reynolds makes Winston-Salem different.

From downtown, its influence ripples out in all directions. Travel west, along Interstate 40, where every third billboard is devoted to Reynolds brands, and the Bowman Gray School of Medicine rises into view. An eminent teaching hospital and research center, it is named for the former Reynolds chairman who bequeathed it. Farther west is the exit for Tangle-wood, a sprawling park donated to the county by the brother of R. J. Reynolds, William. "Mr. Will," as he is still known forty years after his death, made it clear that Tanglewood was to be used by the *white* people of the county.

Travel north along Reynolda Road toward the estate of R. J. Reynolds himself—"Mr. RJ," he is called, seventy years after his death. His sprawl-ing mansion, Reynolda House, holds one of the nation's finest collections of American paintings. Its grounds are host to the city's most exclusive country club, Old Town. There's room left over on the estate for the campus of Wake Forest University, which the Reynolds family brought to Winston-Salem from 100 miles away in the 1950s. Along Reynolda Road, the model farm that R. J. Reynolds's wife—"Mrs. RJ"—once set up has been converted into a collection of toney boutiques, along with the offices that administer the public service component of the Reynolds family fortune. The Z. Smith Reynolds Foundation gives millions each year for good works in North Carolina, as does the Mary Reynolds Bab-cock Foundation. A fine French restaurant called La Chaudière is housed in the Reynolds farm's old boiler room and offers Winston and Salem cigarettes to its customers gratis. Many people accept. This is, after all, a town where the occasional sign says, "Thank you for smoking."

The Reynolds influence ripples into the poor side of town as well. Mister Will may have better remembered the white people, but he also donated money to start the Kate Bitting Reynolds Hospital for the blacks. (The hospital no longer exists, but the Kate B. Reynolds Trust distributes one-quarter of the income from its 2.4 million RJR shares to the city's "poor and needy.") R.J. Reynolds High School, in a rich neighborhood, provides the city's best secondary education. But James A. Gray High School—named for a former RJR chairman—for years provided good schooling for the lower strata. On its grounds now stands the North Carolina School of the Arts. RJR donations help maintain this well-regarded fine arts training institute.

On a humid summer morning, when there's no breeze to carry it away, the pungent smell of tobacco still hangs over downtown Winston-Salem, wafting from the company's oldest tobacco factory, still in operation down the hill from the little Empire State Building. It serves as one constant reminder why there *is* a Winston-Salem. A few blocks away, in front of City Hall, stands another: the statue of Richard Joshua Reynolds riding into town on horseback.

He rode into Winston-Salem in 1874, a twenty-four-year-old Virginian attracted by some of the best tobacco-growing land in the country. At six feet two inches, R. J. Reynolds cut an imposing figure as he moved through the dusty streets of the burgeoning town. He had grown up sixty miles north in Rock Springs, just across the state line. His father owned a chewing-tobacco factory there, and Reynolds spent his youth learning the business. Business wasn't easy in the hardscrabble world of the post–Civil War South. Cash was scarce and hard-driving ingenuity was required. The young R. J. Reynolds had just that, showing a brilliant talent for bartering. Sent out on the road with a wagonload of chewing tobacco, he returned with an even bigger wagonload of goods in exchange: beeswax, cowhides, sheep pelts, ginseng, carpets, and furniture, along with three or four horses and mules hitched on behind. Back at Rock Springs, it was all auctioned off for a 25 percent profit.

Although R. J. Reynolds had grown up in the Old South—as a child he hid family horses in the woods to escape marauding Union troops—he was a creature of the emerging New South: less agrarian and more entrepreneurial, less rooted and more restless. The day he rode into town, Reynolds had big plans. He knew the flue-cured leaves in the nearby fields were increasingly popular with tobacco chewers. He knew the town had an auction house that would give him access to supply. And he knew a railroad line there could connect him with markets. Within days he bought a plot of land from the Moravian church for $388, and began building a factory. A year later, in 1875, the RJ Reynolds Tobacco Co. was in business, along with its share of competitors: In this bustling town of 2,500, there were already fifteen tobacco companies.

Even in this crowded field, R. J. Reynolds distinguished himself. He innovated, becoming the first to devise a way to make chewing tobacco sweeter, by blending in saccharin. He expanded aggressively, always keeping the capacity of his factory well ahead of current production, and he worked hard, for years living above the factory floor. He played hard, too, drinking deeply, gambling heavily, squiring around different women. He literally drove himself hard, making his way through the countryside with a double team of horses for extra speed. (At an 1890 meeting of the Reynolds board, directors authorized spending $240 a year for Reynolds's horse team, the equivalent of today's corporate jet.) The only thing R. J. Reynolds did slowly was speak, in an effort to overcome a lifelong stutter.

The combination of Mr. RJ's business acumen with the area's tenacious Moravian work ethic laid the foundation of the Reynolds corporate culture for decades to come. The Moravians had arrived here in 1753 to settle 100,000 acres of land they bought from Lord Granville of England. These Czechoslovakian immigrants sought not only religious freedom, in the Piedmont region of central Carolina, but also economic self-sufficiency. They were a stubborn, industrious people, skilled at manufacturing and trading and making do. They made Salem important enough that by the 1800s a railroad line ran westward to it from the larger town of Raleigh.

To a great extent, the policies of Reynolds Tobacco mirrored strong Moravian values. The Moravians believed in the individual subsuming himself for the good of the community, in being conservative in personal bearing as well as in finances. They founded a solid bank called Wachovia, named after a region in the old country, and, when the two towns merged a few years later, gave Winston-Salem a feeling unlike that of other Bible Belt towns. It was more progressive, for the Moravians were great believers in education. They established Salem Female Academy, the first women's college in the region. R. J. Reynolds and his Moravian workers made a great team, and by the 1890s their company was the clear leader among the area's many tobacco companies.

In fact, Reynolds Tobacco grew fast enough that it came to be coveted, as it would a century later, by a ravenous Northern suitor. The 1890s saw the rise of James B. ("Buck") Duke's national tobacco trust, which grew by gobbling up regional tobacco companies like RJ Reynolds. Buck Duke's roots were down the road in Durham, North Carolina, but he had moved his American Tobacco Company to New York to develop the financial contacts that would enable him to expand nationwide. As he became more successful, Duke modeled his tobacco trust after John D. Rockefeller's Standard Oil and soon effectively controlled the nation's fledgling cigarette market. Buck Duke then turned his attention to taking over the chewing-tobacco business.

R. J. Reynolds saw the threat and vowed to fight. "If Buck Duke tries to swallow me he will have the bellyache the balance of his life," he vowed. Then, inexplicably, Mr. RJ made a secret trip to New York in 1899 and cut a deal that gave Duke's trust a two-thirds stake in Reynolds Tobacco for $3 million. Apparently Reynolds agreed to sell out because he felt he needed more capital to grow and because he was guaranteed operating control of his company. Buck Duke might think R. J. Reynolds was working for him, but Mr. RJ had other ideas. Under the trust's control, he went on a buying spree, snapping up a host of local competitors and becoming the biggest employer in North Carolina. The price of that expansion was a regimen of quarterly trips northward to report to Buck Duke's people, the detested "New York crowd."

R. J. Reynolds may have hated Yankee control, but there was no question he thrived under it. He now dreamed up the idea of a nationally distributed pipe tobacco. After supervising its secret mixture, he picked a name for it—Prince Albert, after the popular prince of Wales, who had become the British monarch, Edward VII—and personally hunted down a suitable picture of the prince (at a tea party with Mark Twain) to be used as the model for the label. For the first time, the company retained a big New York agency, N. W. Ayer, to conduct a national ad campaign. In *The Saturday Evening Post, Collier's,* and other magazines, Prince Albert was proclaimed as the "Joy Smoke" that "can't bite your tongue." In a full-court press on distributors and retailers, Reynolds offered sweet discount incentives for them to load up on Prince Albert and threatened dire consequences if they didn't. Customers would be very unhappy if they didn't stock it, the company warned, because "we control the process that takes the tongue blistering bite out of tobacco—so there can't be even a near substitute." Much like Nabisco's experience with Uneeda Biscuit, Mr. RJ's plan to go national was a huge success. Annual production of Prince Albert grew from 250,000 pounds in 1907 to more than 14 million by 1911.

But the far bigger news that year was the demise of the carpetbagger, Buck Duke. After years of attempting to break Duke's stranglehold on the tobacco industry, Teddy Roosevelt's "trustbusters" finally succeeded. When a U.S. Appeals Court granted Reynolds Tobacco its independence, there was unrestrained joy in Winston-Salem. Reynolds salesmen were told of the trust's dissolution in a letter headed "News of Freedom."

"Now watch me," a gleeful Mr. RJ told his Moravian executives, "see if I don't give Buck Duke hell." A few days later, just as darkness fell over Manhattan, a giant new electrical advertising display was switched on. There, towering over the city, was Prince Albert himself in a great glow, with these words at his feet: "The Nation's Joy Smoke, R.J. Reynolds Tobacco Company, Winston-Salem, N.C."

Free from the grip of Northern interlopers, Mr. RJ immediately moved to ensure that his company would never again fall into the hands of "the New York crowd." He began force-feeding Reynolds stock to its employees. "You should have an interest in this company," he told them as he arranged for bank loans to buy stock. Never mind that many workers didn't want to go into hock; Mr. RJ said he knew what was best, and he did. As the value of Reynolds stock ballooned in coming years, Winston-Salem came to be known as "the city of the reluctant millionaires."

Soon Mr. RJ went even further, creating a "Class A" stock—known locally as anticipation stock—designed to put all voting power in the hands of the workers. It paid an extraordinarily rich dividend: 10 percent of all profits in excess of $2.2 million. Workers clamored for the new issue, and many used their salaries to buy all the Class A they could. The annual dividend payment became a kind of local holiday, a time local car dealers and luxury purveyors eagerly awaited. The story was told of a Winston-Salem tyke who received a horde of presents on Christmas morning, only to begin weeping uncontrollably. He said he'd had his heart set on Class A stock. From the early 1920s until the IRS disallowed the Class A in the 1950s, Reynolds employees controlled the majority of the company's stock.

In return for its security, Reynolds took special care of its workers. The company loaned employees up to two-thirds the value of their property, operated lunchrooms at cost, and always had ice water on hand in the steamy tobacco factories. It provided day care for the children of women workers—one for the whites, of course, and one for the blacks. Reynolds even ran a supervised rooming house for country girls who came to Winston-Salem to work, and provided housing for another 180 families at cost. Many of these reforms were personally orchestrated by Mr. RJ's young wife, Katharine.

In the context of its age, Reynolds was a remarkable institution. At a time when the South was desperately poor and mired in an agrarian economy, here was a company taking an indigenous agricultural product and making it a major industrial business. At a time when southern businesses were generally controlled by absentee Yankee owners, here was a company under local control raining cash on its community. By 1913, a quarter of Winston-Salem's 25,000 residents worked at RJ Reynolds.

It was in that year that Mr. RJ, then sixty-three, took his biggest gamble yet on a new product: the cigarette. At the time, there was little demand for manufactured cigarettes in packages because smokers preferred to roll their own. The only brands on the market were regional and weren't thought to taste very good. But Mr. RJ, fresh off Prince Albert's success, thought a cigarette with an appealing taste just might sell nationally. Riding herd on the project himself, he experimented with a wide variety of tobaccos before coming up with just the right mix, an exotic blend of locally grown, Kentucky-grown burley, and Turkish tobaccos. Playing up the latter's mysterious Eastern connotation, he called it Camel, and when the Barnum & Bailey Circus came to Winston-Salem that year, a photographer snapped a picture of a dromedary for the pack.

Camel got an added boost from N. W. Ayer, which applied the same gusto to it that it had with Prince Albert and Uneeda Biscuit. Ayer introduced the cigarette into each market with a series of teaser ads: first the word "Camels," then "The Camels are coming!" with the dromedary picture, then "Tomorrow there'll be more Camels in this town than in all Asia and Africa combined!" and finally "Camel cigarettes are here!" with a description of the cigarette's virtues and price. It was breathless and brazen and, by modern standards, hokey. But it made the first national cigarette a major event. Reynolds sold twenty Camels for a dime, undercutting other brands by a full nickel. Soon, its nearest three competitors wallowed and died; Camel was a phenomenon. Within a year, Reynolds was selling 425 million packs a year. Camel became the first cigarette brand to be sold by the carton. Reynolds secured the exclusive concession on shipping cigarettes to the American troops fighting World War I in Europe. Mr. RJ had scored again, redefining and revolutionizing the tobacco business.

Furious competitors tried everything to kill Camel. Buck Duke's American Tobacco was suspected of spreading rumors that workers in the Camel factory had leprosy and syphilis. Another rumor, that there was saltpeter in Camels, received some currency. Outraged, Mr. RJ fought back, offering $500 rewards for identification of the stories' source. "The

Stench of a Contemptible Slanderer is Repulsive Even to the Nostrils of a Buzzard," one of his combative posters proclaimed.

It was his last great fight. In 1918 Mr. RJ succumbed to cancer of the pancreas. But as he was dying, he was pleased with what he had done and confident that, if run correctly, the company would never again slip into the hands of scalawags. "I have written the book," he said. "All you need to do is follow it."

The company's management soon fell out of family hands. Mr. Will became chairman, but preferred to devote his time to breeding horses. Mr. RJ's first son, Dick, took more to politics than business, becoming mayor of Winston-Salem and treasurer of the Democratic National Committee. His second, Zachary Smith Reynolds, was a noted playboy and aviator. He married a torch singer named Libby Holman and was shot to death, at age twenty, under strange and scandalous circumstances. His wife was indicted for murder but never tried. His name now graces the Winston-Salem airport.

The burden of running Reynolds Tobacco fell to a succession of locally grown executives, several handpicked by Mr. RJ before his death. The first was Bowman Gray, a family favorite. Gray was a details man who had neither the dynamism nor the imagination to ignite real growth, but he did keep Reynolds on an even keel, slipping into his downtown office well before dawn each day and staying until well after dusk. His brother, James Gray, was a top banker at Wachovia, and the bank's interests became indistinguishable from Reynolds's. (Gray would later come over to run Reynolds.) Wachovia's executive committee, a select group of Reynoldses and Grays and Moravian elders, became the town's ruling elite. Its members belonged to the prestigious Old Town Club and summered at Roaring Gap, in the mountains sixty miles away. They married in a tight circle, until the various branches of family trees became thoroughly entangled.

This, of course, fostered a virulent strain of parochialism that haunts Winston-Salem to this day. A top Reynolds executive during the 1930s got that way in part by marrying Will Reynolds's niece; he got fired in part because he wouldn't live in Winston-Salem. Insulated from the outside world, the company was slow to pick up on trends, most seriously when it overlooked an emerging market for women smokers (even though the bank robber Bonnie Parker was known to be a Camel devotee and once toured its factory while on the lam). As a result, Camel forfeited its lead in the cigarette business and was passed as the nation's best-seller by American Tobacco's Lucky Strikes in 1929. Aided by a small New York ad agency headed by William Esty, Reynolds launched a furious counterattack and recaptured the top spot in the 1930s. The Reynolds-Esty alliance kept the company's brands competitive for more than fifty years.

The little burg was enormously proud of its big company, calling itself "Camel City." Factory workers in overalls walked into stockbrokers' offices with paper bags full of cash and "buy" orders for Reynolds Tobacco. A factory worker named Hobert Johnson was one of the company's biggest shareholders for years, snapping up all the Class A stock he could afford every time some became available. Shares were handed from one generation to the next, with an admonition: "Don't you *ever* sell that Reynolds stock."

The community's Moravian values became, if anything, even more imbued in the company. *Work:* Competitors' tobacco buyers returned home and goofed off after the eight-month tobacco-auction season. Reynolds's were assigned to cull the tobacco leaves they had bought, forcing them to contemplate the quality of their labors. *Thrift:* Reynolds workers were expected to turn in the stub of a pencil to get a new one. A young manager running a small fan in his office on a sultry summer day was admonished to unplug it. A waste of electricity. *Ingenuity:* The company developed a way to recycle scraps and stems of tobacco to greatly increase the usable amount of each leaf—and greatly increase profits. "Reconstituted tobacco," as it was called, was considered classic Reynolds: a blend of its manufacturing know-how and its waste-not, want-not culture.

This was not, to be sure, paradise on the Piedmont. After Bowman Gray died in the mid-1930s, Reynolds endured more than a decade of tepid management. Among the workers there had always been minor grumbling: W-S, as Winston-Salem was sometimes abbreviated, stood for Work and Sleep, they joked. During the forties, the factory work force was briefly unionized; Reynolds spent much of the decade trying to break the union's back, succeeding only when its leaders were tarred as communists. The distraction cost them, however, as sales fell behind those of archrival American Tobacco.

But not for long. Under the leadership of Mr. Will's nephew, John Whitaker, Reynolds entered a new golden age in the 1950s. Having run one of Reynolds's first cigarette machines years before, Whitaker reinstated the sense of family in the company after the difficult union years. He liked to wander the factory floor, greeting workers by name and inquiring after their families. "I remember some mornings pulling up beside Mr. Whitaker in his little brown Studebaker," a former employee recalled. "He'd give me a wave and I'd give him a wave back. We were going in to work together. We were all after the same thing." (There was an unwritten rule that Reynolds executives didn't drive anything bigger than a Buick. Even years later, when David Rockefeller came to Winston-Salem for a speech, an assistant asked that he be provided with a limousine. One couldn't be found in the entire city.)

Under Whitaker, Reynolds in 1954 introduced Winston, the first major filtered cigarette; 6.5 billion sold in its first nine months. It followed that triumph with the first mass-marketed menthol cigarette, Salem, which also sold in the billions. In 1959 the two new brands, benevolently named for the city that spawned them, enabled Reynolds's sales to surge past American Tobacco's. In Winston-Salem, they danced in the streets.

Whitaker continued the Reynolds tradition of taking care of its town and its workers. He paid them better than union wage and set up one of the most generous corporate health programs in the country; for a nominal fee, employees and their families got free medical and dental care at a company-sponsored clinic. In the mid-fifties the company and the Reynolds family teamed to move Wake Forest University from its campus 100 miles to the east. The American Tobacco heirs had moved a college to Durham and renamed it Duke University; Reynolds made sure Winston-Salem got the same treatment.

Life was good then. Reynolds's Winston, Salem, and Camel were three of the top four bestselling cigarette brands, Prince Albert remained the top-selling pipe tobacco, and a brand called Days Work was the top chewing tobacco. Americans were smoking like chimneys. In 1960, 58 percent of all men and 36 percent of all women smoked. It was often said that Reynolds's only problem was how to turn out cigarettes fast enough and how to ship all that money back to Wachovia Bank.

In one respect, it was true. From a corporate executive's point of view, Reynolds had too much cash on its hands. In 1956 the company amended its charter to allow it for the first time to buy nontobacco businesses. Two years later, it came close to buying a pharmaceutical company named Warner-Lambert. But when Charley Wade, a senior vice president and board member, visited Warner headquarters in New Jersey, he made a shocking discovery: Warner-Lambert's chairman sailed a company-owned yacht. "I came back and said, 'This is not for us; these are not our kind of people,'" recalled Wade. The deal died. Others recall it being more complicated than that, with directors also fearing that Warner-Lambert's unionized work force would prove to be a plague on Reynolds. But the picture captures the mind-set of that era's Reynolds: frugal, suspicious of outsiders, protective of the status quo, profoundly antiunion. "You just had small-town thinking," says one retired executive, remembering that some directors "wanted nothing to do with Yankees and unions."

During the fifties, Reynolds was one great, happy family. Its executives never forgot that their company was run by the people who got up in the dark of the North Carolina countryside each morning, hopped into pickup trucks, and drove to the Reynolds factories, where they took pride in selecting the right tobacco leaves and knew the innards of each packing machine by heart. When Reynolds had to answer the all-important question of whether a new cigarette would sell, it turned to a panel of 250 of its own employees. The right formula for Winston was selected only after each worker smoked more than 250 trial mixtures. Finally Bowman Gray, Jr., the sales chief at the time, took the final puff. "This is it!" he cried.

Gray succeeded Whitaker in 1959. He was a typical Reynolds executive of the day. The son of Mr. RJ's right-hand man, Bowman Sr., he smoked four packs of Winstons daily and had worked for Reynolds since he was eleven, when he spent summers trimming tobacco leaves. After selecting Winston, he trusted his own smoking taste above all. "I do believe if a cigarette appeals to me—I'm a pretty average fella—it might appeal to the population," Gray told *Time* magazine in 1960.

But during the next decade the population was forced to question whether it wanted to smoke *any* cigarette. Ever since tobacco was first rolled into cigarettes, there have been people opposed to smoking. King James I of Great Britain called it "the lively image and pattern of hell" and slapped an import tax on tobacco. Louis XIII of France and Czar Michael I of Russia decreed penalties for smoking ranging from death to castration. Pope Urban VIII threatened excommunication for anyone found smoking in church or on church premises. But America's love affair with tobacco went largely unopposed until 1964, when surgeon general Luther Terry issued his landmark report linking cigarette smoke with cancer. Cigarette sales, which had risen an average of 5 percent a year, fell sharply.

Growth eventually resumed, but Reynolds saw and heeded the warning. Gray began buying businesses outside the tobacco industry, mostly in the food business, which Reynolds executives saw as an easy mark for their marketing acumen. Anyone who could sell a product linked with cancer, Reynolds executives were fond of saying, "can sell anything." Reynolds compiled a mixed bag of brands: Hawaiian Punch, Vermont Maid maple syrup, My-T-Fine pudding, Chun King Chinese food, Patio Mexican food.

Its parochial nature, however, kept Reynolds from pursuing an opportunity that a newfound rival, Philip Morris of New York, was busily exploiting: overseas markets. Philip Morris was making millions selling its lead brand, Marlboro, around the world. Cocky after years of market dominance, Reynolds executives liked to say that from the twenty-second floor of headquarters they could see everything the company owned. "If somebody out there in the world wants a Camel," they joked, "let them call us."

But by the late sixties the days when Reynolds could rest on its laurels were coming to a close. Gray, the last direct link to Mr. RJ's mantle, died in 1969. Two senior executives considered likely successors also died, and Gray was succeeded by his cousin, a weak-willed financial executive named Alex Galloway. Galloway proceeded to lead Reynolds on a disastrous diversification campaign that, in a deterioration similar to Nabisco's, would have far-reaching effects on the company's core tobacco business.

At the suggestion of a former Winston-Salem businessman named Malcolm McLean, Galloway bought Sea-Land, a shipping company McLean owned. Given a seat on the Reynolds board, McLean next suggested that Galloway buy a small oil company named Aminoil, which Reynolds acquired the next year. The idea was that Aminoil's oil would be transported aboard Sea-Land's tankers. The next year Galloway, in a move to reflect the company's diversification, changed the company's name to RJ Reynolds Industries and, over the next decade, poured more than $2 billion into Aminoil and Sea-Land, building the latter into the world's largest private shipping line. Taken for granted, the tobacco factories slowly fell apart.

During his short caretaker reign, Galloway was largely under the sway of McLean and other powerful outsiders. The question of his successor became a matter of interest to one of them, a Reynolds director named J. Paul Sticht. Sticht was a rare outsider on the board: there were only two others when he joined in 1968. Rarer still, he was a Yankee who grew up in a boardinghouse outside Pittsburgh, the son of a German-immigrant steelworker. Sticht worked in the mills during high school and, after attending a nearby liberal arts school named Grove City College, went right back. He became a shop steward in the union and rose to become foreman. But behind his soft-spoken demeanor and blue-collar background, the fires of ambition burned as hot as any factory furnace.

Sticht soon left for the white-collar world, taking a job in personnel at Trans World Airways and, later, at Campbell Soup. There he quickly climbed the corporate ladder and by the late 1950s joined Federated Department Stores, the big Cincinnati retailer. By the mid-1960s, he was president and chief operating officer. Then, blocked from getting the top job—some say he was fired—Sticht took early retirement in 1972 at the age of fifty-five.

He had joined the Reynolds board at the request of Charley Wade, who had befriended him years earlier while comparing notes on union-busting tactics. Now, in 1972, Sticht lobbied against replacing Galloway with his heir apparent, a financial man named David Peoples. After consulting the board's three other outside directors, Sticht told Galloway they would all quit if Peoples was chosen. A search committee was formed to select a new successor, and Sticht, with time on his hands, was named its chairman. After months of exhaustive searching, Sticht's committee decided on a surprise choice to lead Reynolds into the late seventies: Paul Sticht.

Actually, Sticht would be the number-two executive, but in a new, hydraheaded executive structure he would come to wield influence far beyond his station. His titular superior, a homegrown tobacco man named Colin Stokes, was a classic Reynolds executive: his father had been head of the leaf-drying house under Mr. RJ. A chain-smoking forty-year Reynolds veteran, Stokes had worked his way up from the factory floor and knew everything about cigarettes, but next to nothing of the world outside North Carolina. Stokes proved to be putty in Sticht's hands.

The difference in the two men who steered Reynolds through the 1970s was symbolized in their attitudes toward corporate jets. The company had kept a pair since the 1950s, when it painted one the color of a Camel pack and the other a Salem pack. They were used so sparingly that one veteran pilot recalled logging only thirty-seven minutes of flight time one month, long enough to get a jet aloft and make sure it was in working order. It reflected not only Reynolds's egalitarian spirit but its executives' preference to stay home. Stokes and his friends particularly hated going to New York, and Larry Wassong, one of the company's New York ad men, would go to great lengths to ease the pain, arranging for Reynolds executives to be met at the airport, to have reservations at their favorite restaurants, to make sure they didn't end up on a Manhattan street corner befuddled. Mostly Wassong went to Winston-Salem himself.

Sticht, however, was born for corporate jets. He had phones installed on them, and personally made sure they had ample food and drink. Sticht took it as his mission to show Stokes new, far-flung places like Chicago and Boston. He formed an international advisory board, which included men such as Bunichiro Tonabe of Mitsubishi and Hermann Abs of Deutsche Bank. Twice a year these and other foreign business titans were brought together with Reynolds executives to discuss global issues in exotic locales. Sticht was determined to wrench some of the provincialism out of Reynolds.

It was a dream-come-true for an ambitious man: one day an out-of-work retailer, the next a captain of industry. Sticht loved rubbing shoulders with the corporate elite at the Business Round Table in New York and U.S. Chamber of Commerce in Washington. He loved dropping the names of the people he hobnobbed with. Some muttered that he was more interested in the trappings of business than doing business.

For all his whirl of motion, Sticht procrastinated terribly on decisions and tried to sidestep executive-suite conflicts. He preferred to come off as being above the fray: part statesman, part Dutch uncle. His voice was soft, his manner reserved. He remembered chauffeurs' names and asked after pilots' wives. In his courtly style and worldly ways, Sticht in some ways was a perfect bridge from the old, parochial Reynolds to the modern world.

But as an outsider, he was never well received by Winston-Salem's old guard. Sticht, a nonsmoker, would occasionally light up a pipe, but it seemed more for effect than pleasure. On weekends a Reynolds jet would fly him to his Palm Beach home in winter and his New Hampshire home in summer. His wife, Ferne, was rarely seen in Winston-Salem. It was something of an insult to people who expected Reynolds top brass to be at the center of the town's civic and social life. Sticht wasn't at first admitted to the upper-crust Old Town Club, and was relegated instead to the new-money crowd at Bermuda Run.

Dominating Colin Stokes, Sticht navigated Reynolds through the tumultuous 1970s, a period that would transform the company from a family-dominated business into something approaching a modern conglomerate. He consolidated his power by ousting three top executives in a Watergate-era scandal involving illegal political contributions. Sticht took control of that mess and another that broke on its heels—$19 million in illegal rebates paid by Sea-Land overseas—and in the process cemented his control over the company.

There was a terrible foreboding, among some, that the fall of the company's good Moravian standards and the rise of Paul Sticht meant ruinous change. "You watch," warned Stewart Robertson, a local stockbroker. "We're going to have a bunch of Yankee carpetbaggers come in here. They'll have never seen this much money, and they won't know what to do with it."

The next thing anyone knew, Reynolds was overrun with Yankees. The company had been under growing pressure during the seventies from its chief rival Philip Morris, whose Marlboro brand was growing in leaps and bounds, and Sticht was convinced that more sophisticated marketers could beat back the challenge. For the first time, he brought a slew of outsiders to Winston-Salem, including Jim Peterson, the former president of Pillsbury, to head the domestic tobacco business; Morgan Hunter, a senior vice president of American Cyanamid, to be president of Reynolds Tobacco; Bob Anderson, a Lever Brothers executive, to head tobacco marketing; and J. Tylee Wilson, a Chesebrough-Pond vice president, to run first the food businesses and later the company's long-overdue entry into overseas markets.

The newcomers, Northerners almost to a man, stood out painfully at Reynolds. "It's not the end of the earth," they joked of Winston-Salem, "but you can see it from here." They mistook gentility for weakness, slowness of pace for lack of acumen, and Southern accents for dimwittedness. "They would treat brilliant people as backwater rubes," recalled Larry Wassong, the ad executive.

For all their self-assuredness, the New Guard proved astoundingly inept at selling cigarettes. When cigarette ads were banned from the airwaves in 1971, Reynolds had to scrap its catchy jingle, "Winston tastes good like a cigarette should." For years Sticht's new hires flailed about to find a proper substitute, torturously reworking the line for print ads: "There's a lot of good between 'Winston' and 'should.' " Bob Anderson compounded the problem by yanking Reynolds's brands off billboards, a crucial source of cigarette advertising.

A succession of ad agencies was thrown at the problem, each with its own ideas, each with a new direction, each doomed to fail. Cigarettes are sold on image, and for years Reynolds executives held their brand images sacrosanct. Philip Morris had gained millions of Marlboro smokers by sticking with the same cowboy image since the 1950s. Now Reynolds tried a macho counteroffensive, with campaigns portraying loggers and sailors. It tried a "working men of America" campaign, trying to celebrate the blue-collar brand it had become. Nothing worked.

Marlboro was also winning the battle on the factory floor. The entrenched traditions that kept Reynolds on top for twenty years now kept it from changing with the times. The reconstituted tobacco long embraced by Reynolds manufacturing executives saved money but sacrificed quality. It produced a hot, harsh taste that was popular with blue collar workers but that, by the 1970s, was being rejected by more sophisticated and youthful palates. Marlboro, by blending a smoother cigarette, won converts. Philip Morris did it by pouring money into new plants and equipment, while Reynolds stood pat. After dominating the cigarette business for so long, the Reynolds line executives had grown complacent. "Ah, what do those guys on Park Avenue know?" they said, doubting the judgment of anyone that distant from the factories and tobacco fields.

In the mid-seventies both Philip Morris and Reynolds had a shot at purchasing a first generation of electronic cigarette-making machines that would greatly speed production. But many Reynolds mechanics weren't literate enough to handle them; they chose to stick with older, more reliable machines they knew how to take apart and reassemble. Philip Morris jumped at the new devices. By the time Reynolds realized its mistake, all the manufacturer's production was committed to Philip Morris plants. It was the final straw. In 1976, Marlboro passed Winston as America's bestselling cigarette, a position it holds to this day. Reynolds held onto its lead in overall cigarette sales by a hair.

The problems weren't confined to the old brands, as a new-product fiasco shook Reynolds further. It was a time when "all-natural" products were popular, and shortly after losing the number-one position to Marlboro, the company decided to roll out an all-natural cigarette. They named it Real. As usual, they ignored local skeptics. "What are we doing trying to sell to the health conscious?" muttered one dissenter. "People who smoke don't give a shit about their health." But Reynolds' executives were so confident of Real's success they bypassed test markets and took it directly national. They spent millions on ads showing ruddy-cheeked young bucks enjoying a Real and passed out packs by the gross on street corners. Real, of course, was a real disaster.

In the late seventies, Sticht officially became chief executive upon Stokes's retirement, and Reynolds left its fifty-year-old downtown headquarters for a sprawling, glass-enclosed building erected several miles away. Reynolds, one executive declared, had arrived at "the age of mass, class and glass." But the intrigues soon spawned within the new building would give it a far more colorful nickname: "The Glass Menagerie."

His only mistake, Paul Sticht would later say, was that he had gotten too old too soon. He was past sixty by the time he became chief executive, and he no sooner had the job than speculation began about his successor. The early favorite was Tylee Wilson, a man with two years' experience running the company's overseas business and the only one of the original New Guard to make it into the 1980s. Sticht named Wilson president in 1979. As Sticht's number two, Wilson was responsible for the company's entire tobacco operation. He had initially gained Sticht's notice shepherding Reynolds's ragtag, money-losing food businesses, bringing them to heel and managing to turn a profit. As president, Wilson began pouring billions into the gargantuan task of revitalizing Reynolds's aging factories.

He soon rubbed the genteel Sticht the wrong way. Wilson was a cold tactician and technician, a straight-ahead tank of an administrator who rolled over everything between him and his current objective. As a young man, he had been an Army instructor, and he brought that blunt, Prussian style to the executive suite. Wilson had a humorless laugh and a knack for tortured syntax. A Wilson sentence might begin, "I would opine that . . ."

Sticht's succession, it was clear, would be a horse race. The second entry in that race was Edward A. Horrigan, Jr., president of Reynolds's main tobacco business. Ed Horrigan, who would leave his own indelible mark on Reynolds, was a combative fireplug of a man who liked to brag he was "born in a three-point stance." Horrigan was typical of the new-generation executive Sticht had brought in; he ran a tobacco business without ever having smoked in his life. He had made his career marketing liquor, joining Reynolds in the seventies and, unlike many of the New Guard, fitting in well in Winston-Salem.

He was born in Brooklyn, the son of an accountant who was hard-pressed to find work during Horrigan's Depression-era childhood. He got into the University of Connecticut on a football scholarship; although only five foot seven, by his own admission he "liked to hit people." Horrigan got through UConn working summer construction jobs, then joined the army. In Korea, Horrigan led a platoon of 200 men at the battle of Old Baldy. The North Koreans were dug in on a hill, mowing down Americans as they tried to take it. But the young lieutenant kept regrouping and finally led his decimated unit on one final assault. Horrigan took out a machine-gun nest by himself, and his platoon took the hill. He won a Silver Star for valor, but his wounds knocked him out of combat for the duration.

After Horrigan came home, he marched through a succession of marketing jobs, until being lured to Reynolds by Tylee Wilson after heading the Buckingham liquor unit of Chicago conglomerate Northwest Industries. At Reynolds the two old soldiers were natural allies, at least at first. Together they commiserated over drinks about Reynolds's plodding ways. Horrigan chafed at Reynolds's gentlemanly, Southern work ethic. "We need a stronger sense of urgency here," he told his troops. Horrigan was brimming with pep talks for the troops: They were going to fight Philip Morris on the beaches, in the air, at the convenience-store racks, everywhere. When they began to make progress, Horrigan got a good measure of the credit. Subordinates didn't question him without risking a tirade; behind his back, they called him "Little Caesar." These were not the gentlemanly qualities Sticht preferred. Nonetheless, Horrigan was a contender.

A third candidate for Sticht's crown was Joe Abely, the suave chief financial officer recruited from General Foods. Abely most looked the part of a chief executive, with a distinguished silver mane. He also had the best pedigree, with law and business degrees from Harvard. He was on the Council of Foreign Relations, which appealed to the statesman side of Sticht. But Abely had a personality that made Wilson seem warm. While he didn't meet the gentility test, Abely worked closely with Sticht on acquisitions and performed the useful task of bringing financial systems out of the dark ages. (Sea-Land's accounting system, it was discovered, consisted of stuffing invoices in shoe boxes.)

After a century of "one-for-all," the Sticht succession scramble split Reynolds into warring camps. No longer did people pull together for the company. Now they looked after the interests of the executive they hitched their star to: Wilson, Horrigan, or Abely. Preparing for a financial analysts' meeting, Wilson and Abely quarreled over who would speak first, a squabble Sticht finally had to settle. At a rehearsal for presentations to a companywide conference, Abely had run over his allotted time when Horrigan stomped into the room. "What's that cocksucker doing up there?" he stormed. "It's my time." Abely ordered a feasibility study on spinning off Sea-Land. Wilson, to whom Sea-Land reported, got wind of it and confronted John Dowdle, the treasurer, who was doing the study. "I'm sorry, I can't tell you about that," Dowdle said. "Abely will fire me if I tell you." Horrigan hired a public relations firm to get him nominated for the right kinds of business and humanitarian awards to enhance his résumé. Horrigan's big score: a Horatio Alger Award.

The succession mess would have a lasting effect on the business, fueling an insidious practice known as "loading." Loading wasn't unique to Reynolds; every tobacco company did it to some extent. Just prior to its regular semiannual price hikes, Reynolds regularly offered huge volumes of cigarettes to its customers—wholesalers and supermarket chains—at the old prices. Customers loved it because they could sell low-cost cigarettes at the new, higher prices. Reynolds loved it because it cleared away unwanted inventory, kept the factories humming, and, most important, produced large, artificial, end-of-quarter profits.

The problem, of course, was that loading was as addictive as nicotine. In order to top profits aided by loading, the company had to load even more—and so on, *ad infinitum.* It created huge inventories in the hands of wholesalers and retailers. When those inventories couldn't be sold, one of two things happened, neither of them good. The cigarettes could be shipped back to Reynolds for credit, forcing the company to swallow the expense of reprocessing the tobacco into fresh cigarettes and, likely as not, reloading them. Or they could sit around for a few months, growing stale. As Reynolds grew more and more addicted to loading, more and more smokers were drawing on stale Winstons. Many would switch over to Marlboro.

With Reynolds gripped in bitter political squabbling, Sticht struggled to find a successor he could recommend to the board. A director named Ronald Grierson came to him with an idea. Grierson was a distinguished

Briton, vice chairman of British General Electric. In Europe, Grierson told Sticht, companies often went to handwriting experts when confronted with tough decisions like this. And so an oracle on such matters in Switzerland was consulted. She looked at writing samples of the successor candidates and shook her head morosely at each: not competent . . . couldn't be trusted . . . and so on down the line.

Sticht stalled. Some believed he didn't want to make a decision. He was in his mid-sixties, but felt as if he were in the prime of his late-blooming career. Then, just as those inside the company held their breath waiting for his final decision, Sticht made an even more startling announcement: He had agreed to buy a company named Heublein for $1.2 billion. What he got was a good liquor business (Smirnov, Inglenook Wines), a mediocre fast-food business (Kentucky Fried Chicken), and Heublein's chief executive, Hicks Waldron, a fourth succession candidate. Waldron had spent most of his career at General Electric, a breeding ground for modern managers, and had a patina of polish Sticht found lacking in the others. Waldron wasn't unmindful of the succession war gripping Reynolds. There were only a few key terms to Heublein's sale, as far as Waldron was concerned: a price of $63 a share and a promise that Tylee Wilson wouldn't be made chief executive.

Now the succession situation grew even more complex. In October 1982, Sticht turned sixty-five and told the board he couldn't yet recommend a candidate to replace him. Instead he asked for and received permission to stay on an extra year. There was little doubt his request would be approved: Since the mid-seventies, Sticht had been packing the board with his supporters.

In an era when many American companies favored weak-willed, rubber-stamp boards, Reynolds directors were unusually strong-minded. Among their most outspoken members was John Macomber, chief executive of Celanese, the chemical company. Macomber was chairman of the board's compensation committee, which was looking after the succession matter. He was Eastern Establishment through and through—Yale undergraduate, Harvard Business School, Lincoln Center board, International Chamber of Commerce—and close to Sticht. Sticht was on the Celanese board and had been on the search committee that installed Macomber in his job.

As far as the Reynolds succession went, Macomber was an anybody-but-Wilson man. Celanese did $25 million of business a year with Reynolds, selling it material for cigarette filters. But Reynolds bought twice as much from Eastman Kodak, and when Macomber lobbied Wilson for more business, Wilson—no corporate politician—bluntly told him: "You're our secondary supplier for two reasons: quality and service." Macomber simmered. "I will *not* be on the board of a company run by Tylee Wilson," he declared.

Vernon Jordan, the former Urban League president, was another director tight with the Macomber–Sticht axis. He, too, served on the Celanese board. As a partner in the Washington law firm of Akin, Gump, Strauss, Hauer and Feld, Jordan was well disposed to any chairman who put him on his board. Sticht would often have Jordan along as his guest at Bohemian Grove, the exclusive northern California corporate retreat, a superb place for the lawyer to do some rainmaking.

Juanita Kreps also owed Sticht. A longtime professor and administrator at Duke, Kreps was the token woman on Reynolds's board even before attaining modest fame as Jimmy Carter's secretary of commerce. Sticht had gotten her on the board of Chrysler, where he was a director. Sticht had Reynolds make handsome contributions to the Duke University Endowment, of which Kreps was a trustee. Kreps got credit at Duke for the gift; Sticht's name got attached to the largesse. At Duke there was a J. Paul Sticht chair for international studies and a J. Paul Sticht fellowship for graduate business-school study, for a deserving alumnus of his alma mater, Grove City College.

Another Sticht supporter was Grierson, who Sticht also maneuvered onto the Chrysler board. Sticht could also count on Albert Butler, of Winston-Salem, who headed a family textile business and, for many years, a Moravian good-works foundation. Butler was a creature of the local establishment who summered at Roaring Gap, golfed at Old Town, and sat on the boards at Wachovia and Wake Forest. Butler had been thrilled to be tapped for Reynolds's board and was utterly passive once on it.

Bill Anderson, chairman of NCR Corporation, was the kind of international businessman that Sticht could only pretend to be. Anderson had grown up in Shanghai and spoke several Chinese dialects. He had spent four years as a Japanese prisoner of war during World War II, and afterward was chief witness at a war crimes trial that sent thirty of his Japanese captors to prison. He had seen heavier scenes than the succession mess, at which he seemed slightly bemused.

It was a powerful board and squarely in Sticht's pocket. But if the directors pampered Sticht, they felt no obligation to treat his subordinates—or his successors—the same. Reynolds executives seethed at the way board members put them through the second degree. "Paul had his own bevy of directors; they knew everything and management knew nothing," Ed Horrigan recalled years later. "He and they were using the company as a vehicle for self-aggrandizement." Horrigan's hostility was apparent to all—some board members called him "that trigger-happy whiskey salesman"—hurting his chances for the top spot. "Always remember, they're only in it for themselves," the personnel chief, Rodney Austin, told colleagues. "They're mostly whores, pimps, and panderers."

The succession scramble had been dragging on for two years when, in the wee hours of a Saturday morning in early 1983, Austin awoke Horrigan with a phone call to pass along a tip from one of the directors. Stuart Watson, the former chairman of Heublein and now a Reynolds director, had gone before the succession committee and made a case for his man, Hicks Waldron. The committee had bought it, Austin said; it looked like Waldron, the dark horse, had the job.

As Horrigan raged at the development, Austin suggested it wasn't too late to recover. "But your only hope is to get together with Ty and Jerry Long [tobacco's number-two man] right now and stop it from happening."

That weekend Horrigan, Long, and Wilson met and agreed: Waldron had to be stopped. The best way to do that, they reasoned, was to use themselves as leverage. If they could bury the hatchet and form a united front behind either Wilson or Horrigan, they could derail the Waldron express.

On Monday, Wilson met with Sticht and delivered him a handwritten letter. "We cannot accept Hicks Waldron as chairman or as CEO," Wilson wrote on behalf of the three men. "We believe the selection of Waldron as your successor would be an unnecessary sellout. We assume the committee believes the retention of the proven successful principal executives of this company is vital to its future. However, the selection of Waldron would result in the three of us leaving the company." It wasn't right that someone with no tobacco experience should get the job, the letter went on. Especially because the best candidate was right under the board's nose. "We respectfully conclude that I am the most qualified candidate to succeed you," Wilson wrote.

As much as Sticht detested their demands, the trio had him in a corner.

He couldn't lose his top three tobacco executives, not with Philip Morris poised to pass Reynolds as the nation's top tobacco company. Sticht sent the succession committee copies of what was already being called, by the few who knew of it, "the midnight letter." The directors were also furious, and they were also in a corner.

As they thrashed about for an answer, Macomber was even advanced as a possible compromise candidate; it wouldn't be the last time he would do so. Debate ran on for weeks. During a marathon parley after the April annual meeting, there was still strong sentiment for Waldron. Finally in May, at a Saturday meeting of the succession committee in Winston-Salem, Sticht made his recommendation. The board reluctantly consented. Sticht flew to Heublein headquarters in Hartford, Connecticut, to break the news to Waldron. "Hicks, I'm going to do something that I'm afraid isn't in the best interests of the shareholders, but I've got to do it," Sticht said. "I'm naming Ty chief executive."

———

Elevated to chief executive in 1983, Tylee Wilson set to work reshaping Reynolds. Like many in the New Guard, Wilson's background had been in consumer products, and it was there he believed the company's future lay. He spun off Sea-Land to shareholders in 1984, and sent Joe Abely out to sea with it, ridding himself of a potential challenger. Wilson sold Aminoil the same year for $1.7 billion, just before oil prices went into free fall. Wall Street analysts praised the changes and issued "buy" recommendations on Reynolds stock. *Business Week* chimed in with a laudatory cover story, declaring "The Consumer Drives R.J. Reynolds Again."

They were smart moves. After its troubles during the seventies, Reynolds's tobacco business had begun what would become a long decline. In 1983 cigarette sales had crested and would fall a steady 2 percent each year to come. The rise of the antismoking movement—the "antis," Reynolds partisans spat—was taking its toll. By the early eighties, less than a third of Americans smoked. Federal excise taxes on cigarettes were doubled in 1983, to 16 cents a pack. Tobacco remained a fabulously profitable business—prices were still raised twice a year—but even diehard industry partisans saw the twilight ahead. By diversifying, Wilson was simply readying Reynolds for the inevitable.

Horrigan was named Wilson's president and chief operating officer. Their alliance was a shaky one, but Wilson owed Horrigan for his role in drafting the midnight letter. Now, much as Wilson had grated on Sticht, Horrigan grated on Wilson. When he had questions about the tobacco business, Wilson bypassed Horrigan and went to his henchman Jerry Long, who replaced Horrigan as president of the domestic tobacco business. A stickler for detail, Wilson criticized Horrigan for his weekend trips to Palm Springs, where the Horrigans had a home. Even though Horrigan often took along other executives, Wilson thought the trips more personal than corporate, and challenged Horrigan's use of a corporate jet.

"Ed, you're really, really stretching," Wilson said.

Horrigan bristled. "You're challenging my integrity." When internal auditors later forced Horrigan to reimburse Reynolds for some trips—at the going rate of twice first-class airfare—Little Caesar threw a fit.

Wall Street may have liked Wilson's ideas about remaking Reynolds, but they were greeted somewhat less enthusiastically by Paul Sticht: Wilson was, after all, undoing a decade of his work. On his retirement, Sticht remained a powerful board member—maybe the most powerful—and kept close tabs on Reynolds's inner workings. Wilson did everything possible to freeze him out. Sticht's life revolved around the corporate jets, but when Wilson felt his trips were for personal business, he made sure Sticht was charged for them. A retired chairman was entitled to an office and a secretary, and Sticht got one—but in the old headquarters downtown, away from his beloved Glass Menagerie. "Sticht is going to be my sexual consultant," Wilson was heard to say. "When I want his fucking advice, I'll ask for it."

But Sticht simply couldn't let go. He called department heads with questions or observations. He took calls from Hicks Waldron, passing along his former Heublein colleague's complaints. One of the sorest points was the head of Del Monte's fresh fruit division, Sammy Gordon. He was a favorite of Sticht, who liked the business and whose son worked for Gordon. Sticht used the talkative Gordon to disseminate anti-Wilson gossip, Wilson thought. Sticht defended Gordon for running his business like the freewheeling banana trader he was.

Gordon's style ran counter to Wilson's bedrock belief in what he called "process and procedure." Wilson lived for the trappings of bureaucracy: When it came to corporate decision making, he was confident that if one went through the right steps and approvals, the right conclusions would follow. "Process," Wilson told a gathering of senior executives shortly after taking office, "can speed the smooth and orderly flow of most routine activities and permit us to devote valuable management time to exceptional or unanticipated concerns." As a maiden speech, it was an earnest declaration of principles. But it betrayed a rigidity and coldness that wouldn't win Wilson allies when he most needed them.

Wilson would sometimes wander around headquarters, trying awkwardly to make small talk with middle managers. But he couldn't shed his brusque nature. When he thought the executive dining room was being cluttered by too many lower-level types, he ordered higher admission standards. "R.H.I.P.," he crisply explained, then translated: "Rank has its privileges."

From the outset, Wilson's relations with the Reynolds board were shaky. None of the directors condoned his strong-arm tactics in winning the chairmanship, and his treatment of their friend Sticht wasn't appreciated. Wilson tried to build bridges, in his fashion. He sent directors briefing papers between board meetings. He scheduled one lunch a year with each director, during which he took copious notes as his guest aired whatever was on his mind; Wilson kept the notes in little books, one for each director.

But where it mattered most, Wilson fell hopelessly short. John Macomber was still pestering him for business and getting rebuffed. When Vernon Jordan pressed for more legal work, Wilson would coolly reply that, as a nonlawyer, he couldn't judge whether there was anything appropriate; he referred Jordan to Reynolds's general counsel. In contrast to chief executives such as Paul Sticht and Ross Johnson, who played their boards like a personal symphony orchestra, Wilson had a tin ear.

He further alienated Sticht and the board by diminishing an institution dear to their hearts, the International Advisory Board. Since its formation in the seventies, it had become a prime junketeering vehicle for Reynolds directors. Wilson cut the meetings back from two a year to one and removed Sticht as the board's chairman, making the job a staff-run function. Wilson knew all the changes weren't met with pleasure by Sticht or his board cronies, but both profits and the stock price were up, and he couldn't conceive of anyone arguing with his results.

After unloading Aminoil and Sea-Land, Wilson began preparations for his biggest move yet, an acquisition that would fulfill his grand vision to mold Reynolds into a consumer-goods superpower to rival Procter & Gamble. Wilson set up a task force of Reynolds staffers and representatives of the company's longtime Wall Street investment bank, Dillon

Read & Co., to sift through and rank the candidates. After many months and countless computer studies, they came up with three recommendations.

Second runner-up was PepsiCo, which scored seventy-five on Wilson's acquisition-lust scale. Wilson approached it first, in part because he knew its chief executive, Wayne Calloway. But Wilson found Calloway as ice-cold as a Pepsi. "There's no way I'll discuss that with you, and if you come at me hostile I'm going to fight you all the way," he said. Wilson backed off.

First runner-up, with a score of seventy-six, was Kellogg, the cereal giant. But half its stock was controlled by a trust, and Wilson doubted the trust would sell. That left the company that was number one, with eighty-one points. Wilson demurred only briefly, because he didn't know the chief executive. According to his task force, Reynolds's ideal marriage partner was Nabisco Brands, headed by a breezy, likable Canadian named Ross Johnson.

———

"Oh, yeah, I know who you are," said Johnson, who had bumped into Wilson a few times over the years.

The two chief executives met the following week over sandwiches at Johnson's midtown Manhattan office, and Wilson laid out his plan. Reynolds, he explained, needed a major acquisition to ease its reliance on tobacco, and he thought Nabisco fit the bill perfectly. As they spoke, the two men leafed through each other's annual reports.

Relaxed and chatty, Johnson played it coy, not responding immediately. Wilson suspected Johnson would be receptive: He had picked up rumors that Nabisco and Philip Morris were sniffing at each other, and he thought Johnson would be motivated to sell. To make certain, Wilson threw in a sweetener. The two of them were the same age, Wilson noted, but he had no plans to remain chief until sixty-five. Wilson told Johnson he planned to retire in two or three years, and hinted strongly that Johnson would get first crack at replacing him as head of their combined companies. The two talked terms and agreed that if they chose to pursue a merger, a tax-free stock swap made sense. They parted with plans to meet again in several weeks. Both had board meetings in the meantime, and each could get word on whether to proceed.

Wilson had left Johnson's office sky-high, his grand vision apparently within reach, but when he met with his directors in late April 1985, he found them cool to the idea of merging with Nabisco. Some were downright angry. This would be the biggest deal in Reynolds history: Why hadn't the board been told about it beforehand? The reason, Wilson noted testily, was that he and Johnson had had only the most preliminary of chats: no money on the table, no obligations, just a first date. What about this business of promising Johnson a shot at the chairmanship? the board members protested. Succession was their prerogative. The directors didn't like the idea of a tax-free merger, either; if any deal was done, Reynolds ought to do the buying. In a stern rebuke, they ordered Wilson to back off.

Wilson remained confident. "This is still going to happen; it makes so much sense," he assured Horrigan over lunch. "But the next time Ross Johnson isn't going to have so much power. We'll be the acquirer. All he'll get is vice chairman."

The talks, in fact, rekindled within weeks. A small army of Wall Street lawyers and investment bankers were brought in, and, the directors having been convinced, Reynolds agreed in principle to acquire Nabisco for cash. The lone sticking point was the price. Then, during the negotiations, Nabisco stock began rising, a sure sign that word of the talks had leaked.* Johnson took it as an opportunity to wheedle more money out of Wilson. At $80 a share, Wilson said he could go no further. "Well," Johnson said, "you're not gonna get a deal at eighty bucks." The logjam broke when Wilson agreed to throw in preferred stock, which brought the price to $85 a share, or $4.9 billion, at the time the largest merger ever to take place outside the oil industry.

Johnson, sensing Wilson's hunger for the deal, drove tough bargains on side issues. Despite Sticht's love of corporate jets, Reynolds's perks trailed those of Nabisco. Most everything was negotiable, Johnson said, but not the perks. Wilson thought company apartments for all the top officers of a cookie-and-cracker company was ridiculous. But he wasn't giving up his dream over Johnson's petty concerns; he gave in. Johnson insisted he be named president and chief operating officer, number two behind Wilson. He characterized it as a signal to Nabisco people that they wouldn't be forgotten; Wilson gave in to that, too.

---

* Only later would Johnson and Wilson learn, to their embarrassment, that one of the investment bankers involved in the negotiations was funneling inside information to the arbitrager Ivan Boesky, who fueled the run-up by loading up on Nabisco stock.

The problem, of course, was that by elevating Johnson he would be forced to demote the proud, tempestuous Horrigan. Wilson broke the news to him gently, promising to give him a sweet contract, the post of vice chairman, and a place in a new, three-man office of the chairman. Horrigan, seeing he had no choice, relented, taking solace in the fact he would be part of a troika ruling a vast new empire.

On the last day of May 1985, the Reynolds board met in a teleconference to wrap up the details. Horrigan, en route to Australia to inspect Reynolds troops there, stopped by Del Monte's San Francisco offices to listen in. Wilson, in New York for the negotiations, ticked off the final terms item by item, leaving the management structure for last. "Ross Johnson will become the president and chief operating officer," he said. "Ed has agreed to accept the position of vice chairman."

"I want to hear from Ed on this," John Hanley of Monsanto asked. "Is that acceptable to you?"

Horrigan made a gracious little speech—wholly out of character, some thought—that he had written for the occasion. For several minutes he rhapsodized about the need to sacrifice his ambitions for the greater good. Afterward Wilson came back on the line. There would be an "office of the chairman," he announced, consisting of Wilson and Johnson. He didn't mention Horrigan.

In San Francisco, Horrigan was dumbstruck. Wilson had waited until the conclusion of his self-effacing speech, then stolen the one sop Horrigan felt he had been thrown in the entire deal. Horrigan listened in a fog of rage as the directors finished the meeting. "Ty," he said, "when this call is over, I want you to call me."

"Very well, Ed," Wilson said in his clipped manner.

For a minute, Horrigan sat alone. He began to cry, his fury and frustration producing tears that were streaming down his cheeks in torrents when Wilson finally called.

"I don't believe what you just said in that goddamned call," Horrigan stormed. "We had an agreement that I was in that office." He raged on about how he had a good mind to resign; how dishonest a son-of-a-bitch Wilson was; how he had been played for a patsy in front of the whole board.

"Now calm down, Ed, calm down."

"I am not going to calm down," Horrigan shouted. "Unless you change this and put me in that office of the chairman, I will recant everything

I just said to the board. I will blow this whole thing out of the water. I'm not budging from this phone until you call back and get our deal back."

Wilson called Johnson and told him it would be necessary to include Horrigan in the office of the chairman. Johnson, wholly ignorant of Wilson's deception and of Reynolds politics in general, readily agreed. Wilson relayed the message to Horrigan, singing praises of Johnson's willingness to compromise. But Horrigan held Johnson equally accountable for the slight; he knew all about how Johnson had seized power at Standard Brands and Nabisco. Horrigan figured Johnson was angling to purge him even before the merger was completed. "Ty, I wish you a lot of luck," Horrigan said. "Ross Johnson will have your job in eighteen months. Just remember that."

"The hell he will," Wilson retorted. "We made a deal. He'll get the job when I retire."

"Deal, hell," Horrigan snorted.

When the merger was completed several days later, a delighted Wilson was in Washington for a Ford Theater gala, where he ran into Johnson's good friend, Jim Robinson of American Express. Robinson was Atlanta born and bred, occasionally summered at his mother's home in Roaring Gap, and knew both Nabisco and Reynolds well; Johnson, in fact, had consulted Robinson at length during the merger negotiations. "You'll like Rawss," Robinson said in his soft Southern accent. "He's a good guy, and I know you'll get along well together."

For the most part, the first weeks following the merger went smoothly, though there were undercurrents of uneasiness that would resurface. Because Reynolds had acquired Nabisco, news of the merger was greeted favorably in Winston-Salem, where the locals took pride in gaining control of a great Northern company. The lone dissenting voice was Horrigan, who settled into a black Irish funk. Horrigan groused constantly to Wilson about the Nabisco executives' perks, about how Laurie Johnson was always traveling with Ross, when that was forbidden by company policy. "Ross Johnson is a snake, a low-life slime," he declared to anyone who would listen. "We'll rue the day we hooked up with that character." When Ty and Pat Wilson gave a brunch to welcome the Johnsons to Winston-Salem, Ed and Betty Horrigan were conspicuous in their absence.

Johnson was soon down on Horrigan, too, although he was incapable of hating as Horrigan did. "There's no way I will ever have Ed Horrigan reporting to me," he told friends. "I don't like him and I don't trust him."

Sometimes Johnson mused about whether Horrigan was on the take from the liquor distributors who did business with Heublein, a unit that reported to Horrigan. The more Johnson learned about Horrigan, the less use he had for him. "Ed's a dead man when I'm running this company," Johnson vowed.

Apart from Horrigan, Johnson was initially well received at Reynolds. Alone among senior Nabisco executives, Johnson moved to Winston-Salem, where he bought a large house off an Old Town fairway. He was reported to be a thoroughly winning fellow, a smiling, backslapping yin to Wilson's tight Prussian yang. "I know what they said about this guy, but I don't find it to be true at all," gushed Rodney Austin. "I think he's great." In his first weeks in Winston-Salem Johnson made an all-out effort to fit in, driving around in a Jeep Wagoneer, inviting people over to dinner, and joining the board of the North Carolina Zoological Society. Most in Winston-Salem were impressed, but not all. Ginny Dowdle, the wife of Reynolds treasurer John Dowdle, sized up Johnson with a single phrase: "A used-car salesman."

Below the top ranks, deep differences in the two organizations were soon apparent. When Reginald Starr, head of the Reynolds shareholder services department, flew to New Jersey for a first meeting with his Nabisco counterparts, he was met at its Morristown hangar by a pair of white limousines with smoked windows. "I don't know, it looked like Mafia to me," Starr, a thirty-year Reynolds veteran, said. "It was so ostentatious. I was ashamed to be seen in one of those things . . ."

Wilson's first meeting at Nabisco went no better. As he stepped off a Reynolds jet into the Morristown terminal, he was smoking a cigarette. "Hey! No smoking in here," barked Nabisco's flight operations chief, Linda Galvin. Startled, Wilson dropped the cigarette to the floor and crushed it out. If that weren't enough, the Reynolds contingent found the Nabisco people patronizing. On the return flight Nancy Holder, Reynolds's meetings planner, took Wilson aside. "Ty, be careful," she said. "Standard Brands merged with Nabisco, and now there's no Nabisco left." Paul Bott, a top planner, scoffed: "Nancy, don't be silly. Ty's too smart for that."

Even the two companies' products were an uneasy—some said unnatural—mix. Early on, Horrigan learned that one of Nabisco's brands, Fleischmann's Margarine, had developed a joint marketing campaign with the American Heart Association that, among other things, urged consumers not to smoke. Horrigan hit the roof; the campaign was soon dropped. Johnson, of course, made light of combining wholesome Nabisco and the "Death Merchants" at Reynolds. "Mom and apple pie meet the skull and crossbones," he chuckled. But to Nabisco's Old Guard, it was no laughing matter. If the stolid Nabisco bakers had derided Standard Brands's liquor managers as "the booze boys," they were even more horrified at joining a tobacco company. In Washington, RJR Nabisco created two political action committees, one for Reynolds, one for Nabisco. Nabisco employees didn't want their contributions going to the tobacco lobby.

Johnson, who for the most part enjoyed wonderful relations with the Nabisco and Standard Brands boards, immediately sensed the tensions between Wilson and the Reynolds directors. After the first meeting of the combined board, he got a strong impression of cliquishness and peevishness. Off to one side, Sticht, Macomber, Jordan, and Kreps huddled to discuss something secretively. Out of earshot, Wilson complained about the directors and some imagined slight. "[Wilson] didn't like them and they didn't like him," recalled Johnson. "It was clear there was a lot of scar tissue there."

Five Nabisco directors, including Andy Sage, were named to RJR Nabisco's twenty-person board. One, Charles Hugel, the amiable chief of Connecticut-based Combustion Engineering, lunched with Wilson shortly after coming aboard, and was stunned to hear him openly criticize other directors. Wilson railed at each in detail as Hugel stared in wonder. *Why is he telling me this?* Hugel thought. *How did he expect to win me over by telling me how his board was a bunch of jerks? What kind of instincts does this guy have, anyway?*

As far as the actual business was concerned, the theory behind the merger was that by combining Reynolds's huge line of products with Nabisco's, the new company could command greater sway with buyers, demanding more and better shelf space in supermarkets and deeper discounts from wholesalers. Wilson was certain that, by following his beloved process and procedure, success was inevitable. He set up task forces to study joint marketing arrangements, cross-fertilization of management, and other ways to exploit what must be tremendous potential. If it was Sticht's aspiration to walk with kings, it was Wilson's to be the hero of a Harvard Business School case study.

Johnson's Merry Men, of course, thought Wilson was nuts. To a man they remained at Nabisco in New York, where they found themselves powerless to fight bosses in far-off Winston-Salem. Under Wilson, any strategic move, from advertising to changing a cookie box, required multiple sign-offs and weeks of waiting. The Nabisco people could believe neither the size of Wilson's staff nor the obtuseness of its exercises. One task force studied how to assemble a telecommunications and computer system that would tie together the whole empire. To Wilson it was a grand-scale means of achieving efficiencies. To Nabisco it was a nightmare. Said John Gora, a Nabisco candy division executive: "It was like we'd been bought by the federal government."

Isolated from Johnson, many of his longtime aides grew restless. After just six months under Wilson's regime, several were poised to leave. Ed Robinson, Nabisco's chief financial officer, was on the verge of taking a high-level post at A&P, the grocery chain. Peter Rogers had made up his mind to resign as well, and Andy Barrett, Nabisco's personnel chief, was headed for a job in his native England. Bob Carbonell was complaining about how "you had to raise your hand to go to the bathroom." Martin Emmett had left before the merger, although he remained on the payroll as chairman of Nabisco Canada.

Johnson traveled to New York and urged his friends to be patient. Things would change, he assured them. But he knew it wouldn't be easy to hold them much longer; they hardly bothered to hide their alienation and sense of a separate identity. At the Dinah Shore Golf Tournament following the merger, a retired Del Monte executive was introduced to Ed Robinson and tried to make pleasant conversation.

"Are you from the RJR side of the company or the Nabisco?" the man asked.

"Neither," Robinson replied. "Standard Brands."

As the Merry Men's sense of despondency grew, Johnson directed his p.r. man, Mike Masterpool, to stage a banquet to commemorate the tenth anniversary of Henry Weigl's overthrow. Held in May 1986 at the Brook Club in New York, it brought together a dozen of Johnson's coconspirators as well as their board supporters from that fateful day in 1976. The Merry Men took turns reading the board minutes, to great cheers; rose to tell Weigl stories, to great laughter; and, of course, drank mightily. Johnson capped the evening by handing everyone a paperweight inscribed with the numerals "10-5-1." The meaning: ten years since the Standard Brands overthrow, five years since the Nabisco merger, one year since the

Reynolds merger. The upshot: This subjugation, too, would pass.

Johnson, meanwhile, was doing his best to ingratiate himself with Tylee Wilson. It wasn't easy; the two men were complete opposites, and Wilson, unlike Bob Schaeberle, was no pushover. Wilson asked each senior executive to submit his daily schedule for the next three months; Wilson himself was personally scheduled to the minute for the next quarter. Johnson's schedule, if it could be called that, was subject to change by the minute. On the spur of the moment, he might leave Winston-Salem in late afternoon and fly to New York for dinner. Wilson preferred to unwind with solitary weekends on his boat. Johnson liked rounding up an entourage of his celebrity friends for an all-weekend party, inviting a grocery executive or two along so he could write the whole shindig off. Wilson cringed at Johnson's expense account. When he got a tab for a $13,000 weekend at a Colorado country club, he asked Johnson whether all the hoopla was really necessary. Johnson could always spin a superb rationale about how piddling the cost was compared to the goodwill his party had engendered with grocery executives. "A few million dollars," he quipped, "are lost in the sands of time."

For his part, Wilson worried that Johnson had the style of one of those television pitchmen shouting, "We will not be undersold!" He was forever coming up with new ideas, independent of Wilson's beloved channels. Some were intriguing, although Johnson would likely have moved on to a whole different notion by the next day.

At least one of Johnson's ideas Wilson found disquieting. Soon after the merger had been completed, a spate of new lawsuits were filed against tobacco companies, charging they had caused smokers' deaths. Reynolds's stock, which had been marching steadily upward, fell more than ten points into the mid-twenties. Johnson came bursting into Wilson's office. "You know, Ty, we really ought to be thinking about doing an LBO."

Wilson eyed Johnson coldly; he knew all about leveraged buyouts and didn't like them a bit. "Ross," he said, "I don't think much of that idea." Wilson gave Johnson a lecture on how the industry would win those suits, how the tobacco stocks would recover. "I know this is a frustrating time," he said, "but it's only a temporary setback."

For all their differences in style, Wilson and Johnson rarely disagreed on business matters, and Wilson came to appreciate Johnson's quick mind. Johnson was especially useful to his boss in handling the planned consolidation of Nabisco and Del Monte. Johnson also made points by firing Sammy Gordon, the banana trader close to Paul Sticht. After most major mergers some businesses must be sold; Johnson and Wilson easily agreed which ones. Canada Dry was one; Del Monte frozen foods another. Johnson did his usual masterful job of selling them.

Wilson, in fact, was so pleased with Johnson that he encouraged him to get to know the board members. Sticht, who initially tagged Johnson as a slippery character, shared a transatlantic plane flight with him and later told a luncheon companion, "You know, he's not a bad sort." Other directors were even more taken. Much as it had with Henry Weigl a decade before, Johnson's easy charm contrasted sharply with the prickliness of his boss. Wilson plowed through a five-point discourse on why Canada Dry didn't fit into the strategic plan and therefore must be divested. Johnson simply told directors, "You could walk on water with that business, and holy hell! There's the boys from Coke and Pepsi waiting for you on the other side."

Behind his back Johnson made fun of Wilson, whom he called "Jiggerballs." Nobody knew what that meant exactly, but it clearly didn't fall into the category of affectionate nicknames. On trips to New York, Johnson spun great tales of Wilson and the faltering tobacco business for his despondent chums. "Why, if you listened to our guys, you'd think we were kicking the shit out of Philip Morris," Johnson told them. "It reminds me of the boxer who's getting beat up something awful and going back to his corner at the end of the round saying, 'He never laid a glove on me.' The trainer says, 'Well, keep an eye on the referee, because somebody's kicking the shit out of you.' "

After eight months in Winston-Salem, Johnson was dying for a dose of the old glitz, and he arranged to get a double shot that March in Palm Springs. For the Reynolds executives and directors, their first Dinah Shore was a mindblower. Attendees gained admission to events by flashing the $1,500 Gucci watch each was given. That year's "Night with Dinah" gala featured Frank Sinatra crooning, Bob Hope joking, and Don Meredith emceeing. "That's an awful leak you've got out there," cracked Meredith, referring to the fountain out front. "But don't worry; Ross will throw enough money at it to fix it." Albert Butler, the Winston-Salem patrician, found himself paired with golf star Pat Bradley and baseball legend Johnny Bench and prayed he wouldn't shank the ball in the crowd à la former president Gerald Ford, who was also playing.

The Reynolds crowd had never seen anything like it. Over the years the company had sponsored sporting events, but it leaned toward stock-car racing. The weeklong orgy of golf and glamour concluded with more gifts—Nabisco golf shoes and tennis shirts, Polaroid cameras, and compact disc players—all that each invitee's complimentary suitcase could carry. "We were all flabbergasted," recalled Butler. It was at the Dinah Shore that the strained relationship between Wilson and Sticht finally fell apart when Sticht was unable to land a seat on an RJR jet home. He blamed Wilson. Sticht was still simmering three months later when, on a morning drive into his downtown Winston-Salem office, he noticed a new building going up near the Whitaker Park cigarette plant. "What's that?" Sticht asked his driver, Eddie.

"That's where they're going to work on that smokeless cigarette," Eddie said.

"What?" Sticht asked in amazement.

Sticht immediately confronted Wilson, who admitted the company had been secretly trying to develop a breakthrough product, a new high-tech, "smokeless" cigarette. Wilson said he had been planning to mention it to the board soon. Sticht was aghast; that such a product could be developed without consulting the board was unthinkable.

"How long have you been doing this?" he asked.

"Since 1981," said Wilson. Five years.

"Why didn't you come to the board with it sooner?" asked Sticht.

"Because it's had to go through years and years of testing to get to the point where we could even think about its being viable," Wilson replied.

What Wilson didn't say was that he hadn't trusted the board to keep the project secret. Nor did he mention that he had funded its development by dribbling out appropriations in increments small enough to avoid having to obtain the board's approval.

Project Spa, as it was code-named, was indeed a revolutionary product. Later named Premier, the smokeless cigarette was Wilson's secret weapon to turn the tide on the antismoking movement, smite Marlboro, and reverse the tobacco industry's decline. Premier itself resembled a normal cigarette. Inside, though, it held only a smidgen of tobacco. A smoker lit a carbon tip on the end, heating, not burning, the tobacco and "flavor beads" inside. The process produced almost no smoke and no tar at all—only a fraction, in fact, of the compounds that had been linked to cancer. Wilson hoped it would keep smokers from quitting and draw ex-smokers back to Reynolds.

Whatever its chances of success, the board was incensed that Wilson would attempt such a mammoth undertaking without its approval. He was summoned to explain himself at a July 1986 board meeting in New York. Wilson came fully armed, his tobacco executives giving a full presentation on all of Premier's features. Wilson offered to let the directors smoke one. Albert Butler did, and didn't think it tasted or smelled very good. But it soon became apparent Wilson had bigger problems than foul-smelling cigarettes.

"Why didn't you tell us about this sooner?" Juanita Kreps demanded. Wilson repeated the explanation he had given Sticht, but Kreps didn't buy it. "You trust hundreds of company people working on this project; you trust dozens of people at an ad agency you're working with; you trust outside suppliers and scientists; but you don't trust us," she said. "I, for one, absolutely resent that."

One by one, the other directors echoed Kreps's concerns, and added more of their own. Stuart Watson of Heublein, for example, was steamed that Wilson was planning to sell Kentucky Fried Chicken. He didn't feel the board had been consulted on that, either. "Don't you trust us?" Watson asked. "Don't you trust us?"

A pair of Sticht allies, Ron Grierson and John Macomber, chimed in from their perches on the audit committee. The $68 million Wilson had secretly authorized for Premier's development far exceeded his spending limit set by the board. Why, the two asked, hadn't it been brought to the audit committee? Soon Sticht jumped in personally to deliver his licks, as well. The meeting droned on so long that New York police ordered the directors' limousines, which were lined up along Grand Army Plaza, to pull away. When the session finally ended, Project Spa had tentative approval to proceed—it had gone so far it hardly seemed worth canceling—and Tylee Wilson had used up what little political capital he retained with his board of directors.

After a year of working elbow-to-elbow with Wilson, Johnson now struck like lightning. Out of the blue he telephoned several directors and told them he planned to leave RJR Nabisco, possibly to head a British food company, Beecham PLC. No, Johnson told each board member, don't try to stop me. There wasn't anything they could do; he felt his work was done after having successfully merged the two companies. Only one man could be chief executive, Johnson suggested coyly, and Wilson was clearly the board's choice. It was time to move on.

75

"Not so fast," said one director, Charlie Hugel, just as Johnson knew he would. "Maybe you can run this place."

Hugel invited Ross and Laurie Johnson to his New Hampshire summer place on Lake Winnipesaukee. The two men sat on the back porch nearly all night talking. They examined all Johnson's options. They analyzed each board member. They sipped drinks. They decided, at 4 A.M., that Johnson should take a run at Tylee Wilson.

The following weekend, Hugel invited over Paul Sticht, who had a nearby home. They, too, had a long heart-to-heart on the back porch. Hugel wasn't surprised to find Sticht receptive. Johnson made a personal pilgrimage to follow up with Sticht, flying to New Hampshire in a borrowed American Express jet to avoid alerting Wilson. "Well," said Sticht when Johnson walked in, "we've wondered why it took you so long to get here."

Soon Sticht enlisted Macomber, who thought Wilson's ouster a positively bully idea. He and Sticht would pursue Johnson's case with other old-line board members. Hugel would work the Nabisco side of the aisle, though the likes of Andy Sage, Bob Schaeberle, and Jim Welch hardly needed convincing. They were old Johnson partisans.

Having planted the seed, Johnson laid back to watch. Sticht and Macomber dutifully carried his case to the other directors. "We can't afford to lose Ross," Macomber said, pointing out that without Johnson the company had only Ed Horrigan to fall back on in an emergency. "How could we ever fire Ty if we did that?" Then, in the first week of August, Johnson told Wilson he planned to resign. Wilson was alarmed, although for the wrong reasons. He, too, hated to lose Johnson. Thinking fast, Wilson noted a compensation committee meeting the following week, where, he said, he would be glad to discuss moving up his retirement date to the middle of 1988, the end of 1987 if necessary. Then, satisfied the matter would hold a week, Wilson flew to his Florida Keys home for a few days off.

There Wilson began receiving disquieting calls from allies in Winston-Salem. His enemies, he heard, were massing for an assault, which would install Johnson. Worried, Wilson called John Medlin, the chairman of Wachovia Bank, one of only two directors Wilson had put on the board. "Yes, something's going on," Medlin said. "I wish I could help, but you've got a problem."

Wilson next called Hugel, who he knew was orchestrating the pro-Johnson movement. Should he call Sticht? Wilson wondered.

"He's not going to be any help," Hugel said cryptically.

Macomber? "There's no point in it," Hugel said. He gave it to Wilson straight: "You don't have the votes."

Wilson tried one last call to Vernon Jordan, but it was no use. "This one's lost," Jordan said. "You'd better cut yourself a deal and get out."

Wilson saw the writing on the wall. At the following week's meeting, he resigned. To go quietly, Wilson received a princely pact: a lump-sum payment of $3.25 million, continuation of his annual salary and bonus of $1.3 million until his official retirement at the end of 1987, and annual retirement pay totaling about $600,000 thereafter. The directors even threw in some perks: an office and secretary, a security system for his house, a car phone, and use of corporate apartments. Directors concocted a cover story for the public announcement. His departure, they announced, was in keeping with Wilson's long-standing desire for early retirement.

Following the meeting, the full board made the change official in a conference call. After the slightest of efforts, Ross Johnson was named chief executive of RJR Nabisco, America's nineteenth largest industrial company. "Well," Tylee Wilson muttered afterward, "they got me."

CHAPTER

3

Ross Johnson's rise to the helm of RJR Nabisco had proceeded with blinding speed: CEO of Nabisco in 1984, the Reynolds–Nabisco merger in 1985, CEO of RJR Nabisco in 1986. If he had stopped there, kicked back, and assumed the life of North Carolina gentry, history might have looked very differently on his career. But Johnson, a man who devoted his life to shaking things up, had no intention of changing his ways. Reynolds Tobacco churned out $1 billion a year in cash, enough to fund the wildest schemes and cover the worst mistakes. "A billion dollars," Johnson sometimes said reverentially. "You can't spend that much money in a year."

But in sleepy Winston-Salem Johnson was a Ferrari revving in a badly clogged parking lot. Under Wilson he had kept a low profile and avoided stirring up the locals. After he took control of RJR Nabisco in the fall of 1986, Johnson's honeymoon proved short. One of his first moves was dealing with Ed Horrigan. Just days after Johnson took the top post, Horrigan walked into his office and offered to resign. After a year of internal sniping, he figured he would quit before Johnson fired him. Johnson shocked Horrigan by refusing to accept the resignation. "No," Johnson said, "I need you."

Because Johnson still knew next to nothing about tobacco, he had to have a man who did and, whatever their past disagreements, he was determined it would be Horrigan. Horrigan had raged about the luxurious New York apartments Johnson's Nabisco chums had; Johnson now made sure Horrigan got the most luxurious of all, in the Museum Tower above the Museum of Modern Art. Wilson had made Horrigan pay for his weekend excursions to Palm Springs. Not only would RJR Nabisco foot the bill for the trips, but Johnson gave Horrigan his own personal Gulfstream G-3 jet, the top of the line in corporate aircraft, to use as he wished. Johnson even encouraged Horrigan to lease a company car in Palm Springs, and Horrigan happily obliged, selecting a Rolls Royce. Horrigan was given free rein to run Reynolds Tobacco and, to the shock of local gossipmongers, appeared to become fast friends with Johnson.

Next Johnson began to purge the ranks of the Reynolds Old Guard. Gwain Gillespie was fired as chief financial officer and replaced by Ed Robinson of Nabisco. John Dowdle, the treasurer, accepted an early retirement package and was replaced by Nabisco's Mack Baines. Rodney Austin was fired as personnel chief and replaced by Andrew Barrett of Nabisco. Public relations chief Ron Sustana thought he was a survivor when Johnson told him he would move to New York to better oversee the entire company. But Horrigan despised Sustana, and when Johnson found out, he had Sustana fired. Mike Masterpool of Nabisco replaced him. All down the line, Reynolds people were thrown into the streets to make room for Johnson's Nabisco cronies.

Johnson's troubles began when Winston-Salem began to notice the strange goings-on. Things the locals hadn't paid attention to when he was Wilson's number two were now held against him. No Reynolds executive in history had had a bodyguard, but at Old Town and Bermuda Run they whispered that Johnson hired one. He did. His name was Frank Mancini, a stocky ex–New York cop. The natives called him "Lurch."

Mancini was merely the vanguard of Johnson's effort to beef up Reynolds security. Tylee Wilson was alarmed one day to see a man with a gun on his hip skulking around in front of his home. When Wilson demanded an explanation, the man said he was an off-duty policeman handling security in the area, where Paul Sticht also lived. "Well, I don't like you parked out in front of my house," said Wilson. "I'm not scared of anything." Those who knew of the incident were baffled. Winston-Salem just wasn't that tough a town.

As Johnson consolidated his control, he shed his small-town poses and reverted to the Johnson of old. Most every weekend he jetted off to some far-flung golf club, tended to his tan in Florida, or hit Manhattan with Frank Gifford and other friends. Sticht had begun the process, but under

Johnson RJR Nabisco was finally torn loose from the old-fashioned Reynolds value system. Out went Moravian: Make way for bacchanalian.

Over the years the unassuming largess of Reynolds senior executives had created institutions such as the Bowman Gray School of Medicine. Johnson's idea of good works was the Pro-Am Golf Tournament he organized to benefit the Wake Forest golf team. He brought in Dinah Shore and Don Meredith to kick off the local United Way drive. He went on the North Carolina Zoological Society's board and headed a fund-raising campaign. But he raised eyebrows by descending on a function there in a helicopter: this in a town where Cadillacs were considered ostentatious. In a community of seersucker, Johnson pranced about with a puff handkerchief peeking jauntily from his jacket pocket.

The capper was his wife. At Old Town, the matrons would draw close at the luncheon table: Have you heard the *latest?* They called her Cupcake. Laurie Johnson was a gorgeous blond in her early thirties. The proper Reynolds wife wore conservative clothes and lots of makeup; Laurie bounced around in jogging suits, looking like the California girl she was. The proper Reynolds wife played bridge; Laurie was an ace golfer who could drive a ball as far as a man.

She tried to fit in. She found some charities as pet causes and became a trustee at the North Carolina School of the Arts. When the International Advisory Board met in Winston-Salem, Laurie led a shopping expedition to the outlet malls in nearby Burlington. The corporate wives from around the world, including a Norwegian princess, came back laden with shopping bags. Trump Tower it wasn't, but if there was one thing Laurie Johnson was good at, it was shopping.

It was hopeless, and the Johnsons didn't help matters any by flouting local mores. The gossips had a field day after Johnson took a top Wake Forest golfer under his wing and into his home. When the young golfer moved into the Johnsons' basement, rumors spread that he and Cupcake had been caught in the Jacuzzi in flagrante. Every time Johnson left on a business trip, tongues wagged that Cupcake was sleeping with the Old Town golf pros. When the rumors got back to the Johnsons, Laurie called her New York friends in tears. A lot of them couldn't possibly understand the cruelties a small town could inflict. Jim Robinson's wife, Linda, did. The Robinsons and Johnsons had vacationed together in Roaring Gap, a good place to learn about Winston-Salem's establishment. "If we don't like someone in Winston-Salem, we make them sweat," one Roaring Gap matron was overheard to say. "We made the Johnsons sweat for everything."

Tensions flared into the open that November, when a *Winston-Salem Journal* editorial took frowning note of the company's name change and management upheaval, wondering just who had acquired whom. "Looks as if someone may have underestimated the cookie monster's appetite," it said. For Johnson, it was one of the last straws. "I don't have to take this shit," he said. Although he had done his best to disguise the fact, he hated small-town life. This wasn't what he had spent his career struggling to escape the Canadian provinces for. He loathed the petty politics that had sprung up since the merger. Corporate staff at the Glass Menagerie were constantly warring with the tobacco people downtown: Johnson quickly tired of moderating their disputes.

But the worst part was simply living in Winston-Salem. "You keep running into the same people over and over," he told his New York friends. And few of the locals did Johnson relish seeing. He longed to light up a cigar with Jim Robinson or Marty Davis or Rand Araskog of ITT. Peers. Horrigan was good for a few laughs; at least he could hold his Scotch. And there was John Medlin of Wachovia. But that was it. None of the Merry Men, city-bred Yankees and foreigners, would move south. Their loyalty only went so far.

"You had a town of one hundred and forty thousand people, where you've got seventeen thousand people working for the company and ten thousand retirees and you can't breathe," Johnson recalled.

To Johnson there seemed only one conclusion: move. Relocating RJR Nabisco's headquarters would kill Winston-Salem, drive a dagger right through its proud, provincial heart. Johnson knew it, and began laying his groundwork carefully. First a cadre of close advisers began discreetly evaluating new sites. New York was an obvious candidate, although so far afield that it would inevitably jar the board, to whose feelings Johnson remained acutely tuned. Reynolds veterans would never move there, and some had to be retained, if only to avoid alarming the board. Dallas was Johnson's kind of town, bursting with new money and rootless people and centrally located to Palm Beach and Vail, where Johnson maintained retreats. But he sensed it was a city in decline, what with the oil bust and the Dallas Cowboys beginning to lose football games.

Atlanta also intrigued Johnson. Like Dallas it was nouveau riche and rootless—and deliciously overbuilt. Top-of-the-line office space was going begging, ready for instant occupancy. It was near enough to Winston-Salem to be politically plausible. Then while in London one evening that fall, Johnson ran into an old acquaintance, Don Keough, the president of Coca-Cola, at a dinner given by Ambassador Charles Price for the Queen. As Keough's wife shushed them to listen to Her Highness, Keough heartily endorsed Atlanta.

Atlanta it was. His site chosen, Johnson began working the board. "Corporate and tobacco are armpit to armpit in this town," he told Albert Butler. "It's not a healthy situation." Butler was won over. Johnson also won over John Medlin. Wachovia had just bought a major Atlanta bank and was trying to maintain a jury-rigged two-headquarters setup; Medlin well understood the pros and cons of each city.

The biggest problem figured to be Sticht. The Glass Menagerie was his pride and joy. It was Sticht's secret hope, Johnson suspected, that the building would one day be named after him. Money could ease the pain; Johnson boosted Sticht's consulting contract to $250,000 a year from $185,000. Prestige could do the rest. Johnson made Sticht chairman of the International Advisory Board and promised to restore it to its pre-Wilson glory. A $6 million donation for the J. Paul Sticht Center on Aging at the Bowman Gray School of Medicine helped. Sticht soon came around. With the three local directors backing Johnson, the rest of the board's support seemed assured.

But before the board could make the move official, the *Atlanta Constitution* broke the news, triggering the predictable fire storm in Winston-Salem. The *Winston-Salem Journal* implored the board to stay put, noting that local workers had built the company and local men had led it to greatness. "The corporate soul and mind can flourish only where the heart, the roots, and the heritage are," said the front-page editorial. "For the soul to survive, the head belongs with the heart."

Overnight Johnson became a local pariah. One man had brought Reynolds into Winston-Salem on a horse; another would take it away on a Gulfstream jet. A country music station had a local hit with a ballad excoriating Johnson. Hobert Johnson, the factory worker cum major shareholder, marched into Johnson's office seeking an audience; the steaming-mad octogenarian cooled his heels for half a day before heading home and composing an angry letter. "We built the foundation for this company," he wrote Johnson, "when you were in your knee pants."

Johnson tried to defend himself in a speech to the Winston-Salem

Rotary Club. But those who attended didn't so much remember the words as the aftermath. A phalanx of bodyguards surrounded Johnson and hustled him out on a freight elevator. One word that was remembered was *bucolic,* which was how Johnson described Winston-Salem in an interview with the *Atlanta Constitution.* Bumper stickers began appearing around town: "Honk if you're bucolic." Another had "RJR" on the left with a thumbs-up, "Nabisco" on the right with a thumbs-down.

Savage new gossip about the Johnsons made the rounds. Rumors had Ross beaten up by local toughs. Cupcake had run off with a golf pro. Cupcake had run off with a tennis pro. Amid the turmoil, Johnson attempted to do something nice for his embattled wife. The wife of Johnson's friend Dwayne Andreas, the chairman of Archer Daniels Midland, was a trustee at a small Florida college named Barry University. Johnson arranged for the RJR Nabisco foundation to make a fat donation to Barry for a new gymnasium; in return, the university would bestow Johnson with an honorary doctorate. When Johnson insisted his wife get one, too, Barry agreed. Now the couple's critics took to calling Laurie "Dr. Cupcake."

Hundreds of workers who wouldn't make the move to Atlanta would be fired. Reynolds veterans who never before worried about losing the shelter of their fatherly employer now lived in daily fear of finding pink slips on their desks. In some cases, entire departments were summoned for what amounted to mass executions. The tension was unbearable. "Shoot me between the eyes," a man in the tax department cried out one day, "but don't keep me in suspense like this." The Reynolds work ethic died hard. A group of four secretaries fired one afternoon stayed past midnight to complete a project.

Gallows humor flourished. Bob Carbonell, Johnson's Latin American hatchet man, was said to have been recruited from a Salvadoran death squad. Photocopying machines worked overtime producing underground cartoons. In one Johnson was depicted climbing the miniature Empire State Building à la King Kong. In another he was depicted as a missing child. The caption: "Happiness is when you wake up and see Ross's picture on the milk carton." Among the most bitter was one showing a rat, identified as F. Ross Johnson, feverishly humping another rat, labeled RJR Tobacco, as it lay helplessly pinned in a trap. The trap was labeled Bucolic Traps Inc.; the bait was an Oreo. A group of other rats ran eagerly out of a boardroom to watch. "Hey Ross," asked one, "what does the 'F' mean?"

83

Johnson, a man with almost no roots, couldn't fathom the emotions he had unleashed. "Jesus Christ," he said, "Exxon takes seven thousand jobs out of New York and nobody bats an eyelash. I move a few hundred jobs out of there and I'm Attila the Hun."

His reaction said a lot about Johnson, a man who felt aides didn't have a job but an assignment, who felt the moment he established an organization it started to decay, that standing still was a sucker's play. Why, he wondered, couldn't Winston-Salem see the plodder's day was past? The world was changing; you had to keep moving, or you were passed by. "Ross is addicted to action, to a constant dynamism," said O. C. Adams, a Connecticut psychologist who consulted with Johnson on personnel matters. "He can't always see what effect that has on others."

The backlash made no difference. The meetings with Winston-Salem's mayor and North Carolina's governor did nothing to change Johnson's mind. Even before the move was officially announced, he and Laurie had picked out a new million-dollar home in Atlanta. The only sign of real trouble came when Sticht changed his mind about the move. Few in Winston-Salem knew how Johnson had come to replace Wilson, but most suspected it had somehow been orchestrated by Sticht. When news of the Atlanta move broke, Sticht was suddenly called to account and forced to field tough questions about the man he had supposedly chosen to run Reynolds. Sticht had voted in favor of the move, but under mounting pressure, walked into Johnson's office with Albert Butler and tried to stop it.

Johnson held his ground, but the incident gave him pause to reconsider Sticht's power, especially among his fellow board members. He had seen what Sticht and his allies had done to Wilson and was determined to avoid the same fate. No, Johnson told himself, Sticht had to be made an ally. After all the grants and raises he had lavished on Sticht, Johnson decided to do something more: He would name him chairman of RJR Nabisco. It would be a largely ceremonial position—Johnson would retain real power as president and chief executive—but the move would thrill Sticht.

"Don't do it; he'll only cause you trouble," Ed Horrigan said.

"Don't do it; you don't need him," Charlie Hugel said.

"You're kidding me," said Wilson, when Johnson replaced him with Sticht. "It's your company, so you do whatever the hell you like. But it's a sham, and you'll regret it." Weeks later Sticht was named chairman, and Wilson was right: Johnson came to regret it.

When the move to Atlanta was officially announced in mid-January 1987, Johnson put the best face on it. Only the corporate headquarters was moving. Some of the thousand staffers would be offered jobs in Atlanta. Some would be transferred to tobacco. The 12,000-plus people at RJ Reynolds Tobacco would stay put, and only a few hundred jobs in Winston-Salem would be lost. (That, in fact, was how it worked out.) Johnson made one final gesture to soothe Winston-Salem's pain, donating the Glass Menagerie to Wake Forest.

Atlanta awaited, its throngs of boosterish businessmen thrilled to welcome a major *Fortune* 500 company to their ranks. But if the city thought it was getting a warm corporate benefactor eager to put down roots, it soon discovered the truth about restless Ross Johnson. Johnson took over eleven floors in an unremarkable glass tower at a suburban shopping center named The Galleria. In his maiden public speech, he suggested that his skeletal headquarters staff should not be reckoned as a dispenser of corporate largess. "I told them I can't support every organization from the United Way to the Seven Jolly Girls Athletic Club Beanbag competition," Johnson later said to an interviewer. "If it pisses them off, I can't help that."

It was hardly the attitude city fathers had hoped for. "Don't worry, Winston-Salem," said the *Atlanta Constitution* headline the following day. "RJR move here was no great loss."

Just weeks after moving to Atlanta, Johnson again shocked RJR Nabisco partisans. At a meeting of securities analysts, he mentioned almost in passing that he was thinking of transforming Reynolds Tobacco from a corporation into a limited partnership. In Winston-Salem, shareholders panicked: What was a limited partnership? And how would it affect their beloved stock? Inside the company, people rolled their eyes. No one could tell whether it was a certainty or just another half-baked idea sprung from Johnson's unpredictable mind.

The announcement, in fact, signaled a change in Johnson's corporate focus. As takeovers swept Corporate America during the 1980s, Wall Street investment bankers had long salivated at Reynolds's massive cash flow; it begged to be put to use in acquisitions. But they had never gotten to first base with Wilson, who relied for financial advice on solid, conservative Dillon Read. When Merrill Lynch bankers suggested looking at an

LBO, Wilson's chief financial officer, Gwain Gillespie, sent them packing.

But Johnson was another matter. Here was a man the Wall Streeters could talk deals with. Big deals. Exotic deals. The companies Johnson ran were in a state of constant flux, buying, selling, and reshaping their parts in tried-and-true Pesketteer fashion. His door had always been open to discuss possibilities, whether the caller was Tylee Wilson, Bob Schaeberle, or a Wall Streeter with a briefcase full of ideas. The move to Atlanta brought investment bankers streaming south like june bugs to a light on a hot Georgia night. To Horrigan, the growing tide of Wall Street callers resembled "a steady stream of salesmen calling on the boss. It was because Ross was so open to it. It just got his juices flowing."

Sometimes it got to be a bit much: Of the forty or so phone messages Johnson accumulated on an average day, more than half would be from investment bankers. Johnson had always had his share of harebrained schemes, but now friends joked that Johnson and the bankers formed an "idea of the week" club. His Monday Night Wrecking Crew long since broken up, Johnson enjoyed "bullshitting" with the bankers. He regarded their constant flow of ideas as free advice. "Why have a dog and bark for yourself?" he would ask.

The limited partnership idea had come from one of Johnson's most determined pursuers, a wild-eyed Wall Street dealmaker named Jeffrey Beck. Beck worked for Drexel Burnham Lambert, the sharp-elbowed investment house whose Beverly Hills–based junk-bond chief, Michael Milken, almost single-handedly transformed the takeover business in the mid-1980s.* On Wall Street they called Beck "Mad Dog." Although he sported a bow tie and horn-rim glasses, Beck more closely resembled a cross between a stand-up comedian and an assassin.

A true character, Beck styled himself the ultimate wheeler-dealer, a rock-'em-sock-'em, behind-the-scenes operator, one of Wall Street's top

* In early 1987 Drexel Burnham and Michael Milken came under federal investigation for violating securities laws as part of the Ivan Boesky insider-trading probe. Drexel ultimately settled sweeping charges of wrongdoing with prosecutors in December 1988; Milken was indicted the following spring.

seven dealmakers—he could name the other six—a bit of hubris not terribly far from the truth. "Rock and roll!" he would shout to greet good news, "lock and load" before entering a tense meeting. Beck served as informal adviser on the movie *Wall Street* and even took a cameo role, delivering an angry, improvised speech as an investment banker readying his troops for a hostile takeover.

While other bankers specialized in analysis or combat tactics, Beck made a career out of fast talking and histrionics. When one of his biggest deals, the LBO of a Chicago food company named Esmark, was topped by another bidder, Beck pleaded with Esmark's chairman, Donald Kelly, to pay him for setting events in motion.

"You got to do something for me; you got to do something for me," Beck moaned, lying spread-eagle on the floor of an Esmark office. Kelly, who intended to give Beck a fee, decided to play a joke on him by pretending to ignore his pleas. "He'll go crazy," Kelly told an aide, "It'll be fun to watch." Beck was called into Kelly's office and given the bad news. "Oh my God; oh my God; you can't do this to me," moaned Mad Dog, who proceeded to open Kelly's office window. "That's it! I'm going to jump out the window! I'm going to kill myself." Kelly, breaking up in laughter, yelled, "Don't jump!" For his work, and his dramatics, Beck received a $7.5 million fee.

Beck courted Johnson with his usual intensity. When, shortly after their initial meeting, the Johnsons were vacationing in the south of France, Beck sent the couple a bottle of Roederer Cristal and flowers. "Have a good vacation," the card read, "from the Mad Dog." Johnson instantly took to Beck's frat-house mien. At their second meeting, he brought along a box of Milk Bone dog biscuits, a joke on Beck's nickname. Then, while discussing restructuring plans with the chief of America's nineteenth largest industrial company, the Mad Dog ate the whole box.

In late 1986, Beck was peddling the notion of a master limited partnership for Reynolds Tobacco. Johnson had long been worried that RJR Nabisco's stock price was unfairly penalized because of the company's tobacco operations. He believed investors never factored in Nabisco, choosing only to focus on tobacco's bleak future. Beck's partnership idea, code-named Project Alpha, was intended to combat that perception. Holders of common stock typically receive small cash dividends. But by replacing much of RJR Nabisco's stock with partnership "units," a portion of Reynolds's extraordinary cash flow could flow directly to the unit holders, allowing them to wallow in huge payouts while avoiding the corporate tax on common stock. Beck's hope was that the sky-high trading values of the partnership units would rub off on RJR Nabisco's remaining common stock, making everyone richer. Johnson thought the idea was impossibly complicated, but went along when Beck offered to do the work for free. The Mad Dog knew his favor would be paid off in more business later.

Johnson was an idea man, not a details man. As ideas like Beck's began to pile up, he handed them off to an informal group of advisers he took to calling his "financial R&D department." Johnson looked to the group, headed by his old friend Andy Sage, to separate the wheat from the chaff and perhaps come up with a few financial tricks of its own.

Sage, who had sat on Johnson-run boards since the Weigl coup, was the son of a Wall Street stock specialist. He had been kicked out of the elite prep school St. Paul's, and his higher education was a trade school. But Sage had a certain eclectic brilliance that enabled him to fly planes, master the piano, and rise to the top of Lehman Brothers. He became managing partner and then president. But it had been years since he was very active on the Street and, at age sixty, was considered practically a museum piece. He came across as an absentminded professor, given to wearing rumpled old suits.

But Sage was that rarest of Wall Streeters, less interested in selling businesses than tending to how they ran. Over the years he had been active in the restructuring of International Harvester, an architect of the Alaska pipeline financing, and, as chairman of the American Motors executive committee, helped steer that company through the shoals. He was a peripatetic figure, shuttling between homes in New York, Jackson Hole, and Palm Beach, where he had kept the home he bought from Johnson years before. When Reynolds acquired Nabisco, Sage added Winston-Salem to the list of places he hung his hat. There he would borrow an office and spend hours going through balance sheets and income statements.

To pore over Johnson's ideas, Sage hired a Washington-based consultant named Frank Benevento, whom Johnson took to calling "Sir Francis." Benevento was an odd choice. At thirty-nine he had limited Wall Street experience: four years at Lehman Brothers. He had been a Washington lawyer before that and an energy-industry investor and executive since. Sage was a mentor to Benevento and an occasional investor in his ventures. The two talked for hours about what they called "financial architecture." Johnson thought the pair was top-notch; when their work surfaced months later, his Wall Street friends would wonder why.

Benevento lived to untangle financial knots, and at Sage's direction, he plunged into Drexel's Project Alpha with gusto. Limited partnerships had proven somewhat successful in the oil and gas industry, and in meetings with Johnson and Sage, Benevento would prattle on for hours about new ways to reshape their architecture. He reminded Johnson of a mad scientist.

Still, Project Alpha ultimately died. Benevento wasn't convinced the idea would help the stock, and Johnson, always wary of bureaucracy, recoiled at the paperwork it would require. "Holy God," he said when they killed it. "We'd have to get another tower here full of people doing everybody's tax returns. It's two hundred dollars of labor to save a dollar of material." Two months after riling Winston-Salem and Wall Street by mentioning the limited partnership, Johnson announced he was no longer considering it.

Beck was undaunted. He promptly came back to Johnson with reams of computer printouts and another idea. Why not split up the company, spinning off Reynolds to shareholders and allowing management to acquire Nabisco in a leveraged buyout? Johnson passed the idea to Sage, who came up with his own twist. It involved redeeming all of RJR Nabisco's stock for a package of cash and stock; management could then acquire Nabisco in an LBO valued at around $6 billion. Sage liked the idea enough that he assigned it the code name Project Sadim—*Midas* spelled backward. Benevento, too, got excited and passed his thoughts on to Johnson.

Johnson yawned. In an executive suite noted for "ideas of the week," Benevento's scribblings were yesterday's news by the time they crossed his desk. Johnson himself had a new plan. It involved constructing a "third leg" for RJR Nabisco in the media business, a fascination that dated back to his friendship with Gifford. The immediate object of his attention was ESPN, the all-sports cable-television network of which RJR Nabisco already owned 20 percent; Johnson had become intrigued with the idea of buying the 80 percent of ESPN owned by Capital Cities/ABC. Don Ohlmeyer was brought in to evaluate the company, and Johnson for once followed through, offering to buy out Cap Cities for $720 million. He was turned down flat.

Benevento was also left flat. He had hoped Johnson would broach their LBO idea at a board meeting in Palm Springs in late March. But as Benevento sat by idle, Johnson focused instead on ESPN, never mentioning any of financial R&D's schemes. Later Johnson told Benevento to forget about LBOs for now. For all his free-spending ways, the fact was Johnson remained a prude about corporate debt, the core of any LBO. He remembered the backbreaking trips to GSW's bankers twenty years before and cringed. Banks didn't understand the need for golf tournaments and corporate jets. They cramped his style. No, he told Benevento, he'd take a pass on an LBO.

Jeff Beck proved tenacious. He knew what made Johnson tick; at Drexel, one of Johnson's nicknames was "Starfucker." Hearing RJR Nabisco might be interested in media properties, Beck arranged a dinner at a posh New York restaurant, La Côte Basque, for Johnson to meet the actor Michael Douglas, a friend of Beck's who was looking to start his own production company. Nothing came of it, although Johnson had a marvelous time, as always.

————

His power consolidated, Johnson relaxed and began to enjoy himself. Freed from the constraints of Winston-Salem, RJR Nabisco was a blank canvas Johnson now set to painting. The order of the day was having fun, and for Johnson that meant two things: movement and perks.

From his new office above The Galleria, Johnson played the role of master puppeteer, keeping the company and its officers in a constant state of reorganization. Some of the changes seemed like sheer mischief. Johnson would order that two business units change buildings, knowing that one would wind up bursting at the seams, while the other would be rattling around looking for ways to grow. The joke at Nabisco offices in New Jersey was that Johnson owned a piece of a company called Quirk Moving Systems, which did all the moving. In the blink of an eye he would order reporting relationships inverted, with the subordinate becoming the boss. "If my boss calls," the joke went, "ask him for his name and number."

While Johnson chuckled at the helm, his whipsawed junior executives found the constant shuffling no joking matter. A case in point was the July transfer of a Nabisco unit, Planters/Life Savers, to Winston-Salem, where it reported to Horrigan. The official reason for the move was that the distribution system of nuts and candies coincided with that of cigarettes; they were all so-called front-of-the-store items, sold in racks near cash registers. The real reason seemed to have more to do with padding Horrigan's empire, soothing Winston-Salem's pain, and providing new jobs for out-of-work Reynolds employees. Planters's president, Martin Orlowsky, protested the move so vehemently that he was replaced by a Horrigan favorite. Scores of other Planters executives left rather than move to Winston-Salem and work with the Reynolds Death Merchants.

John Greeniaus, Nabisco's up-and-coming forty-two-year-old president, also fought the move bitterly until Johnson cut him off. "Hey Johnny," he said, "stop taking things so seriously. Maybe it's right; maybe it's wrong. So what? We'll find out." The exchange captured both the slapdash spirit of the day and Johnson's continued ignorance of the pain his whims were inflicting. But the Planters move also demonstrated the hazards of Johnson's impetuous nature. Having donated the Glass Menagerie to Wake Forest, there was no office space in Winston-Salem in which to put the incoming workers. RJR Nabisco was forced to lease the building back from the college.

For his part, Johnson stayed clear of Winston-Salem as much as possible. He remained a marked man in North Carolina. That summer Reynolds announced an early retirement program in an effort to trim 2,800 more people from the payroll. As always, Johnson got the blame. A story, widely believed, made the rounds in Winston-Salem that Johnson had gotten into a fistfight with Jerry Long, the domestic tobacco chief. Long had been defending the interests of Reynolds workers, the story went, and had given Johnson a fat lip. Both men denied it, explaining that the rumor began on a day Johnson cut himself shaving and Long arrived for work in a cast following minor surgery. But it was a tough story to kill, because everyone in Winston-Salem wanted so badly to believe it. Later, after Long was purged from Reynolds, he ran for the county commission. When he was elected, some political observers gave credit to the lingering story of the Johnson fistfight.

When Johnson returned to play in a Reynolds-sponsored golf tournament, the Vantage Pro-Am, he took hell from the gallery. He invited some of the abuse, arriving at the course in a helicopter and tooling around in a golf cart with his name on it. "Go back to Atlanta, you bucolic bastard," someone shouted. Even Johnson's playing partner, Arnold Palmer, couldn't escape the invective. "Nice drive, Arnie," someone yelled. "Too bad you have to play with that son of a bitch." The *pièce de résistance*, though, came as Johnson was carefully lining up a putt. Suddenly a voice bellowed from the gallery: "It breaks south, you bastard, toward Atlanta."

His estrangement from Winston-Salem may have contributed to Johnson's continued pampering of Horrigan. Having buried their old enmities, the two were actually growing close, as were their wives: Betty Horrigan was Canadian, and she could keep up with Laurie Johnson on the fairways. Johnson continued to give Horrigan everything he wanted and some things he didn't ask for, including exclusive use of a lavish new home the company had bought at the Loxahatchee Country Club outside Palm Beach.

He even indulged Horrigan's fetish for limousines. And not just any limo. When traveling, Horrigan insisted on a white stretch. He grew apoplectic if it was anything else, or if a chauffeur wasn't on hand at all times. Horrigan even insisted one be on hand to drive the few hundred yards between the Atlanta headquarters and the Waverly Hotel. The 1980s had introduced limos to Winston-Salem, and, with Johnson's approval, Horrigan switched the Reynolds fleet from black Lincoln Town Cars to maroon Cadillacs, with matching uniforms for the drivers. Maroon was Horrigan's favorite color.

Johnson would roar with laughter at Horrigan's peccadilloes and his craving for perks, but he granted every one. "I didn't care about the $50,000 for a chauffeur," Johnson said years later. "I cared about the $1.2 billion [tobacco cash flow]." As Johnson was distracted by other matters, he came to depend more and more on Horrigan to run tobacco, still the largest source of RJR Nabisco's profits. "The only question is," Johnson would say, "is the screwing I'm getting worth the screwing I'm getting?"

One evening the Horrigans had the Johnsons over for dinner. Talk turned to the burgeoning LBO phenomenon. "Oh hell, we'll never do a buyout," Johnson said. "Just think of all the people that would be affected; we can't do that. Do we want to have to fire thousands of people? Can we live with that?" Besides, he added, "We have the best jobs in America."

It was no lie. RJR executives lived like kings. The top thirty-one executives were paid a total of $14.2 million, or an average of $458,000. Some of them became legends at the Waverly for dispensing $100 tips to the shoeshine girl. Johnson's two maids were on the company payroll, and Johnson's lieutenants single-handedly perked up the upper end of Atlanta's housing market.

No expense was spared in decorating the new headquarters, highlighted by the top-floor digs of the top executives. The reception area's backdrop was an eighteenth-century $100,000 lacquered Chinese screen, complemented by a $16,000 pair of powder blue Chinese vases from a slightly later dynasty. Visitors could settle into a set of French Empire mahogany chairs ($30,000) and ogle the two matching *bibliothèque* cabinets ($30,000) from the same period. In each was an English porcelain dessert service in a tobacco-leaf pattern ($20,000). The visitor might be ushered in to see Bob Carbonell and pad across his camel-colored $50,000 Persian rug. Or, if the visitor was lucky enough to see Ross Johnson, they could jointly admire the $30,000 worth of blue-and-white eighteenth-century porcelain china scattered throughout his office.

If the visitor was really lucky, he was an antique dealer in town to take more orders. RJR was the toast of dealers in London, Paris, and New York. Laurie Johnson personally supervised many purchases on European jaunts with her decorator. Despite the $50 million cost of moving the headquarters, multimillion-dollar decorating projects were also underway at the old tobacco headquarters and the new Washington office. "It was the only company I ever worked for without a budget," gasped one grateful vendor.

It was, literally, the sweet life. A candy cart came around twice a day, dropping off bowls of bonbons at each floor's reception areas. Not Baby Ruths but fine French confections. The minimum perks for even lowly middle managers was one club membership and one company car, worth up to $28,000. (For serious luxury cars, executives had to kick in some of their own money.) The maximum, as nearly as anyone could tell, was Johnson's two-dozen club memberships and John Martin's $75,000 Mercedes.

Sweet as the surroundings were, the new headquarters developed a clear caste system. About a third of the 400 people working there had moved from New Jersey. Many were Standard Brands veterans. Another third were Reynolds people from Winston-Salem. The remaining third, mostly secretaries and support staff, were new hires from Atlanta. The Reynolds veterans felt they shouldered much of the menial work. Some began calling themselves "the mushroom farmers" because they worked in the dark and just kept shoveling manure.

An inescapable air of the transitory pervaded the new headquarters. Instead of the grand old tobacco building in Winston-Salem, or even the Glass Menagerie across the street from a cigarette factory, Johnson had moved RJR Nabisco into a spec office building in a mall-hotel-office park complex that overlooked a highway cloverleaf. Some of Johnson's lieutenants—Ed Robinson and Andy Hines, the controller—hadn't even bothered to sell their houses up north. Ward Miller, the corporate secretary, hadn't even moved to Atlanta. Everything about RJR Nabisco said, "We're just passing through."

But it was at nearby Charlie Brown Airport, where corporate Atlanta housed its jets, that the air of new money and restlessness found its ultimate expression. There Johnson ordered a new hangar built to house RJR Nabisco's growing fleet of corporate aircraft. Reynolds had a half-dozen jets, and Nabisco a couple of Falcon 50s and a Lear, tiny planes an executive like Johnson wouldn't be caught dead in. After the arrival of two new Gulfstreams, Johnson ordered a pair of top-of-the-line G4s, at a cool $21 million apiece. For the hangar, Johnson gave aviation head Linda Galvin an unlimited budget and implicit instructions to exceed it.

When it was finished, RJR Nabisco had the Taj Mahal of corporate hangars, dwarfing that of Coca-Cola's next door. The cost hadn't gone into the hangar itself, but into an adjacent three-story building of tinted glass, surrounded by $250,000 in landscaping, complete with a Japanese garden. Inside a visitor walked into a stunning three-story atrium. The floors were Italian marble, the walls and doors lined in inlaid mahogany. More than $600,000 in new furniture was spread throughout, topped off by $100,000 in objets d'art, including an antique Chinese ceremonial robe spread in a glass case and a magnificent Chinese platter and urn. In one corner of the ornate bathroom stood a stuffed chair, as if one might grow fatigued walking from one end to the other. Among the building's other features: a walk-in wine cooler; a "visiting pilots' room," with television and stereo; and a "flight-planning room," packed with state-of-the-art computers to track executives' whereabouts and their future transportation wishes. All this was necessary to keep track of RJR Nabisco's thirty-six corporate pilots and ten planes, widely known as the RJR Air Force.

The aviation staff presented the plans for all this to Johnson with some trepidation. He had said state-of-the-art, but this cost $12 million. He had wanted everything a corporate-jet hangar could possibly have, but this came out to 20,000 square feet. Johnson looked over the drawings, heard out the architects, and made his recommendation: add another 7,000 square feet.

The RJR Air Force was a defining symbol for Johnson. It was all about restlessness and restiveness. It was also about dispensing favors. Frank Gifford got rides home from "Monday Night Football" games. Gifford and his talk-show host bride, Kathie Lee, were whisked away to their honeymoon on an RJR Nabisco jet. (Johnson was best man at the wedding.) When Roone Arledge needed a lift from Los Angeles to San Francisco, an RJR jet was dispatched from Atlanta. Johnson's old buddy Martin Emmett, long gone from the company, racked up more miles on Johnson's jets one year than nearly anyone still employed.

The jets were also a symbol of the increasingly fuzzy line between what constituted proper use of a corporate asset and what constituted abuse. Some thought the case of Johnson's German shepherd, Rocco, fell in the latter category. At the Dinah Shore that year, Rocco bit a security guard, setting off a flurry of concern in the Johnson household.

Would he be seized by the authorities and quarantined, or worse? Rocco, it was decided, had to go on the lam. He was smuggled onto a corporate jet and secretly flown out of Palm Springs to Winston-Salem, one jump ahead of the law. Escorted by a senior vice president named Dennis Durden, Rocco was listed on the passenger manifold as "G. Shepherd." It wasn't the only Rocco adventure: The company would later pay an insurance claim for a bite inflicted on the Johnsons' gardener.*

The RJR Air Force was Johnson's ticket to the high life. Each weekend the planes disgorged Don Meredith from Santa Fe, or Bobby Orr from Boston, or the Mulroneys from Canada. The jocks of Team Nabisco were frequent flyers on Air Johnson. The Pope took excellent care of them, paying more for occasional public appearances than for an average senior vice president: Meredith got $500,000 a year, Gifford $413,000 (plus a New York office and apartment), golfer Ben Crenshaw $400,000, and golfer Fuzzy Zoeller $300,000. The king was Jack Nicklaus, who commanded a $1 million a year.

Johnson claimed his jocks yielded big benefits in wooing supermarket people, but the line between corporate and personal services was a blurry one at RJR Nabisco. LPGA pro Judy Dickenson gave Laurie Johnson golf lessons. Gifford emceed benefits for Johnson's favorite charities like the

* Johnson denies the trip was made just for the dog.

New York Boys Club. A pair of retired New York Giant fullbacks, Alex Webster and Tucker Frederickson, maintained offices at the Team Nabisco office in Jupiter, Florida; Frederickson ran an investment counseling business from his.

For all the money Johnson doled out for Team Nabisco, some of the athletes weren't easily managed. Nicklaus was notoriously difficult. For one thing, he didn't like playing golf with Johnson's best customers, which was his highest and best use. And he considered himself above the task of working the room solo at some Nabisco function. Although he was making more money than anyone at RJR Nabisco except Johnson and Horrigan, the "Golden Bear" growled at doing more than a half-dozen appearances a year. After several run-ins with subordinates, an arrangement was struck where only Johnson and Horrigan could personally tap Nicklaus's services.

Then there was the O. J. Simpson problem. Simpson, the football star and sometime sports announcer, was being paid $250,000 a year, but was a perennial no-show at Team Nabisco events. So was Don Mattingly of the New York Yankees, who also pulled down a quarter million. Johnson didn't care. Subordinates took care of those and most other problems. He was having a grand time. *"A few million dollars,"* he always said, *"are lost in the sands of time."*

———

As RJR Nabisco's titular chairman, Paul Sticht was appalled by Johnson's free-spending ways. A lover of the finer things himself, even Sticht now thought things had gone too far. To him, RJR Nabisco in its shiny Atlanta headquarters fairly screamed of opulence, waste, and nouveau-riche excess. Johnson was so busy flitting around between golf tournaments and trips to Manhattan that Sticht, his own chairman, couldn't get in to see him.

At his annual Bohemian Grove outing in August 1987, Sticht was openly critical of Johnson with every corporate titan there who would listen. "Hipshooter" was the word he kept using. He also groused to fellow directors and Grove denizens John Macomber and Vernon Jordan. Maybe it was time for another change of command, he suggested. Macomber was all ears. He had just sold Celanese to the German company Hoechst and had time on his hands. He would always deny it when asked, but he seemed forever intrigued with the idea of running RJR.

Johnson moved swiftly to quash the possibility of a coup. On August 31, he met with Sticht. "Look, Paul, you're turning seventy in October; this isn't working out," he said. "I'm going to make a change." Always alert to shifting political winds, Johnson sensed that Sticht's power was finally waning. Just as he had earlier wooed him, Johnson now cut Sticht off at the knees. After he was removed as chairman, the aviation department was told that if Sticht asked for a jet, it would have to be personally authorized by Johnson. When Sticht found out, he stopped asking.

True to Johnson's instincts, there was no ground swell of protest from Sticht's board allies. In contrast to their treatment under Wilson, the directors found that all their needs were now attended to in detail. Bill Anderson of NCR slid into Sticht's chairmanship of the International Advisory Board and was slipped an $80,000 contract for his services. Johnson disbanded RJR Nabisco's shareholder services department and contracted its work out to John Medlin's Wachovia Bank. Juanita Kreps was given $2 million to endow two chairs at Duke, one of them named after herself. For another $2 million, Duke's business school named a wing of a new building "Horrigan Hall." (Johnson was named a Duke trustee.) Ron Grierson was also being fussed over lovingly; on his visits to Atlanta, Grierson spent so much time on the phone Johnson took an alcove and marked it "Ronnie Grierson's office."

Holdovers from Johnson's Nabisco board did especially well. Bob Schaeberle was given a six-year, $180,000-a-year consulting contract for ill-defined duties. Andy Sage received $250,000 a year for his efforts with financial R&D. In an unusual move, Charlie Hugel took Sticht's post as the ceremonial "nonexecutive" chairman of RJR Nabisco, for which he received a $150,000 contract. By naming him chairman, Johnson hoped Hugel would cement his increasingly close ties with the board.

At the same time, the number of board meetings was slashed, and directors' fees were boosted to $50,000. Wilson had allowed board members to use company jets only for official business. Johnson encouraged them to use the RJR Air Force anytime, anywhere, at no charge. "I sometimes feel like the director of transportation," he once sighed after arranging yet another director's flight. "But I know if I'm there for them they'll be there for me."

At one point, Johnson badly wanted to sell Heublein, mostly because a British conglomerate, Grand Metropolitan PLC, had offered $1.2 billion for it. The problem was Stuart Watson. The retired Heublein chairman, still on RJR Nabisco's board, had balked at selling Kentucky Fried Chicken and would no doubt raise a ruckus at the idea of selling his old company to the Brits. Heublein's chief executive, Jack Powers, was in Winston-Salem for meetings one week, and Johnson took him out for dinner at the Old Town Club.

"Jack," he asked, "what does Stuart Watson want more than anything in the world?"

Powers thought a moment. Watson was retiring from the board in several months and would hate to give up the trappings of corporate power. "More than anything?" Powers asked. "An office and a secretary."

"You tell him he has an office and secretary wherever he wants it," Johnson replied. "Zaire; you name it." The Heublein sale went through without a hitch.

Johnson thought he had the board in the palm of his hand, but Horrigan wasn't so sure. He saw how, when Johnson's language turned blue, their heads sometimes jerked back as though they had been slapped in the face. He wished Johnson would quit wearing gold necklaces and open-collar shirts at board social occasions. Horrigan finally warned him. Maybe it was just his "natural Irish suspicion," Horrigan said. "But this isn't your board, Ross. They're just waiting for you to make a mistake."

Most people were waiting for Johnson to make his next move. Every year he seemed to come up with something new, whether the Reynolds–Nabisco merger, the move to Atlanta, or the half-cocked limited partnership idea. Johnson's Ferrari had one of America's largest engines—$1.2 billion in tobacco cash flow—and a clear highway ahead. The question was, where did he want to go?

For a year after moving to Atlanta, Johnson made do trimming RJR Nabisco, selling Heublein and a host of small companies. Out went the venerable Prince Albert pipe tobacco, Mr. RJ's first national product, along with the rest of the Reynolds pipe tobaccos, Carter Hall, Apple, and Royal Comfort. A line of cigars called Winchester was also sold. In Canada, Emmett was selling businesses as fast as they could go: a half-dozen divisions for $350 million.

As money from these and other divestitures poured into RJR Nabisco's coffers, Johnson used it only to pay down bank debt. Investment bankers pestered him constantly to put the funds to better use. Buy something, they urged. Put your imprint on the company. But Johnson wasn't interested in building anything.

One recurrent rumor had him buying part of Beatrice, the Chicago food giant taken private in 1986 by the leading LBO boutique, Kohlberg Kravis Roberts & Co. Johnson, in fact, was mildly drawn to Beatrice's Hunt Wesson unit, because some of its businesses would be a snug fit with Del Monte. And Beatrice's La Choy Chinese food might fit well with Nabisco's Chun King. But his interest was desultory at best.

Johnson knew Beatrice's chief, a witty Irishman from Chicago's South Side named Don Kelly. Kelly had transformed the old Swift meat-packing business into a high-flying conglomerate known as Esmark. He had sold out to Beatrice, then reemerged as that company's chief executive after Kohlberg Kravis took the company private The $3 billion profit they projected to turn had stunned the financial world. Johnson was getting tired of hearing Kelly brag about how rich they all were becoming.

Eric Gleacher, an investment banker who headed Morgan Stanley & Co.'s merger department, had been badgering Johnson for months to meet with Kelly and the lead partner at Kohlberg Kravis, Henry Kravis. Finally, Johnson agreed. But when Gleacher arrived at RJR Nabisco's New York offices at Nine West Fifty-seventh on the appointed morning, he found Johnson had changed his mind.

"We're not going to do it, Eric," Johnson said. "It's such crap we're not even interested. We don't want to embarrass Henry, but these are marginal businesses at best. Why waste their time and ours?"

"Then why have you been going through the motions?" Gleacher wondered.

Johnson said he was just trying to be polite to Kelly. "Anybody that buys this stuff from Kelly is going to be a real fool," he told Gleacher. "I'm not going to be Don Kelly's patsy."

Then Ira Harris came into the picture. Harris was the dean of Chicago investment bankers, and had known both Johnson and Kelly for years. A poor kid from the Bronx, Harris had risen through the ranks of stockbrokers to become one of America's premier deal makers. He was rotund, always fighting a weight problem, and loved to play golf. For years, as Salomon Brothers's man in Chicago, he had played matchmaker to the Windy City's biggest companies. After a falling out with Salomon Chairman John Gutfreund, he had quit for a spell of leisure, ending it in 1987 to join another Wall Street firm, Lazard Freres & Co.

Now, as the summer wound down, Harris called Johnson and suggested a round of golf at one of Johnson's favorite clubs, Deepdale, on Long Island. Kelly had never played there and wanted to see it, Harris said, and Johnson agreed. They hit the links at a quarter past twelve one day in the first week of September, three big spenders playing a $3 Nassau. With his ten handicap, Johnson was the best golfer of the group. But Kelly made good use of the extra strokes his fourteen handicap afforded and won the entire $9 pot.

Afterward they sat on the clubhouse terrace, downing a round of drinks while Kelly talked about the incredible benefits of LBOs, especially one with Henry Kravis. "Ross," he said, "you'd be doing exactly what you're doing as a CEO, but you're making a helluva lot more money."

Johnson knew that. As part of his earlier LBO studies, he had had Frank Benevento calculate Kelly's cut of the Beatrice profits. It came out to $400 million. Still, Johnson reacted coolly to the idea of an LBO at RJR Nabisco. "I'm happy doing what I'm doing," he said, "and money's no big problem for me."

Besides, Johnson said, look at the size of RJR Nabisco. At $6.2 billion, Beatrice was the largest LBO ever. In recent days RJR Nabisco stock had traded in the low seventies. "Good God, if you want to do that you're talking in the eighties or nineties," Johnson said. "To have any kind of premium, you're talking a helluva lot of money." Some quick arithmetic told how much: $90 for each of RJR Nabisco's 230 million shares outstanding. Twenty billion dollars!

"You should meet Henry," Kelly persisted. "He's curious to meet you. I could set up a dinner with him." Johnson was intrigued. Kravis, whose name was practically synonymous with LBOs, was a legend on Wall Street. Kohlberg Kravis controlled more than two dozen companies it had acquired, using borrowed money, since its founding in 1976. It wasn't every day, Johnson mused, you got the chance to meet a legend.

Ten days later Johnson arrived at Kravis's Park Avenue apartment, where he found Kelly waiting. Johnson stared goggle-eyed at Kravis's sumptuous quarters. He thought he spied a Renoir or a Monet on the wall. *Hell,* Johnson told himself, *the guy could live well off the liquidation value of his living room.* They dined in an alcove off the dining room, which was dominated by a massive John Singer Sargent portrait of the 6th Marquis of Londonderry.

Kravis was a small, intense man with silvery hair, just forty-three. He spent much of the dinner extolling LBOs, how pouring on debt made a company tighten its operations, how executives could reap millions from little extra effort. "If you're interested, maybe we could get together," Kravis said. "If you'd like, we could send out people to look at your numbers."

"Well, who would run this thing?" Johnson wondered. "How does that work?"

"Ask Don," Kravis said, motioning to Kelly.

As if on cue, Kelly rhapsodized about his wonderful, hands-off working relationship with Kohlberg Kravis, which, after all, owned majority control of Beatrice. Johnson was skeptical, although he kept his tongue. "I didn't just fall off the turnip truck," he would recall. "You knew goddamned well that if somebody puts in that kind of money, they're going to be up your ass to make sure that what you say you're going to do, you're going to do." Johnson wasn't interested in working for anyone other than himself.

When the talk got a tad specific for Johnson, he switched subjects, spending much of their remaining time heralding the soon-to-be-introduced Premier. Kravis listened politely, but clearly had other matters on his mind. Dinner soon ran its course, and Johnson rose to leave after scarcely ninety minutes. He left feeling Kravis was a bright, steady young man. He also felt sure they could never do business.

The following Monday morning, Johnson sat down with Benevento and Sage at Nine West and took another look at the possibility of an LBO. Benevento had dusted off Project Sadim and run the numbers through the computer once more. The basics of an LBO were relatively simple and familiar to all three men. A firm such as Kohlberg Kravis, working with a company's management, buys the company using money raised from banks and the public sale of securities; the debt is paid down with cash from the company's operations and, often, by selling pieces of the business.

Sitting in Johnson's corner office, Benevento showed Johnson how a buyout of RJR Nabisco could work. Factoring in a $90-a-share purchase price, Benevento estimated the company's cash flow over the next five years, then compared it to the debt necessary to buy the company. To make it work, he cautioned, they would have to sell off everything except Reynolds Tobacco.

Johnson scanned Benevento's work, paying particular attention to the coverage ratios, the cushion between cash flow and debt payments. They were simply too thin. Post–LBO companies were run in a notoriously spartan manner to conserve cash. As much as he tried, Johnson simply couldn't drum up any enthusiasm for cutting costs, not to mention his precious perks. "I don't like it," he said. "There's just not enough cash coverage here for me to be comfortable. Christ, you can't run the company on this basis."

The lure of personal wealth was strong, but Johnson couldn't see risking his already-lush life-style just to get more. "I already consider myself a very lucky man," he said. "I started off with practically nothing. I have more money than I ever dreamed I would have, and I'll be drawing a $700,000 salary when I retire. Who needs the aggravation?" Sage agreed.

Johnson turned to Benevento. "Frank, forget about the goddamned LBOs, you're chasing the wrong horse. Let's throw some business Drexel's way for bringing us some of these ideas, but let's just take care of our own business now."

For the rest of their ninety-minute session the trio discussed other ideas, including selling the ESPN stake and buying a British candy business. As they rose to leave, Johnson walked over to his window and looked south over midtown Manhattan. In the distance he could barely see Wall Street. For now, the lure of its fancy schemes failed to grip him. "You know," he said, gazing out, "I hope that five years from now the three of us are still here being the strategic brain trust of this company."

CHAPTER

4

Good, bad, or indifferent, you're always thinking, you're doing, you're extending yourself. If you don't do that, the place becomes a bore. You've got to create some excitement.   —ROSS JOHNSON

On October 19, 1987, the stock market crashed. Like the rest of the financial world, Johnson tuned in his Quotron and slipped into a state of shock. RJR Nabisco, which had been trading in the mid-sixties the week before, plunged into the low forties by midday. In the crash's wake, the stock languished there for weeks.

It was the beginning of Johnson's road to ruin, for the low stock price would haunt him for months to come. In December the company posted a 25 percent profit increase, and the Street ignored it. Even when food stocks rose that winter, RJR Nabisco remained in the dumps. No matter what Johnson did, buyers treated his stock like a tobacco stock, even though 60 percent of its sales came from Nabisco and Del Monte.

In Atlanta, Johnson simmered. Like many chief executives, he considered his stock price something of a report card. As he watched other food stocks soar, Johnson felt like a wallflower at the orgy. If the business he knew best was hot, Johnson was determined to be a player. He began pondering the possibility of linking up with a food company.

His first thought was Pillsbury. It was an unstable situation, his favorite kind, with takeover speculation swirling around a chief executive just come out of retirement. Buying the company, though, ran against Johnson's grain. He was a seller, not a buyer. He considered a joint venture. Why not combine Pillsbury and Nabisco, sell its stock to the public, and thereby highlight the remaining food assets inside RJR Nabisco?

Johnson tossed the idea to Sage and Benevento, who were hugely unimpressed. Pillsbury was a dog, they said, its core businesses anemic. "Why would you want to own part of a so-so food business rather than one hundred percent of a great one?" asked Benevento. As Sage typed what they called a "stick-it-in-your-ear" memo to Johnson, Benevento looked over his shoulder. A thought struck him. General Motors, faced with a similar problem, had created separate classes of stock for the parent company and its Hughes Aircraft and Electronic Data Systems units. If Johnson was worried that tobacco was dragging down the price of his food stock, why not make them trade as separate securities? If GM could have an H stock for Hughes, why couldn't RJR have an F stock for food? They tacked it on the end of the memo. When Johnson saw it he shrugged, then gave Benevento the go-ahead to look at the dual-stock plan. It was just another idea.

Johnson wasn't the only one who noticed RJR Nabisco's low stock price. In January the syndicated columnist Dan Dorfman mentioned the company as a takeover candidate. Johnson pooh-poohed the notion, although some of his aides, including Ed Robinson, grew worried. Then, as February's board meeting broke up, Paul Sticht approached Johnson. The two hadn't talked much since Sticht's ouster six months earlier. "Ross, are you going to be down in Florida this weekend?" Sticht asked.

"Yeah," Johnson replied, "I've got to go down and do my dad's taxes."

"Are you going to have any spare time?"

"Really, I'm not," Johnson said, eager to avoid any invitation from Sticht. "I'm up to my tail."

"Well, there's a very important shareholder, and you should get to know him," Sticht said. "He's got some ideas, and he's going to be down in Lost Tree. His name is Spangler." Johnson reluctantly agreed to meet Sticht and his friend Spangler the following Saturday in Jupiter.

Clemmie Dixon Spangler, Jr., was the president of the University of North Carolina. Before taking its helm in 1986, "Dickie" Spangler had been a bona fide big wheel in North Carolina business circles: president of C. D. Spangler Construction Co. of Charlotte, and chairman of the Bank of North Carolina, which, when it was sold to giant NCNB Corp.

in 1982, made him a rich man. His family was also one of RJR Nabisco's largest shareholders.

Spangler had been incensed when Johnson pulled the headquarters out of Winston-Salem. He had called an old Harvard Business School classmate, Richard H. Jenrette, chairman of The Equitable Life Insurance Society, one of the nation's largest insurance companies. Dick Jenrette was a native North Carolinian and knew the Spangler family well. Spangler wanted to know if The Equitable, among the nation's most powerful institutional investors, would be interested in backing some sort of shareholder vote in an attempt to reverse the move to Atlanta.

"You think we could get enough votes to stop that from happening?" Spangler asked.

Frankly, Jenrette replied, "No."

Jenrette put the call out of his mind. Then, several months later Spangler called again. "Dick," he said, "what would you think about forming a group to do a leveraged buyout of Reynolds? I think it can be done." Spangler mentioned that he planned to approach Paul Sticht and also hoped to interest Jim Robinson of American Express, with whom he had prepped at Woodberry Forest in Virginia.

Jenrette mulled the offer for several days before deciding it would appear unseemly for a major insurance company—one that doled out millions each year to cancer victims—to invest in a cigarette maker. "I've got to back off on it," he told Spangler.

Spangler stewed as RJR Nabisco stock plummeted during the crash. He blamed his losses—and North Carolina's—squarely on Ross Johnson. He approached Sticht through a mutual friend, John Medlin of Wachovia. "If I could get the funds to take control of the company, would you be interested in helping me put things back the way they were?" Spangler asked.

Sticht played coy. "Gee," he said, "I don't think that's possible or practical." But when Spangler invited him to an exploratory meeting in New York, Sticht accepted. The meeting turned out to be with a group of Citibank executives. Spangler had interested the mammoth bank in financing an LBO of RJR Nabisco.

Sticht was impressed. He was also practical. LBOs weren't a hostile device. If Spangler's group wanted to buy RJR Nabisco, they would have to involve Johnson. "Can you arrange for me to meet with him?" Spangler asked.

And so Johnson found himself on a Saturday morning in late February unlocking the Team Nabisco office in Jupiter. Seeing Sticht was keeping him from his golf game, and he hoped they could wrap it up quickly. When he was introduced to Spangler, Johnson's first thought was that he and Sticht made a splendid pair. Dickie Spangler's slicked-back hair and clear-framed glasses were straight out of the fifties.

"I really don't have anything to do with this," Sticht began. "Dick has come to me. He has some ideas. And I think he should talk to you."

RJR Nabisco was a great company, Spangler began. It had great prospects, though it remained undervalued.

Blinding glimpse of the obvious, Johnson thought.

Spangler prattled on about how he felt silly he hadn't sold his stock at seventy and how he felt bad that it now languished at fifty. His family was peeved with him for not selling.

"I can't tell you when it's going back to seventy," Johnson said, "all I can do is run the company." He was dying to get on the fairway.

Spangler proceeded to his idea: an LBO, at $70 dollars a share or so. He and Sticht had already met with Citibank about it, Spangler said, and the bank was enthusiastic.

Johnson was stunned. He and Sticht had *what?*

"Now my role is strictly advisory," Sticht interjected.

Johnson looked at Sticht and thought: *Your role is strictly ambushing, you old dinosaur.* But Johnson wasn't built for confrontation, and fighting with these two wasn't going to get him anywhere, so he smiled. "Seventy dollars is okay by me, Paul." It was a vintage performance.

Johnson would be the key, Spangler continued. He would own 15 percent of the company, with other managers owning another 10 percent. "Ross, I know a lot of wealthy people," Spangler said. "You could be a billionaire."

Johnson left the meeting "in a state of goddamn shock": What did Sticht think he was doing? He might be an old fool, Johnson told himself, but as a former chairman, he was a dangerous old fool. His presence lent credibility to even a crazy proposal like Spangler's. Didn't Sticht know Citibank's chairman, John Reed, was a director of Philip Morris? If this got out, it could be dynamite in a competitor's hands.

Johnson dashed back to his condo and put out a flurry of calls. "Holy smokes," he told Andy Sage, who was in Jackson Hole. "I've been blindsided. Spangler wants to buy the company!" He called Jim Robinson. "All

I know is he's got a lot of money and he's very close with Dick Jenrette," Robinson told him. Johnson grew alarmed; he knew what kind of firepower The Equitable had. "Get the goddamn executive committee together," he told Harold Henderson later that day. Johnson was due at an International Advisory Board meeting in Palm Springs Monday. "I've got to talk with them as soon as I get back," he said.

Johnson and his directors caucused Tuesday. They agreed that a conversation with Citibank was called for, if only to see how far Spangler had progressed. Johnson called John Reed and arranged a meeting. Reed confirmed that the matter had come up, and suggested the bank was willing to pursue it further. "The bank is here to serve," he told Johnson.

The following week Johnson picked up Spangler in North Carolina and flew to New York. En route, Spangler showed him a computer printout of various financial projections. It assumed that the company could be held intact, that the necessary savings could come from slashing capital expenditures. Johnson wasn't impressed: *Amateur hour,* he thought.

For Johnson, the meeting at Citibank proved to be a huge relief. The bank thought an LBO could be done at $65 a share, with Johnson taking a 10 percent cut. It was clear they hadn't done much work. Johnson was openly cool toward the idea. On the flight back, Spangler was apologetic. The matter, it was clear, would be dropped.

Johnson returned to Atlanta, dashed off "thanks-but-no-thanks" letters to Citibank and Spangler, and sat down with Henderson to figure out what to do about Sticht. He simply couldn't be allowed to keep meddling in RJR Nabisco affairs. The next day Henderson flew to Winston-Salem and read Sticht the riot act. There were only two board meetings before he was scheduled to retire in May. Sticht attended neither, much to Johnson's satisfaction. "We shipped him his silver tray, wrote all the right things, and that was that," recalled Johnson, certain he had seen the last of Paul Sticht.

After the Spangler affair Johnson redoubled his efforts to boost his sagging stock price. At the March board meeting, he gave directors two options: buy Hunt Wesson, which would further emphasize the company's tilt toward food, or buy back more stock. Having fewer shares outstanding should buoy the price of the stock. The directors, none of whom shared Johnson's growing concern about the stock price, chose the latter.

Johnson had the buyback supervised by Ira Harris's firm, Lazard Freres.

In late March, RJR Nabisco announced it would purchase up to 20 million of its shares at prices between $52 and $58 a share. A month later it bought even more—21 million shares—at $53.50 each. RJR Nabisco, which had traded around $52 a share in anticipation of the buyback, immediately fell back into the mid-forties. Johnson had spent more than $1.1 billion buying stock, and its price was lower than ever.

———

By the spring of 1988, Wall Street still hadn't recovered from October's stock market crash. Individual investors had fled the market in droves. Trading volume dropped. As demand flagged, Corporate America lost interest in floating new stock offerings. With all its other businesses wallowing, Wall Street turned to its one guaranteed source of income: takeovers.

Mergers and acquisitions—M&A—were the ultimate creature of Wall Street because win, lose, or draw, they produced fees: fees for advising, fees for divesting unwanted businesses, fees for lending money. Just as they had fueled the Street's mushrooming growth throughout the 1980s, takeover fees would again prop up the securities industry's profits that spring.

After three months of eerie silence following the market crash, January had brought the beginning of an unprecedented burst of takeover activity, as domestic and foreign companies alike fed on the bargains afforded by newly lowered stock prices. More than a dozen major takeover contests ensued, peaking with the $6 billion fight for control of Paul Sticht's old company, Cincinnati-based Federated Department Stores. More takeovers were attempted during the first half of 1988 than in all of 1985, itself a very good year. Wall Street, in short, became addicted to deals. And the offices of RJR soon became the deal junkies' newest shooting gallery.

At the crest of the takeover wave that spring was the merger department at Shearson Lehman Hutton, the fast-growing brokerage unit of financial giant American Express. With its acquisition of E. F. Hutton that winter, Shearson was poised to challenge Merrill Lynch as the preeminent Wall Street brokerage. Its merger department was headed by a pair of veteran deal makers who, after a decade operating in the shadow of better-known colleagues, were now eager to make names for themselves.

Steve Waters was a nut for organization, an ex-Vietnam helicopter pilot who still had an air of the military. He thought of Shearson's M&A

group as the Marines, fast and hard-hitting. Yet his edges were appealingly soft. Waters wasn't ashamed to be a bit square; he and his wife taught Sunday school classes at their Presbyterian church in Connecticut. If he wasn't the consummate takeover tactician, Waters's easygoing manner, forthright attitude, and sincerity—a rarity among his ilk—made him a favorite of Johnson, whom he had known since Standard Brands.

J. Tomilson Hill III, Harvard College, Harvard Business School, was the warrior of the pair, a zealot for the Wall Street trenches. To enemies—and he had a few—Tom Hill came across as an oiled-back Gordon Gekko haircut atop five feet, ten inches of icy Protestant reserve. Hill was well tailored and proud of it; "the best-dressed man on Wall Street" a competitor called him, and Hill wore his dark Paul Stuart suits like armor. His office was all cool modern art and Lucite-encased tombstones commemorating past victories.

Hill could be charming but rarely glib; sometimes it seemed as if he chose every word from a dictionary. Around Shearson he wasn't popular. "Found a single person who likes the guy?" more than one colleague asked. A longtime coworker described Hill as "the ultimate heretic. You can't believe he's devout about anything. He's like a jungle fighter . . . capable of being a really nasty guy." To colleagues, Waters and Hill made an unlikely pair.

That spring Hill's tactical skills were in demand as never before. He helped call the shots in the defense of Federated and engineered a raft of Shearson-backed hostile offers, including a Black & Decker bid for the big toilet-seat maker, American Standard. But as Hill's prestige rose— later that year he would be profiled in *USA Today*— Waters found himself embroiled in a nasty internal battle to gain better bonuses for their troops. At a meeting of Shearson's top managers, Waters roundly denounced the bonus structure, revealing that he had urged some of the department's brightest associates to consider leaving if they weren't better paid. The speech angered many at Shearson, most importantly its chairman, Peter A. Cohen, who believed Waters was inciting unrest in the ranks. When Waters offered his resignation, it was accepted.

Waters wasn't surprised to learn that Hill had been quietly assuring senior Shearson executives he could handle the department on his own. As he cleared out his office on his last day at Shearson, Hill walked in, offering his hand in farewell. Waters left it there, hanging in the air. "I wouldn't treat someone the way you treated me," he said. When he left

Shearson that spring, many on Wall Street suspected Tom Hill's fingerprints were on the dagger protruding from Steve Waters's back.

With his partner gone, Hill moved fast. Waters had brought in many of Shearson's best clients, and it was now Hill's job to make certain none of them followed him out the door. At the top of Hill's damage-control list was RJR Nabisco. Ross Johnson was one of the department's five most lucrative relationships, and Hill had a hunch he was ripe to do a deal. He brought out RJR Nabisco's balance sheet. Any fool could see the tobacco business was throwing off cash that had to go somewhere. *This one's a live wire,* he thought. *Something's going to happen.* Hill dialed Andy Sage and set up an introductory meeting.

After leaving Shearson, meanwhile, Waters talked through his options with a number of his clients, including Johnson, who offered office space during his search. Another client who helped Waters scout job opportunities was Henry Kravis. One day that spring Waters spoke to Kravis and found him in a good mood. "I just found a new friend this morning," Kravis said.

Tom Hill had called. Waters knew the two men didn't get along: Kravis had taken it personally when Hill had bad-mouthed a Kravis offer to Federated's board three months before. "Suddenly I'm the nicest guy in the world," Kravis said in mock wonder, relating Hill's conversation, "and he's got the most interesting ideas in the world. Funny how things like this work."

Waters ultimately accepted an offer from his old friend Eric Gleacher at Morgan Stanley. On his second day in his new job, Waters sat down in Gleacher's corner office to discuss what clients they could hope to snatch from Shearson. Johnson topped the list.

"Listen, every two or three years he does something big," Waters said. "We really want to stay close to that situation. Something big is going to happen. I can feel it." With Gleacher's go-ahead, Waters formed a team of investment bankers whose top priority was generating ideas to run past Johnson.

By late spring the word was all over Wall Street that Ross Johnson was ripe to do a deal. Jeff Beck knew it; he continued to push Johnson to do an LBO. Ira Harris knew it. So did Hill and Waters. Each had his own ideas on how best to twist The Pope's arm.

As the bankers circled, Johnson remained transfixed by his stock price. It was like a scab at which he constantly picked. Most chief executives wouldn't have bothered; many companies live with low stock prices all their lives, and almost no chief executive thinks Wall Street gives his stock its due. RJR Nabisco's directors weren't concerned. Profits were up; sales, too. But Johnson couldn't leave well enough alone. The old urges to action were returning, and the stock price was simply their latest manifestation.

Months later, when friends would ask him why he chose his ultimate course, Johnson would speak of stock multiples and capital structures. He would recite all the steps he had taken to get the stock up: the profit gains, the pristine balance sheet, the stock buy backs, and Premier. It was all true, but it was intellectual window dressing for something much deeper. He could never leave well enough alone. There was shit to be stirred.

In the name of boosting his stock, Johnson had sorted through dozens of schemes. Benevento had gotten pumped up about his General Motors dual-stock idea, but Johnson killed it at a May 31 meeting. Benevento loved the plan's mad complexities. But to Johnson it was just more paperwork. "Holy God," he exclaimed, "it's just too complicated."

Johnson clung to the idea of a joint venture with Pillsbury, directing Dean Posvar's planning department to do an exhaustive evaluation of the company. He had Beck noodling out possible approaches. He took Jim Welch to visit Pillsbury's chief executive, Bill Spoor. Spoor entertained the idea, but demanded all kinds of standstill agreements to ensure Johnson couldn't take control of the company.

When the Pillsbury talks fell through, Johnson had Ira Harris check on possible approaches to Quaker Oats. Maybe, he reasoned, the two companies could combine their grocery-products businesses. But Quaker's chief executive, Bill Smithburg, was an ardent antismoker who wanted nothing to do with RJR Nabisco. Steve Waters tried to get Johnson interested in a takeover of Kraft, the Chicago food giant. Johnson passed; Kraft was too big, too expensive, and its brands wouldn't fit well with Nabisco. Tom Hill also proved energetic in his pursuit, making presentations on a number of possible takeover candidates. Johnson was happy to browse, but found them all too expensive.

There were other ways to boost the stock price, of course. Johnson had high hopes for the smokeless cigarette, Premier, which was due in test markets by fall. Premier had been wheeled out for public display the previous September in an elaborate press conference at New York's Grand

Hyatt Hotel. Rumors swept the stock market the week before that the company was developing a revolutionary new cigarette, and the stock had shot up three points. Premier was judged to be "material" news to RJR Nabisco's shareholders forcing a public announcement. A Reynolds executive named Dick Kampe used a pointer and a cross-sectional diagram to explain Premier to the press. In a separate room, Horrigan took the message to financial analysts. "Simply put," a beaming Horrigan declared, "we think this will be the world's cleanest cigarette."

What neither man mentioned were some lingering problems. Horrigan's people, in fact, hadn't wanted to introduce the product so soon—it was far from market-ready—but their hand had been forced. For one thing, Premier was flunking its taste tests. In its U.S. research laboratories, Reynolds scientists found that fewer than 5 percent of smokers liked its taste. In Japan, another team of researchers quickly learned to translate at least one sentence of Japanese: "This tastes like shit." It had a very basic problem for a cigarette: It tasted awful if lit by a match instead of a lighter. The sulfur in a match reacted badly with Premier's carbon tip. It also made it smell awful—"like a fart," as Johnson delicately put it. If all that weren't bad enough, the cigarette was hard to draw on—darned hard. Inside the company, they called it "the hernia effect."

Privately, line executives knew they needed years to iron out the glitches. Even in limited production, Premier's carbon tips had a habit of falling off. Internal projections determined that Premier couldn't be ready for test markets before 1991, 1990 at the outside. Yet Horrigan had promised the world it would be out in 1988.

But then, the company's top executives had refused to listen to reason for some time. When Washington lobbyist Paul Bergson doubted the wisdom of Project Spa, warning of regulatory problems, he was ousted by Horrigan in favor of a Winston-Salem lawyer named Champ Mitchell. Charlie Hugel thought the idea of a smokeless cigarette was nutty and said so: People *liked* to blow smoke, tap ashes, watch their cigarette burn. Nonsense, Johnson argued. Premier was just what was needed to combat the country's rising health concerns, especially the issue of "passive smoke" that had led to smoking being banned in many public places. "Throw it out there," Johnson argued. "Let the consumer decide."

As Premier moved toward its fall introduction, further new hopes for boosting the stock arose in June. In a New Jersey federal court, the widower of a lifelong smoker named Rose Cipollone was suing a number of tobacco companies for contributing to his wife's death. Reynolds wasn't a defendant, but its fate was tied to that of its fellow tobacco companies. The case mounted by Anthony Cipollone was considered among the strongest ever brought against the tobacco industry; the plaintiff's lawyers had unearthed a raft of damaging documents. A tobacco victory, Johnson reasoned, would give his stock a real pop.

When the jury finally delivered a verdict, it broke tobacco's unbeaten streak—but just barely, clearing the industry of conspiracy and awarding only $400,000 in damages. "A tip for Tony Cipollone," Johnson chortled, and waited for RJR Nabisco's stock to spike up. It didn't. Johnson's office became a wailing wall where everybody came to cry about the injustice of it all. Horrigan was particularly bitter; he had predicted the stock would climb at least six points. "The market is never going to give us its due," Henderson complained. "The equity markets just aren't a suitable capital structure for some companies." Arguing to take stock from public hands was in fact the intellectual basis for an LBO, although no one openly advocated it at the time. Horrigan thought Johnson would never go private. "The problem with the company going private," he said to himself, "is that nobody would pay any attention to him."

———

Investment bankers weren't the only new faces in RJR Nabisco's executive suite that summer. After fifteen years, Johnson's band of Merry Men was breaking up. Peter Rogers had rotated through three senior jobs at Nabisco and was poised to leave in the fall. Bob Carbonell, who as vice chairman functioned as Johnson's right hand in Atlanta, got into repeated fights with Horrigan and was exiled to head Del Monte in Miami. In their places Johnson's closest friend became an executive vice president named John Martin.

At forty-six, Martin was part of the Frank Gifford connection. During the seventies he had been one of the bright young men at ABC Sports. As logistic chief for "Monday Night Football," Martin had become Howard Cosell's surrogate son. As an ABC programming executive, he hammered out three Olympics contracts. Martin was television smooth, with a low, soothing voice that inevitably made a good first impression. "He meets well," it was said of Martin. He dressed so well friends at ABC called him "Suits." He was also a scratch golfer and had once been club champion at Winged Foot, one of the New York area's prestigious country clubs. Martin joined RJR Nabisco in January 1988 from Ohlmeyer Communications, and he and Johnson were soon inseparable.

They became so close that Martin lived in Johnson's basement for months before finding a home in Atlanta. When he selected one, only a nine-iron shot down the street, he remained in the basement while Laurie Johnson decorated it. The three were constantly together, playing golf, traveling, and watching televised sports for hours on end. On organizational charts Martin didn't appear to wield much power, but he had Johnson's ear, and he began acting as his gatekeeper. Nobody was more jealous of Martin's rise than Horrigan, who sneered that the well-tanned Martin reminded him of the actor George Hamilton.

Some chuckled that the well-connected Martin was Johnson's pimp for celebrities. He did bring in new faces. One was Martin's longtime friend, baseball commissioner Peter Ueberroth. Martin was also a friend of boxer Mike Tyson's manager, Jimmy Jacobs, and handled the champ's endorsements in his spare time. It was only a sidelight, but it gave Johnson entrée to the fight game. In June, he invited Atlanta's business and political elite to watch the Mike Tyson–Michael Spinks fight on television at headquarters. Gold-engraved invitations clasped in red leather boxing gloves were sent to a select 100 people. As guests arrived at the top floor, they were greeted by white-gloved waiters offering Dom Perignon. Sometimes Martin was a bit careless in making introductions. While in England the previous June, he had brought Johnson together with a merry Scotsman who was a gofer for ABC Sports in London. Johnson was quite taken, and invited the fellow to stay in his Atlanta home. Once there, the Scot was offered a job by Johnson as a bodyguard. The man happily accepted, and began living with Johnson; the two men got on famously. But that fall, during his visa review, Johnson and Martin learned the fellow had been part of a gang that blew open safes throughout Scotland. He had served several prison terms, including one for forgery. The merry Scot was hurriedly given a one-way ticket back to Glasgow.

A number of friends thought the dismissal of trusted advisers such as Carbonell underscored some unsettling changes in Johnson. For the first time, he was attracting media attention. *Fortune* profiled him in a puffy cover story that summer as "America's Toughest Marketing Man." "He specializes in taking break shots at neatly racked old cultures and replacing them with an organizational mix of turbulence, vigilance and guts," it gushed. "In three reorganizations, he sent 2,650 corpocrats back to line jobs or out into the wilderness." Johnson, it went on, "has been shoving the noses of his managers up against the window of the future."

Business Week was less impressed. It noted RJR's low stock price, its fuzzy long-term outlook, and the tobacco company's declining performance. The magazine at first looked like it was headed for an even tougher story, spotlighting Johnson's lavish spending and questioning his operating ability. But the company put on a full-court press to squelch it. Martin told editor-in-chief Stephen Shepard a biased reporter was out to do a hatchet job and threatened to withhold future access to RJR. The story appeared in tamer form, and Johnson was bothered by only one line. It noted that he would routinely press a $50 bill into a wine steward's hand. "Christ," said a distressed Johnson, "it's been years since I tipped that little."*

Johnson's friends came to rue the two pieces. The man was beginning to believe his reviews. "America's toughest marketing man," they feared, was really becoming America's most out-of-touch marketing man. He was fond of bragging that his relations with the grocery trade were worth four or five market share points—hundreds of millions of dollars. But the only supermarket executives he spent much time with these days were a group of three ex-jocks with whom he loved to play golf. Johnson called them "the Buffaloes."

At the same time the man who had made a science of stroking directors was growingly cavalier about his board meetings. They were fewer and farther between—only one would be held between May and October 1988—and were increasingly sloppy affairs. Staffers would arduously put together slide presentations on the financials, only to see Johnson scrap them. "Screw the slides," he would say. "We'll tell them the numbers are good." Scrapped, too, was Johnson's habit of rehearsing for the meetings.

As he had at Standard Brands and Nabisco, Johnson seemed to be losing interest in operating the company. More and more he concentrated on only two things: having fun and goosing the stock. A new catch phrase replaced the old "BGO" on Johnson's lips. "Ah," he took to saying, "fuck it."

In July, Ed Robinson and Harold Henderson, worried that the company's continuing low stock price made it vulnerable to a takeover, got permis-

---

* Shepard denies the magazine was influenced by company pressure, saying any changes in the story were the result of normal editing.

sion from Johnson to approach Shearson Lehman about shoring up its takeover defenses. They wanted a "top-drawer" study, an array of plans that could be erected at the first sign of a hostile raider. Johnson considered a takeover unlikely, but Henderson insisted they be prepared for the worst.

Shearson was the logical choice to do the study. Johnson was on the American Express board, and he knew both the Shearson chief, Peter Cohen, and the American Express chief, Jim Robinson. "Let's go to Shearson with every study and piece of crap we've got, have them look at all the scenarios, and see what they have to say," Johnson said. "If somebody wants to buy us, what would they buy us for and what would we do."

American Express's July board meeting was breaking up when Johnson first approached Cohen with the plan. "Andy Sage is going to be giving you a call," he said. "He wants to have a very private conversation with you about the company." In late July, Andy Sage and several Johnson aides met with Cohen in his lower Manhattan office overlooking the Hudson River. They wanted all options explored: a wide variety of recapitalization plans as well as partial and full buyout proposals. Sage insisted on strictest secrecy. The mere hint of the project's existence, he knew, could prove a self-fulfilling prophecy. Word a company was worried about a takeover invited speculation, which inevitably drew speculators. Only five Shearson executives, including Cohen and Tom Hill, were cleared to work on the plan. Hill came up with a code name whose irony wouldn't be clear until months later: Project Stretch.

At the same time, Johnson got the RJR Nabisco board to approve a set of antitakeover provisions Robinson and Henderson had drawn up with the help of a Wall Street law firm, Davis, Polk & Wardwell. The board also approved severance arrangements known as "golden parachutes" for each of the company's top ten officers. Most large U.S. companies have similar pacts, which are often considered part and parcel of antitakeover contingencies. The only thing unusual about RJR Nabisco's was their size: all told, they were worth $52.5 million.

One thing puzzled staffers in the company's treasury department. At Johnson's direction, money for the parachutes was placed in protective trusts known as "rabbi trusts." Under the trusts' terms, if RJR Nabisco changed hands, the new owner couldn't touch these funds. To the treasury staffers, it almost looked like Johnson was preparing for something.

As they searched for solutions to Johnson's concerns about the stock, everyone who analyzed the problem mentioned the possibility of a leveraged buyout. It was a standard solution to any company whose stock drooped. An LBO, of course, wasn't so much a solution to the problem as an end to it. Going private simply took the stock out of the public's hands. Every investment banker urged Johnson to consider it.

Soon LBO ideas were arriving, uninvited, over the transom. Dillon Read proposed a partial LBO it called Project Tara. Johnson's old Standard Brands sidekick, Ruben Gutoff, suggested a scenario his consulting firm called Project Reo. The subject even came up one night when Johnson was sitting with neighbors around a pool. "Gee," one said, "why don't you take your company private?"

To each, Johnson replied he wasn't interested. "No way," he told a gathering of lieutenants in July. "Why would I want to do something like that? I've got a great life; I've got a great company just the way it is." But at least one of the men at lunch that day thought Johnson's denial rang hollow. Peter Rogers had known The Pope too long. When Johnson thought an idea dumb, he would dismiss it with a withering one-liner. Rogers, walking out with John Greeniaus after lunch, said, "Methinks the lady doth protest too much."

For the time being, though, Johnson seemed curious about every possible scheme but an LBO. His grandest occurred to him in July. For months he had been trying to interest Philip Morris in combining the two companies' international businesses into a joint venture. Philip Morris had expressed interest in acquiring RJR Nabisco, but Johnson suggested a joint venture instead. Horrigan, of course, hated the idea. Consort with the enemy? Run up the white flag? But at Johnson's urging, he had met with his opposite number at Philip Morris. After months of on-again, off-again talks, Johnson had scrapped the idea. Even if they came to terms, he suspected that foreign governments would object to the merger on antitrust grounds.

Now, in late July, Johnson called Philip Morris's chief executive, Hamish Maxwell, with a new idea. Unlike their predecessors, the two men got along well; Johnson, it seemed, could get along with anyone. They met for dinner at RJR Nabisco's suite at the Regency Hotel in New York. In deference to his host, Maxwell smoked a Winston while listening closely as Johnson laid out his plan.

"Let's face it," Johnson said. "Diversification isn't working for us, and it isn't working for Philip Morris. We still both trade as tobacco stocks."

It was only half true. In their core tobacco businesses, Maxwell was running the *Queen Mary* and Johnson the *African Queen.* Philip Morris's lead brand, Marlboro, had an ever-widening lead over Reynolds's brands, fatter profit margins, and cash flow that dwarfed RJR Nabisco's. Institutional investors—the big pension and mutual funds who could make or break stocks—typically chose just one tobacco stock for their portfolios, and more often than not it was Philip Morris. With their support, Philip Morris stock had risen 25 percent since the beginning of 1987, while RJR Nabisco's, after spiking up and down, was flat. Portfolio managers liked Philip Morris's predictability. They thought they knew where Maxwell was going. They *never* knew what Johnson was up to.

As Maxwell listened, Johnson proposed that Philip Morris and RJR Nabisco combine their respective food businesses—Nabisco and General Foods—into a publicly traded joint venture. RJR Nabisco would own 37.5 percent, as would Philip Morris; the remaining 25 percent would be traded publicly. The great value attached to the public stock, Johnson said, advancing Jeff Beck's old theory, would heat up both parents' stocks.

"I think we can create an eighteen-billion-dollar company with a lot of zip in it," said Johnson. Then he laid down the capper. "And I'll run it for you."

Once the two food companies were combined, Johnson proposed to resign as chief executive of RJR Nabisco, leaving the remaining tobacco company for Horrigan to manage. It was an outlandish proposal, but Johnson was betting Maxwell might go for it.

"Ross, it's a brilliant idea," Maxwell said when Johnson finished, "but joint ventures have problems." The logistics alone were daunting: so many people being thrown together from so many companies. Even if Johnson and Maxwell got along, he went on, was there any assurance that their successors would? Still, Maxwell told Johnson he would give it some thought.

Two weeks later, in mid-August, Maxwell called back. Sorry, he said, Philip Morris isn't interested. There were simply too many problems. Johnson tried to shrug it off. It wasn't as if he had nothing else up his sleeve to boost the stock. There was always Premier. For now, though, he wanted to take a break from the whirlwind of ideas he had stirred up, as well as from the muggy summer heat draping Atlanta. He boarded a jet for a couple of weeks of work and play in Colorado.

———

The Castle Pines Golf Club is twenty-five miles south of Denver and, to golf enthusiasts like Johnson, just this side of heaven. It is a beautiful setting for a golf course, a natural valley framed by Castle Rock, Pike's Peak, and the snowcapped Rockies. Its fairways twist through verdant mountain meadows crowned with ponderosa pine.

Ranked one of the country's thirty top courses, Castle Pines was designed by Jack Nicklaus, and the Golden Bear made the ninth hole among his toughest: a 458-yard par four, a tough driving hole with water on the right, trouble left, and a blind uphill second shot to a mean green. Back in the pines off the left side of the fairway is a cluster of three-story villas. RJR Nabisco owned one as a corporate retreat, and it was there, on the weekend of August 21, that Johnson threw one of the most memorable parties of his career.

That weekend Castle Pines played host to a professional golf tournament, the International, and Johnson had invited a pack of his best pals to help him enjoy it. Peter Ueberroth and Roger Penske were there, as was Roone Arledge, up from the Republican convention in New Orleans. Jack Meyers, the retired publisher of *Time* magazine, showed up, as well as Johnson's three Buffaloes, including Floyd Hall, president of the Grand Union supermarket chain. Charlie Hugel and Ira Harris also arrived, as did Martin Emmett.

It was the kind of weekend Johnson lived for. He could play golf in the morning, watch the pros in the afternoon, and enjoy world-class schmoozing at night. The RJR Air Force stood by if needed, whisking Harris off to a Chicago wedding at one point. Saturday night a pair of Team Nabisco pros, Fuzzy Zoeller and Raymond Floyd, joined the group for dinner, as did Ben Crenshaw, who was in the thick of contention in the International.

That evening Johnson had an after-dinner surprise for his guests at the villa. Had they heard about Reynolds's new smokeless cigarette? he asked. Most had. Ed Horrigan rolled out a videotape that showed how Premier worked. After an hour of explaining its science, Johnson broke out packs of Premier and passed them around. Tell us what you think of everything, Johnson invited: the taste, the packs, the marketing, the pitfalls.

———

He had kept the affair casual, but Johnson was eager to hear what his VIP friends had to say about Premier. He and Horrigan watched intently as Ueberroth and the others began inspecting the cigarettes closely, eyeing the little holes in its carbon tip, feeling how its hard casing compared with that of a normal cigarette. Slowly they began lighting up. The odor was unmistakable and unpleasant.

"Smells like burning lettuce," someone cracked.

"Boy, this is hard to draw on," said someone else.

They take some getting used to, Johnson conceded. "We're saying in the ads to try them for a week," he said.

"I don't know if I could get through a pack," someone said.

Looking for something positive to say, Penske praised the technology. Arledge wondered who the spokesperson would be on television news shows; Premier was bound to create a splash when introduced. Johnson admitted he hadn't given the matter much thought. You'd better, Ueberroth interjected. The media is going to be very interested in this and will be asking tough questions. Like: "If this is a safer cigarette, aren't you admitting that your others are unsafe?"

"That's a problem," Johnson admitted. "It is a safer cigarette, but you can't really say it."

As the session stretched on, Johnson could tell Premier had bigger problems than he had feared. No one liked the taste—Johnson at least expected them to enjoy the menthol brand—and they puckered like prunes trying to inhale its smoke. He and Horrigan had remained optimistic through all the poor test results. If only 5 percent of smokers found Premier palatable, Johnson figured, it would still be a big hit. He simply couldn't believe it wouldn't do great things.

But as he listened to Ueberroth, Arledge, and the others, Johnson realized that his own staff's conservative projections were accurate: Premier would need years, rather than months, before it could be considered a success. Any chance of an overnight hit evaporated in the pithy comments of his high-profile friends—and with it Johnson's last, best hope for revving up his stock.

The International ended the next day, and the RJR Air Force spirited Johnson's friends to all points of the compass. Johnson stayed on to play golf, but scheduled a meeting of senior aides the following Monday to discuss the Premier situation. Horrigan, Henderson, and Martin all came, as did a bevy of tobacco strategists and outsiders, including Stanley Katz, head of a Reynolds ad agency, FCB Leber/Katz, and Herb Schmertz, Mobil Oil's ex–public relations chief.

Rather than address the key problems of taste and smell, the group tackled the issue of how to package Premier for the press. Who, for instance, would be their primary spokesman? Horrigan favored Johnson. Others demurred. He may have been chief executive of America's second largest cigarette company, but Johnson was no cigarette expert, and he was apt to say whatever popped into his head. "Christ," he liked to say, "you get more carbon monoxide from a New York bus going by you than from a cigarette." The consensus selection was Dick Kampe, who was heading the Premier development team. Horrigan and Martin got into an argument about the best way to prep Kampe for his appearance on "Nightline."

The meeting ended by midafternoon, and all but Horrigan and Henderson left. The next morning Johnson and Horrigan sprawled in easy chairs in one of the villa's living rooms. Their tee time was at ten o'clock; Henderson was already out taking practice swings.

"Ed, I've got to tell you what I think," Johnson said, returning to the problem of Premier. "We may have the p.r. squared away now, but I think this is going to be one long haul. We're going to stay with it. We're going to hold its hand. But I have a feeling those test markets are going to give us trouble."

What really bothered him, Johnson went on, wasn't Premier's progress so much as its inability to move the stock. "Here we are," said Johnson, "sitting with food assets that are right through the bloody roof—Del Monte worth eighteen times earnings, Nabisco another twenty-two to twenty-five times, and it doesn't make a bit of difference. We're still going to trade at nine times. We're still a tobacco company. Now it looks like Premier isn't going to have any effect. If anything, it's going to be negative in the short run." Life as a tobacco company, they agreed, was unfair. No matter what they did, Wall Street gave them no credit. The stock stayed down. "Where the hell do we go?" Johnson asked.

In the middle of Johnson's soliloquy, Henderson walked in from the practice tee. "Ross, the market is never going to give it its due," said Henderson, picking up his old theme. "This should be a private company."

"Well," Johnson said, "what are the mechanics from a legal standpoint? How would you go about exploring an LBO?"

Henderson outlined the basics, as best he could. After management proposed a buyout, a special committee of board members was formed to consider it. At some point, they would have to make the offer public. And when they did, other companies, even Wall Street raiders, would be free to top it. Therein lay the risk.

"What are the practical realities of operating under an LBO structure?" Johnson asked.

Henderson posed his answers as questions. First, could you raise the kind of money it would take to buy RJR Nabisco? At a glance, it was clear it would be the largest LBO, the largest takeover, ever attempted. How many businesses would have to be sold to pay down debt? Could they keep the Atlanta headquarters, or would they be forced to move back to Winston-Salem to save money? Could they afford to bring out Premier?

If they were at all interested in an LBO, Henderson went on, they would need help. He mentioned some Wall Street lawyers he knew. "Okay," Johnson said, "maybe we'd better seriously see what Shearson's got for us, too."

It'll never happen, Horrigan thought as they headed for the links. He had seen too many of Johnson's "ideas of the week" come and go to generate any real enthusiasm for an LBO. Henderson, too, doubted Johnson was serious. He thought an LBO demanded too much attention to detail for Johnson's tastes.

For his part, Johnson remained ambivalent. Life was good, as the past two weeks had reminded him. A company home on a great golf course. A raft of adoring VIP friends. A jet awaiting his next command. Yet the siren song of action beckoned. "Sure I could have taken the idea of the LBO, stuck it in my lower left-hand drawer, and gone on my merry way," he would later say. "But I would have known it was there." The itch was there, and Johnson couldn't help but scratch it.

A few days later Johnson called Andy Sage at his Wyoming ranch and asked him to stop by Castle Pines on his way east. As they strolled the fairway one afternoon, Johnson brought up his latest idea. "Everything we thought we'd try, nothing happened, nothing happened, nothing happened; the stock just sits there," he said. "Andy, I'm trying to figure out an alternative structure that will serve everybody's interests."

Sage wasn't at all sure an LBO was the solution to RJR Nabisco's problems, and as a general matter, he didn't enjoy seeing America's great companies replace good, old-fashioned shareholder equity with bank debt.

One of American industry's great strengths, Sage and men of his generation felt, was its capital base. At a time when the country faced stiff competition in world markets, he hated to watch that advantage being squandered. Business, he felt, should be creating jobs and new products, things it couldn't do if it was focused on paying back debt. More to the point, he wasn't at all certain Johnson's free-spending style could be reconciled with the rigorous demands and cost cuts demanded by high levels of debt. Still, he kept his doubts to himself.

Johnson told Sage to call Shearson and light a fire under Project Stretch. Hill's team had already begun the arduous task of cataloging the values of RJR Nabisco's businesses; Johnson wanted the homework done by mid-September so they could quickly begin looking at the possibility of an LBO. Sage called Benevento and directed him to pull out the old LBO studies again. Still, Sage, like Horrigan, tried not to dwell on their new tack. Johnson's mind, like the New York weather, was susceptible to change at the slightest notice.

Later that week, Johnson called Charlie Hugel, mentioning the Shearson study almost offhandedly. "Incidentally," Johnson said, "we're having them take a look at whether there's any merit in an LBO. I don't know how much an LBO is worth, but they're doing it. What do you think?"

Frankly, Hugel said, not much. At sixty, Hugel was three years older than Johnson, but a world apart in outlook. Hugel was old line, a man who had risen through the ranks at AT&T before leaving five years earlier to head Combustion Engineering. He was a believer in business fundamentals, and didn't put much stead in faddish Wall Street inventions such as the LBO. At Combustion, Hugel was a hands-on executive working hard to open new markets abroad. Set down in Moscow's notoriously spartan hotels, he mopped the floors himself. It amused him when Johnson, traveling to Moscow for trade ceremonies, tried to order a suite.

"Ross, why do you want to do that?" he asked. "You haven't really completed everything you've been working on. Why would you want to abandon that now?"

"Well, I find it hard to be enthusiastic" about running the company, Johnson admitted. He reiterated everything he'd tried to improve the stock. Hugel himself had confronted far tougher problems than a low stock price, and to him, proposing an LBO was like shooting someone to rid them of a hangnail.

"Ross," he said, deciding to hit Johnson where he lived, "you might have to cut back on the jets, the headquarters, the whole way you live. Do you really want to do that?" They spoke a while longer, and by the time he hung up, Hugel thought he had talked Johnson out of pursuing an LBO.

When Johnson returned to Atlanta after Labor Day, it was only for a day. The next morning he headed to London, where he and John Martin had a whirlwind schedule set up: a General Electric board meeting, a powwow with the international tobacco people, and a tête-à-tête with David Montagu of Rothmans International, a British tobacco company interested in buying pieces of international tobacco. On the flight over, Johnson mentioned the LBO idea to Martin. He wanted to get some sleep, he said, but they could talk about it in the morning.

They never got the chance. As Johnson dozed over the North Atlantic a few minutes before two o'clock Wednesday morning, September 7, a policeman in suburban Westchester County, New York, pulled off the Saw Mill River Parkway. He had spotted a 1987 Nissan, crushed and overturned, about 300 feet from the road. The car had apparently hit a traffic sign before skidding out of control and flipping. Nearby, authorities found the bleeding body of Johnson's twenty-six-year-old son, Bruce. Unconscious, he was rushed to a nearby hospital.

Johnson had just checked into London's Inn on the Park when Laurie called with the news. It wasn't clear whether Bruce was dead or alive. Johnson and Martin hopped on the first Concorde back. On the flight, Johnson lit up a Premier in the No Smoking section. "It'll be interesting to see if anyone notices," he told Martin. By the time Johnson arrived at the Westchester County hospital, his son was in a coma. Doctors weren't sure when, if ever, he would regain consciousness. The Johnsons stayed at Frank and Kathie Lee Gifford's home in Connecticut. Gifford was a rock: his son Kyle had once suffered severe head injuries in an accident.

On Thursday, Jim Robinson visited. The two friends took a long walk around the hospital grounds. "Rawss, all you can do is make sure you're getting the best medical attention you can get," Robinson said. "Other than that, and hoping, there's not a lot of value you can add."

"I know you've been through a similar situation," Johnson said.

"You just have to keep your focus and perspective," Robinson advised, "and go on about your life."

On Friday, Johnson stared at his open briefcase. Mail was piling up at the office. He knew he had to get himself together, get back on track. He decided to take Robinson's advice and plunge back into work. Monday morning he visited Bruce's hospital room, then drove to Manhattan, where he met with Sage and Benevento.

Walking into his office, Johnson brought out a sharp pencil, a calculator, and an accounting spreadsheet, the kind he learned to use at General Electric thirty-five years before. All around him, on the floor and the furniture, he piled reports from his planning department, blue-book statements, studies from investment bankers, and computer printouts. He wanted to see for himself if an LBO made sense, for he no longer trusted investment bankers or computers to give him the answer. As Benevento looked on in wonder, Johnson hunched over the spreadsheet and went to work. "Nobody," he said, "is better at this than me."

Benevento knew what Johnson must be going through; he had three sons of his own. For the first time, Johnson submerged himself in the possibilities and challenges of an LBO. For five hours he and Benevento waded through the numbers, dissecting cash flows, market shares, profit, and sales projections for every RJR Nabisco business. From time to time, Johnson stood and called Atlanta or Winston-Salem to get up-to-date figures.

Johnson wanted to value each business, determine what it might sell for. That, plus tobacco's future cash flows, would go a long way toward determining what price, if any, he could offer in an LBO. By Monday evening he had a feeling: Not only could he raise enough to try a buyout, but he was ready to give it a serious look. Walking to his apartment that evening, Johnson thanked God for giving him something to take his mind off his son.

The next morning a Shearson contingent led by Peter Cohen and Tom Hill arrived at Nine West. The two Shearson executives handed Johnson some how-to materials to scan while thinking about a buyout, and Johnson asked them to study all aspects of an LBO. Johnson was well aware the project they were contemplating could lead to an LBO three times larger than any seen before.

"Peter, is this something you think is doable and viable?" Johnson asked Cohen. "Because you're talking about a pissload of money here. Just a pissload of money."

"Yeah," Cohen said confidently. "We can do it."

The next day Johnson returned to his son's hospital room. Earlier he had canceled a meeting of the executive committee scheduled for Thursday, citing Bruce's accident. Besides, he told Hugel, there really wasn't anything pressing to discuss.

Jeff Beck was perplexed. He couldn't reach Johnson.* Every time he tried, Jim Welch called back. The two men had a running joke. Welch, a courtly Nabisco veteran, had politely objected to Beck's calling him "Jimmy," saying he was too old for that. Beck, of course, ignored him. So Welch had taken to calling Beck "Jeffy."

The last time Welch returned one of his calls, Beck had subtly probed for signs of a shift in Johnson's outlook.

"You know, Jimmy, we have all the money you need if you want to do this deal." Beck didn't have to mention the word buyout; he had been pushing the idea so long Welch understood what he meant.

"I know that, Jeffy."

"Well, you know, shit happens. And I find it peculiar that you're answering all of Ross's phone calls."

"We don't know anything," Welch said. "Nothing's going on."

Something was going on; Beck could feel it. It crossed his mind that Johnson might be attempting an LBO, but he dismissed the notion. Drexel had gotten nowhere recommending that approach for two years now. Still, something had changed. *Maybe they're preparing some kind of restructuring,* Beck thought.

On September 12, he took his suspicions to a man he had courted just as fervently as Johnson: Henry Kravis. Beck had helped Kravis with a number of deals, including his largest, Beatrice. When he arrived at Kohlberg Kravis's offices, ironically just six floors below RJR's New York offices, Beck got right to the point.

"I think it's time to do something about RJR," Beck said.

"Why is that?" Kravis wondered.

"For some reason Johnson's stopped taking my calls. He's having Jim Welch call me back. We ought to just have a meeting and make an offer."

"You're probably right," Kravis said. "Get me the numbers and set something up."

---

* Nor could he reach Andy Sage, who stopped returning Beck's calls after Johnson began looking at the possibility of an LBO. "I couldn't tell the truth," said Sage, "and I didn't want to tell him a lie."

Beck agreed. "There's a problem, though. You won't give Ross what he wants."

"What's that?"

Beck had talked with Johnson's people long enough to know their concerns about LBOs. Johnson simply wasn't interested in working for someone else. "For one thing," he told Kravis, "they'll want control of the board."

"That's true, we won't give him that," Kravis said. "That's a problem."

The two men talked a while but came to no resolution. Nothing could be done, it was clear, without speaking to Johnson first. "Try to set something up," Kravis said, "and we'll discuss it at a meeting."

Later, Beck got back to Welch about setting up a conference between Johnson and Kravis. Welch was noncommittal, but suggested they might get together in the last week of October or the first week of November. The Mad Dog didn't know it, of course, but by then his request would long be moot.

CHAPTER

5

Outside the Metropolitan Museum that blustery September evening, there was all the anticipation of a Hollywood opening. Through a phalanx of photographers and reporters the cream of New York society hustled inside, the ladies clutching their hair against the wind, the men dapper in tuxedos, flashing invitations by one account "as stiff as Sheetrock." In went the Saul Steinbergs, Carol and Punch Sulzberger of *The New York Times*, Jonathon and Laura Tisch, and a hundred others.

Few even in this social stratum had the connections to throw a private party at the museum, but greeting their guests inside the wrought-iron gates of its Medieval Court was a couple who had muscled their way in with a $10 million donation: Henry Kravis and his stunning, fashion-designer wife, Carolyne Roehm. No more than five-foot-six, Kravis wore a tuxedo and a tan. He had a ready smile, rheumy blue eyes, and a voice that held the faint echo of his Oklahoma childhood. But it was Roehm, as always, who attracted attention. Three inches taller than her husband, agonizingly thin, her gleaming dark hair pulled back, she wore a strapless gown of emerald green satin Charmeuse, and a necklace of glistening cabochon emeralds. At social events, she clung to her husband's arm.

After champagne and cocktails the guests gathered around a small stage and, as the lights went down, were bathed in the dulcet strains of the teenage violinist Midori. Kravis and Roehm, who took seats in the front row at the far right, had invited the young Japanese to play after enjoying a private recital in their palatial Park Avenue apartment. Roehm sat rapt, her hands clasped to her chest, Kravis silent beside her.

Afterward the Kravises guided their guests past foliage-crowned trellises into the specially decorated Blumenthal Patio, its stone balconies draped with giant tapestries, lush green vines twisting through its columns and balustrades. Atop the dining tables, which were covered with hunt tapestries trimmed with heavy bullion fringe, were centerpieces of miniature fruits in gilded baskets, each surrounded by gilt candlesticks with green shades. The wines, a Louis Latour Mersault 1985 and a Château Beychevelle 1979, accompanied a dinner most notable for the inclusion of rabbit pie, which some shunted aside with a round of nervous jokes. "Who maimed Roger Rabbit?" someone quipped. Dessert was a baba au rhum served with great silver bowls piled with a colorful display of miniature fruits and sorbets. The evening was topped off by a special showing of the museum's new, 160-piece Degas exhibit, which the guests toured thoughtfully.

"Oh, what is so rare as the perfect party?" wrote the society columnist Suzy days later. "The evening was superb from beginning to end, the one to be measured against by any host and hostess seeking to entertain with wondrous taste and big dollops of flair."

The affair was, in fact, an unofficial coronation of sorts for its hosts, Kravis and Roehm, the prince and princess of the newly moneyed set dubbed "Nouvelle Society." Married just three years, they had rocketed to the fore of Manhattan society, capturing the imagination of social climbers everywhere. Their $5.5 million Park Avenue apartment, laden with Renoirs and French antiques, was practically legend on the charity circuit. Stories of Kravis's lavish gifts to his wife were told and retold in hand-clapping, cheek-clasping awe.

Yet for all the attention, Kravis himself remained something of an enigma. Friends inevitably described him as kind, gentle, and upbeat, a caring father and husband who wrote long, ardent love letters—qualities, of course, that never quite came across in his business dealings. Often characterized as even-tempered and controlled, he nevertheless had a mean streak, a tendency to dismiss a competitor like Ted Forstmann as "having an Avis complex," or to remark cruelly about an overweight associate. There was a steely glint in his eyes that made one want to believe the stories of unbridled greed and ambition. And there was an air—maybe it was his cool, boarding-school reserve—that hinted at something tightly coiled beneath: a sense, however slight, of menace.

His rise on Wall Street had been swift, even by the standards of the high-flying eighties. Practically unknown just five years before, Kravis and his secretive firm had ridden Wall Street's leveraged buyout wave to prominence in the mid-eighties. Years later, the mystery of how Kravis had shunted aside his longtime mentor, Jerome Kohlberg, remained the stuff of drawing-room speculation. If it were ranked as an industrial company, the businesses Kohlberg Kravis controlled, from Duracell batteries to Safeway supermarkets, would place it among the top ten U.S. corporations. Now, with $45 billion in buying power, Kravis was the unquestioned king of Wall Street acquisitors, his war chest greater than the gross national products of Pakistan or Greece, his clout rivaling that of any in financial history.

No one really knew what made Kravis run. The best guess was it had something to do with his diminutive stature or his father, who had made, lost, and regained a fortune by the time Kravis was born in 1944. Little in Kravis's early years foretold greatness. He grew up rich in postwar Tulsa, remembers riding his bicycle a lot, loved golf, and wasn't too keen on classes at Edison Junior High.

His father, Raymond Kravis, was the son of an English tailor who emigrated to Atlantic City at the turn of the century. After working in a Pennsylvania coal mine, Ray Kravis moved to the Southwest, where he became wealthy in the roaring stock market of the 1920s. He lost everything in the crash of 1929, and, having borrowed heavily on margin, worked for years afterward to pay off his margin calls. After the war, he began a second career as a petroleum engineer, estimating oil reserves for Wall Street firms such as Goldman Sachs and managing to amass a second fortune

When Henry was thirteen Ray and Bessie Kravis sent him off to follow his older brother, George, to a boarding school named Eaglebrook in the hills of northwest Massachusetts. Moving on to the Loomis School in Connecticut, "Hank" Kravis was a popular student: vice president of the student council, scrappy captain of the wrestling team, dorm monitor. Teachers remember him as mature, purposeful, controlled.

Kravis was a small boy, and sometimes seemed driven to prove himself among the bigger kids. Years later he relished the touchdowns he scored as a high-school halfback after the coach said he was too puny to play. One of his favorite memories was of his first job at seventeen, working in the mailroom for the Sunray DX Oil Company in Tulsa. After a few days he had been given his first big assignment, distributing the mail for the entire company. But when he woke up on the big morning, he couldn't see. His new contact lenses hadn't been fitted correctly; the pain felt like needles being driven into his eyes. Unable to remove the lenses, his parents out of town, Kravis got in his car and, practically blinded, managed to navigate the empty, early-morning streets of Tulsa to get to work. Afterward his eyes had to be bandaged. "But I got the mail out," Kravis recalled proudly.

An economics course at Loomis persuaded him to pursue a business career, and he majored in finance at tiny 600-student Claremont Men's College in California. (He had applied and was accepted to his father's alma mater, Lehigh, just to show he could get in.) At Claremont, Kravis spent his freshman year majoring in golf, beach, Las Vegas, and the racetrack at nearby Santa Anita. His junior year he captained the golf team. By his senior year he was focused on a Wall Street career. His senior thesis was on convertible debentures.

Ray Kravis knew the people at Goldman Sachs, the old-line Wall Street firm, and each summer during college his son worked there, beginning as a runner. Plunked down amid the shouting, red-faced men on the trading floor, Kravis decided he couldn't see himself among them at age forty. For one thing, he wanted an office. His senior year Kravis secured a post-graduation internship at the Madison Fund, one of Wall Street's hot money management firms. There he made a name for himself as a stock picker. These were the "go-go years," when every stock seemed to be rising. Friends joked he could have done as well using a dart board.

In the fall of 1967 Kravis enrolled at Columbia Business School and immediately regretted it. He missed the action on Wall Street. His father persuaded him to stick with it, but Kravis called his boss at Madison, a man named Ed Merkle, who let him continue working while he completed his studies. Going through the motions, he graduated two years later, at the height of student riots, with an undistinguished record of *B*s and *C*s.

Wall Street beckoned. Madison had acquired a small railroad, Katy Industries, and Merkle, impressed with Kravis's drive, put the young Oklahoman in charge of diversifying its businesses. Kravis settled on an industry he knew, oil field services, and, working for the first time with corporate "finders," spent a year traveling the backroads of Louisiana buying mom-and-pop companies for Katy: a barge and tugboat outfit and a dredging company. It was good, nuts-and-bolts experience.

As Katy grew, Kravis selected the father of a business school friend, a man named Jacob Saliba, to be its new president. Together they rented a suite at Manhattan's Delmonico Hotel—Saliba took the bedroom, Kravis the living room—and continued buying a string of companies for Katy. Eventually Katy was sold, and Kravis, at twenty-five a young man in a hurry, looked for a new challenge. Goldman Sachs was too hidebound, too structured, so Kravis joined a small firm named Fahaerty & Swartwood, where he hoped to begin a venture-capital operation. It didn't pan out and, after a year, he left. Out of work, he turned for help to his cousin, George Roberts.

Just a year older, Roberts had grown up in Houston. His father and Kravis's mother were brother and sister. The grandfather Kravis and Roberts shared was a Russian Jew who fled to America in the late 1890s rather than fight in the czar's army. After his name was changed by an Ellis Island clerk, "George Roberts" joined people from his native village in Muncie, Indiana, where he eventually owned a dry goods store and the Roberts Hotel, which still stands. After losing everything in the Depression, he entered the oil business in Tulsa, and eventually died of a heart attack, alone in an oil field tent.

His son, Louis Roberts, grew up to be a freewheeling oilman in Houston, where he made and lost several fortunes in the Texas oil fields. During the 1950s Lou Roberts often took his teenage son George along to business meetings. At an American Petroleum Institute conference one year, father and son sat by a dirt-caked wildcatter in cowboy boots while listening to a speech by the chairman of Humble Oil, the predecessor to Exxon.

"Which one of those two men would you like to be?" Lou Roberts asked his son afterward.

"I'd rather be like the guy up on the stage, the businessman," young George answered.

The businessman, his father explained, had 50,000 employees to watch over, a long, tiring workday, and could expect a pension of several hundred thousand dollars on retirement. The wildcatter, on the other hand, had maybe 30 employees, several dozen oil wells that pumped away while he slept, and was probably worth $5 million.

"Now who would you rather be?" Lou Roberts asked.*

George Roberts, who grew to be as introverted as his father was garru-

* Lou Roberts died in 1977.

lous, never forgot that lesson about the importance of being your own boss. After attending Culver Military Academy in Indiana, he had been a year ahead of Kravis at Claremont. When George was twenty-one, Ray Kravis had landed him a summer job at Bear Stearns, the big Wall Street trading house. Arriving most mornings before his peers, Roberts—quiet, steady, hardworking—struck up a friendship with the head of the firm's corporate finance department, Jerome Kohlberg. After law school at the University of California-Hastings he went to work for Kohlberg full-time.

Bear Stearns was a cutthroat place, even by Wall Street standards. Run by its hard-charging chief, Salim ("Cy") Lewis, Bear was essentially a loose group of private fiefdoms. At Lewis's encouragement, competition rather than cooperation was emphasized, and jealousy and internal politics flourished. Roberts enjoyed working for Kohlberg because the older man sheltered him from the incessant turmoil. But he soon grew tired of New York. He was raising a family and longed to return to California. When Kohlberg arranged a transfer to Bear's San Francisco office, Roberts, who would continue working for Kohlberg on the coast, nominated his cousin Henry Kravis as a replacement.

Friends joked that Kravis's new boss, Jerry Kohlberg, had one suit (dark) and one tie (yellow, painfully narrow). A forty-four-year-old graduate of Swarthmore and Harvard Business School, he was a quiet, balding family man who loved tennis, the trumpet, his three children, and books. Like Roberts before him, Kravis was taken under the wing of Kohlberg, who ignored, for the moment, his protégé's penchant for raising a little hell. Kravis had grown into the kind of young man who, at his thirtieth birthday party, rode one of his gifts, a Honda motorcycle, around his Park Avenue apartment. He stopped only when the band complained.

For the most part, Kravis's work under Kohlberg was the routine stuff of investment banking: private placements, fairness opinions, stock underwritings. But in his little fiefdom, Kohlberg had also developed a profitable sideline: something known as "the bootstrap deal."

Leveraged buyouts, as bootstrap deals came to be known, began as a kind of aid to the elderly. By the mid-sixties, many of the men who had founded family-owned companies and prospered during the postwar economic boom were growing old As they looked for ways to avoid estate taxes, yet allow their families to retain control of their firms, they had three options: remain privately held, sell shares to the public, or sell out to a larger company. Each approach had drawbacks. Remaining private ignored the problem. Going public exposed the founder to a fickle stock market. Selling out usually meant losing operating autonomy.

Kohlberg saw the LBO as "the missing link," a way for aging executives "to have their cake and eat it, too." His first deal, in 1965, was the $9.5 million acquisition of a Mount Vernon, New York, dental products maker named Stern Metals. It remained his blueprint for years. Kohlberg formed a shell company, backed by a group of investors he assembled, to buy Stern from its seventy-two-year-old family patriarch, using mostly borrowed money. The Sterns retained a stake in the business and continued to run it. Eight months later Kohlberg sold some of his stock—which he had bought for $1.25 a share—to the public for $8 a share, using the proceeds to retire debt. Kohlberg then took the company on a buying spree, snapping up a California dental supply company, an Ohio X-ray firm, and a European maker of dental chairs. When the original investors sold off their $500,000 investment in the transformed company to the public two years later, it was worth $4 million.

The approach was refined in subsequent deals. As the vast conglomerates of the 1960s shed businesses in the face of a declining stock market in the early 1970s, Kohlberg branched out to buy their cast-off divisions. He liked basic industry, companies that made things like bricks and wires and valves, whose management, products, and earnings were solid and reliable. Because he borrowed heavily to buy companies, getting a fix on future earnings and cash flows was crucial if Kohlberg was to avoid having his loans called. Balance sheets were his tarot cards, cash flow projections his crystal ball. Once Kohlberg got his hands on a company, he ruthlessly cut costs and sold unwanted businesses, freeing up every extra dollar to pay debts. In most cases he gave management stock incentives, which he found did wonders for their ability to run the business more efficiently. When he was done, the leaner, meaner result was usually worth more than when he bought it. In their most basic guise, LBOs have worked the same way ever since.

This was grimy, street-level work, and as "Jerry's boy," Kravis pursued it with abandon. For the buyout of a Rockwell International division named Incom, Kravis compiled a seventy-five-page prospectus, crammed with balance sheets, operation summaries, and debt projections, and sent it to major insurance companies. One spring morning a handful of potential investors assembled in Quincy, Massachusetts, where Kravis escorted them through Incom's Boston Gear plant. Piling into three limousines, the group continued on to Holyoke to tour Acme Chain, then to Fairfield, Connecticut, to see Helm Bearing. Finally they caught a plane to Cleveland to visit Incom's Air Maze and Morse Control divisions. It wasn't glamorous, but it worked.

By 1973, after three years of tutelage, Kravis was ready to call the shots on his first deal. Like Stern Metals and other Kohlberg targets, Boren Clay Products, a small North Carolina brick maker, was owned by a strong-willed, elderly founder looking to cash out before his death. Orten Boren, then in his early seventies, didn't have much use for Yankees or, for that matter, Jews.

"Boy," Boren said at one of his first meetings with Kravis. "What faith are you?"

Kravis clinched. "Well, I'm Jewish."

"I thought so." A pause. "You Jewish boys are pretty smart, aren't you?"

Kravis gritted his teeth. If anti-Semitism was the price of success, it was the price he would pay. Over the course of a six-month courtship, Kravis would pay plenty more. At one point, Boren showed Kravis through one of the company's brick factories.

"Henry, see those kilns?" Boren asked, pointing to the giant containers where bricks were baked. "Those are just like the ovens the Germans used." He repeated the remark for emphasis.

Kravis forced a smile.

"Boy," Boren urged, "come on over here, a little closer, and see 'em."

"Oh, no," Kravis replied. "I can see them fine from here."

After buying Boren Clay, Kravis moved on to Providence, Rhode Island, where he began negotiations to buy a tiny, family-owned jewelry maker, Barrows Industries. "I always had the impression Henry just wanted to show he was doing better than his father," recalled its retired chairman, Fred Barrows, Jr. "He always set very strenuous goals for himself. . . . Even then you got the sense Henry was getting too big for Jerry Kohlberg to stomach. Henry was just so aggressive. Jerry was much more conservative."

The Barrows buyout, Kravis's second deal, ended three years later after a series of rancorous disputes. Kravis charged that company executives were "playing games with the figures" to enable them to obtain incentive bonuses. Fred Barrows remembered the falling out differently. "Very frankly, I thought they were milking the company," he says. "They wanted directors' fees, but they weren't directing. And then they had what they called maintenance fees. I said, 'Look, why do we need all this expense?' . . . It just went against my Yankee grain."

In the end, Barrows bought out Kravis and his investors, giving Kravis a 16.5 percent annual return on his money, little better than a certificate of deposit. Kravis was disappointed, but ultimately better off: Gold prices shot up shortly after, and Barrows eventually went out of business.

In fact, Kravis and Kohlberg's experience with Barrows wasn't all that unusual. After three successful buyouts in the mid-sixties, Kohlberg had yet to discover the Midas touch that would later bring Kohlberg Kravis to prominence. A graph of the returns from the fourteen buyouts he completed between 1965 and 1975 would start high on the left, then plunge straight down, ending in a series of low hummocks.

When stock prices turned down in the early 1970s, Kohlberg's returns turned dismal, at least by later standards. Eagle Motors Line, an Alabama trucking outfit acquired in 1973, was a disappointment and had to be merged with another trucker. Boren Clay, Kravis's first deal, hit a long slump before rebounding nearly a decade later. By far Kohlberg's most spectacular failure was his sixth buyout, in 1971, the $27 million acquisition of a California shoemaker, Cobblers Industries. Three months after George Roberts closed the deal, the company founder and creative genius walked up to the factory roof during a lunch break and committed suicide. "Jerry called me and screamed, 'The fucker jumped off the roof!' " recalls Robert Pirie, a Cobblers investor. Rudderless, its Jamestown, Pennsylvania, factory washed away in a subsequent flood, Cobblers ultimately went bankrupt. Kohlberg and his investors lost their entire $400,000 investment.

As Kohlberg and the two young cousins spent more time on their buyouts, it took them away from the bread-and-butter business of corporate finance, prompting grumbling among many at Bear Stearns, including their boss, Cy Lewis. "Cy was a legend," says Bob Pirie. "Legendarily difficult." Lewis was also a trader, and traders are notoriously short-term oriented. Decisions on the trading floor are made in a split second, profits on fractions of a point. Kohlberg's buyout business, in contrast, was based on returns that took three, four, five years to realize, an eternity to Bear's dominant trading culture. "Overnight was long-term for Bear Stearns," Kravis liked to say. Cy Lewis thought Kohlberg was spending far too much on his silly buyout sideline. It simply took too long to make a buck, when it made a buck at all.

Matters came to a head in 1976 in the wake of Kravis's disastrous decision to invest in a Hartford, Connecticut, direct marketing firm named Advo. Initially he and Kohlberg had turned down the deal as too risky, but reconsidered when Travelers, the big insurance company, suggested they do it together, offering Kravis 40 percent of the $7.5 million acquisition for just $200,000. "Hell," Kravis said, "how can we lose?" Easily, it turned out. Advo's business headed downhill fast. Kohlberg removed the president, leaving Kravis the interim chief for three weeks. Cy Lewis hit the roof when he found a Bear Stearns partner running a sputtering direct-mail outfit instead of producing income for the firm.

"What the hell are you doing up there?" Lewis demanded in a phone call. "Goddamn it, you should be at home drumming up new business. Forget this deal. We've got our fee, let's go on with the next deal."

"But Cy," Kravis protested, "that's not the way it works. You've got to stick with it a while."

Kravis stuck with it long enough to unload his backers' $200,000 investment for half that. Advo was a nightmare for him. If his losses weren't bad enough, Bear Stearns and several Bear partners, including Lewis, had invested alongside them in the deal, further widening the gulf between Kohlberg and his colleagues.

As the political infighting worsened, Kravis threatened to quit. "Everyone, some of the partners, was telling me, 'do this, do that,' and I didn't like anyone telling me what to do," Kravis recalled. Kohlberg urged him to stay the course. He proposed to Lewis that the three of them—Kohlberg, Kravis, and Roberts—set up a freestanding LBO group within Bear Stearns. Lewis said no.

"After that Jerry's position within the firm really deteriorated," Roberts recalled years later. "They were going to make life very difficult for him. Some administrative people were going to be put over him. It was clear he was going to be put in a box." After much gnashing of teeth, Kohlberg repeated his request to begin an LBO group. Again Lewis refused.

Kohlberg and the two cousins began talking among themselves of resigning. With a nest egg of $5 million or so, Kohlberg had little incentive to remain. Roberts, anxious to follow his father's lead into private business, pushed Kravis to leave, too. The two estimated how much money they could make at Bear Stearns over the next decade, compared to going their own way. Bear won. Kravis left anyway.

When Kohlberg announced their intention to resign, Roberts flew in from San Francisco to tell Cy Lewis personally. The chairman of Bear Stearns was a large, imposing man, and as Roberts delivered the bad news, Lewis leaned way over his huge desk. "You know, young man," he said, "you're making a terrible mistake. No one has ever left this firm and been successful."

Then things got nasty. A few mornings later, Kravis walked in and found his office emptied, its door locked. A tall man in paratrooper boots stormed up to him.

"You vill not be in that office," the man said in a German accent.

"What do you mean?" Kravis said. "I'm a partner here."

A similar "hit man" arrived in San Francisco. The contents of Roberts's office were saved only by the timely intervention of his West Coast colleagues. Dumbstruck, Kohlberg and Kravis confronted Lewis: "What the hell's going on?"

Lewis had declared war on the traitorous trio. On their departure, he demanded that Bear Stearns retain control of all Kohlberg's deals, even though the three had millions of their own money sunk in them and, in most cases, controlled the companies' boards. Lewis attempted to apply pressure through Kohlberg's investors, including insurance giant Prudential and the midwestern bank First Chicago. "But the Pru told him to 'shove it,' and so did First Chicago," Kravis recalled. Eventually lawyers were brought in and, in a long, difficult negotiation, the trio kept control of its investments.

They set up shop in the old Mutual of New York building on Fifth Avenue. Kohlberg preferred a low profile, so for years there was no name on the door. Roberts continued to work out of San Francisco. For overhead they raised $50,000 from each of eight investors, including Ray Kravis and the Hillman family of Pittsburgh. Kohlberg Kravis Roberts & Co. would take 20 percent of the profits from every deal, and charge a 1 percent management fee (later 1.5 percent).

For five years they stuck to Kohlberg's guiding tenets: the deals were always friendly, always with management, always careful. They identified many of their targets with the help of a Los Angeles finder named Harry Roman. It was difficult, uphill work. LBOs were still Greek to most people, and the trio spent much of its time explaining how three unknowns and a handful of executives could borrow enough money to buy an entire company. Their own low profile didn't help. "Investment bankers, everyone, looked at us and said, 'KKR, what is that, a delicatessen?'" remembered a Wall Street executive who worked for the firm in the seventies.

Despite the physical distance between them, Kohlberg remained close to the sobersided Roberts, closer than with Kravis, who was still prone to sowing his wild oats. Roberts, quieter and, many believe, smarter than Kravis, had known Kohlberg longer and was considered his intellectual equal. When one of Kohlberg's sons had problems as a teenager, Roberts took him into his California home. Kravis, on the other hand, seemed to be regarded by Kohlberg as a hardworking subordinate. The two men had little in common besides their work. On weekend outings Kohlberg would wear chinos and hiking boots. Kravis would come in Italian slacks and Gucci loafers. After working side by side for sixteen-hour days, Kohlberg headed home to sleep, but Kravis headed out on the town with his wife. "Jerry would see Henry going out and remark dryly, 'Oh, off again, Henry?'" said a former Kohlberg Kravis associate.

The deals came in spurts: three in 1977, none in 1978, three more in 1979, including the first buyout of a major publicly held company, Houdaille Industries. Then, after a small deal in 1980, Kohlberg Kravis went on a tear in 1981, completing six deals and generating the first spate of press coverage for the tiny firm.

During this period the trio fine-tuned its craft. They found larger companies could be acquired as easily as small ones, for the simple reason that they had larger cash flows; by diverting that money to pay down its debt, Kohlberg Kravis was able to use a company's own strengths to acquire it. They began accumulating pools of money from investors, allowing them fast access to larger amounts of cash. Beginning with a $30 million fund in 1978, they raised a series of steadily larger pools, eventually reaching $1 billion in their fourth fund in 1983. The size of the deals grew in lockstep, reaching a peak during this period with the $440 million buyout of a Hawaiian construction company, Dillingham Corp.

After a company was acquired, Kohlberg, Kravis, and Roberts kept a close watch on its budgets, but otherwise gave its management more or less free rein to streamline and meet its mountainous debts. In most cases it worked like a charm. When it didn't, as in the firm's second buyout, an oil field services firm named L. B. Foster that ran into the teeth of an industry slump, heads rolled, and new management was swiftly brought in. After five to eight years they resold their companies, or took them public again, often getting three, four, five, even ten times their original investment. By 1983 Kohlberg Kravis claimed an average annual return of 62.7 percent to their investors. Their own 20 percent stake made the three men rich.

For six years they plugged along, quietly dominating their obscure little niche of finance. Then, as so often happens on Wall Street, someone noticed. In 1982 an investment group headed by William Simon, a former treasury secretary, took private a Cincinnati company, Gibson Greetings, for $80 million, using only a million dollars of its own money. When Simon took Gibson public eighteen months later, it sold for $290 million. Simon's $330,000 investment was suddenly worth $66 million in cash and securities.

It was a fluke, an accident of timing, but it turned heads on Wall Street. Gibson Greetings became its equivalent of gold at Sutter's Mill. Suddenly everyone wanted to try this "LBO thing," even though few knew how it worked. And try it they did. Measured by the total sales of acquired companies, the LBO phenomenon increased tenfold between 1979 and 1983. By 1985, just two years after Gibson Greetings, there were eighteen separate LBOs valued at $1 billion or more. In the five years before Ross Johnson decided to pursue his buyout, LBO activity totaled $181.9 billion, compared to $11 billion in the six years before that.

A number of factors combined to fan the frenzy. The Internal Revenue Code, by making interest but not dividends deductible from taxable income, in effect subsidized the trend. That got LBOs off the ground. What made them soar was junk bonds.

Of the money raised for any LBO, about 60 percent, the secured debt, comes in the form of loans from commercial banks. Only about 10 percent comes from the buyer itself. For years the remaining 30 percent—the meat in the sandwich—came from a handful of major insurance companies whose commitments sometimes took months to obtain. Then, in the mid-eighties, Drexel Burnham began using high-risk "junk" bonds to replace the insurance company funds. The firm's bond czar, Michael Milken, had proven his ability to raise enormous amounts of these securities on a moment's notice for hostile takeovers. Pumped into buyouts, Milken's junk bonds became a high-octane fuel that transformed the LBO industry from a Volkswagen Beetle into a monstrous drag racer belching smoke and fire.

Thanks to junk bonds, LBO buyers, once thought too slow to compete in a takeover battle, were able to mount split-second tender offers of their own for the first time. Suddenly LBOs became a viable alternative in every takeover situation; because they held out the promise of operating autonomy and vast riches, Kohlberg Kravis and other firms were swamped with requests from chief executives to become "white knight" rescuers of their raider-besieged companies. It was a symbiotic relationship repeated in deal after deal: raider seeks target; target seeks LBO; and raider, target, and LBO firm all profit from the outcome. The only ones hurt were the company's bondholders, whose holdings were devalued in the face of new debt, and employees, who often lost their jobs. In the sheer joy of making money, Wall Street didn't pay too much attention to either group.

No sooner did LBOs blossom than critics took aim. The vast debt assumed by post-LBO companies worried many, including those in government. In mid-1984 the chairman of the Securities and Exchange Commission predicted that "the more leveraged takeovers and buyouts now, the more bankruptcies tomorrow." A Republican SEC commissioner decried LBOs as "little more than a charade." Proponents, of course, argued that LBOs actually strengthened the business community by cutting corporate flab and building leaner companies.

Curiously, the loudest outcry came from the raider-ravaged corporate community, where Main Street executives saw the mounting power of LBO buyers as the next plague to be unleashed by Wall Street. A top executive of Goodyear Tire & Rubber, for one, labeled the LBO "an idea that was created in hell by the Devil himself."

———

As the spiritual leader of the LBO community, Jerry Kohlberg by 1983 was growing uncomfortable with changes in the industry he helped spawn. He still favored small, friendly deals initiated by pull-up-a-chair talks with older gentlemen. The new breed of LBO buyer was typified by the young, hard-charging investment bankers who now flocked to Kohlberg Kravis with ideas for new deals. Kravis and Roberts, then in their late thirties and coming into their own as deal makers, were magnets for these men.

"This is really a young person's game," says Richard Beattie, a Manhattan lawyer who had worked closely with Kravis since Boren Clay. "By now

Jerry is fifty-three, fifty-four. Investment bankers don't call Jerry. They call Henry and George. They're the same age. Jerry begins to feel left out. He's not part of the action anymore."

As the LBO game grew faster, Kravis and Roberts took on more and more of the firm's deal-making responsibility. In 1984 they completed the first $1 billion LBO, and took Kohlberg Kravis on a spree of other large deals. As buying opportunities mushroomed, the pair pushed to enlarge the firm and add staff. New men were added, but Kohlberg blocked hiring even more. Kravis and Roberts pushed for more and larger deals, and Kohlberg blocked many of those, too. Inside the firm, Kohlberg acquired the inevitable moniker, "Dr. No." Kravis complained that Kohlberg was stuck in the sixties. Behind his back, the two cousins began to grouse that Kohlberg was holding them back. "Jerry was older, and he never wanted to work as hard," Roberts recalled. "The reason Jerry was so negative was that he wasn't reading and understanding what was going on."

As the firm grew—by 1983, it had eight deal makers, by 1988, fifteen—tensions rose. Factions developed. Junk bonds produced an ever more complicated stream of Rubik's Cube financial structures. Kravis and Roberts were so busy Kohlberg could no longer keep abreast of every deal. Outside parties began shouldering more and more of the daily work, and Kravis and Roberts soon were orchestrating small armies of investment bankers and lawyers. "Jerry began to pull back," says his longtime friend George Peck, a Kohlberg Kravis consultant. "He was less comfortable with all that. He was starting to get a real sense of despondency."

Then, in late 1983, Kohlberg began experiencing mysterious dizzy spells. Tests found a blood clot in his brain, and in early 1984 he underwent surgery at New York's Mount Sinai Hospital to have it removed. During his hospital stay, a friend says, "Jerry [got] a little offended because [Henry and George didn't] visit him very often." Afterward, Kohlberg, impatient to return to his normal routine, insisted on convalescing at his home in St. Croix. After the flight down, a blood clot in his lung was found. Rushed to the hospital, two close friends say, Jerry Kohlberg nearly died.

He attempted a return to work in mid-1984 but, plagued by headaches and lethargy, gave up and remained away for months. When Kohlberg finally returned to work again, he was unable to handle his former workload. Tired, medicated, he left many days by noon. Other days, said Peck,

"Jerry would get up, plan to come in at seven-thirty, then have a splitting headache and have to stay home."

"Healthwise, Jerry was not ready to come back," said Paul Raether, a former investment banker who was named the firm's fifth general partner in 1986. When "Jerry comes back in 1985, he's in the flow, but he's not in the flow. He's working maybe twenty-five hours a week. He can't keep up in the day-to-day work. That created tensions. Things start to pile up because Jerry's behind. Decisions aren't made as fast as they should be, and that creates more friction. Another problem was Jerry wasn't always there. He lost his train of thought easily. Jerry doesn't believe it. If you told him I said that, he'd say I'm full of shit. But it's true. It's just a fact. Sometimes he just wasn't there."

The tensions between Kohlberg and his two partners broke into the open during the fight for Beatrice, when Kohlberg opposed their plan to launch a hostile tender offer. There were awkward scenes when Kohlberg demanded to attend a meeting or strategy session to which he hadn't been invited. "The person that has the greatest problem with all this, of course, is Jerry himself," says a Kravis intimate. "He develops a great deal of anxiety about being left out of the business, walking into people's offices at the wrong time, always asking what's going on. He begins insisting for the first time on formal lines of communication."

It was a difficult period for Roberts and Kravis, who realized they might not be able to continue as they had before. After Beatrice, Kohlberg forced the issue by insisting that his responsibilities within the firm be defined. It was a painful dialogue for all involved.

"What should I do?" Kohlberg would ask.

"What do you mean, 'What should I do?' " Kravis would reply. "I don't have to tell George or the others what to do. Doesn't that tell you maybe it's time for a change?"

They had the same arguments over and over. You want it the way it was in the old days, Kravis would say, and it can't be. It just can't be. Times have changed.

"But we were partners when we started," Kohlberg said.

"That's true," Kravis said. "But life changes. The business has changed."

The simple fact was, Kravis and Roberts no longer needed their former mentor. In his absence they had completed a number of difficult, high-profile deals, including the $2.4 billion buyout of Storer Communications.

"George and Henry said, 'Hey, we're doing pretty well,' " says George Peck. " 'If Jerry's not in today, no big deal. Things are being taken care of.' That just killed Jerry." Says Roberts, "As we needed less and less help, Jerry wanted to help more and more."

In the months to come, the gap between Kohlberg and Kravis was widened by the stark difference in their life-styles. Kohlberg was a homebody, married to the same woman for forty years. Money hadn't changed him. He dressed simply, led a quiet family life, and spent his free time playing tennis or reading thick volumes of fiction or biography. His idea of entertaining was tossing a softball around on a Sunday afternoon and retiring early to read. "Getting Jerry to go out to a cocktail party," says a friend, "is a major event."

Kravis, on the other hand, lived for the lush life. His first marriage on the rocks, Kravis began seeing Carolyne Roehm, and the couple quickly became a fixture of society pages. Every night, it seemed, they were photographed at some black-tie function or another, laughing with flashy friends such as the Donald Trumps. Kohlberg didn't think it was the way a grown man ought to act; it was ostentatious, and it gave the firm a bad image. "It came to bother Jerry a lot," says a Kohlberg friend. "It came between them to the point where Jerry couldn't stand to go to Henry's apartment on Park Avenue, there was so much wealth."

Rather than confront Kravis, Kohlberg took his complaints to his kindred spirit, Roberts. Roberts counseled restraint. "Look, Henry is happy," he told Kohlberg. "Carolyne is a fashion designer, and fashion designers need publicity. You know Henry has always been more a social animal than you and me. Let's not try to be running everyone's lives."

For months the debates on Kohlberg's future dragged on. Kravis thought Kohlberg was being egged on by his son James, a former journeyman tennis player now working for Roberts in San Francisco. Much of the time the three principals communicated via their friends, Beattie and Peck, who tried to keep them together.

It was no use. In the end, the crux of their disagreement came down to two things: money and power. To Kravis and Roberts, Kohlberg wanted too much of both. On the firm's founding, they had agreed that Kohlberg would take about 40 percent of the profits, with Kravis and Roberts taking about 30 percent apiece. As other partners joined, their shares came out of Kohlberg's take. It was painful for the two cousins to tell Kohlberg he wasn't pulling his load. But as a result, they felt he shouldn't be allowed to remain an equal partner. "It just wasn't fair," Roberts recalled quietly.

The firm's charter provided for majority rule among the trio. According to Roberts, Kohlberg now demanded it be unanimous, in effect giving him veto power over major firm decisions. It was the final straw. "We were prepared to give him a large interest, to let him stay, to treat him with due respect, but we wouldn't give him veto power," says Roberts. "It just wasn't right."

There was talk of Kohlberg becoming chairman emeritus, but he wasn't ready to retire. Eventually tempers flared. "There were scenes, you know, when Jerry said, 'I founded this firm. You guys wouldn't be here without me,'" Raether recalled. "None of us liked the way it worked out in the end."

When Kohlberg suggested he might leave, neither Kravis nor Roberts argued with him. Both sides hired lawyers, and a severance agreement was negotiated over a period of months. By the spring of 1987 it was completed and, in June, Kohlberg's departure was announced to the firm's investors. The rift between the partners was hinted at but never explained. Kohlberg and his son, along with George Peck, soon founded their own LBO firm, Kohlberg & Co., which pointedly concentrated on small, strictly friendly deals. Kohlberg almost never spoke of the rift, and when he did he hinted of his disapproval of Kravis and Roberts's growing appetite for larger fees and bigger, more aggressive deals. "I won't restrict myself to small transactions," he told *The New York Times* in 1987, "but I'll stick with deals where reason prevails." Kravis and Roberts read the comments and thought Kohlberg was erecting a smoke screen to hide the real reasons behind his departure.

"It makes me sad," Roberts said in a mid-1989 interview. "It's like a divorce. Of the twenty-four years I worked with Jerry, nineteen were idyllic. The last five were not. . . . I feel like I lost a good friend. The decision we made for him to leave was best. But personally, it was very tough on me. Still is."

By the time Jerry Kohlberg left Kohlberg Kravis, his office had lain empty so long it was regularly used by visiting lawyers. With its Talmud and collection of Lucite tombstones, the lawyers dubbed it "the LBO library." When the offices were remodeled in 1989 after a fire, Henry Kravis had it turned into a stairwell.

Long before he became a major force on Wall Street, Kravis was a fixture of New York society circles, thanks to his extended courtship of Carolyne Roehm. Before the creation of Carolyne Roehm, fashion designer, there was Jane Smith, specialist in Sears polyester sportswear. The only child of a pair of teachers, little Janey enjoyed an idyllic childhood in tiny Kirksville, Missouri. At five she saved her money for her first fashion purchase, a rhinestone necklace from the Sears catalog. At thirteen she saw Susan Hayward in *Back Street* and decided she wanted to be a fashion designer.

Jane Smith was a skinny, bright, energetic fashion student at Washington University in St. Louis, the kind of "good girl" who wore pearls and nice skirts to peace rallies and who once called her mother when she couldn't find her way back to the sorority house. Upon graduation she journeyed to the fashion capital of the world, New York's Seventh Avenue, only to quit her first job after two days when her supervisor suggested she clean the bathrooms. Moving on to another firm, she rode the subway each day and scraped by in a tiny apartment, always making sure to have plenty of fresh flowers and a bubble bath. "Beauty and glamour," she liked to say, "are a state of mind."

After paying her dues in polyester for eleven months, Jane Smith got up the gumption to take her portfolio to her idol, Oscar de la Renta. De la Renta wasn't terribly impressed, but she was persistent. She signed on as a design assistant, and soon twenty-four-year-old Jane Smith was playing Eliza Doolittle to the famed designer's Henry Higgins. She took cooking and riding lessons, learned French, and tried hard to be a charming dinner partner. At the office she was sweet and innocent, a crier not a yeller, still the ideal prom date who talked about themes in gift wrapping.

The earliest casualty of her self-transformation was her first name. She would introduce herself as Jane Smith and hard-bitten Seventh Avenue types would say, "Yeah, and I'm Tarzan." A boyfriend suggested she go by her real first name, Carolyne, and it stuck.

So, unfortunately, did the boyfriend. Axel Roehm, heir to a German chemical fortune, was tall, dark, handsome, European, and rich; in short, her fantasy of the ideal husband. They married and, as Carolyne Roehm, she moved to Darmstadt, Germany, to lead the life of a wealthy, lonely hausfrau. After a year of domestic boredom Roehm ran back to de la Renta in tears, the marriage a failure. De la Renta gave her responsibility for his lower priced "Miss O" line and the traumatized young divorcée threw herself into the work with a vengeance.

A year later, in 1979, she met Kravis at a party. It wasn't love at first sight. Kravis was too short, for one thing, and he had a boring job on Wall Street. He was also married, although separated from his wife of nine years. After a Christmastime skiing date in Vail—Roehm's mother chaperoned—they began seeing each other. Theirs was not a storybook love affair. Roehm, coming off a tough divorce, was a reluctant target. "It was a friendship," Roehm recalled. "Being together with Henry was like putting a wonderful salve on a bad wound. . . . [My recollection] is not clouded by the romance of the beginning, because there wasn't one. We were friends for a long time before I thought of him as a lover."

Kravis's marriage had been on the wane for years. In 1970 he had wed Hedi Shulman, the daughter of a Brooklyn psychiatrist. The Kravises, with a Park Avenue apartment and rented summer homes in Greenwich or The Hamptons, had always been social climbers. But by most accounts, Kravis, his later riches still a dream, balked at his wife's spending habits.

"Hedi always wanted to buy the biggest and the best, the most," recalled a family friend. "Henry didn't like to spend money at that time. Hedi was driven by the dollar. It drove Henry crazy. It was personally embarrassing to him to have to explain to people out in North Carolina why his wife was going off to a summer home with their staff."

One summer evening Kravis stepped off the train in Greenwich to find Hedi waiting expectantly. "Henry, I've found the most wonderful house to buy!" she enthused. She drove Kravis out a lonely road where mansions lay a mile apart. Down a long, wooded lane she led him, emerging before a virtual castle. Kravis, unnerved, didn't even want to get out of the car.

Kravis attacked the courtship of Roehm with all the zest of a major takeover contest. On their way to a formal dinner one night, he insisted she test a pair of new tennis shoes; he despised the ratty old sneakers she had worn for years. Roehm, trying her damndest to slip into a red lace dress, finally relented and took a shoe. In its toe she found a diamond necklace.

"As far as romance goes, Henry has fantasy," Roehm says. "It's not Oscar Wilde, but of all the business types I've gone out with, he's by far the most romantic. Every anniversary, every Christmas, every birthday, he writes me these sweet, long letters about what he's feeling. You know, 'My faith, my love, my belief in you.' They're very touching letters. I've kept all of them."

They were partners in business before marriage. In 1984 Kravis agreed to invest several million dollars to bankroll Roehm in her own design business. She rented half a floor in the Seventh Avenue building that also housed Lauren, Beene, and Blass. Unveiled in a show seven months later, Roehm's first collection of elegant evening wear and sprightly day wear was a triumph. When she strolled out for the standing ovation, a teary Roehm waved to the man who made it possible, Henry Kravis. He was crying, too.

Roehm was ready for marriage, but Kravis, after finally getting a divorce in 1984, apparently was having second thoughts. One day, as she frantically prepared for her first showing, Roehm broke down in tears before her mentor. "I don't think Henry will marry me," she said. De la Renta, ever the father figure, called Kravis. "You're going to tell me this is none of my business, and it is none of my business," the designer said. "I understand that you've had a bad divorce and may not be in the mood to marry again. But I've got to tell you: I will be very disturbed if Carolyne becomes the mistress of an unmarried man. I think she's better than that. I will use all my influence to break the relationship."

When Kravis finally asked for her hand, Roehm wavered. They were in Italy, where Roehm was shopping for new fabrics for her next collection. "I said I had to think about it," she recalled. Crestfallen, Kravis pestered her about it all evening and into the next day. "He kept saying, 'I can't believe you said that, I can't believe it.' Every five minutes it was, 'What's your decision?' He kept at me all the next day until finally, around three, I said, 'Well, okay.'"

Days before their wedding the couple moved into an apartment whose elaborate furnishings immediately became the talk of the town. English and French antiques from Louis XV to Empire filled the "public rooms," where rich, silken draperies fell in puddles onto the floor. On the living room's celadon walls hung a Renoir, across from a Monet landscape. In his library Kravis preferred English horse paintings. A drawing room held a Sisley, a second Renoir, and Dutch flower paintings. The apricot and yellow damask dining room, with its massive Sargent, conjured up visions of a grand English manor house. Coral damask lined the walls and silk festoon shades adorned the windows. To one side was a *faux-marbre* dining alcove, where Roehm would place a trio—two violinists and, say, a harpist—to play softly for dinner guests.

Four years later *GQ* would enshrine the Kravis–Roehm wedding, along with that of Charles and Diana, as one of the "twenty weddings of the century since 1980." Their vows, exchanged at the apartment, were followed by dinner for 101 and a toast by Kravis's father. "Henry's always been impatient," said Ray Kravis. "He was born premature, and he's been in a hurry ever since."

The newlyweds cut a wide swath through Manhattan society. Kravis, already on many of the "right" boards—New York City Ballet, Mount Sinai Hospital, the exclusive Spence School—leapt onto the coveted Metropolitan Museum board and had a museum wing named after him. Roehm, whose dresses cost up to $8,000 and are worn by the likes of Barbara Walters and Sigourney Weaver, attained the New York Public Library board of trustees and orchestrated memorable galas for the Metropolitan Opera and the New York Winter Antiques show. The Kravises added a beach home in The Hamptons, a ski chalet in Vail, and a pre-Revolutionary manor in Connecticut, where Roehm gardened and rode horses and Kravis sometimes raced around on a Honda four-wheeler. Despite his burgeoning fortune—variously estimated at between $200 million and $350 million—the Kravises continued to work grueling twelve-hour days, traveling constantly.

When in New York they went out nightly, becoming mainstays of *W* and *Women's Wear Daily*, in large part because Roehm, threatened by up-and-coming designers like Donna Karan, made a conscious decision to seek the social limelight. Her clothes were intended for women like herself—tall, thin, and rich—and she saw the society pages as her best bet to stand out in a crowded field. *W* noted wryly that in her quest for publicity, Roehm appeared "on the cover of every imaginable publication, including real-estate listings." It wondered: "Is *Pravda* next?"

In many ways it was a storybook life. Summers in Salzburg. Holidays in Vail. Weekends hunting pheasant in Connecticut. Evenings at glittering charity balls. Mornings with Roehm strolling through the Renoirs, an aria on her lips. Their West Highland terrier, Pookie, walked each day by a liveried servant. Of all the stories, the one told most often was of the night Kravis surprised his wife in bed with an eye-popping emerald necklace. When she wore it to a Council of Fashion Designers cocktail party, it was the talk of the crowd.

"Where did you get those?" asked a longtime friend.

"I found them under my pillow," Roehm replied.

"And where have you been sleeping?"
"In the right bed."

By 1987 the LBO industry, once the exclusive hunting ground of Kohlberg Kravis and a handful of other boutique firms, was getting crowded. Attracted by the tremendous returns seen in Gibson Greetings and Beatrice, institutional investors poured billions of dollars into scores of firms, hoping to get a piece of Kravis's action. Two of Wall Street's largest concerns, Morgan Stanley and Merrill Lynch, each raised more than $1 billion to do LBOs, and most other firms, including Shearson, planned similar thrusts. Kravis and Roberts hadn't even finished spending their $2 billion 1986 fund—by far Wall Street's largest—before one of their rivals, Forstmann Little & Co., unveiled a $2.7 billion fund. Suddenly the sound of footsteps Kravis had been hearing became a thundering posse, charging into his corral.

Now deals where Kravis could once have quietly negotiated a buyout agreement became bidding contests. "Done deals" unraveled in the face of higher bids, sometimes wasting months of work. When Kravis did carry the day, prices were sky-high. "A lot of guys want to do deals just to do them," complained Paul Raether. "They want to put scalps up on their walls. They say, 'I gotta do this deal because it'll make me a player. It'll put me on the map.' "

For Kravis, a startling case in point came during the fall 1986 bidding contest for Jim Walter, a Tampa construction firm. A Kohlberg Kravis bid was topped by PaineWebber, a firm with no track record in LBOs. When Kravis, alarmed, asked the firm's chairman, Donald Marron, what he thought he was doing, Marron pointed out that his firm had a lot of money and talent committed to merchant banking and needed to put them to use. It wouldn't be the last such conversation Kravis had.

If Kohlberg Kravis were to reassert its dominance in LBOs, it somehow had to rise above the competition. The only place to go was up. In early 1987 Kravis and Roberts made a conscious decision to go after the megadeals, the $5 billion and $10 billion buyouts that few others could attempt. They had laid the groundwork by completing a string of mammoth LBOs: the $6.2 billion Beatrice deal, the $4.4 billion buyout of Safeway Stores, and the $2.1 billion buyout of Owens-Illinois in 1987. Now they would push into higher, uncharted territories.

" 'Who else could do a ten-billion-dollar deal' was the reasoning," recalled Raether. "Nobody. The only possible competitor at those levels was corporations. And most likely you won't get competition from corporations at that price level."

Erasing the competition wasn't the only attraction of the megadeal. Kravis and Roberts knew from experience that it took little more work to complete a large LBO than it did a small one. Whatever the size of the transaction, however, their percentile fees remained the same. It didn't take a genius to see they could make more money working on $10 billion deals than "puny" $100 million deals. On Beatrice they had taken a $45 million fee, plus $60 million apiece on Safeway and Owens-Illinois. That money went straight into the partners' pockets.

The vehicle to attain these new heights was a new fund, their largest ever. Even before spending the 1986 fund, Roberts began lobbying to raise another, bigger one. "We don't have to finish the 1986 fund," he argued. "The money is available now. Let's get it while we can." Recalled Raether: "By 1987 everyone had a pot of money. We wanted to have by far the biggest pot. That would differentiate us from everybody else. It would be clear we had more power than anyone else, and everyone would know it. Everyone would know the big deals were ours."

They began raising the new fund in June 1987, using publicity from the Beatrice deal to whip up interest. As an incentive to investors to re-up, Kravis offered to waive the management fee for all deals done before 1990. It worked. When the fund closed just four months later, Kravis and Roberts sat atop a $5.6 billion war chest, more than two times the size of its nearest competitor's. Of the estimated $20 billion in equity poised for LBO investments worldwide, the two grandsons of a Russian immigrant controlled one dollar of every four. Fully leveraged, it gave them an unprecedented $45 billion in buying power, enough money, *Fortune* pointed out, to buy all ten *Fortune* 500 companies headquartered in Minneapolis, including Honeywell, General Mills, and Pillsbury. Wall Street had never seen anything like it before.

Wall Street didn't know the half of it. For the first time, Kravis and Roberts had sought and received permission from their investors to secretly accumulate stock in their targets. These so-called toehold investments, a mainstay of corporate raiders like Boone Pickens, would give Kravis negotiating advantage with chief executives and allow the firm to profit from the inevitable run-up in a target company's stock. A reaction to its new competitive environment, this tactic, more than any other, took the firm away from Jerry Kohlberg's fireside chats and institutionalized its new, more aggressive bent. Arm-twisting, rather than friendly discussion, would now lead to most of the firm's deals.

But this approach required Kravis to walk a fine line. Most pension funds, the major source of Kohlberg Kravis's money, were either barred from, or leery of, hostile takeovers. Just a whiff of hostile action could scare off investors and irreparably damage their franchise in strictly friendly LBOs. If Kohlberg Kravis were branded a raider, what chief executive in his right mind would want to work with it? It made Kravis, thin-skinned by nature, acutely sensitive to public criticism.

As stock prices plummeted in the crash of October 1987, Kravis and Roberts made their move, swooping in and secretly buying vast chunks of several major U.S. corporations. In 1988 they brought the LBO idea to one of those companies—its identity still secret—and were rejected. At the end of March, Kravis unveiled a 4.9 percent stake in Texaco, then under pressure from its largest shareholder, investor Carl Icahn. For two months Kravis and Roberts attempted to talk the oil company's officials into a buyout or major restructuring. "We tried everything in the world to get them to do something with us," Raether recalled, "and they wouldn't." The firm eventually sold its stock at a profit.

The problem, it soon became clear, was that Kohlberg Kravis was all bite and no bark. With one eye trained on their pension-fund investors, Kravis and Roberts couldn't bring themselves to make an outright hostile bid. And everyone knew it. In mid-September, the firm made an unsolicited, $4.64 billion bid to acquire Kroger, the Cincinnati-based grocery chain that had days before rejected a similar offer from the Haft family. Kroger twice rejected Kravis's overtures, leaving him with a nice profit on his 9.9 percent stock position and egg on his face.

It wasn't just new deals that were turning sour. After shedding many of its businesses, Kravis was finding it impossible to sell the remainder of Beatrice. The problem was a nasty knot of liabilities that no buyer wanted to take on. After being perused by every food industry buyer from Ross Johnson to Heinz, Beatrice, for the moment, belonged to Kravis. By midyear, not only hadn't the $3 billion profit they had hoped for materialized, Kravis and his investors were little better than break-even.

It had been a rotten year. Rejected by his targets, competitors nipping at his heels, Kravis couldn't be blamed for falling into a foul mood. When

Jeff Beck mentioned approaching RJR Nabisco, Kravis hadn't thought much of it. Kravis sent out dozens of similar feelers every month. On October 5, Kravis breakfasted with one of his favorite investment bankers, Steve Waters of Morgan Stanley.

"What's going on with RJR?" Kravis asked. He hadn't talked with Johnson since their meeting a year before.

Waters said he knew of nothing new. The last time the two had discussed RJR Nabisco, Kravis had been worried about the tobacco industry's mounting legal problems. After the *Cippollone* case his worries had subsided. "I've rethought some of my objections about tobacco liability," he told Waters. "Maybe we should see if Ross might want to talk."

Waters telephoned Johnson later that day. Jim Welch returned his call. "Henry has changed his mind about tobacco liability, Jim," Waters said. "He'd really like to sit down with you guys."

"Well, that's interesting," Welch replied. "Ross is busy now. Let us think about it. We'll crank through the numbers and get back to you."

Waters's call should have been a warning. Johnson ignored it.

CHAPTER

6

The history of merchant banking, with the exception of RJR Nabisco, is that I stayed out of it.   —PETER A. COHEN

As his sleak Gulfstream jet descended through the clouds over Atlanta that Friday evening, Peter Cohen pondered the weekend ahead. The following morning, October 8, Cohen was to meet with Ross Johnson for the first time in nearly a month. Tom Hill's team had been assembling data for weeks, although Johnson still hadn't signaled whether he would go through with an LBO. Cohen hoped they would find out in the morning.

It had been a long flight from Zurich, where Cohen had ended a two-week European business-and-pleasure trip, and he was tired. Cohen was a short man, his skull gripped by a tight cap of brown hair. He liked to joke about writers' descriptions of him: always small, dark, and, a real favorite, intense. *Institutional Investor* once compared his looks to those of Al Pacino as Michael Corleone in the *The Godfather, Part II.* Cohen looked like a tough guy, and for years that's pretty much what he was. As a longtime aide to one of Shearson's founders, Sandy Weill, he had earned a reputation as a hatchet man. If he were an animal, Cohen would be a wolverine.

Turning forty and taking the reins at Shearson had mellowed him, or so it seemed. Friends talked of how much Cohen had "grown" in recent years, meaning he no longer referred to a tiny competitor like Dillon Read as a "peanut," as he had in one published interview. Nor he did he publicly label critics "assholes," as he once had. At the urging of Jim Robinson, his boss at American Express, Cohen had taken strides to become more statesmanlike, making the rounds in Washington, talking loftily of the globalization of the securities industry, and nurturing friendships with heavy hitters like European industrialist Carlo De Benedetti.

He had taken pains to hone his sharp edges. Gone from his office was the sculpted chain saw and the statue of two pin-striped legs cut off at the calves. In their place were family pictures and his children's finger paintings. Years before it became faddish, Cohen was making an effort to present a kinder, gentler image.

The son of a clothing manufacturer, Cohen grew up on Long Island and attended public schools and Ohio State University. As a teenager he loved poring through the *Fortune*s and *Dun's Review*s to which his father subscribed. The elder Cohen bought his son T. Rowe Price mutual funds, and Cohen had been fascinated by the stock market ever since. He worked odd jobs through high school, and at Ohio State made a small fortune brokering kegs of Colt 45 beer to the fraternities.

If hustling came naturally to Cohen, school didn't. As a finance major he was a solid *C* student. At Columbia Business School, Cohen haunted the midtown brokerage offices, watching the market and investing the proceeds from his beer-brokering days. He canceled plans to enter the family business when his father wouldn't pay him what Cohen thought he was worth. Instead he headed to Wall Street.

Cohen had married young, at twenty-two, and by his late twenties had two children. As Weill's assistant he was the one who stayed late, his office light burning deep into the night. He was an administrator, never a trader or an investment banker. In tough negotiations it was Cohen who played the bad cop. He was good with threats. He had no time to learn about wine, art, travel, and the other fine things Wall Street executives seemed bred for. For years he traveled the world's great cities ignorant of all but their airports. Now, when in Rome or Madrid, Cohen tried to take half a day to take in the things he had missed. At forty he discovered the Louvre, the Musée d'Orsay, the National Museum in Taipei. He improved his tennis and golf games. Friends thought Cohen worked very hard to learn how to relax.

In the early 1980s Shearson, the successor to a long line of smaller houses, had been a scrappy, fast-growing wirehouse; that is, it made its money handling transactions for individual investors by wire. It had no investment banking arm to speak of. But just a year after taking over from Weill in 1983, Cohen stunned Wall Street by buying its oldest partnership, Lehman Brothers Kuhn Loeb, a topflight, blue-blooded investment bank that had all but disintegrated after a civil war among its quarreling partners.

It was a strange marriage. Lehman was sterling silver cigarette boxes, fresh flowers, Impressionist paintings, and dusty bottles of Petrus and Haut-Brion in the wine cellar. Shearson was empty pizza boxes, half-empty cartons of Chinese noodles, and coffee in a Styrofoam cup. "Shearson taking over Lehman," an old Lehman partisan quipped, "is like McDonald's taking over '21.'" Much like its chairman, the combined firm of Shearson Lehman came to be marked by a peculiar blend of elegance and streetwise chutzpah: brass knuckles in a velvet glove. Amid the cultured quiet of its nineteenth-floor executive offices, tastefully decorated with Audubon prints and Oriental rugs, visitors were greeted by a gentleman named Gus, who, while leafing through the New York *Daily News,* gave directions in a thick New York accent: "Go true dose dubble dohrs," he would say.

Backed by the tremendous firepower of American Express, which had acquired majority control of Shearson in 1981, Cohen had looked for ways to put his firm's capital to work for years. By the mid-1980s competitors such as Morgan Stanley and Merrill Lynch were thrusting into LBOs and, in efforts to compete with Drexel's junk-bond capabilities, had begun lending their own money in interim takeover financings known as "bridge loans." These loans were typically refinanced, or bridged, by the later sale of junk bonds. The trend was collectively known as merchant banking, a highfalutin term that basically meant investment banks were putting their money where their mouths had been for years.

Shearson's entry into merchant banking had been both late and lackluster. Lehman's active takeover business gave Cohen access for the first time to a wealth of investment opportunities. But for all its eagerness, Shearson backed into the LBO business. After the Lehman merger, a number of senior Lehman partners jumped to other firms, and Cohen was determined not to lose any more. In late 1984 he flew to England with a proposition for the chief of Lehman's London office, Stephen W. Bershad. His idea was intriguing: Would Bershad come back to New York and devise a means to generate profits to line top executives' pockets? "The idea was, let's get these guys richer," Bershad recalled. "Just make money however you can."

Bershad came up with an answer: LBOs. But after a number of false starts, he managed only one buyout of any size, and that proved a nightmare. Six months after the $482 million buyout of Sheller-Globe, a Toledo-based auto parts maker, news accounts reported that Cohen and fourteen Shearson executives had been slapped with subpoenas as part of an insider-trading probe by the Securities and Exchange Commission. Cohen denied any wrongdoing, and an investigation never turned up any, but it was a mortifying experience. "The deal that's dragging Shearson into the spotlight," *Business Week* called it.

It was a tough introduction to LBOs. "Cohen had never really been around corporate finance," recalled Bershad, who resigned after a tiff with Cohen during Sheller-Globe. "Peter knew what he read in the magazines, but he had about as much experience in investment banking as my father," who had advised Bershad to stay away from Wall Street.

Bershad's replacement, hired in June 1986, was a controversial figure named Daniel Good, who as merger chief at E. F. Hutton had built a thriving business backing corporate raiders. Good, so boundlessly optimistic he was sometimes called "Dan Quixote," didn't back four-star investors like Carl Icahn or Boone Pickens. His clients were little-known "wanna be" raiders, third-tier greenmailers such as Asher Edelman, a Fifth Avenue arbitrager, and Herbert Haft, the pompadoured scourge of the retail industry.

Instead of LBOs, Cohen chose to funnel Shearson's money into bridge loans for Good's raiders. With a wink and a shrug they could call this merchant banking, but for the most part, Good's clients were interested only in hounding Corporate America's sick and wounded until they either bought back their shares or sought a merger elsewhere. Either way Shearson profited.

A number of Shearson executives were violently opposed to Good's hiring, especially the M&A team, Hill and Waters, who considered Good a glorified shakedown artist. Good's raider clients, Hill argued, would stain Shearson's reputation and prevent it from establishing contacts with the blue-chip corporate giants it needed to build its traditional merger-advisory business. Hill campaigned tirelessly against Good, a crusade that didn't stop even when he joined the firm; he and Waters took to keeping a list of Good's mistakes. "Hill," said a colleague, "was out to cut off Dan's balls from the beginning."

But after Good's first deal—Paul Bilzerian's 1986 raid on Hammermill Paper—produced a fat $6 million fee, Cohen's doubts vanished. It was the easiest money Shearson had ever made. "Jesus," enthused George Sheinberg, a Shearson vice chairman, "this is great!" For fifteen months Good's clients kept fees pouring into Cohen's coffers, as Shearson backed raids on several companies, including Burlington Industries and Telex.

Over time, though, Cohen began to lose confidence in Good. The sale of junk bonds is normally among the most profitable aspects of merchant banking. But because Good's raiders rarely bought anything, Shearson's junk-bond department sat idle, atrophying. When Asher Edelman finally managed to snag a company—the steakhouse chain, Ponderosa—Shearson's junk-bond offering was a disaster, and the firm took steep losses. Cohen steamed. Good took the blame.

The final run of Shearson's raider express began on Black Monday, October 19, 1987. As the market crashed, scores of pending takeovers unraveled, and Cohen and Sheinberg panicked. For the first time they realized that the firm could actually lose the hundreds of millions of dollars it was lending. When a buoyant Dan Good appeared before the investment committee a week later seeking approval for a Bilzerian raid on Singer, the former sewing-machine maker, he received a rude shock. Instead of the $100 million down payment he had expected, Cohen demanded Bilzerian put up $250 million. "If he can't come up with it, fuck him," Sheinberg said. "I don't give a shit. The rules of the game have changed."

No one was more shocked than Cohen when Bilzerian came up with the money, dragging Shearson kicking and screaming into its last great corporate raid. When Singer quickly capitulated, Bilzerian was forced for the first time to raise the money to buy a company, not an easy task given Wall Street's postcrash sobriety. It was a long, uphill fight, and before it ended Sheinberg and Good nearly came to blows. At one point, Good fled New York for a Caribbean vacation, and Sheinberg brought in his sworn enemy, Tom Hill, to bargain with Bilzerian. With what one imagines must have been unparalleled glee, Hill began to play hardball with Good's best client. "When the deal started falling apart," Hill would later boast, "I had to come in and break Bilzerian's legs."*

---

* In September 1989, Bilzerian was convicted of numerous securities law violations and sentenced to four years in prison. Shearson wasn't accused of any wrongdoing.

Eventually Bilzerian acquired Singer, but the deal was Good's Waterloo. Although Singer generated well over $30 million in fees, he had lost all credibility within the firm. "Good already had two guns at his head," Hill recalled. "And then Peter Solomon put one in his mouth."

Solomon, formerly Good's superior as cohead of investment banking, was a boisterous, bullying Lehman veteran who coveted Good's domain as a way to exert control over the latest evolution in Shearson's merchant-banking drive: an LBO fund. Cohen's long-overdue decision to raise a fund was a reaction to competitors' success with similar funds and to Black Monday. Investing other people's money, any fool could see, was far safer than investing one's own.

Cohen and Solomon, however, had wholly different visions of the fund, which was to raise more than $1 billion. At other firms, LBO funds are semiautonomous, but friends say the ambitious Solomon saw Shearson's as a chance to establish a personal fiefdom and get rich at the same time. He sought to claim a sizable piece of the fund's profits, something to which Cohen was staunchly opposed. Cohen regarded the fund as just another Shearson department, and couldn't see why Solomon should receive "a special deal." Both men were headstrong and temperamental, and by the spring of 1988 they were barely speaking. Bob Millard, Shearson's suave head of arbitrage trading, became the reluctant conduit through which they communicated. It was hardly an auspicious start for Shearson's drive into LBOs *

With Solomon and Cohen at loggerheads, Tom Hill was riding to his greatest glory. Four days before Steve Waters's resignation that March, Hill unveiled his flashiest takeover attempt yet, a $1.27 billion hostile tender offer by a British firm, Beazer PLC, for a sleepy Pittsburgh company named Koppers Co. But this particular deal had a twist: Shearson owned 45 percent of the acquisition vehicle, Beazer just less than half. Never before had a major investment bank taken a high-profile position in a hostile takeover vehicle. Shearson was stepping over an invisible line, and Hill was practically giddy at the prospects the innovative deal might have for his business and, presumably, his reputation. He was convinced the deal would be an easy victory—"a slam dunk," in Wall Street parlance.

He couldn't have been more wrong. Koppers's defense became a cause

---

* Cohen later froze Peter Solomon out of the RJR Nabisco deal. He made the decision, Cohen later said, after Andy Sage demanded it. Incensed, Solomon fled the city for a New York Yankees fantasy baseball camp. Sage denies making any such request.

célèbre in Pittsburgh. Shearson and American Express were publicly attacked by everyone from Pittsburgh's mayor to the Pennsylvania State treasurer, who cut off all state business with both firms. Koppers employees posed for pictures cutting their American Express cards in half, and sent letters to other companies denouncing American Express's support for the bid.

No one was angrier than Jim Robinson, who felt he hadn't been adequately consulted about the move. "It created a lot of heat for Jim Robinson, and heat from Jim Robinson shoots through from the fifty-first floor to the nineteenth floor pretty fast," said a Cohen confidante. "It was a painful experience for Peter."

Although its client ultimately won the battle, the Koppers deal had a profound effect on Shearson's merchant-banking effort. Suddenly hostile deals, the backbone of its recent successes, were badly out of favor. That summer Cohen turned down the chance to back a pair of hostile takeover attempts, the Rales brothers' raid on St. Louis–based Interco and underwear magnate Bill Farley's run at a Georgia textile concern, West-Point Pepperell.

At the same time, Shearson's earnings began to sag. The entire securities industry suffered in Black Monday's wake, but few firms more so than Shearson, which had dramatically increased its overhead by acquiring a faltering brokerage, E. F. Hutton. Although there had been layoffs—and Cohen planned more—he badly needed a fresh stream of profits. Merchant banking had become Wall Street's most active and profitable business; now more than ever, it was critical that Shearson plunge into it. And with hostile deals all but ruled out, that meant one thing: LBOs.

When Ross Johnson switched course and began contemplating LBO scenarios, it looked like the answer to Cohen's prayers. An $18 billion buyout could wash away a lot of problems. The mere fact they had carried it off, the largest LBO in history, would instantly catapult Shearson into the top ranks of merchant banking firms. Afterward anyone considering a major LBO would have to consider working with Shearson. It would be a magnificent debut for the fund. The residual benefits for Hill's merger business would be tremendous. The bonds Shearson would sell to finance the deal could, in one fell swoop, revive Cohen's moribund junk-bond department. And all before they took a single fee.

Oh, the fees! The upfront fees alone—for advising and money lending and a "success fee," maybe $200 million in all—would be a gigantic boost to Shearson's flagging earnings. And it wouldn't stop there. For years afterward the money would continue to stream in. There would be fees for refinancing, fees for advice, and fees for simply minding the shop. M&A alone could count on tens of millions in fees from the divestitures they planned as RJR Nabisco's unwanted businesses were chopped up and sold to meet debt payments. And all before they even thought about returns on their investment: Hill was projecting an annual return of at least 40 percent. On a $500 million investment, that was $200 million a year—for five years or more!

It was enough to make Cohen's head swim. Even though he had masterminded Shearson's own acquisitions, Cohen had worked on only one LBO in his entire career, Sheller-Globe, which until RJR Nabisco remained Shearson's largest. But Johnson's friendship with Jim Robinson, combined with the deal's potential impact on Shearson, compelled him to take an active interest in the current deliberations. Johnson was dangling before his eyes a dream deal, quite literally the deal of a lifetime. And as his plane touched down in Atlanta that evening, it was all within Peter Cohen's grasp.

Saturday morning Cohen had breakfast at the Waverly with Tom Hill and Jack Nusbaum, Shearson's lead attorney. One of Cohen's closest advisers, Nusbaum, a common-sensical counsel with the face of an angst-ridden bulldog, had learned of the brewing deal while on vacation in Morocco. He had flown to Atlanta two days early to hear a presentation on tobacco liability from Ed Horrigan and Harold Henderson and came away convinced the legal quandary wasn't bad enough to prevent an LBO. Hill and a veteran Shearson banker named Jim Stern went down a day early, laying the groundwork for Saturday's meeting and letting Johnson's people know what to expect if they went forward. So far, so good, both men agreed. Johnson seemed to be on track.

After breakfast, the Shearson team shuttled across the parking lot to headquarters in twos and threes to avoid arousing suspicion. Upstairs, they settled into Johnson's office overlooking a sea of Georgia pines. Johnson, accompanied by Horrigan, Sage, and Henderson, had brought along the newest member of his team, Steven Goldstone of the Wall Street firm of Davis, Polk & Wardwell.

At forty-two, Goldstone was a curious choice to advise the RJR Nabisco executives. Slight and balding, the New York–raised son of a lingerie merchant, he was a rarity among Wall Street lawyers. Most specialized in advising merger clients or litigating court cases, but Goldstone did both. As a tactician he was virtually unknown. For a decade he worked on the bread-and-butter underwriting and mid-size acquisitions on which the securities industry is built. He had met Johnson when Davis Polk helped install RJR Nabisco's poison pill that summer.

As a litigator, Goldstone had gained notoriety for his role in what *American Lawyer* called "the most talked-about district court ruling" of 1987. Defending the Wall Street firm Donaldson Lufkin & Jenrette in a San Diego lawsuit, Goldstone inexplicably defied a court order to produce a key witness, prompting the judge to declare a default judgment against his client, a move that left Donaldson Lufkin vulnerable to a $100 million loss. Adding insult to injury, claims against three codefendants were thrown out four months later. Hiring Goldstone had been Henderson's idea.

From the outset it was clear this would be no ordinary LBO. The talk in Johnson's office that day was cordial and covered a variety of issues: price, profits, and plans of attack, among other things. Until then their discussions had been largely theoretical and over the phone: No one was sure Johnson would actually go through with it. "What do you think the chances are he'll do it?" Nusbaum asked Goldstone at one point. Goldstone pondered the question a moment. "Less than fifty-fifty," he said.

For all their uncertainty, Tom Hill was surprised to find how thoroughly Johnson's people understood LBOs. The pupil, in fact, was about to tell the teacher how class would be run.

Central to the success of most LBOs is a ruse known as the "gun-to-the-head" strategy. In it, a group of senior corporate executives secretly works with a Wall Street firm such as Shearson to assemble financing. Once the financing is lined up and an offering price agreed on, the chief executive presents the bid as a take-it-or-leave-it proposition to his board. Hill had even drawn up a ten-week schedule the Johnson–Shearson group could follow in approaching its own buyout. It might have been called "Ten Steps to a Successful LBO":

WEEKS ONE THROUGH THREE: Preliminary work on values and price discussions.

WEEK FOUR: Meet with banks to discuss loans.

WEEK FIVE: Banks work to refine a loan structure.

WEEK SIX: Management decides whether to pursue LBO.

WEEK SEVEN: Directors are quietly informed and asked to secretly form an "independent" committee to analyze any LBO proposal.

WEEK EIGHT: Management prepares a merger agreement.

WEEK NINE: Management makes an initial proposal to the board. Negotiations begin with the independent committee. A press release is issued stating the board is "considering a buyout proposal."

WEEK TEN: An acquisition agreement is executed and announced publicly.

The idea is to keep the entire process secret until a deal has been cut, ending the bidding before it can begin. Placing a gun to the board's head, in Wall Street parlance, is intended to leave directors with few options. Disclosing the overture prematurely tends to put the company "in play" for corporate raiders and risks frightening off a certain offer from management. For years boards capitulated and signed merger agreements with the "ambushing" management. Many still did. Wall Street strategists such as Hill consider it crucial to sneak up on a board with a fully financed offer ready to be launched. He naturally assumed Johnson felt the same way.

Johnson wouldn't hear of it. He had seen this board exact its wrath on Tylee Wilson for lesser transgressions; hell hath no fury like this board scorned. Nor was he willing to let Shearson arrange financing or do anything else that, if leaked, would anger directors. Johnson had it good in Atlanta, and until he made up his mind to pursue the LBO, he wasn't going to risk it all by letting Shearson get ahead of him. On the other hand, Johnson had supreme faith in his ability to make a pitch. If an LBO was the best approach, he knew he could sell it to the board—but only if it was an idea, not an ambush.

Diverting from accepted LBO strategy made Cohen and Hill uneasy, but they had no choice; without Johnson, they had no deal. If the board chose to publicly announce their overture, it would blow their tactical advantage. In a worst-case scenario, it would put them on equal footing with any party who might wish to top their bid. But no one—Cohen, Hill, or Johnson—was particularly worried about that happening. RJR Nabisco was simply too big for all but a handful of firms in the world to think about attacking. That day Hill ran down the possibilities:

- Hanson Trust PLC, a British conglomerate with a huge appetite for U.S. companies. Its chairman, Lord Hanson, had built its empire around a core tobacco company.

- American Brands, the Connecticut-based cigarette company whose brands included Pall Mall and Lucky Strike, had pulled off a daring defense against a hostile takeover raid earlier that year.

- Forstmann Little, Wall Street's number-two LBO firm, had shown itself willing to charge into heated takeover battles with multibillion-dollar offers. But a $20 billion LBO, Hill suggested, was probably out of Forstmann Little's reach.

All were dark horses. Everyone in the room knew the only one strong enough to put up real competition was Henry Kravis. Of all the world's conglomerates and investors, only Kravis had the combination of power, confidence, and money to mount a serious counterbid. Johnson's office was filled with opinions and purported intelligence. Someone mentioned they thought Kravis was on an African safari and might not be able to react fast enough. But it was when Johnson talked that Shearson Lehman Hutton listened. They all knew Kravis had courted him a year earlier.

"Henry won't do anything," Johnson said confidently. "I just don't think he's interested in tobacco." Andy Sage echoed his boss's feelings.

It was a critical assertion, one that Johnson repeated several times in coming days. He knew of Kravis's overtures via Beck and Waters and didn't take them at all seriously. He purposely avoided mentioning them to Shearson. "No reason to," Johnson would later say. "They'd have just run around in a flap saying, 'We've got to do this and we've got to do that.' These are not cool people in this business. I didn't want them to lose any objectivity."

In fact, Johnson was lulled by the same fundamental fallacy embraced by the Shearson executives. For all the talk of possible competitors, most of them were convinced their bid, if launched, would be unopposed. They felt certain that no one, not even Kravis, would attempt a buyout this size without the help of a management team to identify the best ways to cut costs. Even if tempted, they believed, Kravis would no doubt be put off by the daunting complexities of tobacco litigation. Cohen and Hill, in effect, considered Johnson to be their shield against any competing bids. As the group's primary strategist, Hill had ways to test Kravis's appetite, but later said he felt handcuffed by Johnson's insistence on secrecy.

Asking questions, he knew, could prompt interest in the wrong quarters.*

Just as Shearson took it on faith that Johnson could handle his board, Johnson took it on faith that Shearson could raise enough money to buy the company. In fact, the firm had never attempted anything like it and had even discussed the possibility of bringing in a major junk-bond power such as Drexel or Merrill Lynch to help out. The idea was quickly dropped: Seeking help would be an admission that Shearson couldn't do the deal itself. Cohen was confident that, with American Express behind it, Shearson could do the job.

Price was never a matter of serious debate. Both Hill and Johnson thought a bid around $75 a share made sense. It was higher than the stock had ever traded—around $71—although not by much. The $75 a share worked out to $17.6 billion, nearly three times the size of the Beatrice deal. The $15 billion or so they would need from commercial banks was more than twice the largest sum ever lent on a takeover; Shearson's Jim Stern had spent hours calculating whether that much takeover money existed in the *world*. "Seventeen billion dollars," Johnson said. "Fuck, I'll be going around on my hands and knees like a monkey with an organ grinder to find seventeen billion dollars."

It could go higher, Hill warned. The board would try and negotiate a better price, perhaps as high as the low $80 range. It was all part of the elaborate stage play performed in most LBO situations. A management group bid low on purpose, knowing the board would want to coax a few dollars more. The ruse allowed directors to claim they had pushed for the best price. It was good public relations, but was even more useful in defending directors against the inevitable shareholder lawsuit.

Johnson got visibly queasy when talk turned to paying more than $75. The higher the price, the more debt had to be piled on. The more debt, the more the corporate belt had to be tightened. Johnson was a man with absolutely no stomach for cost cutting, certainly not if it meant cutting back the RJR Air Force or other perks. He felt Shearson, like most lenders, was obsessed with what he called "nits and grunts" budget watching. Johnson insisted that, if the LBO went forward, both Premier and the Atlanta headquarters be held sacrosanct from any budget cutting.

* When Hill learned of the Waters call months later, the color drained from his face. "You're kidding; I can't believe that," Hill said. "If I'd ever known Kravis was trying to get ahold of Ross, that would have totally changed our strategy. It would have had a lot of significance." Alone among Johnson's strategists, Peter Cohen insists he never doubted Kravis would contest their bid.

"I'm telling you, we're not going to start running a pushcart operation here," Johnson declared. "I don't want a bunch of your guys coming around saying we should have five jets instead of six, that sort of thing. I realize if we do this I'll have to work my ass off a while. I don't mind that. But I don't want my life-style to change. I've got a great company, a nice life, I don't want to change the way I live."

A more seasoned LBO player might have laughed at the idea of a painless LBO. Cohen and Hill went along, although privately Hill felt certain that both Premier and the headquarters would ultimately be sacrificed. Both men were bent on making the process of an LBO as easy for Johnson as possible; nothing would be done to spook their prize stallion from charging out of the gate at the board gathering the evening of October 19, just ten days hence. They readily acceded to each of Johnson's "demands"; the future of Shearson's LBO effort depended on keeping him happy.

Steve Goldstone, hired to protect Johnson's interests, sensed that Shearson might be painting an overly rosy picture for his client. "Look," he told Nusbaum at one point, "are you guys telling Ross that he is going to have to pay top dollar here, and that he will have to make a competitive bid?" Both Nusbaum and Hill swore they were telling it straight.

The last, and most important, point of discussion that day was a management agreement. As the central document defining Johnson's relationship to Shearson, it would lay out how RJR Nabisco would be run, who would control it, and how the profits would be split.

Within the LBO community, executives who throw in their lots with the likes of Henry Kravis have clearly defined roles. As leaders of publicly held companies, they were ardently wooed by LBO firms; a Kohlberg Kravis can knock on the door, but in most cases it can't get in without being invited. In return, LBO firms typically permit them to put up their own money to buy 10 to 15 percent stakes in the companies they previously ran as professional managers. But while the CEO remains nominal head, and often retains operating autonomy, there is no mistaking who calls the shots: firms such as Kohlberg Kravis and Forstmann Little control every board, approve every budget, and retain the power to remove senior executives at their whim. LBOs are not democracies: each executive in a Kohlberg Kravis–owned company answers to Kravis and Roberts.

Johnson didn't care much for conventional wisdom. What he had in mind amounted to nothing less than a total reversal of the traditional roles of the executive and the LBO firm. Why, Johnson wondered, should Shearson control the board? After all, wasn't he the one putting his job on the line? Why shouldn't the managers, the men who knew this company best, call the shots? To Shearson's amazement, he had demanded control of the board and a veto over major strategic decisions, both during and after the deal. He suspected correctly that Shearson would want to cut Premier, the headquarters, and the RJR Air Force. A veto was his insurance RJR Nabisco would be run his way, not Shearson's.

"For Christ's sake, I'm not going to have a bunch of bloody investment bankers on my board telling me what I can do and what I can't do," he told Cohen. "You've got to have faith that I know how to do it. I don't need a bunch of kids looking at screens all day trying to figure it out for me. That's the way it's got to be if I'm going through all this horseshit and put myself through five more goddamn years of agony instead of retiring."

Henry Kravis would have told Johnson to jump in a lake. But Cohen and Hill had already made up their minds to concede to his demand. Again they felt they had no choice. Johnson made it clear: No veto, no deal. "It was," Hill would later acknowledge, "the price of admission" to a club Shearson badly wanted to join.

But Cohen had so far balked at Johnson's most outrageous demand. Andy Sage had determined that Shearson had promised the investors in its new fund a 40 percent return on their money. Fine, Sage said, Shearson could have 40 percent; he insisted Johnson and his people receive everything left over. That worked out to 20 percent or more of the stock in a post-LBO RJR Nabisco. Without arguing, Hill had let Sage know he considered the request excessive. As evidence, he had brought to Atlanta a sheaf of management agreements from other LBOs; in Beatrice, for example, Kelly and his people had bought a 12.5 percent share.

But Johnson not only wanted a far larger percentage of the profits, he wanted it on a far larger deal. Hill had calculated a 20 percent share of the profits could be worth $2.5 billion to Johnson's group in five years. In a September 30 memo to Cohen, Jim Stern had noted that Johnson's suggested cut, or promote, "seems very large, particularly when one considers the size of this deal compared with [previous] ones. In absolute terms, the level of management's promote dwarfs those in other deals."

The matter was discussed again Saturday. But when the group adjourned around three o'clock, little headway had been made. So much progress had been gained on other fronts it hardly seemed necessary to muddy the waters with a lengthy negotiation. Johnson assured Cohen the question of splitting the profits wouldn't be a problem, and Cohen, thrilled with their progress, felt certain he was right. Sage agreed to discuss it with Hill the following week.

Before returning to New York, the Shearson bankers tried once again to persuade Johnson to sit down with a group of commercial banks to discuss financing. Johnson refused. Shearson, he said, could approach only two banks, and then only for preliminary discussions. Find out if there's enough money to do this deal, Johnson told Cohen, and limit it to that. They would have plenty of time to negotiate bank agreements in the weeks to come.

Monday was Columbus Day. Cohen reached Charles Sanford, chairman of Bankers Trust, at his home. "Charlie, I have to talk to you about something that is of great importance to both of us. The sooner we can do this the better. Once we talk about it, you'll understand why we can't do this on the phone . . ." Cohen reached Citibank's chairman, John Reed, the next day. "John, I've got a tremendous opportunity for you . . ."

The following morning, Wednesday, October 12, a Shearson team led by Jim Stern met separately with senior representatives of Bankers Trust and Citibank. To ensure secrecy Stern demanded that both banks limit their credit analysis teams to no more than four bankers. Within two days he heard back that both were ready to commit to the transaction. This was going to be easier than anyone had hoped, Stern thought.

Bob O'Brien, the head of takeover lending for Bankers Trust in New York, found analyzing Shearson's proposal among the most fascinating exercises of his career. There was no question that any bank would jump at the opportunity to lend money for the LBO of a blue-chip company like RJR Nabisco. The central dilemma was this: Was there, as Jim Stern had already wondered, enough takeover money in the world to do it?

In most large takeovers, loans are parceled out, or syndicated, to banks around the globe. O'Brien's team canvassed each of his department's fifty or so salespeople worldwide. Country by country, bank by bank, they totted up the dollars available for LBOs. The lending practices of banks in Ireland, Belgium, Denmark, and Greece were assessed. How would the Union Bank of Finland react to the buyout of an Atlanta conglomerate? How would the unpredictable Japanese banks feel about tobacco?

In the end, O'Brien concluded there was a total of $21 billion world-wide that could be committed to a single buyout. From there he worked down. Not all the money, of course, would come. Some banks won't like tobacco, he reasoned, because the chairman had smoke blown in his face one day. Of the $21 billion, O'Brien was willing to bet he could put his hands on $16 billion. It was an aggressive guess. In its calculations Shearson penciled in $15.5 billion—roughly three-quarters of all the LBO money in the world.

———

For a man whose life had been one long party, there was a curious lack of merriment about Johnson in the days leading up to October 19. Andy Sage was struck by the fact he wasn't getting the buoyant, late-night calls from Johnson that had accompanied all their previous adventures. It struck more than a few amateur psychologists that Johnson might be doing the whole thing to fill the void caused by his son's accident. Bruce Johnson remained in a coma.

As the board meeting approached, Johnson seemed to grow ambivalent toward the whole idea of an LBO. Part of it, of course, was that so many of Johnson's longtime pals wouldn't be taking the trip with him. In a long, teary dinner, Johnson told Bob Carbonell he wouldn't be part of the seven-man group making the bid; if they won, Del Monte was to be sold. Of those included, Ed Horrigan was the most enthusiastic. According to Johnson and others, Horrigan was positively giddy at the prospect of LBO riches. He scurried about, working and reworking a list of those to be included in the group on a yellow legal pad.*

If Johnson was salivating over the millions he stood to make, no one saw it. Nor did he seem concerned by the inherent conflict of interest faced by executives engaged in LBOs. To Johnson, buying the company wasn't a conflict of interest but a wondrous convergence of interests. In an LBO, he believed, everyone would win. The stock problem would be solved. Stockholders would get a $75 payout: "We wouldn't hit that level for four or five *years* running the company the way it was," he said, as if four or five years were an eternity. Shearson and his friend Jim Robinson would get a great feather in their caps. And Johnson and his friends would

* In addition to Johnson and Horrigan, the group included Sage, Henderson, Ed Robinson, John Martin, and Vice Chairman Jim Welch.

get rich beyond their wildest dreams.

Monday-morning quarterbacks would attribute Johnson's decision to proceed to greed. But it was more complicated than that. First and foremost the LBO seemed to satisfy Johnson's cravings for action: He wasn't letting this organization decay. If his justification—the stock problem—was overblown, Johnson had shown himself incapable of ignoring a dilemma other CEOs would dismiss as minor. And while Johnson liked the prospect of an instant fortune as much as any man, he loved giving as well as receiving. This would be the ultimate gift to everyone. "Ross," his psychologist friend O. C. Adams observed, "created a situation where [he thought] there was a chicken in every pot."

On Thursday, October 13, Johnson tracked down Charlie Hugel at a hotel in Seoul, South Korea, where Hugel was peddling nuclear plants. Terrified someone would overhear the conversation on an unreliable overseas connection, Johnson tried to talk in a sort of code. "You remember the project we were looking at?" he asked.

Yes, Hugel said. He thought he had talked Johnson out of pursuing an LBO a month before.

"Well, Charlie, it's beginning to look the other way. There may be a lot more meat to this thing than when I talked to you before. It's something the board has to look at."

Hugel was stunned.

"We're going to go for it," Johnson said. "It's important that you get back and be there for this meeting."

Hugel searched his mind for something to explain Johnson's turnabout. Bruce's accident, maybe? He began to try and talk Johnson out of it, but stopped. The distance combined with Johnson's resolve sealed his lips. Before hanging up, Johnson asked if Hugel would head the independent committee that would evaluate his offer. Hugel accepted.

Johnson had assured Cohen that negotiating the management agreement would be no trouble. But Andy Sage had his own ideas. He was no fool: If Shearson wanted to do this deal, it would do it by Johnson's rules. The Saturday session had already demonstrated that. Now Sage was prepared to drive that message home by taking a hard line on Johnson's cut of the profits. "Andy," Steve Goldstone said at one point, "Shearson will never agree to this stuff."

"Look," Sage replied, "it's already been agreed to in principle."

"I'm telling you," Goldstone warned, "they won't agree to it. They'd be giving away way too much."

Sage was adamant. "I'm telling you, this is the deal. They'll take it."

Tom Hill and Jim Stern walked into Sage's ambush at RJR Nabisco's Manhattan offices Thursday morning. From the first words, the meeting was to be drastically different in tone than the gathering in Atlanta. Gone was the good ol' boy, putting-green folksiness of Ross Johnson. In his place was an icy, bullying Andy Sage.

In the dramatic setting of RJR Nabisco's glass-walled New York board-room, the Shearson bankers listened as Sage laid down the law. If Shearson wanted Johnson to go forward, Shearson would have only two of seven board seats; Johnson would take three, with the remainder going to a pair of independent directors. Johnson's executives would put up no money for their stake in the business; Shearson would loan them the funds to buy their stock, which could be repaid through the use of incentive bonuses. Shearson would even pay Johnson's taxes. In effect, management would take its cut for free. And, Sage repeated, management would settle for nothing less than 20 percent of the profits.

Hill was speechless. He had expected tough negotiations, but nothing like this. He didn't even know where to start objecting. When Hill and Stern attempted to reason with Sage, he made it clear Johnson stood ready to scrap the whole project, or, worse, take it to another investment bank.

To Hill, Sage seemed to have no regard for the way LBOs were done. "Andy," Hill argued, "we're putting up all the money. We're taking all the risk. Get off it." Asking Shearson's investors to settle for a straight 40 percent return was ludicrous; money managers placed their money with Shearson for the "upside" well beyond 40 percent. Johnson's cut, Hill felt, shouldn't top 10 percent.

But Sage wouldn't budge. For two days Hill and Stern slugged it out with the former Lehman banker. The negotiations grew emotional, until the three men began shouting at each other. Both Shearson bankers would later recall them as the toughest of their Wall Street careers. Throughout, they kept in touch with Cohen, who was attending a meeting of senior American Express executives in Tucson that week.

"Sage is being totally unreasonable," Stern told Cohen late Thursday. As the talks progressed, his judgments grew harsher. "Peter," Stern said, "it's a fucking nightmare."

More so than Hill, Jim Stern was amazed at Sage's behavior. As a junior investment banker at Lehman in the seventies, he had worked with Sage on Standard Brands, and considered him an old friend. But now, during a heated exchange, Sage accused Stern of acting unprofessionally, an accusation that struck a nerve. "That's it; I'm outta here," Stern said, rising to leave. Sage quickly apologized.

Part of his intransigence, Sage would later acknowledge, was his somewhat outdated understanding of how banking relationships worked. During Sage's days on Wall Street, the client was the boss, the investment bank the hired help. But Shearson, which would invest hundreds of millions of dollars in an RJR Nabisco buyout, wasn't hired help; it was a full partner. Sage failed to grasp the distinction. "They weren't supplicants for business anymore; they were players," he would later say.

Sage was also driven by disdain. He didn't feel Hill and Stern were up to the grand old Lehman standards, and he appeared to want to teach them a lesson about negotiations. "Andy," Johnson said later, "felt these guys were jackasses. He just didn't feel they were sharp at all."

Groping for allies against Sage, Hill called Goldstone. The Davis Polk lawyer remained skeptical of Sage's demands and for the first time told Hill so. "Look," Goldstone said, "if our clients convince you they're entitled to this, great. But if there's a way I can be helpful here, I'll try."

Goldstone regretted the conversation when Hill, at a crucial point of the negotiations, mentioned to Sage that even Davis Polk supported Shearson's position. Afterward Goldstone endured a thorough chewing out from an angry Sage. Who are you representing? Sage pointedly asked the lawyer. Goldstone stayed out of the fray after that.

As the negotiations wore on, Hill, with Cohen's approval, began to concede key points. Yes, Shearson would take just two board seats. Yes, Shearson would pay Johnson's taxes. But handing management 20 percent of one of the country's largest companies for free? Not only would Sage's demands chew into Shearson's profits, they would look awful to the public.

"Andy, you're setting yourself up for a big, big negative p.r. issue," Hill warned. "Look at the raw dollars. . . . People are going to say management is ripping off the company." Sage countered: We'll worry about that when the time comes.

Nothing Hill came up with worked. And at every turn, Sage threatened to walk. One part of Jim Stern wanted to call Sage's bluff; another wanted to tell him to go screw himself. Stern gained a small compromise when Sage agreed to the idea of granting management extra stock for meeting certain performance incentives, or "bogeys." There would be bogeys for completing a divestiture program, for targeted operating profits, for reaching certain rates of return.

But the Shearson bankers couldn't persuade Sage to back off his central demands, that those bogeys would march Johnson's cut up to 20 percent. At one point, Stern, in an effort to convince Sage the agreement was too rich, ordered up a computer run showing returns on an LBO priced in the upper $80-a-share range. Sage scoffed at the premise. "You're crazy," Sage said. "No one would bid that."

After two days, Hill and Stern threw up their hands and appealed to Cohen. "Peter, you're going to have to deal with Ross yourself," Stern said, washing his hands of Sage. "This guy's crazy. He's impossible to deal with."

Sage, too, had had all he could stand of Shearson. That weekend Stern refused to return his calls. By Sunday Sage was ready to dump Shearson and call up another firm, probably Drexel. "Let's get rid of these guys and go back to scratch," he complained to Johnson, who was in Florida with Goldstone for the weekend.

Johnson wasn't worried. Every negotiation was a fight, he felt, and some fights were just worse than others. Anyway, Shearson wasn't dealing from strength. In three days Johnson was to go before his board and make the pitch. He knew how badly Cohen wanted this deal and doubted Shearson would spike the entire effort over this one negotiation.

"Oh, they'll come around," Johnson assured Sage. "If they don't, there's no deal."

———

Charlie Hugel had a long flight back from Korea to think about the call from Johnson. Somewhere over the northern Pacific, he took out a pad and began jotting down things he had to do. He decided the special committee should have five members. Some had three, but Hugel had planned a trip to Moscow next month and didn't want just two directors left behind. He wanted people who had been CEOs, who understood the way companies worked. He also wanted people who had the time, who wouldn't be griping about missed dinners during the long hours of deliberations sure to come.

———

Returning to his Connecticut home Sunday night, Hugel called Johnson, who had returned to Atlanta. They talked about whom to put on the special committee. In effect, Hugel was letting Johnson help name his own judges. They agreed on Marty Davis of Gulf + Western. Johnson's old friend, named a director that spring, knew more about corporate restructurings than anyone on the board, having shaken up his own company repeatedly over the last five years. They agreed, too, on Bill Anderson, the former NCR chairman whom Johnson had blessed with an $80,000 consulting agreement. At least one of the directors, they agreed, should come from Winston-Salem. They decided on John Medlin. The most curious selection was John Macomber. After their earlier run-ins, Johnson didn't trust the former Celanese chairman. But he and Hugel agreed it would be better to place Macomber on the committee than risk his stirring up trouble among other directors.

"Another thing, Charlie," Johnson said, reminded of something Goldstone had told him. "You'd better make sure the board has a lawyer. We want it to be like Sani-Flush ran through there."

Hugel had already put "lawyer" on his list. His selection of counsel would be crucial, for it would be up to the committee's lawyer to make certain that the directors acted within the bounds of their complex legal and fiduciary duties. On Monday morning, Hugel began putting out help-wanted calls to some of New York's most prestigious law firms. He grew alarmed when the first three said they had conflicts, a sure sign that outside banks or investment bankers were already working on the deal. Suddenly Hugel realized Johnson had gone further than he'd let on.

Peter Atkins glared at the airport monitor in disgust. His American Airlines flight to Albuquerque was to be delayed indefinitely, the airline announcement said. Chicago's O'Hare Airport was fogged in.

Atkins picked up his briefcase and strode through the crowds at La Guardia to a pay phone. He needed to be in New Mexico by late afternoon for an important meeting. At forty-five, Atkins spent more time traveling than he liked. It wasn't the jet lag that bothered him. His colleagues at Skadden, Arps, Slate, Meagher & Flom marveled at his constitution. When other lawyers tired in postmidnight negotiating sessions, the well-dressed Atkins "always seemed to look like the cover of *GQ*," said one of his partners. "The rest of us would be hanging over lamp shades, but not Peter." The son of an engineer born in the Flatbush section of Brooklyn, he was one of Wall Street's top securities lawyers. Skadden Arps was the nation's third-largest law firm and by far the most active in the budding field of takeover law.

Atkins picked up a phone and called his secretary to make new reservations. There was, she said, a message from a Mr. Hugel. The only Hugel that Atkins knew, and only vaguely, was chairman of Combustion Engineering. He'd call him later, Atkins told himself.

Atkins's secretary made reservations aboard a United flight to Albuquerque via Denver's Stapleton Airport. He ran for the gate. When he arrived, Atkins found this flight, too, was indefinitely delayed. Denver was socked in. As he cursed his luck, he heard his name paged. He walked over to a courtesy phone and called the operator.

There was a message from a Mr. Hugel: "Tell him he's going to miss the biggest deal ever."

Hyperbole, Atkins thought, his mind only on getting a flight to New Mexico. His secretary checked again for alternate flights and reserved him a seat on a Continental Airlines flight via Dallas.

This time Atkins sprinted for the distant Continental gate. He arrived, out of breath but triumphant, just as the plane was boarding. As the line inched forward, Atkins took out the cellular phone he carried and dialed the insistent Mr. Hugel. Twenty minutes later Peter Atkins was in the air flying west, and Charlie Hugel had himself a lawyer.

On Monday, just two days before the board gathering, Johnson began to grow nervous. Every hour he checked the stock price, half expecting to see it rise. He stood prepared to kill the entire deal if the stock so much as burped.

He was already on edge because of *Business Week*'s latest "Inside Wall Street" column. "Smoke signals say: Buy RJR Nabisco," the headline advised. Citing the huge gap between the company's liquidation value and its stock price, the article quoted a money manager as saying, "RJR is a big restructuring or buyout play waiting to happen." It went on to speculate: "Whispers have it that to avert a takeover, management plans to take the company private and then sell the tobacco unit." Only half right, Johnson thought; food would be sold, as he and Benevento had decided, and tobacco, with its huge cash flows, would be kept. He tried to put the item out of his mind.

The real shocker, though, came that afternoon a few minutes before six o'clock when news crossed the Dow Jones News Service that Philip Morris was launching a surprise $11 billion tender offer for Kraft. In vivid contrast to Johnson's plans, Hamish Maxwell had chosen to expand his empire rather than dismantle it. His announcement prompted the usual flurry of calls from investment bankers wondering if Johnson might be interested in topping the bid for Kraft. By now their song was familiar. *This is a once-in-a-lifetime opportunity. . . . Kraft is a great business. . . . You ought to take a look. . . . You ought to move fast.*

The only call Johnson noted came from Steve Waters of Morgan Stanley. Waters got through to Jim Welch, asking about Kraft. Before hanging up, he brought up the matter he'd mentioned to Welch just twelve days earlier. "Where are you on KKR, by the way?"

"Well," Welch said, "we're thinking about it."

That day Johnson began calling directors, urging them to attend Wednesday night's dinner. When board members asked why, Johnson was cagey. "It's important," was all he said. To those earmarked for the special committee, he asked whether they might be willing to serve as part of a group to study restructuring alternatives. Davis was grouchy but said he would do it. Macomber was agreeable. Hugel got through to Anderson, who accepted. Only John Medlin backed off. "I'm just too doggoned busy," he told Hugel. Privately, he was uncomfortable with the potential conflict of interest of sitting on the committee while heading one of RJR Nabisco's major banks. "Couldn't you get somebody else?" Medlin asked. "What about Albert Butler?"

The docile Butler was Hugel's only choice. "Has Ross already talked to you about this?" he asked Butler later that day. "No," Butler said, "but he did tell me a few weeks ago about the study of alternatives."

Butler agreed to join the committee. Just one thing, he said. A few weeks before, Johnson had graciously asked him to remain on the Reynolds Tobacco board past his seventieth birthday in May. "That doesn't have anything to do with this, does it?" Butler asked.

An alarm went off in Hugel's mind. "How deep did he go into this?" he asked.

It had been a definite offer, Butler said.

"Let me get back to you."

Hugel hung up, miffed. He knew tobacco would be the surviving core of the post-LBO company, and he didn't like the idea of Johnson's offering a seat on its board to a current director. Directors were supposed to be neutral in this process, and that kind of offer might not look right. He called Johnson and told him so.

"Albert got confused," Johnson said. "At the time I was talking to him, I hadn't even decided to go forward with this. What I meant was that I wanted him to go on the tobacco board" as it was.

Hugel wasn't so sure Butler was confused. "You know, Ross, you've got to be careful on this," he warned. "This is bad stuff."

Johnson then said something that Hugel would never forget. There would be, he noted, a couple of slots on the post-LBO board for independent directors. "It's something I'd like you to consider, Charlie. You'll have to make up your own mind, and we've got to get the deal done first. But we've worked so well together, I'd like you to come over. And as a director, you'd have the ability to get equity." A piece of the action.

"Well, how are you handling equity?" Hugel asked, suspicious.

Johnson laid it out. Hugel could get the same sweet deal management would be getting. He would get a loan to buy stock from Shearson, Johnson said, then watch it grow like Topsy. A $5 million stake would probably be worth $20 million in five years.

Hugel didn't know what to say. Did Johnson know what he was saying? Did he realize he was offering, in essence, a bribe? Was he scheming or merely naive? With Johnson you never knew. "I can't do that," Hugel said hurriedly. "I'll be chairman of the special committee."

Confused and more than a little worried, Hugel ended the conversation, suggesting Johnson call Butler to straighten out his board seat. Later he called Butler himself. "I wouldn't say anything about this," Hugel said, "to anyone."

Johnson was at home Monday night when Andy Sage called. Sage was beside himself. That day junior lawyers had tried to bang out a compromise on the management agreement. Shearson had just faxed him a draft copy, and it was all wrong. From Sage's point of view, Shearson was reneging on several major points. "Come on over to the house," Johnson said, "and we'll get everyone together."

Johnson was irritated. With less than forty-eight hours to go until the meeting, it was silly to have crucial matters like this unresolved. He decided to gather the group and call Shearson and settle it, once and for all. Laurie Johnson started working the phones, tracking people down. Goldstone had returned to New York for the evening, but she reached his Harvard-trained assistant, George ("Gar") Bason, Jr., finishing a Wendy's hamburger in his hotel room. In Goldstone's absence, the baby-faced thirty-four-year-old would be their negotiator. Horrigan was tracked down at the Waverly, dining with two tobacco executives. John Martin came from down the street. Benevento and Henderson were located having dinner together.

By the time they assembled at Johnson's house, it was past ten o'clock. As Laurie got the group Diet Cokes, Johnson sat at the desk in his study down the hall and dialed Peter Cohen in New York. While the phone rang, he gazed at the celebrity-studded pictures on the study wall.

To his surprise, Jim Robinson answered the phone. The Robinsons had just slipped into bed at their Manhattan apartment. Johnson realized he had hit the wrong speed-dialing number. "Oh shit, Jimmy. I was trying to reach Peter."

What's wrong, Robinson asked.

Johnson's voice was uncharacteristically angry. "These jackasses at Shearson," he said, "they're trying to screw us to the wall. They're just being totally unreasonable. These items they're changing on us just seem like birdshit to me, and I'm fed up with 'em."

Robinson, who hadn't been following the group's progress in detail, didn't understand everything Johnson said. He extricated himself from Johnson and dialed Cohen at his Fifth Avenue apartment. "I don't know what the hell is going on," he told Cohen, "but apparently Jim Stern and Tom Hill have managed to piss off The Pope. Could you settle things down?"

Cohen dreaded calling Johnson. He had hoped Hill and Stern could handle the management agreement themselves. Besides, he was scheduled to get up at the crack of dawn for an interview on "Good Morning America." Reluctantly, he picked up the phone and reached Atlanta. Can't we do this another time? Cohen wondered. It's late.

"No, this has got to be done now," Johnson said. "Come on, let's get this baby done, Peter. From my standpoint, you know, this thing is just ridiculous. It's just a bunch of birdshit. Peter, either we get this goddamn thing solved tonight, or we pack up. If I have this kind of trouble with you now, what'll it be like later?"

Cohen backed off; Johnson sounded upset. We'll work something out, he said. Cohen hung up and summoned his personal assistant, Andrea Farace, to his apartment. Farace lived just three blocks north and was at Cohen's door within minutes. He also got Jack Nusbaum on the line. Soon all three men were on the phone with Gar Bason, who had taken a seat in Johnson's study. "Love the chair," he told Johnson.

"If you get this deal," Johnson said, "I'll buy you one."

On the other end of the line, Cohen found himself in a difficult position. He remained uncomfortable with the sheer size of the cut Johnson was demanding. He knew how much Shearson was giving away, both in terms of control and money. But it was clear some accommodation had to be reached quickly if the deal was to be salvaged. Somehow Johnson had to be placated.

It was over in less than two hours. Cohen capitulated to virtually every demand Bason put on the table. Typed up by Sage's secretary that night, the management agreement gave Johnson's seven-man group 8.5 percent of the equity, complete with a tax-compensated loan from Shearson. If Johnson hit all his "bogeys," the group's stake could easily march up to 18.5 percent. The package's total value could go as high as $2.5 billion in the coming years. Johnson was free to divvy up his share of the pot as he chose; his personal 1 percent share—Horrigan also took 1 percent— could be worth as much as $100 million in five years, according to Steve Goldstone. Johnson also received a veto and control over the board. It was unlike any major LBO agreement ever signed.

Cohen allowed himself to rest somewhat easy, having wrested from Johnson the understanding that the pact would be renegotiated if the price topped $75 a share, as it almost certainly would. For the moment, though, both sides got what they wanted. Johnson had history's richest management agreement. Cohen kept the ball rolling and was able to tell his colleagues that nothing was final.

When Jim Stern learned of Cohen's compromise, he was incensed. "Fuck it!" he shouted, banging his fist violently onto his desktop. "I'll do this at seventy-five, but not one penny more. At seventy-five-oh-one, *it's over!*"

At RJR Nabisco headquarters, workers began to notice changes in the air. One day Ed Robinson ordered $40 million immediately deposited into the golden-parachute "rabbi" trusts, prompting curious looks among the financial people. Johnson and the others seemed constantly distracted. Rumors began flying. A couple of secretaries even consulted psychics. "Your job does not look secure," a seer told one. "I would recommend applying to something more stable, like the government or IBM."

The second woman's psychic was even worse. "I don't see this as the job for the rest of your life," the psychic said.

"What do you see?" she asked.

The psychic closed her eyes and appeared to concentrate for a long moment. Then she said, "It just kind of goes . . . poof."

Johnson waited nervously Tuesday, checking the stock every hour. The next morning he invited Goldstone, who had returned from New York, to his house for breakfast. The lawyer, growing nervous, still didn't know whether Johnson would recommend an LBO or simply discuss the possibility. Johnson ran through his speech, adding that he would indeed recommend the LBO. "Just lay it out for them," Goldstone said. "It's their choice."

After breakfast Johnson went to the office and again checked the stock. Still quiet. He made the final rounds of the inner circle, checking with each man to make sure he remained comfortable with the furies they were about to unleash. Sage, for all the Sturm und Drang of his negotiations with Tom Hill, remained ambivalent; he would support Johnson whatever happened. Ed Robinson was all for the project. "Go for it," he told Johnson. John Martin was also on board. "Pay your money," he said smiling, "and take your chances."

Horrigan, eager to enter battle, again reminded Johnson to be wary of the board. Just because Johnson kept a jar on Marty Davis's desk brimming with Fig Newtons didn't mean Paul Sticht's old allies were going to hand him the company. "Guys like Bill Anderson are creatures of the establishment," he warned. "They aren't going to like LBOs. Albert Butler is as Old Guard as they come. Macomber is a whiner, a second-guesser."

Johnson had mentioned that Dillon Read, Reynolds's longtime investment banker, and Lazard Freres would be excellent choices to serve as the board's investment bankers. He thought it would be great to throw Ira Harris a piece of business. Horrigan couldn't believe it. "In doing this with

Shearson, you're about to give Ira Harris the biggest screwing of his life," he said. "His ego is going to get such a bruising. He's not going to be your friend; he's going to be your archenemy." Johnson's odd mixture of naïveté and Machiavellian wiles never ceased to amaze Horrigan.*

Wednesday morning Hugel and Atkins flew to Atlanta aboard a Combustion Engineering jet. After checking into the Waverly, Hugel walked next door to caucus with Johnson, as he did before most board meetings. He found him in his usual jolly mood, maybe even a bit bouncier than normal. It was clear Johnson hadn't changed his mind; the buyout was on. Hugel wanted to know how Johnson planned to approach the board that evening, and the two men walked through Johnson's speech.

Hugel mentioned that Peter Atkins planned to attend the board meeting. Johnson appeared surprised. He half-heartedly suggested that maybe public disclosure of the matter could be put off, but didn't pursue it. Afterward Hugel walked back to Atkins's hotel room and directed him to draw up a press release to be issued the following morning, if necessary.

"Oh, God."

Goldstone groaned when he heard Hugel had brought along Atkins. Until that moment he had held out some hope the board wouldn't disclose Johnson's presentation that night, giving the management group a chance to finish its negotiations in secrecy. Now he knew an announcement was all but certain.

The clincher was Atkins's past. Just two months earlier, the Skadden Arps lawyer had had his knuckles rapped by a Delaware judge for his role in the buyout of Fort Howard, a Wisconsin paper company. The company's management had used a textbook gun-to-the-head strategy to prod its board into a merger agreement. Atkins, representing the board, allowed talks with the buyout group to remain secret until the last minute, opting for disclosure only when the company's stock began rising.

Atkins had been selected to advise Fort Howard by the company's chief executive, the man making the bid, a fact that troubled the court and called into question Atkins's actions in favor of secrecy. "It is obvious that

---

* Johnson doesn't remember this exchange.

no role is more critical with respect to protection of shareholder interests in these matters than that of the expert lawyers who guide sometimes inexperienced directors through the process," the court said. "A suspicious mind is made uneasy contemplating the possibilities when the interested CEO is so active in choosing his adversary." Atkins's choice of secrecy, the judge noted, was "a source of concern to a suspicious mind."

The opinion all but accused Atkins of selling out his neutrality to a buyout group. Goldstone guessed he was still stinging from the rebuke. Jack Nusbaum concurred. "It was clear Atkins was going to be living down Fort Howard," Nusbaum recalled. "We figured he was going to be holier than Caesar's wife."

———

After Hugel left, Johnson welcomed John Greeniaus, the young Nabisco president, just down from New Jersey. Although few knew it, Greeniaus was to have been Johnson's successor. Three months earlier, Johnson had sat with him and mapped out plans for his future in detail. Greeniaus would move to Atlanta from New York in early 1989 to become an executive vice president. He would be put on the board at the annual meeting in the spring. Then, at a mere forty-five years old, he would become chief executive on Johnson's retirement in 1990.

Greeniaus had done nothing but thrive under Johnson. Although never one of his inner circle, he had followed Johnson through his career, rising from liquor marketing manager at Standard Brands Canada to CEO of Nabisco in just ten years. Greeniaus was as serious and introverted as Johnson was devil-may-care. He wasn't without a sense of humor: he kept an anvil in his office. But he always wore starkly conservative suits. He was wholly incapable of rousing his salesmen with stirring speeches. While Johnson was out carousing at night, Greeniaus would be planted in his office catching up on paperwork. He didn't play golf. He wore lifts. But Greeniaus delivered results, and Johnson had brought him along rapidly. Envious rivals whispered it was because Greeniaus was Canadian.

When he walked into Johnson's office at four o'clock, Greeniaus was unaware of the cataclysm about to engulf RJR Nabisco. He hadn't been made part of the buyout group for the simple reason that Nabisco, like Del Monte, would be sold to finance it. Greeniaus didn't know it, but he was about to go from heir apparent to outcast.

———

"Johnny," Johnson said, greeting Greeniaus excitedly, "I'm going to do a leveraged buyout!"

Greeniaus sunk into a chair and a state of shock. He absorbed phrases and, gradually, meanings. Johnson was working with Shearson and a group of executives. *But not me*, it dawned on Greeniaus, *not me*. He looked at Johnson as his one-time mentor prattled on about the incredible opportunities available to everyone in an LBO. *He's blowing up Nabisco. I'm out of a job. My people are screwed.*

He sat there, silent, numb. Finally, he ventured a question. "Why didn't you have everybody part of the management team?"

Johnson explained it was because Nabisco would be sold. But, he added, Greeniaus could help find the right buyers. Johnson kept saying what a great opportunity this was for him. "You've got a wonderful watershed in your life, Johnny. If you don't like what the new situation is, somebody else will want you. You're young, you've got a lot of opportunity. The world is your oyster."

And if for any reason he didn't like Nabisco's new parent, Johnson pointed out, he could resign and receive three years' golden parachute pay. Together with his 50,000 shares of restricted stock, Greeniaus could walk away with more than $7 million.

"Johnny," Johnson announced, "I'm gonna make you rich!"

Greeniaus walked out of Johnson's office an hour later, destroyed. He walked to the Waverly, wondering if he was dreaming. He went to his room and sat for several minutes in silence. He would have to do something, he thought. Just have to.

Afterward Johnson remained in his office, alone. Outside, the warm autumn afternoon was fading into darkness. In little more than two hours, he would make the biggest speech of his life. He sat at his desk jotting down notes on a yellow legal pad. He selected his words carefully. It was just like the practice tee, he thought; concentrate, make the necessary adjustments, and everything will work out fine.

CHAPTER

7

Johnson rose early the next morning, the memory of Wednesday night's board meeting still fresh in his mind. He was due at headquarters for the compensation committee meeting at eight o'clock, to be followed by a gathering of the full board. A press release announcing the LBO effort was due to go out at nine-thirty. As he read his morning papers, Johnson came down with an attack of the giggles. There, on the front page of the *Atlanta Constitution*'s business section, was a story headlined "Analysts say RJR isn't likely to be involved in any merger."

The newspaper had concluded that RJR Nabisco would remain on the sidelines in the latest round of food-industry takeovers. In addition to Philip Morris's run on Kraft, Grand Metropolitan had launched a hostile bid for Pillsbury. "Well," Johnson told his wife, "they sure have us figured out again."

Before leaving the house, he took a congratulatory call from Ronnie Grierson, then a worried one from Hugel. Several of the directors had huddled after dinner last night, Hugel said, and some, including John Macomber and Vernon Jordan, were concerned about what the LBO might mean to their $50,000-a-year pensions; it might make for a difficult comp meeting. When Johnson arrived at headquarters, he found Hugel was right.

That morning the committee was to have taken up the matter of lifetime pensions for board members, a sweetening of their current ten-year deals. Now, of course, any such move might look as if Johnson were attempting to influence the board. He urged that they table the matter, and they did, although Johnson got a distinct feeling of displeasure from several directors. Johnson also fielded questions about the board's other perks, including cut-rate auto insurance. What would become of them? Irked, Johnson said they'd have to wait and see.

Horrigan was in Atlanta that morning and raised a fuss about the release. As drafted, it said Johnson was leading the buyout group. Horrigan insisted his name be added, saying he feared his people in Winston-Salem would revolt if they thought Johnson was running off with the company. "We have to say it's Johnson and Horrigan," he told Harold Henderson. "There can't be any doubt left that I'm in this with him." Henderson, who could see red creeping into Horrigan's face, gave in.

All hell broke loose when the announcement crossed the Dow Jones News Service at 9:35. RJR's public relations chief, Bill Liss, had risen that morning thinking the day's big news would be the third-quarter earnings report and the board's approval of a new Planters peanut factory. Moments after the release went out, the first of hundreds of calls began flooding the switchboard, from wire services and newspapers, radio and television stations. They came from Ames, Iowa, and Altoona, Pennsylvania, from overseas reporters and overwrought shareholders. The local television stations were soon set up outside, and a helicopter hovered overhead, its occupants peering through the upstairs windows. Liss hadn't had a day like it since his years handling skyjacking crises at TWA. But to each of the callers, he and his four-person staff could only say the same thing. Beyond the press release, no comment.

At noon, a reporter outside headquarters told his television audience he planned to question Johnson as he left the building to go home for lunch. At the house on Whitewater Creek Road, the Johnsons' maid was watching. "Oh, Mrs. Johnson," she called to Laurie. "Mr. Johnson is coming home for lunch." Laurie called her husband, puzzled. "Are you coming home for lunch?" she asked.

Johnson couldn't have gone home if he wanted to. The building remained under media siege all day. Even local reporters knew a $17.6 billion LBO would be the largest corporate takeover in history. It was the biggest story of the day, soon to be the biggest business story of the year. The trendy shopping center on Atlanta's north side was suddenly the center of the business world.

Thursday morning Jim Robinson was at his mother's home in Atlanta, preparing for a board meeting at Coca-Cola, which he pronounced the Southern way: *Co-Cola.* Atlanta raised and Harvard trained, at fifty-two Jim Robinson had been called Corporate America's secretary of state. The company he had headed for ten years, American Express, was one of the world's true financial superpowers, overseeing $198 billion of other people's money. Twenty-eight million members used its credit cards. When Jim Robinson spoke, heads of state listened; his plan to settle the Third World debt crisis had created widespread interest the year before. Robinson's manner was formal, a cross between southern planter and establishment banker. His wife, Linda, a power in her own right, headed her own New York public relations firm.

At seven o'clock Robinson took a call from Peter Cohen, who told him of the impending news release. Robinson was surprised. Although he hadn't kept up on details, he hadn't expected any announcement until at least the following week, if then.

"How did this happen so quick?" Robinson asked.

"The lawyers felt it was far enough along," Cohen said, "and the board concluded that they had to put out an announcement."

It wasn't an auspicious beginning, but neither man was too worried. They weren't expecting any trouble.

October 20 dawned clear and cool on Wall Street. Two blocks north, commuters hustled from the bowels of the World Trade Center, past the corner Burger King and down Broadway to the brokerage offices beyond. Talk on the street that morning was of the presidential elections just two weeks away and the World Series, which the Los Angeles Dodgers were poised to win.

A year after Black Monday, Wall Street was still nursing its postcrash hangover. The disastrous downturn so widely predicted hadn't materialized, but neither had a recovery. Instead, Wall Street was mired in a funk. A malaise pervaded the executive suites, and brokerage earnings were down. Investors who had fled the market in droves showed no sign of coming back; securities transactions of all types were down 22 percent.

Since the crash, some 15,000 Wall Streeters had lost their jobs. Shearson wasn't alone in contemplating layoffs; rumors swept the Street daily of impending purges at other firms. Those who weren't scared were bored. On trading floors across lower Manhattan traders swapped bad jokes more often than shares of stock. The only thing flying high was paper airplanes.

As it had been all year, the lone source of optimism remained the merger business, especially merchant banking. Peter Cohen was not alone: Merchant banking was on the minds of every Wall Street chief executive. Merrill Lynch bragged that its LBO portfolio generated returns of 100 percent a year. "Not since the heyday of J. P. Morgan," *Business Week* noted in a June cover story, "has Wall Street been buying so many corporations."

The Street's lingering slump lent a new edge of desperation to the merchant-banking game: Windfall profits from LBOs and bridge loans were the fastest way to shore up a brokerage's sagging profits. A single deal could generate upfront fees of $50 million or more, enough to save a firm's quarter. In June, Morgan Stanley posted a $120 million pretax gain from the sale of its 10 percent stake in a Texas chemical company; the entire firm posted record profits of $230 million in the entire year of 1987. With those kinds of numbers being thrown around, even the laggards in merchant banking—firms such as Goldman Sachs, trading colossus Salomon Brothers, and little Dillon Read—began scanning the Street for investment opportunities.

At the vanguard of merchant banking was the merger crowd. Most every investment bank has a merger department, and its inhabitants are a close and incestuous lot. Their predecessors in investment banking had forged decades-long friendships with their corporate clients, attending to private placements and underwritings in a tidy, gentlemanly fashion. In the late seventies, with the proliferation of hostile takeovers, there rose a new breed of investment banker. They were mercenaries, warriors clad in $2,000 Alan Flusser suits, form-fitted Turnbull & Asser shirts, Bulgari watches, and Hermes silk ties from the airport shops at Paris and Brussels. To men like Shearson's Tom Hill and to their cousins the takeover lawyers almost any takeover is a good takeover, for every takeover produces a fee. To say Wall Street's merger advisers have shifting allegiances is a misstatement. They have no allegiances, period—except to their firms and themselves.

"All these guys," says the chairman of one of Wall Street's largest firms, "have three balls. Loyalties one, two, and three are to themselves. Loyalties four and five are to their buddies in the deal business. Loyalty six or so is to their client."

In their world, takeovers are "deals," and the top producers are "players." The top players juggle work on several deals at once. At any given time, on any number of deals, they may be simultaneously teamed with and opposed by their closest friends. While the merger makers are often compared to mercenaries, cynics might find a more apt comparison in professional wrestling: a squad of high-priced grapplers traveling from venue to venue, leaving onlookers wondering whether all that spitting and fighting was actually for real.

At the merger crowd's core is an elite clique of a dozen or so top deal makers who have been fast friends and competitors for more than a decade. When they call themselves anything, it's simply The Group. They grew up together, their careers intertwined in hundreds of now-forgotten takeover contests. Most graduated from college in the late 1960s, became friends while pioneering merger work in the mid-1970s and threw surprise fortieth birthday parties for one another in the late 1980s, as players in the white-hot crucible of the decade's largest deals.

In addition to Hill, The Group's members are Bruce Wasserstein and Joseph Perella, the first superstars of the merger era, who left their long-time firm, First Boston, in a huff to form their own merger boutique, Wasserstein Perella & Co., in early 1988; Eric Gleacher, the bantam merger chief at Morgan Stanley; Donald Drapkin, a former attorney who became vice chairman of takeover-minded Revlon Group; Michael Goldberg* and Morris Kramer, a pair of attorneys at Skadden Arps; Jim Maher, a Wasserstein intimate who replaced him as First Boston's new merger chief; Stephen Schwarzman, the fast-talking president of The Blackstone Group, another leading merger boutique; and Allen Finkelson, an attorney at Cravath Swaine & Moore. "These guys are all guys I would stake my life, my entire career, on," says Drapkin. "We all have a habit of finishing each other's sentences."

Although its members are scattered among several Wall Street firms, The Group sprang almost entirely from a pair of investment banks, First Boston and Lehman Brothers, and a pair of major law firms, Skadden Arps and Cravath Swaine & Moore. Most were run-of-the-mill underwriting specialists or mortgage attorneys who longed for something exciting; they

---

* Goldberg joined First Boston in 1989.

thrived on the adrenaline they found in corporate combat.

In one regard, American corporate merger activity can be viewed as a running chess game between these old friends. Wasserstein, in many ways the center of the group, is the acknowledged grandmaster; the brother of playwright Wendy Wasserstein, he introduced innovations in merger strategy and tactics that could fill volumes. For years Gleacher, who first rose to prominence in the Bendix–Martin Marietta battle, was his chief rival. By 1989 he had ceded that position to Hill, who had left First Boston a decade earlier rather than face a power struggle with Wasserstein.

"In almost any deal," said Hill, "one of these guys is going to be there. Our lives are constantly crisscrossing. We're able to cut through a lot of the dancing that takes place." Says Mike Goldberg: "You see Tom Hill and Joe and Bruce and First Boston on every deal. You know each of these people and what they might do in a given situation. And believe me, you don't want to be the new man at a poker game that's been running for years." Adds Allen Finkelson, who made his career on legal work doled out by Wasserstein: "People ask me, what do I account for my success? It's a certain amount of coming of age, turning forty. The other thing has to be with my whole group coming of age. All of us are turning forty. And we help each other."

The Group's patriarch is Joseph Flom, a takeover lawyer of legendary proportions on Wall Street. Most of The Group learned the merger business at Flom's elbow; to several he remains a father figure. Semiretired, gnomelike, Flom is adviser to practically all The Group's members on matters professional and private, the moderator of their disputes, and, from time to time, their toughest competitor. "The fact that it's a small fraternity is good for discipline," Flom says. "I see this in small-town legal bars. You fight harder because, it's like, who's going to win the chess game? It keeps you honest because everybody knows each other. Everybody knows what everybody's doing. There are no secrets."

That kind of inbred thinking helped spawn the insider-trading scandals that swept Wall Street in the late eighties. To The Group, the investigations represented a jarring wave of McCarthyism. Almost without exception those convicted were their friends and colleagues. The first to be named in the scandal, a high-flying Drexel Burnham investment banker named Dennis Levine, had been hired and supervised by Gleacher after leaving Smith Barney under the disapproving gaze of its merger chief at the time, Tom Hill. By far the toughest blow was the indictment of investment banker Martin Siegel, a close friend of Wasserstein's and several other group members. Unlike Levine, a fast-talking upstart, Siegel was respected, Harvard trained, one of them. "Everybody who's not in The Group," jokes Gleacher, "is in jail."

Does The Group's friendship come at the expense of their clients? Only a grand jury would know for sure. Even when on opposing sides in a billion-dollar takeover contest, its members are constantly talking to one another; these "back-channel" communications have become a staple of their deals. For all the camaraderie, though, the evidence indicates they are competitors first and friends second. Men like Hill, Wasserstein, and Gleacher, the first to proclaim themselves great friends, are also the first to spread gossip about the others' failures. Their multimillion-dollar bonuses often depend on knowing and beating each other.

There are, of course, other important deal makers in Wall Street circles outside The Group: Felix Rohatyn, the conservative dean of establishment bankers at Lazard Freres; Ira Harris, Chicago's Lord of LaSalle Street; Jeff Beck, the Mad Dog of Drexel; Geoff Boisi, the investment banking chief at Goldman Sachs. Like several members of The Group, they would each be drawn into the vortex of RJR Nabisco.

It had been a hectic week for Kravis.

Philip Morris's sudden attack on Kraft presented him with a perfect opportunity to ride to the Chicago company's rescue. He had been bird hunting in Spain but had managed to get a call through to Kraft's chairman, John Richman. Kravis offered his services should Kraft seek a friendly merger, and Richman had seemed interested without appearing threatened. Even now Kohlberg Kravis associates were running the numbers on a Kraft LBO. It could be the largest in history, topping $13 billion. Kravis was also eyeing Pillsbury, which had begun talking to possible merger partners to fend off Grand Met. That afternoon Kravis was scheduled to take in a presentation on Pillsbury's financial situation at Skadden Arps.

But as busy as Kravis's week had been, it was about to get far busier. He was on the phone in his corner office, which overlooked Grand Army Plaza forty-two floors below, when his secretary put a note in front of him.

"RJR going private at 75 a share."

Kravis nearly dropped the receiver. For a second he was speechless. It couldn't be true.

Paul Raether, Kravis's right-hand man, wandered in moments later. "Have you heard?" Kravis asked quickly.

"Heard what?"

"Ross Johnson is going private at seventy-five."

Raether paused for a moment as the enormity of the news sank in. "Holy Christ," he said. A second thought raced through Raether's mind: *That's too cheap.*

Kravis began to grow angry. "I can't believe this," he fumed. "We gave them the idea! He wouldn't even meet with us!"

High above Radio City Music Hall, Eric Gleacher's corner office was lined floor-to-ceiling with green-framed photos of his family. Their pastel clothes and rough-hewn good looks made his walls appear to be one big advertisement for Ralph Lauren's Polo clothing line. A humidifier percolated behind a green plant in one corner.

Gleacher was leaning back in his desk chair when he saw the headline cross his computer screen. In a flash he swung forward and stabbed at his telephone console. "I don't give a shit what you're doing," he barked. "Get down here right now."

Steve Waters was in Gleacher's office within seconds. Both men were stunned as they stared at the screen.

RJR? A deal? Without Morgan Stanley?

Look at the price, Gleacher said. At $75, they quickly agreed, Johnson was stealing the company.

That morning Gleacher and Waters acted as if by reflex. Both men knew the drill, the questions that had to be answered: Was this a done deal? Who was advising Johnson? Who was advising the special committee? And, most important, how could Morgan Stanley get a piece of the action?

Before they could move, however, Waters had to dart down the hall to answer his ringing phone.

"What the hell is going on?" Paul Raether demanded.

"I don't know, Paul. As soon as we find out, I'll get back to you."

The moment Waters replaced the receiver, the phone rang again. This time it was Kravis himself.

"What the hell is going on?"

"Henry, you'll know as soon as we do."

"Who is it? Who's doing the deal?"

"I don't know. We're trying to find out. It could be Shearson."

Gleacher and Waters hit the phones. After several minutes, during which news of Shearson's involvement crossed his screen, Gleacher reeled in the first fish: Andy Sage. Gleacher knew this was no time to come on strong. "Hey, Andy," he joshed, "what are you gonna to do with all that money?"

Sage mumbled something noncommittal.

"I gotta tell you," Gleacher said. "I was a little surprised we didn't get a chance to represent the special committee. Did Shearson do something to prevent us from getting hired?"

No, Sage said. Andy Sage was a pro, and Gleacher got little out of him. Later Gleacher reached Jim Welch. Welch vaguely assured him that Morgan would somehow get its foot in the door. Down the hall, Waters managed to collar Dean Posvar, Johnson's planning chief. Posvar told Waters the deal was all but finished. "We're just fleshing this out," he said. "We're rushing it as fast as we can, and it ought to be a done deal by the middle of next week."

A window of opportunity existed, Waters concluded, but not a big one. Anyone who wanted this company would have to move fast.

Jeff Beck was at Skadden Arps when he heard the news.

For weeks Beck and a small army of strategists from four separate investment banks had been devising defenses for Pillsbury to fend off Grand Met. That day he and other Pillsbury bankers were holding talks with a number of potential merger partners.

Beck was floored by Johnson's announcement.

An LBO? Without Drexel? Without me? It made no sense.

He rode downtown in a car with John Herrmann, a Shearson banker he knew from their days at Lehman. Herrmann was beaming, going on about what a coup the deal was for Shearson.

"This is going to be the greatest deal ever," he said as Beck stepped out of the car at his lower Wall Street office.

The Drexel banker could barely contain his anger. "I don't think so, John. I don't think so."

Upstairs, Beck took a call from Kravis. "What the hell is going on?" Kravis said.

"I don't know, Henry. You know we wanted to meet with them. Let me call and get the lay of the land and I'll get back to you."

Beck quickly called Johnson in Atlanta but was stopped by Johnson's secretary, Betty Martin. "They're all in a board meeting," she said.

Beck was fuming. *Lock and load!* He simply had to talk to Johnson. "Betty, if you don't get these guys out of that boardroom, you know, I'm just taking names at this point. This goes beyond being urgent."

Minutes later, Johnson came to the phone.

"Hey man, what's going on?" Beck asked, the exasperation clear in his voice.

"Well," Johnson said. "We're going to buy the company."

"You know, it's nice to read about it on the tape, Ross. I don't understand you." Beck wasn't even trying to hide his irritation.

It was Johnson's turn to show his irritation. "We've already got our primary partners on this, Jeff. And that's that."

The Mad Dog had been muzzled.

One of the first calls Kravis took that morning was from Dick Beattie. In the merger world, Beattie was known as Kravis's *consigliere.* For fifteen years he had been one of his most trusted outside advisers. Having held positions in the Carter administration, Beattie was also a fixture in New York Democratic circles, a friend of Mayor Ed Koch and, more than a few of the city's movers and shakers believed, a possible future candidate for mayor himself. A former Marine fighter pilot, at forty-nine Beattie had the sandy hair, baby-blue eyes, and soft voice of a kindly uncle, yet the steely gaze of an ex-Marine.

Kravis's interest in RJR Nabisco was no secret to Beattie. For more than a year his firm had been compiling analyses of tobacco litigation to fathom its impact on the company.

"Did you see this?" Beattie asked.

"I sure as hell did," Kravis said.

"I don't believe it. We've got to find out what the hell is going on."

"Dick, I don't understand it. We talked to Ross. Why didn't he come to us? This doesn't make any sense. *I* gave him the idea."

"I know," Beattie said. "It's crazy."

"Why in the world is he doing this with Shearson, of all people? They've never done a deal."

Dick Beattie knew that all too well. After Kohlberg Kravis, his second largest client was Shearson Lehman Hutton.

Bob Millard, Shearson's arbitrage chief, wasn't over his initial shock at the announcement when he took a phone call from Peter Cohen. Cohen had spent the morning in his office, pacing back and forth, watching the headlines on his Quotron. RJR Nabisco stock was skyrocketing; it would finish the day at $77.25, up more than twenty-one points.

"God, Peter," Millard said, "this is really terrific."

But the trader, who made his living following takeovers, was curious why Cohen had chosen this approach. Why hadn't Shearson tried to sew up the deal before its public disclosure, as Morgan Stanley and others so artfully did? "Why are you leaving yourself so vulnerable?" Millard asked.

"Well," Cohen replied, "it had to be done this way."

"What makes you so sure no one else is going to top it?"

No other company has the muscle, Cohen said.

"What about other financial buyers? What about KKR?"

"KKR won't do it," Cohen said. "Henry won't give Ross Johnson the deal we gave him."

"So what?"

Millard reminded Cohen that Kravis had moved unilaterally in recent months against targets like Texaco and Kroger. "Just because they don't have management, Peter, doesn't mean they won't bid for it. Why wouldn't they bid for it?"

"Well, because they won't give Johnson the same deal we did," he repeated.

"But if they buy it," Millard said, "Johnson will take whatever deal he's given." It was clear Cohen didn't understand what Millard was driving at. The trader suggested Shearson might want to feel out Kravis to see where he stood. "You'd better go talk to them," he said.

Cohen didn't seem to be listening.

By Thursday afternoon the Johnson camp realized it might not be healthy to have an angry Drexel Burnham rattling about Wall Street looking for an entry into the deal. Jim Welch called Beck, who was still steaming.

"This is crazy, Jim," Beck said. "The price is crazy. I don't understand what you guys think you're doing." Why, he argued, doesn't Johnson team up with Kravis? "Why should we work at cross purposes?" he asked.

Welch tried a half-hearted appeal for Beck to remain on the sidelines. "We want Drexel to applaud this deal, to be our friends," he said.

Beck was surprised by Welch's naïveté. "Well, Jimmy, I can assure you that we will applaud this transaction. But not the way you're thinking."

"Why?"

"We've been trying to get you to do this deal for two and a half years! If you think we're going to sit back now, not be a part of the biggest deal in history, I mean, you leave me speechless. I don't know how to respond."

"Well, would you consider going in with us?"

"Jim, we've got other obligations."

Welch called Beck twice more in attempts to snare Drexel, but Beck remained irate at Johnson's snub. As a result, Drexel, the largest piece of financial artillery on the Wall Street battlefield, was free to be used by a competing bidder. Beck had no doubt who that would be.

———

Thursday afternoon Kravis and Raether set aside their consternation and took in the Pillsbury presentation at Skadden Arps. Afterward Kravis pulled Beck into a conference room.

"What's going on with RJR?" he asked.

"I don't know. They've cut off communication at this point," Beck said. "I don't know what's going on. But you know we've got to do this deal. Are we retained?"

"Don't worry about it," Kravis said. "There's going to be a role for you."

The assignment would ultimately be worth more than $50 million to Drexel. Money aside, Beck couldn't help thinking how much fun it would be beating the pants off Ross Johnson.

———

On the seventeenth floor of an anonymous-looking office building tucked near the Staten Island Ferry in lower Manhattan, a chubby investment banker named Bill Strong was on the phone. Strong sat in a cramped cubicle along a wall of identical small offices: the somewhat lowbrow setting, absent the mahogany and Oriental rugs of other merger departments, reflected the historical neglect of Strong's employer, Salomon

Brothers. For years Salomon had made its millions on the trading floor, not the boardroom.

Half-listening to one of his major clients, Strong stared intently as details of Johnson's curious proposal inched into the public domain. As the news sank in, Strong did what any good investment banker would do. "Would you be interested?" he asked the client on the phone.

No, came the answer.

Strong had to be audacious. Salomon was the sick man of investment banking. Despite all the dire predictions, only one major LBO, the Revco drugstore chain, had gone belly up, and it was a Salomon deal. When the market crashed a year earlier, only one major junk-bond offering, for Dallas-based Southland Corporation, had been repeatedly rejected as unsafe by institutional investors; Salomon was its cosponsor. Only one major bridge loan, to a Norfolk-based chain of television stations named TVX, had collapsed. Salomon again. For three years the firm had been struggling to enter merchant banking; the results had been a string of public humiliations. Strong and his colleagues had been scrambling to pick up the broken glass ever since.

On Wall Street, Bill Strong was not a big name, having just made partner two years earlier. But he was hardworking and energetic, possessed of an earnest Midwestern work ethic. A former accountant, he was from Indiana and proud of it. Strong looked clients in the eye and said he prided himself on honesty and integrity, traits he didn't believe were terribly widespread in investment banking. A lot of investment bankers had the same spiel. Only Strong actually seemed to mean it.

Like every other banker on Wall Street, Strong was intrigued by the possibilities opened by Johnson's proposal. By Thursday evening he had assembled a stack of RJR Nabisco annual reports and 10-K financial reports filed with the Securities and Exchange Commission. A cursory read convinced Strong that $75 was way too low. These guys were stealing the company.

He got excited. Salomon had had more than its share of merchant banking disasters, but this deal, if done right, could erase a lot of bad memories. And Strong had the ideal partner in mind: Hanson Trust. An avid shopper of American companies, it had developed a U.S. arm that, were it independent, would be among the country's largest corporations. Using Salomon's financial firepower and Hanson's marketing expertise, Strong thought, they would be an unbeatable team.

Friday morning he pitched his idea to John Gutfreund, Salomon's autocratic chairman. As Strong outlined it, RJR Nabisco was a unique deal. It had once-in-a-lifetime brand names up for grabs, he explained. Tobacco's cash flow was a torrent so strong it could virtually pay for the entire deal. "This one," Strong told Gutfreund, "has everything."

Gutfreund, often skeptical of his enthusiastic young deal makers, listened with interest. "Fine," he said. "Make the call."

At ten Strong called his contact at Hanson. He explained the situation, running down a handwritten list of RJR Nabisco's chief attractions. Tremendous cash flow from tobacco. Unmatched food brands. Undervalued stock.

"You put in a billion five, we put in a billion five and jointly acquire it," Strong said. And just one thing: "I need a quick response."

The call came back at two o'clock.

"Done," the Hanson aide said. "We'll do it."

Strong was jubilant. A meeting to flesh out details was set for Monday morning. In the meantime Strong had plenty of work to do. He called Gutfreund and brought him up to date. The chairman sounded encouraging. Strong then assembled a team of ten bankers and analysts to pore over RJR Nabisco data that weekend. It was a smallish group for such a gigantic project. But Strong wanted to keep a low profile and avoid leaks. He wanted to be ready to move first thing Monday morning.

By Thursday afternoon RJR Nabisco's executive suite was swarming with people. The Shearson bankers—Tom Hill, looking cool in a blue suit, and Jim Stern, relaxed after a morning jog—stood around with little to do. Directors milled about, drinking in the excitement. Teams from Lazard Freres and Dillon Read, summoned by Hugel the night before, arrived around eleven o'clock. Felix Rohatyn of Lazard was there, his great salt-and-pepper eyebrows dancing as he spoke. With Rohatyn was Ira Harris, down from Chicago, and Luis Rinaldini, a hard-driving Argentinian. A pair of well-starched Dillon Read bankers, Franklin W. Hobbs IV, who everyone called Fritz, and John H. Mullin III, Tylee Wilson's old banker, arrived with them.

"Hi, Johnny!" Johnson cried when he spied Mullin. He came over to shake the bankers' hands as if it were a backyard barbecue rather than an LBO. To the bankers, yet to grasp the enormity of the task before them, Johnson seemed without a care in the world.

"Well, boys," he crowed, "we're off to the races! Whaddya think?"

Quite frankly, they didn't know what to think, especially when escorted into a conference room to meet with Hugel. As chairman of the special committee, Hugel briefed first the Lazard bankers, then the Dillon pair, on events to date. Both banks agreed to represent the committee for a fee of $14 million apiece. Their job would be to analyze any bid from Johnson and advise the committee whether it was fair to shareholders. They would do the same in the unlikely event other bids cropped up.

Several of the bankers' antennae rose when Hugel insisted on bringing the process to a quick conclusion. He suggested their review could be wrapped up in ten days, a time period Rohatyn and Harris thought ridiculously short. Speed favored Johnson, and the two bankers immediately wondered whether Hugel was in Johnson's pocket. For now, they kept their suspicions to themselves.

The crowd on the twenty-first floor began to thin when the meetings broke up in midafternoon. Horrigan flew to Winston-Salem to explain the news to his tobacco troops. Johnson sat alone in his office, opening mail and tending to paperwork. For the moment, there was little else to do. "Gee," he told Martin, "I feel like I brought my harp to the party and nobody asked me to play."

Goldstone and the other Wall Streeters were smuggled out an underground passage to avoid the reporters waiting outside. Along with Peter Atkins and a pair of directors, Marty Davis and John Macomber, he boarded an RJR Nabisco jet for the trip to New York. Atkins huddled with the directors for most of the flight. As they neared New York, Goldstone found himself crouching behind the cockpit entrance with Atkins.

"Look at this," one of the pilots said.

The two attorneys peered through the windshield. Below, they could see past the Verrazano Narrows bridge up the length of New York Harbor to Wall Street. The setting sun bathed the harbor and much of lower Manhattan in a stunning display of blues and reds. Goldstone thought it was among the most beautiful things he had ever seen. For a moment his lawyerly demeanor dropped and he felt part of some great, romantic adventure.

He smiled. "Well, Peter, this is going to be very interesting."

"Yes," Atkins said. "I'm sure it will be."

CHAPTER

8

Friday afternoon Tom Hill sat mired in another interminable Pillsbury strategy session at the midtown law firm of Skadden Arps. In the time since its British suitor, Grand Metropolitan, launched a hostile tender offer, Pillsbury had hired half of Wall Street to erect its defenses. They had looked at LBOs, defensive recapitalizations, poison pills, spin-offs, everything. So far nothing had worked.

One problem was that there were simply too many cooks. Hill represented Shearson. Jeff Beck headed a Drexel team. Bruce Wasserstein anchored the Wasserstein Perella contingent. Investment bankers from First Boston were also flitting about.

For all of Pillsbury's woes, Hill couldn't take his mind off RJR Nabisco. The waiting game had begun. The special committee had been formed and, with any luck, would be up to speed on the company's values in two or three weeks. At that point, Hill was betting, Ross Johnson's management group would belly up to the negotiating table, haggle with directors over an offering price, and, ultimately, agree to buy the company for a price a few dollars a share more than $75, maybe as high as the low $80 range.

In the meantime, Shearson was on full alert to any sign of a competing bid. It was just thirty hours since Johnson's initial announcement, but Hill knew every investment banker on Wall Street would be looking for ways to top their $75 price. So far, no one had; with any luck, no one would. Hill hated the waiting. It made him uneasy.

As the Pillsbury meetings droned on, Hill noticed Jeff Beck and Bruce Wasserstein ducking in and out of the conference room. Both men seemed especially busy today. Hill wondered what they were up to. He found himself reflecting on something Beck had told him earlier that day about RJR. "You're way off on price," the Mad Dog had assured him. "There's going to be competition."

All at once Tom Hill realized what all the scurrying about and Beck's warning must mean.

Kravis.

It couldn't be. Henry Kravis wouldn't try something on this scale without a management team in his camp. Besides, Johnson had said repeatedly that Kravis wasn't interested in RJR Nabisco.

Hill had to find out for certain. Excusing himself from the meeting, he headed for a telephone and dialed Kohlberg Kravis's number from memory. When Kravis came on the line, Hill forced his voice to brim with good cheer.

"I'm wondering whether you guys are interested in Kraft," Hill said. "We thought maybe we could help you with it." It was a transparent excuse for a call: Kraft had been in play a full four days, an eternity in the takeover business. If Kravis were to move on the company, no doubt he already would have retained a banker.

Kravis could barely contain his anger. "A lot of people have talked to us about Kraft, Tom. We may do something with one of them. But it's not going to be you. . . ."

In a split second Hill knew the truth. In Kravis's venomous tone he recognized the realization of his worst fears. Henry Kravis wanted RJR Nabisco, and he wanted it badly. "Henry came right through the phone," Hill recalled later. "He was loaded for bear."

Kravis's message was brief. "You know, Tom, you've just floored us on this RJR thing. We're the ones who gave Ross Johnson that idea. We've had an excellent relationship with you, Tom. I'm surprised in a deal this size there wasn't an opportunity to do something together. This is one we can't just sit on the sidelines on."

The conversation was over quickly. Hill hung up, stunned.

Something had gone horribly wrong. He had to think fast.

Quickly he called Peter Cohen at Shearson and relayed news of the Kravis call. To Hill's surprise, Cohen didn't seem especially worried.

"So what's he pissed off about?" Cohen asked.

"Why don't we meet with him and find out?"

"Why don't we find out and then meet with him?"

Hill thought through his options. Maybe they could head Kravis off. Maybe they could placate him. Whatever the case, they had to meet with him, if only to more accurately gauge his intentions. Cohen didn't think a meeting with Kravis was necessary. This was Shearson's deal; they didn't need him.

Hill had to make Cohen realize the significance of the call. Henry Kravis wasn't someone you simply stonewalled.

"Peter, you have to understand. . . ."

———

A half hour later, Hill called Kravis again. "Peter and I would like to meet with you," he said.

It was getting late. Kravis suggested they meet Monday.

Hill sounded nervous, jumpy.

"Nah, nah, let's meet right now. I think we should."

"Tom, it's late."

"Henry, I really want to have this meeting."

All right, Kravis agreed.

———

At six sharp, Hill hustled through a drizzle into the lobby at Nine West. As he entered, he ran into Jeff Beck and an associate on their way out.

Hill forced a smile. "I know where you guys are coming from." *So Kravis has hired Drexel,* he thought. This was getting worse by the minute.

Upstairs, Hill waited for Cohen, who had been delayed in the Friday afternoon traffic. Cohen finally walked in at around six-thirty.

"Henry," he said jauntily, "what are you doing here at six-thirty on a Friday night? You ought to be off skiing or something."

"Well, Peter. You're here, aren't you?"

The two men shook hands. As Cohen took a seat, Hill turned to Kravis. "I wanted to have this meeting, Henry, because I sensed you're very interested in RJR," he began. "I thought it would be useful to see where that interest lies."

"Yes, I do have a very real interest," Kravis said. "And this interest goes way back."

"But this is our deal, Henry," Cohen interjected. He tried to make Kravis understand why RJR Nabisco was so vital to Shearson's future. He explained the importance he placed on merchant banking and its place as the cornerstone of Shearson Lehman's drive into the LBO industry. Hill was coming into his own as a merger adviser, enabling Shearson to review more opportunities than ever before. "You see, we have to be involved," Cohen said. "It's a natural for us. We have a built-in flow of business."

"That's all fine," Kravis said. "You're now our competitors." The intimation was clear: If Shearson went ahead with RJR Nabisco, it could forget ever again doing business with Kohlberg Kravis. "I find it surprising that you're doing this," Kravis continued. "We've given you a lot of business. I guess clients don't mean that much to you anymore."

"Henry, we've got to be in this business," Cohen said. "It's our future."

Cohen reflected on a conversation he had had with Kravis the previous February. The two men had skied together in the Shearson-sponsored American Ski Classic in Vail. It was no accident they found themselves on the same team. While they had waited to compete in a slalom, they had chatted about the changing face of the LBO industry.

That day Kravis had been concerned about newfound competitors such as Morgan Stanley and Merrill Lynch. "What's going to happen, Peter?" Kravis had asked. "Who else is coming in? And what are you guys going to do?"

Cohen had responded with a broad outline of Shearson's desire to enter the merchant-banking field as well. He didn't have to mention that the stock market crash last October had wreaked havoc on Shearson's other businesses. "Given the new pressures on margins in our other businesses," Cohen had said, "it's an obvious way to use our capital. Clients are asking us to do it. We can do it all for them. It just makes sense." As Cohen recalled the conversation, Kravis had then suggested the two firms ought to stay out of each other's deals.

Cohen now threw the remark back at Kravis.

"Henry," he said, "this is Shearson's deal. This is exactly what we talked about eight months ago. I thought we had an agreement. You said we would stay out of each other's deals. Well, here it is."

"We never agreed on anything like that, Peter."

Cohen's little speech sent shivers through Kravis. *So this is what it's come to,* he thought. Every investment banker with an extra nickel in his pocket thinks he ought to go into LBOs. After five years of steadily mounting competition, Kravis was sick of it. Morgan Stanley, Merrill Lynch, firms he had never heard of, all wanted a piece of his business. Now it was Shearson Lehman. The entire idea behind Kohlberg Kravis's 1987 fund was doing deals too large for anyone else to handle. Once and for all, Kravis had hoped, his firm could leave the competition behind. Now, just as they had carved out a territory for themselves, here came Peter Cohen, a man who probably didn't know the difference between LBO and BO, claiming he had a right to do an $18 billion deal! Kravis couldn't believe the ingratitude, the gall. One part of him wanted to teach all of them, particularly Peter Cohen, a very rough lesson.

"I regard Shearson as a firm we've given business to," Kravis repeated. "I have a relationship with you. This would have been the perfect deal to bring to us."

"But we've raised this money," Cohen repeated. "We have a responsibility to investors in the fund to put that money to work."

"This deal is so visible, so big," Kravis warned. "It has all the right cash flow characteristics, I can't lay off. We have to be in on this deal. And we will be in this deal."*

Tom Hill, watching and listening, thought Cohen's notion a bit strange. Did Peter really think Henry Kravis would stay out of a $20 billion deal because of a conversation on a ski slope? He could see, in any case, that neither Cohen nor Kravis was going to budge. Each man seemed to believe it was his blood right to own Ross Johnson's company. Hill tried to play the peacemaker, occasionally throwing in a "What can we do?" or a "How can we work that out?" He was getting nowhere. These two were just building up steam.

"I'd be very surprised if you end up buying this at seventy-five," Kravis said.

"Why?" Cohen asked.

"We've been looking at this company for a long time, and we know it well. This bid is just cheap. It's really very cheap."

"This is really Ross's deal," Cohen said defensively. "We're just financing it."

---

* Kravis denies having told Cohen and Hill he had to be involved in a deal for RJR Nabisco. Newspapers reported that Kravis vowed to protect his "franchise," a word Kravis denied having used.

"Well, you're his partners now."

"It's Ross's deal, and he's very close to the board."

Kravis didn't miss Cohen's message: Johnson had his board in his back pocket.

"What do you intend to do?" Kravis asked.

"What do *you* intend to do?" Cohen shot back.

"I don't know what I'm going to do."

"Well," Cohen said, "what do we do about it?"

"Well," Kravis said finally, "maybe there's a role for both of us." Kravis had anticipated this confrontation. There were, he suggested, three options. "We can compete," he said. It was a notion neither Kravis nor Cohen relished. A drawn-out bidding battle could send the price of the company skyrocketing and, because higher purchase prices inevitably meant higher debt levels, would all but guarantee the winner a Pyrrhic victory.

Or, Kravis continued, Shearson and Kohlberg Kravis could team up in a joint bid for the company. Neither Kravis nor Cohen, their egos fully intact, relished that idea either. For his part, Cohen regarded a partnership with Kravis—or anyone else, for that matter—as an admission that Shearson couldn't manage the deal itself. Selling off a piece of equity to an investor was one thing; he expected to do that. A fifty-fifty deal was another thing altogether. A partnership, at least between these two men, seemed unlikely.

Or, Kravis concluded, Shearson could sell RJR's food businesses to Kohlberg Kravis, taking tobacco for itself.

Cohen was noncommittal. He would have to check with Johnson and others before seriously talking about any joint venture with Kohlberg Kravis. "It may make sense for us to do something together, Henry. But what does that say about the future? I don't know the answer to that. What does it all mean? I can't tell you that now."

The meeting was winding down. Maybe, Cohen suggested as he got up to leave, they should talk more next week.

Afterward Cohen and Hill retreated to Hill's Upper East Side apartment. There they called Johnson and relayed the news. Cohen played down the confrontation, insisting that he planned to meet again with Kravis on Monday.

When they finished, there was a long silence.

"What do you think it means?" Johnson asked.

"One way or another," Tom Hill said, "Henry is coming."

Cohen also relayed news of the meeting to his boss at American Express, Jim Robinson, who was at his Connecticut farm.

Robinson listened with interest. As Cohen laid out the confrontation with Kravis, his interest turned to worry. Henry Kravis was not someone to be trifled with.

Maybe, Robinson suggested, he should call and reason with Kravis himself. "Maybe we can work together on this thing," he said.

Cohen discouraged that idea, explaining that he believed it would be interpreted as a sign of weakness.

Robinson wasn't so sure. But he decided to bow to Cohen's on-the-scene expertise. No good second-guessing the executives you place in charge of day-to-day matters, he told himself. He knew how much this deal meant to Cohen and to Shearson's future. Cohen wasn't giving up a single piece of RJR Nabisco without a fight.

Still, Robinson reasoned, talking with Kravis only made sense. The man was simply too powerful to needlessly provoke.

"Give me one more shot at Henry," Cohen asked. "Give him a chance to do his homework, and I'll get back to you Monday morning after I talk to him." Jim Robinson agreed.

Kravis wasn't waiting around for Peter Cohen.

By Friday evening he had assembled a team of investment banks to advise and finance a competing offer for RJR Nabisco. Heading the list was Drexel Burnham, Jeff Beck's employer. Drexel's powerful junk-bond network was still remarkably intact despite being the focus of a two-year federal investigation stemming from the Ivan Boesky insider-trading probe. Still, Drexel's future was a question; an indictment was rumored to be near. And if it hit in the middle of the coming contest, it could have catastrophic consequences for Kravis. To cover himself, he decided to hire Merrill Lynch as a backup fund-raiser.

Morgan Stanley, the bank of Steve Waters and Eric Gleacher, was a natural choice for the routine number-crunching and advisory work Kohlberg Kravis would need. Waters was a Kravis favorite, and Kravis knew the banker's career could use a boost after his abrupt fall from power at Shearson.

Three investment banks made for a cumbersome, not to mention expensive, team. It would be the largest array of advisers ever assembled on a Kohlberg Kravis deal. Even so, Kravis decided to hire a fourth: the red-hot merger boutique, Wasserstein Perella. Wasserstein, arguably Wall Street's most brilliant takeover tactician, would be invaluable in any major deal. But advice was not what Kravis needed from him. Hiring him was purely a defensive move: He wanted Wasserstein out of circulation. Left out of the deal, Wasserstein could prove a dangerous agitator. Better to hire the roly-poly deal maker and lock him in a closet than allow him to run loose and perhaps assemble a competing bidding group.

Hiring the investment banks had gone smoothly. But Kravis had encountered a rude surprise when he began assembling the team of commercial banks he would need to raise the $10 billion or more of permanent financing. On Thursday he had called Ronald Badie, the head of West Coast operations for Bankers Trust, the big New York bank that was a leading source of takeover financing. Badie, Kravis's longtime banker, promised to start work the next day after clearing the assignment with his bosses in New York. But when Badie called back on Friday he sounded strangely calm.

"Henry, there's a problem," the banker said. "I've got to be honest. Right now I don't have clear-cut permission to go forward with you. But I'll try to work something out over the weekend."

Kravis was floored. Nothing like this—certainly not on this scale—had ever happened before. The only possible reason Badie couldn't commit, Kravis knew, was that Peter Cohen had already hired Bankers Trust on an exclusive basis, an exceedingly rare and cutthroat move. This was a crisis of the first order. Cut off from its regular source of bank money, Kravis's army had no bullets.

"You can't be exclusive with someone else!" Kravis exploded. "You can't be!"

All day Saturday Kravis pondered what to do about RJR Nabisco. The more he stewed, the more worried he became. Cohen and Hill, although no veterans of buyouts, weren't stupid. Unless he heard otherwise, Kravis had to assume they had bank financing in place and were on the brink of sewing up the deal. The way Cohen sounded the night before, the board of directors must surely have been in Ross Johnson's pocket.

The situation with Bankers Trust was an unexpected crisis. It not only threatened to cut Kravis off from his most reliable source of funding, but was regarded by him as clear evidence Shearson was trying to prevent the major banks from funding a competing bid for Johnson's company. On top of that, Kravis had learned that the American Express board was scheduled to meet on Monday. That could mean only one thing: Shearson needed its corporate parent's approval for the massive bridge loan it required to fund the buyout.

Everything pointed to Shearson and Johnson's wrapping up this deal quickly. And if they signed a merger agreement, Kravis knew, it would be difficult to break. On Saturday night Kravis consulted with Bruce Wasserstein. Wasserstein, known for his aggressive tactics, counseled a blitzkrieg approach. If Kravis was seriously worried about Johnson's locking up the deal, he said, the only way to proceed was to attack—and fast. Any delay gave Johnson time to sign a merger agreement with a board of directors apparently packed with his cronies.

Wasserstein, also trained as a lawyer, paraphrased former Supreme Court justice Louis D. Brandeis. "Sunlight is the best of all disinfectants," he told Kravis. If Kravis was worried about Johnson stealing this deal in some darkened back room, Wasserstein argued, he should shed some sunlight on the process. And the best of all illuminations, he continued, was an immediate tender offer.

A meeting of the entire Kravis team was set for the next day.

Fast, fast, fast, Kravis thought. *Everything had to move fast.*

Around the world there are thousands of commercial banks. In the takeover world, only three count.

Citibank, Manufacturers Hanover Trust Co., and Bankers Trust formed a powerful triumvirate with loose control over the spigots through which flowed the billions of dollars in money necessary to fuel Wall Street's takeover machine. Junk bonds sold by Drexel Burnham and others were important means of supplementary financing, but without the Big Three banks, the takeover world would come to a screeching halt.

So powerful was this trio, and so eager were they to lend money for takeovers, that by the late 1980s all three were acting as "common carriers" for merger money. That is, they saw nothing wrong with lending simultaneously to any number of bidders seeking the same prey. Like their distant cousins the investment banks, the commercial banks erected "Chinese Walls" of secrecy to maintain the confidences of each bidder.

From time to time, of course, this notion angered the banks' longtime clients. Gillette, the Boston-based razor-blade maker, cut its long-standing ties to Citibank when an arm of the bank agreed to back a hostile bid for control of the company. Other examples abounded. All in all, the banks found lucrative takeover fees more than outweighed the lost business of a few churlish clients. As much as Corporate America disliked the practice, the fact remained that the banks' power and influence were simply too pervasive to be challenged.

It was possible, although rare, to hire one of the Big Three on an exclusive basis for a major takeover. It was also expensive. Henry Kravis's suspicions to the contrary, Shearson hadn't in fact demanded an exclusive arrangement with either Bankers Trust or Citibank. Not foreseeing competition, Peter Cohen hadn't thought they would need exclusives. Jim Stern, Shearson's liaison to its banks, had brought the matter up informally with Bob O'Brien of Bankers Trust, but O'Brien had allowed the matter to be left vague. O'Brien would later acknowledge, however, that he had allowed Shearson to operate under the impression that his bank wouldn't lead a competing bank group. There remained an implicit understanding that Bankers Trust was working for Ross Johnson alone.

Thus when Ron Badie had asked for clearance to back Kravis, O'Brien's New York superiors, caught off guard, had blocked it until the matter could be cleared up. All weekend Badie tried in vain to secure approval to work with his largest client. The snag wouldn't be untangled until the following week, well after it had already had an effect on Kravis's actions.

Until Saturday evening, the Kravis camp hadn't been in touch with the other two members of the banking triumvirate. Dick Beattie, Kravis's attorney and confidant, was relaxing in his Manhattan apartment Saturday night when he took a call from Mark Solow. Solow, head of acquisition finance at Manufacturers Hanover, was a canny banker, well respected among Wall Street's takeover set.

Solow explained that he was trying to reach Peter Solomon at Shearson. He knew Beattie was also one of Shearson's closest outside advisers. Did Beattie have Solomon's home number?

"What do you want to talk to Peter about?" Beattie asked.

"I probably shouldn't tell you," Solow responded. "But I need to talk to someone at Shearson Lehman right away." What Solow didn't say was that he had been contacted by Bob O'Brien of Bankers Trust about joining the Shearson bank group, and wanted to talk to someone at Shearson before accepting.

1. Adolphus Green: the father of Nabisco products like the Oreo, Fig Newtons, and Animal Crackers, he called his work force "a great family."

2. R. J. Reynolds: Near death, "Mister RJ" told followers, "I have written the book. All you need to do is follow it."

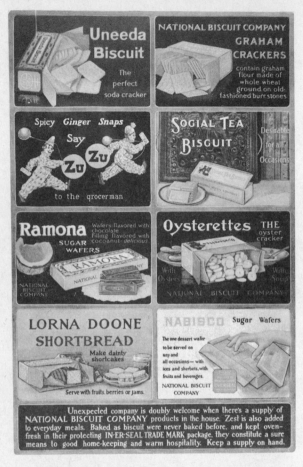

3. Early Nabisco advertisements: Savvy marketing transformed both Reynolds and Nabisco into early corporate giants.

4. Camel: the first mass-marketed cigarette, "Mister RJ's" greatest triumph.

5. Reynolds longtime headquarters: The Empire State Building on Main Street, Winston-Salem, North Carolina. From its top floors, parochial Reynolds executives bragged they could see everything the company owned.

6. "The Glass Menagerie": Inside the later Reynolds headquarters intrigues were spawned that weakened the company and laid the groundwork for Johnson's coup.

7–8. The young Ross Johnson: During twenty years of Canadian obscurity, he was best known for creativity in light bulbs and expense accounts.

9–10. Johnson and Henry Weigl in the 1975 Standard Brands annual report: Spiked with private detectives, tales of extramarital liaisons, and a climactic boardroom face-off, their power struggle ranked among the nastiest in corporate history.

11. Johnson, with Nabisco's Bob Schaeberle: After combining their two companies, the upstart Canadian effected an internal takeover so smoothly that his ascendancy to CEO was a formality.

12. Tylee Wilson, center, with Ed Horrigan and Johnson: Once in Winston-Salem, Johnson ingratiated himself with Wilson, then struck decisively at his weakest moment. Horrigan's hostility was overcome with a fancy New York apartment, limitless limousines, and a corporate jet.

13. Frank Gifford, Laurie Johnson, and Johnson on an early corporate jet: RJR Nabisco's vast "Air Force" was an abiding symbol of Johnson's extravagant corporate style.

14. Johnson so loved rubbing elbows with ex-athletes he was known as a "jock sniffer." Team Nabisco, 1982 (*left to right*): David Marr, Reggie Jackson, Bobby Orr, Alex Webster, Frank Gifford, Don Meredith, Rod Laver.

15. Johnson, Peter Ueberroth, and Gerald Ford at the Dinah Shore: The Nabisco-sponsored golf tournament attracted swarms of celebrities, much to Johnson's delight.

16. Johnson in his element, at an NFL alumni golf tournament (*left to right*): Richard Currie (president of Loblaw Companies, Ltd.), Charlie Hugel, Don Meredith, David Mahoney (former CEO of Norton Simon), Martin Emmett, Ed Horrigan, Ross Johnson, John Martin, Peter Eby (vice chairman of Burns Fry, Ltd.), Frank Gifford.

17. Johnson with Jack Nicklaus: The Golden Bear growled often at Nabisco executives who asked too much of him.

18. Paul Sticht: A Yankee who came south to run Reynolds and found he couldn't leave, Sticht undertook a series of machinations that were an enduring thorn in Johnson's side.

19. Steve Goldstone: An odd choice to be Johnson's closest Wall Street adviser, the lawyer warned that their secret project could encounter unforeseen hazards.

20. Andy Sage: To some a relic of a Wall Street gone by, Johnson's old friend demanded history's richest LBO agreement and scoffed at suggestions it might appear greedy.

21–26. The board's special committee (*clockwise from upper left*): Bill Anderson, who deplored latter-day Wall Street; Albert Butler, who felt the heat in Winston-Salem;

Charles Hugel, who came to doubt Johnson's word; John Macomber, who never cared for Johnson; and Martin Davis, who was Johnson's friend but no one's patsy.

27. Jim and Linda Robinson, Wall Street's premier power couple: He was Johnson's well-mannered senior adviser, while she initiated secret talks with Henry Kravis.

28. Jack Nusbaum: As Cohen's most trusted confidant, he played a vital role in the drama's waning hours.

29. Peter Cohen: After knuckling in to Johnson's demands, the tough-talking Shearson chief never saw the coming ambush.

30. Tom Hill: The merger world's rising star, he was shunted to a subsidiary role in favor of the inexperienced Cohen.

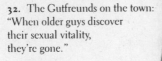

31. John Gutfreund: Leery of Johnson's secret pact, the powerful chief of Salomon Brothers put more emphasis on selling bonds than Oreos.

32. The Gutfreunds on the town: "When older guys discover their sexual vitality, they're gone."

33. Tom Strauss: A novice to the takeover world, the executive's speech spelled doom for a hard-won peace pact.

Nevertheless, Beattie realized the call had to be about RJR Nabisco. Solow obviously didn't know about Kravis's interest and certainly wasn't aware that Beattie was representing Kravis in a brewing fight with Shearson.

Beattie thought fast. The developing situation with Ron Badie made him especially sensitive toward bank matters. He had to cut Solow off before he got to Shearson.

"It's funny you should call, Mark, because Henry Kravis wants to talk to you. Can I have him call you?"

"Sure."

Beattie told Solow he couldn't find Peter Solomon's number and hung up. He immediately dialed Kravis and explained the situation.

Kravis reached Solow early the next morning. "Is Manny Hanny working on an exclusive basis for Shearson?" he asked.

"No, we're not working on an exclusive basis with Shearson or anyone else," Solow said.

Kravis was relieved to hear Solow was available. In that case, he told the banker, Kohlberg Kravis wants to hire Manufacturers Hanover on an exclusive basis for a bid on RJR Nabisco.

Solow was surprised. "Jeez," he said. "We've never done that before."

"Well, you're going to do it this time," Kravis said. "We'll make it worth your while."

For Kravis it was a rare piece of good news. Manny Hanny was one bank Peter Cohen wouldn't get his hands on.

It was during that weekend that the first boxes of financial data began arriving at Lazard Freres and Dillon Read, the vanguard of a wave of numbers the bankers would receive in coming weeks to help them determine RJR Nabisco's fair price. Inside they also found a half-dozen financial studies authored by outsiders, most sent in attempts to cajole Johnson into some type of restructuring.

At Lazard, Luis Rinaldini hustled into a colleague's office that Saturday with a handful of studies. "Have you seen these?" the Argentinian asked in amazement. At his Chicago apartment, Ira Harris received the documents Saturday morning and was shocked by what he read.

Not a single valuation put RJR Nabisco's value below $80 a share. Most were closer to $90. Dillon Read's Project Tara put a price tag on RJR

Nabisco of $81 to $87 a share, an average of $2 billion more than Johnson's $75 suggestion. Ruben Gutoff's Project Reo noted that private market valuations of the company went as high as $96 a share. All the bankers knew RJR Nabisco had fat to cut—Johnson's RJR Air Force was notorious on Wall Street—but they hadn't expected to see valuations like this.

While the bankers sifted through Johnson's data, a curious package was delivered anonymously to Charlie Hugel in Connecticut. Inside Hugel found an RJR Nabisco planning document, apparently generated by Dean Posvar's people. Titled "Corporate Strategy Update" and stamped CONFIDENTIAL, it was dated September 29, just three weeks before Johnson addressed the board.

Hugel read the document carefully. It gave an overview of the stock problem, outlined ways to fight Philip Morris, and suggested tobacco liability concerns probably made the company an unlikely takeover candidate. But what drew his attention were the valuations put on the company. Step-by-step, the document built a case for placing a price tag on RJR Nabisco of as low as $82 a share and as high as $111 a share. "A strong case," it concluded, "could be made for RJR Nabisco refusing to accept any offer below one hundred and eleven dollars per share."

Hugel was confused. *As low as eighty-two?* If Johnson's own people said the company was worth $82 to $111, what the hell was he doing bidding at $75?

Equally curious was the source of the document. There was no note attached, no clue to the sender's identity. But one thing was clear: Someone, almost certainly a high-level RJR Nabisco executive with access to confidential documents, was out to get Ross Johnson.

"We're interested in a tobacco company," Kravis began, eyeing Bruce Wasserstein, "but I'm not sure I want to tell you which one yet."

Kravis smiled. Everyone in the crowded boardroom knew Wasserstein was waist-deep in the Philip Morris bid for Kraft.

On Sunday afternoon the investment bankers had trickled in in pairs, driving in from weekend homes or strolling through the leaf-strewn paths of Central Park to convene in Kohlberg Kravis's boardroom at four o'-clock. Kravis and his people had arrived by noon and had spent much of the afternoon studying various analyses of the values locked inside RJR Nabisco.

From his seat at the side of the great table, Kravis surveyed the troops he had assembled for his assault. To his left, in his customary position, sat Dick Beattie, pale blue eyes steady, jaw firmly set. To Beattie's left was Casey Cogut, the lawyer's boyish second in command. Cogut supervised much of Kohlberg Kravis's legal work at Beattie's direction. The two lawyers had driven in together that morning from their Connecticut homes.

Next was Ted Ammon, a former lawyer, now a senior Kohlberg Kravis associate known for devising creative solutions to thorny financial problems. Wasserstein sat beside Ammon. Despite his genius, and the endless variety of ideas he brought to Kravis, Wasserstein had never been able to crack the inner circle at Kohlberg Kravis: Kravis and his aides found his meandering speeches tiresome. Some of them, especially George Roberts, were never quite sure where Wasserstein's loyalties lay.

Beside Wasserstein sat Eric Gleacher, Morgan Stanley's bantam merger chief. Two of the most prominent names in the takeover business, Gleacher and Wasserstein would prove to be an endless source of comic relief for Kravis and his aides. At meetings the pair took turns delivering the first speech, never forgetting who had gone first the last time. Inevitably they offered the same advice, sometimes so similarly that Kravis would roll his eyes. Beattie assumed the two conferred before each strategy session as, in fact, they had this day. George Roberts took to calling Wasserstein and Gleacher the "Siskel and Ebert of investment banking."

On the table's far side sat Steve Waters and Mack Rossoff, a baby-faced Wasserstein aide who had become a favorite of Kravis's with his crackerjack work during the recent Macmillan auction. Off to one side stood the Drexel contingent: Jeff Beck and Leon Black, the savvy financing expert who brought life to many of Mike Milken's ideas. Paul Raether completed the circle, along with a pair of his hardworking junior associates, Scott Stuart and Cliff Robbins.

After bringing the meeting to order, Kravis briefed the group on the current situation. "We understand Shearson is trying to get commitments from major banks to lock them up," Kravis concluded. "If that's the case, we've got to do something right away to prevent that from happening."

A lengthy debate ensued on the values inside RJR Nabisco that would come spilling forth in a successful leveraged buyout. There were no real differences of opinion. Everyone knew there was money in Ross Johnson's cookie jar. The question was how best to get at it. Cliff Robbins had laid out their options in a memo for the "Project Peach" team that day.

There were three. First was a so-called bear hug letter to the board. In it, Kravis would signal his interest to pay more than $75 a share but stop short of an outright offer. Under the "Advantages" column, Robbins noted, a bear hug would probably get them access to confidential RJR Nabisco financial information, a must if they weren't bidding with a management team. It would also stall the management group's drive to quickly sew up the deal. Under "Disadvantages," Robbins worried that a threatening letter would only lead to an extended auction. Bidding, the memo noted, "would go to the edge of the envelope." They might win, he concluded, but it could cost them billions in the process.

The second option was a meeting with Shearson and Johnson, perhaps to discuss a joint bid. "Shows weakness?" the memo asked. Third was a tender offer, the blitzkrieg approach counseled by Wasserstein. The upside: "Seizes timing advantage . . . stalls management deal." The downside: "No information . . . hostile . . . financing hurdles."

When it came time for the advisers to speak, Eric Gleacher went first. His speech was almost military in tone, the kind of talk one delivers to a boot camp or at halftime of a crucial football game. Gleacher, a jock and proud of it, had the macho intensity characteristic of some small men.

"You've got to do a tender offer," Gleacher said. "The risk here is that Shearson'll have some kind of contract with the board before we can do something. If you call 'em back and say, 'Yeah, we're interested,' we end up getting pushed around. A tender offer puts us on even footing. We have to be firm here. It's very important from a symbolic point. . . . We've got to move fast. We've got to blow 'em out of the water. Just blow 'em right away."

Across the table Dick Beattie grinned. It was vintage Gleacher.

Wasserstein went next, essentially repeating the message he had given Kravis privately the night before. The discussion continued, with the pros and cons of each move pored over in detail. Drexel's Leon Black sounded a cautionary note. "Gee, what's the hurry? Why don't we just wait and top it?"

"Then you're the bad guys," Gleacher said.

They talked further, but it was clear which way the group was leaning.

"What price?" Kravis asked.

"Maybe we should do it at seventy-five," Gleacher suggested.

Wasserstein shook his head. "Somewhere in the nineties, I think." Competitors joked that Wasserstein's pocketbook was always open, at least when it was a client's money he was spending. His clients regularly bid so high traders spoke of a "Wasserstein Premium."

Kravis turned to Steve Waters, who knew Johnson better than anyone at the table.

"How do you read Johnson?" Kravis asked.

Waters rattled through Johnson's track record, concluding, "Ross never bought anything. He's always been a seller." A $90 tender offer would immediately put him on the defensive. For one thing, he wouldn't want to match it. But more important, compared to the $75 proposal already on the table, a $90 bid would make it appear Johnson was stealing the company. If so, they could hope to drive a crucial wedge between Johnson and his board.

"If we come on strong," Waters added, "he might fold."

Last, Kravis turned to the Drexel contingent. Could enough bonds be sold to buy RJR Nabisco? Was there enough demand in world markets? They all knew the bond offerings under consideration would dwarf the largest in Wall Street history. And there was still the consideration that a Drexel indictment could have disastrous consequences for both the takeover and the bond offerings.

"We can place the junk," said Leon Black. "Don't worry about our problems. We'll be able to do it." Black's reputation was such that few were concerned that his routine assurances were hollow.

As the discussion wound down, Kravis took Paul Raether and the associates and retired to his office. It was decision time. Left behind, the advisers took the opportunity to raid the Kohlberg Kravis kitchen and order pizzas. As Kravis closed his office door, no one realized that a very similar meeting was taking place that moment, just six blocks north.

———

John Gutfreund closed his grip around his three-year-old son's tiny hand and stepped off the curb onto Madison Avenue. Father and son had been out shopping, and Gutfreund clasped a package under one arm. Across the way, he could see Bill Strong and another Salomon investment banker trying in vain to locate a parking place. Gutfreund waved.

The meeting at his Fifth Avenue apartment that evening, Gutfreund knew, could well be among the most important in his long and spectacular Wall Street career. Salomon Brothers was among Wall Street's most powerful trading houses. Through its massive trading floor overlooking New York Harbor more than $20 billion in securities flowed daily, a sum greater than that of the New York Stock Exchange itself. But now, after three years of unfulfilled promises, Gutfreund was finally ready to move his firm away from the trading floor and to invest its hard-won capital in a major merchant-banking deal. And the way Gutfreund's investment-banking department wanted to do it—and the amounts they proposed to use—would stagger all those who said Salomon would never amount to anything in the LBO business.

Gutfreund himself was a newcomer to the takeover world. Wall Street had always been split into two, sometimes warring, camps: investment bankers—smooth, dapper, trained at Andover and Harvard—and traders—red-faced Jewish and Irish kids who went to City College and made their living hollering at each other on the trading floor. By training and attitude, Gutfreund was a trader.

From his desk on the trading floor he had ruthlessly steered Salomon Brothers through a decade of growth, until it had become the largest and most profitable firm in its field. In 1985, *Business Week* crowned him "King of Wall Street." To many involved in finance John Gutfreund *was* Salomon Brothers. His word was law inside the firm, and subordinates literally trembled when he stalked into a room, waving one of his giant cigars. Short and fond of dark, three-piece suits, Gutfreund had a round face, thick, sensuous lips, and a jack-o'-lantern smile that often looked forced. Ross Johnson, who knew him from Standard Brands days, called Gutfreund "Old Potatohead."

At fifty-nine, Gutfreund had discovered a new life, marrying a second wife, fathering a son, and cutting a social profile that set tongues wagging across Wall Street. Susan Gutfreund, a former Pan Am stewardess in her early forties, had transformed her husband's drab existence into a series of black-tie fund-raisers and society parties. Married in 1981, the Gutfreunds were soon fixtures in the social pages of *W* and *Women's Wear Daily.* Susan had sealed their rise in New York society by snaring the honor of throwing a sixtieth birthday party for Henry Kissinger. Months later the guests were still talking about the green apples of spun sugar Susan's chef had prepared for dessert.

When the Gutfreunds acquired an eighteenth-century mansion on Rue de Grenelle in Paris, Susan spent more time in France, and Gutfreund began taking the Concorde back and forth on weekends. Not surprisingly, when Salomon Brothers first encountered problems in the mid-1980s, many thought Susan Gutfreund deserved some of the blame for diverting her husband's attention from weightier matters. "It's my theory that Susan Gutfreund has had a lot do with John's problems," a Wall Street friend told *New York* magazine in early 1988. "When older guys discover their sexual vitality, they're gone."

As Salomon grew, tensions had arisen between its dominant trading culture and its small investment-banking arm, long considered a neglected stepchild within the firm. By 1987 those tensions had erupted into something approaching open warfare, as the bankers demanded a greater voice inside the firm and, not incidentally, sought to push more aggressively into mergers and merchant banking. The intrigues hatched within Salomon spawned comparisons to a Florentine palace during the rule of the Medicis, with Gutfreund playing the role written by Machiavelli. A man who had ruthlessly frozen out his own mentor and who seemed to take pride in firing challengers to his power, Gutfreund found himself spending much of his time suppressing internal revolts. As he did, profits and morale plummeted. A series of ill-advised restructurings led to a spate of high-level resignations, including those of Chicago deal maker Ira Harris and economic guru Henry Kaufman. At his lowest point, Gutfreund narrowly escaped a takeover attempt by the investor Ronald O. Perelman.

For nearly two years Gutfreund leapt from crisis to crisis, his firm a simmering cauldron of unrest. Now, as he strolled with his son toward his home, Gutfreund, defying the doomsayers, seemed to have put the worst behind him. Many of the troublemakers inside Salomon had been purged, profits were again up, and Gutfreund and his wife had all but vanished from the pages of *Women's Wear Daily.* For the first time Gutfreund, a man who sometimes referred to takeovers as "trades," was taking an active interest in investment banking, even tagging along with bankers to pay courtesy calls on prospective clients. Trading was still profitable but Gutfreund was learning what every other Wall Street chief executive had known for years: The real money these days was in merchant banking.

RJR Nabisco was to be the test of Gutfreund's resolve. His entire investment-banking department, he knew, was pumped up to get a piece of the action Ross Johnson had created. Gutfreund was skeptical, attributing their passion to "deal heat," the state that occurs when an investment banker finds the takeover of a lifetime. In most "deal guys," Gutfreund had observed, the symptoms cropped up every month or two. The bankers, Gutfreund recognized, believed they had stumbled on their Holy Grail: the deal that could Bring Us Back. RJR Nabisco was to be Salomon's salvation, the deal that would, in one fell swoop, rewrite history, wipe out their past embarrassments, and instantly establish Salomon as a major force in the LBO field.

An admirable goal, Gutfreund thought, but an unlikely one. And certainly risky. From what Bill Strong had told him about RJR Nabisco, Ross Johnson's company seemed attractive—good brand names, super cash flow. But Gutfreund had to look at the bigger picture. The amount of capital they would need—maybe several hundred million dollars—would place an enormous burden on the firm. Salomon's trading operations used its funds to scoop up massive amounts of stocks and bonds, selling them at thin margins for huge profits. Any deep cut in the firm's capital could cause the rating agencies to review Salomon's credit ratings. Any downgrading could cost Gutfreund millions in higher trading costs. More important, a downgrading was just the kind of thing that could rekindle discontent in the ranks. Gutfreund couldn't afford to delude himself: If he didn't handle this right, he could have an open revolt on his hands.

After parking his car Bill Strong, and later a half-dozen other investment bankers, met Gutfreund at the threshold of his apartment. Inside they were escorted into a soaring, two-story foyer paneled with stone. To one side hung one of Monet's water-lily paintings. The six-bedroom apartment had cost the Gutfreunds $6.5 million—before its top-to-bottom renovation—and every dollar seemed to be hanging on the walls. For their "public" rooms, the Gutfreunds favored a palatial eighteenth-century French atmosphere, including a plant-filled room adorned with antique painted panels and trellises. The society matrons at Mortimer's loved to joke about how French Susan Gutfreund had become during her time in Paris. *"Bonsoir, Madame,"* she had said when introduced to Nancy Reagan.

The Gutfreunds had moved to Fifth Avenue after a dispute with their former neighbors at the posh River House. Susan insisted on having a twenty-two-foot Douglas fir as a Christmas tree. When the tree proved too large for the building's elevator, she simply had a crane positioned on the roof and had it winched up—without, unfortunately, having obtained permission of the penthouse tenants. There was a nasty scene, followed by a $35 million lawsuit. The Gutfreunds soon moved to larger quarters on Fifth Avenue.

After a guided tour of the sumptuous apartment, Strong's group was shown into Gutfreund's darkened, leather-walled library. "All right," Gutfreund said, "tell me what I need to know about this thing."

Strong was nervous. This would be the biggest presentation he had ever made, that he might ever make. He was asking Gutfreund for an unprecedented commitment, one that could reshape the entire future of the firm. Quickly he outlined the structure. It was simplicity itself, Strong explained. Salomon and Hanson would act as "pure partners," splitting stock, costs, and control fifty-fifty. Salomon brought the financial expertise, Hanson a background in operations. What was unusual was how Strong proposed to wedge Salomon into the deal.

Working through the weekend, Strong's Salomon team had come to the same conclusion as Henry Kravis. To make a move on RJR Nabisco one needed to move aggressively. Strong proposed that Salomon quickly and secretly accumulate a large position in RJR Nabisco stock—a toehold—with an eye toward launching an unsolicited takeover bid. This would give Salomon bargaining leverage, Strong argued. It had the added advantage that, even if Salomon failed to ultimately gain control of the company, the firm would almost certainly realize a massive gain on its stock holdings.

What Strong described was exactly the strategy that corporate raiders such as Boone Pickens and Carl Icahn had been using for years. For a major investment bank to try the same approach was unheard of, an order of magnitude beyond what Tom Hill and Shearson had sprung on Koppers that spring. But unusual deals, Strong argued, required unusual tactics. With Gutfreund's approval, Strong wanted to begin acquiring RJR Nabisco stock on Monday morning and keep buying until they had spent $1 billion.

Strong didn't make the suggestion lightly. All weekend the bankers had debated the point. The strategy seemed brilliant, the target a once-in-a-lifetime collection of name brands. It was exactly the kind of aggressive move they thought Salomon should be making. The more they discussed it, the more enthusiastic they became. Just one question remained on everyone's lips: Would Gutfreund do it?

"No way: He'll never do it," a banker named Charles ("Chaz") Phillips said. Gutfreund talked a good game, Phillips argued, but down deep didn't have what it took to push the button. Some of the bankers grew depressed. If Gutfreund wouldn't approve the RJR Nabisco deal, they moaned, he would never approve anything. "If we can't find a way to do this," a veteran banker named Ronald Freeman said, "my fifteen years at Salomon mean nothing."

Now, as Strong finished his presentation, Gutfreund attacked, a fighter firing jabs into their case, looking for any weakness. His style was to put the bankers on the defensive, make them justify the move a hundred different ways. Before he gambled a dollar on this deal, Gutfreund said, he wanted to hear everything that could possibly go wrong. "You guys are being pretty goddamn easy with my shareholders' money," he challenged. "What makes you think it'll work?"

At first the bankers couldn't tell whether he was hostile or simply asking the right questions. What about tobacco litigation? Gutfreund asked. "Not a problem," the bankers assured. To Chaz Phillips: "Is the bond market large enough to handle all the paper?" "Yes," Phillips shot back.

They went through it again and again until, after an hour, Gutfreund placed a call to one of Salomon's most influential directors, Warren Buffett. Buffett was renowned as one of Wall Street's most intelligent investors. His prognostications could move markets, and often did. He wasn't a quick-buck artist—no raiding for Warren Buffett. Buffett invested the old-fashioned way: buy and hold. He had bought a 12 percent holding in Salomon the previous fall, rescuing Gutfreund from the hostile overtures of Ron Perelman.

When Buffett came on the line, Gutfreund put him on a speaker phone and laid out the situation in detail. What should they do?

Go for it, Buffett advised. Once one of RJR's largest shareholders, he knew tobacco and liked it. "I'll tell you why I like the cigarette business," he said. "It costs a penny to make. Sell it for a dollar. It's addictive. And there's fantastic brand loyalty."

Would Buffett himself like to join forces with Salomon? No, the investor said, not this time. Cigarettes were a fine investment, but owning a tobacco company, with its social baggage and all that Death Merchant business, wasn't a burden Buffett felt he was ready to bear. "I'm wealthy enough where I don't need to own a tobacco company and deal with the consequences of public ownership," he said.

To the bankers in Gutfreund's library, Buffett's blessing seemed to erase the last of their chairman's doubts. If drastic action were required,

Gutfreund agreed, then drastic action would be taken.

The bankers left Gutfreund's apartment that night in various stages of euphoria. One of Gutfreund's doubters, Chaz Phillips, took the bus to his Fifth Avenue apartment feeling high. Phillips was sure he had just witnessed one of the single most important moments in the history of Salomon Brothers. He couldn't believe it.

Gutfreund actually did it.

Into the wee hours the Salomon bankers exchanged congratulatory phone calls. None could believe their good fortune. Finally, after years of talk, Salomon Brothers was actually going to *do* something.

"Whoa, whoa, wait a minute," George Roberts said. "Why do we have to do this tonight? I'll take a plane and get there tomorrow."

"We could do that," Kravis said, "but by tomorrow it may be too late."

Put on the speaker phone in Kravis's office, Roberts had been caught off guard by the suggestion of an immediate tender offer. Although kept up to date on Kravis's preparations, he hadn't expected anything like this. Sitting in his home south of San Francisco, all Roberts had to whet his appetite was a single computer run sent out from New York two days earlier. Naturally cautious, Roberts wanted to hear a lot more before he committed to the first unsolicited tender offer in the firm's history.

Kravis laid out all the reasons for expeditiousness. Banks were being locked up. The American Express board was meeting tomorrow, no doubt to approve the bridge loan necessary to cement the deal. If they didn't move fast, Kravis said, Johnson could sew this deal up within days, if not hours. A tender offer, he argued, was the only way Kohlberg Kravis could be certain of getting its foot in the door. For one thing, it guaranteed a response from the board. Federal securities laws mandate that any target of a tender offer must formally reply to the offer within ten days. The board couldn't ignore them then, Kravis said.

Moreover, he continued, it wouldn't be an outright hostile bid. For one thing, Johnson had already put this company in play. And Kravis intended to make completion of the tender offer conditioned on approval of RJR Nabisco's board. That way, he said, they obtained the time advantages of a tender offer without launching a full-fledged hostile bid.

Bruce Wasserstein and Eric Gleacher were brought in and repeated their militant pitches for Roberts. Roberts was less than impressed by the two bankers' arguments, although he didn't say so in their presence. Wall Street, Roberts knew, was full of Wassersteins and Gleachers trying to push Kohlberg Kravis into hasty deals whose chief benefit seemed to be the creation of multimillion-dollar advisory fees. Wasserstein was particularly bad, always pestering Henry with new takeover ideas. Roberts took them all with a grain of salt, lumping them together with everything else he hated about New York. After a while Roberts asked the two bankers to leave the room.

It was an enormous decision. This deal was three times larger than anything they had ever done before. It was also the first time they had launched a bid without the aid of a friendly management team. If they wanted RJR Nabisco, it appeared they would have to fly solo.

Nevertheless, Roberts felt himself slowly bowing to Kravis's on-the-scene instincts. Isolated in California, he saw it was fruitless for him to second-guess everyone in New York. "Well," Roberts said. "Let's sleep on it, then look at in the morning. If neither of us has any real reservations, we'll go ahead."

The meeting broke up around 10:15. As Kravis began to think about leaving, Gleacher and Wasserstein walked into his office. "We'd like to talk to you about the fees," one of them said.

Kravis was irritated by the request. Kohlberg Kravis generally waited until further along in a takeover, even after its completion, before negotiating fees with its investment bankers. Kravis considered it a matter of trust that the firm would take care of its advisers. He cast a stern glance at the two men: little boys asking for a raise in their allowances.

"Why should we talk to you about the fee now?" Kravis said. "We've never had any problems with that before."

The two advisers figured that both Morgan Stanley and Wasserstein Perella should receive a fee of $50 million each. It was an awesome number. The largest fees negotiated to that point had been in the $50 million-to-$60 million range—and those were for deals that required massive bridge loans and billion-dollar capital commitments. Wasserstein and Gleacher wanted the same amount just for their advice.

This is ridiculous, Kravis thought. Here he was about to launch the largest takeover battle of his career—indeed, in the history of Wall Street—and his advisers were more worried about their compensation than their tactics.

"You're just not even close," Kravis told the pair. "We're not even going to talk about it. This is the last time we'll talk about it."

"Well, fine," Gleacher said after a moment. "But this is important to us, Henry. We'll just have to trust you on it."*

Later, Kravis took a car home to his Park Avenue apartment. He was pleased by the evening's events. A tender offer felt like the right thing to do. He was 75 percent sure he would do it. Doubts lingered, of course. How would investors in their funds see it? How would the newspapers play it? Far more important, how would RJR's board regard it? The directors had to be convinced it was not a hostile bid.

Kravis wanted to sleep on it. In the morning he would talk with Beattie and Roberts, maybe with Peter Cohen.

Then he would make his final decision.

For all Henry Kravis's feverish preparations, the management group itself had taken the weekend off. Early Sunday evening Johnson, amiably oblivious to the storm gathering before him, breezed into Jim and Linda Robinson's apartment high above the Museum of Modern Art. Johnson was in a fine mood, looking tanned and well rested in a cotton sweater and casual slacks. On the flight up from Atlanta that afternoon he had stopped in Chattanooga, Tennessee, and, with Laurie and John Martin in tow, played a round of golf. The Honors golf course there, owned by his friend Jack Lupton, a former Coca-Cola bottler, was one of Johnson's favorites. They had all played well, Laurie teeing off from the short tees, Johnson from the middle tees, and Martin from the back tees.

Johnson hadn't worried about the threat from Kravis. In fact, he hadn't spent much time worrying about anything since Friday. He had slept until noon Saturday and watched college football all afternoon with Martin. Monday he and Laurie planned to visit Bruce, who still lay in a coma after his accident more than a month before. Tuesday they would meet with the commercial bankers, the first step toward raising the $15 billion or so they needed for the deal. That's when the real work would start, Johnson figured.

As for Kravis, well, Cohen could take care of him. Kravis would calm down; everything would work out. Cohen said he had things under control

---

* Wasserstein says he doesn't recall this conversation, but says it is "perfectly plausible. . . . We basically deferred to Morgan Stanley on the fee discussion. You're better off talking to Eric." Gleacher says he doesn't recall the conversation.

and, until he was informed otherwise, Johnson was inclined to believe him. Anyway, what could Kravis do? He certainly wasn't going to bid $18 billion for this company without management, Johnson felt.

Jim Robinson wasn't so blasé. All weekend he had agonized over whether to call Kravis himself. Cohen said he had everything under control, but Robinson couldn't shake the feeling that he might be able to help out. He and Johnson spent much of the evening sorting through options on the phone with Cohen.

Around eleven o'clock, the Johnsons and Martin retired to the Johnsons' Fifth Avenue apartment, next to the Pierre Hotel. When they arrived, Martin was surprised to find a message from his assistant, Bill Liss. Returning the call, he found Liss near panic.

He had just received a call from a *Wall Street Journal* reporter, Liss explained. "Henry Kravis is going to make a tender offer in the morning at ninety dollars a share."

Martin and Johnson exchanged bemused looks. "That's crazy," Martin told Liss.

"That's nuts," Johnson echoed. "Who the hell would pay ninety?"

Takeover rumors, the two men figured. In a deal this size there were bound to be hundreds of bizarre stories floating around. Still, John Martin passed on the rumor to Linda Robinson.

———

Peter Cohen was just about to put down the book he was reading and join his wife in bed. Tomorrow, he knew, would be a rough day. Henry Kravis had to be dealt with.

It had been an uneventful weekend. After meeting with Kravis on Friday evening, Cohen had come home exhausted. Saturday he endured six hours of French lessons. Cohen needed the tutelage—he also was taking Italian—for his new friendship with Carlo De Benedetti, because he had recently joined De Benedetti-controlled boards in France and Italy. Cohen assured his tutor he would pursue his studies more diligently than he had the previous spring. "I promise it'll be different this time," he said, having no idea it would be his last French lesson for months. Late that afternoon he took in his son's peewee football game. On Sunday Cohen lay around the house all day. He talked several times with Jim Robinson and Tom Hill. All agreed Shearson should pursue its dialogue with Kravis. Cohen didn't have the slightest idea where the talks would lead, but it seemed smart to try and head off Kravis before matters had a chance to escalate.

Cohen's phone rang. It was Linda Robinson, relaying news of John Martin's call and the disturbing rumor that Kravis was launching a tender offer for RJR Nabisco.

"I have trouble believing that," Cohen said. "Someone's just playing around with you." Like Johnson, he tossed it off to the usual rumors that accompany any large takeover bid. Linda Robinson thought that sounded plausible.

Less than an hour later, Robinson called again. She had gotten a call herself from a reporter, passing along the same rumor.

"That can't be right, Linda," Cohen repeated. "We're supposed to meet with Henry tomorrow. Why would he do something like that without the benefit of another conversation? It doesn't make any sense. It's just rumors."

Before the night ended, Linda Robinson made a final call to Johnson and passed on the news of the second reporter's call. She assured him he didn't need to worry. "Myron says it's impossible," she told him, using her pet nickname for Cohen. "They're going to be meeting in the morning."

For the first time, though, Johnson allowed himself a moment of concern. "Holy Christ, she got a call, too," he told Laurie after bidding Linda Robinson good night. "This is strange. . . ."

Could it be real? Johnson thought. No, it had to be rumors. It just didn't make sense. Hell, he mused, even if Kravis were going to top their proposal, he wouldn't do it by $15 a share.

Nah, couldn't be. . . .

Bill Strong, the Salomon Brothers banker, rose early Monday morning at his Summit, New Jersey, home, psyched up for the day ahead. Today was the day the deal makers at staid old Salomon Brothers entered the twenty-first century.

At twenty minutes past five Strong slipped into his black BMW 735ii and headed for a nearby newsstand. Twenty minutes later he was cruising toward the Holland Tunnel, a pile of newspapers lying unread on the passenger seat, when his car phone rang. It was a Salomon associate,

David Kirkland. Kirkland had just heard on CBS Radio that Henry Kravis had announced a $90-a-share tender offer for RJR Nabisco.

"Oh, Christ," Bill Strong said.

———

Johnson's attorney, Steve Goldstone, was pulling on a pair of sweatpants at six A.M. when the phone rang. The lawyer had recently moved into an apartment at United Nations Plaza. He had taken to using the downstairs gymnasium to work off stress.

"KKR has launched a tender offer," Tom Hill said matter-of-factly, quickly outlining what few details of the offer were known.

At first Goldstone didn't understand. "Tell me what it is again?"

Hill repeated what he knew.

"And the price?" Goldstone asked.

"Ninety dollars a share."

Goldstone was shocked. Never, in all their weeks of preparation, had he heard anything to prepare him for so high a number. Shearson had said it didn't expect the deal to go for more than $80.

"Say that again? Ninety? Nine-oh?"

"Yes."

"I'll come down to your office right away."

Goldstone numbly slipped off his gym clothes. "That call," he would remember months later, "literally knocked my socks off."

———

The Monday editions of both *The Wall Street Journal* and *The New York Times* carried the news that Kohlberg Kravis was set to launch a $90-a-share tender offer for RJR Nabisco. Dick Beattie's jaw dropped when he picked up the papers. Somewhere there had been a leak. It was the worst breach of confidence he had witnessed in twenty years on Wall Street. Someone, probably an adviser Kravis was paying millions of dollars, had leaked the biggest move of Kravis's career. Beattie was still agog when Kravis called around seven o'clock.

"Have you seen this fucking story in *The Times?*" he asked, practically screaming.

"Yeah, I'm damn mad about it."

"It's that goddamn Beck!"

"No, Henry. . . ."

"Yes it is!"

Kravis, homing in on a reference to Drexel Burnham in *The Times* story, had instantly fingered Jeff Beck as the culprit. For years he had put up with Beck's silly high jinks, the dumb jokes, the hysterics. Now Beck would have to pay.

Kravis was still livid when he arrived at his office a half hour later. Whatever reservations he had harbored toward the tender offer were now moot. The leak had forced his hand. He had to go forward with the offer. He directed that the bid be formally announced at eight o'clock.

Trying to set aside his blinding anger at Beck, Kravis scribbled down a list of people to call. It was short, just five names: Charles Hugel, Ross Johnson, Jim Robinson, Peter Cohen, and Ira Harris, now working with the special committee.

The first four Kravis couldn't immediately reach. At twenty minutes to eight he reached Ira Harris at his Chicago apartment. Harris, who constantly battled a weight problem, was slogging aboard a treadmill when Kravis called.

"Oh my God!" Harris exclaimed when Kravis disclosed the looming tender offer. The Chicago deal maker reminded Kravis that, as an adviser to the board, he was strictly neutral in this takeover. But any bid that boosted the payout to shareholders was bound to be good news to RJR Nabisco's board.

"Henry," he said, "that's great."

Peter Cohen rose early Monday morning, ducking into his chauffeured limousine by seven-thirty for the drive to Shearson's downtown headquarters. After dropping off his children at school, Cohen's car was cruising down Park Avenue when his wife, Karen, rang. "Henry just called looking for you."

Cohen, who hadn't yet read the papers that morning, reached Kravis minutes later. In all their conversations—at dinner parties, openings, even on the ski slopes—he had never heard Kravis's voice so tense.

"Peter, I'm just calling to let you know we knew what you were up to all weekend. Because of it, we're announcing a tender offer at eight o'clock to buy RJR at ninety dollars a share."

"Henry," Cohen said, fighting back his irritation, "what exactly was I up to all weekend?"

"You know, trying to lock up the banks and all that. We knew about that. We know about the board meetings, too."

"I don't know where you got that stuff, but nothing remotely like that took place. Those board meetings have been on the calendar for months. Henry, what are you doing? I was going to call you. Have I ever said something and not done it?

"Let me tell you something," Cohen continued. "You're making a mistake, Henry, and I think you're underestimating us." Cohen made no effort to hide his disgust.

Hanging up, Cohen's anger quickly gave way to shock, then worry. As the limo whisked him downtown, Cohen tried to figure out what had happened. Something had set Kravis off. He dialed Shearson's lead attorney, Jack Nusbaum.

"Why are they doing this? I can't understand it! This is crazy," Cohen said, his voice rising. "He was supposed to get back to me."

Neither man could guess what had gone wrong. Nusbaum said there had to be more to it. If it was a tender offer, it wasn't much of one. For one thing, Kravis couldn't have arranged $20 billion in financing in three days.

"How on earth can they make a tender offer, Peter?" Nusbaum said. "They've got no financing. It's got to be illusory. And he wouldn't dare do a hostile deal."

Ross Johnson was just about to sit down to his normal breakfast of toast, bacon, an English muffin, and a single egg over easy when John Martin burst into the apartment. "The Kravis thing," Martin said, "we're getting it from too many sources. It's true."

No, Johnson said. No, it couldn't be true, he stammered. It made no sense. Ninety dollars a share! It was insane!

But it's true, Martin said.

Johnson immediately thought of Cohen's meeting with Kravis. Something must have happened Friday night to set him off. Something he wasn't told about.

"Somebody's sure pissed off somebody," Johnson said. "I'm going to get to the bottom of this."

Other than their abortive meeting a year earlier, Kravis didn't really know Johnson. He called Eric Gleacher at Morgan Stanley to arrange a telephone conversation.

"Henry," Gleacher said in mock wonder, "I'm reading about you in the papers." He laughed, unable to resist taking a shot at Jeff Beck, his competitor. "Can you believe these Drexel guys?"

"Goddamn it," Kravis fumed, "I've never been so mad in my life. Can you believe this? I almost dropped Drexel right out of this deal."

Chuckling to himself, Gleacher phoned Johnson in Atlanta. Johnson returned the call minutes later from his New York apartment. The Morgan Stanley banker was surprised to find Johnson in his usual high spirits. If Kravis's offer had thrown him for a loop, Johnson wasn't letting it show.

"Goddamn, what a price!" Johnson exclaimed. "Boy, this is crazy. But what a great job we've all done for shareholders."

Gleacher didn't know what to make of Johnson. Did the guy really not care that he was losing his company, maybe his job?

When Johnson called Henry Kravis a few minutes later, Kravis, too, was surprised by the onslaught of cheerfulness from RJR Nabisco's president. Johnson sounded anything but shaken by news of Kravis's move.

"My God, Henry!" Johnson said. "I knew you were rich, but I didn't know you were that rich! That's one hell of an offer. . . ."

In contrast to Johnson's inexplicably sunny greeting, Kravis's tone was calm, businesslike: "Ross, I just wanted to let you know, as a courtesy. We'd like to buy the company. And we'd be happy to sit down and talk with you and see if we can get together. We'd love to have you run this company."

"Well, let's see how things work out," Johnson said. "I'll get back to you."

It was over that quickly.

Later that morning, after relaying similar messages to Jim Robinson and Charles Hugel, Kravis phoned and confronted Jeff Beck. If he could have reached through the telephone line and strangled the Drexel banker, he would have.

"I can't believe you did this to me," Kravis seethed.

Beck immediately grew panicky. "I didn't do it. Henry, you gotta believe me. I didn't do it!"

"These articles sure lead me to believe you did," Kravis said icily. "I don't want anyone around that can't be trusted. I don't want anyone on this team who's out for their own selves. We've got no use for that. That's it, Jeff. I don't want you at any more meetings."

Beck became hysterical. He had a multimillion fee, not to mention his reputation, on the line. "Henry, it wasn't me," he said. "I didn't do it! I didn't do it! You gotta believe me! It was Wasserstein! It had to be Wasserstein!"

Beck pleaded and begged, but Kravis quickly grew tired of the panicked denials.

All that day, every thirty minutes or so, Beck phoned Kravis, but not a single call was returned. Beck pleaded with Paul Raether and the others, swearing his innocence, and even turned to newspaper reporters to back up his story, to no avail. For days Beck would hang in limbo, unable to sleep, unsure of his standing with Kravis.

At one point that day, Beck heard that Eric Gleacher was spreading the story he was behind the leaks. He called Gleacher's partner, Steve Waters.

"Tell Eric," Beck said, "that if he says it one more time, I'll break his fucking neck."

———

The leak's true source proved a topic of enduring debate within Kohlberg Kravis.

For several weeks Jeff Beck was exiled from all strategy meetings as he remained in Kravis's doghouse. Eventually, Beck was taken back into the fold when Kravis came to believe the Drexel banker had cleverly been set up by the real Deep Throat: Bruce Wasserstein.

Kravis aides theorized that Wasserstein leaked the story to the press to force Kravis into a prolonged fight for RJR Nabisco. The perceived motive: Wasserstein's desire to prevent Kravis from bidding for Kraft instead. Wasserstein was advising Kraft's suitor, Philip Morris, and was deathly afraid he would lose his prey to Henry Kravis. "He wanted to give us that last little shove over the edge," said Paul Raether. In fact, Kravis had been in touch with Kraft's chief executive, John Richman, about exactly such a move as late as Sunday afternoon.

To cover his tracks, Kravis believed, Wasserstein shrewdly planted references to Drexel Burnham in that morning's *New York Times* story, knowing it would draw speculation to the loquacious Beck.

Months after the deal's completion, Kravis and Raether again amended their theory. After checking Kohlberg Kravis phone records for that Sunday night, they claimed to have identified phone calls to reporters for *The Wall Street Journal* and *The New York Times*. Kravis came to believe there were dual sources for the leaks, Beck and Wasserstein, one for each newspaper. Beck's motive, they surmised, was pure ego: He wanted to take credit for the deal. Whatever the truth, both Beck and Wasserstein fervently denied being the sources of any leaks.

The leak controversy would have consequences for Kravis far beyond that day. From that morning on he faced a simple fact: He couldn't trust his advisers, men to whom Kohlberg Kravis would ultimately pay well over $500 million. For the remainder of the RJR Nabisco battle, Kravis, Roberts, and their aides largely worked alone. Although they continued to seek financial analysis from the bankers—they wanted something for their $25 million—both men tended to share their true thoughts only with Kohlberg Kravis colleagues. At times they intentionally misled their own bankers, hoping a Wasserstein or a Beck would inadvertently spread misinformation.

Kravis's announcement went off like a bomb in John Gutfreund's lap. RJR Nabisco's stock skyrocketed on news of the Kravis bid, forcing Gutfreund to put Salomon's plan to buy RJR Nabisco stock on hold. At eleven o'clock, Bill Strong and Chaz Phillips met with Hanson representatives at the British firm's midtown offices and were told the bid was being reconsidered. By three o'clock it was dead.

By evening the previous night's meeting had receded into the Salomon bankers' consciousness like a bad dream. Gutfreund toured the bankers' seventeenth-floor offices, intently questioning the strategy they had pushed on him so avidly the evening before. At one point he suggested the bankers had been "cavalier" with Salomon's money. On his departure several of them, in a black mood, dubbed themselves "The Cavaliers," a nickname that stuck for some time.

"Last night we were brilliant," a brooding Chaz Phillips said. "Now all of a sudden we're stupid assholes."

Ross Johnson sat in his apartment across Grand Army Plaza from Kravis's office and tried to make sense of the morning's events. Gone was the brave front erected for Kravis and Gleacher. In its place was a face few of Johnson's friends had ever seen: The Merry Prankster with vertigo.

"As far as I'm concerned," Johnson told John Martin, "this is all over."

CHAPTER

9

Theodore J. Forstmann slipped into his white terry cloth bathrobe and padded down the gently curving staircase to breakfast. Bright shards of morning light streamed through the windows of his duplex apartment high above the East River. Far below, Monday-morning commuters poked their way through the traffic snarl on Franklin Delano Roosevelt Drive.

In the kitchen Forstmann could hear his maid, Noemi, readying his usual breakfast of coffee, bagels, and half a grapefruit. He looked forward to a leisurely breakfast. It gave him time to read the morning papers.

At forty-nine, Ted Forstmann maintained the solid build and broad shoulders of an ex-athlete. His tennis game was better than it had been as a teenager—so good, in fact, he sometimes volleyed with professionals. His Mediterranean features were highlighted by olive skin, a gift from his Italian mother, that crinkled around his eyes in dark folds. His hair was going gracefully gray.

Beneath the dining room's French rock-crystal chandelier, Forstmann was encircled by tall shelves of leather-bound volumes. His toes caressed the soft Turkish rug as he settled into a tiger-patterned velvet chair. Over his left shoulder gazed the asymmetrical eyes of a Picasso. Forstmann's address was among Manhattan's most exclusive: His neighbors included Rex Harrison and Greta Garbo.

Here, anyone would say, was a man who had everything. One of New

York's best-known bachelors, a Republican party fund-raiser of national repute, Ted Forstmann lived in a world of chauffeured Mercedes, corporate jets laden with fresh fruit and gold-plated bathroom fixtures, and plush, liquor- and television-stocked helicopters that whisked him over Manhattan traffic. Through hard work and a dash of luck, his ten-year-old firm, Forstmann Little & Co., a specialist in leveraged buyouts, now owned firms boasting $8 billion in revenues, throwing off enough cash for Forstmann to maintain second homes near Southampton and Aspen. His office held a smattering of Western art, a drop-dead view of Central Park, and a photo of Forstmann clasping hands with Ronald Reagan. In his spare time he bankrolled an Afghan rebel group.

His wealth, it seemed, had bought Ted Forstmann everything but serenity. For Forstmann was a deeply angry man, burning with a resentment that friends and business associates knew best to steer clear of. At the drop of a name—*that* name—he would launch into an impassioned, ten-minute denunciation. Friends had heard the speech a hundred times. On Wall Street, Forstmann knew, some were calling him a Cassandra; holier than thou, competitors sneered behind his back. Forstmann didn't care. He read Winston Churchill's biography and identified with the statesman's lonely campaign to warn the world about Nazi Germany.

That morning Forstmann was to be reminded yet again of his obsession. Unfolding *The Times*, his eyes were drawn immediately to the headline at the upper right corner of the business section. "KOHLBERG BID IS SEEN FOR RJR." He scanned the story intently.

Those fucking assholes, Forstmann said to himself. *They're doing it again.*

The Kohlberg Kravis bid for Nabisco was worthless, Forstmann could see. Ninety dollars a share was a meaningless price. It might as well have been pulled out of thin air. *Hell,* Forstmann told himself, *the little fart could bid twice that much for all his junk bonds are worth.* Once more, Henry Kravis was using a thimbleful of cash and a wheelbarrow load of debt to attempt the takeover of a great American company. Forstmann checked the article again. Of course there were no details of Kravis's financing—*there wouldn't be*—or much other relevant information.

What the Kravis bid did have, Forstmann saw, was an unusual number of conditions: financing and the approval of RJR Nabisco's board, among others. *Oh, it's a bid,* Forstmann reasoned, *that is, if Kravis doesn't get a cold, if the Dodgers win the World Series, if his wife makes fourteen more dresses. . . .*

He could feel the anger welling up inside him. It was a familiar feeling. Ted Forstmann had been angry for five years now.

Wall Street had been taken over by a cartel, Forstmann believed. A junk-bond cartel. A cartel whose guru was Michael Milken of Drexel Burnham Lambert and whose most powerful member was Henry Kravis of Kohlberg Kravis. A cartel that now had the upper hand in the looming battle for RJR Nabisco.

The cartel's product, the high-yield, or "junk," bond, was by 1988 being used to raise money—usually for takeovers—by virtually every major investor, brokerage house, and leveraged-buyout firm. Ted Forstmann fervently believed junk bonds had perverted not only the LBO industry, but Wall Street itself. Almost alone among major acquirers, Forstmann Little refused to use them.

To Forstmann the junk bond was a drug that enabled the puniest acquisitors to take on the titans of industry, and he held it responsible for twisting the buyout world's priorities until they were unrecognizable. No longer, Forstmann believed, did buyout firms buy companies to work side-by-side with management, grow their businesses, and sell out in five to seven years, as Forstmann Little did. All that mattered now was keeping up a steady flow of transactions that produced an even steadier flow of fees—management fees for the buyout firms, advisory fees for the investment banks, junk-bond fees for the bond specialists. As far as Ted Forstmann was concerned, the entire LBO industry had become the province of quick-buck artists.

The junk bond itself wasn't to blame, Forstmann held. In its normal form it could be a useful financing tool. What he objected to were the mutant strains that seemed to crop up with each new transaction: securities that paid interest only in other bonds (called pay-in-kind, or PIKs), stocks that were crammed down shareholders' throats (known artlessly as "cram down"), and bonds whose interest rates escalated until debt service choked a company to death. Forstmann derided these securities as "funny money," "play dough," and, his personal favorite, "wampum." In speeches to institutional investors, he took to waving a piece of Indian jewelry to make his point.

Sooner or later, Forstmann knew, the economy would turn down and all the junk-bond junkies would go belly-up when they couldn't make their mountainous debt payments. They were like those "no-money-down" real estate investors with no money in their pockets when their debts came due. When that happened, Forstmann feared, the use of junk-bond debt would be so widespread that the entire U.S. economy might be dragged into a depression.

Of all Drexel's junk-bond clients, by far the most nettlesome to Forstmann was his archrival Kohlberg Kravis. Kravis not only used more junk bonds than any other, but it did so in Forstmann Little's front yard, the LBO industry. The longer Ted Forstmann stewed over the junk-bond menace, the more the focal point of his anger became Henry Kravis.

Ironically, they had once been friends. Now Kravis was Ted Forstmann's obsession. Forstmann saw the contrast in terms that approached the apocalyptic. To him Kravis was nothing less than a Wall Street Faust who sold his soul for a pile of junk bonds and a new takeover every Monday morning. At the mention of his name, Forstmann would snort in derision, roll his eyes, and heave a deep sigh. Words such as *fraud* and *liar* spewed from his lips. In his worst moments Forstmann referred to Kravis as "that little fart" or "the little bastard."*

Those attempting to research Kohlberg Kravis and the LBO business inevitably received an earful of anti-Kravis vitriol from Forstmann. A snort, a sigh, a roll of the eyes, and Forstmann was off. His face would go white. His tone was incredulous, the voice of a man who couldn't get others to see the obvious.

"It's like Alice in Wonderland," Forstmann would say in exasperated tones. "The reason Kravis can pay these incredible sums is that *his money isn't real.* It's phony. It's funny money. It's wampum. These guys are getting away with murder, and nobody knows it."

The companies Kohlberg Kravis owned, Forstmann would rail, aren't half as healthy as they claim. The returns Kravis paid his investors, Forstmann insisted, weren't a fraction of Forstmann Little's. And every new Kohlberg Kravis deal furthered a machine that Forstmann feared was threatening the economy.

Many who knew both men considered that Forstmann's rage was fueled by envy. Certainly that was part of it. Occasionally, after attacking Kravis for twenty minutes, Forstmann would deny he held a personal

---

* Forstmann had been a sometime escort of Carolyne Roehm's before her marriage to Kravis. A friend of her first husband's, he had been an usher at Roehm's first wedding. Roehm insists she and Forstmann were "just friends."

grudge. "It's more than personal," he would say. Kravis wasn't his enemy: He was simply the most egregious symptom of a disease that infected all Wall Street and ruined the industry Ted Forstmann helped build. It was a distinction few outside Forstmann Little could appreciate.

Sometimes it seemed that Ted Forstmann had been born angry. His grandfather, an autocratic, 300-pound German immigrant, founded a textile company that made him one of the world's richest men before World War II. Ted's father, Julius, inherited the family company, Forstmann Woolens, and raised his children in splendor in a Greenwich, Connecticut, mansion complete with tennis courts and a private baseball field. For all its wealth, the Forstmann household was far from idyllic. Julius Forstmann was an abusive alcoholic. The Forstmanns owned guns and young Ted, the second of six children, grew up in physical fear of his father. Many nights the Forstmann home echoed with the sounds of screaming fights, sometimes sparked by Forstmann's mother challenging whether her husband had been drinking against doctor's orders. It took decades for Julius Forstmann's offspring to work out the problems of their turbulent youth: As adults, Ted and his brother Tony wouldn't speak for a period of ten years.

In his teens, Ted Forstmann channeled much of his anger into sports. By sixteen he was ranked among the East Coast's top junior amateur tennis players. His joy in the game, though, was slowly crushed under the pressure of his diminutive, ambitious mother. "A tennis mother" he called her. "She pushed me too hard." By seventeen, Forstmann's promising career was over. Tied 5–5 in the finals of a major junior tournament at Forest Hills, he disputed a key call. Overruled, Forstmann's competitive fire flickered. He lost the set 7–5; the next was a 6–0 washout. "I just couldn't take it anymore," he recalled, and would not walk onto another tennis court for seventeen years.

Hockey was Forstmann's other love. An able goalie, he had first stepped before the net at the age of eight because he couldn't skate. He liked the independence afforded by the big goal at his back, the feeling that his success turned on no one but himself. At Yale, Forstmann became a straight C student and an All-East hockey goalie. After graduation, Forstmann turned down an invitation to join the U.S. national team at the world championships, without ever knowing quite why. Instead, he wandered for a year through a succession of minor jobs, teaching gym at a reform school, working for a Washington law firm. He was, he would later say, a "mixed-up kid" attempting to come to grips with his childhood. Then his father died.

Julius Forstmann's fervent wish had been for his second son to attend law school, and Ted Forstmann enrolled at Columbia three months after his father's death. But the money from his father's estate began to dwindle soon after. Forstmann Woolens had failed and was sold. His father's estate, while paying for tuition and books, gave Forstmann a paltry $150 a month. To live as he was accustomed, the rich kid from Greenwich took to high-stakes bridge games. Always a good card player, Forstmann was soon living in a $350-a-month apartment in midtown Manhattan.

Upon graduation he joined a small Manhattan law firm, and for three years Forstmann endured the minutia of corporate legal work. Many days he sneaked out by four P.M. to a bridge game where, on a good night, he could rake in $1,500. Forstmann detested the long hours spent in law libraries doing research for senior partners, but he had too little self-confidence to leave—until the day the small firm reeled in a major Wall Street bond underwriting and presented the young lawyer with the ultimate menial job. "Forstmann," the senior lawyer had proudly intoned, "*you* will be our liaison with the printer." At that moment, Ted Forstmann made up his mind to flee the restraints of the legal world.

He landed with friends at a small Wall Street firm, where he learned the ins and outs of stock underwritings and other sundry financial tasks. Soon he chafed at that as well, impatient for more responsibility and outraged at what he considered his underpayment. Forstmann spent six months at another small investment firm, Fahaerty & Swartwood, where he toiled side-by-side with a hardworking young Oklahoman named Henry Kravis. Forstmann soon left, joining still-another obscure, now-defunct investment firm. For three years there, he dabbled in underwriting, investment banking, and merger work. In the end, though, it was the same old story: Forstmann found the constraints of office work under senior executives' watchful eyes suffocating. "The fact is, I was never a good employee," Forstmann said. "I never did what I was told, and I always screwed up the chain of command."

In 1974 Forstmann was thirty-five years old, out of work, and running out of money. He was too proud to ask his mother for more, and cringed at the idea of soliciting his older brother, Tony, who had founded a successful money-management firm, Forstmann Leff Associates. After selling his car, Forstmann had $20,000, which he figured would last a year.

To pay the rent he hustled at the bridge table and on the golf course and worked sporadically attempting to arrange deals among his Wall Street friends. Approaching middle age, Ted Forstmann was a Wall Street refugee, a minor-league playboy, and a sorry bet to ever make his mark in life.

One thing Forstmann had, though, was a seat on the board of directors at Graham Magnetics, a small Texas company he had helped take public in his last Wall Street job. Running out of options, he convinced the company's president not only to sell his firm, but to let Forstmann handle the auction. With no office, Forstmann conned his brother's secretary at Forstmann Leff into taking his phone calls. He promised her a mink coat for telling callers he was in a meeting and quickly relaying messages to his apartment.

It took eighteen months to sell Graham Magnetics—"I was very inept," Forstmann would recall—but when the deal closed he was $300,000 richer. He took an office at Forstmann Leff and tried putting together more deals. Forstmann would try anything, at one point even attempting to peddle spare furnace parts to the Shah of Iran's government.

Among Forstmann's golfing buddies at Long Island's exclusive Deepdale Country Club was Derald Ruttenberg, then president of an industrial company named Studebaker Worthington. Forstmann was forever attempting to arrange deals for Ruttenberg, so when Forstmann's younger brother Nick, then working at a start-up firm named Kohlberg Kravis Roberts & Co., said he wanted to arrange a meeting with the executive, Forstmann, smelling a commission, did so promptly.

It was a meeting that changed Ted Forstmann's life. In it, he and Ruttenberg listened to Henry Kravis and Jerry Kohlberg propose something they called a leveraged buyout. Forstmann was familiar with the concept, but had never attempted anything like it during his own Wall Street career. Ruttenberg heard them out politely, then turned to Forstmann after the pair left.

"Isn't that kind of what you were talking about?"

Forstmann wasn't quite sure what Ruttenberg meant. "Well," he said guardedly, "yeah, sort of."

"Well," Ruttenberg continued, "what do those guys have that you and I don't have?"

"Nothing."

"Okay. How would you go about doing this?"

"I would need some money first."

The conversation led to Ruttenberg's proposing to bankroll Forstmann in a new firm. The executive and a group of his friends would chip in, and Forstmann and his brother would try their hand at leveraged buyouts. Ruttenberg told Forstmann something the younger man would never forget. "I have a reputation, it's all I have, and I don't want to lose that reputation," he said, and Forstmann embraced that principle as a creed. Teaming up with a former investment banker named Brian Little, Forstmann Little & Co. opened its doors in 1978: three men, two salaries—Ted didn't take one for years—and one secretary.

Forstmann Little was among the first LBO firms to raise money directly from giant pension funds, a practice pioneered by Kohlberg Kravis. Like a real estate salesman, Ted Forstmann's pitch was simple: reputation, reputation, reputation. Crisscrossing the country on money-raising tours, Forstmann—bluntly honest, at times self-righteous and a bit naive—perfected a spiel that became his trademark. It was endearing to partners, irksome to allies, and outrageous to opponents. It began with The Reputation—"the best on Wall Street, ask anyone"—escalated into a discussion of Forstmann Little's financial strengths and old-fashioned ways, and, especially in later versions, climaxed with an all-out attack on the evils of junk bonds.

For all the bluster, Forstmann Little's returns were first-rate. In three to five years it sold the companies it bought for four to ten times the purchase price. By the mid-1980s only one firm's pioneering success overshadowed Forstmann Little's: Kohlberg Kravis Roberts.

The first signal that Forstmann Little's world was changing came in 1983, when the firm won a bidding battle to acquire Dr Pepper Co., the Dallas soft-drink franchiser. Forstmann's opponent, Castle & Cooke, was backed by Drexel Burnham's Milken, then an obscure California bond trader. Forstmann Little's management-supported cash bid was faced by a Castle & Cooke junk-bond bid, but won after a long, drawn-out fight.

Though Forstmann won that battle, he soon lost the war. His next scrape with a member of Milken's junk-bond coterie would not only be his most bitter defeat but also would lead to a fateful shift in Wall Street's power structure. In 1985 Revlon, the international cosmetics giant, came under attack from little-known Philadelphia investor Ron Perelman. Perelman's principal asset, a grocery store chain named Pantry Pride, was a fraction of Revlon's size, but he was armed with Drexel Burnham junk bonds. Its defenses crumbling, Revlon's management rushed to the open arms of Forstmann Little, saving their jobs, it seemed, and raising the specter of untold personal riches. But Perelman won out when a Delaware court, in a precedent-setting move, ruled that key components of Forstmann's merger agreement unfairly discriminated against Pantry Pride.

Revlon was the first hostile takeover of a major public company by a junk-bond-backed buyer, and it opened the gates for a string of similar battles, including a string of attacks by raiders such as Paul Bilzerian and Sir James Goldsmith. In an odd way, Ted Forstmann held himself responsible for the carnage junk-bond-financed raiders wrought on Corporate America.

The triumph of junk bonds was more than an affront to Forstmann's morals, of course. It was laying waste to his business as well. Because the use of junk bonds allowed corporate raiders to raise money cheaply and easily, it tended to drive up the prices of takeover targets. Forstmann found himself being outbid for companies where once he had no competition. In many cases, he refused to enter a takeover battle when junk-bond buyers had driven up prices beyond reason, and as a result, he found himself completing fewer and fewer deals. Finally, the unthinkable happened. In 1987, after raising a then-record $2.7 billion buyout fund from investors, Forstmann Little failed to propose a single new leveraged buyout. What should have been the height of Ted Forstmann's power on Wall Street was, instead, its nadir.

At first Forstmann directed his anger at Drexel Burnham. Once, a Milken lieutenant visited Forstmann Little and, in a meeting arranged by a young Forstmann associate named John Sprague, suggested the firm jump on the junk-bond bandwagon. Forstmann chatted politely with the Drexel banker, shook his hand farewell, and then called Sprague into his office. "John," he told the younger man, "you've got a long and profitable life ahead of you here. But don't ever bring another piece of slime like that in here again."

Forstmann's alarm grew as other Wall Street brokerages, initially cool to junk bonds, flocked to grab a piece of the burgeoning market. "Imagine ten debutantes sitting in a ballroom," Forstmann told a gathering of Securities and Exchange commissioners. "They're the heads of Merrill Lynch, Shearson Lehman, and all the other big brokerages. In walks a hooker. It's Milken. The debutantes wouldn't have anything to do with a woman who sells her body for a hundred dollars a night. But this hooker is different. She makes a million dollars a night. Pretty soon, what have you got? Eleven hookers."

Never before had Forstmann known such frustration. Only during periodic disruptions in the junk-bond market was Forstmann Little able to compete on an equal basis for large takeovers. The firm succeeded in grabbing its largest prey to date, a California defense contractor named Lear Siegler, after the market for junk bonds temporarily dried up following disclosure of the Ivan Boesky insider-trading scandal in November 1986. Again opposed by a Drexel Burnham client, Forstmann took his crusade right to Lear Siegler's board.

"Before I tell you who we are," Forstmann told the assembled directors, "let me tell who we are not. We are not, nor will we ever be, a client of Drexel Burnham Lambert." Forstmann detected an audible gasp from the direction of a Drexel banker present. "We have not, and we will not, issue crazy paper to put the companies we buy in jeopardy. We are real people with real money." Forstmann recalled that the directors then applauded.

Remarkably, Forstmann had gone head-to-head with Kravis in just one deal, but it was a deal that left an indelible mark on Forstmann's psyche. In the spring of 1988, six months before the RJR Nabisco fight, Kraft put its Duracell battery unit up for sale. Forstmann had ardently and successfully wooed Duracell's management. So close did he grow to Duracell's president, C. Robert Kidder, that the executive took the extraordinary step of pleading with Kraft's senior management not to sell Duracell to a junk-bond buyer such as Kohlberg Kravis. Kidder warned in a letter that such a move would ruin the company. With Forstmann's fingers tightly crossed, Kidder made the same plea to Kravis, who also coveted Duracell. Kravis not only rejected the executive's plea, he upped his offer for the company, swamping a bid by Forstmann Little and leaving Ted Forstmann to rage anew.

Through the summer and fall of 1988, Forstmann's ire rose unchecked. He looked on, aghast, as Kravis broke one of the LBO industry's most sacred tenets, secretly accumulating stock positions in Texaco and Kroger, much as a hostile raider would. The aggressive tactics forced Forstmann into an agonizing reappraisal of his own beliefs. *Maybe I'm wrong,* he wondered in quiet moments. *Maybe I'm the one who's missing the dawn of a new financial age.* His younger partners suggested he rethink his opposition to junk bonds. His girlfriend urged him to "forget Kravis," quit worrying, and enjoy his riches. Forstmann tried to relax, but found his long-held convictions only grew stronger.

Just weeks before the RJR deal broke, Forstmann finally vented his feelings publicly, taking friends' advice and authoring an anti-junk-bond diatribe for *The Wall Street Journal*'s editorial page. The article was to appear Tuesday, October 25.

"Today's financial age has become a period of unbridled excess with accepted risk soaring out of proportion to possible reward," Forstmann wrote. "Every week, with ever-increasing levels of irresponsibility, many billions of dollars in American assets are being saddled with debt that has virtually no chance of being repaid. Most of this is happening for the short-term benefit of Wall Street's investment bankers, lawyers, lever-aged-buyout firms and junk-bond dealers at the long-term expense of Main Street's employees, communities, companies and investors."

LBO specialists would recognize key passages of Forstmann's article— criticism of investments in such cyclical industries as oil and forestry, for example—as thinly veiled attacks on Henry Kravis. "Watching these deals get done," Forstmann concluded, "is like watching a herd of drunk drivers take to the highway on New Year's Eve. You cannot tell who will hit whom, but you know it is dangerous."

Monday morning, as he looked out over the East River, Ted Forstmann knew what he had to do. Suddenly the Nabisco deal wasn't just a big deal. It wasn't just another Henry Kravis deal-of-the-week. It had become *the* deal. It would, he realized, be the culmination of his five-year crusade to show the world the truth about junk bonds and Kohlberg Kravis Roberts. It would be Ted Forstmann in the white hat against Henry Kravis in the black. This, Forstmann vowed, would be the deal in which Kravis would be revealed as the fraud he was.

But first he had to get his foot in the door. The articles laid out on Forstmann's antique dining table held few details of Ross Johnson's buy-out proposal. But what he saw he liked. Reading between the lines, Forstmann guessed Johnson's group had been forced into premature disclosure of its deliberations. If so, that meant they could be days, or even weeks, from putting together a formal offer and lining up the banks necessary to finance it. That gave Forstmann Little some time.

The presence of Shearson was also encouraging. Although he knew almost no one at the firm, he realized that Tom Hill's troops had no great expertise in leveraged buyouts. On top of that, they would probably need a boatload of money to complete any deal. Forstmann Little's $9 billion of buying power could be invaluable.

Ross Johnson was another plus. Forstmann knew Johnson and his young wife, Laurie, and liked them both. He had first run into Johnson in the early 1980s when Forstmann Little considered buying the Fleischmann's division of Standard Brands. Their talks at the time left Forstmann with the impression that Johnson was sharp, although a bit of a salesman. Later Forstmann recommended Johnson for membership at Deepdale, where Forstmann sat on the board of governors. (Ironically, it was the same club where Don Kelly would later woo Johnson into meeting with Kravis.)

Several years later, Forstmann had called Johnson seeking an investment in a Forstmann Little buyout fund. Johnson was eager to help and was effusive in his praise. "My God, what an opportunity!" Forstmann recalled Johnson shouting into the phone. "How phenomenal. We'd love to!" Forstmann hung up thinking RJR's president was an okay guy, even if he came off a bit like a game-show host.

As he pored over the papers that morning, the makings of a plan formed in Ted Forstmann's mind. He recalled a conversation he had had four days earlier with his most trusted investment banker, Geoff Boisi of Goldman Sachs & Co. Boisi, one of Wall Street's top deal makers, was attempting to arrange a consortium of Goldman's blue-chip clients to mount a third-party bid for RJR Nabisco.

"Do you have a problem with owning a tobacco business?" Boisi had asked.

"Yeah, why?" Forstmann had replied.

"What's the problem?"

Forstmann's reply had been off-the-cuff. "I don't want to be selling cancer."

When Boisi had persisted, Forstmann had said he'd think about it. Afterward Forstmann had touched base with his partners and found that they, too, harbored a vague distaste for the tobacco business. His brother Nick, like Forstmann a reformed smoker, was chortling as he added up the money Shearson and others would make from Johnson's deal. He calculated that the fees alone would top the value of a $500 million buyout Forstmann Little was considering. "It's like throwing a hundred pounds of bloody meat into a shark pool," he mused.

Still, the prospect of tackling history's biggest buyout was an undeniable attraction. To cover himself, Forstmann had phoned his longtime lawyer Stephen Fraidin at the lower Manhattan firm of Fried, Frank, Harris, Shriver & Jacobson. "Don't do anything with anybody else before you talk to me," Forstmann had said. He had left the matter unsettled when he left the office on Friday.

After breakfast, Forstmann slipped into his black, chauffeur-driven Mercedes and headed to his office in the General Motors building across from the Plaza Hotel, just a stone's throw from the Kohlberg Kravis headquarters at Nine West Fifty-seventh Street.

"Get me Jim Robinson," he told his secretary.

"Look, Jim," Forstmann said, when Robinson called back later that morning, "I don't know what's going on. But you know my reputation. . . ." He was off on the Forstmann Little pitch.

Robinson interrupted before he got too far. "Teddy, I know all that," he said. "I'll have somebody call you."

Forstmann was satisfied. It was a first step. The showdown was fast approaching; he could feel it. It was time to make a stand.

But there was something else, some other emotion Forstmann wasn't proud of and whose existence he wouldn't admit to himself until months later. Down deep, Ted Forstmann knew he wanted to hurt Henry Kravis.

Fuck them. This is not going to be the next KKR deal, Forstmann vowed to himself. *I know Ross Johnson. I know Jim Robinson. Henry Kravis will not run off with this deal.*

CHAPTER

10

Pandemonium reigned at Shearson Monday morning. Amid the Audubon prints, green plants, and fine Oriental rugs of its nineteenth-floor executive offices, the stunned members of the management group gathered. Rather than face the obvious folly of their earlier preparation, Cohen, Hill, and the others directed their anger toward Kravis. Everyone had a theory why Kravis had jumped the gun.

Johnson stalked in and took a seat at the long table in Shearson's boardroom. Dumbstruck, he demanded an explanation for Kravis's ambush attack. Wasn't Cohen supposed to meet with him? What on earth could have propelled Kravis into this course of action?

"Something's gone haywire here, Peter," Johnson said, citing Cohen's initial meeting with Kravis. "Somebody must have pissed off somebody. You don't get from a meeting like that, franchise or no franchise, to a meeting scheduled on Monday unless somebody put their finger up somebody's ass. I mean, there must have been something that happened at that meeting on Friday to make him do this."

This was a different Ross Johnson than many at Shearson had seen. The shock of Kravis's bid was evident on his face and in his voice. It was the first time Steve Goldstone had seen cracks in his client's sunny facade. Hill thought Johnson "looked like he'd been hit by a load of bricks."

"I thought everything was okay," Johnson repeated. "I thought you were going to meet with the guy. What the hell happened?"

Cohen, after talking with Hill and Jack Nusbaum, thought he knew the answer: It was Bruce Wasserstein and the other Wall Street advisers. They must have pushed Kravis into a premature bid with harem-scarem tales about Shearson locking up the banks.

Each of Kravis's advisers, Cohen explained to the group—Drexel, Morgan Stanley, and Wasserstein Perella—had its own reasons to want Shearson's big deal crushed. The junk-bond offering to follow RJR's buyout would no doubt be history's largest, and could instantly turn Shearson into the greatest challenger yet to Drexel's hammerlock on the junk-bond market.

No doubt Morgan Stanley similarly regarded Shearson's bid as a challenge to its own growing power in the LBO market. Cohen was willing to bet that Steve Waters, bitter about his forced departure from Shearson, was gunning to embarrass his old partner Tom Hill. And Hill's emergence as a major deal maker was a direct threat to Wasserstein's reputation. "The fact of life here," Cohen went on, "is that everybody who advised Henry probably told him to 'go for it.' It's in everybody's interest that we fail. . . . Those piranhas were probably nipping at his fingers and toes all weekend."

Johnson didn't particularly care about the intricacies of Shearson's Wall Street rivalries. And as Cohen and Hill began plotting a counterattack, he was too shaken to listen. "Well," Johnson said. "I guess this is over. This is the end. I mean, who can compete with that kind of offer?"

Steve Goldstone could tell it was time to explain some things to his client. Johnson's interests weren't necessarily the same as Shearson's. If Johnson played his cards right, he might yet come out of this with a buyout he could live with. He had a number of options, including joining forces with Kravis, a fact Goldstone was sure Cohen was well aware of. There was another reason to spirit Johnson out of Shearson's offices: He and Cohen appeared headed for a major blowup. Goldstone sidled up to Johnson and took him by the arm.

"Ross, look, let's go back to Davis Polk," the lawyer said. "There are things we need to talk about."

———

There was a surreal, Alice-in-Wonderland quality about the procession Goldstone led for three blocks to Davis Polk's offices at Chase Manhattan Plaza.

For Johnson, the whole thing had become a bad dream. He couldn't shake the feeling they had left the real world behind in Atlanta. They had stepped through the looking glass to a place where reality was suspended, where the old numbers, the old rules, the old financial reasoning, simply didn't apply. Money was paper, and paper was money, and people got paid $25 million for lying to you.

At Davis Polk, Goldstone parked Johnson, John Martin, and Harold Henderson in a thirty-eighth-floor conference room and walked up to his office to retrieve something. He immediately drew a crowd of curious colleagues. *My God, what happened?* they clamored. *Steve, are you okay? What'll you do now?*

Goldstone stared out his office window north toward the art-deco spire of the Chrysler Building. "The outlook is not good," he said slowly. "Everything has changed. . . . Either we'll reach an agreement with Henry, or . . ." Or what, he didn't know. Kravis had caught them totally off guard. To fight him would mean throwing out every financial and operating assumption of the $75 bid and starting over from scratch. He wasn't at all sure Johnson was willing to do that.

When Goldstone returned he found Johnson pacing up and down. The group with him looked shell-shocked. The enormity of what had befallen them was sinking in. The prospect of instant riches had vanished, gone in the four-bell ring of the Dow Jones ticker announcing Kravis's arrival on the scene.

"At this point, this is over," Johnson was saying. "I mean, if this is right, this is ridiculous. If they've got the money, it's all over." Again and again he wondered what Cohen could have done to set Kravis off.

Goldstone tried to swivel Johnson's focus from the past to the future. Kravis's ambush drastically raised the stakes: If they were going to fight, they now would have to top $90 a share. Running a post-LBO company at $90 a share, Goldstone said, would be radically different than running one bought at $75. The added debt would require wholesale cuts of the kind Johnson dreaded. The planes, the Atlanta headquarters, even Premier, would have to be reassessed.

"Ross," Goldstone said, "you've got to decide whether you are willing to operate this company above ninety. If you're willing to do that, then the next decision is Shearson's. The decisions are now Shearson's to make. It's not your money."

First, Johnson said, he wanted to know a lot more about Henry Kravis's bid. What did Kravis really want? Could they get rid of him somehow? How on earth could Kravis get $90 of value, when Shearson only got $75? No, Johnson said, he wasn't going to decide anything until he heard more from Kravis. Cohen would talk to him and find out what had happened. Then, and only then, would they decide their next move.

Goldstone emerged from the conference room at one point to find Tom Hill loitering outside. The lawyer smiled to himself. It was obvious Hill had come over to keep tabs on Johnson and make sure he didn't do anything drastic.

Like talk with Henry Kravis.

The Kravis camp emerged Monday afternoon to assess the damage from its morning announcement.

In the days to come Dick Beattie would be Kravis's most effective source of intelligence. Over the years the soft-spoken lawyer had built a loyal circle of Wall Street friends. His work with Shearson gave him especially good contacts among Cohen's troops.

The best was Bob Millard, Shearson's head of risk arbitrage trading. The two were old friends, and Millard was half-expecting Beattie's call that afternoon. It was the first of many conversations the pair would have in coming weeks, and they would prove to be invaluable to Kravis. Millard, also a close friend of Cohen's, would function as an unofficial conduit for the Shearson chief, passing on Cohen's thoughts and threats in a cordial atmosphere with no risk of confrontation. Beattie, while arguing Kravis's ideas, usually got a good sense of the Shearson group's strategy. For security reasons, the lawyer never told Kravis of Millard's identity.

That day the two spoke in the tones people sometimes use when attempting to reconcile mutual friends. "Peter says he's got a winner because he's got Ross Johnson," Millard said.

"You know that's not true," Beattie retorted. "Bob, you have to explain to Peter that the best deal will win on this. It's not who has Ross Johnson. Can't he see Henry is ready to do this deal without Johnson?"

Millard had to agree. He had told Cohen the same thing the previous Thursday. But so far Cohen hadn't listened. Both Beattie and Millard realized the obvious solution was for Kravis and Cohen to get together and divvy up Johnson's company. A bidding battle could cost the winner billions of dollars and generate ugly publicity. But whether the egos involved would permit a joint effort was another question.

Bob Millard suggested Beattie give Peter Cohen a call.

Kravis's bid was Cohen's nightmare come true. But unlike Ross Johnson, Cohen wasn't giving any thought to surrender. It simply wasn't in his nature.

As information on Kravis's bid trickled in that day, Cohen and Hill realized it wasn't as formidable as they first had feared. For one thing, the bid wasn't all cash. Kravis had put up just $79 a share in cash, with the remainder coming from securities Kravis valued at $11 a share. Cohen and Hill seized on the structure as a rallying cry. Look, they said, Kravis only topped our cash by $4 a share. Shearson, Cohen figured, could counter by adding "paper," too. Johnson's opposition to securities would have to be overcome, of course, but that shouldn't be a problem if it presented their only recourse.

Amid the confusion, one other fact was becoming clear. Shearson couldn't fight Kravis alone. A bid north of $90 would require an equity investment—a downpayment—in the neighborhood of $2.5 billion. Even with money from American Express, Cohen knew it wouldn't be practical for Shearson to shoulder so large an investment itself.

That afternoon Cohen took a call from one of his closest friends, Thomas Strauss, president of Salomon Brothers. Strauss was the trading house's number two executive behind John Gutfreund; his office overlooked its trading floor. The Strausses and Cohens often vacationed together, once sharing an African safari, and were frequent guests at each other's homes. Strauss wondered whether there might be a role for Salomon in Shearson's deal. Similar calls poured into Cohen's office all day, but Strauss's was among the few he accepted. They agreed to meet the next day for lunch.

The universe of possible partners, Hill advised Cohen, was small and shrinking fast. Already Kravis had snapped up the obvious ones: Merrill Lynch, Drexel, and Morgan. "We have a choice: Sally or First Boston," Hill said. "Sally has more capital, but it's not a factor in the LBO market. In fact, they're a disaster in the LBO market. They don't have much depth in their merger practice, either." First Boston had better junk-bond operations and more merger depth, Hill said, even with the recent departures of Wasserstein and Perella. Hill preferred First Boston, but knew it was a wasted exercise. Friendships counted for a lot on Wall Street, and Cohen wasn't likely to pass up the chance to work with his buddy Tom Strauss.

———

Dick Beattie reached Peter Cohen around four o'clock that afternoon.

The lawyer was in an awkward situation. His firm, Simpson Thacher & Bartlett, had represented Lehman for forty years and was, along with Jack Nusbaum's firm, one of Shearson's two primary law firms. Although Nusbaum was his closest confidant, Cohen also considered Beattie a valued adviser. Cohen had been incensed when he heard Beattie was working with Kravis in the fight for RJR Nabisco and thought that Beattie at least owed him the courtesy to ask approval.

When Cohen came on the line, Beattie tiptoed around the issue, formally alerting the Shearson chief he was representing Kravis but stopping short of seeking Cohen's approval. "Peter, I'm calling because we'd like to try and keep the channel of communications open, if we can," Beattie said. "This tender offer doesn't mean we can't still work together."

"Why, if Henry Kravis wants to talk, did he launch the tender offer? He didn't have to do that. Why didn't he call? I was going to call him. This is ridiculous."

Beattie tried to calm Cohen. "Peter, for any number of strategic reasons, it appeared best to do it that way. But we should still talk. This is no reason to close off that option. You ought to talk to Henry."

Maybe, Cohen said. Before agreeing, he ran the idea past Johnson, who busied himself at Nine West that afternoon returning phone calls, answering mail, and reviewing new computer runs.

"Lookit, Peter," Johnson said, "this isn't a cockfight here. This is serious, and Henry is a serious guy. You guys have got to get together, and you've got to test how serious he is."

A meeting between Cohen and Kravis was set for Tuesday morning.

———

Jim Robinson's alarm grew as he read a copy of Johnson's management agreement for the first time Monday afternoon. It was worse than he had feared: the veto, the free ride, the incredible total all bothered him. But what worried the chairman of American Express most was what Wall

Streeters called the "cosmetics" of the deal: From a public point of view—and Robinson had no doubt the document would ultimately be disclosed—the agreement simply looked awful. In a reporter's hands it would be turned into a document of greed incarnate. To Robinson the prospect of seven men's sharing up to $2 billion was a public relations disaster waiting to happen.

Changes would have to be made, he could see, and not just for the sake of cosmetics. The pact was simply too rich; much of the money promised to Johnson would now have to be channeled into a bid high enough to beat Kravis. As his closest friend on Wall Street, Jim Robinson was the natural choice to carry the difficult message to Johnson.

On Monday night Robinson sat down in Johnson's office and tried to break the news as gently as possible. "Rawss," he said in his Atlanta lilt, "we've got to reappraise things in a way that is more appropriate, given what's going on."

What do you mean? Johnson asked, bridling a little. He remembered Steve Goldstone's cautionary words about the management agreement: "These guys are going to try and screw you down and down and down. . . ." Johnson trusted Jim Robinson, to a point.

"I hope you're not here as the advocate of Peter Cohen," Johnson said, "because they're not going to take us down and just give it all back to Shearson."

"No, Rawss, this is how I feel. I'm here as a friend."

"Totally different, totally different," Johnson said. "What do you want to do?"

"How many people are going to share in the management agreement?" Robinson asked.

"It could be eight, it could be twenty," Johnson said. He said he hadn't given the matter much thought.

"I thought maybe you might want to better define what it is," Robinson suggested.

"I don't give a goddamn," Johnson said. "I've always thought that a lot of employees would share it. I want to get it to as broad a group as possible."

Robinson explained that it might be a good idea to set that idea in motion. Maybe the best thing to do would be to get Davis Polk and Champ Mitchell's law firm working on an employee stock ownership plan.

Johnson agreed. Later he would say that it had been his intention all along.

Whether or not employees would actually share in Johnson's riches, of course, was beside the point. What mattered here was cosmetics. Jim Robinson couldn't throw out the management agreement. But he could make damn sure that, once revealed to directors and a skeptical public, it would be easier to swallow.

He hoped.

――――――

"OFFERS FOR RJR PIT KKR AND SHEARSON IN A BATTLE FOR TURF," read the front-page headline in *The Wall Street Journal* on Tuesday morning.

Kravis read the article with disgust. Both major papers, the *Journal* and *The New York Times*, reported his Friday meeting with Cohen in detail. Both, Kravis thought, made him out to be the heavy, the overlord of LBOs attempting to smite an upstart competitor. He was especially irked at quotes attributed to him about protecting his *franchise*, a word Kravis would later deny having uttered. Whatever the truth, it was apparent to Kravis that Shearson was using the press to strike at his Achilles' heel, his public image.

Kravis had to laugh, though, when he read Cohen's remarks to the *Journal.* Playing the wounded innocent, Cohen complained that Kravis was muscling in on his deal after promising to meet with Shearson. "We ski together and socialize together," Cohen said of Kravis, "and I thought there was a higher level of conduct called for here."

Kravis couldn't believe it. He didn't consider Cohen his friend. Why, he told friends, he hardly knew the man. They had skied together once— at "some Shearson ski boondoggle" in Vail—and hardly "socialized" outside occasionally bumping into each other at Wall Street functions. *The nerve of the guy. . . .*

――――――

The atmosphere at Tuesday morning's breakfast between Cohen and Kravis was no worse than that inside any commercial meat locker.

Cohen arrived first and surveyed the ground. They had chosen a neutral venue, the dining room at the Plaza Hotel. Cohen asked the maître d' for an isolated table, one where he and Kravis could talk discreetly, and was led into an uncrowded corner of the dining area. Kravis walked in minutes later and took a seat across from Cohen. After ordering coffee, the two men got straight to business.

"Henry, I said I was going to call you, and I would have called you," Cohen said. "I believe I'm a person who keeps his word. Now you've escalated this thing."

If Cohen was combative, he was also a realist. A drawn-out battle with Kravis was one Shearson could well lose. He pitched a compromise. "We're open-minded about this, Henry. We never intended to keep all the equity in the transaction to ourselves. It's simply too big. We're looking for a sensible transaction. If we can do a sensible transaction that will help everyone's objectives, we ought to try. Now, why don't we try and do something together?"

"Like what?" Kravis asked.

"A split. Fifty-fifty."

"That's not going to happen," Kravis said. Kohlberg Kravis never did fifty-fifty deals. "That's too much."

"I don't think it should be at anything other than fifty-fifty," Cohen said.

"No, no." He wouldn't discuss it further.

Kravis brought up the management agreement. He had been thinking about what Jeff Beck said a month before. *They want control of the board.* If Johnson didn't want the Kohlberg Kravis kind of buyout, what kind did he want?

"It's your normal deal," Cohen said. Nothing special.

"What's that mean?" Kravis asked. "Is that five, ten, fifteen, thirty percent, what?"

"Yeah, in that range. . . ."

Cohen pointedly failed to mention Johnson's veto power or the $2 billion management agreement he had demanded and received. "If we do something," Cohen said, "we'll obviously make that all available to you."

As they talked, Kravis attempted to size up Cohen. The man was out of his element, he decided. Kravis knew Cohen had attempted no more than one or two buyouts in his career; Eric Gleacher was calling him "Peter Cohen, Boy Investment Banker." Yet Cohen seemed to think he was dealing from strength. *He's feeling pretty good,* Kravis thought. *He thinks he has all the cards because he has management. He thinks the presence of Ross Johnson will stop us.*

Well, Boy Investment Banker, Kravis told himself, you're in for one hell of a surprise. "What Cohen didn't know," Kravis recalled months later, "was that we were charging right through the rice paddies, not stopping for anything and taking no prisoners."

———

While Cohen and Kravis glared over their coffee cups, Johnson decided to take matters into his own hands. He simply had to know if the Kravis bid was real and, if so, what it meant for his management group. Johnson was nothing if not a quick read: He could tell Cohen was less than enthusiastic about sharing the deal of his life with Kravis. Both times Cohen and Kravis had spoken they had gotten into spit fights. Maybe it made sense to try some kind of partnership with Kravis. The only way to find out for sure, he reasoned, was to meet with Kravis himself.

Scanning his phone messages, Johnson saw Steve Waters's name. Perhaps the former Shearson investment banker, now working for Kravis, would be a good conduit. Minutes later, Waters picked up the phone in his office at Morgan Stanley and was surprised to hear Johnson's laughter. "I thought I'd get through to you," Johnson said, chuckling.

"Ross," Waters bantered, "you know I always talk to you."

Johnson mentioned he might have an interest in speaking with Kravis. "You really should see Henry," Waters said. "He's not such a bad guy. It clearly makes sense for you guys to be talking to each other."

Johnson agreed. Next he tracked down Jim Robinson at American Express. He wanted to touch base before striking out on his own. "Listen, Jim, I think I'm going to meet with Henry, just to hear what he has to say. What do you think?"

Robinson listened as Johnson made his case.

"I just think the more people talking the better. Maybe it's right, maybe it's wrong, but I'd like to hear their position myself. Jim, you're a highroad guy, and so am I. I think there's a highroad here." He left the obvious unspoken: Cohen's "low-road" arguments with Kravis were getting them nowhere. "Jimmy," he concluded, "I want to bring in the varsity team, not the JV."

When Robinson agreed, Johnson got back to Steve Waters. A meeting with Kravis was set for four o'clock that afternoon.

———

After his breakfast with Cohen, Kravis crossed the street and caucused with Beattie and Roberts, who had flown in the night before, in his forty-second-floor office overlooking Central Park. Peter Cohen, they agreed, was the only thing standing in the way of their owning RJR Nabisco. There was no earthly reason for Shearson to be in this deal. Ross Johnson had the management expertise. Kohlberg Kravis had the buyout expertise. Cohen had an appetite for big fees, an eye on making it big in LBOs, and a bad attitude.

"They don't bring much to the table," Roberts said.

"No, they don't," Kravis agreed.

There had to be a way to get rid of Shearson. The obvious solution was to offer it some lesser role in the deal. Kravis favored some kind of advisory fee and maybe a chance to buy a piece of the action. But he wasn't going to give up a large share of the stock, certainly nothing approaching fifty-fifty control. Maybe 10 percent, he suggested.

Beattie wasn't so sure. Ten percent sounded pretty puny. After all, Shearson had put this deal together. The lawyer didn't say much, but he felt certain that Cohen would view the offer as an insult. Equally clear, he could tell, was the fact that Henry Kravis didn't give a damn.

––––––

While Cohen lunched with Tom Strauss and John Gutfreund of Salomon Brothers and attended a Shearson board meeting, Johnson met with a gaggle of gray-suited commercial bankers at Nine West to raise funds for the Nabisco deal. With their niggling questions about cost cuts, the bankers were a nuisance, and Johnson tried to push them off on Jim Stern of Shearson. In turn the bankers, led by Bob O'Brien of Bankers Trust, felt Johnson didn't understand the importance of their role. For $13 billion, they thought he ought to sit still for their questions.

But Johnson had more important things on his mind, most notably his meeting with Kravis. A few minutes before four o'clock Johnson stepped into the elevator alone for the ride six floors down to Kohlberg Kravis. As the elevator doors closed behind him, he realized he had forgotten which floor Kravis was on. He punched forty-four and got off there, only to realize his mistake. He tried forty-two and wandered around a few minutes before finding the firm in a back corner.

Inside, he was ushered into Kravis's corner office and met George Roberts for the first time. The atmosphere was cordial: Johnson had no ax to grind, and Kravis badly wanted Johnson's management expertise. Taking long drags on a Premier, Johnson soon was outlining how he would run a post-LBO RJR Nabisco. The conversation was general: The three men wanted to feel one another out. When Kravis and Roberts talked about their operating philosophies, Johnson was impressed. They seemed to know much more about financial structures and money raising than Cohen's people. Johnson replied with observations about his company, which the cousins, thirsty for information about their prey, listened to intently.

Johnson fished for more, openly curious about the possibilities of working with Kohlberg Kravis. "Now, Henry," Johnson said, "if you guys get this, you're not going to get into chickenshit stuff about planes and golf courses, are you?"

"That's not important to us," Kravis said. "If you take an extra plane ride, that's up to you." Talk to Don Kelly, Kravis said. "Well, that's pretty good," Johnson said, nodding.

Roberts, however, wasn't as flippant. A man sometimes described as a "cold fish," George Roberts was beginning to dislike Johnson's breezy, putting-green manners. "Well, we don't want you to live a spartan life," he said. "But we like to have things justified. We don't mind people using private airplanes to get places, if there's no ordinary way. It is important that a CEO set the tone in any deal we do. Check with Peter Magowan." Magowan was chief of the KKR controlled Safeway Stores chain and a friend of Johnson's.

"Well, I did," Johnson said. "I guess the deal we're looking for is a bit unusual." Johnson explained that he was looking for a structure in which he would retain significant control of his company.

No, Roberts said, shaking his head, Kohlberg Kravis didn't operate that way. "We're not going to do any deal where management controls it," Roberts stated. "We'll work with you. But we have no interest in losing control."

Why is that, Johnson wondered.

"We've got the money," Roberts said, "we've got the investors, that's why we have to control the deal." From the look in Johnson's eyes, Roberts could tell it wasn't the message he wanted to hear.

"Well, that's interesting," Johnson said. "But frankly, I've got more freedom doing what I do right now."

The subject of cost cutting, one of the keys to a successful LBO, was raised. To Roberts's surprise, Johnson said he didn't care much for wielding a budgetary ax. Anyway, he explained, cutting costs was an overrated procedure. "Any Neanderthal can go in there and whack away and cut costs," he said. "Show me a guy that can spend money."

He went on. "I've run as spartan an operation as anyone. But we're bringing in a first-class management team here. We're not profligate. I don't want a bunch of nerds telling me whether to take a limo or not. That's all chickenshit. What you need to worry about is the price of tobacco or the price of assets I'm selling. I want to deal with the big issues."

What was important were things like Premier. Johnson began talking about the smokeless cigarette, its strengths and weaknesses, the status of its test marketing. The secret, he told them, was that it warmed rather than burned the tobacco. Suddenly Johnson flicked his Premier onto Kravis's antique Oriental rug.

George Roberts, horrified, looked down at the smoking tube at Johnson's feet. "See, it doesn't burn anything," Johnson said, retrieving it with a grin. He thought Roberts was about to jump out the window.

They had been talking about an hour when Johnson trotted out to take a call. He returned a minute later, apologizing. "That was Jimmy and Peter. I'm late to meet with your buddy Ted Forstmann." Johnson smiled. It didn't hurt for these two to know he had options. "Yeah, we know Teddy," Kravis said, smiling in return. *So Forstmann thinks he's going to get in this deal.*

The information struck Roberts cold. But then everything about Ross Johnson struck Roberts cold. The man didn't seem to be a serious businessman. Now he was going to meet with Ted Forstmann? George Roberts wasn't a man who liked being toyed with.

As he left, Johnson brought up the prospect of further talks with Shearson. "I hope you can work things out," he said. "Just be fair. Make a fair deal. No one party should be looking to get some great edge over the other party. Work things out, you know. So we can get on with things."

When Johnson walked out a few minutes past six, Kravis and Roberts agreed it was time to make their move.

Jim Robinson silently cursed cellular phones.

After Robinson had emerged from a meeting of the New York City

Partnership, a group of top corporate executives working to improve conditions in Gotham, he was surprised to find inside his limousine a phone message from Henry Kravis.

As his car pulled away from the curb, the only thing worse than the late afternoon traffic was the reception on Robinson's portable phone. When Kravis came on the line, the transmission came in fits and starts. But his message was crystal clear.

I want to make you an offer, Kravis said.

The proposal: Kohlberg Kravis would acquire RJR Nabisco. In return, Shearson would receive a one-time fee of $125 million from Kohlberg Kravis and an option to buy a 10 percent stake in the company. Kravis said he'd like an answer by midnight.

Jim Robinson wasn't the type of man to get excited at the sight of another man's wallet. "Henry, that sounds a little thin," Robinson said, but promised to get back to him.

Minutes later, Cohen emerged from the Shearson board meeting to hear the same offer. Cohen said little, but from the tone of his voice Kravis knew he wasn't being greeted with open arms.

Where was Ross Johnson?

Ted Forstmann had been waiting for nearly two hours, and there was still no sign of the man.

After a full day of deliberations, Forstmann was ready to begin his crusade against Kravis and the junk-bond scourge. Forstmann Little's computers had chewed through every available piece of public information on RJR Nabisco. Teams of analysts from Goldman Sachs had pored over the resulting printouts, and their conclusions only buttressed what Forstmann already knew: Even at $90 a share, RJR Nabisco was a good deal.

Forstmann Little's strategy was clear, at least its first step. Kravis's rash tender offer opened the door for the firm to step in and "rescue" RJR Nabisco. Kravis was already taking a beating in the press for his "franchise" speech, and Forstmann's advisers were determined to take advantage of it. "We've got to cloak ourselves in apple pie and motherhood," Geoff Boisi told Forstmann, a plan to which he agreed wholeheartedly.

Now all they needed was Ross Johnson.

Accompanied by Tom Hill, Johnson finally arrived at Forstmann Little at half-past six. After shaking hands, Forstmann noticed a third man behind them.

Forstmann took Hill aside.

"Who is this fucking guy?" he whispered, motioning to the third man. Hill looked sheepish. "Well, without going into great detail, he travels with Johnson. He has nothing to do with this."

A bodyguard, Forstmann thought. Bodyguards were not Forstmann Little's style. It was not a good sign.

Forstmann led Hill and Johnson into a conference room whose informal furnishings gave it the atmosphere of a family room rather than a boardroom. Twelve black leather chairs ringed a wooden table. A television sat in one corner. The walls were lined with the Depression-era posters Forstmann favored.

Johnson, a broad smile pasted across his face, took a seat at the head of the table.

"I've just come from the competition," he began.

Ted Forstmann flinched. "What?"

"I've just come from talking with Kravis."

Forstmann couldn't hide his irritation. "What are you doing that for?"

Tom Hill intervened. "It's something that we had to do, Ted," he assured Forstmann. "It's nothing, really. I'd attach no importance to it." Johnson was merely covering all his bases, Hill suggested.

The mention of Kravis's name set Forstmann off on The Spiel. For nearly half an hour he pontificated on the evils of junk bonds, the sins of Henry Kravis, and the way Forstmann Little could save Wall Street. He made a special point to mention his article in *The Wall Street Journal* that morning. Johnson listened, secretly amused.

This guy's cock is really stiff over this Wall Street Journal *article,* he mused. Johnson thought he understood Forstmann's world view. *Henry Kravis is a devil. Ted Forstmann is an angel. His clients are perfect. He's not interested in fees. This guy is doing the Lord's work for people who want to go private. . . .*

Oh, I see.

When Forstmann finished, Nick Forstmann and a partner, Steve Klinsky, began asking Johnson questions about his company. What was the outlook for tobacco? Which businesses could be sold? In his rambling replies, Johnson seemed almost hyperactive. Clearly the pressure of the deal was wearing on him, Forstmann thought.

Tom Hill left the room to take a call. It was Cohen, relaying news of Kravis's $125 million offer. "That doesn't sound like my idea of a partnership," Hill said.

"Mine either," Cohen agreed.

Yet Hill could see it was attractive. A fee that size was nearly half of Shearson's total merger-advisory revenues for the entire 1987 year. Shearson's fourth-quarter earnings were expected to be down, and Hill knew Cohen was under enormous pressure to save them. A one-shot injection of $125 million would be tempting.

"Needless to say," Hill said, "if we take it, it would be the end of our merchant-banking business. It would be an admission that there's a price where we will stand down. Even if we dressed it up, it would be clear. There's no way we can take it."

"That was them again," Hill announced when he returned to the conference room. "We have received the most insulting offer."

Forstmann was confused. It was clear Hill meant Kravis. Was Hill negotiating with Kravis on *his* phone? What was going on here? Lost in his thoughts, Forstmann couldn't have grasped the irony of the poster over his right shoulder: "Don't waste my time," it read. "Idle talk earns nothing."

"We have to talk about this," Hill was saying to Johnson, "because this offer isn't as insulting to you as it is to us."

Johnson and Hill soon left, leaving the Forstmann brothers perplexed. Was Johnson negotiating with Kravis? If so, why was he talking to Forstmann Little? Maybe they would find out later: Hill had invited Forstmann's crew over to Nine West that evening to talk about joining forces.

As they ran through details of the meeting, Steve Klinsky came up to Ted Forstmann. "Are you sure that guy is all there?" he asked.

Forstmann put Johnson's strange behavior down to excitement. He had seen the phenomenon many times: a chief executive, secure in his corporate environment, bewildered by the blinding pace of Wall Street. "He's under a lot of pressure," Forstmann explained. "He's in a difficult position, you know. I have sympathy for CEOs in this world."

Klinsky wasn't so sure. "I think the guy is totally insane."

An hour after Kravis lofted his $125 million offer, Dick Beattie was on the phone to Bob Millard at Shearson.

"Have you heard about our offer?" Beattie wondered.

Millard passed on the news Beattie expected. Cohen, the trader said, was bouncing off the walls at Kravis's offer. He was insulted; he was outraged; he had never seen anything like it.

"He's calling it a bribe," Millard said.

"I knew it," Beattie said with a sigh.

Johnson returned to his forty-eighth-floor offices to find Cohen in a rage at the Kravis offer. Hill soon joined him. As he stomped about cursing Kravis, Tom Hill's face turned so red Johnson thought he was going to have a heart attack. Jim Robinson was also there.

For all the sound and fury, the Kravis offer brought into the open the unacknowledged rift between Shearson and Johnson, which had now lasted nearly two days, since Kravis's announcement the previous morning. Johnson still hadn't openly reaffirmed his commitment to go ahead with the Shearson offer. Robinson and Cohen, although they hadn't pressed the matter, were clearly worried by Johnson's meeting that afternoon with Kravis. Would Johnson stay with Shearson or leap to the Kravis camp?

"Ross, if you want to go with them, you're perfectly free to do it," Robinson now told Johnson. "We won't stop you." Cohen echoed Robinson's sentiments.

"Oh, hell," Johnson said. "Let's just everybody calm down. I've got to talk about this with my people first. Then we'll decide what we're going to do."

By nightfall the forty-eighth floor was overflowing with people: teams from Shearson, Davis Polk, Jack Nusbaum's law firm, and RJR were all busily reworking weeks of analysis in preparation for topping Kravis's bid. Johnson gathered his executives in his office. Horrigan, Henderson, John Martin, and the others draped themselves over the cream-colored furniture and lined the walls.

"This is the situation," Johnson said, explaining Kravis's offer. "I'm not going to make a unilateral decision here. We're going to vote on it. I'll do what you guys want to do. I want each of you to tell me how you feel.

Now you can go any way you want to go. But fellows, you're voting your careers. We can go with Henry, or we can go with Jim."

Johnson looked around the room at the men he had chosen to pursue the Great Adventure. You all know what working for Henry Kravis would be like, he explained. There were nods all around. They knew. But the odds of winning with Shearson were hardly any better, Johnson cautioned.

"You realize, if we go with Shearson," he said, "you're probably all gone." Shearson's chances of beating Kravis seemed that remote; no one was even sure Cohen's people could raise the money necessary to do battle. If they went with Shearson and lost, they'd all lose their jobs.

Listening to the speech, Ed Horrigan knew Johnson was serious in encouraging them to reconsider their allegiances. The two men had earlier spoken privately, and when Horrigan asked about Johnson's meeting with Kravis, he had been startled by Johnson's apparent ambivalence. "Boy, they're great guys," Johnson had said of Kravis and Roberts.

"They are?" Horrigan said, incredulously.

Horrigan had questioned Johnson closely about what had happened six floors below. At one level, the feisty tobacco chief was suspicious about what kind of deal Johnson, acting as a free agent, might have cut for himself. At another, he was baffled: How could they suddenly go from regarding Kravis with fear and loathing to embracing the SOB? Maybe hang-loose Ross Johnson could make that flip-flop. But not hang-tough Ed Horrigan.

"I don't know what you talked about," Horrigan said, "but I don't like it."

"I don't understand you," Johnson replied. "I'm making the biggest deal in the world and you're not impressed."

Horrigan tried to make it simple for him. For one thing, he said, think about how all this will look to the board. How on earth could the management group maintain it was trying to serve shareholder value if it was cutting a deal with Kravis that would no doubt hold down the company's selling price? "The board will shove it right up our butt," Horrigan declared.

Johnson disagreed. With the $90 floor established by Kravis, shareholder value had already been served. Now, he said, it was important to make sure this bidding contest didn't get out of control, that it didn't get to the point where the debt they piled on would make it impossible to run the company.

Horrigan didn't want to hear any more about consorting with Kravis. "They're the enemy," he had said. "I don't see how we can work with them."

Now, as they went around the room one by one, Horrigan again decried Kravis and his methods. Staying with Shearson was the right thing to do, no matter what the chances of victory. "You go home with the guy who brung you," Horrigan said. "We win with Shearson or we go out with Shearson."

The others—Henderson, Ed Robinson, Sage—agreed. "Look, we're in. We're with you," John Martin said. "We picked our partners and we'll stay with 'em."

The crisis had passed. When the group adjourned, Johnson summoned Cohen. "I know you had some doubts about us," he said. "You made a very generous offer to free us up. I appreciate that. I just want to reaffirm that we're with you."

Cohen was clearly gratified. "I appreciate the vote of confidence. Let me tell you, we'll stick with you to the end."

———

At the height of the evening's chaos, Ted Forstmann arrived on the forty-eighth floor. The moment he emerged from the elevator, Forstmann had a bad feeling. The place was crawling with people. Most of them seemed to be lawyers. Forstmann groaned. *Too many cooks. . . .*

Forstmann had brought along his brother Nick, his lawyer Steve Fraidin, and Geoff Boisi of Goldman Sachs. They, too, noticed the disorder. Boisi, accustomed to dealing with investment bankers, was puzzled to see senior executives such as Cohen and Robinson darting about. *Who's in charge here?* he wondered.

The Forstmann group was escorted into a windowless conference room dominated by a single cherry table and packed with more than a dozen lawyers and investment bankers. Johnson was there, as was Cohen. Immediately the Shearson troops began pelting Forstmann with questions, most of them variations on a single theme: How do you fight Henry Kravis? Forstmann brushed the questions aside. There was no sense in talking about that, he explained, until they were sure they were on the same wavelength. For at least the second time that day, Forstmann launched into The Spiel.

First came the denunciations of Kravis. No junk bonds. No bridge loans. Forstmann was gathering steam when he noticed Johnson duck out. No hostile tender offers, he continued. None of that crazy shit. On and on he went. After a bit Cohen followed Johnson out the door. "I don't fuck around," Forstmann concluded. "We don't say yes to many things. But we're there on this one. Are you there?"

Forstmann looked around. Suddenly it struck him that the conference room had emptied. Only three of the original group remained. As Forstmann scratched his head, a junior Shearson banker began suggesting ways that junk bonds could be wedded to Forstmann Little's goals without sullying the firm's moral views.

Forstmann was annoyed. Hadn't this guy heard anything he'd said? Hadn't he bothered to read the article in *The Wall Street Journal* that very morning? Didn't he know who he was talking to? "Wait, wait, wait," Forstmann said in exasperation. "You guys don't understand. I don't do that stuff."

Then, distracted, he paused. "Where did everybody go?" he asked.

No one knew. When the remaining Shearson bankers left, Forstmann wasn't sure what to do. He waited. For more than an hour there was no sign of Johnson, Cohen, Jim Robinson, or Tom Hill. Geoff Boisi began to get mad. "Something funny's going on here," he warned.

All evening Cohen had been trying to reach Kravis. It was important, he and Johnson agreed, to send a message back to him that his $125 million "bribe" was entirely unsatisfactory. John Martin suggested a dead fish might get the idea across. Cohen left messages at Kravis's apartment. He called Dick Beattie: Did Beattie know where Kravis was? The lawyer knew, but he wasn't telling Cohen.

As they spoke, Kravis was in fact enjoying a lavish black-tie dinner at a nearby restaurant, La Grenouille, given by the agent Swifty Lazar for Henry Kissinger. There he chatted with Felix Rohatyn, the Lazard banker now working with Charlie Hugel's special committee, and with Salomon's John Gutfreund. The room, of course, was abuzz with gossip on the RJR Nabisco deal. Gutfreund sat at Kravis's table, smiling to himself as his tablemates quizzed the diminutive financier. Not once did Gutfreund let on that Salomon was on the verge of joining the battle against Kravis. His dinner chatter with Kravis was limited to a comment about Kravis's newfound press exposure.

"I think," Gutfreund said, "this is the first time I remember a financial guy has been on the front page of *The Wall Street Journal* and *The New York Times* in the same day."

Henry Kravis smiled; he didn't much like John Gutfreund.

After dinner Kravis returned to his apartment and waited for Cohen's call. From his library window he could see the forty-eighth floor of Nine West ablaze with light. *They're still up there*, he thought.

At 12:15 the phone rang. It was Johnson.

Johnson's normally ebullient air was gone. "Henry, I'm disappointed in you," he said. "That's a lousy offer you made to them. I thought you were going to be fair. That wasn't fair at all. That's not right."

There was still room for a dialogue, Johnson explained, but not on those terms. If Kravis had something better to propose, he was still welcome to do so.

Kravis wasn't surprised. Beattie's intelligence, as always, had been on target. "Fine," Kravis said. He was in no mood for a debate. "If that's the way you feel. . . ."

Johnson put down the phone and looked at Goldstone. The two men were seated in the anteroom just off Johnson's office. Cohen hovered outside the door.

Goldstone wasn't pleased with his client's performance. Johnson's personality simply wasn't built for confrontations. The guy was too cheerful for his own good.

"Ross, look, if you're intending to give the message to Henry that you're not going to switch sides here, you didn't give him that message," the lawyer said. "I think you should call him again and give him the message more clearly."

"Maybe I didn't make it clear enough."

"I think that's right," Goldstone said. "It sounded kind of vague."

"Maybe I ought to call him back."

"Yeah, I think you ought to."

Five minutes later Johnson phoned Kravis again.

"Henry, maybe I didn't make one thing clear. Let me tell you I'm staying with Shearson. I don't want you to think in any way we're not partners. You can't expect me to abandon the people that are my partners."

Kravis wondered why Johnson was calling a second time. Someone was pulling Johnson's strings, he decided. He wondered who was really in charge of the management group.

"I wouldn't expect you to," Kravis said. "Ross, let me make one thing clear. Nobody's given a thought to splitting you two. That's not what we're about."

It was a lie, more or less. But this was no time to alienate Ross Johnson. Kravis hung up, worried, and quickly conferred with George Roberts and Dick Beattie. Rejection of their offer was not good, not good at all. A $90-a-share tender offer looked fine in the papers. But Kravis was acutely aware that he had never made a major takeover bid without the analytical help of a management team that knew its company inside and out. He didn't like to admit it, but one thing was clear: He needed Ross Johnson. Besides, a bidding war at these levels could cost the winner billions of dollars. Kravis and Roberts agreed a second approach was called for.

Kravis dialed Johnson at Nine West. After a minute Cohen came on the line.

"Peter, I think it's probably good for us to talk," Kravis said. "You know we're not trying to split you up. I just think we should talk about this."

Fine, Cohen said. Let's talk.

"Why don't we meet in the morning?"

"No, if you want to meet, let's meet right now." Cohen didn't mention that he had Ted Forstmann cooling his heels in a back room.

"Peter, it's twelve-thirty at night. . . ."

"No, if you have something to say, say it now. Tomorrow might be too late."

Kravis called Dick Beattie minutes later.

"They want to meet."

"What time tomorrow?" Beattie was ready for bed.

"Tonight."

"Tonight?"

Beattie pulled on a light jacket, walked out of his Fifth Avenue apartment and hailed a cab. On the way he picked up Roberts at the Carlyle Hotel, then Kravis at his Park Avenue apartment. The cab made good time moving through the empty streets. When the trio pulled up outside Nine West, they were surprised to find a long line of limousines parked outside.

Kravis shook his head. "Geez," he said, "the whole world must be upstairs."

George Sheinberg, the Shearson vice chairman, saw Kravis come off the elevator a few minutes past one o'clock. An accomplished photographer, Sheinberg had brought along a camera. He started to raise the camera to snap a picture—this was history in the making—but stopped. Normally not a superstitious man, Sheinberg didn't want to jinx the meeting.

Shearson's Jim Stern waved as Kravis, Roberts, and Beattie emerged from the elevator. Stern had spent much of the evening updating a team of Salomon investment bankers in a conference room just eight feet from the one where the Forstmanns sat. A pair of locked doors was the best bet the two groups wouldn't run into each other. Hurrying back to the Salomon people, Stern couldn't help thinking what a three-ring circus the evening was turning into.

The air was electric inside Johnson's office as the Shearson group awaited Kravis's arrival.

Cohen and a half-dozen others, including Jim Robinson and Tom Hill, paced the room nervously. Among other things, Shearson's chief was deathly afraid Kravis would somehow run into Ted Forstmann. God only knew what would happen then.

Johnson's office was, literally and figuratively, a smoke-filled room. A cigarillo hung from Johnson's lower lip, and Cohen puffed one of his ever-present cigars. A layer of smoke hung low in the stale air. No one seemed to mind. This was, after all, a cigarette company they were trying to buy. On a shelf behind Johnson's desk was a copy of Sun Tzu's *The Art of War;* there was no evidence Johnson had ever read it. Windows ran the length of one wall: Outside the view looked south past the darkened RCA building and the red neon letters of PaineWebber to the twinkling lights of lower Manhattan beyond.

Kravis, Roberts, and Beattie were escorted into the executive suite, past Andy Sage's empty office and rows of burl-paneled cabinets and into Johnson's office. Pleasantries took several minutes in the crowded room.

Jack Nusbaum ribbed Beattie, who looked as if he had thrown on a jacket over his pajamas: "Dick, you look like you just tucked in for the night."

The smoky air immediately bothered George Roberts, who instinctively began waving the haze from his face. His eyes stinging, Roberts attempted to make light of his discomfort. "I'm glad you guys don't make cigars," he said as he met Ed Horrigan. "Cigar smoke drives me nuts."

It took a moment for the irony of Roberts's remark to register. Johnson and Horrigan exchanged astonished looks. *Did he say smoke bothered him?* It seemed an incredible admission from a man looking to buy one of America's great cigarette companies; Roberts's faux pas set the tone for what would be a bewildering evening for all concerned.

"If it really bothers you," Cohen said, motioning to his lit cigar, "I'll put it out."

"Yes, it does," Roberts said.

"This is fucking beautiful," Horrigan muttered.

Cohen left the room, returning seconds later with an unlit cigar. Holding it in his hand, he moved behind Johnson's empty desk. Earlier, Cohen and Jim Robinson had agreed that it would best if the American Express chief made himself scarce when Kravis arrived. Cohen knew the Robinsons and Kravises were horseback riding buddies, and he didn't want Robinson's judgment blurred in a confrontation with his friend.

Now Robinson and Johnson rose to make their exit. "We're going to let you banker types talk," Johnson told the group. "I hope you guys can put something together. It'll be better for everybody. We'll be down the hall if you need us."

"Let's all keep in mind that a lot of people are watching this process, including Congress," Robinson said.

"We wouldn't want to hurt the business that we've grown to love and admire," George Roberts said wryly.

As Robinson and Johnson left, Cohen instinctively knew how he and Hill would handle their opponents. It was the same in every Wall Street negotiation, he felt: The senior partner tended to play the statesman's role, the "good cop," while the junior partner inevitably played the enforcer, "the bad cop." For years Cohen had played Sandy Weill's bad cop, a role he played so well it became second nature. Tonight Cohen would try out his new role as diplomat.

Still angry about Kravis's "bribe," he started out poorly. Standing behind Johnson's desk, Cohen emphasized that Shearson remained "open-minded" to a partnership with Kohlberg Kravis. But although his tone was even, Cohen's combative instincts soon took over. "This is our deal," he said. "We're not going to go away. We're not going to take a subsidiary role, to you or anyone else. We've got Ross on our side, and that gives us an obvious advantage."

As for Kohlberg Kravis's offer, Cohen went on, "We're not interested in taking any bribes. You couldn't pay us twice what you've offered. It's insulting, and it's arrogant." (Later, Cohen himself would acknowledge, "No one's ever going to confuse me with a statesman.")

George Roberts, sitting on the couch beside Beattie, spoke coolly, his hands never leaving his lap. "Peter, we've come here to talk about this in a businesslike manner. Why don't you give us some idea of a way we can work together? We'd like to explore these possibilities, see what we can work out."

But Shearson wasn't done yet. Tom Hill—cool, well tailored, clearly unintimidated—weighed in as the bad cop. "Management has now made the decision to stay with Shearson Lehman," he began. "We are now entering a realm where, absent a deal between us, we will be competing."

Hill wanted to make clear the risks facing Kravis in an all-out fight. "Henry, you're entering uncharted territory. This is unique. You don't have management on your side. That raises a whole host of questions, chiefly your ability to get at the right numbers."

Now Hill bore in. "This all raises the question of how you will be perceived, friendly or hostile. This is a hostile bid, and your investors will have reservations about this deal. It also has real implications for how future managements will want to deal with you. In addition, as you know, RJR has its operations in the South and in the Carolinas. These are constituencies where there are some very strong legislators, including Jesse Helms. I'm sure Jesse Helms would take a very active interest in the future of this company and its community."

The threats were unmistakable. When Hill paused, everyone spoke at once. Kravis was infuriated. "Tom," he said, "if that's a threat, that's ridiculous. I'm not going to sit here and listen to you threaten us."

"If you want to call Jesse Helms, Tom, go ahead, be our guest," Roberts said. "It's a free country."

Dick Beattie, palms outstretched, tried to head things off. "Tom, that's not going to get us anywhere."

Cohen interrupted before anyone built up a head of steam. "Hey. Hey.

This is ridiculous," he said. "This is not what this meeting is about. We're here to see how we can go in together."

Beattie, glad for Cohen's olive branch, didn't miss the fact that the Shearson chief had waited until Hill finished to intervene.

It was past two o'clock when a messenger stuck his head into the conference room where the Forstmanns sat waiting. Ross Johnson wanted to see them. "Should I bring Fraidin?" Forstmann asked.

"No," the man said, "no lawyers."

Wearily, Ted Forstmann and his brother Nick pulled themselves from their seats and followed their guide past darkened rooms into Ed Horrigan's corner office. Inside sat Johnson, Jim Robinson, and Horrigan. Robinson wore a rumpled tuxedo with the tie pulled down.

"What's going on?" Forstmann asked.

Jim Robinson spoke. "Ted, I want you to know what's going on. There's no other way to tell you but the truth."

"What's that?"

"Our side is meeting with Henry Kravis in another conference room."

Forstmann stared at a spot somewhere above Robinson's head. It was as if someone had socked him in the stomach. For a moment Forstmann searched for words. He took a seat on a couch beside his brother.

Disappointment wasn't a strong enough word for Forstmann's feelings at the moment. It bordered on betrayal. He had so hoped these people had principles. He had wanted so badly to believe they could see through Kravis, as he had. Now, he realized, he had been wrong.

Slowly, a stream of profanity, like some earthy ticker tape, began scrolling through Forstmann's mind. *Son of a bitch,* he thought. *Son of a fucking bitch. What did I ever come here for? Of all people, they're talking to that little bastard Kravis.*

Forstmann said nothing.

Robinson continued. "Teddy, what we've done is the best thing, not the right thing. It's the smart business thing to do."

Forstmann remained silent.

"We don't think it's going anywhere," Robinson said.

Johnson piped up. "No, we don't think it will. It's not going to go anywhere. Management is not going to go with these guys."

Forstmann thought, *Then why are you down there talking with them?*

Oh, how he hated to hear the lies. He wanted to shout *"You bastards!"* but held his tongue. He had always told his partners that once you lose your temper, you lose the deal.

He looked at Jim Robinson. "Well, it's none of my business," Forstmann said, "but I really don't agree with you."

He wanted to leave it at that, but knew he couldn't. "I think that they're really third-rate people," he ventured. "They've proven themselves over and over again to be third-rate people."

Again, Forstmann looked at Jim Robinson with imploring eyes. It was an awkward moment. "We're friends socially, Ted," Robinson said. "We only know them socially." He paused. "Anyway, there's nothing to really worry about, because it's not going to work out."

"Jim," Forstmann said, "whether it works out or not, why are you doing this? I just don't get it. I mean, how can you do business with these guys when you have us? Our money costs nine percent. You don't need junk bonds. You don't need Kravis. I would never have done what they did. I would never have lobbed in ninety dollars. If KKR hadn't come along, we would have just cheered you on from the sidelines."

They talked for a while longer, awkwardly passing the minutes talking about tennis and golf. "Well," Forstmann finally said, "thank you for at least telling me."

"Yeah," Johnson said, "you got to give us some credit for at least telling you."

"Yeah," Forstmann said. "Thanks."

Forstmann returned to Boisi and Fraidin a defeated man. "You guys are never going to believe this," he began.

"Let's go," Fraidin said when Forstmann relayed the news. There was no reason to stay and try to work with people who treated you like this, the lawyer said. Forstmann would never pull such a stunt, Fraidin added, and he shouldn't work with people who did. "I don't want you around here," the lawyer told him.

Fraidin sounded like a kindly uncle after a playground fight. But after eight years he had developed a strangely protective attitude toward Teddy Forstmann. In many ways his client was naive about Wall Street, Fraidin knew. He didn't run with people like Cohen and Kravis, and as much as he criticized them, deep down he didn't really understand them. Forstmann trusted people to be as upfront as he was, and that sometimes led to rude surprises, like tonight.

"Let's get the fuck out of here," Forstmann agreed, and made to leave.

Geoff Boisi stopped him. "Hold it, Ted. Eventually we all want to get out of here. But this is a situation that could turn to our advantage. That is, if you'll stay."

The Goldman banker had taken note of the chaotic atmosphere, the bewildered faces, the confusing presence of top executives such as Cohen and Robinson. He saw an opportunity in the air of desperation he sensed about the Shearson team.

"These guys are floundering," Boisi suggested to Forstmann. "If they can't work out something with KKR, they're really going to need us. We could dictate our own terms."

Forstmann was torn. He badly wanted to fight Kravis and show the world the truth about junk bonds. But Johnson didn't seem to be able to tell the difference between right and wrong, between Forstmann Little and Kohlberg Kravis, and that bothered him.

They waited.

Across the forty-eighth floor, talks in Johnson's smoke-filled office were going nowhere. In theory, it was in both sides' interest to negotiate some form of partnership. Everyone had too much to lose in a long, public fight. But "partnership" clearly meant different things to different people. Cohen rejected Kravis's offer of a 10 percent equity stake as an insult. Kravis wanted no part of a fifty-fifty split. "We've never done that before," Kravis said, "and we're not starting now."

"Well, there's always a first," Tom Hill said. "I mean, how many twenty-billion-dollar deals come around? There's plenty for all of us."

Kravis, still seething at Hill's invocation of Jesse Helms, glared at the banker. "We're not going to do a deal where we give up control. We just can't do that. That's the way it works."

For an hour they swerved from issue to issue, never finding agreement, never mushrooming into outright confrontation. "Well," Kravis said to Cohen, "what role do you see for yourselves?"

"We'll do the financing. We'll do the whole deal."

Kravis rolled his eyes. "Why don't you just let us do the deal? You guys can come in as equity partners. What do you care? You'll get your fair share of fees."

At one point, Kravis and Roberts asked again about Shearson's deal with Johnson. "There's no sense talking about the management deal until we can work out our deal," Cohen said.

"How can we cut our deal without knowing your deal?" Roberts shot back. Cohen outlined the deal in the vaguest terms.

They were getting nowhere.

George Roberts attempted a Solomonic compromise. The Shearson group could acquire RJR Nabisco outright, he suggested, then agree to sell Kohlberg Kravis its food businesses. It was a complex proposal involving a maze of tax benefits that took a few minutes to explain. Roberts asked Tom Hill how much Shearson would want for RJR's food businesses. "Oh, fifteen, fifteen and a half," he said. Fifteen and a half billion dollars.

"Well," Roberts said, "we have a problem right there. That business isn't worth more than fourteen billion." Cohen and Hill left the room and caucused a few minutes before rejecting the idea out of hand.

And so it went. There was no shortage of matters to disagree on. The question arose, for instance, which investment bank would supervise the posttakeover bond offerings. Besides the return on an LBO investment, "running the books," or leading, those offerings was the plum assignment for an investment bank in an RJR Nabisco buyout. Kravis saw Drexel, the firm that had created and long dominated the junk market, as the natural choice.

"We're not going to take a backseat to Drexel," Cohen said. "That's not even negotiable." Not to mention the fact that Drexel was about to be indicted. "Who knows what could happen to them then?" he said.

By three o'clock it was obvious that no agreement would be reached. As Kravis and Roberts rose to leave, Cohen took Dick Beattie aside.

"Look," Cohen said, "to the extent you have any influence here, we should get together before this gets too crazy. This could get really out of hand."

Downstairs, Kravis and Roberts hailed a cab.

As it pulled away from the curb, Henry Kravis's only thoughts were on strangling Tom Hill. The Jesse Helms remark still incensed him, and no amount of Dick Beattie's soothing words could calm Kravis down.

"Can you believe that guy, threatening us?" Kravis said.

George Roberts thought Hill was simply one of the worst of a bad breed. "Knowing Tom Hill," he said, "you could almost have scripted what he was going to say."

Ross Johnson expected to return to his office and find the situation with Kravis defused. He was shocked to find the talks had fallen through. Cohen was pacing about, uttering foul things about Kravis. "It's absolutely impossible," he told Johnson. "We can't do business with them."

Johnson couldn't believe it. In four separate conversations now, Cohen hadn't been able to reach some kind of compromise with Kravis. What was going on here? A man who prided himself on getting along with anyone, Johnson couldn't fathom why Cohen was unable to strike a deal, especially at a time when it seemed so vital. Kravis and Cohen were like inert chemicals that exploded when mixed. Having met with him that afternoon, Johnson knew Kravis wasn't that difficult to deal with.

Johnson listened as Cohen railed about how unreasonable Kravis had been. From the tone of his voice, Johnson suspected Cohen was almost glad the talks had gone nowhere; it gave him an excuse to stiff-arm Kravis and keep the deal for Shearson. Johnson, more worried about his company than Wall Street rivalries, began to have serious doubts about Cohen's brand of machismo. *Jesus,* he thought, *something is really wrong here.*

Johnson's reverie was interrupted when someone stuck his head into the room and said Ted Forstmann was about to leave.

"Oh my God," Jim Robinson said. "Teddy's still down there."

As Cohen and the others hustled out to head off Forstmann, Johnson and Robinson remained behind. "I feel like keepers of the asylum," Johnson said.

Geoff Boisi hadn't been able to stand the waiting a minute longer. Forstmann's combative investment banker got up from his chair and left the windowless conference room like a man on a mission. Outside, no one was in sight. He checked a number of deserted offices before he found what he was looking for.

Inside an office, a pair of Shearson executives, Jeff Lane and George Sheinberg, sat on a desk, talking. Boisi stuck his head in the door.

"I just want to tell you guys one thing. I've been in this business eighteen years, and this is the most atrocious behavior I've ever seen. It's simply outrageous. We will not be treated this way. I simply won't stand for it anymore."

With that, Boisi stormed out.

————

Ted Forstmann had had enough. He and his trio of advisers picked up their coats and began to look for someone to whom to say good-bye.

Suddenly, down a long corridor, Forstmann saw Cohen and a retinue of a half-dozen people trotting toward him. The two groups came face-to-face outside the conference room where Forstmann had been cooling his heels for most of the evening.

"Hey, partner," Cohen said, extending his arms in welcome toward Forstmann. "Let's go. Let's talk."

Forstmann realized instantly what had happened: The talks with Kravis had fallen through, and Cohen now needed Forstmann Little.

For the second time that night, Forstmann wanted to scream. He looked at Cohen and knew exactly what he wanted to say. *You make me sick.*

But Forstmann couldn't leave. It was, he would later reflect, a moment quite similar to ones he had experienced in high school romances. With every girl there was a moment before you broke up when you knew—you just knew—that if you left her right then, you would never make up. Forstmann knew if he left RJR Nabisco's offices at that moment he would never return. Henry Kravis would gain the biggest prize in history as a result. And nobody would know the truth. Nobody would know the emperor had no clothes. The two groups filed back into the conference room.

Inside, Forstmann tried to keep calm, but as usual, did a poor job of it. Before they went any further, before they could even consider being "partners," he had to make Cohen understand what Forstmann Little was about. He had to make them understand the fundamental differences between Forstmann Little and Kohlberg Kravis.

"You can't mention Forstmann Little and Kohlberg Kravis in the same breath," Forstmann said. "We are not comparable. When I started this business ten years ago, I said I wanted to be the best. I didn't care about being the biggest. If you think the biggest is the best, go away. You belong with Kravis. Our returns are three and four times the returns they lie about getting."

Jim Robinson cut him off before he got too far into The Spiel. "We know all that, Ted. We know that's true. That's why we're all here."

A few minutes later Ross Johnson joined the gathering. Forstmann turned to him. "What I'm saying is, if you have any ambivalence about KKR, you can't be for me. You just can't." It had to be all or nothing, Forstmann said. He wouldn't be partners with anyone who would even consider joining forces with Kravis.

Geoff Boisi thought he knew what was needed. "We need to hear you guys say that, if we're going to go forward, you will not deal with these people anymore." He repeated the same message two or three times so it would sink in.

Boisi looked at Johnson, who slouched down in his chair, his head in his right hand just inches above the tabletop. He appeared exhausted. From time to time Johnson sipped from a glass of clear liquid. Steve Fraidin, who noticed Johnson seemed to be slurring his words, wondered whether the glass held water or vodka.

"Ross," Boisi continued, "I think what Teddy's saying is, he wants to be sure you're through with Kravis. I think he wants you to look him in the eye and tell him you've made up your mind. Tell him you're finished with this other business. If you're not, we'll leave right now."

Forstmann interrupted. "Is it over? 'Cause if it isn't over, we're over."

Finally Johnson spoke. "There's no deal with those guys. That was something we had to do. It had to be done, and now we're finished. We need your help. We'd like to work with you."

There was some more talk, about strategy and tactics and how best to deal with a hostile Henry Kravis. And then somebody said it was four in the morning, and didn't everyone have plenty of work tomorrow? Soon they rose and shook hands and headed for the elevators. As they did, Ted Forstmann couldn't help thinking that no one had apologized for letting him sit in a room alone for more than three hours.

The cool morning breeze blew hard against their faces as the Forstmann group emerged from Nine West. For a few moments, the four men stood in silence on Fifty-seventh Street, each lost in his own thoughts.

Boisi broke the silence. "Are you sure you want to do something with these guys?" he asked Forstmann.

"Geoff," Forstmann said, "it's where the management is. It's where we should start. We need to at least try to work with them. Don't you agree?"

"Speaking as an adviser, and I'm an adviser now," Boisi said, "I have a thought. I want you to tell them that you're upset. I mean it. We need to tell them we didn't like what happened in there."

It was clear where Boisi stood. He wanted nothing to do with Peter Cohen. But then Boisi had his own agenda. Several of Goldman's best clients, including Procter & Gamble, were chomping at the bit to get a piece of this deal. "Teddy, don't you feel you have an alternative?" Boisi wondered. "I mean, why don't you do something with us?" With Goldman Sachs.

"Geoff," Forstmann said. "I have three alternatives. I can join up with these guys. I can go team up with you. That's certainly doable. Or I could do nothing."

Fraidin laughed, as if to say the idea of doing nothing in Wall Street's fee-driven atmosphere was something only Ted Forstmann could imagine.

"Geoff, you do take me seriously, don't you?" Forstmann said. "About doing nothing? I mean, if there's nothing there, I won't do anything."

"I think you ought to tell Cohen that," Boisi said.

"That's the type of thing an adviser should do," Forstmann replied. "I want as little as possible to do with this Cohen guy."

CHAPTER

11

The peace talks off, Cohen's troops prepared for war. With Kravis forging ahead with his $90 tender offer, every assumption underlying the management group's $75 bid had to be thrown out. A small mountain of revised analysis was already underway. New divestiture estimates were calculated, and talks aimed at securing $15 billion from the bank group were restarted. In the spirit of men bailing out a sinking ship, the gnomes at Shearson quietly tossed each of Johnson's corporate playthings overboard to make possible a higher bid. "All the planes, the penthouses, Premier, the country clubs, the Atlanta headquarters," recalls Tom Hill, "had to be napalmed."

Not only had Shearson been badly outmaneuvered, it now found itself outmatched by the financial sophistication of Kohlberg Kravis and its advisers, Drexel and Merrill Lynch. Kravis's introduction into the bidding of PIK preferred stock, which represented a full $11 a share, or nearly $2.5 billion, of his $90 bid, was a masterstroke Shearson couldn't easily equal. Two years of backing Dan Good's corporate raiders had left Cohen's junk-bond department sadly lacking in the expertise it now needed. The worldwide market for PIK stock, which is convertible into junk bonds, then stood about $2.5 billion; Kravis's offer would easily double its size. That kind of confidence didn't come overnight. As hard as he tried, Tom Hill couldn't see how the market could absorb much more than $5 a share; later he would revise that number to $8 a share.

For the moment, Cohen put off dealing with Forstmann. Already Forstmann was pestering him with calls. *We have to move fast! Do you think Kravis is waiting around?* It was impossible to talk with the man without enduring twenty minutes of why Kravis was ruining the world.

Bringing Salomon into the deal as a full partner topped Cohen's list of priorities Wednesday morning. Johnson slept late that day, then hustled down to Shearson's offices in Battery Park City to meet with Cohen and the Salomon chieftains, Gutfreund and Strauss. Afterward, Cohen asked Johnson for permission to bring Salomon into the fold.

"I have to rely on you for this." Johnson asked, "What do they bring to the party?"

"They bring a lot to the party," Cohen replied, principally $3 billion in capital. The bidding was reaching heights where the equity alone was more than Shearson could safely assemble itself. If Johnson's team won, Salomon could also prove valuable in the critical sale of bonds to finance the bid.

"Any objections to them coming in?" Cohen asked.

"No, not at all," Johnson said. "And you need the money."

If Forstmann Little and Shearson were to join forces, a lot of work had to be done. That evening Nick Forstmann strode across Grand Army Plaza to RJR Nabisco's offices to begin what he hoped would be a profitable partnership.

Nicky Forstmann, eight years his brother's junior, movie-star handsome, and well tanned year-round, shared his brother's distaste for junk bonds and Henry Kravis. He was walking toward Nine West's glass-enclosed lobby when he spotted Kravis and Roberts inside, coming toward him. Kravis saw Forstmann and smiled; he knew where Nicky was going. As Forstmann entered the revolving doors, Kravis suddenly held them, temporarily trapping the younger man. Kravis wore a wide smile; he loved toying with his rivals.

Released a moment later, a red-faced Forstmann stepped into the lobby. "What are you doing here, Nicky?" Kravis chided him. "What do you want to be involved in this thing for?"

Kravis snickered as he watched Forstmann head for an elevator bank far from the one to Johnson's floor. Kravis thought he was trying to throw them off. "He should know better than that," Kravis said, smiling.*

---

* Forstmann denies attempting to mislead Kravis by heading for the wrong elevator.

On Wednesday evening Johnson emceed a benefit honoring Charlie Hugel as Boys Club's Man of the Year. Johnson had worked with the charity since his early years in New York; he had suggested Hugel for the award.

Johnson was the perfect dinner speaker, cracking jokes and needling Hugel, the man whose committee would determine the future of Johnson's buyout effort. A number of those involved in the deal were there: John Greeniaus and Jim Welch from RJR Nabisco, Ira Harris of Lazard Freres, Marty Davis of Gulf + Western. "Welcome to the special committee meeting," Johnson said, opening the dinner.

Afterward, Johnson retired to Jim and Linda Robinson's apartment, where the two men talked late into the night. Looking down on the city below, Johnson, a drink cradled in his hand, enjoyed a moment of rest. He hadn't been comfortable bidding in the low eighties; now that they were looking at bids in the low nineties, he was having a hard time generating enthusiasm for the work. At those levels the debt payments would be crushing. Atlanta, Premier, the apartments, the planes—he shuddered to think. If winning meant giving up everything he loved about corporate life, he would rather lose.

"How high is this thing going?" Johnson wondered aloud. "We're talking serious money here, now. Jimmy, you know, basically, the business can only produce what the business can produce. No matter how good it is, if you pay too much, you'll lose."

When Johnson had shared his fears with Steve Goldstone, the lawyer had tried to break the truth about Shearson to him gently. "Ross, it's their money," Goldstone said. "If they want to spend it, let them spend it."

Now, as he sipped his drink and hashed out things with Jim Robinson, Johnson couldn't shake the feeling he was losing control of his Great Adventure. "Jimmy," he asked the chairman of American Express, "how much insanity is there?"

Plenty.

As Johnson's troubled mind wound down, a scene of minor chaos was being played out at RJR Nabisco's forty-eighth-floor offices. There, investment bankers from Shearson and Salomon met with Nick Forstmann and a Goldman Sachs team led by Geoff Boisi. After a month of work, Tom Hill had definite notions about how to proceed, about what businesses should be sold, about what Johnson would and wouldn't do. Boisi, it was clear, had his own ideas. More assets should be sold off, he said, and quicker. Hill bridled. The two bankers' voices took on edges, and soon sparks were flying.

Nick Forstmann could tell the room wasn't big enough for both bankers' egos. Boisi was trying to bully Hill. And Hill was threatened that a competitor was trying to run his deal. Forstmann rose and took Hill aside.

"Look, Tom," he said, "this thing is not a turf issue, all right? It's about how we can get this thing done." Forget the intramural squabbling, Forstmann suggested.

Later, when Forstmann took the elevator down with Boisi, it was clear the Goldman banker was incensed by the *ex parte* conversation with Hill. "What did you do that for?" Boisi demanded. "What did you tell him?"

Forstmann had no patience for investment bankers' macho mind games. "Geoff, this is not a turf thing," he repeated. "The idea is to get the deal done."

Thursday morning Tom Strauss was in John Gutfreund's art-deco office off Salomon's trading floor, talking with a pair of his investment bankers about RJR Nabisco. Gutfreund had flown to Madrid the night before to open a branch office, leaving Strauss the senior Salomon executive on the deal. The takeover game was new to Strauss, a man who made his career trading government bonds. Most days he sat near Gutfreund in a desk on the trading floor. There, among the shouting men moving billions of dollars in bonds, Strauss felt most at home. These days he was relying heavily on his bankers' advice.

Gutfreund's phone rang. "It's Henry Kravis," a secretary said. Before Strauss could take the call, a second line rang. It was Gutfreund himself calling from Europe.

Strauss hollered that he would take Gutfreund's call first. He picked up the phone expecting to hear the chairman's gruff voice but instead heard Henry Kravis. Somehow he had picked up the wrong line.

Before Kravis said a word, Strauss knew it would be an unpleasant conversation. The two men had known each other for twenty years, but these days their friendship was strained. In the 1970s Tom and Bonnie Strauss had been close friends of Henry and Hedi Kravis. "When Henry divorced Hedi," says one of Strauss's closest friends, "Tom and Bonnie lived through the whole thing. They stayed close with Hedi. When Henry remarried, there was a break." As a result, the friend says, "Henry felt betrayed by Tom and Bonnie."

In hindsight, Strauss acknowledged the breach, saying, "It's natural for the wives to stay close in these things." He downplayed its effect on his performance in the RJR Nabisco deal, saying, "I think Henry's too big for that."

Friends of both men disagree. The tension between Strauss and Kravis was to have an effect on several of the deal's key negotiations. "When the deal was over, a lot of broken friendships were mended," says one observer. "But the relationship between Tom and Henry will never be the same."

That morning Kravis wanted something from his old friend Tommy Strauss. He was smooth and conciliatory, every inch the old pal.

"Tom, I understand you all are thinking about getting in the middle of this thing," Kravis began. "I'd appreciate your not doing that. We're good friends, and I'd sure like it if you didn't complicate things."

Strauss couldn't believe Kravis's gall. RJR Nabisco represented Salomon's best chance yet to make the leap into merchant banking. And hadn't Kravis just hired four separate investment banks for the deal—not one of them Salomon? Strauss's irritation went beyond RJR Nabisco, of course. "KKR had shit on Salomon for years," recalled Chaz Phillips. "They've given out five hundred million dollars of investment-banking fees, and Salomon's gotten about one percent of it. And what Salomon got, the others didn't want."

Strauss was too much of a gentleman to curse Kravis that morning. "This looks like a transaction that makes a lot of sense for us, Henry," he said briskly. "It doesn't preclude our doing something with you."

Strauss beat a retreat as fast as he could. Gutfreund was still holding on the other line.

Ingrate, Kravis said to himself, putting down the phone.

Here he had channeled several major projects to Salomon in recent years, and Strauss wouldn't give him the time of day. Strauss wouldn't even afford him the courtesy of a call before entering battle against him.

Kravis tried to put it out of his mind. He had more important things to worry about. His tender offer would officially begin the next day,

Friday. It wouldn't be long, Kravis knew, until Cohen and Johnson regrouped and put their own bid on the table. When that happened, Kravis would have to be ready to bid higher. Before he did, he needed to know a lot more about Johnson's company. And without Johnson in his camp, Kravis remained at a severe disadvantage. What he needed was someone who knew RJR Nabisco. A wise man.

A few days earlier he had taken a call from Jim Walter, founder of a Tampa company Kravis had acquired in 1987. Walter sat on the board of Anchor Glass with Tylee Wilson and suggested to Kravis that Wilson might be of help analyzing RJR Nabisco. Kravis hesitated; he didn't know Wilson. But as the week wore on and the chances of joining forces with Johnson diminished, he changed his mind.

He now dialed Wilson in Jacksonville, Florida, where the former RJR chief had moved after his ouster. "Oh, I know he'll want to talk to you," Wilson's secretary said, promising that the executive would return the call immediately.

Minutes later Wilson ducked out of an American Heritage board meeting to return Kravis's call. "Maybe we could get together," Kravis said after introducing himself. "It could make sense."

"That's great," Wilson said. A meeting was arranged for Friday morning at ten o'clock.

Smith Bagley wasn't easily moved to rage. The most prominent member of the R. J. Reynolds family's scattered remnants, he was an affable patrician who moved comfortably in the civilized circles of Georgetown salons and Nantucket beach houses. He compensated for his imposing six-foot, six-inch height by walking slow, talking slow, and stooping slightly so, it seemed, as not to alarm anyone. His hair, just now turning to gray, was perennially tousled, like a schoolboy's.

But now Bagley was mad. As the grandson of R. J. Reynolds and the owner of more than 1 million shares of RJR stock, he saw himself as the inheritor of the Reynolds family mantle. Damned if he was going to sit by and watch Ross Johnson steal the company his family worked so hard to build. Wednesday afternoon Bagley strode around his lawyer's office, waving his arms and violating the dignified hush of Arnold & Porter's Washington office.

"Those little bastards; those little *managers*," Bagley shouted. "This little guy could take the company from the shareholders to make all that money for himself. That money belongs to the shareholders. It's so *wrong.* We have to do something."

But what? Until now, Smith Bagley hadn't exactly taken an active interest in the company. He had grown up in Greenwich, Connecticut, a few doors down from Ted Forstmann's family. He hadn't cared much for Winston-Salem, which he considered a cultural backwater. For much of his life, Bagley had steered clear of the business world. His experiences in it hadn't been pleasant; in the seventies, he headed a company named Washington Group, but it wound up in bankruptcy proceedings and Bagley, in court, charged with stock manipulation. Acquitted, Bagley became a philanthropist, active in the affairs of foundations that used the proceeds from their RJR stock. He had been president of the Z. Smith Reynolds Foundation. He was also vice chairman of the Democratic National Committee's finance committee and, as such, in the thick of the final weeks of the Dukakis presidential campaign. Johnson's power grab couldn't have come at a worse time.

But Bagley was determined to derail him. It was, he felt, his duty as a Reynolds. His mother, Nancy Reynolds, R. J.'s third child, had cared deeply for the company long after severing formal ties to it. In the early seventies she had fought a proposal to take "Reynolds" out of the company name, writing letters to board members that said, in effect, "Over my dead body." In the mid-1980s she pressured Tylee Wilson's people to publish an authoritative company history that had been gathering dust for twenty years. Some had thought the book a bit *too* authoritative and suppressed it, but Nancy Reynolds lived to see it published in 1985, the year she died.

Like his mother, Bagley made it a point to get together with the company's reigning chief executive from time to time to talk. He had lunched with Tylee Wilson about once a year and liked him. After a year of trying to arrange a meeting, Bagley had finally met Johnson at the Democratic National Convention that summer. He wasn't impressed. "That bastard," Bagley cried now. "He moved the company to Atlanta and now he's cashing out."

But what to do? Bagley had already conferred with a lawyer in Winston-Salem about blocking the LBO legally, but was told he had a better chance of organizing a competing bidding group. Now he sorted through the possibilities with Arnold & Porter lawyers. RJR Nabisco employees and retirees held maybe 5 percent of the stock. Could they be rallied into an anti-Johnson block? Possibly, the lawyer said. What about the family? Reynolds family members controlled another 5 to 8 percent. The idea of marshaling those shares into a family-backed bid appealed to Bagley, although he knew it would never happen. Aside from the dabblings of Bagley and his mother, the family hadn't been active in the company's affairs for decades.

Bagley didn't want the company sold at all, although he confessed to mixed feelings as he watched the stock soar. But if it were to be sold, he wanted it to be at the best price for shareholders, not at the best price for Johnson. In that regard, Johnson's publicly disclosed flirtation with Henry Kravis was downright scary.

Bagley had met Kravis years before and had a favorable impression of him. If he could bring Kravis the imprimatur of the Reynolds family and the aid of a man who knew the company inside and out, could he forestall a sweetheart deal with Johnson? It was a long shot, but Bagley had little to lose.

He returned to his office and quickly got through to Kravis in New York. What are you up to? Bagley wondered.

"Well, I'm doing some work with the family company," Kravis said, and they agreed to meet for breakfast on Saturday in New York.

Next Bagley called his friend Tylee Wilson in Jacksonville. "Look, we've got to get involved in this," Bagley said. "Would you have any interest in seeing me and my lawyer?"

Was Tylee Wilson interested? The man who had sat atop a $15 billion corporation now ran two things: a one-man consulting firm and a faltering marina. For two years Wilson had taken phone calls from his old corporate allies whispering about Johnson's latest escapades. It galled Tylee Wilson to see that breezy playboy trashing a fine American company.

Wilson had come to rationalize his sacking as a principled refusal on his part to play corporate politics with the board. "I wouldn't kiss their ass in Macy's window," he told friends. He had used a portion of his severance pay to buy a new boat he named *The Integrity*. Now the folly of installing Johnson had been laid bare. It gave him some grim satisfaction. It would give him a lot more satisfaction to ride back in, the man given up for dead, and save the kingdom from this corrupt reign.

Was Tylee Wilson interested? So bad he could taste it.

"How about tomorrow?" he asked Bagley.

Bagley agreed. There was just one logistical question.

"Will you have a limo?" Wilson asked.

"Ah, sure," Bagley replied.

Bagley and his lawyer flew to Jacksonville the next day, arriving *en limo* at six. Wilson greeted them in shirtsleeves and a tie and, it being cocktail hour, asked if they would like a drink. A few minutes later, Kravis called to say he would send a jet for Wilson in the morning. That night the two men dined at Wilson's club, and Bagley got an earful from RJR's former chief. Wilson went on and on about the waste under the Johnson regime: The words *appalling* and *sickening* were used a lot. "It's a great company with great traditions that's being run down," he said.

"Kravis needs you as a credible manager," Bagley said. "You could give him the management, and I could give him the family. We could beat Johnson."

An alliance was formed. That night, Bagley returned to Wilson's house, where Tylee's wife, Pat, joined them. Into the night they drank and swapped old Reynolds war stories. Wouldn't it be great, they mused, to strap on the guns again.

Friday morning, as he waited for Wilson to arrive in New York, Kravis was startled to read in *The Wall Street Journal* that Kohlberg Kravis had hired Wilson as a special consultant.

"Where the hell could this have come from?" he asked Roberts. Neither man had a clue. As far as they knew, Wilson was already on a jet heading north. The airplane pilot, maybe?

Kravis and Roberts were still puzzling over the leak when a call came in from Charlie Hugel. Kravis put him on the speaker phone. Hugel had just read of Wilson's hiring, too.

"Henry," Hugel said, "if you're really going to do that, let me tell you one thing. Don't. If you do, everybody will quit. They'll go right out the door. If you're worried about management, there's a lot of good people in this company. I'll even help you find them. But you're making a big mistake hiring Tylee Wilson."

Kravis thanked Hugel for the tip. Later that morning he and Roberts met with Wilson for two hours. They found his knowledge of the company outdated and his zest for revenge apparent. The leak, they concluded, had come from Wilson himself. *Leaks!* Kravis was sick of them and wanted no part of a chief executive who wasn't. When Wilson left, Kravis and Roberts quickly made up their minds to wash their hands of the man. Tylee Wilson's career as a Kohlberg Kravis consultant was over before it started.*

————

Thursday afternoon Peter Cohen slipped into a limousine and swung by to pick up Tom Strauss for a trip uptown to see Ted Forstmann. Salomon had agreed to join the Shearson group as a fifty-fifty partner; an announcement would go out that afternoon. On the way uptown, Strauss related in mock wonder his call from Kravis.

Ushered into Forstmann's office, Cohen strolled about, inspecting its motley collection of art, family photos, and books. Forstmann realized Shearson's chairman was sizing up the place. As a chance to make new friends, the gathering was a failure. Forstmann, impatient to join the fight, spent much of the time preaching against Kravis. Strauss thought Forstmann would never get off the soapbox.

Geoff Boisi was also there. Tom Hill had passed his suspicions about the Goldman deal maker on to Cohen: Boisi and his people had shown a keen interest—too keen, Hill thought—in obtaining confidential information about Nabisco businesses. Hill didn't know about Boisi's contacts with Procter & Gamble and others, but suspected the Goldman banker had other interests at work than strictly advising Forstmann. Already Hill had directed his people not to share too much of their data with their Goldman counterparts.

For his part, Cohen hadn't appreciated Boisi's bullying style during their first meeting on Tuesday. Now he quizzed the banker about his job as Forstmann's adviser. When Boisi seemed to equivocate, Cohen realized Hill could be right: Boisi might be playing along just to get his hands on information that would aid a Goldman-led bidding group.

Cohen and Strauss left Forstmann's office that day deeply suspicious of Geoff Boisi's motives.

————

Friday morning Boisi read the news as his chauffeur-driven car nosed through Manhattan traffic on the way in from his Long Island home. The

* Wilson denies being the source of the leak.

286

papers were full of what a great partner Salomon would make for Shearson, but there wasn't a single mention of Forstmann Little. Coming after the fiasco Tuesday night, to Boisi it was more evidence that his client was being treated shabbily.

From the car phone he dialed Forstmann, waking him from a sound sleep. It was time to talk to Cohen. "We better let this guy know absolutely that they're not treating us correctly," he told Forstmann. "This guy's looking at you as financing. He uses the word *partner,* but he doesn't know what being a partner means. It's time they know how you treat a partner."

Cohen was at home, pulling on his overcoat and heading for the front door when the phone rang. He jogged into the kitchen to get it and immediately heard the steel in Boisi's voice. "Teddy doesn't have to do anything here, Peter," he said. "Unless this thing starts going in the right direction, we can just walk away. . . . You know, you're losing this guy. Don't be sitting there thinking he doesn't have any alternatives, because he does. We are perfectly capable of helping him."

"What are you saying?"

"I'm saying we have alternative courses of action here if we don't do this deal with you."

"Whoa, whoa," Cohen said. "You have alternative courses of action? What does that mean?"

Cohen knew exactly what that meant. Hill had been right: Goldman wanted to make a run at RJR Nabisco itself. To Cohen, the Goldman banker was a mole attempting to insinuate himself into the upper reaches of Shearson's strategists. Cohen, in his own words, "went nuts."

"Listen. We don't need you," he told Boisi. "We don't need Teddy. We don't need anybody! We can go our own way, too, you know. . . . We've shared all our data, all our secrets, with you. Now you're telling me you have alternative courses of action? That's absolutely one hundred percent contrary to what you have told us to date."

Cohen hung up knowing it wouldn't be the last heated exchange he would have with the Goldman banker. Later that morning, Cohen called Forstmann, who was due at Shearson only a few hours later.

"Who are you going to bring down?" Cohen asked.

Forstmann ticked off his brother, Boisi, and Steve Fraidin, the owlish lawyer.

"Can't we do it without Boisi?"

"Gee, Peter, he's our adviser, you know."

"Well, all right, if you have to. But I don't need to get any more phone calls from this guy. I don't like the way he talks."

Cohen was still fuming when the Forstmann group arrived at Shearson that afternoon. They took seats in its sumptuous nineteenth-floor library, and turning to Boisi, Cohen came right to the point. "I want to know whether you guys have signed the confidentiality agreement," Cohen said. "Are you free to go out on your own? Otherwise, I don't know how you can be sitting here in this room with us."

No, Boisi said, neither Forstmann Little nor Goldman has signed any such agreement. But Boisi assured Cohen he had no intention of divulging any of Shearson's secrets. "Peter, you have my word on that."

"I want to hear that from a lawyer."

Boisi stiffened. "Let me understand, Peter. You're saying my word isn't good enough?"

"I just want to hear it from a lawyer."

Cohen turned to Fraidin, who sat on a couch across from him.

"Hey. Lawyer."

Fraidin, who was taking notes, didn't seem to hear him.

"Hey you. Lawyer. I'm talkin' to you."

Fraidin, blinking through his professor's glasses, looked up. He knew Cohen was trying to intimidate him. "Are you talking to me? What's the question?"

"Does the confidentiality agreement permit you to make an offer separate from management's?"

Fraidin was silent for a moment. When he spoke his tone was calm. "I have two answers. First, I am not your lawyer. I would not presume to give you legal advice. You should ask your own attorneys that question. Ask Jack Nusbaum. He's a fine attorney. As regards the other, I have advised my client, of course, they are free to pursue another venture."

Cohen showed no reaction. A minute later he excused himself and left the room.

Forstmann couldn't believe the exchange. *"Hey you, lawyer?" Who does this guy Cohen think he is? Little tough guy with that big cigar. A psychiatrist would love this guy.*

It was clear to Forstmann that Cohen was confused. Forstmann Little had signed a confidentiality agreement with RJR Nabisco barring it from divulging any of the company's secret data. There was no such agreement with Shearson, nor with any member of the management group. Nor would there be.

Cohen returned several minutes later with a set of photocopied computer runs. This is how we think a Shearson–Salomon–Forstmann Little offer would look, Cohen said, handing Forstmann a copy of the document.

Forstmann leafed through it, but the numbers inside meant nothing to him. Everywhere he looked there were junk bonds, page after page of gobbledygook. Somewhere among the figures he found Forstmann Little's $3 billion sandwiched between layers of junk bonds. It made his skin crawl.

It got worse. It was clear Forstmann Little didn't control the bidding group, and the Shearson proposal seemed to contain clause after clause whose sole purpose was blocking that from ever happening.

Cohen could tell Forstmann didn't like what he was reading. "Don't think this is a hard-and-fast proposal," he said. "We're perfectly willing to accommodate you on this."

Forstmann was shaking his head. This won't work, he said. He tried to make Cohen understand that, under Forstmann Little's guidelines with its investors, the firm would end up controlling the bidding group. A full 37 percent of every Forstmann Little deal was promised to its lenders. Another 10 to 15 percent was sold to management. Even if they split the remaining 53 percent, Forstmann and his backers would have majority control. Guidelines preventing that made no sense. "No hard feelings, Peter, but this just won't work."

"That's all right," Cohen said. "We'll just rework it." He got up and left the room.

When Cohen left, Forstmann turned to Boisi. "Geoff, what can we do about this? We can't even talk about this. You can't turn chickenshit into chicken salad. There's nothing to negotiate. You know? They just don't get it."

The four men caucused. Maybe, they agreed, Forstmann ought to propose his own capital structure to Shearson. Forstmann thought it was a great idea. Besides, he was worn out from forty-eight hours of nonstop analysis. He rose and went looking for Cohen. He found him down the hall, chomping a cigar in a smoke-filled boardroom. Lawyers and investment bankers clad in shirtsleeves lined the walls.

"Peter, look, this is impossible," Forstmann said. "I'm exhausted. I'm going back uptown. We don't even have a starting point here. Let us put something together and send it down to you."

Cohen agreed.

Outside, Forstmann and Boisi climbed into the backseat of Forstmann's black Mercedes. The two were already deep in conversation as the car pulled into traffic on the West Side Highway. Suddenly Boisi noticed Forstmann's eyes widen. Forstmann saw the oncoming car and wanted to yell, *Geoff, duck!* but it was too late. The Mercedes shuddered as a car plowed into its left rear end.

No one was hurt in the fender bender, but the other driver had no insurance. They waited for what seemed like hours for a policeman to arrive. It just didn't seem like Ted Forstmann's week.

———

His Spanish outing a success, John Gutfreund had a terrible time returning to New York. His flight to Paris was diverted because of bad weather. He was offered a chance to land at Lyon but turned it down. London was fogged in. Finally the plane landed at Brussels. Gutfreund caught the one-thirty Sabena flight to New York, landing at Kennedy International a few minutes before six.

Clad in corduroy slacks and a sports shirt, Gutfreund boarded a helicopter arranged by Shearson and arrived at Salomon's lower Wall Street headquarters in fifteen minutes. There he was met in the boardroom by a pair of advisers, Peter Darrow, his lanky longtime lawyer, and Mike Zimmerman, a fast-talking Salomon investment banker. In their hands were copies of Johnson's management agreement.

"You're never going to believe this," Zimmerman said.

Gutfreund took a copy and read it. He was startled. The agreement was far more lucrative than Cohen had hinted. If he was interpreting it correctly, Johnson's seven-man group was entitled to $1 billion, maybe more, free of charge. Darrow ran through the agreement with Gutfreund, point by point. It was important they realize what they had gotten themselves into.

Arriving at Shearson a half hour later, Gutfreund didn't wait long to bring up the management agreement with Cohen. "I am going to have an enormous amount of difficulty, and we as a team will have an enormous amount of difficulty, unless that package can be reworked at a lower level," Gutfreund said. "Peter, it's just *unseemly.*"

"John, I promise you, it will be dealt with," Cohen said. But, he added, it made little sense to revise the pact until they had a better sense of what levels the bidding might rise to.

Relieved, Gutfreund agreed. It could wait.

Teams of Shearson and Salomon bankers worked late into the night Friday and all day Saturday. Both firms mobilized traders and salesmen in London and Tokyo in the scramble to obtain funding commitments from an array of foreign banks. Another team, led by Jim Stern, was attempting to construct a compromise capital structure acceptable to Forstmann.

Cohen spent much of Saturday looking for Forstmann. He called his office and his home. Forstmann was at lunch; then he was out during the afternoon. Cohen knew he was getting the messages. All week Forstmann had bugged him to move faster, always faster. Now, when he was needed most, he couldn't be found. Cohen guessed Forstmann was trying reverse psychology, playing hard to get.

"He's just trying to act cute now," Cohen told Tom Strauss.

As the phone messages from Cohen stacked up, Forstmann ignored them. He took a long lunch, and that afternoon played tennis across the East River in Queens. Loping across the court, he reflected on Cohen and RJR Nabisco. He wasn't comfortable with the way this deal was going.

I think we're out. We're wasting too much time. You think Kravis is wasting his time? We've got to move!

As Forstmann walked off the court, he couldn't shake the feeling that had plagued him for three days. As much as he wanted to whip Kravis, this didn't feel like a Forstmann Little deal. *It's gotta feel right.*

Forstmann returned to his apartment to find the phone ringing.

"I've been trying to get you."

The tone of Cohen's voice instantly conveyed his irritation. Cohen was saying something, but Forstmann wasn't listening. *I don't want to be on board with a guy like this. I don't like this guy. Why can't he be more like Jim Robinson? You're trying to make a hooker into a dream girl,* Forstmann told himself, *and it just won't work.*

"Peter, I got the messages," Forstmann said. "But I've been out all day."

Cohen apologized for the misunderstanding. "I've got some good news for you," he said. "I'm out at Tommy Strauss's house. I really think we've figured out a way to accommodate your strictures. We can do this. I know we can." Cohen and Strauss had breezed into the Salomon executive's Armonk, New York, home in the middle of an informal dinner party, and Cohen had ducked out to call Forstmann.

Forstmann heard dogs barking and children giggling in the background. He heard someone, maybe Cohen, jokingly say, "Get that dog outta here."

Forstmann warmed to Cohen at that moment, chastising himself for so harshly judging the Shearson executive. *This is more like it,* Forstmann thought. *Dogs and kids. This is good, this is like a family. This is more like Forstmann Little.*

Cohen outlined a new capital structure to Forstmann. Salomon and Shearson would each contribute 25 percent of the group's equity. Forstmann Little would take the remaining 50 percent. Control of the company would be split the same way, with Forstmann Little taking half. The proposal downplayed the junk-bond aspects of the earlier proposal and promised Forstmann Little a greater voice in the future management of RJR. Just as important, Forstmann Little would receive senior debt rather than junior debt—roughly the difference between an American Express card and an IOU.

"How's that, Ted?" Cohen asked.

Forstmann was genuinely surprised. "Peter, that's a gigantic step forward," he said. "That's great."

"Let's get together tomorrow," Cohen said.

All evening Forstmann's people analyzed Cohen's proposal. It looked promising, they agreed. Forstmann tracked down Boisi at a Long Island dinner party after midnight and excitedly passed on the news.

That evening Forstmann's partner, Brian Little, arrived in San Francisco after a Far Eastern vacation. Little had avidly followed the goings-on at RJR Nabisco at stops in Hong Kong, Thailand, and Bali. Soon after his plane touched down, he was on the phone with Forstmann, who brought him up to date on the talks with Cohen.

Little was immediately turned off by the idea of teaming up with Shearson. "Geez," he said. "This would be a real departure from anything we've done before, working with these guys."

Little's reservations went deeper than balance sheets. He had known Cohen for a decade. The two men had weekend homes near each other in the Hamptons. Little thought Cohen represented the very worst of Wall Street, an abrasive, fee-hungry overreacher. He found the notion of working with the man repulsive.

"Teddy," Little said, "the guy's a thug."

Forstmann assured him the deal they were considering would be "a Forstmann Little deal." But Brian Little still couldn't generate any enthusiasm for the partnership, and before hanging up, aimed at Cohen the ultimate insult a Forstmann Little partner could muster: "I'd almost rather be in business with Henry Kravis."

———

Most U.S. companies employ spokespeople who are paid to parrot the company line, whether it be on toxic wastes or quarterly dividends. To reporters they are derisively known as "flaks" whose main duties consist of peddling press releases. But on Wall Street, with its steady flow of gossip and inside information, a score of public relations professionals have managed to achieve considerable power. Their rise is understandable: As the business press devoted more space to the great takeover battles of the 1980s, the importance of manipulating its coverage grew. By the end of the decade, each entrant into a takeover fight routinely hired a p.r. firm to work alongside its investment banker and attorneys.

For years Wall Street public relations has been dominated by a single firm, Kekst & Co., and its well-connected founder, Gershon Kekst. Kekst spokespeople can be found in every major takeover, dishing dirt on that day's enemy alongside their formal, routine press releases. It was on Gershon Kekst's advice that Kohlberg Kravis managed to stay out of the headlines for nearly a decade.

Then in the late 1980s came the first serious challenger to Kekst's rule in years. Linda Robinson was no ordinary flak. She was a tall, willowy strawberry-blond with a knowing smile, a grueling work schedule, and an obvious love of gab. Raised in California, the daughter of the actor who played Amos in radio's famous "Amos 'n' Andy" serials of the 1940s, she was a former debutante who spent the 1970s in a failed marriage and an array of jobs, including one at an acupuncture clinic.

A die-hard Republican, she finagled a job as deputy press secretary to Ronald Reagan's 1980 presidential campaign. Later she went to work for a company run by the former transportation secretary, Drew Lewis, where she met and married Jim Robinson. After she founded her own New York firm with a group of friends, Linda Robinson's affection for her husband began to be displayed publicly, and regularly. "Isn't he cute?" she asked one female reporter, insisting that the woman fondle Jim Robinson's biceps.

In no time she became a force to be reckoned with, although she bristled at any suggestion that it was because she was Jim Robinson's wife. Her clients included Texaco, whom she advised in its drawn-out struggle with Carl Icahn, and Michael Milken of Drexel. Her friends included Tom Brokaw, Diane Sawyer, and Barbara Walters, and her attendance at the marriage of *The Wall Street Journal*'s managing editor was noted by the paper's staff. "At 35," the *Journal* observed in a front-page profile in 1988, "she appears poised to wield a degree of behind-the-scenes influence approaching that of a few superlawyers and image makers, invariably men."

Hired by Ross Johnson within hours of his initial LBO announcement, Linda Robinson found her old friend's p.r. effort in disarray. It had no theme, no rhyme, no reason. The first week on the assignment she spent keeping up with the avalanche of hostile phone calls. As the chief spokesperson for Johnson's management group, she was constantly on the phone, ladling out inside details to reporters.

Her activist style quickly alienated Bob Baker, a genteel South Carolinian who was Salomon Brothers' senior public relations specialist. Baker thought Linda Robinson talked too much. He had argued against a *New York Times* piece Robinson had helped arrange that profiled Cohen and other Wall Street figures involved in the RJR and Philip Morris deals. "That's what you do when the deal is over," Baker insisted. "Linda, it's going to look like a bunch of silly fucking yuppies."

Matters came to a head when Baker suspected Robinson was plotting to put Cohen on a Sunday morning news show, "This Week with David Brinkley." The Salomon spokesman, trying to conjure a high profile for his own firm's deal makers, had arranged for Salomon's Ron Freeman to appear alongside Ted Forstmann, and didn't want his man replaced by Cohen.

"Linda, we at Salomon are deferring to you because you work for management," Baker said. "Far be it from me to suggest that because you sleep with the chairman of American Express you would tilt to Shearson's interest. On the surface, there would appear to be a conflict of interest here. I'm not suggesting that. This is not a threat. Just remember, there is life after this deal."

Although she nearly lost her temper with Baker, Linda Robinson tried to avoid wasting time on bureaucratic squabbling. She had bigger fish to fry. The Robinsons led a busy social life, packed with formal galas of one sort or another; she joked that they tried to spend a night and a half at home together every two weeks. Among the Robinsons' closer friends were the Henry Kravises. The two couples' Connecticut spreads were only twenty minutes apart, and Linda had managed to get Kravis interested in the thoroughbred business. The two had just bought their first horse together. They had named it Trillion, although in the weeks to come Kravis would give it a nickname: Cookie Crumbles.

Since Kravis first announced his bid, Linda Robinson had been quietly lobbying him to team up with Johnson. "Linda has always cuddled up to Henry," says one of Kravis's aides. "You have to understand these people. They all want to be friends with each other. So Henry starts getting calls from Linda every day. And he starts talking to her. She was playing matchmaker."

Linda Robinson's conversations with Kravis were a closely guarded secret. Other than her husband and Johnson, only Steve Goldstone knew of them. Goldstone grew worried: Of all the Wall Street firepower at their disposal, was it wise to have a public relations person as the primary conduit to Kravis?

"Linda, you ought to be careful here," Goldstone ventured at one point. "You don't want to be saying anything that the group hasn't agreed upon in advance."

Linda Robinson told the lawyer not to worry. She knew what she was doing.

Salomon's Ron Freeman, a veteran investment banker but no expert on LBOs, appeared pasty faced and nervous as Sam Donaldson bore in for the kill on Sunday morning television.

"Talk about the morality, if you will, of what's going on with these LBOs," Donaldson urged. "In the old days, companies were built to prosper and hire people, and make a profit for the stockholders. . . . Now a lot of people get into this business simply to break up companies, to make the maximum money, and to leave town. Is that moral?"

"I think that's not the only description of the LBO phenomenon," Freeman replied. "Corporate restructurings occur to vast degrees of difference. For example, some of the largest and best known corporations in the United States have restructured themselves with amazing success. Atlantic Richfield would be a good example of that. AT&T would be another. The extreme cases are only one small part of this overall restructuring movement."

"I grant you it's not the only description," Donaldson said. "But there certainly are cases where people say in advance, 'We're going to get in there, we're going to break up the company, it's worth more in its separate parts than it is together, we're going to get the money and we're going to run.' Mr. Forstmann, is that a good thing?"

Forstmann's only condition before appearing on the Brinkley show was that he wouldn't discuss the RJR Nabisco deal. Although his interest had been reported in the newspapers, no one outside the talks knew how deeply involved he was.

"Well, sometimes that's a good thing to do," Forstmann said. "It's not always a bad thing to do."

"What about the workers, Mr. Forstmann?"

"Well, they—"

"Who are they, anyway? I mean, if they're out of a job."

"No, that's not the point at all," Forstmann said. "Again, in my article, I said that without discipline, workers are one of the groups that may suffer. Discipline is the—investment discipline is the phrase that's got to come back and be talked about. In the beginning the innovators of this idea, of whom I was one, had a great deal of discipline. . . . What has happened is imitators by the hundreds have gotten into this business and as imitators flocked in, discipline has eroded, and as a result, breakups that didn't make sense have occurred."

"I'm not pointing the finger at you," Donaldson said a moment later. "I guess I'm pointing the finger at the people you yourself brought up, these so-called imitators. Now, why should they have a free ride with no regulation?"

"Well, I don't think it's a free ride. And if we had more time and we could get into it. . . . What's gone wrong here is that people have created a new source of money which is commonly called junk bonds . . ."

After the taping, Forstmann asked Freeman back to his apartment, and the pair watched themselves on television. Freeman called his mother-in-law. "That other man on with you was so cute," she told the Salomon banker. "Is he Jewish?"

Over coffee, Forstmann brought up RJR Nabisco. His enthusiasm of the night before was beginning to wane. "Ron, I don't know if we can get together. You guys are doing this all wrong. All these junk bonds, PIKs and Zeros, this and that. It's crazy. And what is this deal with Johnson?"

"I just don't know," Freeman said. "We're really not in control here. We're kind of silent partners."

"Well, here it is, the biggest deal of all time. And Kravis is going to take it."

Thanks to a pileup on FDR Drive, Forstmann was running an hour late when he arrived at Shearson that afternoon, accompanied by his brother Nick and Steve Fraidin. The trio was escorted through milling groups of investment bankers to the boardroom, where they were joined by Peter Cohen and John Gutfreund. Forstmann had tactfully left Boisi behind.

As they gathered, Forstmann didn't know whether the day's talks would end with a joint agreement to fight Kravis or a one-way ticket out of the deal. Within minutes the picture cleared.

"First, I want to say I misspoke last night," Cohen began the meeting. "I was a bit confused. Let me give you the correct terms now."

Cohen laid out Shearson's proposed capital structure. It was nothing like what he had suggested the night before. Among other things, Forstmann Little was to be junior debt rather than senior. The changes were enormous. Forstmann didn't believe Cohen had intentionally misled him—no one would do that—and chalked it up to inexperience.

"Well, Peter, this is quite different from what we talked about last night," Forstmann said when Cohen finished. "Not that I hold it against you. It's just different."

"Yeah, I know."

Ted Forstmann was the picture of accommodation, but inside he suspected this was the last straw. Still, Forstmann found himself listening as Cohen for the first time went through specific details of the management agreement. As Cohen explained it, each side seemed to have veto power over everything the other sides did. If he heard correctly, Johnson and his management team could practically veto their own firing.

This is insane, Forstmann thought. *The absolute amateurs of all time are playing in the World Series. They're putting up billions of dollars and they can't even get rid of the management. And they actually think I'll do the same.*

When Cohen finished, there was a moment of silence. "We think we can do a lot better," Gutfreund said. "This is just where we are now."

Salomon's chairman turned to Fraidin. "What do you think, Steve?"

Fraidin thought Gutfreund and Cohen had no idea how their arrangement with Johnson would look to outsiders. They were missing the big picture. "Because of the size of this transaction," Fraidin said, "I think there's going to be a tremendous amount of political and congressional scrutiny. I think that reaction is going to affect every institution in this room. And I think we ought to keep that in mind."

He continued. "By my calculation, this management contract is worth about two billion dollars. Is that right?"

"No, no, no," Forstmann interrupted. "That's not right." What he meant was: That *can't* be right.

"I think it is," Fraidin said.

Gutfreund looked around the room. "Is that right?"

They totted up the numbers. If all the incentives were met, the deal could be worth as much as $1.9 billion.

"That certainly is a very big profit for management," Fraidin observed.

Yes, they agreed, it was. Cohen emphasized again that the agreement would need to be reworked.

"Tell me about the fees," Ted Forstmann said.

Gutfreund chuckled. "Oh, we knew Teddy would get to that."

Cohen began reading. First came a success fee. Shearson and Salomon would receive $120 million if the takeover was successful. Next came a 5 percent fee paid to everyone who put up equity.

"What's that for?" Forstmann asked.

"Oh, you get part of that," Cohen said.

"Oh," Forstmann said.

Shearson was projecting an estimated $103 million in fees for auctioning off RJR Nabisco assets after the LBO. There was a fee—$23 million—for committing to the mezzanine debt. Forstmann Little would receive a $30 million fee for its share of the mezzanine debt.

Forstmann thought the list would go on forever. He asked questions but only pretended to write down the answers. At his side, Fraidin had some questions for Cohen.

"Are you going to be getting a spread when you do the junk bonds to take out the bridge?" the lawyer asked.

"Oh, yes," Cohen said, "we get a three and a half percent fee on that." That came to about $425 million.

Fraidin saw the Forstmann brothers exchanging bewildered glances. "Is there a bridge fee?" Fraidin asked. Multibillion-dollar bridge loans, he knew, don't come free.

Cohen nodded.

"What the hell is that for?" Forstmann asked.

Jim Stern was standing in the corner. Shearson's junk-bond chief looked as if he hadn't slept in a week. "If you would like to take the risk on a billion five," he said, "we'd be delighted to let you take it."

Forstmann didn't miss the sarcasm. He glared at Stern.

"I don't know who you are, but—Peter, who is this guy?" Forstmann was so mad he felt the blood drain from his face. "Maybe you don't know who I am," he said to Stern. "But you're talking about taking the underwriting risk on one point five billion. I'm talking about putting in three billion forever." Forstmann's anger was rising, and no one in the room wanted to get him started on The Spiel.

Cohen intervened. Pointing to Stern, he said to Forstmann, "You want him outta here? You want him to leave the room?"

Forstmann thought Cohen sounded like a Mafia don. "No, no," he said. "He can stay."

The fee discussion resumed. "Well," Fraidin asked, "what about the bank fees?"

"Yes, of course," Cohen said. "There's bank fees." Shearson was assuming payment of a 2.5 percent fee to its commercial banks—about $375 million.

"Two-and-a-half percent, huh?" It was Nick Forstmann, rolling his eyes at his brother.

"Two-and-a-half percent," Fraidin repeated. It sounded like a lot of money.

Cohen wasn't through. "And we've estimated seventy-five million dollars for legal fees." He turned to Fraidin. "So I guess you really want this deal to go through."

"Well," Fraidin said, "that's not how I operate."

At one point, Nick Forstmann halted the proceedings. "Hold it, hold it. Wait a minute," he said. "Peter, what are we paying for this company?

I don't understand this. If I'm calculating right, it seems to me you're borrowing too much money."

When Nick Forstmann ran the numbers, they didn't add up. If he heard right, Shearson proposed raising $19 billion after their downpayment. But it seemed to need only $16.5 billion to buy RJR Nabisco. "It looks like we're raising two and half billion too much," Nick Forstmann said. "Why are we doing that?"

"Is that right?" John Gutfreund asked.

Nick Forstmann glanced over at Steve Fraidin. He didn't need to say anything. *Do these guys know what they're doing?*

They took a break. Nick Forstmann retreated to a conference room to hash out the arithmetic with a dozen Shearson and Salomon bankers. His brother and Fraidin caucused in a hall outside the conference room. To Fraidin it was obvious that Cohen's presentation left little room for agreement.

Fraidin returned to the room alone. "Look, Teddy may want to reconsider some aspects, including the fees, the capital structure, the Ross Johnson situation, and the governance issues."

In short, everything.

"I'm also concerned that the preferred is a PIK preferred, which you may know he's never used."

"Okay," Cohen said.

Later, after Cohen and Tom Hill reviewed more of their strategy, the Forstmanns walked outside to their waiting car. Fraidin wondered aloud what their next step was.

"Well," Ted Forstmann said, "let's go uptown and call Boisi and tell him where we are."

"Where are we?" Fraidin asked.

"You know where we are, Steve," Forstmann said. "We're out."

CHAPTER

12

In one way, an LBO is a lot like buying a used car.

A target company's annual report and public filings can be compared to a classified ad. Like an advertisement, they contain useful information, although a savvy buyer knows the numbers can convey anything a clever accountant needs them to.

The car buyer wants to know more than just what's in the ad. He wants to talk to the owner, check under the hood, go for a ride around the block. For LBO buyers, a thorough inspection is equally crucial. More so than any takeover artist, the LBO buyer must know his prey. His success depends on determining exactly how much debt the target company can take on, and figuring precisely what budgets can be cut and what businesses sold to pay down that debt quickly. To take the used car analogy a step further, the LBO buyer must estimate, in precise detail, how many miles the car has left, how many spare parts he will need, and how much maintenance will be required. His margin of error is so thin that a worn crank shaft or a blown gasket could prompt the bank to call his loan. Similarly, in an LBO, a wrong calculation or an inaccurate projection can bring both buyer and seller down in an avalanche of debt.

But what if you're Henry Kravis, and the fellows driving the car won't even let you kick the tires?

This was the dilemma Kravis now faced. In a bidding contest, Johnson and Cohen would hold all the cards. Not only did they have access to every piece of confidential information, they had a management team to analyze it. They knew where every last dollar was stored, which budgets could be slashed without hurting the business, which plants could be mothballed without slowing production. Information was the key to success, and Kravis was on the outside looking in.

One of the special committee's most important duties was helping Kravis learn about RJR Nabisco. The bankers of Lazard and Dillon were the referees charged with creating "a level playing field" on which Kravis, at least theoretically, could compete equally with Johnson. In practice, this proved a difficult task.

The process by which LBO buyers inspect a target company is known as due diligence. When Kravis worked with a management group, due diligence was a breeze. Confidential documents were instantly produced, and executives were always available to brainstorm on the best ways to improve cash flows and reduce overhead. Kravis had teams of accountants, lawyers, and investment bankers crawl all over a target company until he was satisfied they knew its every nook and cranny and had earmarked every asset to be jettisoned, pared, or retained. It was a methodical, unexciting chore, but in many ways it was the key to Kohlberg Kravis's success in the LBO business.

On Thursday, October 27, Kravis and Roberts had met with Charlie Hugel and received assurances they could promptly begin due diligence. RJR Nabisco executives, including members of Johnson's group, would be produced for interviews. Like many public corporations RJR was chartered in Delaware, and under Delaware case law the board was compelled to produce its executives for Kravis's scrutiny. But, as Kravis would find out, there was no law saying they had to be cooperative.

The special committee had arranged for Kravis to begin interviewing RJR executives at New York's Plaza Hotel Monday morning, October 31. The interviews would go on for two days. Johnson wouldn't be called—fruitless, Kravis figured. And Ed Horrigan had refused. Kravis's team spent all weekend preparing.

Johnson's executives were to run an unusual gauntlet. Kravis planned to greet each man in a sitting room, brief him on his firm's operating philosophy, and encourage him to stay on if Kravis won. Afterward he would escort each executive to a separate room, where he would be grilled by Paul Raether and a handful of Kohlberg Kravis associates. Raether was in a foul mood even before the interviews began. The first boxes of RJR financial data had arrived from the special committee only that morning, giving him no time to prepare intelligent questions.

At nine-thirty the first executive, John Polychron, president of Planters, appeared. When Kravis shook Polychron's hand he noticed a second man behind him, one of Harold Henderson's lawyers. Kravis, alert for signs of tampering or intimidation by Johnson, was immediately suspicious. Was the man a spy? Was he sent along to intimidate those interviewed and prevent them from spilling secrets? Kravis couldn't tell, and after a few moments the man departed, leaving Polychron on his own.

The next pair, John Greeniaus, the Nabisco head, and Bill McKnight, an aide, arrived at one o'clock. Kravis went through his speech, trying to make the pair comfortable. He was surprised when Greeniaus remarked, "Look, you gotta understand, I'm not part of the Ross Johnson group. I'm not one of these seven guys."

"Watch this guy," Kravis told Raether as he escorted Greeniaus into the interviewing room. "Maybe there's a wedge here we can use. He just might be helpful."

Raether was hopeful as Greeniaus seated himself at the interview table. But just as they began, a young Lazard associate came in with a message. "When you're finished," he told Greeniaus, "you're supposed to go across the street to the forty-eighth floor." It broke the mood. Raether suspected that the message from Johnson was meant to intimidate Greeniaus. It was all a mind game. Greeniaus, like Polychron before him, went on to answer questions politely and appeared helpful—but not too helpful.

Harold Henderson was scheduled to be questioned at five o'clock. Henderson, with his detailed knowledge of tobacco litigation, could be especially useful. A few minutes before five, Kravis and Dick Beattie ran into him in the hall outside the interview room. The lawyer introduced himself and shook Kravis's hand.

"Can I talk to you, Mr. Kravis, a minute?"

The two men stepped into a vacant suite while Beattie waited outside. Kravis emerged from the room a minute later and watched Henderson walk off down the hallway.

"That's the damndest thing I've ever heard."

"What?"

"The guy made it absolutely clear: I'm with Ross, win, lose, or draw. He won't talk to us. That's the first time that's ever happened."

By Monday evening Raether was growing irritated. Johnson's men seemed to be suffering from collective memory loss. The easy questions they answered. But when Raether probed for a judgment, an opinion on where a budget could be cut, they clammed up with an "I'll get back to you on that."

The parade of Johnson executives continued on Tuesday. That afternoon a trio of senior executives led by the domestic tobacco chief, Dolph von Arx, came in. Von Arx had been quoted in *The Wall Street Journal* the day before saying he would leave the company in the event of a Kravis takeover. As a result, Kravis had little use for the man.

"You've undoubtedly heard most of what I have to say in these speeches," Kravis said. "And well, Mr. von Arx, there's not a lot to talk about with you. You're leaving, or so I read in the paper, along with your top eight guys."

"Oh, no," von Arx protested. "Reread that quote. I'm not speaking for them; they have to make their own assessment."

"Are you gone if I buy this company?" Kravis asked.

"I'm loyal to management, as you would expect," said von Arx. "But I would have to reassess my position."

Interesting, Kravis thought, how quickly these people switched allegiances. As for the others, a few, such as Bob Carbonell of Del Monte, were pleasant and mildly cooperative. Others couldn't seem to remember their names.

Ed Robinson was the worst. Johnson's chief financial officer should have been a treasure trove of information. His intimate knowledge of the company's European and offshore funding operations could have been invaluable.

Shown in on Tuesday at five o'clock, Robinson clearly wanted nothing to do with Kravis. Hostility radiated from the man like summer heat from a city street.

"Do you want to hear what I have to say?" Kravis asked.

"No," Robinson said. "I know enough."

In the interview room, Robinson was openly antagonistic. To most questions he either pleaded ignorance or said he would find the answer and send it on later. At one point, Raether asked about the company's leasing subsidiary, whose existence he had learned of only through an unsolicited letter to Kravis offering to buy it.

"What leasing company?" Robinson said.

And so it went. After a series of particularly evasive answers, one of

Raether's aides, Scott Stuart, threw up his hands. "Do we want to continue this charade," he asked Raether, "or can we go home now?"

Robinson was issued out. The last to be questioned, Dean Posvar, the planning chief, was little better. It was like interrogating prisoners of war, Raether thought, and he half expected Posvar to give his name, rank, and serial number. When the last session ended, Raether stormed out.

"This is useless," he muttered to Josh Gotbaum, a Lazard Freres banker monitoring the interviews. "These guys aren't saying anything."

After making farewell phone calls to Cohen and Gutfreund Monday morning, Forstmann told himself he wasn't sorry things hadn't worked out. Dealing with Shearson had been as frustrating as any experience of his career. Working with junk bonds made him want to wash his hands. His only regret was that, without a serious challenger, Kravis would probably waltz off with the largest prize in history. Shearson couldn't stop him. The two sides would probably end up as a team, Forstmann figured. Good riddance; they deserved each other.

Then Geoff Boisi called. Boisi wasn't about to give up on RJR Nabisco. He had three of Goldman's best clients chomping at the bit to get a piece of this deal. Procter & Gamble badly wanted RJR's biscuits business. Ralston Purina of St. Louis coveted a host of food brands. And David Murdock, the chief of Castle & Cooke, parent of Dole fruits, was dying to get his hands on Dole's archrival, Del Monte. As seriously as his clients sought pieces of Johnson's company, no one wanted this deal more than Boisi.

Much like Shearson, Goldman Sachs was about to unveil a multibillion-dollar investment fund. The Goldman fund, though, was to be earmarked for bridge loans. For the first time it would allow staid old Goldman to compete head-to-head with moneyed megafirms such as Shearson and Merrill Lynch. The fund was Boisi's baby; an RJR Nabisco bid would be its debut.

The consortium Boisi envisioned would be a dream team. All he needed to complete it was someone interested in buying the tobacco operations. That someone was going to be Ted Forstmann. Forstmann just had to be convinced. And Boisi knew all the right buttons to push.

All that day he hammered at Forstmann, reminding him of the reasons they had attempted this deal in the first place. Kravis had to be stopped,

Boisi insisted, before he jeopardized every *Fortune* 500 company. "If KKR wins this, there'll be no stopping them," he argued. "They'll be bigger than Boone Pickens, Carl Icahn, and all the raiders wrapped into one."

Corporate America would stand up and cheer a challenger to the junk-bond cartel, Boisi told Forstmann. Whoever beat Kravis would emerge the true hero of this mud-wrestling match. That hero, Boisi suggested, had to be Ted Forstmann. Only Forstmann had the right combination of skill and power to pull it off.

"You don't realize how strong you are," Boisi said. Forstmann Little's "cheap" money gave it an edge over all other competitors. "You just don't realize how powerful your money is. It's the key to the whole deal."

Soon Forstmann began to nibble at Boisi's bait. The lure of striking a blow against Kravis and the junk-bond junkies was too strong. And no one could deny the appeal of working with blue-chip companies such as P&G. Forstmann allowed himself to think out loud.

"If we do our due diligence, and this really is economically viable, these guys you've rounded up are going to be aggressive participants," he mused. "Everybody is a real money player. Nobody comes from the other world. No one's part of the cartel. Boy . . . wouldn't that be a wonderful thing?"

Yes, Boisi said, and it wouldn't have to be risky. "I know you're not going to do anything risky. I know your parameters. But think of this: If this deal could meet your standards, think of what we could accomplish. These junk-bond guys have had their way for three, four years. We could turn the tide."

Forstmann found himself thinking of the Revlon deal. The junk-bond cartel had risen to power on Ron Perelman's takeover of Revlon. He again felt a pang of responsibility for that loss and the damage the raiders had wrought. He had been defeated in that fight. But now . . .

An image began to form in Forstmann's mind. *The junk-bond hoards are at the city gates,* Forstmann thought. *We could stop them, once and for all. This is where we could stand at the bridge and push the barbarians back. Wouldn't that be phenomenal?*

He would do it.

Screw Cohen. We don't need him, Forstmann said. Cohen is so inexperienced he's bound to fail. This would be Forstmann versus Kravis. The good guys—P&G, Ralston, and Castle & Cooke—versus the junk-bond hoards of Drexel Burnham and Merrill Lynch.

"You know the conditions," Forstmann told Boisi. "No junk paper. None of that crazy shit. And we have to be invited to bid."

"Okay," Boisi said. He would have pledged his left leg and his bonus at that point.

And, Forstmann added, Forstmann Little must have a veto over the bidding group's moves. Boisi agreed to that, too.

Slowly Johnson's group moved toward assembling a bid of its own. Johnson, who had spent the weekend in Atlanta, returned to New York Monday afternoon and met for an hour with representatives of Texas investor Robert Bass, one of several parties Cohen was considering bringing into the fold. Afterward Johnson, Horrigan, and the other RJR Nabisco executives met for dinner with the Shearson and Salomon teams in one of Shearson's paisley-wallpapered dining rooms.

Two schools of thought were forming as to the best way to approach the bid. The Salomon team, led by Gutfreund and Strauss, was leaning toward an immediate bid, something that would show the world and the board they were for real. Something around $92 a share, just enough to top Kravis's $90. It was a trader's instinct: Bid fast, top the other guy by a fraction of a point, and wait to see what happened next.

Another faction, led by Steve Goldstone and Tom Hill, judged that approach shortsighted. Topping Kravis now, they argued, would only lead to a drawn-out bidding war that would send prices spiraling upward. An auction was the last thing they wanted. Somehow they had to bring a swift end to the process: a single, sharp, decisive blow that would knock out Kravis and secure the board once and for all. A bid of $100 a share wasn't out of the realm of possibility to Hill and Goldstone. By evening's end, Goldstone felt the group was leaning toward his position.

Tuesday morning Goldstone took a call from Peter Atkins, the attorney working with Hugel's committee. It had been a week since Kravis's bid, and with his due diligence underway, Atkins was curious as to when he could expect a bid from Johnson. Goldstone decided to try an idea out on him. If we gave you a massive bid—a preemptive bid—Goldstone said, would the board consider entering into a merger agreement? It would allow the board to lock in a high price, Goldstone suggested, while in effect setting a bidding floor. Atkins didn't seem to give the proposal much thought. His message was clear: Just make your bid, Steve. Make your bid.

Afterward, Goldstone chewed over the idea further. A blockbuster bid in return for a merger agreement. He liked it. Johnson, too, thought it sounded like a sensible approach. But how to get Atkins to take the bait? Goldstone got an idea from Johnson.

From conversations with Hugel, Johnson knew the board was deathly afraid the management group would cut a deal with Kravis, eliminating the competition, and, Hugel feared, leading inevitably to a lower bid. Maybe, Goldstone reasoned, the board would leap at the chance to seize a high bid as a way of spoiling any chance of further talks between the two sides.

Goldstone talked to Atkins again Wednesday morning. "Here's what I have in mind," Goldstone told the lawyer. "We would like to negotiate a merger agreement with you. It'll establish a floor. I can tell you, if you're willing to proceed on that basis, we will give you a very, very good bid. A preemptive bid."

"Look," Atkins said, "why don't you just give me the bid now. The board is very interested in receiving your bid." Atkins thought: Hadn't he heard this before?

"But Peter, it's not that simple," Goldstone countered. "Why should we give you a bid if there's no quid pro quo? We're not getting anything back. Right now we have the opportunity to negotiate with our competition. If we do, and we're successful, you'll see a bid much lower than this. I'm not going to throw a bid out to you now until we're through talking with our competition."

It was a bluff. Goldstone had no idea whether Johnson's group could work something out with Kravis. As heated as the public rhetoric had become, the chances seemed low. But Atkins didn't know that. Goldstone had to use his own fear against him.

"Oh, I see the leverage," Atkins said. "You're really giving us an incentive." Goldstone almost heard the light bulb click on over the lawyer's head.

"That's right."

"I see," Atkins said. "Now you've given us something to think about. Well, I'll discuss it with the appropriate people and get back to you. Do you have a proposed merger agreement in mind?"

"Yes, I do."

"Why don't you send it up to me."

Goldstone was excited. He instructed Gar Bason to send over an agreement that afternoon, and late, he rushed over to lunch at Shearson.

The Salomon chieftains, Gutfreund and Strauss, were already waiting in Cohen's office when Goldstone arrived. They repaired to Cohen's dining room for lunch, where Goldstone briefed the group on his conversation with Atkins.

Gutfreund was immediately skeptical. A preemptive bid? Goldstone's strategy, he said, would push the group into a bid well above $90 a share. Why go so high? "Aren't we wasting our money?" Gutfreund asked. "Why should we do this? Can you tell me we'll actually get a merger agreement if we do this? What are the chances it'll work?"

"I'd say less than fifty-fifty," Goldstone admitted.

Goldstone was baffled. Hadn't these people told him just two nights ago they were in favor of a preemptive bid? The lawyer tried to read Cohen, but couldn't. He thought Jack Nusbaum shared Gutfreund's concerns about overpaying.

After lunch Goldstone returned to his office, worried. He didn't call Atkins back. For the first time he realized he was making promises his group, especially Gutfreund, had no intention of keeping. He was irritated. Gutfreund didn't seem to understand even the most fundamental bidding strategy. Now, Goldstone knew, he had to move very carefully. He may already have gone too far.

On Tuesday evening, the due diligence sessions completed, Kravis returned from the Plaza to his office in a black mood, ready to discuss with Roberts the plan for their next move.

Their bid was at a crossroads. After seizing the initiative from Johnson's group a week before, they were losing momentum. Nothing seemed to be going right. Due diligence had been a disaster. Short of a miracle, Kravis and Roberts were facing the biggest deal of their lives with little more financial guidance than that available to an RJR Nabisco retiree.

If that weren't bad enough, Kravis was hearing ominous rumblings among his investors. Friday had seen a spate of newspaper stories suggesting that some of Kohlberg Kravis's largest backers were uneasy about the aggressive tack Kravis had taken. The involvement of state pension funds in a "hostile" bid spawned headlines and partisan political squabbles in

Oregon, Michigan, and Massachusetts.* Kravis and his people tried to calm their investors, but the pressure on them was mounting. He'd even had Eric Gleacher ask Hugel to assure his investors he wasn't a hostile bidder.

Kravis suspected Tom Hill and the management group were behind some of the trouble in his rear, and he was right. One of Kravis's most influential backers was Doug LeBon of Los Angeles–based Wilshire Associates, a pension fund adviser that called the shots for a number of Kravis's largest investors, including the states of Massachusetts, Oregon, and Iowa. LeBon's clients accounted for roughly 25 percent of the money behind Kravis. No sooner had Kravis announced his tender offer than Wilshire's clients came under pressure from all sides to denounce the move. LeBon himself got angry phone calls from RJR Nabisco executives, including Harold Henderson, who heatedly pointed out that Wilshire's agreements with its clients forbade backing hostile deals.

Of all his woes, though, none bothered Kravis more than the press. Kohlberg Kravis was getting killed. Following a week of controversy over Kravis's "franchise" remarks, Monday had brought the first full burst of major media attention. "The Debt Binge: Have Takeovers Gone Too Far?" blared the cover of *Business Week*. *Time* weighed in with a hand-wringing report, "Big-Time Buyouts." Major business leaders seemed to be popping out of every boardroom with pithy denunciations of LBOs and dire predictions of an America drowning in debt. Every story seemed to take a shot or two at Kravis. *Newsweek* was the worst. Its coverage included a sidebar on Kravis and Roehm—"The 'High Voltage Life' of a New York Supercouple"—that contained such juicy details as Oscar de la Renta's threat to Kravis to make Roehm an honest woman.

The press attacks deeply wounded Kravis. George Roberts, who led a private life in California, also found the coverage unnerving. Friends sidled up to him at cocktail parties and asked him whether his business was really good for America. Remarkably, in thirteen years of public life it was the first time the two cousins had been pulled into the glare of a major bidding contest. While Kravis had long been a fixture of the society columns, color pictures and articles in *Newsweek* and *Time* were another thing altogether. This kind of publicity could ruin their business. It could

---

* Both Michigan and Massachusetts ultimately declined to back Kravis in the RJR Nabisco deal, citing RJR's investments in South Africa.

also bring down the wrath of Washington, a fact never far from Roberts's mind.

"You people in New York are crazy," he said. "This is a terrible environment. We're taking a real beating."

Kravis had to agree.

"I can't wait to get back to San Francisco," Roberts said. "This town is crazy."

The due diligence, the worried investors, the press—there had to be a way to end this. Maybe, the pair agreed, it was time to jump start talks with Johnson. As they discussed it, Kravis found himself rationalizing the benefits of a joint bid. "We like Jim Robinson," he said. "We like Peter Cohen, I guess. It wouldn't be so bad when you think about it . . ."

His contempt for Johnson aside, Roberts found himself warming to the idea. Shearson doesn't run food companies for a living, he thought. Cohen will lose interest once he has his fees. Give him half the deal now, Roberts suggested, and we'll probably be able to buy back the rest later on.

However distasteful he found approaching Johnson on bended knee, Kravis knew it was the right thing to do. Depressed by the prospect, he looked at his list of telephone messages. As usual there were several calls from Linda Robinson. Jim Robinson's wife seemed to have Johnson's ear. Linda had no obvious ax to grind here; that had to account for something. He picked up the phone.

———

Linda Robinson was glad to hear from Kravis. As far as she was concerned, the whole fight—the name-calling, the finger pointing, everything—was getting out of control. There was no earthly reason Kravis couldn't do this deal with Shearson and Salomon. There was every reason he should.

It was all about egos, Linda Robinson knew. She considered herself finely attuned to the ways of her swaggering Wall Street clients. As so often happened, Peter Cohen and Tommy Strauss and Henry Kravis and the rest had totally lost sight of their real objective, RJR Nabisco. Their disagreements had nothing to do with shareholder values or fiduciary duties. It was all a test of wills among an intensely competitive clique of macho, Park Avenue bullies in pinstripes. At this point, she was well aware, Cohen would never give in to Kravis, or vice versa. Kravis certainly wasn't going to cut a deal with Strauss. Each was determined to be King of the Sandbox.

Someone had to cut through all the bullshit, she told herself. Absent the built-up emotions, the knot ought to be easy to cut. What this takeover fight needed was, well, a woman's touch.

"I know we can work something out," she told Kravis. "Don't give up on Ross. We've just got to get you guys in the same room. We've got to get you guys together."

"Linda, I don't know," Kravis said. "We're just nowhere right now. There's a bid and an ask that are just so far apart."

Linda Robinson pressed. "There's just got to be a way to get together. Ross is just a great guy. I know you two would get along great. This is just crazy."

Kravis agreed. "All right. Maybe it does make sense for us to get together," he said.

"I'll try to set something up" Linda Robinson said.

———

Linda Robinson called Johnson Wednesday morning, excited. "I think we should give it one more try. I think something could happen. What do you think?"

Johnson liked the idea. He too saw no reason not to join forces with Kravis. No matter what Cohen said, Kravis wasn't a devil. They all had too much to lose not to join forces. And frankly, Johnson was losing confidence in Shearson's ability to put together a viable counterbid. Andy Sage was bird-dogging the bankers' progress and thought they were going nowhere.

"Sure," Johnson said. "Why not?"

Carolyne Roehm was having a showing of her spring fashions at the Plaza at two o'clock, Linda Robinson pointed out. "I'm probably going to see Henry at the fashion show. What should I say?"

"Tell Henry it's gotta be done at a high level. We made a mistake the last time when Jim and I weren't in the room. It should be Jim and me—no one else. Try that out on him, and let's give it one last gasp."

Oh, and one other thing, Johnson said. "This has to be totally confidential." No one else must know about the approach. No one, Johnson emphasized, not even—and maybe especially—Peter Cohen. Cohen and Hill were simply too volatile to be brought into the process at this point. Johnson wouldn't even tell Steve Goldstone.

Before giving Linda Robinson the go-ahead, Johnson called her husband at American Express. Quickly Johnson explained the rationale behind the meeting. Jim Robinson agreed.

A few minutes before two o'clock, Kravis took the elevator down to Fifty-eighth Street and walked across to the Plaza. Inside the hotel's Grand Ballroom, Kravis found the crowd gathering. Flashbulbs exploded across the wide room, a sea of flashing teeth and violently teased hair. A sense of anticipation pervaded the air as the crowd awaited the unveiling of Roehm's spring collection. All the right people were there: Kravis saw Jerome Zipkin, the professional party goer, to one side, and society matrons Anne Bass and Blaine Trump sitting together.

But Kravis had more than fashion on his mind. He surveyed the room a minute before finding Linda Robinson. In addition to counting her a friend, Jim Robinson's wife also adored Carolyne Roehm's clothes. Kravis discreetly guided the tall strawberry-blond into a corner. He looked around, taking pains not to be noticed.

"So," he asked. "How's it going?"

"I'm working on it," Linda Robinson said. "I think it can work. I just know you and Ross can work together. I've got to set something up with just you, George, Ross, and Jim."

"Fine. That sounds constructive."

"Now," Robinson chided. "If we do this, I want you to be rational. I'm going to tell our guys to be rational, too."

Kravis assured her he would be on his best behavior.

"And Henry," Robinson said, "I hope this isn't just going to be bullshit, because if it is, you can do it through some other channel."

The show was about to start. Kravis excused himself and took a front-row seat by Oscar de la Renta. Linda Robinson slipped into a chair behind them. As the lively music pulsed—"Georgia," "Hit the Road, Jack"—Roehm's models bounced down the runway in a group of red, navy, and white short-skirt suits, pantsuits with boxy jackets, and jumpsuits topped with crop jackets or sweeping capes. The strength of Roehm's collection, as always, was her nightwear, elegant bias-cut dresses in solids or striped silk; slender wool crepes with chiffon godets; lean tuxedo dresses and spare strapless slivers. Only her accessories would turn off the critics—"pins that overpowered," *Women's Wear Daily* fretted the next day, "scarves that overwhelmed and handbags that are best left off the runway."

Kravis thought it all grand. Beaming with pride, he chatted and laughed with de la Renta throughout the show. As the models made their last turns, Roehm herself came out, took a turn, and waved at her husband. She looked ravishing, tall and thin, as she acknowledged the applause. Kravis waved back.

Throngs of photographers hovered around Kravis throughout the show, snapping his picture from every conceivable angle. At one point, Linda Robinson leaned over and whispered in his ear.

"When you do a really big deal, Henry," she purred, "just think how many photographers there's going to be then."

Leaving behind the airy kisses and popping flashbulbs, Kravis crossed the street and returned to his office. During the fashion show Roberts had canvassed the other partners to gauge their enthusiasm for renewed talks with Johnson. The feeling was positive. The two cousins established what they wanted from any meeting with Johnson, then called Linda Robinson, who had returned to the forty-eighth floor after slipping backstage to congratulate Roehm with a kiss on the cheek.

"Look," Kravis began, "there's no point in us getting together at all if we can't deal with some of these issues ahead of time."

"Okay," Robinson said. "What are the issues?"

Kravis wanted majority control of the equity and the board, but soon consented when Robinson insisted on evenly splitting both. It was the price he would have to pay for peace. But on a third issue he refused to compromise. Drexel had to run the books on the bond offerings, he said. It was the only way Kravis could guarantee a deal this size could be completed.

"Linda, listen," he said. "This is very, very important. You've got to understand this. Drexel is going to play this role. It's just got to happen. If that's going to be a problem, this deal is not going to happen."

"You know there's real sensitivities on the Drexel thing from the Salomon side," Robinson said. The two firms were archrivals at the top of the fiercely competitive bond-trading business. "Look," she told Kravis. "Ross wants to do this deal. He wants to go with whoever's best. It shouldn't be a problem."

Three points, three agreements. Both Kravis and Robinson were encouraged by their swift progress. Before hanging up, Kravis tried to haggle a minor point. Linda Robinson thought he was backsliding.

"Henry, you know, every time we make a little progress here, you can't just go back on it."

"All right," Kravis said. "Enough's enough."

"Do I have your word on that?"

"Yes," Kravis said. "Do I have your word on it? Are your people good with you on each of these issues?"

"Yes," Linda Robinson said. "There should be no problem."

What was needed now, they agreed, was a summit.

Johnson liked what he heard as Linda Robinson related her conversation with Kravis. The conditions seemed reasonable. Hell, he thought, Kravis was caving in on the equity, going up to fifty-fifty from 10 percent just a week before. A meeting was set for six o'clock. "Henry says it has to be absolutely confidential," she told Johnson. "They're not telling their investment bankers. They're not telling anybody."

Johnson nodded. It was the way he wanted it, too. He was taking no chances that this would end up like the disastrous Cohen–Kravis sessions. Johnson was coming to admire the way Kravis handled his investment bankers, who were kept ignorant and more or less docile. The less they knew, Johnson figured, the less they could screw up. Sometimes he wished he could handle Cohen and Gutfreund the same way.

There was only one hitch, Linda Robinson continued, a matter of social scheduling. "Tonight," she said, "Jim and I have to go to a party at the Gleachers. What do we do?" If Gleacher found out about a summit meeting, they both knew, the news could spread like wildfire.

"Don't do anything," Johnson said. "Just call 'em about eight o'clock and tell 'em, you know, that something came up. You can't tell ol' Gleach. He'd go off like a skyrocket if he knew something was going on."

Although she hated to be rude, Robinson agreed it was the only solution. "Now," she said, "you have to call Henry."

First she called Kravis herself. "Now, Ross is going to call you and confirm these things with you. Are we square?"

"I'm not going to have any surprises, am I?" Kravis said.

"No, you're not."

"Good."

Minutes later Johnson placed his call.

"Henry," he said, "let's give this thing one more go." It was to be Johnson and Robinson for the management group, Kravis and Roberts for themselves. "All right," Kravis said. "But no one can know. If I hear one word, I'll know it came from your side. Because it's not coming from mine."

They agreed to meet at the Plaza. When Johnson relayed news of the meeting to Jim Robinson, the American Express chief insisted that Cohen be included. It just wouldn't do, he suggested, for Cohen to see his boss and his boss's wife scurrying around his back arranging meetings with his nemesis. Johnson reluctantly agreed.

Afterward, Johnson called Cohen. This had to be handled carefully. "I've talked with Henry," Johnson said. "He wants to meet. What do you think I should do?"

"Go do it," Cohen said. "You owe it to yourself and your people. It's the right thing to do."

Cohen and Robinson reached Nine West shortly before six o'clock. As the trio walked into the Plaza, Johnson wanted to make sure Cohen checked his ego at the door. "I want this kept on a very low key basis," Johnson warned the Shearson chief. "I don't want any powder kegs going off."

———

Kravis and Roberts were the first to arrive in the fifth-floor suite. It was beautifully redecorated, the pride and joy of the hotel's new owners, Donald and Ivana Trump. The Plaza was packed to the gills that night, but Kravis had wangled the suite out of Ivana by promising to be out the next morning by eight, when a photographer was due in to shoot the room for a promotional brochure.

As they waited, Kravis paced the room nervously. At one point, he thought he heard noises. A chirping, maybe. Kravis walked into the bedroom and found a pair of caged parakeets. He would listen to their chirping throughout the meeting.

Johnson, with Cohen and Robinson in tow, arrived at six. Roberts greeted them with a surprise for Cohen. As an icebreaker, and a play on his earlier comments, he presented the Shearson chairman with a box of fine Montecruz cigars.

"A peace offering," Roberts said as he handed the box to Cohen. "But I wish you wouldn't smoke them in here."

Cohen smiled. "I'm going to sit back here in the corner and smoke them so the smoke doesn't bother you," he said.

It was a good start.

"Listen," Johnson began, addressing the group. "Let's see if we can get back to square zero here. . . . This thing is getting ridiculous. It seems to Jim and me—and Peter—that we can work out some compromises that make a lot of sense. It's not going to be everything you would want. It's not going to be everything we would want. But it's going to be good. No one person is going to end up with everything they want to get."

In thirty minutes they had the outlines of an agreement. Control of the RJR Nabisco board would be split fifty-fifty: Neither side would have outright control. The stock would likewise be split down the middle, with Johnson's share coming out of Shearson's take. If Cohen, unaware of Linda Robinson's secret peace initiative, was surprised by the quick consensus, he didn't show it.

As for fees, Kravis said he planned to pay each of his four investment banks $25 million. In addition, Kohlberg Kravis intended to take its customary fee of one percent. No one had to do the arithmetic: It amounted to more than $200 million, three times the size of any previous merger fee in Wall Street history.

Hold on, Robinson interrupted. He remained acutely aware that the eyes of the world were on them. They mustn't appear too greedy, he cautioned. Surprisingly, Kravis agreed in theory to reconsider his fee.

Kravis brought up Drexel, insisting that the junk-bond powerhouse lead the bond offerings necessary to finance the deal.

Cohen stiffened. "Why Drexel?"

"Look, Peter," Roberts said. "If we're putting out two billion in equity, well, we wouldn't put that kind of money on the table if the takeout of that bridge wasn't certain." Roberts had no confidence that Salomon, or even Shearson and Salomon combined, could do the job. "If we were doing this deal ourselves"—without Shearson—"we wouldn't even consider you for it."

Cohen didn't like the idea of selling bonds under Drexel's yoke and said so. "You know how they are. When Drexel comanages a deal, they hog the deal. They won't give you anything."

"This isn't going to be that way," Roberts assured him. "You'll get half the fees. If you don't sell a single bond, Peter, you get half the fees. All right?"

Cohen quit arguing.

Other issues came up. Shearson would want to handle the auction of all RJR Nabisco assets to be sold, Cohen said. Tom Hill was projecting $103 million in fees from that alone.

"That makes no sense," Roberts argued. "You ought to parcel out each business to an investment banker seasoned in that industry."

"Well, at least we'd want to be coadviser," Cohen said.

"Why pay twice?"

"No, no, no," Cohen said. "You don't understand. That's not what's important. What's important is getting your name on the tombstone." The rankings of most active merger advisers were compiled from the names of firms listed on the "tombstone" advertisements that accompanied all major acquisitions. Cohen wanted to get credit for the sales even if Shearson didn't get a fee. The matter was left unsettled.

In an hour they were finished. The three major issues had been agreed to. All that remained was for the lawyers to join them and pound out final details.

Johnson was thrilled. The logjam was broken! Thanks in large part to Linda Robinson, he finally had a deal. It wasn't perfect, Johnson told himself, but it sure beat losing—or winning at some level that made it impossible to run his company.

As they headed for the door, there were smiles all around. On the way out, Robinson sidled up to Kravis, his wife's horsebackriding partner. "You better send a big bouquet of flowers to my wife for this," Robinson said, smiling. "She went way out on a limb for you."

———

So far only a half-dozen people knew of the secret summit.

Downtown, Steve Goldstone was growing suspicious. He couldn't find Johnson. Or Cohen. No one seemed to be at Nine West. He called Tom Hill at Shearson.

"You haven't heard anything, have you?"

"No," Hill said. "Have you?"

"No. But something is going on . . ."

———

Roberts and Kravis, who remained behind in the suite, were in high spirits. Kravis phoned Dick Beattie, who, with his partner Casey Cogut, met the pair downstairs in the Oak Room for dinner. The lawyers ordered fish, Kravis and Roberts celebratory steaks. Roberts, a finicky eater, found his too peppery and pushed it aside. As they ate, Kravis hurriedly briefed the lawyers on where the talks stood. The group was scheduled to reconvene upstairs in an hour.

"It's not the ideal solution," Roberts told the lawyers. "But it's a solution."

Returning upstairs, Kravis took a short call from Cohen.

"That's funny," Kravis said, putting down the phone.

"What?" Beattie asked.

"He's bringing Tommy Strauss. You'd think he'd bring Gutfreund."

"Strauss?" Beattie was surprised. "Why the hell is he bringing over Tommy Strauss? What the hell does he know about this business?"

Kravis didn't have to say how he felt. To Beattie it was clear he'd just as soon not have to deal with his former friend.

Roberts took a second call. An attendant at the Oak Room wanted to know why a Mr. Roberts was charging his dinner to that room. "We show a Mr. Brown registered to that room."

Roberts had to smile. Mr. Brown was the code name they had used in registering. "Just put it on the room," he said.

Across the street at Nine West, Johnson was growing worried about the size of the group that would return to the Plaza. Goldstone had been called, and would need to be brought along. So had Gutfreund and Strauss, who clearly expected to go as well. Johnson wanted to keep the meeting small, both for secrecy's sake and because so far large contingents of people seemed to lead invariably to large arguments. Besides, he sensed Kravis didn't much care for either of the Salomon chiefs.

Johnson asked Jim Robinson to see to it that only one of them went along. Somehow, Strauss was chosen. Along with Shearson's attorney, Jack Nusbaum, that made six. Johnson was happy.

When Goldstone arrived, Johnson enthusiastically described the afternoon's talks with Kravis. Everything was going great, Johnson said. "Now we're to the point where Henry is going to want to see the management agreement."

Goldstone was immediately suspicious. For two weeks he had jealously guarded the pact's secrecy. Goldstone, like Jim Robinson, was under no illusions about how it would appear if leaked to the press. You're taking a big risk showing this to Kravis, Goldstone warned. If these talks fall apart, he said, Kravis could use it to crucify us in the papers.

"Jesus Christ," Johnson said, brushing Goldstone's concerns aside. "They're going to be our partners here. You're gonna be partners, you gotta have everything on the table. If there are problems, they gotta be worked out." Johnson told Goldstone he was being paranoid. At his client's insistence, Goldstone agreed to show Kravis a copy of the agreement. But he didn't like it one bit.

The six members of Johnson's group hustled back to the Plaza around nine o'clock. After twenty minutes things were going smoothly, and Johnson, with no appetite for lawyerly details, was growing restless. As best he could tell, it was all over but the fine print. "Is there anything else you need me for?" he asked Goldstone.

"No reason for you to hang around that I can see," the lawyer replied.

Exhilarated, Johnson returned to Nine West, wolfed down a sandwich, and briefed Sage and Horrigan on the evening's events. Then he walked the two blocks to his apartment, showered and shaved, and threw on a sports coat. He prepared to head back to his office, where he planned to do some serious partying.

"Why don't you come on over?" Johnson asked his wife, Laurie. "You've just got to come. It'll be an interesting experience. You'll have some fun."

Peter Darrow, the lead attorney for Salomon Brothers, was unwinding at his Brooklyn Heights home when Salomon's Mike Zimmerman called around ten o'clock. "Gutfreund's up at Nine West," Zimmerman said, "and he wants you up there, right away."

Darrow made it to RJR Nabisco's offices in no time. He found the forty-eighth floor deserted except for a seething John Gutfreund. Salomon's chairman was clearly in no mood to party. He was, in fact, as mad as Darrow had ever seen him.

"I don't know what's happening, Peter," Gutfreund said. "There's a meeting over at the Plaza. I've been excluded. I don't know why. I want you to get into the meeting, *right now.*"

"Sure, John, no problem," Darrow said, not having any idea how he would gain entrance to a closed meeting to which John Gutfreund hadn't been invited. Gutfreund handed him a slip of paper with the room number of Kravis's suite.

Darrow strode across Fifty-eighth Street and took an elevator to the hotel's fifth floor. He checked twice for the room number Gutfreund had written down. It didn't exist. Darrow found himself wandering aimlessly until he saw a very large man standing outside a pair of double doors.

"This is Henry's suite?" Darrow said on a hunch.

"Yes sir," the man said, opening the doors. "Go right in."

Darrow walked in to find Tom Strauss in the middle of a heated discussion with Kravis and Roberts. He didn't know it at the moment, but he was witnessing the first cracks in Ross Johnson's carefully won $20 billion peace pact.

"This is our capital," Strauss was saying. "We're not prepared to put in these amounts when anybody other than us controls the exit."

Strauss's speech was impassioned, his plea direct. Salomon and Shearson simply must run these bond offerings, he said. Salomon was ready to run them, was willing to run them, had the expertise to run them, and demanded the right to run them. They had worked weeks in preparation, and to hand their assignment to Drexel wouldn't be fair.

"We've just got to do this thing," Strauss said. "Why don't you try us?"

Irked, Kravis explained the importance he placed on Drexel's handling the bonds. "Look," he said, "Drexel has done a first-rate job for us every time. They did Beatrice when everyone said it couldn't be done. They're the best. They're cheap. This is the biggest deal ever. We can't afford to take any chances."

Strauss may have been arguing for the sanctity of Salomon's capital, but everyone in the room knew what he was really objecting to. Salomon hated Drexel. To lose history's largest bond offering to its archrival would be a profound embarrassment to the firm. For five years Salomon, strong in every other kind of bond, had tried in vain to break into the highly specialized—and highly profitable—field of junk bonds. But its efforts, plagued by internal politics, had resulted in a series of disasters. Drexel's hammerlock on the market was a source of continuing frustration to Gutfreund.

"Not to knock you, but you guys don't really do this stuff," Kravis told Strauss. "You guys haven't done anything here."

At one point, Strauss mentioned that Salomon had had sixty bond salesmen in over the weekend to hash out the best ways to sell these bonds. What am I supposed to tell them? he asked. Kravis and Roberts rolled their eyes. "So what if your guys were there all weekend?" Kravis said. "That doesn't mean anything. We ought to go with the best, most qualified people."

Peter Cohen found himself in an awkward position. Having more or less approved Drexel's selection earlier, he row weighed in with what seemed a halfhearted endorsement of Strauss's stance. Cohen, in fact, had his own reason to distrust Drexel. For five years Shearson had been locked in litigation with Drexel over tin contracts that Cohen believed Drexel had reneged on. Drexel's refusal to make good on the contracts had forced Cohen to take a $50 million charge against his 1985 earnings. Drexel, he said, simply wasn't the kind of firm Shearson felt comfortable betting its future on.

Soon both Kravis and Strauss were repeating themselves. As their debate wound down, no one was overly worried about Salomon's new-found intransigence. In a deal this large there were bound to be some sticking points in the fine print. Surely they could reach a compromise later on. Besides, there was a more important matter to be dealt with: the management agreement.

Goldstone hauled out a copy and waved it in front of Kravis. "We'd like you to sign off on this," the lawyer said.

"Show it to Dick," Kravis said.

Beattie watched as Goldstone flipped through the pages and stabbed his thumb at the paragraph he was looking for. "This," he said. "I want to make sure you see this and understand it."

It was the control paragraph, stating that Johnson would have full control over the deal. Standing beside Goldstone, Beattie thought it an insignificant detail. If they struck a deal, he knew, Kravis was going to call the shots. It was as simple as that.

Without saying anything, Beattie took a copy of the agreement and retreated to a corner with Casey Cogut to scan it. Goldstone was nervous. "I want your word that you won't use this document for any reason other than evaluating this transaction," he said, "and that you won't disclose it to anyone."

After a few minutes, Beattie motioned to Kravis and Roberts, and, with Cogut, the four retreated into an adjacent bedroom. "You're not going to believe this," Beattie said. The lawyer had read the document quickly, but what he saw was incredible: The control, a veto in Johnson's hands, and, most alarming of all, the astronomical returns Shearson was promising Johnson. "You can't live with this thing, Henry," Beattie said.

Cogut agreed. "If we sign up to this deal, Ross will run the whole thing. You're not going to agree with that."

Kravis was shocked. He knew Cohen was hungry to get into merchant banking. But giving Johnson control of the deal? It was unlike any LBO he had ever seen. "This is just crazy," Kravis said. "How could Cohen do this?"

Cogut and the Salomon lawyer, Peter Darrow, were neighbors on a one-block street in Brooklyn Heights. They had joked that the RJR Nabisco drama would be "a good deal for the street," meaning Garden Place, not Wall Street. Cogut emerged from the bedroom and, as the meeting showed signs of breaking up, motioned to Darrow. The Salomon lawyer slipped into the bedroom where Kravis and the others were caucusing.

"Have you seen this?" Beattie asked Darrow.

Darrow nodded.

"Are you on board with this thing?"

The Salomon lawyer had expected this. As soon as Goldstone brought out the agreement, he had called Gutfreund to ask how to handle it. Darrow had to walk a fine line. If Salomon were to be partners with Kravis, it was important to signal its discomfort with what Gutfreund called the "unseemly" agreement. But if the talks somehow fell through, Kravis would no doubt use Salomon's displeasure as a club to publicly maul the management group.

Darrow conceded to Beattie that the document had "obvious problems" and would likely be rewritten. He mentioned that Gutfreund and Warren Buffett opposed it. It was all he had to say. A few minutes later, Beattie stepped back into the living room and took Goldstone aside.

"How many people did you say are involved in this?"

Only seven at the moment, Goldstone said, but Johnson had in mind that hundreds of employees would also share in the riches.

"Well, this is pretty rich, you know."

"You should talk to Ross about that."

"Well," Beattie said, "we've obviously going to reserve opinion on this. We can't say yea or nay until we have some time to look at this thing."

Goldstone nodded, but suggested they consider the document closely. "You'll need to get things resolved, because it's very important."

The meeting adjourned with plans to reconvene at RJR Nabisco's offices an hour later. In the confusion, neither Goldstone nor Jack Nusbaum retrieved the management agreement from Beattie.

"They never asked for it," said Casey Cogut. "So we kept it."

When Kravis, Roberts, Beattie, and Cogut stepped from the elevator onto the forty-eighth floor, they were surprised to find the place packed with people. Scores of people with nothing to do with the negotiations were rushing to and fro. Linda Robinson was scurrying about with a draft copy of a press release. Kravis was nonplussed to be introduced to Laurie Johnson. He spied Johnson, scotch in hand, looking relaxed and refreshed, a puff handkerchief peeking jauntily from a chest pocket. Kravis was also introduced to Ed Horrigan, who looked natty in a white tennis sweater. Expecting to resume a set of tough negotiations, the Kravis group was startled to encounter something more akin to a fraternity mixer.

Kravis and Roberts were escorted into Johnson's office, the sight of their first tangle a week earlier. In fine spirits, Johnson offered the cousins a drink, which they declined. Beattie slipped Johnson's secretary a draft agreement he had hastily scribbled out and asked that it be typed. There was no sign of Cohen or Strauss.

As Kravis and Roberts waited, they listened to Johnson ramble on about the businesses they were all about to co-own. In a wide-ranging soliloquy, Johnson—upbeat, casual, laughing—skittered through a number of subjects, including Premier, the Atlanta headquarters, and the outlook for Nabisco businesses they would sell. He was glad for the time to get to know his new partners. Jim Robinson and Ed Horrigan sat by, listening and chatting occasionally.

For nearly an hour they discussed the fine points of RJR Nabisco. At one point, Gar Bason, the terrierlike Davis Polk lawyer, poked his head into the room. "What are you doing in this room without another lawyer?" Bason challenged Beattie. He was merely being protective of his client, but it broke the mood.

Kravis noticed they had been waiting a long time. "What's holding everything up?"

"I don't know," Johnson said. But then, he wasn't especially concerned; these finishing-up sessions always took time.

Cohen came in shortly after. He had been working with Strauss and Gutfreund on a way around the bond-offering problem.

"Where do we stand?" Roberts asked.

"We're still trying to thrash this thing out," Cohen explained.

In fact, Cohen was getting nowhere. For an hour he had tried to fathom Salomon's objections to Drexel and searched in vain for a compromise. Cohen hadn't come from a trading culture like Salomon's, and sometimes didn't grasp the fine points of Gutfreund's arguments. It was taking time, and he was tired.

Later, everyone who participated in the long night's deliberations would emerge with different versions of what came to be known as The Drexel Problem. Jim Robinson would point to Drexel's expected indictment. Salomon's official line was its concern about placing its capital in another firm's hands—a curious explanation, because it planned to do exactly that with Shearson. Johnson would suggest, mysteriously, that Kravis had somehow come under the control of Drexel.

Months later Tom Strauss acknowledged the central controversy. It lay in the esoteric world of the bond trader. When more than one bank agrees to underwrite a bond offering, a lead bank must be chosen to run the books. The key records of bond sales reside physically at that bank, which generally calls the shots and parcels out bonds over the course of the offering. The lead bank is so noted by placing its name first—on the left side—of the subsequent tombstone advertisements that pack *The Wall Street Journal* and other financial publications. Being "on the left" of the tombstone thus has powerful symbolic significance in the bond world.

Before Kravis's entry, Strauss and Cohen had agreed that Salomon and Shearson would corun the books. Shearson would be on the left, Salomon on the right. The books would rest physically at Shearson. That arrangement didn't bother Salomon, Strauss explained, because Salomon's power in the bond world so overshadowed Shearson's that everyone would know who had really run the deal.

The same structure, however, would send an entirely different message with Drexel on the left. While Salomon could tower over Shearson from a position on the right, the same wouldn't be true of a bond-trading power such as Drexel. "With Drexel on the left," Strauss said, *"we would have been perceived as an afterthought."*

In the end, then, perception was the issue. Perception about who was running a set of bond offerings that, to Johnson or any other acquirer, was a detail. For despite its status as a full partner in Johnson's deal, despite all the high talk about merchant banking, Salomon's principal mission wasn't owning Oreos. It was selling bonds. And it was willing to sacrifice Johnson's interests—indeed, his entire deal—to avoid the perception that it was taking a backseat to its hated rival, Drexel. Through all the machismo, through all the greed, through all the discussion of shareholder values, it all came down to this: John Gutfreund and Tom Strauss were prepared to scrap the largest takeover of all time because their firm's name would go on the right side, not the left side, of a tombstone advertisement buried among the stock tables at the back of *The Wall Street Journal* and *The New York Times*.

By two o'clock Cohen was shuttling between Kravis and Roberts in Johnson's office and a Salomon contingent, which remained in the "fishbowl" conference room around the corner. Desperately he sought a middle ground. Whatever doubts Cohen might have had about sharing his bounty with Kravis, that night he tried his best to reconcile the two sides.

But no compromise seemed acceptable to Gutfreund. "In no way will we defer to Drexel," Salomon's chairman intoned. "Glad to have 'em as a partner, Peter. But we haven't gone this far to give this deal up to Drexel."

Time after time, Cohen attempted to pull his friend Strauss off to the side for a heart-to-heart talk. Each time, Mike Zimmerman or one of the other Salomon bankers would trot out and join the conversation. Cohen began to think of the Salomon executives as sausages, linked together wherever they went. It was impossible to get a moment alone with any one of them.

Only once did Cohen lose his temper. Zimmerman made another of his group's pronouncements about Salomon's reputation. "We are Salomon Brothers," he said. "Who do they think they are to treat us this way?" It was too much for Cohen, who proceeded to jump down the banker's throat. "What are you talking about? You guys didn't exactly blow out the lights on Southland and Revco, you know. They have reason to be concerned. I mean, do you even understand what we're doing here?"

Cohen tried every alternative he could imagine. Reimbursing Kravis for the extra cost of hiring Salomon. Setting up a trading room at a neutral site where all three firms could manage the offering together. He held his breath whenever he saw movement in the Salomon position. Each time they seemed to be nearing an agreement, a Salomon banker popped off about Drexel. "What are we doing?" one would say. "These guys are crooks. They're crooks!" And the whole group would set off on a spree of Drexel bashing.

It was as frustrating as anything Cohen had attempted. A man who prided himself on his stamina, Shearson's chief had to admit he was exhausted. For two weeks he had been fighting nonstop. He needed sleep. Negotiating the most important issues of history's largest takeover at two in the morning—it made no sense. Why were they here?

As the night wore on, Johnson, who continued to be impressed with Kravis's financial sophistication, began to lean perceptively toward his position. Why not go with Drexel, Johnson asked, if in fact they were most reliable? "Peter, we should have the best people doing this, I don't care who they are," Johnson said. "If it's a better idea, let's use the better idea."

Johnson's behavior emboldened Kravis. Why don't you go out there and bang out a compromise yourself, Kravis asked Johnson at one point. After all, wasn't Johnson the client here? Couldn't he simply demand that his own investment bankers go along with his wishes? Johnson said he'd give it a try.

He left, then returned twenty minutes later. "Well, I talked to 'em."

And? Kravis wondered.

"Well, I still don't know what's going on."

"Who the hell is making decisions around here?" Kravis said, his anger growing.

"Well, I don't know," Johnson replied. "There's all these guys from Salomon out there . . ."

Jim Robinson, who had kept his counsel through most of the evening, thought he saw a solution. Gutfreund, he suggested, hadn't liked being excluded from their discussions at the Plaza. "I think his feelings are hurt," Robinson said. "Why don't you guys sit down and talk with him?"

"Fine," Kravis said. "Why don't you go get him."

Word came back that no one could find Gutfreund. He had vanished. "Where the hell is he?" Johnson asked, stalking out of the room. He checked first with the security guards, who said they thought Gutfreund had gone out for a walk.

If Gutfreund was pouting, Johnson figured, it would probably only make things worse to send a minion after him, so Johnson went to retrieve him himself. He found him on Fifty-seventh Street, smoking a cigar. Gutfreund appeared to be lost in thought.

"Come on, John, you gotta get upstairs and spend some time with Henry," Johnson said. "This thing seems to be moving along."

Around three o'clock Kravis and Roberts sat down with Gutfreund in the small anteroom off Johnson's office. "We're trying to be reasonable here," Kravis said. "Now why is it so important that you guys run this deal?"

"Because I think we're competent," Gutfreund said. "Because our people have spent a considerable amount of time on this. We are perfectly capable of doing this job, and we should do it. . . . There are any number of reasons we should do this deal. . . . Our firm has taken a terrible beating in recent years." Kravis knew: It was one reason they didn't want Salomon running the books. "Now I've got the most respect for Mike Milken," Gutfreund continued, "but this is how we at Salomon Brothers want to proceed."

Gutfreund, it was clear, wasn't budging, but neither was Kravis. When Gutfreund left the room, Roberts sank into a dark mood. He stood talking with Kravis beside Johnson's wet bar for several minutes until Dick Beattie walked in.

"Look, this is crazy," Roberts said. "We've spent all night arguing who's going to be on the left and right of the underwriting tombstone. How are we going to work out agreement on the real issues? How are we going to work with these guys even if we do this deal? Everyone's interested in everything except doing a business deal. It's all jockeying for ego and position."

He was growing more depressed just talking about it. "I came in here thinking we were going to do a deal," Roberts said. "Now . . ."

"I believe you, George," Kravis said, nodding his head in agreement. "You're absolutely right."

Beattie shared his clients' discouragement. "You know, there's a lot of issues in the management agreement we put off, too. If we can't get this behind us, we'll never get anything behind us."

"Let's just go home and get some sleep," Roberts said. "This is crazy."

Kravis took Cohen aside and told him they should resume after daylight. As for the bond situation, Roberts and Kravis planned to talk through compromises at a seven o'clock breakfast with Drexel's Peter Ackerman, the trader stepping into Milken's shoes. Maybe Ackerman could come up with something Gutfreund could live with.

"Call me at home when you're ready to reconvene," Cohen said.

As the Kravis contingent headed for the elevator, Gutfreund came scurrying after them. "Dick, Dick, hold it a second. Let's talk this over." Beattie tried to calm the Salomon chairman. "We're just not making any progress, John."

Kravis and Roberts paused while Beattie walked back to speak with the Salomon bankers milling about in the fishbowl. A dozen questions pelted the lawyer as he entered. "Why are you guys so protective of Drexel?" someone asked. "They're big boys. They can take care of themselves."

"Look," Beattie said, "all night Peter Cohen has been defending you guys. The Drexel guys are our partners. They've been good to us. We're not going to desert them."

Beattie didn't belabor the fact that Salomon had repeatedly bungled its attempts to enter the LBO field. Or that Kravis would sooner have his mother handle this offering than Salomon. Or that Kravis felt Strauss had betrayed him. It was all so complicated.

By the time Kravis and Roberts departed, Johnson had already left. Gar Bason had a memorandum of agreement between the two sides ready to sign, and Johnson initialed it on his way out. The impasse between Kravis and Salomon, he was certain, would be solved by daylight. Frankly, he liked Kravis's approach better than Shearson's. But he would be satisfied with whatever approach they chose. These last-minute details were just so tiresome.

Many of the Shearson group stayed and stewed over the night's events until five A.M. Two members of the Salomon contingent, Peter Darrow and Mike Zimmerman, emerged into the dawn to find their cab had been waiting for eight hours. The meter was still running.

"Excuse me, sirs?" the driver said as he dropped the pair off in Brooklyn Heights. "Would you mind initialing this voucher? No one's going to believe this."

Dawn was gathering when Cohen dragged himself into his Fifth Avenue apartment. He thought about going to bed, but knew he was too wound up to fall asleep immediately. In the bedroom his wife, Karen, woke up and asked how it went. Rarely had Cohen felt so frustrated. For the first time in his career he hadn't been able to build a bridge between warring factions. It was an ability he prided himself on. They sat on the bed, husband and wife, for nearly an hour, sorting out the night's events, slowly unwinding, before quietly falling asleep.

The ringing phone beside his bed jarred Cohen from a deep sleep. Through bleary eyes he stared at the clock. It was eight o'clock. Tucking the receiver to his ear, Cohen heard the cool voice of Henry Kravis. They were ready to meet.

Cohen wasn't looking forward to seeing Kravis again; for some reason he couldn't seem to shake his head clear. He called Jim Robinson. "Whatever you're doing," Cohen said, "drop it. Come on up and meet me at Nine West."

Next Cohen called Jeff Lane. Shearson's number-two executive hadn't been deeply involved in the RJR drama so far, for he had his hands full running the company in Cohen's absence. Now Cohen needed him. "I'm really worn out here," he told Lane. "I may not be thinking as clearly as I should. I need someone with a fresh head."

By nine o'clock a small group had reassembled in Johnson's offices. Only Gutfreund and Strauss made up the Salomon contingent. Kravis and Roberts showed up a few minutes later, ready to talk. Cohen suggested they return downstairs to their own offices until Johnson turned up. When Johnson hadn't arrived fifteen minutes later, someone called his apartment and discovered he was still asleep. Around nine-fifteen Cohen went down to Kravis's offices, so tired he could barely see straight, and found Kravis and Roberts with Dick Beattie. At breakfast, Peter Ackerman had offered to back out of the deal if Kravis wished. Kravis wanted no such thing. Asked for a compromise, Ackerman came up with something he thought Gutfreund could live with. The bond offerings would be split: Drexel would head the first portion, with Shearson on the right, and Salomon would head the second, also with Shearson on the right. Similar ideas had been batted around the night before, but Kravis thought it sounded reasonable.

Cohen tried his best to listen, not sure he fully understood the proposal. Less than a half hour later he returned upstairs to explain Kravis's compromise to a group that now included Jack Nusbaum, Jim Robinson, and Steve Goldstone. Johnson still hadn't shown up. When Gutfreund and the others began questioning him about Ackerman's plan, Cohen found himself short of answers.

"Look, I give up," Cohen wearily told the group. "Maybe somebody else can crack the code here. Maybe somebody else should go down and see what you can do."

Jeff Lane and Jack Nusbaum were chosen to make the second sortie. Downstairs Kravis sent the pair into another room and had Ted Ammon explain again the compromise he had in mind. Kravis was alarmed. Lane and Nusbaum didn't seem to have the slightest grasp of what they were talking about.

In her apartment above the Museum of Modern Art, Linda Robinson was awakened by a call from her secretary. "Henry Kravis just called. He says it's important."

Robinson hadn't been asleep for more than three hours. When her head hit the pillow at six A.M., she had hoped the deal would be struck by the time she woke up. She called Kravis and was passed through quickly.

"How'm I doing, coach?" Kravis asked.

"I don't know, Henry," Robinson said sleepily. "It's nine-thirty in the morning. What's going on?"

"We just had a meeting. Things went okay, but we couldn't really tell." Kravis was fishing, Robinson figured.

"I don't know what happened," she said, "but I'll find out and call you back."

Linda Robinson put down the phone, then called the group at RJR Nabisco. Kravis insisted on keeping Drexel in the deal, she was told, and the talks were collapsing. Everyone was blaming it on Kravis. *Oh, no,* Robinson thought.

She called Johnson. He was still at home and knew nothing about the rapidly deteriorating situation at Nine West. Johnson was a late sleeper, and hadn't let a $20 billion negotiation change his habits. "Things sound really bad," Robinson said. "They're way off track."

Finally she called Kravis back. "Everybody is really mad. What the hell went on when you met with our guys?"

"Your guys were really tough."

"Well, they say you were backsliding on all this stuff."

———

When Johnson finally reached his office around ten o'clock, he found Cohen, Gutfreund, and the rest in an uproar. Not only was Kravis insisting that Drexel corun the books, they said, but he had now raised questions about the management agreement and other new issues. "They hate your management agreement," Cohen said. "They're taking a whack of that, too."

Johnson could always tell when someone was trying to get a rise out of him. Cohen, it was clear, wanted him mad at Kravis. Confused and growing angrier by the minute, Johnson took a seat in the large conference room where the group was debating how to handle Kravis. Mostly they seemed to be cursing him.

They're trying to take the whole deal! We're getting fucked! They're fucking us! They're fucking us!

It made no sense to Johnson. As best he could tell, it all boiled down to who got the most fees. When he asked questions, the answers came back in Wall Street gobbledygook that only made the issues more difficult to comprehend. Half the time Johnson couldn't tell if he was supposed to be upset. "I just bloody don't understand what the problem is," he said.

Strauss tried to explain that splitting the bond offerings would be a logistical nightmare. "Goddamn it," Gutfreund railed, "what they're looking for is preposterous. We should just go out on our own. We'll never be able to live with these people."

Disgusted, Johnson retreated to his office. He wanted no part of what he viewed as trivial arguments. He couldn't believe the agreement would fall apart over something as silly as which bank would run a bond offering. People shuttled in after him, complaining that the deal wasn't working. Johnson grew testy.

"This is all horseshit," he snapped. "Nobody gives a shit about the company. Nobody gives a shit about the employees. Jesus, we've got a goddamn company to run. I've got 140,000 people to worry about. We've got to get going!"

As the morning wore on, Johnson waited for something—anything—to happen. The peace treaty couldn't fall apart. It just couldn't. This too, he figured, would blow over.

Inside the fishbowl, matters deteriorated quickly. If Kravis insisted on using Drexel, they agreed, there would be no joint deal. If there was no deal, it was time to bid. It had been ten days since Kravis announced his $90 offer, Gutfreund and Strauss argued, and still the management team had no bid. They proposed to immediately loft a $92 counterbid.

"It makes us real," Strauss argued. "We need to be penciled in as a player. We need a bid on the table." The price got no argument from Cohen or Jim Robinson. Of those present, the only serious opposition came from Steve Goldstone.

To Goldstone, it was clear what this tactic was about: It was what traders called a "fuck you" bid. Simply put, Cohen and Gutfreund were so mad at Kravis they wanted to shove an offer right in his face. Goldstone silently cursed these men and their giant egos.

He stood beside the great table and denounced the idea of a new bid, his voice rising as he spoke. He had been pleading with Atkins for a merger agreement, promising that management would come through with a blockbuster bid. If Shearson bid $92, he said, that argument would be moot. A $2 bump wouldn't bust many blocks. Once a bid was out, they lost their leverage with the special committee. Atkins and Hugel would know they had management on the hook and would pull for all their worth.

"This won't scare Henry off," Goldstone argued. "Henry won't walk away from this thing. It will only infuriate him. All you're doing is pissing off Henry and losing our leverage with the special committee. We're throwing away our strategic advantage. It's a wasted bid."

Gutfreund didn't think much of Goldstone's argument and said so. Ross Johnson may write the check, Gutfreund suggested, but it was still Salomon and Shearson's bankbook. "It's not your money," he snapped. "We know how we're going to proceed."

For several minutes Goldstone and the Salomon executives locked in a heated discussion of bidding strategy. Goldstone wished Tom Hill, who was in Minneapolis for a Pillsbury board meeting, were there to add heft to his argument. Finally Goldstone's partner, Dennis Hersch, leaned over and whispered into his friend's ear.

"Hey, cool it," Hersch said. "They've made up their minds. You're not their counsel."

Goldstone stormed around the corner into Johnson's office. Spitting mad, he briefed Johnson on the situation, adding that the bankers were prepared to launch a counterbid. "It's a serious, serious mistake and it's going to hurt us," Goldstone said. "But I can't stop them. They're completely hostile. They're not listening to me."

Johnson listened as Goldstone went on about Gutfreund. Still he remained unconcerned. This was a negotiation, and all negotiations get heated. Sooner or later, he told himself, they would calm down.

Robinson, Cohen, and Nusbaum were appointed to make the final trip downstairs to Kohlberg Kravis around eleven o'clock. Escorted into Kravis's office, Robinson did the talking.

"We appreciate your negotiating in good faith," he said. "We both tried to cut a deal. Everybody worked hard. We seem to have problems that can't be overcome. If you can't move off that point, there's no point in discussing this any further. We'll have to go our separate ways."

Kravis was nonplussed. "What's the response to our proposal that we gave to Peter this morning?" he asked.

Robinson was every inch the diplomat. It just wouldn't work, he said, not going into details. Then he dropped the bomb.

"We'll be submitting an alternate bid," Robinson said. "We're putting it on the tape right now."

"What?" Kravis said, amazed. As far as he was concerned, they were still in negotiations. "Why?"

"We may win or we may lose," Robinson said, "but if we lose it'll be with a structure that is best for our company and investors."

When Robinson's group left, Kravis erupted, as did George Roberts. "Goddamn it," Roberts groused, "Ross Johnson didn't have the balls to come down here and look us in the eye and tell us that himself. I'm glad we didn't hook up with those guys. It never would have worked out."

Cohen stepped out of Kravis's office, picked up a phone in Kohlberg Kravis's waiting room, and called the group upstairs.

"Go ahead," he said. Minutes later news of the management group's $92 bid crossed the Dow Jones News Service.

Kravis wasn't the only one stunned by the management group's bid. Johnson was floored. Brooding in his office, Johnson had figured the debate going on in the conference room was theoretical. Despite Goldstone's warning, he didn't believe anyone would actually launch a new bid. Not with a deal with Kravis so close. And certainly not without his approval.

"What are we doing?" Johnson railed at Goldstone when he saw the news cross the tape. "This is stupid as hell! This is asinine! If all the negotiations have broken down, what the hell use is there in making an offer? You're not going to get a merger agreement." It would only anger Kravis.

Linda Robinson arrived on the forty-eighth floor and talked with Kravis on the phone at noon. He was livid. "I can't believe they did it!" Kravis raged. "Why didn't they try harder?" He went on for several minutes, his anger flowing unchecked. Linda Robinson could only listen, irritated and a bit embarrassed at her own side's behavior.

Johnson remained in his office, shocked at the turn in events. He couldn't talk to Gutfreund or Cohen; they seemed too pleased at having shown Kravis the price of messing with them. He couldn't talk to Kravis, who, in Johnson's words, was "pissing fire." Just seventeen hours earlier, he had managed to get a peace treaty. He hadn't wanted to invite Strauss or Cohen or any of the Wall Streeters. The whole thing had fallen apart over greed—pure and simple greed. And now, the *pièce de résistance*, his own partners were launching a $20 billion bid without even bothering to tell him. He felt like the man who entered the casino in a tuxedo one night and emerged the next morning in rags. Far worse, Johnson realized, he had lost all control of his fate.

As Johnson moped, Goldstone reluctantly dialed Peter Atkins to inform him of the group's new bid. Atkins was pulled from a special committee meeting at Skadden Arps to take the call. Goldstone fought to disguise the displeasure in his voice. After their discussion of a preemptive bid the day before, he was almost ashamed to speak to Atkins. A blockbuster, Goldstone had vowed.

As he broke the news to Atkins, Goldstone thought he could hear the surprise in the lawyer's voice. He wanted to explain, but knew he didn't dare. When he finished, there were several moments of awkward silence. He knew Atkins must be struggling with how to deal with the surprise of such a low bid.

"Okay," Atkins finally said. "I hear you."

Goldstone wasn't the only one unhappy with the management group's $92 bid. In Minneapolis, Hill stepped out of a Pillsbury board meeting to hear the news from Cohen. "I think it's a mistake," Hill told his boss. Now they were in an auction, and in an auction the auctioneer has control over all the bidders. "Once we stepped forward with a bid," Hill recalled months later, "the board knew they had us by the short hairs."

Afterward, everyone scattered. Cohen spent the afternoon in a New York Stock Exchange board meeting. Strauss and Gutfreund boarded a plane and flew to Palm Beach for a weekend outing with Salomon clients. Johnson simmered in his office. Linda Robinson stopped by Kravis's suite on her way out of the building.

"We've got to do something," she said. "We've got to get it back on track."

"I don't see how we can get it back on track," Kravis said. He was resigned to the fact; it was over. In the middle of negotiations, Peter Cohen had pulled a gun and sprayed the room with bullets. How do you negotiate with people like that?

"You've made your bid," Kravis told Jim Robinson's wife. "You're on your own at this point."

———

Financial studies were Frank Benevento's life. As a consultant to Johnson and Sage, Benevento loved to use terms such as *financial engineering* to describe his number crunching. Lately Benevento had been busy studying the fee structures of major Wall Street advisers. On Thursday afternoon he walked into Johnson's office with the results of his latest study. According to the percentile fees currently prevailing on Wall Street, and in light of the tremendous fees being paid the investment bankers and lawyers in this deal, Benevento said, he had compiled his own bill.

It came to $24 million.

Johnson nearly fainted. Everyone, he reflected, was out to get something for themselves. The directors, with their petty concerns about pensions and auto insurance. Kravis and his investment bankers and their fees. Salomon and its bonds. And now Frank Benevento wanted $24 million.

There was no bloody way Benevento was getting anywhere near $24 million, Johnson thought. He told him to bill the company for whatever he wished. The matter would be dealt with when things returned to normal.

Depressed, the Johnsons left New York on Friday morning, flying north to a hospital outside Albany. That afternoon Johnson sat in his comatose son's hospital room for four hours. Bruce Johnson wasn't doing well. His condition had deteriorated seriously on the trip to Albany from Westchester. The Westchester doctors insisted it would be safe, but their Albany counterparts felt he probably shouldn't have been moved. Bruce's temperature soared. Johnson passed the day talking with the doctors, but there was little to say.

Similarly, Kravis spent Friday with his own son. It was Parents Day at the exclusive Middlesex school in Massachusetts, and Kravis drove up for the occasion. Afterward he retired to his country home, hoping to escape the rigors of all-night negotiations and the *rat-a-tat* of press criticism. The media attacks had left him feeling besieged. At his darkest moments, it was enough to make him question how badly he really wanted to own RJR Nabisco. Was it worth the cost of being a pariah?

Friday afternoon Kravis suffered by far the worst blow from the press so far. "KING HENRY," blared the cover of *Business Week*, out that day. The headline inside read, "Why KKR's Kravis may be headed for a fall—even if he wins the battle for RJR Nabisco." Carolyne Roehm saw the cover at her Seventh Avenue office and cringed.

Kravis reacted as if he'd been publicly labeled a child molester. He withdrew into himself, morose. All weekend Roehm tried to cheer him up, but it was no use. She tried silliness and teasing and laughing. She joked they should enlarge it to poster size and hang it up. Linda Robinson called and passed on her condolences. Nothing worked. Kravis was stricken.

Then, at his lowest ebb, something happened that should have made him feel better. Kravis didn't know it, but the tides of public sentiment were about to shift, strongly, in his favor.

For all the debate over its contents, the copy of Johnson's management agreement that fell into Kravis's hands hadn't changed much in two weeks.

Despite Gutfreund's complaints about its "unseemly" aspects, despite Jim Robinson's suggestions, and despite the fact that virtually everyone involved agreed it would be renegotiated, so far it hadn't. Peter Cohen had more important things to worry about. He passed responsibility for it to Jack Nusbaum, who passed it on to an associate at his firm. Negotiations would be messy and time-consuming, and everyone was busy battling Kravis.

Gutfreund, having received assurances it would be cut back, was in no hurry. The keepers of the agreement, Johnson's attorneys at Davis Polk, were in no hurry. Steve Goldstone, curiously, left it to Johnson to renegotiate the management agreement. "Ross is a grown-up," Goldstone said later. "He knew he had to give it up. It was up to him."

Day-to-day responsibility for the agreement remained in the hands of Goldstone's assistant, Gar Bason. Bason saw his job as looking out for no one's interests but Johnson's and was determined to hold the agreement sacrosanct, no matter what Cohen had promised Gutfreund. For a week following Salomon's entry into the fray, Bason badgered Gutfreund's aides to approve it. "Have you signed off on it yet?" he asked. "Have you signed off?"

Frustrated, Bason complained to Goldstone. "They're just fucking us over!" he snapped. Irritated by Bason's demands, Salomon's lead attorney, Peter Darrow, also took complaints to Goldstone. "Your guy Bason keeps hammering me on this thing," Darrow said. "He seems to think there will be no changes. Well, there will be changes."

Goldstone had no interest in fighting. "Agreed," he said. It could wait.

Among the few who wanted the agreement changed quickly were Jim and Linda Robinson, the two members of the group most keenly attuned to public relations. Both had recognized the agreement's potential to explode in Johnson's face. But Jim Robinson, the one who could have pressed for a change, didn't. As a result, nothing happened. The agreement simply lay in state, a time bomb ticking away. Friday afternoon it went off.

Linda Robinson took the call. A veteran *New York Times* reporter, James Sterngold, was preparing a story on the management agreement for Saturday's paper. From what Sterngold told her, it was clear he knew everything: the $2 billion, the free ride, even Salomon's opposition. Linda Robinson's first impulse was to come clean and discuss the agreement openly, but she was overruled by a press-wary Goldstone. When she informed her husband of Sterngold's call, Corporate America's secretary of state had a succinct reaction: "Oh, shit."

Late Friday afternoon Peter Cohen sat in the back of a limousine cruising home. It had been a long, frustrating week, but despite breakdown of the peace talks, he still held out hope he could get Johnson and Kravis together. No permanent enmity existed between the two sides, and the clash between Drexel and Salomon seemed too silly to keep them apart.

When he heard of the developing *Times* story, Cohen instantly realized the repercussions. If the pact had leaked, it could only have come from one place. Cohen immediately called Dick Beattie.

"What the hell happened?" Cohen demanded.

"I don't know, Peter," Beattie said. "I have an idea how it happened. But it didn't come from me."

"You leaked that agreement to Sterngold!"*

"Peter, I didn't. I couldn't have. It's right here in my briefcase." The briefcase lay open at Beattie's feet. "Peter, I'm not in control of everything," Beattie said. "Henry hands out everything to everybody."

In fact, Kravis had convened a meeting of his investment bankers Thursday afternoon, where terms of the agreement were aired in detail. Kravis hadn't trusted his advisers to keep their mouths shut for a moment. The management agreement, though, seemed like just the kind of thing they ought to know about. Any one of a dozen advisers, Beattie knew, could have been the leak's source.

Cohen hung up, incensed. The battle for RJR Nabisco was escalating. The winds were changing, and they were beginning to blow hard in Peter Cohen's face.

By Friday Ted Forstmann's bidding group was ready to surface. At first, Hugel's special committee, wary about giving sensitive financial information to the company's toughest competitors, had balked at welcoming Forstmann's group. But Geoff Boisi's persistence had won the day. Boisi had agreed to a difficult due diligence process, in which each document

---

* Cohen recalls having taken a less combative stance; this version is largely Beattie's recollection.

the group received was to be color coded for review by only certain members.

What broke the logjam, though, was Hugel's realization that Forstmann Little represented a fallback position in case Johnson and Kravis teamed up. Hugel was certain the two would join forces: It made too much sense. If so, Forstmann's presence would keep the bidding alive.

Forstmann, of course, ensured it would be a difficult birth. Friday he spent the day at Lazard's Rockefeller Center offices negotiating a press release announcing his group's formation. He insisted that the release note that his group had been "invited" to bid; it was vital if Forstmann were to wear the white hat. Peter Atkins refused. The board, after all, was supposed to be neutral. No matter how much it wanted Forstmann in the bidding, it couldn't be seen as playing favorites.

But Forstmann was adamant. "I have to be invited. Don't you understand?" he told the Lazard advisers. "Either it's there or I'm not."

All afternoon they argued. Then, with Forstmann on the verge of storming out, Atkins finally relented. How about *welcomed?* the lawyer suggested. The board would *welcome* Forstmann's interest. Forstmann agreed.

During a break, Forstmann contacted his office and discovered a message from Jim Robinson. Minutes later he called and heard Robinson's soft Georgia drawl come on the line.

"Teddy, you know the respect I have for you," Robinson began. "You run your business, and I run mine. Now, I'm not telling you how to run your business. But I want you to know that the rumor down here is that you and Geoff Boisi are trying to put something together. I want you to know our guys are jumping up and down stiff-legged about this."

Forstmann wasn't familiar with the phrase, but got the message that Cohen was irate. "They feel," Robinson continued, "they had a statement from you that if you didn't do something with us, you wouldn't do anything at all. They said you had agreed to sit on the sidelines."

Forstmann took a deep breath. "Jimmy, this is very tough. I know you know I'm an honest guy." He told Robinson how he had stressed to Cohen that Forstmann Little had three options: joining forces with Shearson, going it alone, or dropping out. "Quite frankly, the last alternative was my preference—I just wanted to forget it. Now I'm not sure what we'll do."

"I know that," Robinson said. "But you said yourself you'd sit on the sidelines."

Forstmann attempted to explain what he meant by the sidelines remark. He could tell it was no use. "Listen, Jim, we don't know what we're going to do yet. When we do, you'll be the first to know."

Two hours later, Forstmann called Robinson again. He read the American Express chief the press release announcing formation of the new bidding group.

Robinson laughed. "Gosh, my phone call sure had some impact." Forstmann hadn't given Robinson's earlier objection a second thought.

"Good luck to you guys," Forstmann said.

"And you," said Jim Robinson.

Johnson slept late Saturday morning at his Atlanta home. Padding downstairs he picked up the *The New York Times*. Scanning the business section, his eyes were immediately drawn to a story at the bottom left-hand corner.

"NABISCO EXECUTIVES TO TAKE HUGE GAINS IN THEIR BUYOUT," the headline read.

Johnson, who never viewed the management agreement as the symbol of greed others did, thought the story was so wild it wouldn't have any credibility. It suggested the pact might be worth as much as $2 billion, a figure Johnson considered absurd. Only if every incentive was reached might they have reaped that much, but now, with bids pushing into the low nineties, that would never happen. Besides, everyone knew the agreement was to be renegotiated.

"This is absolutely fucking ridiculous," he said aloud. No one would believe this. Would they?

He reached Jim and Linda Robinson in Connecticut. "No reasonable person is going to believe this shit," he told them. "This is goddamn asinine."

Linda Robinson didn't think the story was so far off the mark, but didn't tell Johnson that. "Ross, it's not a p.r. problem you're dealing with," she said. She had to make Johnson grasp the scope of the dilemma they now faced. "It's a factual problem. You don't understand. You can't just tough this out. You're going to get killed on this thing."

Johnson's phone rang off the hook that day. One of the first to call was

Andy Sage, the architect of the management agreement. Sage had read *The Times* story and, remarkably, hadn't thought much of it. "Oh, that thing," Sage said. "That's all conjecture; nobody's going to take that seriously."

Sage wanted to talk about the bank situation. He was concerned that Shearson wasn't making progress toward assembling bank financing. "I can only beat their heads so long," Sage said. "I just don't think they're doing the job."

It was all Johnson needed to hear. Coming on top of everything else, he was beginning to realize the limitations of his partners, Shearson and Salomon. "Having watched and listened to George and Henry," he told Sage, "I would say we're a little overmatched here."

Charlie Hugel, who read *The Times* story that morning at his Connecticut home, was also getting calls. His were from angry directors, demanding an explanation from Johnson. If *The Times* report were true, the board risked looking like fools for not knowing about the agreement. Hugel himself was also curious, although he was too contemptuous of the press to grant it any accuracy. He called Johnson in Atlanta.

"Oh, Charlie, listen," Johnson said. "It's horseshit. Don't believe a word of it."

The two men discussed the article's alleged inaccuracies for some time. "Listen," Hugel finally said, "will you get me a letter on it, because I'm getting some calls."

Sure, Johnson said. The next day Goldstone authored a letter to Hugel, which Johnson signed. "Saturday's *New York Times* incorrectly implied that I and a few other members of management could earn excessive amounts under our group's buyout proposal," it began. "This simply is not the case, and I would like to set the record straight."

Johnson went on to suggest that his group's compensation arrangements were typical of LBOs. Furthermore, he wrote, much of the equity the group would receive would be distributed to large numbers of employees. "When we reached agreement with our financial partners on the allocation of equity," Johnson wrote, "I asked our lawyers in New York and Winston-Salem to analyze ways in which this stock could be distributed to our employees, and they are actively engaged in this analysis."

Charlie Hugel read Johnson's letter carefully. In three weeks of conversations with Johnson—including the talk in which Johnson offered him a share of the purse—it was the first time Hugel had heard any mention of employees receiving stock. Not even the day before, when Johnson had *The Times* story in hand, had he mentioned anything about this.

Hugel thought Ross Johnson was lying.

———

Among the more surprising elements of *The Times* story was a passage suggesting that Salomon had misgivings about the management agreement. Gutfreund called Johnson Saturday to deny this and to assure him that no Salomon executive had talked to the reporter. "Well, I tell you, Johnny, you got some kind of canary in there somewhere," Johnson said. He left it at that; Johnson simply wasn't built for confrontations.

Steve Goldstone was. When Goldstone read the Salomon reference he went berserk. The first thought that crossed his mind was that Salomon had leaked the management agreement to force the changes it wanted. He put the thought aside.* Not even Gutfreund, he said, was that stupid.

"We've got to get Sally in line," Goldstone complained to Cohen that afternoon. "If there's some changes we have to make, let's get to it. But this kind of public bickering shows a terrible division in our camp. They simply have to be brought in line. This is going to kill us."

Cohen insisted Salomon would be no problem, but Goldstone wasn't so sure. Later he had Gar Bason send Cohen the draft of a letter he was considering sending:

Dear Peter,

We have become increasingly concerned at press reports in recent days that suggest that the management group's financial partners are not fully supportive of Ross and the management equity arrangement that all of us have reached. Ross and his group are confident, based on your and Tom's [Strauss] assurances, that this [is] not the case. Nonetheless, the continuing rumors that surface in the newspapers are damaging to all of us. As a consequence, I am writing to ask that each of Shearson and Salomon write a brief note to me indicating that you are supportive of our existing arrange-

———

* "If I thought they were, I would take out my knives and kill them personally," Goldstone said later. "It would be one of the stupidest moves in all of Wall Street history."

ments. Naturally we understand that as we go forward with any new proposal, those arrangements will be a subject for discussion among all of us.

Sincerely yours,

George R. Bason, Jr.

On Saturday Ted Forstmann tried in vain to contact Johnson to formally notify him of his new group, and finally resorted to phoning Jim Robinson in Connecticut. "Jim, I'd just like you to know I'm trying to reach Ross. I don't have all his numbers. Would you mind telling him I was trying to get hold of him?"

"I think you ought to call him yourself." Robinson seemed in good spirits.

"Gosh, I'd love that."

Robinson mentioned Forstmann's new group. "Would you still work with us, Ted? I mean, could we try to put something together? Is it even possible?"

An idea struck Forstmann. Why couldn't Johnson join the Forstmann group? Shearson could even have a role. Instead of shoehorning Forstmann Little into Shearson's cockamamy structure, why couldn't Forstmann find room for Shearson in his "real money" deal?

"Absolutely, we would work with you," Forstmann said. "No problem at all. We'd have to do it the Forstmann Little way. No junk shit. No bullshit. But we'd love to have you."

Robinson gave him Johnson's number, and Johnson returned Forstmann's call Saturday afternoon. "Ross," Forstmann began, "I hope you understand what I'm doing is altogether permissible. I wanted to tell you the true story of what happened. But I haven't been able to see you. Christ, I haven't been able to talk to you."

Johnson brought up *The Times* story. "My deal has been leaked to the press," he said. "You wouldn't know anything about that, would you, Ted?" Forstmann didn't miss the implication.

"Ross, I didn't hear that . . . I give you my word I didn't do it. I abhor that. That's a dirty, fucking thing to do."

"Well," Johnson said, "I will have a way of dealing with Mr. Kravis if that's who did it."

Forstmann brought the conversation back to his group. "You know, Ross, I think we're the best people in this business. We're your kind of people. You know where I get my money. GM, IBM, GE."

"Yep, John Welch, John Akers," Johnson said, ticking off the CEOs of General Electric and International Business Machines. "I play golf with 'em."

"I don't blame you for going with all these junk bond guys," Forstmann said. "But in my deal there's no junk bonds, no funny money."

Johnson laughed. "I don't have any junk bonds in my portfolio."

Forstmann allowed himself to get excited. This sounded promising. "Now," Forstmann said, "Jim asked me if we could do this together. I said yes. I'm not trying to cut anyone out of anything. I'm not trying to do anything funny. We've got a reputation to protect."

"I know your reputation."

"Ross, you ought to seriously consider what I'm talking about. Talk to Jimmy. He's a very straight guy. He'll tell you. If we could get together, it would be great. You're the key to making this thing happen. I hope you'll be with us."

"Teddy, I'll give some thought to that."

Forstmann garnished his appeal with a personal touch. "Ross, I wanted to tell you I'm very sorry about your son. Goddamn it. I'm really sorry about that." After Johnson thanked him, Forstmann continued, "You know, we'll both be around after this. There are more important things than who buys RJR Nabisco."

"You're right."

"It's important we remain friends."

"Betcher ass."

Johnson had no intention of joining forces with Ted Forstmann's new group, which he labeled "the five-legged elephant." As far as he was concerned, Forstmann didn't have a chance in hell of winning this deal.

On Sunday they rested. In Atlanta, Johnson curled up with a stack of newspapers and watched football and golf on television. In Connecticut, a morose Henry Kravis wondered aloud whether the board had noticed the curious story in *The Times*. He paid little attention to Forstmann's new group; consortia, in his experience, were too cumbersome to win. In New Jersey, Peter Cohen took his son to a New York Giants game, and was probably the only father at the Meadowlands that day to sleep through the entire four quarters.

That evening a group of bankers and lawyers gathered at Cohen's Fifth Avenue apartment to plot strategy for the following week. Cohen was outraged at Geoff Boisi and Ted Forstmann, who he felt had given him repeated assurances they wouldn't pursue RJR Nabisco on their own. The possibility of a lawsuit was batted about, then dismissed. Jack Nusbaum suggested they write a letter expressing their displeasure. Goldstone and Peter Darrow saw no point in it, but Cohen seemed determined to exact his pound of flesh.

Sunday evening Ted Forstmann was at his East River apartment enduring a vigorous rubdown from a masseur once employed by the Italian national tennis team. Forstmann kept getting interrupted by worried calls from his outside public relations adviser, Davis Weinstock. From the hostile tone of reporters' inquiries that day, Weinstock said, it was clear Shearson was displeased with Forstmann Little. "They're claiming you did something," Weinstock said. "I don't know what."

Forstmann thought for a moment. He must be getting blamed for leaking the management agreement. *If that fucking Kravis has convinced people I leaked this thing . . .*

As Forstmann kept hopping up to take Weinstock's calls, his masseur grew frustrated. "How can I give you a massage if you keep getting up?"

"Maurizio," Forstmann said. "I know you have problems. But I have bigger problems."

Finally Forstmann decided to find out what was happening. He called Johnson in Atlanta. Laurie Johnson answered the phone at the house on Whitewater Creek Road. "Hi, Laurie. It's Ted Forstmann."

"Ted, how are you?" She seemed genuinely pleased to hear from him.

"Fine, fine. Is Ross there?"

"He's on a conference call."

"It'll only be thirty seconds. Could you ask him to pick up?"

Laurie Johnson left the phone for a minute, then returned. "Ross says he'll call you as soon as he gets off the conference call." Before he could hang up, she said, "How's the weather up there?"

Talk of the weather quickly turned to the condition of the greens at Deepdale. They chatted for nearly ten minutes. Forstmann hung up thinking what a nice wife Johnson had.

As Laurie spoke with Forstmann, her husband was on the other line with Cohen and Goldstone. Both were alarmed when he mentioned the call from Forstmann. That could mean only one thing: Like Kravis before him, Forstmann was making a play for Johnson.

"Look, I'm with you guys," Johnson insisted. "I'm not cooperating with anyone you don't want me to cooperate with."

"Why don't we call Ted and express those things so you don't have to?" Goldstone suggested. He was worried that Johnson wasn't capable of dealing with Forstmann firmly.

"Fine, you guys do what you think is best."

Goldstone quickly called Gar Bason with another job for the baby-faced hatchet man.

Thirty minutes later Ted Forstmann's phone rang. He already knew what he was going to tell Johnson. *Ross, I want to assure you I know nothing about this dirty leaking business. We don't do things like that. We abhor that.*

But when he picked up the phone, a voice he didn't recognize said, "This is Gar Bason of Davis Polk and Wardwell. We represent Mr. and Mrs. Johnson, and I am authorized to tell you to stop annoying them. You are imposing on them by calling them in their home. You will not attempt to reach Mr. Johnson directly anymore. Any communication between Mr. Johnson and you in the future will go through me."

"I don't know who you are," the astonished Forstmann shot back, "but let me tell you something. I called Mr. Johnson to tell him if anything funny is going on, I didn't do it. Mrs. Johnson and I were talking about golf and the greens at a club, where I was on the board of governors and helped Ross Johnson get in. I'll have you know I talked to Mr. Johnson yesterday at the request of Jim Robinson."

Now Forstmann was rolling. All the frustration he felt toward Peter Cohen and his cigars and Henry Kravis and lawyers and junk bonds came boiling forth. "Let me tell you something. I know enough about lawyers to know who cooked this up. It wasn't Ross Johnson. I can tell now the lawyers have taken over. God help everyone. This is what's wrong with the world today. Guys like you and your little concocted schemes."

But Forstmann wasn't through yet. "I regard this as extremely rude. Rest assured that I will be spending time with Mr. and Mrs. Johnson when this is over. And rest assured I will tell them of your rudeness."

And then he hung up.

CHAPTER

13

The RJR Nabisco directors who gathered at Skadden Arps on Monday morning, November 7, were a sullen, irritated bunch. For three weeks they had watched in growing horror as Ross Johnson turned their company into the centerpiece of a $20 billion circus, and more than a few on the board felt like fools for allowing it to happen. Disclosure of the management agreement shocked most of them and, by Monday, a rising anti-Johnson feeling was fast crystallizing on the board. Steve Goldstone had been right: These directors were no longer Johnson's friends, they weren't about to give him favors and they resented him for putting them at the eye of an increasingly public hurricane.

Several, including Vernon Jordan, had called Charlie Hugel over the weekend, horrified at details of the management agreement. John Macomber had been morally offended. "So gross, so unfitting," he had sputtered. Hugel had called Marty Davis himself. "Did you see *The New York Times?*" he asked.

Davis hadn't, but had a copy within reach. He had read the article in mounting indignation. *What the hell . . .*

"Can you believe it?" Hugel asked. "This is terrible. He says it's wrong, it's not true, but I don't know . . ."

News of Johnson's secret pact was the crowning blow for a board already feeling the pressure of an anti-Johnson backlash among employees, shareholders, and the media that would grow to earsplitting dimensions in coming days.

It was coming in a steady drumbeat of newspaper stories: the $52.5 million of golden parachutes; the 526,000 shares of restricted stock given to favored RJR executives, now worth nearly $50 million; the whole no-lose situation Johnson had set up. To make matters worse, the press had picked up on the favors bestowed on the board by Johnson, including the fat consulting contracts and the 1,500 shares of restricted stock each of *them* had gotten. The spectacle of Johnson's apparent greed, combined with the bitter public quarreling among the bidders, struck a nerve in a nation already sick of the unrest wrought by takeovers. From the outset, Hugel had been deluged with anti-Johnson, anti-LBO hate mail.

"This is the ultimate in 'insider' trading," a veteran tobacco worker wrote. "This group of insiders were intrusted [*sic*] with the management of the RJR Nabisco company. In return we are lied to, cheated and used by a small group of insiders for their own gain. I fail to see the difference between what Johnson is doing and armed robbery, except that you will let Johnson get away with it for your own personal interest." Other letters pleaded with Hugel to fire Johnson and the entire management group. "Somehow," a Winston-Salem businessman wrote, "there ought to be a greater value in this world than a stock price."

Anger wasn't confined to RJR Nabisco's communities. A Nashville shareholder wrote, "The greedy SOBs don't have the welfare of the company, its employees or stockholders at heart. Fight them if you can!" From Boston: "What has this group of people done to enhance shareholders during their tenure—nothing compared to their manipulation for their own pockets. What have they done for the community in Winston-Salem other than uproot the loyalties of the community? What have they done to build plants, hire and train more people to sell more and better costing products?"

Directors took special note of a letter from Smith Bagley. The angry Reynolds heir demanded that a blue-ribbon panel be formed to referee the developing auction. He questioned whether the committee could truly "safeguard the stockholders' interests," in light of the "close relationships between certain committee members and Mr. Johnson." Bagley's letter, while never acted on, upped the pressure one more notch when it was released to the press.

On a national scale, the fight for RJR Nabisco prompted new debate on the danger LBO debt held for the country. "Our nation is blindly rushing toward the precipice," warned Martin Lipton, the famed merger attorney, in a memo to clients. "As with tulip bulbs, South Sea bubbles, pyramid investment trusts, . . . Texas banks and all the other financial frenzies of the past, the denouement will be a crash."

Federal Reserve Board chairman Alan Greenspan urged Congress to have banks reconsider how LBO loans would fare in a recession. The comptroller of the currency instructed federal bank examiners to take a closer look at LBO loans. Senate minority leader Bob Dole and other politicians began growling about the need to reform the tax code to curb LBOs.

On consecutive days in mid-November, two major insurance companies, Metropolitan Life Insurance and ITT Corporation's Hartford Insurance, sued RJR Nabisco. The value of both firms' RJR bonds had plunged as the stock had risen. "The value lost by the bondholders will unjustly enrich RJR Nabisco management and other leaders of the leveraged buyout," Metropolitan Life chief executive John Creedon said. (Former Federal Reserve Board Chairman Paul Volcker called him up and said one word: "Bravo.") LBOs were generally "unethical," charged ITT Chairman Rand Araskog, who ordered the company's pension managers to stop investing in LBO funds.

In an editorial headlined, "Why the RJR circus is so dangerous," *Business Week* reflected the business establishment's distress. "This spectacle is not just unseemly—it is dangerous," it held. "It is precisely this sort of behavior that plays into the hands of those who want to shackle the free market with unnecessary regulation. LBOs, including a potential RJR deal, should stand or fall on their financial and economic merits, not on the childish behavior of the principals."

For all the high-level handwringing, few felt the effects of the escalating fight as keenly as RJR Nabisco's employees. In Atlanta, office workers sat during lunch periods glumly reading the daily news summaries the company issued. Isolated, irritated, and uncertain of their futures, the staff spent its days consumed with following the events on Wall Street, its spare time channeled into producing anti-Johnson propaganda. "It all started with a small lemonade stand in Manitoba," read one Johnson parody. "The next thing I knew I had sold my mother. The rest was easy." In truth, the headquarters staff was divided between pro-Johnson Standard Brands veterans and the Reynolds "mushroom farmers." Many of the undecideds stampeded into the Reynolds camp on disclosure of the management agreement. "We have circled the wagons," one disgruntled supervisor quipped, "and the Indians are inside."

An editorial cartoon from the *Atlanta Constitution* was widely circulated. It showed a group of hapless people in a cereal bowl, on the cover of what looked like a Shredded Wheat box. "RJR Nabisco Shredded Workers," it said on the box, "List price: 25 billion dollars."

RJR Nabisco employees across the country looked for ways to save their jobs. Second-shift workers at a Winston-Salem cigarette factory got out calculators and began figuring out what all 140,000 employees would have to kick in to make a bid.* In Chicago, two third-shift Nabisco bakery supervisors took the idea of a $3.8 billion bid for all fourteen bakeries to their superiors.

Nowhere were workers more despondent than in Winston-Salem. It wasn't bad enough that their venerable tobacco company had been put in play by Johnson and Horrigan. The smokeless cigarette the two had sent into the market untested was dying a brutal death. Premier was the first cigarette ever to be returned for refunds. It was the butt of drive-time disc-jockey jokes in St. Louis and Arizona, where it was being test marketed. The product that was to be the great hope for Reynolds Tobacco was being called one of the great new-product fiascoes of all time. And while managers fought desperately to salvage it, Horrigan and Johnson fought their LBO battle in New York.

Ed Horrigan put his house under guard and sent out a memo denouncing *The Times* story as "speculative." A parody of Horrigan's memo received wider readership than the real thing. "We have decided to just 'take the money and run!' " it began, closing, "It has been swell being the CEO to such a fine bunch of chumps. Thanks for making Ross and I rich men. We couldn't have done it without you."

Of the five members of the special committee, Hugel had probably swung the farthest in his judgment of Johnson. Unsure of his friend's motives from the outset, Hugel let his suspicions grow as the weeks wore on, prodded by a series of unsettling events: the piece-of-the-action offer, the management agreement, and the anonymous memo suggesting the company was worth between $82 and $111 a share. When Hugel had confronted Johnson with the memo, Johnson had called it "a lot of hypotheticals," suggesting it was the work of a junior-level staffer. Hugel wasn't so sure.

Hugel's annoyance increased Monday morning when *The Times* car-

---

* They spoke to Smith Bagley, but the effort went nowhere.

ried a story speculating that Johnson's group might sue Forstmann Little over its new bidding group. Hugel felt he had bent over backward to allow Forstmann entrance into this fight; he wouldn't stand for Johnson and Cohen's suing over it. He fired off a letter to Johnson that morning.

"Be advised that this committee is flatly opposed to your group taking any such action," Hugel wrote. "Whatever your grievances may be, this committee considers the Forstmann Little group to be a credible bidder for RJR Nabisco. The interests of RJR shareholders will be best served by the active participation of that group in our process, free from interference by your group. . . . Please confirm to me immediately that your group will not take any such action." Goldstone had written Hugel a half-hearted response, suggesting a suit was unlikely but defending the group's right to bring one, anyway.

Each new disclosure contributed to the revised picture of Johnson developing in Hugel's mind. Hugel was chairman of the board of trustees at his alma mater, Lafayette College. Johnson, he realized, gave little to charity. Hugel had been married to the same woman for thirty-six years, and he wondered whether the changes he saw in Johnson could be attributed to Laurie. The phenomenon of rich, older men taking pretty, young, second wives has been called the Jennifer Syndrome, and Hugel was the kind of solid citizen who thought older husbands often did foolish things to show off for their Jennifers. He felt that ambitious women such as Laurie Johnson, Susan Gutfreund, Linda Robinson, and Carolyne Roehm—in New York they called them "trophy wives"—compared notes on how their new husbands were doing, egging them on to grandeur.

Of the other committee members, the Yale-educated, Brooks Brothers–clad Macomber had long mistrusted the Manitoba-educated, Cassini-clad Johnson. Macomber had walked away from Celanese with a $2 million severance package, and was stunned at Johnson's $2 billion pact. Like Hugel he was an old-school believer in fundamental business values and regarded what Johnson was doing as making all executives look bad. He was also a great believer in the board's prerogatives. He hated having been taken by surprise by Johnson.

Johnson's most nettlesome director found a kindred spirit in the one thought to be his chummiest. Johnson had just put his friend Marty Davis of Gulf + Western on the board earlier that year. But Davis was nobody's patsy. He was a blunt, Bronx-born high-school dropout, who had risen in the movie business from Sam Goldwyn's office boy to head of Gulf +

Western's Paramount unit. He had developed a fearsome reputation for firing and intimidating people, earning him a spot on *Fortune*'s list of "America's toughest bosses." As chief executive of Gulf + Western, he had faced down corporate raiders such as Carl Icahn. He had also overhauled the company from a sprawling conglomerate to a media and financial power. He knew how to value businesses, and he thought $75 a share to be insulting or bungling or both.

Bill Anderson of NCR simply didn't like junk bonds, corporate raiders, or any of the modern folderol that kept business from doing business. At NCR he preached a homespun philosophy of looking after "stakeholders": employees, suppliers, and communities whose lives were intertwined with and dependent on a large company. Anderson had gone so far as to hand out stakeholder literature to other board members. He, too, was growing tired of the entire spectacle.

Of all the directors, Albert Butler felt the heat most keenly. At home in Winston-Salem, he was constantly upbraided by anti-Johnson zealots who felt the board had sold out the town and its workers. He and Wachovia's John Medlin were lunching at a downtown club when an angry Paul Sticht happened by. "How could the board let him do this?" Sticht demanded. "How could it?" Butler and Medlin patiently explained that they had really had had no choice, but Sticht didn't want to hear it.

Neither did anyone else.

By the time the committee met Monday, there was an unstated acknowledgment that things had gotten out of control. It was time, the directors agreed, to take matters into their own hands. At the urging of Davis and Macomber, the board's bankers had begun working on a restructuring plan of their own. In theory, the committee could throw out all bids and restructure the company independently, giving shareholders a big onetime payout from the sale of assets. In practice, the board needed the restructuring as a club to wave before Johnson and Kravis, an alternative in case the two teamed up.

More important on the morning's agenda, Peter Atkins had constructed a set of formal bidding guidelines, laying down procedures for each of the three groups—Johnson, Kravis, and Forstmann—to make its bid. For the most part the rules were standard; each of the bidders agreed to them within days. The key was the deadline: five o'clock Friday, November 18, eleven days away.

When the guidelines were issued that afternoon, Johnson groaned. A formal auction put all bidders on the same footing, meaning his group had squandered the last of its tactical advantage. In a call to Hugel, he tried one last pitch for a merger agreement, but got nowhere. As for the restructuring idea, Johnson thought it was a bluff. "Charlie, you'll get your balls blown off," he told Hugel. "No way you'll get ninety dollars out of a restructuring."

As the anti-LBO backlash rose to new heights, Kravis grew concerned that it might be doing irreversible damage to the firm's reputation. He and Roberts consulted twice with a pair of old friends, Gershon Kekst and Marty Lipton, about what they could do to counter it. The consensus: very little. Headlines attracted congressmen, they knew, and Kravis resigned himself to the possibility of anti-LBO legislation once the battle concluded. He tried not to think about it. "They can't do any more than crucify us in the press," Kravis said, "and that's been done."

Still stinging from the *Business Week* cover, Kravis received lectures on handling the press from his wife, who had suffered her own share of slings and arrows in the quest for publicity. "Henry, whether you like the press or not, you've got to deal with it. So deal with it," Roehm urged. "What you don't understand is that you're letting the press be handled by the other side. You must put out your own side of the story, or it won't get told."

"But—"

"There are no buts," Carolyne Roehm said. "You're being hammered. You've got to get your story out there. Otherwise the story that gets told will be theirs."

On his wife's advice, Kravis and Roberts agreed to see a reporter from *The New York Times* that week. The journalist had in mind an extensive interview, but Kravis, after making sure it was understood that he had never uttered the word *franchise* to Peter Cohen, cut the session off after a few minutes. Tom Daly, a Kekst spokesman, apologized for the "abrupt and frosty" end to the interview, explaining that the two were "stressed out."

The press wasn't Kravis's only worry. He was still searching for a wise man to provide guidance to fathoming RJR Nabisco's depths, and with just eleven days until bids were due, he was growing desperate. At Eric Gleacher's suggestion, he had interviewed Charles M. Harper, the chairman of agricultural giant ConAgra, about running the company; it hadn't worked out. Kravis had two meetings with executives of Pepsi, who wanted to invest in his deal in return for buying several Nabisco lines. While he had no doubt the Pepsi executives could help manage the company later, they couldn't help him now. Then, finally, Kravis heard the obvious name: Paul Sticht.

When Kravis called, Sticht tried to balance his loathing of LBOs with his loathing of Ross Johnson. Sticht considered LBOs "a national scandal [that] produced no good for anybody but a few greedy people." But the rabid anti-Johnsonism of Winston-Salem—even his barber was rooting for Kravis—convinced Sticht that helping Kravis was the right thing to do.

The two men met at Simpson Thacher Monday afternoon at four o'clock. Sticht wouldn't come to Kravis's offices for fear of running into Johnson in the lobby or elevator. Kravis found Sticht a genial retiree, "a real gentleman," with none of the obvious bitterness toward Johnson that Tylee Wilson had evidenced. He obviously cared about the company and its employees. Still, Sticht was out of touch with the new RJR Nabisco; his hands-on knowledge of the company seemed to be five years out of date. In the end, though, Kravis had to face a simple truth: Sticht was all he had. The two men shook hands, and Paul Sticht joined the Kohlberg Kravis team.

"Somebody take Henry's temperature," Johnson said when he heard the news. "He must be running a fever."

Leaked to the press on Monday, Peter Cohen's letter to Forstmann Little read like a shot across Ted Forstmann's bow.

Dear Ted:

I am deeply disappointed, in fact dumbfounded, by published reports that you may be leading a group whose purpose would be to seek to acquire RJR Nabisco, Inc.

You will recall that two weeks ago you approached Jim Robinson, Ross Johnson and me with a view towards becoming an important member of the management-led group which was considering an offer for RJR

Nabisco. I am sure you remember your expressed reasons for wanting to join us.

In view of your strong desire to become our partner, and in reliance upon the specific representations outlined below, we agreed to discuss all aspects of our proposed transaction with you fully and frankly, including our economic models, our detailed financing arrangements, our proposed bidding strategy and our preliminary thoughts regarding possible divestitures. . . .

We allowed Goldman Sachs, as your agent, to participate in our conversations based upon your and their expressed assurances that they would likewise be bound by the terms of the confidentiality agreement which you had signed. It would appear that Goldman Sachs nonetheless induced certain food companies to join your group, presumably using the confidential information which you obtained from us to induce them.

I strongly urge you to very carefully consider your actions. Our business relationship, including our recent discussions, presumes a code of conduct which should not include either ethical lapses or breaches of contractual relations. Shearson and the executives of RJR Nabisco intend to honor the commitments they have made. We expect you will do so as well. . . .

I very much hope that you will carefully consider the contents of this letter.

Very truly yours,

Peter

Cohen's letter had a predictable effect on Forstmann, who fired back a reply the next day.

Dear Mr. Cohen:

Through your letter of November 7, 1988 and your apparent distribution of that letter to the press, you have begun a program of irresponsible and false attacks against the ethics of Goldman, Sachs & Co. and Forstmann Little. By implication, you also attack the ethics of Procter & Gamble, Ralston Purina and Castle & Cooke, which have joined with us in considering the acquisition of RJR Nabisco. As you are aware, by attacking our reputation, you attack that which is most valuable to us. We believe that the motivation for your actions is to drive us out of the bidding process for RJR Nabisco in order to permit Shearson Lehman and certain RJR executives to buy the company at a reduced price. It is particularly disappointing that you should pursue this "tactic" because the RJR Nabisco management with whom you are working is obligated to protect the interests of RJR Nabisco shareholders. . . .

As I am sure you recall, we expressly informed you during the course of our discussions that, if we could not reach agreement with you, we reserved the right to consider our own transaction. We repeatedly made clear to you that we maintained three options: first, to participate in the transaction you were proposing if it were amended to comply with our standards; second, to walk away from any involvement with RJR; or third, to formulate our own proposal if such a proposal was invited by the Special Committee. After the Special Committee indicated to us that they would welcome our group's interest, we determined to pursue the option of considering such a proposal. . . .

The Forstmann Little group's interest in RJR Nabisco works to the clear benefit of RJR's shareholders and has been expressly welcomed by the company's Special Committee. We will not make a proposal if, after careful review, this transaction fails to meet our strict financial standards. However, under no circumstances will we permit your efforts at intimidation to impair the interests of Forstmann Little and its capital partners.

The firm of Forstmann Little & Co. has been built carefully, with the highest possible business standards and with total integrity. We have acted in all respects consistent with those standards throughout this transaction; we need no advice from you in this regard.

I hope this puts to rest the phony controversy which you have manufactured. Unlike you, we do not intend to release this letter to the press.

Very truly yours,

Theodore J. Forstmann

Cohen had sent a similar letter to each of Forstmann's bidding partners, including the respected senior partner of Goldman Sachs, John L. Weinberg. Weinberg's reply read like a senior statesman chastising a junior colleague.

Dear Peter:

I received your letter of November 7, 1988 at approximately the same time I received a call from the press, and thus it is clear to me that your letter was for purposes of public relations rather than communication with us. It is also clear that you don't know me very well; otherwise you wouldn't have wasted your and my time with insults or threats—particularly when you have not gotten your facts straight.

In my judgment your letter is not worthy of reply. However, my colleagues have persuaded me that it is appropriate to give you a written response.

Your letter is factually erroneous and totally unwarranted. Goldman

Sachs has not violated any of the terms of the confidentiality agreements which Forstmann Little signed with RJR Nabisco. As you know, I was not personally present, but I am categorically advised by my colleagues that our clear message to you has been that we might proceed independently of management or Shearson and were actively considering that possibility. Goldman Sachs is not precluded by any agreement with Shearson or RJR Nabisco from pursuing that alternative or making proposals for RJR Nabisco that would be received favorably by the Company and its shareholders.

This view is clearly shared by the Company's committee of independent directors. As it publicly reaffirmed today, the committee has welcomed the potential interest of Forstmann Little, Goldman Sachs and the highly respected companies with which we are working.

I find it difficult, if not impossible, to take seriously your professed interest in good relationships with Goldman Sachs. It is not conducive to any relationship between our firms for you to make charges such as those in your November 7 letter, or to seek to exploit them by releasing them to the press before you have even communicated them to us or received our response. We do not believe it is in anyone's interest to escalate this exchange and therefore we are not planning at this time to send copies of this letter to the press.

I strongly object to the tone and substance of your letter; you have no basis to lecture me, Geoff Boisi or Goldman, Sachs & Co. about anything. Moreover, your tactical maneuvers can only contribute to the negative impression of our industry that many people have. I trust those tactics will cease.

Sincerely,

John L. Weinberg

After reading the letters from Hugel, Forstmann, and Weinberg, Jim Robinson called Cohen and, in no uncertain terms, suggested he didn't care to read any more examples of Shearson's penmanship.

———

Bob Carbonell, chairman of Del Monte, stormed into Johnson's New York office Wednesday morning. El Supremo was as angry as The Pope had ever seen him. "Ross, you won't believe the amateur hour that's going on," he said.

Carbonell explained that he had just returned from being questioned by a squad of Dole executives at The Plaza as part of Forstmann Little's due diligence. From their questions, it was obvious that Dole had some-how gained access to a wealth of Del Monte confidential information: shipping schedules, production forecasts, everything. Del Monte's com-petitive position, Carbonell concluded, had been seriously compromised.

Both men realized the slip must have come from the special commit-tee. Its vaunted security procedures hadn't worked and, as a result, Dole had been allowed to snoop into Del Monte's most secret files. For the first time in a month, Johnson lost his temper. He could put up with fighting Kravis or Cohen. Those were fair fights. But to suffer a blow from pure laziness, pure incompetence—that was too much.

Hugel had flown to Russia the day before, but that didn't stop Johnson. John Martin called Roone Arledge at ABC and had a call patched through to the network's office in Moscow. In Moscow, Hugel hustled out of his hotel, through the dark, winding streets, and up to the ABC office to take Johnson's call. Even in Russia Hugel hadn't been able to escape RJR Nabisco. He ran into a senior Pepsi executive in the lobby of his hotel and discussed ways Pepsi might enter the bidding. At the Kremlin, Hugel met with several top deputies, including the chairman of the USSR's commit-tee of commerce. All wanted to know about the big battle on Wall Street.

Now Hugel listened as Johnson vented his fury at the special commit-tee. "Now I know they're all complete fucking idiots!" Johnson ranted over the transatlantic line. "Here they are getting paid twenty-eight million dollars to jump all over our ass. To not even do the due diligence right. This really, really hurts, Charlie. They don't need all that informa-tion to understand whether the goddamn company is right or wrong. You're going so goddamn hard to pump up these people that you're killing the company! It's not fair."

Hugel said he would look into it, and later a committee aide apologized to Johnson for what he termed a "technical mixup." There was a post-script to the episode. Several weeks later Carbonell received a Federal Express package apparently misrouted by a clerk at Dole headquarters. Inside he found photocopied sheets of Del Monte financial data. To Johnson it was clear Dole was sending the data to its executives around the world. By then, of course, it was too late to do anything about it.

The New York Public Library looms out of midtown Manhattan's grimy streets south of Grand Central Station like the Parthenon. A stone redoubt two full city blocks long, among the best examples of beaux arts architecture in New York, it features an enormous entranceway flanked by a pair of massive stone lions, Patience and Fortitude.

Thursday, November 10, was a special evening for the library, the eighth annual Literary Lions dinner, a fund-raiser that also honored twenty of the literary world's most luminous lights. Between the lions that evening filed the upper crust of New York society, names like Astor and Trump and Bass, as well as the honorees, gifted writers like Art Buchwald, George Higgins, and Richard Reeves. Cocktails were to be served, then dinner in three of the reading rooms, followed by the actor Christopher Plummer reading a Stephen Leacock short story.

As the moon rose, guests and honorees gathered in tuxedos and sparkling dresses in the McGraw Rotunda, a long stone hall running the length of the building's third floor. *Everyone* was there. Nancy and Henry Kissinger strode by. Jacqueline Onassis, looking ravishing in a white-over-black ensemble, was there. John Gutfreund, who served as the library's treasurer, appeared with his wife, Susan, who was stunning in a dress of vintage Balenciaga. Gutfreund waved when he saw Kravis walk in with Carolyne Roehm at his elbow.

Suddenly a murmur trilled through the room. Cameras flashed, and heads craned to see what the commotion was all about. There, amid the revelry, Kravis was talking with, of all people, Peter Cohen.

Smiling for the cameras, the two men strained to make small talk. "This thing's terrible," Kravis said, one eye on the gathering crowd. "You know, it's too bad things didn't work out between us."

Cohen said something about keeping their options open.

"I don't know what we're going to do," Kravis said. "I honestly don't know."

They stood there for a minute, both on their best behavior, frozen in the headlights of New York society.

"It's just too bad things came out the way they did, but so be it," Kravis said. "You do what you have to do. We'll do what we have to do."

Kravis broke from Cohen and, with Roehm on his arm, headed into dinner. On the way he spied Billy Norwich, society columnist for the New York *Daily News*. In September, Norwich had been left off the guest list for the Kravises' Metropolitan Museum party and, in a pique, Norwich had accused the financier of "loathing the press" in his column. Kravis had had all he could stand of the press and particularly didn't like Norwich, whom he thought enjoyed taking potshots at his wife.

Roehm saw the confrontation looming and attempted to steer her husband away. "Come on, Henry," she whispered. "Let's go eat."

It was too late. Seeing Norwich, Kravis grew flushed. When the columnist walked up to him, he and Kravis exchanged words. First Kravis called Norwich an asshole. Then Kravis, raising his voice, said, "I'm going to break both your kneecaps." Several people clearly heard his words and turned their heads.

Just at that moment, socialite Brooke Astor walked up. "Have you had a drink?" she asked.

"Yes, I have," Kravis said.

"I wasn't asking you," said Astor. "I was asking Billy."

Astor's intervention, intentional or not, killed the brewing argument. Kravis stepped away and continued into dinner. Dick Beattie, overhearing the conversation, thought Kravis was joking. Not so Norwich's companion, a British writer named Meredith Etherington-Smith, who told *Women's Wear Daily* of the incident.

"I was absolutely shocked," she said. "You would expect that kind of behavior at a low-life party but not at the Literary Lions."

Tensions grew, too, within the management group. Recriminations were only to be expected, given its sorry performance to date. The Salomon bankers—the Sausages—came to loathe Tom Hill, who made little effort to hide his contempt for his Salomon counterparts. The Sausages complained that Hill didn't return their phone calls. He treated Mike Zimmerman, in one banker's words, "like live-in help." They found Hill so tailored, so Waspy, so condescending, so . . . Tom Hillish.

"This asshole Hill, as you call him, has got the number-one merger department on Wall Street," Chaz Phillips reminded his colleagues one day. "Need I remind you that his department was substantially smaller than Sally's four years ago." The bankers looked at Phillips as if he were crazed.

The Sausages were a constant source of consternation for Cohen. "Do you know who all these people are?" he asked Andrea Farace one afternoon as his office filled with Salomon people. "Where are they from? What the hell do they do?" Cohen would take Gutfreund aside and ask, "Can we have a small meeting?" It was impossible.

Johnson was also amazed by the endless procession of advisers. Cohen seemed to trail aides like a wedding train. "Geez, Peter," he said at one point, "no wonder you people took a wrong turn at the Red Sea."

Gutfreund was growing irritated with Steve Goldstone's handling of the special committee. Goldstone remained the group's sole conduit to Peter Atkins, and Gutfreund was exasperated by his inability to get any guidance out of the Skadden lawyer. Gutfreund had his people look into Goldstone's background; they found he had little reputation to speak of. On several occasions Gutfreund suggested to Cohen that Salomon's counsel, Peter Darrow, be allowed to speak with Atkins. Nothing came of it. The Salomon executives, in fact, were disenchanted with Johnson's entire team. They blamed Johnson for the management agreement fiasco. And as coverage of the greed issue mushroomed, some grumbled that Johnson was more trouble than he was worth.

For Johnson's seven-man management group, life at Nine West was fast approaching the surreal. Johnson, always a security fanatic, was having the offices swept for bugs daily; he turned down an offer to bug Kravis's office. Meetings were often interrupted by high-pitched pings: John Martin's aide, Bill Liss, had insisted that all top executives wear beepers, as did a dozen or so reporters with whom Liss kept in constant touch.

For all the bustle, many of Johnson's aides felt strangely isolated, as Shearson and Salomon took over preparations for the following week's bid. "When a banker is talking about raising money, he's your employee," Sage would say. "When he starts writing the checks, you become his." Sage felt so out of touch he brought a television set into his office to idle away the hours.

Johnson, meanwhile, was growing despondent. Nothing about his Great Adventure had gone as planned: the Kravis ambush, the failed peace talks, the uproar over the management agreement, the Del Monte imbroglio, his daily pillorying in the press. And more and more, Shearson was calling the shots. Nothing about this fight was fun. "Nothing happens until the sun goes down," Johnson groused. "Then in comes all this horseshit food and everybody has dinner and talks and talks. The last place I want to eat is in my office at night."

Most of all, it was the bidding level that bothered Johnson. Even if they won, his great Ferrari would be stripped down to the chassis to pay down debt, and he would be handcuffed to the steering wheel for years to come. Johnson's moping became so tiresome that, during one strategy session, an investment banker took Ed Horrigan aside and suggested he give his boss a pep talk. It simply wouldn't do, the banker suggested, for the group's spiritual leader to give up the fight.

"We can't walk away from this," Horrigan told Johnson. "I'd rather go back beaten, bloody, and bowed than walk away. If anybody knows how to run this company at a higher level, in a way that minimizes the pain, it's you and me. If we have to lose, I want it to be in a pitched battle, not a concession. You gotta win, Ross. You've got too good a reputation to lose."

But if "Battlin' Ed" Horrigan was rising to the fight, Johnson was sinking fast. "You don't understand. We don't have to win at all, Ed," he said. "It's poker. You can't put your pride in front of your mind."

On Thursday, November 10, Johnson left New York for the condo in Jupiter, where he looked forward to a quiet weekend. He didn't bother to stop in Atlanta for the grand opening of the new hangar at Charlie Brown Airport. In fact, the gala celebration they had planned was anything but. Hardly any of the invitees showed up: not city officials, not workers from nearby hangars, not even RJR Nabisco's own top brass, who only wanted to lick their wounds. No one, it seemed, wanted anything to do with Johnson. The evening was cut short and employees took the leftover food home to eat themselves.

That weekend Johnson took a call from Hugel, who was just back from Moscow. Hugel had seen a copy of a new SEC filing made by RJR Nabisco. There, in the fine print, he learned that Johnson had boosted Andy Sage's compensation to $500,000 a year from $250,000. He had grown angry as he read the filing. Hugel was certain the board had never approved the raise.

"The board approved that in July," Johnson said. Hugel checked the notes of the July meeting and didn't find anything. He called Johnson again. This time Johnson explained that the raise had been approved in September, retroactive to the July meeting.

Charlie Hugel didn't believe him. It was the second time in a week he thought he had caught Ross Johnson in a lie.

"I'm going to make you rich, Johnny!"

Johnson's words still echoed, unreal yet undying, in John Greeniaus's mind. The path he had chosen since his fateful meeting with Johnson was radical but, as he saw it, unavoidable. It was a matter of either being loyal to his people at Nabisco or to the man who would set them adrift. *I'm going to make you rich,* indeed. How could Johnson do this, Greeniaus wondered, and think that money would make it all better? It wasn't money that made John Greeniaus tick; it was making Nabisco a well-oiled machine. Now Johnson wanted to take his machine and sell it for spare parts.

First he had been numb. The numbness gave way to anger. It was all so clear now: why Johnson had reorganized Nabisco and Del Monte into separate, bite-size, easy-to-sell operating units; why Johnson had given 300,000 shares of restricted stock to tobacco people that summer and almost none to Nabisco people;* why Horrigan had always gotten his way. Johnson had been setting this up for a long time, Greeniaus decided, lying to them all. Now he was promising to take care of Greeniaus, provide a happy landing in some new corporate haven. He would never believe Johnson again.

Greeniaus hated the very idea of this LBO, yet he hated equally the fact that he hadn't been invited to join the management group. It was a bitter tangle of emotions. Finally, as was always the case with John Greeniaus, hot anger gave way to cold reason. No use getting mad; he would get even.

He had flown back to Nabisco's New Jersey headquarters the day the LBO was announced. Within days he slipped a confidential planning document into an envelope and mailed it to Charlie Hugel, marking it "confidential and urgent."

It was the first part of a plan that may, Greeniaus thought, just be a fantasy. He was almost certain Johnson would get the company. Johnson knew the kinds of things no competitor could find out. He had the board in his pocket. But if a top-secret tidbit helped the directors see Johnson's true colors, Greeniaus would see they got it. If another bidder gave Nabisco a better shake than Johnson, he would aid and abet the enemy.

---

* The big restricted-stock grants actually engendered almost as much ill will in the ranks of tobacco's management as Nabisco's. While the top executives had gotten generous restricted-stock grants, many other managers had been browbeaten in August into surrendering their stock options. The company had offered to buy in options for $53.50 a share; the decision was supposed to be up to each employee. But Ed Horrigan spread word that everybody had *better* tender their options. Those who did lost big when the stock leapt weeks later. He wasn't out to cheat anyone, Horrigan later maintained, noting he had tendered options on 59,000 shares himself. On the other hand, he was receiving 50,000 shares of restricted stock at the same time.

He summoned Nabisco's chief financial officer, Larry Kleinberg, into his office. They were going to dissect Nabisco and reinvent it in revved-up form, he told him. They would dress it up for the big party, showing how money could be saved and cash flow spurred. If other bidders saw Nabisco's true potential, they might up the ante and beat Johnson. And if they won, they might keep Nabisco. It was a long shot, Greeniaus said, but it was their only chance of saving the company. "This is a survival game," Greeniaus told Kleinberg. "Let's play it to the best of our ability."

As he secretly prepared for his guerrilla war, Greeniaus took pains to keep his troops happy. From his office a steady stream of anti-Johnson cartoons and memos poured forth to amuse the depressed Nabisco executives. One cartoon showed a divorce court judge addressing a boy. "Junior, would you prefer to live with a smoking or nonsmoking parent?" Greeniaus's accompanying line: "Who knows—we might just be better off with a nonsmoking parent."

When Kravis appeared on the scene, Greeniaus had begun his campaign in earnest. Introduced to the special committee's bankers at Dillon and Lazard, he had kept them amused with RJR Nabisco "factoids." "Guess how many members of Team RJR Nabisco there are," Greeniaus asked. The guesses came in: eight, ten, maybe a dozen. "How about twenty-nine?" Greeniaus said. "How about a cost of seven to ten million dollars a year?"

He titillated them with the famous—Jack Nicklaus and his million-dollar deal—and amazed them with the obscure. Who *was* Vijay Amritraj and why was he on Team RJR Nabisco? Greeniaus regaled them with tales of the villa in Castle Pines, the compound in Palm Springs, the apartments in New York. There was method to Greeniaus's madness: the more waste the board bankers could see cutting, the higher the "fair" price they would demand.

Finally, after three weeks of teasing the bankers with tidbits, Greeniaus was ready to make his move. He took his idea to Josh Gotbaum of Lazard, who immediately grasped its significance. "We'll tell these things only to the special committee," Greeniaus said. "It can't go to management, to Ross. Some of what we have to say could cost us our jobs." Gotbaum had guaranteed Greeniaus that word of their plan wouldn't get back to Johnson.

Greeniaus was scheduled to address the special committee at Skadden Arps on Monday, November 14. By coincidence, so was Johnson, who had been called in to answer questions as part of the board's due diligence. That morning Greeniaus stopped by Nine West on his way to the board meeting.

"Johnny!" Johnson boomed when he spied Greeniaus. "Come on in with us. We're working on our strategy to handle the special committee."

Terrified, Greeniaus followed Johnson into the fishbowl conference room, where Steve Goldstone and the management group sat around the large, round table in the midst of a spirited discussion. It was to be Johnson's first meeting with the board in nearly a month, and everyone had an idea how they should handle it. Horrigan, as usual, urged a combative approach: Don't give the bastards an iota of new information. Johnson vacillated between cool and courteous. Greeniaus sat frozen in fear he would be found out.

When it came time to go to Skadden, Johnson discovered that no provisions had been made for transportation. He turned to Greeniaus, who commandeered a Nabisco limo. They rode to Skadden together; once there, they sat in a small holding room. When Hugel arrived to escort Johnson into the board, Greeniaus stood, anxious and confused. For all the courage he had mustered, there was no way he was addressing the board in Johnson's presence.

Hugel fixed him with a puzzled look. "John, you're not part of the group, are you?"

"Uh, no," Greeniaus said.

"Well, you wait then," Hugel said.

Relieved, Greeniaus returned to his seat.

"There's a rat fink in this room," Hugel said, striding around the conference room and staring at people accusingly. "There's a rat fink, and I'm going to find out who it is."

As they prepared for Johnson's appearance that morning, the board members were clearly testy. It was day twenty-seven of the LBO crisis, and they all felt as if they were hostages to it. Hugel's ire was directed at press leaks, which had continued nonstop since the committee's first meeting three weeks before. Felix Rohatyn of Lazard urged Hugel to calm down. The leaks could be coming from anywhere, he suggested, and witch hunts would only exacerbate the tension they all felt.

Privately, several directors thought Hugel more than a little hypocritical. They all knew Johnson was talking regularly with Hugel, an advantage other bidders didn't have, and that could leave the committee exposed to lawsuits. Twice board advisers had tried to bring the subject up with him, but had gotten nowhere. Hugel had also gotten his wrist slapped for a series of newspaper interviews in which he suggested, among other things, that the board would look favorably on the bid that contained the most cash, as opposed to junk bonds and other securities. "Cash is cash," he said.

Adding to the snappish air that morning was a letter from Ronnie Grierson, the British director. Grierson, the directors all knew, was keenly worried about his liability in any lawsuit. Patched into board meetings via speaker phone from London, he was forever slowing meetings with questions the others thought nit-picking; Hugel had been forced to cut him off several times. Other directors, however, shared Grierson's concern. All board members had been told not to take notes unless they wanted them subpoenaed at a later date.

Now Grierson was demanding the resignation of Johnson and the entire management group. It was "highly improper," he suggested, for them to continue running the company while attempting to acquire it. Hugel was later able to talk Grierson out of his demands, but for the moment, everyone found them irksome. This was no time for him to break ranks.

The mood didn't improve when Johnson and Horrigan were escorted in to address the board. Asked about the management agreement, Johnson stuck to his line that *The Times* had it wrong, that his share of the profits wasn't out of line with that of other LBOs. Asked for ways to cut costs in the tobacco business, both Johnson and Horrigan stated flatly that there weren't any. Their attitude bordered on hostile, and it made them no points with the board.

At one point, the developing rift between Johnson and Hugel flared into view. The board had repeatedly stated its opposition to the bidders "preselling" RJR Nabisco assets, that is, agreeing to sell its businesses to outsiders before the bidding was over. When Johnson denied his group was doing so, Hugel smiled ironically and said: "Everyone's preselling."

"Are you challenging my word?" Johnson snapped. "That's absolutely wrong. I want you to withdraw that statement. Maybe Shearson's doing it and Sally's doing it, but I can tell you we're not doing it." Hugel backed off, but it was clear to everyone that a number of friendships wouldn't survive this auction.

———

The backbone of any successful LBO is a set of projections: profits, sales, and, most important, cash flow. Because they dictate the amount of debt a company can safely repay, projections are the key to formulating a bid. And the right bid means everything to an LBO: The higher the price, the higher the debt. Too much debt can crush the healthiest companies.

Kravis had hoped to emerge from his due diligence sessions at The Plaza with a set of reliable projections. Stonewalled, his people had fallen further and further into a quagmire of confusion. By Monday, just four days before bids were due, Kravis knew something about Del Monte, a little about Nabisco, and next to nothing about Horrigan's tobacco business.

The job of assembling Kravis's projections had fallen to a thirty-year-old associate, Scott Stuart, a handsome bachelor with a sadly neglected apartment on Manhattan's Upper West Side. Often working eighteen-hour days, Stuart had developed four separate sets of projections for RJR Nabisco, each, at least in theory, more accurate than the last.

He began with numbers obtained from RJR Nabisco via the special committee. Coming straight from Johnson, they were suspect. Normally, Stuart would spend weeks brainstorming with management to refine these numbers and identify areas where savings could be found. But with no management on board, Stuart turned to tobacco-industry analysts at Drexel and Merrill Lynch. Work with the bankers at Morgan Stanley and Wasserstein Perella yielded further revisions. Bit by bit, Stuart had compiled a nice, neat set of white computer runs. He wanted to believe they were reliable, but he feared they were no better than guesswork.

Gaping holes yawned in Stuart's analysis, the result of key figures he hadn't been able to obtain. In a perfect world, Stuart wouldn't have even attempted projections without gathering all the relevant figures. But he had no choice: Time constraints dictated he come up with something. For three weeks Stuart had pestered the bankers at Dillon and Lazard for the figures, but to no avail. At first he thought they, too, were stonewalling him. Later he would realize the problems lay within RJR Nabisco. No one below its highest levels knew the whole picture. Those that did, like Ed Robinson, were giving only name, rank, and serial number.

———

By Monday, Stuart was growing panicky. Every day he searched for the missing numbers, shouting at Dillon Read, shouting at Lazard, shouting at his own accountants and lawyers crawling through the data room in Atlanta. Data room, *hah!* The concept made Stuart laugh. They got data all right: reams and reams of raw numbers that would take weeks if not months to fathom. It might as well have been Chinese.

The numbers he needed weren't complicated: an estimate of RJR Nabisco's available cash reserves, a total debt number, an estimate of payments due Johnson's management group under its golden parachute severance packages. Basic stuff, Stuart thought, yet they formed the foundation from which Kravis and Roberts would determine their bid. Both his bosses, Stuart was uncomfortably aware, were growing impatient with his inability to put finished projections on their desks.

If missing figures weren't bad enough, Stuart didn't completely understand the ones he had. One number in particular puzzled them all. On the initial projections they had obtained from RJR Nabisco was a heading "Other Uses of Cash." Beside it was a row of figures stretching out ten years, each year ranging from $300 million to $500 million. Stuart had no idea what the numbers meant. What the hell was "other uses"? Was it cash flowing in or out? Should he add it? Subtract it? Ignore it? Five hundred million dollars wasn't the kind of sum Kravis liked his people to ignore. The swing between adding and subtracting it was nearly $1 billion, roughly the difference between a bid of $96 a share and $92 a share. For three weeks the figures lay like a row of mysterious coals glowing white on the darkened screen of Stuart's IBM personal computer, a category no one could explain. When they asked Ed Robinson about it at The Plaza, he had pleaded ignorance. No one at the special committee knew what it was, either. The "Other Uses of Cash" now headed the list of mysteries Stuart had four days to solve.

Then, on Monday, Stuart took a call from a Dillon Read associate, Blair Effron. Would you be interested in spending any more time with John Greeniaus? Effron asked. Greeniaus had just finished speaking with the special committee. "I think," Effron said, "this guy wants to give you the real story."

Stuart took the offer to Paul Raether. "Sure, why not?" Raether replied. "They were the only guys who were helpful the first time around."

A meeting was arranged that afternoon at a midtown hotel, the Carlton House. Raether led Stuart and another associate into the meeting room, where they took seats at a round table. Greeniaus was already there, Larry Kleinberg in tow.

"Before we start," Greeniaus began, "I've got a few things I'd like to ask you."

"Fire away," Raether said.

"Are you guys still having conversations with the management group?"

"No."

"With Ross Johnson?"

"No."

"Do you have any plans to have any more conversations?"

"Not as far as I know."

"Good," Greeniaus said. The coast was clear. "I've got a few things I'd like to tell you."

The two-and-one-half-hour speech John Greeniaus embarked on was among the most startling Raether had heard in a decade of LBO work. In one fell swoop Greeniaus laid bare Nabisco operating secrets and strategies, its vulnerabilities and follies.

"Look," he said, "nobody's ever asked us how we'd run this business for cash. Let me tell you, there are a whole lot of things that can be done."

Nabisco, Greeniaus stated confidently, could increase its operating income 40 percent in a single year if necessary. Profit margins could be taken to 15 percent from 11. Cash flow, he said, could be taken to $1.1 billion a year from $816 million.

"Come on—" Raether said in disbelief.

"No, you don't understand," Greeniaus replied. "Our charter is to run this company on a steady basis. There was really no good reason for the earnings in this group to go up fifteen or twenty percent. In fact, I'd get in trouble if they did. Twelve percent is about what I'm supposed to give every quarter. The biggest problem I'll have next quarter is disposing of all the additional cash these businesses generate. The earnings are going to be too big. Christ, I've got to spend money to keep them down." It was all done, Greeniaus explained, because Wall Street craved predictability.

Raether was dumbfounded. "What are you going to spend it on?"

"Product promotion, marketing."

"Is that money well spent?"

Greeniaus chuckled. "No, not really."

He mentioned Johnson's $4 billion plan to modernize Nabisco's bakeries. "Technology for technology's sake," Greeniaus scoffed—an outlet for the tobacco cash Johnson didn't know what to do with. "You don't need to spend all this money," he emphasized. "You're just spending it for nothing."

Greeniaus trotted out Johnson's sacred cows and slaughtered them one by one. Team Nabisco: a waste. The golf tournaments: a travesty. "Should I spend ten million dollars each year on the Dinah Shore? Does that sell crackers? No. But it's forced on me by corporate. It's built into my overhead."

Raether's head was spinning as he left the meeting. This was the break they had been waiting for. "You guys better believe those numbers," he told Greeniaus as they left, "because you may have to deliver them." The implication was clear: If Kravis won, Nabisco would be managed, not sold. Greeniaus left the meeting on cloud nine.

Raether hustled back and reported the meeting to Kravis. "I assume we're not being set up," Kravis said. It crossed his mind that Greeniaus might be a Johnson plant.

"No, I think the guy's real," Raether said.

Kravis thought about what type of man Greeniaus must be. Traitor or hero? "I gotta give this guy a lot of credit," he said. "This is the first chink in their armor."

It was the first piece of good news the pair had heard in nearly two weeks. Raether wasted no time plugging Greeniaus's assumptions into their buyout models. By the next day their impact was clear. If everything Greeniaus said was true, Kohlberg Kravis could boost its bid from the low nineties to nearly $100 a share.

On Tuesday, Johnson flew to Washington for a meeting with the president. Actually, he was one of several executives scheduled to see Ronald Reagan that day, all members of the commission commemorating the bicentennial of the U.S. Constitution. Johnson was vice chairman. Ushered into the office after lunch, he shook Reagan's hand.

"Ross," the president said, "I can't help but notice you seem to be getting some publicity lately."

Johnson smiled. For once he didn't have a ready quip. After posing for pictures, his group met with Kenneth Duberstein, the president's chief of staff, and Colin Powell, the national security adviser. Both men asked about the buyout. Johnson told some jokes about the ways of Wall Street.

But even schmoozing with the president failed to lift Johnson from his growing pessimism. Later, leaving for the plane to New York, he turned to Dwayne Andreas, chairman of Archer Daniels Midland and chairman of the committee. Andreas was a friend; Johnson said he wished they saw each other more often. "Well, Dwayne," he said, "I might have a lot more free time in a couple of weeks."

———

The computer runs on Ted Forstmann's desk told the grim story. At $85 a share, Forstmann was comfortable bidding for RJR Nabisco. The deal could be financed the Forstmann Little way, with cash and no junk bonds. At ninety, it was still doable, though the returns to his investors fell sharply. Institutions put their money with Forstmann Little to get the 35 percent minimum return it promised. To pay much above ninety, Forstmann could see, he could give investors no more than 20 percent. Hell, he joked, T-bills paid 11 percent. It was mortifying.

There was only one way to boost the returns enough to justify a bid. North of ninety, Forstmann could see, they could bid with the aid of a Goldman Sachs bridge loan, which would be refinanced through the sale of junk bonds. Forstmann cringed at the thought, but Geoff Boisi was pushing the idea hard. All week Forstmann, at Boisi's behest, had suffered a crash course in junk bonds. Half the time he couldn't understand what the young Goldman bankers were telling him. "I'm speaking English, and it's like they're speaking Turkish," he complained.

But Forstmann understood enough to realize the risks such a loan entailed. For each quarter Goldman couldn't sell the bonds to refinance the loan, the loan's interest rate rose. And rose. If everything went well, Forstmann could repay the loan through RJR Nabisco's cash flow. But if for any reason Goldman couldn't sell the bonds, Forstmann Little was liable for the entire amount. In effect, Forstmann was forced to bet the entire deal on whether Goldman could unload the bonds, a risky wager given the firm's spotty track record.

Boisi was practically feverish, he wanted the bridge so bad. He assured Forstmann it was safe. There was no more than a one in a thousand chance that Goldman couldn't sell the bonds.

"Sure," Forstmann said, "so write that in there," meaning, in the contract.

"No, Teddy," Boisi explained. "We have to have the right to get out of this thing in the event of an emergency."

It was the worst part of a process with which Forstmann had become increasingly uncomfortable. Discussing tobacco left him feeling slimy. Debating future demand in the teen market made him feel like a drug pusher. At least the bank talks were going well. Sunday afternoon Forstmann had stood before a packed auditorium at Manufacturers Hanover in his blue jeans and exhorted a crowd of gray-suited bankers to put forward the $10 billion or more he would need. From all appearances, they would.

In the end, it always came back to junk bonds. They went round and round and round. At one point, Boisi threw up his hands.

"What are you, a priest?" he asked Forstmann. "Have you got some kind of religious conviction about this stuff?"

Forstmann tried to explain. "Geoff, there's no place to go. I'm a fighter, but I just can't do this stuff." He pulled a copy of the article he had written for *The Wall Street Journal* and shook it at Boisi. "I really believe this stuff, you know."

They were in the thick of debate Tuesday afternoon when Brian Little took Forstmann aside. "I think you and Nicky and I ought to talk." The two men collared the younger Forstmann and retreated to Little's office.

The three partners knew their position was bleak. The returns simply weren't adequate unless they used junk bonds. None of them wanted to do that. But the simple truth was that, even if they had, they couldn't. Forstmann's antijunk diatribes had painted them into a corner. To go with a junk-bond–financed bridge loan at this point would invite public ridicule. "The reality is, it can't be done without junk," Little said.

Their mood was somber. "I guess we should just end this," Ted Forstmann said.

He broke the news to Boisi and his three corporate partners. After the initial furor subsided, he wrote out a long press release citing in detail Forstmann Little's reasons for backing out of the deal. It amounted to an attack on the auction process and on junk bonds; he planned to issue it the following morning. That evening he called Peter Atkins and read it to him.

Atkins immediately realized he couldn't let Forstmann issue the release. It sent the wrong message to junk-bond buyers and to a banking industry already jittery about LBO debt and the possibility of anti-LBO legislation. With just three days until the bidding deadline, this was no time to scare the banks. Forstmann could bow out, but Atkins simply couldn't allow his departure to hinder the remaining two bidders.

Forstmann stuck to his guns, insisting that he had to let the world know he was bowing out on principle. Frustrated, Atkins pulled Hugel from a Combustion Engineering board meeting at the Intercontinental Hotel. "We have to get them to change this press release," the lawyer said. "It looks really bad."

Hugel felt he had bent the rules to allow Forstmann into the bidding in the first place, and, like Atkins, was embarrassed to find him withdrawing. "Our horse was dying," Hugel would say later. "And," Atkins added, "it was dying in public."

Now Hugel himself locked horns with Forstmann. For hours they argued about the release. "I have to put it out," Forstmann kept insisting. Forstmann Little had a reputation to protect, he repeated. Hugel laid down the gauntlet. If Forstmann wouldn't bend to persuasion, maybe blackmail would work.

"What if I put out my own press release?" Hugel suggested.

"What do you mean? What would it say?"

"It'll say you acted in a hostile and unethical way."

"You wouldn't do that."

"Try me," Hugel said. "I guarantee it'll be in the newspapers the next day."

The next morning Forstmann Little & Co. issued a terse, one-sentence press release, bowing out of the bidding for RJR Nabisco with nary a peep of explanation.

CHAPTER

14

On Monday morning, in an upstairs conference room at Skadden Arps, Peter Atkins was steering the special committee through its paces. Around him, the auction framework Atkins had erected was humming smoothly. The three investor groups—Forstmann Little wouldn't drop out till the next day—were moving swiftly toward the Friday deadline, and Atkins was confident their bids would satisfy both the board as well as its increasingly restive shareholders. Confidentiality agreements were in place. Due diligence was marching forward. Everything seemed under control, just the way Atkins liked it, when a letter was carried into the meeting and placed in front of him.

He scanned the document impassively. He could see the proposal was desperate, almost certainly too little, too late. "Vague" and "ephemeral" were words that leapt to his mind.

Atkins had hoped to avoid something like this. The five-page letter beneath the First Boston letterhead was a monkey wrench aimed squarely at the gears of his machine. With any luck, Atkins thought, it could be brushed aside. He had no way of knowing, of course, how difficult that would prove.

Setting the letter down, Atkins faced the assembled directors. "There's something else we have to deal with here," he announced.

As the shotgun marriages of America's largest companies spurred Wall Street's growth through the 1980s, one Wall Street firm initiated more major takeovers and created more tactical innovations than any other. First Boston, founded in 1934 and until the late 1970s a sleepy, second-tier underwriter, rocketed to the fore of major investment banks thanks largely to the brains and chutzpah of Bruce Wasserstein and Joe Perella.

From a warren of cluttered offices inside First Boston's glass-sheathed Park Avenue headquarters, Wasserstein—paunchy, disheveled, shirttails flying—and the tall, erudite Perella became the takeover era's first super-stars. In virtually every major takeover battle of the 1980s—at Getty, DuPont, Gulf—their footprints could be found. The two men helped transform investment banking from a sleepy gentleman's trade by intro-ducing the hustling, cutthroat ethic flourishing on Wall Street today.

On a chilly Groundhog Day in 1988, after months of clandestine maneuvering, Wasserstein and Perella strode into First Boston's executive offices and, reading from notes prepared by their lawyers, announced their resignations. As the pair walked out that morning, they left Wall Street's largest and best-known merger department in disarray. More than twenty top First Boston deal makers—the cream of Wasserstein's hand-picked crop—soon flocked to join the pair's new start-up firm, Wasserstein Perella & Co. Many of First Boston's best clients followed suit.

When Henry Kravis launched his unprecedented tender offer for RJR Nabisco, Bruce Wasserstein was seated firmly at his right hand. By then, every major Wall Street investment bank and a host of minor ones were noisily feeding at the trough of RJR Nabisco. Every firm, that is, except First Boston. Without Wasserstein, First Boston seemed destined to sink into obscurity. King Arthur had left Camelot, it appeared, and the Round Table was no more.

It sure seemed like a lousy time for a joust.

As Atkins handed out copies of the curious letter to board members, the man responsible for his discomfort sat anxiously five blocks away. At thirty-eight, James Maher was in the eighth month of the most torturous period of his life. As cohead of First Boston's investment banking and merger departments, it had fallen to Maher (pronounced *Mah-her*) to pick up the pieces after Wasserstein's departure.

Small wonder competitors likened Maher to the captain of the *Titanic*.

But the scramble to save First Boston was more than business to Maher. Besides being his bosses for a decade, Wasserstein and Perella had been Maher's best friends. Their parting left him angry and confused; the intense competition that instantly sprang up between their two firms only added insult to Maher's injury. Survival now meant daily skirmishes with men who had been his confidants for ten years. Beating their former superiors became the rallying cry of First Boston's remaining deal makers.

Now, eight months after their resignations, Maher was desperate. His brief tenure had been marked by exhilarating highs and devastating lows—mostly lows—and it had all come down to this: First Boston was the only major investment bank not involved in the RJR Nabisco deal. It was worse than humiliating. Sitting on the sidelines during history's largest takeover sent a dire message to every First Boston competitor and client. Maher suffered no illusions: His department's future was at stake.

Coming just four days before the bid deadline, Maher's proposal was a rank long shot. On Friday the special committee expected to receive fully financed offers, a task that had taken Kravis and Cohen weeks; First Boston hadn't yet talked to a bank. But if it could somehow emerge with a piece of the action, Maher knew, he could rescue his department from its decline. If he failed, Maher had no doubt, he would be a laughingstock.

A chain-smoking New Englander, Maher was thought by some to be an odd choice to lead First Boston's 170-odd merger specialists. He was neither a natural leader nor a cheerleader. His primary attribute was a steadiness that was the marvel of his colleagues. Some considered Maher a stoic, although he had a gentle, self-deprecating humor and was prone to rare fits of temper; close friends knew to avoid him when the vein in his jaw began pulsing. Thoroughly unpretentious—a rarity on Wall Street—he wore his hair slicked back in a power cut that looked out of place on his head.

Maher grew up a strapping, middle-class kid from central Massachusetts, his father the president of a local machine-tool maker. He had entered Columbia Business School in 1975 when the bicycle-parts maker where he was sales manager began to slide downhill, prodded by a massive recall of shaky handlebar supports. Later he joined First Boston, taking a spot in the infant merger department after a fast-track colleague turned it down as a dead-end job. He started one week after Wasserstein. In First Boston's culture of gray flannel and maroon suspenders, Wasserstein, hair uncombed, constantly in motion, fascinated Maher. "I didn't know who this character was—I thought he was from another planet," Maher would recall. "Bruce was just this rumpled mess."

As their fame grew, Wasserstein turned to Maher so often for advice on personnel and conflict-of-interest questions he took to calling him "Mr. Judgment." For his part, Maher was one of the few at First Boston who could get away with shouting at Wasserstein. Colleagues remember Maher stomping out of Wasserstein's office from time to time, shouting, "You asshole!" at the top of his lungs. No one could make Jim Maher madder than Bruce Wasserstein.

For all Maher's levelheadedness, Wasserstein never considered him a top-notch deal maker. To Wasserstein, Maher's takeover tactics lacked decisiveness. Time was everything in big takeovers, yet he felt Maher hashed over strategies for hours, even days, before moving. So indecisive did Maher seem at times that, behind his back, Wasserstein and the others called him "Hamlet."

It was inevitable that Wasserstein and Perella's success would lead the pair into conflict with First Boston's management. First Boston was headed by Peter Buchanan, a no-nonsense former trader who drove a station wagon and had lived in the same New Jersey house for twenty years. Many felt Buchanan had a hard time understanding Wasserstein and Perella's fast-track world of Porsches and mansions in the Hamptons. By the summer of 1987, Wasserstein believed, with some justification, that he and Perella were First Boston's most important assets. When Wasserstein pushed for First Boston to channel its efforts away from trading and into his merchant-banking domain, he ignited a powder keg. After an initial blowup with Buchanan and other senior managers, Wasserstein and Perella were, by fall of 1987, mulling the possibility of leaving. It was assumed their inner circle would follow.

With Perella pushing the idea and Wasserstein astride the fence, Maher became the leading voice against their departure. All winter he argued that Wasserstein owed it to himself, and to the investment bankers he had recruited, to stay the course. Privately, he feared Wasserstein wouldn't take the time to properly administer a new firm. Maher also suspected that other members of The Group who didn't have First Boston's best interests in mind—Tom Hill and Eric Gleacher—were encouraging Wasserstein to make the break. A weakened First Boston, Maher knew, presented tremendous opportunities for its competitors.

For Wasserstein the final straw came in January 1988, when Buchanan, revealing the results of a lengthy policy review, declared there would be no shift in the firm's direction. Disgusted, he and Perella made up their minds to leave. For Maher the end came at a Japanese restaurant. Wasserstein and his closest advisers sat for hours debating the pros and cons of setting up their own firm when it happened. Wasserstein drew a line in the sand. "We've got to make a decision," he said. "Who's in?"

One by one, Perella, a bearded deal maker named Bill Lambert, and the circle's fifth member, Chuck Ward, threw in their lots with Wasserstein and the new firm.

Maher didn't pause. "I'm out." He hoped his resistance would dampen Wasserstein's enthusiasm for the idea. It didn't.

"Well," Wasserstein said, after more discussion, "we're going off to get a drink and talk about this." Nobody said anything, but it was clear Maher wasn't invited.

"Well," Maher said, "keep me informed."

"Well," Wasserstein responded. "You're out of it." The words stung like a slap. It was as if eleven years of friendship had been forgotten. It was exactly the kind of thing Maher had come to expect from Wasserstein, a painful example of why he wouldn't follow the two stars into a small firm. Maher would stew over the remark for months to come. "A typical Brucian move," he would term it later.

Chuck Ward had tried one last argument to persuade Maher. "You got to come with us," he had argued, only half in jest. "You're the only one around here who can control Bruce."

When Wasserstein and Perella handed in their resignations that February morning, Maher sat in his forty-third-floor office cleaning out his desk. If Maher wouldn't start anew with his friends, neither did he have any interest in picking up the pieces they left behind. First Boston's merger effort *was* Wasserstein and Perella. It was nothing before they arrived. And when they left, Maher feared, it would be nothing again. Maher didn't know what he would do. But he couldn't stay around these offices any longer.

Maher was pondering a resignation letter when Pete Buchanan called. First Boston's chief came right to the point: He wanted Maher to take Wasserstein's place and lead the firm's investment-banking arm, including the merger department. Buchanan pushed all the right buttons, appealing to Maher's loyalty and to his guilt at leaving behind aimless colleagues. Maher thought it over for a couple of hours. All around him, chaos reigned as news of Wasserstein and Perella's departure spread; he had to move fast to prevent permanent damage. He called his wife. Then, taking a deep breath, he accepted Buchanan's offer.

It had been worse than Maher dared fear. Immediately, more than a dozen of First Boston's leading deal makers followed their mentors to their new firm. Every day for weeks, it seemed, another of Maher's friends walked into his office, resignation in hand. It amounted to a full-scale assault on the department they had built over the last decade. Maher fought back with the usual office morale builders: Friday afternoon beer-and-pretzel parties, scattered pep talks, T-shirts. ("Just say no" to Wasserstein Perella & Co.) For weeks he worked eighteen-hour days, pleading with veteran bankers and young stars not to abandon ship.

Even as Maher battled on that front, Wasserstein laid siege to First Boston's gilded client list. Many hired his new firm, including Time Inc. and investor Ronald Perelman. Gleacher and Hill offered their condolences even as their aides phoned Maher's bankers with job offers and sought his biggest clients with predictions of First Boston's impending decline.

It was inevitable that the turmoil at First Boston would take its toll on the firm's performance in a hectic merger season. In an odd way, it had initially worked to Maher's advantage. He was wounded badly enough, competitors reasoned, to do something desperate, a possibility that had to be factored into any confrontation with a First Boston client. Tom Hill knew it. Shearson's merger chief, representing Black & Decker in a hostile tender offer for American Standard that spring, had been surprised to find Maher leading a last-minute rescue mission. A First Boston client, Kelso & Co., topped the Black & Decker offer and agreed to acquire American Standard. Hill's client had to decide whether to fight or retreat. "Knowing Jimmy's problems, it was clear to me they would stay with it," Hill said. "The deal meant an awful lot to First Boston." After sizing up Maher's resolve, Hill advised his client to bow out of the bidding. For Maher's shell-shocked troops, it was the first tangible sign there might be life after Wasserstein.

First Boston hadn't fared so well in other fights. Maher's Chicago office threw up defenses for an Illinois grain company, Staley Continental, only to see them quickly battered down by a British suitor's hostile bid. One crisis followed another: In June, Maher's entire LBO group quit to form its own firm.

The low point was First Boston's defense of one of its oldest clients, Koppers, that spring. Maher met Beazer's tender offer, orchestrated by Tom Hill, with a spirited defense. His twenty-seven-year-old restructuring whiz, Brian Finn, pieced together a complex defense plan involving the sale of Koppers' businesses to three separate companies. But Koppers' board rejected the plan as too iffy, and caved in to its suitor.

Each night Maher trudged home to his Riverside Drive apartment, exhausted. Few besides his wife and four children saw the signs of his strain. Through it all, Maher was outwardly calm. He remained the department's most sought-after father-confessor, "the pier where everybody's boat wanted to tie up," as one friend put it.

Sniping by his new competitors only made matters worse. Commenting on First Boston's string of takeover losses, an anonymous Wasserstein aide told *The Wall Street Journal* that summer, "When we were there, you'd never see things like that. . . . But nobody at First Boston seems to care as long as the fees keep rolling in." Maher exploded. His best friends were accusing him of selling out. A senior Maher aide, Kim Fennebresque, fired back. "Wasserstein Perella & Co., although a fine firm, is basically a one-product firm," he told *Investment Dealers Digest*, suggesting that its thirty bankers worked to create "the impression that Bruce is really working on [all clients'] deals." (Fennebresque knew the term *fine firm* would rankle the Wasserstein contingent. "In investment banking," he explained, "that's like saying she doesn't sweat much for a fat girl.") For his comments, First Boston colleagues pounded Fennebresque on the back as if he had made a last-minute touchdown.

The response to Fennebresque's remarks was immediate. Maher fielded a call from irate Wasserstein aide Chuck Ward. "Can't you control your own people?" Ward demanded.

And so it went. At one point, a bogus memo to First Boston's junior bankers, purportedly from Wasserstein Perella's Ward, circulated at First Boston. Laced with sarcasm, its clear intent was to persuade First Boston bankers not to defect to the new firm. "There are lots of important bags to carry over here and not many bag carriers to go around," the memo said, adding that applicants were advised to bring along mouthwash, knee pads, and Vaseline. "If you need to ask why," it continued, "you haven't figured out how things work around here."

By fall, while First Boston could point to continued lofty rankings among Wall Street merger advisers, morale was sinking. To fatalists First

Boston remained an embittered polyglot of Wasserstein castoffs, a group of second teamers destined to sink to Wall Street's lower tiers. Seven months after its founders' departure, the department's pipeline of deals-in-the-works was drying up, and competition for new business meant daily combat with the emerging clout of Wasserstein Perella.

Fennebresque, the thirty-seven-year-old banker in charge of attracting new business, became one of Maher's closest confidants. A glib, Waspy lawyer, Fennebresque's impish sense of humor served as a counterweight to Maher's sternness. By fall Fennebresque felt the department had become "a rudderless ship." "There had to be a chance for us to do something dramatic," Fennebresque recalled. "Our captain hadn't encountered rough seas yet. There was concern whether we had the depth we needed."

Then on October 17 came the stiffest blow to First Boston's merger effort since announcement of Wasserstein's departure. Philip Morris's $11 billion tender offer for Kraft, the largest offer of its kind in history, not only startled the corporate world. In choosing Wasserstein Perella as its sole adviser, Philip Morris also landed a haymaker to the jaw of its former banker, First Boston.

Jim Maher was in his office interviewing a job candidate a few minutes before six o'clock that afternoon when a headline crawling across the computer screen beside his desk caught his eye.

"PHILIP MORRIS LAUNCHES BID FOR . . . ," the Dow Jones News Service headline paused.

"Oh, no," Maher said to himself. "Oh no . . . Oh no . . ." For several paralyzing moments, his eyes riveted to the screen, Maher prayed the headline signaled only a minor acquisition.

Then came the full headline: "PHILIP MORRIS LAUNCHES BID FOR KRAFT."

"Oh . . . fuck."

The pain Maher felt was more than knowing First Boston was being excluded from history's largest unfriendly transaction. It was more than being upstaged for the umpteenth time by Wasserstein. To Maher Philip Morris's rejection of First Boston was an acute, personal insult: The tobacco giant was his account. Maher had personally overseen Philip Morris's 1985 acquisition of General Foods. As it sunk in that Wasserstein had snatched one of his largest clients, Maher knew he had only himself to blame. He had worked so hard to keep the department together he had neglected his other responsibilities. It was a body blow to the entire department, a reminder that First Boston could no longer count on its best clients for business.

Maher dialed Ehud Houminer, a top Philip Morris executive he knew well. He strained to hold his temper. "Ehud, you know, this is a real kick in the balls." Houminer made soothing noises but offered no promise of future work. It was the same with every Philip Morris executive Maher called that week.

———————

When news of Ross Johnson's $75-a-share proposal inched down his computer screen, Fennebresque thought for a moment it was a typographical error. His mind flashed to the young computer genius in the movie *War Games. A crazed hacker has invaded my Quotron. This can't be real.*

Maher immediately convened a meeting to draw up an attack plan. Like every other investment bank on Wall Street, First Boston aimed to get a piece of the action, most likely by representing the special committee or a buyer for a major product line. Anything, in short, that might produce a fee.

Over the next few days, hundreds of calls were placed to potential buyers of RJR Nabisco assets. At first Maher didn't worry that First Boston was left out of the mounting drama. Something was bound to break. RJR seemed so big that dozens of companies would hire investment banks to analyze acquisition strategies. Rolling up his sleeves and chain-smoking Marlboros, Maher hit the phones.

He first checked to see if First Boston might represent RJR's board, but Lazard and Dillon had already been hired. He called Tom Hill. Did Shearson need more capital for their buyout? Hill said no. Maher called Ted Forstmann and Geoff Boisi. Neither man offered encouragement. Door after door slammed in Maher's face.

The day after Johnson's announcement, some of Maher's old hands were already grumbling. Late Friday afternoon, Gary Swenson wandered into Fennebresque's office. Swenson was a twenty-year First Boston veteran with a Midwestern sobriety that Fennebresque, a Long Islander, found irresistible.

"You know, we're missing the goddamn boat on this deal," Swenson said.

"What do you mean?" Fennebresque asked.

"Everybody on Wall Street has a horse in this thing except us. We're the only ones not involved. We're getting passed by, I tell you. I know what we need to do. Let's put a group together and do it ourselves. Buy the whole thing. It's just what this place needs. It could really turn this place around."

At first Fennebresque dismissed the idea. It was just too big, too crazy. But as Swenson talked, Fennebresque found his enthusiasm catching. He called in several bankers, including David Batten, a veteran First Boston executive ending his first week in a new post in the merger department.

Batten shared Swenson's concerns. Arriving four days earlier from the firm's London office, he recalled finding "a palpable lack of self-confidence in the air." Batten told his colleagues, "What this place really needs is a shot in the arm. Goddamn it, we're still at the top of the heap. We can accomplish as much as anyone."

The group brainstormed in Fennebresque's office. First Boston could call in its Swiss affiliate Credit Suisse, they reasoned, and the two firms' London joint venture. Together the three firms could canvas the globe looking for money and assemble a bidding group. They owed it to themselves to try.

Fennebresque got excited. He phoned Maher, who walked down from his office. Fennebresque laid out their plan. Did Maher think it could work?

Maher pondered the idea for a moment. "I wouldn't object to that," he said.

Fennebresque found the response, so typical of Maher, maddening. *I wouldn't object to that? What kind of reaction is that? This is a great idea!* It was exactly the facet of Maher's personality his friend found so exasperating. How many times had Fennebresque pleaded with Maher to stand on a desktop and give a stirring speech? The enthusiasm just wasn't in him.

Fennebresque roped together a group and began telephoning LBO buyers who might be interested in forming a consortium to bid for RJR Nabisco.

———

Maher, a man badly in need of good news, finally got some the following week. To his surprise, his pursuit of Philip Morris paid off. The company, although still locked in a fight for Kraft, hired First Boston to analyze a possible bid for RJR Nabisco. Maher knew chances were small that Philip Morris would acquire RJR. But maybe, Maher thought, it might drop its Kraft bid if it cut a friendly deal with Ross Johnson. If so, First Boston could use Philip Morris as the centerpiece of a consortium to buy the company.*

For Maher's closest advisers, the Philip Morris assignment was especially sweet. It held out the prospect of spoiling Wasserstein's coup on the Kraft bid while gaining a share of the RJR Nabisco battle, all in one fell swoop. "This is great!" enthused Fennebresque. "It fucks Bruce on Kraft. It fucks Bruce on RJR. It preserves our relationship with Philip Morris. And it gets us into the RJR deal. Beautiful!"

Fennebresque's group, meanwhile, was having little luck assembling the consortium Maher envisioned building around Philip Morris. Fennebresque had met several times with aides of billionaire investor John Kluge, but the talks went nowhere: Disclosure of Johnson's management contract had lent the deal a patina of greed from which Kluge recoiled.

Several days later, Maher learned that Philip Morris was about to strike a friendly deal with Kraft and thus wasn't likely to chase RJR Nabisco any further. Coming on the heels of the failed Kluge talks, the news struck Maher like a blow to the stomach. His worst fear now seemed unavoidable: First Boston was to be the only major Wall Street firm left out of the deal of the century.

For several days, First Boston's RJR team fell into a funk. Greg Malcolm, the firm's junk-bond chief, jokingly captured the mood. "We're just a dog chasing a bus," he told colleagues. The inference was clear: First Boston, in attempting to join the battle for RJR, was out of its league.

As the bankers' minds idled, doubts about First Boston's direction returned. Fennebresque, plagued with dire visions, flew off to Minnesota to scout a minor acquisition candidate. *Can we ever be the same again?* he found himself wondering. *Bruce made us all feel so special. You couldn't help but bask in his reflected glory. Can we ever regain that feeling that we were special?*

Unlike Fennebresque, few witnessed Maher's demons. To outsiders he remained impassive, steady as ever. Inside, Maher was scared. He had

* During the early days of the deal, Hamish Maxwell had at least one conversation with Ross Johnson about a Philip Morris–RJR Nabisco combination. Johnson would later say he never expected Maxwell to generate any real enthusiasm for an RJR bid. Any merger agreement would almost certainly have been blocked on antitrust grounds.

tried every way he knew to get a piece of the RJR Nabisco deal and had gotten nowhere. He knew what people were whispering behind his back. *First Boston has lost it. They'll never be the same again without Wasserstein.* "Our franchise was on the line," Maher recalled. "It was crucial we get involved in this deal."

Maher wasn't totally without options. One idea particularly intrigued him. Late one Friday afternoon, Brian Finn had burst into his office with another of his schemes. In his excitement, Finn had ordered Maher's secretary to hold all calls.

"If you fucking pick up the phone, I'll kick your ass," a smiling Finn told his boss. "Now shut up and pay attention to me."

Maher harbored a special affection for Finn, one of First Boston's brightest young stars. Finn was Wall Street's version of a computer hacker, a brash numbers cruncher who spent hours alone ruminating about takeover tactics. A fervent New York Mets fan, he developed his love for numbers as a kid computing batting averages. As First Boston's specialist on antitakeover restructurings, Finn patrolled the outer edges of accepted merger strategies, twisting and reshaping corporate balance sheets to mount creative defenses to hostile takeovers. His boyish face, unruly brown hair and rumpled suits, not to mention his lightning-fast mind, reminded some of a young Bruce Wasserstein. In fact, Finn had been a Wasserstein favorite and became the subject of an intense tug-of-war between his departing mentor and Maher. Maher won out after a long evening's talk in which he and Finn drained a bottle of gin. "In the end I just couldn't kick Jimmy when he was down," Finn said.

Finn brought Maher's attention to a two-page memo lying unread on his desk. Finn had sent it that morning after being hit with an idea during the hour-long drive to his new Long Island home. The strategy laid out in the memo was, Maher could see, complex, incomplete, and an incredible long shot.

It turned on an esoteric tax law loophole set to expire December 31, just two months away. In its first step, Finn's plan called for First Boston to acquire RJR's food businesses for a bundle of securities known as installment notes. In theory at least, First Boston could take those notes to a major bank and receive money for them, a process known as "monetization." The beauty of the idea was that, using the loophole, taxes on the notes could be deferred for ten or twenty years, creating a tax savings of as much as $4 billion. In the plan's second step, First Boston would auction off Nabisco, passing on 80 percent of the profits to RJR shareholders and keeping the remainder. RJR's board could save billions of dollars and pass on its windfall to shareholders on a tax-free basis. First Boston would then acquire RJR's remaining tobacco businesses in a conventional $15 billion leveraged buyout.

The installment note loophole, discovered by Wall Street tax counsel in reaction to tax law restrictions in 1986 and 1987, had first been used in the sale of several businesses in the wake of Campeau Corporation's 1988 takeover of Federated Department Stores. So successful was it in saving taxes that Congress eliminated it in September. But legislators made the move effective at year-end, giving First Boston and other corporate buyers a brief window of opportunity. Finn proposed to drive the largest takeover in history right through that window.

Maher was skeptical. To himself he wondered if the idea wasn't just a little too flaky, a little too outlandish for such a high-profile deal. Installment notes had never been tried on such a scale. Hundreds of questions, Maher knew, would have to be resolved before the sketchy plan could be considered a viable alternative.

"There's a lot left to resolve," Finn acknowledged.

"So," Maher had said, "go resolve."

First Boston's search for a bidding partner had stalled after talks fell through with the Kluge group. Then, on November 9, after a week of inactivity, Leon Kalvaria walked into Dave Batten's glass-walled office. Kalvaria was a cigar-chewing Rhodesian who had aided the unsuccessful search for a partner.

"Goddamn it," Kalvaria groused, "let's not just give up." He and Batten hauled out the lists of potential partners and looked at them once more. Had they forgotten to call anyone? The two bankers threw out name after name until they came to one Batten didn't recognize: Resource Holdings.

"What about them?" Kalvaria asked.

"Who is it?"

"It's Jay Pritzker."

Batten wasn't heartened. Pritzker, the respected Chicago investor who owned Hyatt Hotels, had a reputation as being unwilling to pay top dollar for acquisitions. First Boston hadn't even bothered to contact his people. But time was running out. Bids were due in nine days. "Why not?" Batten said. "Make the call."

Later that day Kalvaria reached Jerry Seslowe, Resource Holdings's chief executive. At forty-two, Seslowe, a roly-poly former accountant with Groucho Marx eyebrows, kept a low profile on Wall Street. After eleven years at the Big Eight accounting firm Peat, Marwick, Mitchell & Co., where he worked with Pritzker and other big-name investors, he had begun his own small investment firm. Resource Holdings spent much of its time considering investment options for Pritzker and Denver billionaire Philip Anschutz, the rest for a stable of other investors: Indianapolis shopping mall king Melvin Simon and Cincinnati investor Carl Lindner, among others. On Wall Street, Seslowe was considered a minor leaguer whose client list occasionally enabled him to hit a home run.

Seslowe listened patiently as Kalvaria made his pitch. He liked the young Rhodesian, and he knew First Boston badly wanted a way into this deal. But to Seslowe, Kalvaria's idea smacked of desperation.

"You have to be crazy," he told Kalvaria. "For us to come into this at this late date, it's too little too late. Leon, go home."

Kalvaria persisted, but Seslowe would hear no more. "Forget it, Leon. Go home."

Only later was Kalvaria reminded of Brian Finn's unusual strategy—"Finn's tax thing" as it would come to be called. He tried Seslowe again the next day.

"Jerry, we have an edge. We have a tax structure that could give shareholders eight to ten dollars in additional cash which can't be done by KKR or Shearson. Can we come up and make a presentation?" Seslowe relented. "Okay, come on over."

The next morning Fennebresque and Kalvaria spent an hour going over their idea with Seslowe. The First Boston bankers hinted they had other major clients—they mentioned Pepsi—that might go along as well. Seslowe, impressed, said he would study the idea further. "I wish you guys had called us two weeks ago," he said.

Jay Pritzker listened closely as Seslowe's voice crackled over the line from New York.

At sixty-six, Pritzker headed a family acknowledged to be among America's sharpest investors. He was a small, wiry man still energetic after triple- and quadruple-bypass heart surgery. Grandson of a Russian-born pharmacist who emigrated to Chicago from Kiev in 1881, Pritzker had built over four decades a business empire as notable for its diversity as its profitability. It centered on two businesses, the Hyatt Hotel chain, and Marmon Group, a secretive conglomerate with tentacles into more than sixty businesses, from ready-mix concrete to Ticketmaster. Low-key and headline shy, the Pritzkers made a rare splash in the mid-1980s with a bold attempt to resuscitate bankrupt Braniff Airlines, an effort that ultimately proved disappointing.

That Friday, Jay Pritzker listened skeptically as Jerry Seslowe detailed First Boston's unusual tax strategy. "Ah, Jerry, it's too late," Pritzker said. Formal bids were due in just seven days. But Seslowe persisted. As the two discussed their probable competitors, Shearson and Kravis, Seslowe detected a shift in Pritzker's interest. Pritzker had long been an admirer of Henry Kravis and was impressed by his intense interest in RJR.*

"If Henry is there," Jay Pritzker said, "maybe there's something to it . . ."

———

Billionaires have a way of making friends.

One of Jay Pritzker's closest friends and advisers was Melvyn N. Klein, an amiable Corpus Christi, Texas, investor who, while working on Wall Street in the early 1970s, had become friends with Henry Kravis. In early 1988 Klein had formed an investment fund with Harry Gray, the former chairman of United Technologies. The fund's third partner was a partnership headed by Jay Pritzker. By that spring Gray Klein, armed with $500 million in newly raised capital, had attempted to invest in a number of high-profile takeovers, including the battle for Federated Department Stores.

In February, a Gray Klein limited partner named Daniel Lufkin proposed that Pritzker and Gray Klein investigate an LBO of RJR Nabisco; the plan was dubbed Project Smokescreen. Klein and the Pritzkers spent months analyzing the proposal. None knew Ross Johnson, so Klein had suggested they feel out Kravis about a joint approach. Klein pitched the idea to Kravis at a breakfast May 4. "There's no way he's going to do this," Kravis had said, relating details of his earlier meeting with Johnson. "Just no way." That was the end of Project Smokescreen.

———

* Jerry Seslowe wasn't the first to bring RJR Nabisco to Jay Pritzker's attention. Through a number of intermediaries, Smith Bagley had succeeded in talking with one of the investor's aides. Nothing came of it.

In October, after Johnson's initial proposal was announced, Klein had called Kravis again and expressed interest in acquiring a minority stake in any Kravis buyout of the company. Kravis had said he would think about it.

Friday afternoon Pritzker phoned Klein in Texas. "Mel, what is our obligation to Henry Kravis on RJR?" Klein said he knew of none, but would check. That afternoon, as Pritzker weighed whether to join forces with First Boston, Klein reached Kravis.

"I just want to be up-front with you," he said. "It looks like Jay Pritzker may team up with First Boston on a third-party bid for RJR Nabisco."

"Thanks, Mel," Kravis said. "I appreciate that."

Hope was dwindling fast for First Boston when Maher convened a meeting in his office that Friday afternoon. His only chance of avoiding the ignominy of being left out of the RJR Nabisco deal was Finn's flaky restructuring proposal. He called in Finn and a handful of others to figure out what to do. Outside the sun was setting. As a metaphor it seemed all too apt.

Finn had drawn up a more detailed set of plans for the meeting. Using the installment note loophole to acquire RJR, he projected up to $4 billion in savings on taxes deferred beyond the year 2000. If everything clicked exactly right, Finn figured, First Boston might earn almost $300 million in fees—four times the largest merger-advisory fee ever. But Finn knew Maher was interested in more than fees. "Ancillary benefits," he noted in his memo, included a "dramatic impact on M&A market share" and "immeasurable public relations/franchise benefits." In short, Finn suggested, if they pulled this one off, they would never have to hear about Bruce Wasserstein again.

There were, Finn admitted, some unique problems to be ironed out. For one thing, deferring $3.5 billion in taxes—a conservative scenario— was unprecedented. According to Finn's calculations, this single transaction would boost the annual federal budget deficit by 2 percent. If First Boston proposed it, RJR Nabisco's board would almost certainly have to take into account the political fallout. "It's clear," Finn said, "that Washington would go apeshit."

But the brash young banker argued that Congress was unlikely to intervene. Legislators had specifically extended the use of installment notes until year end. And Congress would be in recess during much of the approaching auction. What were the chances of a special session being called to trash an LBO? "They can't do anything," Finn stated.

Still open was the question of whether First Boston needed partners to make Finn's idea work. Some argued for flying solo. Maher wasn't so sure. A respected partner would add legitimacy, something Maher was acutely aware his team might need.

Maher's wish was about to come true. As darkness fell outside his window, Leon Kalvaria stepped out to take a call. It was Jerry Seslowe. Jay Pritzker's former accountant sounded excited. "Leon, we've talked it over with Jay. We're there. Let's move."

Finn sat in the dingy conference room overlooking Rockefeller Center and fumed. *Why are these guys giving us so much grief? They ought to be happy we're here.*

It was Tuesday morning, just three days before the Friday bid deadline, and Finn and three First Boston colleagues had come to Lazard's offices to present their proposal in detail. Finn was always surprised how ratty Lazard's suite seemed. The floors probably hadn't been carpeted since 1932, he said to himself.

First Boston had pitched its proposal as a restructuring rather than an acquisition. Maher was betting the board might instinctively wish to keep RJR Nabisco independent, and a restructuring, albeit a drastic one, might be an easier pill to swallow than those offered by Kravis or Cohen. First Boston and the Pritzkers were offering to work with the board to sell the food businesses, pass along proceeds to shareholders and leave the tobacco business intact.

As the meeting progressed, Finn sized up the two bankers across the table. Luis Rinaldini of Lazard, Finn knew, was sharp, a good talker, like himself a rising star. John Mullin of Dillon Read impressed Finn as a relic of pre-1970 Wall Street, a stodgy, "white-shoe" banker playing way out of his league in the fast-moving eighties.

"We don't see this board participating in this kind of complicated transaction," Rinaldini was saying. "Not with all this risk from Washington." The Lazard banker was shaking his head. "It's too risky. It's not their style. Of course, we don't want to discourage you in any way."

The hell you don't Finn thought. He realized what was happening.

These guys are offended. They think we're screwing up their process. They think we're making a mockery of the whole thing. Finn suspected he knew what the real problem was. *We're doing their jobs for them. They should've thought of this themselves. They think we're trying to steal their jobs.*

Far from welcoming First Boston's interest, the special committee seemed to be snubbing it. Finn left the meeting fearing this was going to be far tougher than he had hoped.

Maher read Peter Atkins's letter in disgust.

The board wasn't going to allow First Boston a chance for due diligence. If First Boston wanted to bid, it would have to fly blind, its only guide an annual report and a stack of 10-Ks.

It didn't seem fair. "I don't know what we're going to do," a disappointed Maher told Atkins on Wednesday, two days before the bidding deadline. "I expect we'll give you something to think about on Friday, which may or may not make your life easier."

Atkins remained noncommittal. "Do what you want to do."

News of First Boston's odd proposal surfaced in the press Thursday morning. Few details were available, but almost no one seemed to take it seriously. Bruce Wasserstein told anyone who would listen what a joke the First Boston approach was. On Friday an unnamed board adviser savaged the overture in *The Wall Street Journal* as "Mickey Mouse."

At Shearson, Tom Hill had nothing but contempt for the First Boston "offer." *Maher is so desperate he'll do anything,* Hill thought. The installment note scheme, he believed, was a gimmick that would never work in a deal this size. Hill considered Seslowe a lightweight, a real amateur. "They've got everybody in this deal except Abbott and Costello," Hill cracked, "and they're dead."

Hill and the Salomon Sausages saw the wide girth of Ira Harris behind Jay Pritzker's sudden interest in RJR Nabisco. Harris, now advising the board, was so close to Pritzker that Hill called them "blood brothers." Pritzker's entry into the fray was no accident, Hill decided; the special committee needed a stalking horse to replace Forstmann Little, so Harris came up with Pritzker. At Nine West, John Martin took to ranting how

"Fat Ira" was bent on mucking up their deal. In fact, Harris had spoken to Pritzker that Monday and had risen at the special committee meeting to urge listening to what First Boston and the Pritzkers had to say. But even his backing didn't persuade Atkins to give the new group any information.

Two days left.

As the deadline neared, Johnson's malaise lifted a bit. He began to grow worried what effect the onslaught of stinging publicity might be having on the board. Wednesday he called Hugel.

"Charlie," he said, "if you're going to run this, I want your word that, if we give our best bid, you're not going to play games and try to negotiate us all over the place."

"You've got my word."

"Are you going to be opening the bids? I don't want any funny business."

"I'll be right there," Hugel said. "I'll personally open the bids."

If you're worried about the publicity, Hugel continued, why don't you call the directors and explain yourself? Johnson began calling directors the next day. His approach was always the same.

"My conscience is clear," he told each director. "I can sleep at night, because I don't think I've done anything wrong. . . . Whatever happens, the management group has gotten the stock up, and that's what's important." To each he downplayed the management agreement, emphasizing his intention to spread the money around.

In the days leading up to the deadline, Johnson spent long evenings at Jim and Linda Robinson's apartment, hashing through pricing strategies. Most nights Horrigan, who had a company apartment downstairs, would join them, and Linda would scurry around serving drinks. Johnson was a scotch man; Jim Robinson preferred a glass of wine. Horrigan insisted on hard liquor, what Linda referred to as "grown-up drinks." Linda herself sipped berry-flavored Perrier.

A night owl, Johnson usually kept the Robinsons up until two or three A.M. As it grew late, Linda would lay face down on a living room couch, nibbling popcorn or stroking one of her three dogs. Each was named after an "Amos 'n' Andy" character: the King Charles Spaniel was Algonquin J. Calhoun, the two others were Ruby Begonia and Lacy.

When her husband and Johnson disappeared into a back room, Linda knew they were talking about the management agreement. In sharp contrast to its fiery birth, the pact was being gently renegotiated, largely in late-night one-on-ones between Robinson and Johnson. Jim Robinson didn't need to push hard to obtain the revisions he sought; the publicity on the greed issue had done it for him.

By Wednesday, November 16, when the revised agreement was approved in a meeting in Peter Cohen's office, Johnson had agreed to cut two points from his group's stake, to 6.5 percent, and to sharply scale back the incentive bonuses. New, detailed provisions were included for spreading the stock to 15,000 RJR Nabisco workers. Later, members of the management group would defend themselves on the greed issue by pointing to that fact, suggesting Johnson had agreed to trim his share of the bounty.

In fact, he hadn't. "At that point, Ross was really giving away other people's money," says Steve Goldstone. All along, Johnson and Horrigan had each planned to take about a point, or 1 percent, of the equity for themselves. Goldstone valued that point at between $75 million and $100 million over five to seven years. And according to Goldstone, Johnson still planned to take one point under the revised agreement.

Goldstone and Gar Bason jokingly chided Johnson about the talks with Robinson. "Every time you go off with Jim Robinson," Goldstone told him at one time, "you come back with $50 million less." When Johnson told his lawyer he planned to spend the weekend of November 19 at the Robinsons' Connecticut farm, Goldstone groaned. "Don't go out there," he said. "This time you'll come back with nothing."

The Kravis camp's buoyant reaction to John Greeniaus's disclosures was short-lived. Wednesday night Scott Stuart got the answers to many of his remaining questions in a phone call from Dillon Read.

What he heard was startling. Working blind, Stuart had overestimated RJR Nabisco's available cash by $450 million. Golden parachute payments were $300 million more than he had guessed. And his worst fear about the "Other Uses of Cash" column came true: $550 million more cash was flowing out of the company than his projections reflected. Stuart didn't need a calculator to assess the damage: $1.3 billion had to be lopped off their projections. It was roughly $6 a share.

"What happened?" Paul Raether asked in amazement when Stuart brought the news to his office. No one knew. Stuart was deeply embarrassed.

Already unnerved by press criticism, Kravis was shaken anew when he learned of Stuart's revisions Thursday morning. It wasn't just their effect on the projections. Kravis could live with that. The more severe blow was to their confidence. If they could be that far off on fundamental numbers, Kravis wondered, how reliable were the rest of their projections? What else didn't they know? All their analysis to date, nearly a month of work, was suddenly open to question.

All this began to sink in on Thursday, not thirty-six hours before bids were due. It was a very bad time to get cold feet.

———

"Jesus," George Roberts said. "How much do we really know about this company?"

It was a somber group that Kravis gathered in his office Friday morning. The same thoughts were on everyone's minds. Here it was, the biggest bid in history, and what did they really know about RJR Nabisco? They hadn't visited the factories, hadn't talked with more than a handful of executives. All they had was a pile of annual reports, government filings, and stacks of white computer runs—all of which they had lost confidence in.

Their doubts fueled other concerns. Could a deal this size be done safely? Would the banks, already nervous about LBO loans, come through? Would jittery junk-bond buyers want KKR's bonds? Roberts brought up life-style issues. They all lived quiet, tidy lives. Buying RJR Nabisco would mean a wave of publicity, Washington hearings, and an unprecedented commitment to run the company. "This firm's going to be in business for a long time," Roberts said. "Do we really need this aggravation?"

"Do we really want to do this to ourselves?" Paul Raether echoed.

As they talked, they followed a familiar pattern. The discussion began with the most junior, Scott Stuart or Cliff Robbins, and went around the room until it stopped with Roberts. As they completed each circuit, the group grew more and more downbeat. At the outset, Kravis and Raether had been the most bullish. Both were comfortable with a bid in the range of $97 to $98. Roberts was the bear. He wasn't comfortable with anything much above $93. "Why don't we do it at ninety-one or ninety-two?" he suggested. "Why take chances?"

Around two-thirty Dick Beattie stuck his head in. His tone was plaintive: the schoolteacher hurrying children off the playground. "If you guys don't hurry up and give us an answer, you're going to be left out of the bidding. I'm going to have to call over there and get an extension or something."

"Okay," someone said. "Give us fifteen more minutes."

Selecting lawyers to prepare its bid, normally the most routine of tasks, became a problem for First Boston. Every major firm seemed to be up to its elbows in RJR Nabisco. So many rejected him that Maher's aides joked they should call Jacoby & Meyers, the nationwide discount firm. Finally Maher selected a little-known outfit named Winthrop Stimson Putnam & Roberts. The firm's first task would be drafting a formal bid letter to be sent Friday afternoon. The search took so long Finn didn't brief the lawyers until Thursday evening.

The Winthrop team arrived at First Boston with a draft letter at eight o'clock Friday morning. The lawyers waited anxiously while Maher and his lieutenants studied it. In minutes their verdict was unanimous: The letter was a disaster.

"This is shit!" Fennebresque ranted behind closed doors. "This is absolute garbage!" Finn agreed. "It's incomprehensible," he said, shaking his head.

Irked, Maher sent the lawyers and a First Boston team to an upstairs boardroom to rework the five-page letter. It promised to be a difficult task, but Maher wasn't too worried. They had all day.

Upstairs the scene degenerated into bedlam. A half-dozen Winthrop lawyers attempted to recast the letter. A First Boston contingent attempted its own version. Drafts were written and torn up. New lawyers filed in. First Boston people shuffled in and out. By noon Jerry Seslowe and his partners arrived, adding to the rising cacophony. Lunch was brought in. More drafts were written and discarded. Heated discussions broke out over the wording of obscure clauses. Finn's secretary, scribbling down every change and suggestion in shorthand, was an island of calm. As the afternoon wore on, a layer of smoke slowly settled atop the arguing lawyers and bankers. Tempers grew short. Points were made then forgotten; talks moved in circles that no one could keep track of. A paper airplane cleaved the smoky air.

Seslowe had never seen anything like it. First Boston's people couldn't seem to agree on the simplest things. Would they bid for the entire company or the food business? Would it be an LBO or a restructuring? Seslowe retreated to a corner where he shook his head in bewilderment. He thought of Tom Pritzker and the senior Pritzker attorney on the deal, Hank Handelsman, who had remained in Chicago. "I'm just glad Hank and Tom aren't here to see this," Seslowe repeated, mantralike. No one seemed to be in charge. "What a disaster," he muttered.

There was little doubt in Seslowe's mind that if Jay Pritzker walked into the room, he would back out of the deal. "They would; they'd just walk away," Seslowe assured one of his partners. Yet in telephone conversations with Pritzker all that day, Seslowe reassured the Chicago investor all was well. Seslowe was acutely aware it was he who had gotten Pritzker into this deal; he wasn't going to back out until he had to.

As the day wore on, Seslowe found himself worrying whether First Boston was up to the task of a $20 billion takeover. To a partner he confided, "I would feel much more confident with Wasserstein and Perella around. These guys are a shadow of their former selves."

It was two hours before the five o'clock deadline when a copy of the revised letter was delivered to Maher's office. Maher read it in silence. The letter seemed to jump from point to point with no focus; peering through its tangled verbiage, it wasn't clear exactly what First Boston wanted from the board, one transaction or three, a merger or a restructuring.

Maher exploded, kicking the leg of his mahogany desk and slamming his fist violently onto the desktop. "This is the worst piece of shit I've ever seen!" he said. "Can't we do this right? I mean, this is awful."

Maher picked up the letter, strode out past his secretary's desk and up three flights of stairs to the crowded boardroom. To Finn, who knew Maher's moods, there was no mistaking the anger in his boss's clenched jaw. Within moments the room fell silent.

"You guys are missing the point," Maher told the group. "Now, just listen to me. This is what we're going to do." Then, for thirty minutes, Maher dictated a new letter to Finn's secretary. When someone interrupted, Maher raised his voice and talked over him. Seslowe couldn't believe the scene. It was like a teacher disciplining a roomful of second graders. For a while he teetered on the edge of phoning Pritzker and advising him to drop out of the bidding.

As the deadline approached, Maher and the lawyers were still arguing whether to bid for the entire company or just the tobacco operation. "The arguments that broke out weren't just over spelling and syntax," Seslowe recalled. "We were still debating what form the bid would take, what we would bid for."

A few minutes before five, Maher called Skadden Arps and told Atkins the letter might be a few minutes late.

"Keep in mind," Seslowe told Maher after he hung up, "you still have to get this past Pritzker."

It was too much for Maher.

"Chicago! I've got to deal with Chicago? This is just a letter! Give me a break!"

"Jesus Christ, when are we going to get going!"

Ed Horrigan was nearly foaming at the mouth. For two hours Johnson and his entourage had sat around the paisley-wallpapered Shearson dining room while butlers in white jackets took lunch orders and hovered over them with coffee and baskets of rolls. They were supposed to be discussing their bid, but so far all they had done was pass menus.

Johnson couldn't believe the scene. As usual, the room was packed. A full Shearson complement, maybe a dozen people, augmented by a nine-man team from Salomon led by John Gutfreund, plus Johnson and his people. Gutfreund's group, which had downed sandwiches and Styrofoam cups full of soup before arriving, sat at a separate table. "We've come over to watch everybody eat," Gutfreund said in a rare bit of humor.

Johnson, Horrigan, and Sage had walked into Cohen's office that morning and found the Shearson chief standing behind his desk. "Okay, guys," Cohen had said. "What's the price going to be?"

"A pissload," answered Johnson, smiling.

Cohen called his secretary to get someone on the phone. Horrigan wondered what the Shearson chief had up his sleeve. A secret weapon? A moment later, Cohen picked up the phone. "Hello?" he said. Horrigan listened in anticipation.

"Yes, my wife and I have talked it over. Forget the coat. We'll go with the jacket."

Three hours later they still hadn't begun talking about their bid. The lunch went on and on, until by one-thirty even Johnson was growing impatient.

"Let's get on with it, Peter," he said.

"Christ," Sage blurted out, "we need a goddamn number. It's getting late."

"Where is the bid?"

Steve Goldstone could hear the exasperation in Gar Bason's voice. It was past two o'clock and the Shearson group hadn't yet produced a final offer.

Goldstone had left Bason at Davis Polk shortly after noon and gone to check on the discussions at Shearson. He was surprised to find Cohen, Gutfreund, and more than thirty others eating a leisurely lunch, debating bid structures amid a tableau of white tablecloths, hovering waiters, and clinking china. The scene resembled a banquet more than a strategy session.

"Gar, it's aborning."

"Hey, come on," Bason pleaded, his voice strained over the phone line. "We need a number. We're running out of time. Steve, if they don't make up their minds soon, we'll have no bid at all."

Goldstone knew his partner wasn't exaggerating. With less than three hours to go, Bason had been preparing more than a dozen major documents—bank commitment letters, debt documents, and other arcane papers—that couldn't be completed without a final number. Bason had word processors standing by at three law firms.

Bason got his number just after three. Across Manhattan, at a half-dozen banks, law offices, and accounting firms, fingers flew across calculators, totting up interest rates, payment schedules, and other key ratios. By a quarter to four the lawyer could see details of the bank letters were falling into place. But it was also clear the three-inch-thick bid package wouldn't be ready in time for the run uptown to Skadden Arps at Fifty-fifth Street and Third Avenue.

The logistics of time-sensitive midtown deliveries were familiar to all Wall Street law firms. Subways were out. A single smoky track fire could trap a courier for hours in the musty tunnels beneath Lexington Avenue, and portable phones were unreliable. Moreover, Bason knew the nearest subway station on the key Lexington line was four long blocks from

Skadden Arps. He preferred taxis up the crowded parkway along the East River.

At four-twenty the young lawyer ordered Salomon's lead counsel, Peter Darrow, a twenty-six-year-old Davis Polk associate named Richard Truesdell, and two other lawyers into a car for the trip uptown. Several key documents the lawyers carried were incomplete, so the four attorneys were to pencil in the remaining numbers in the cab. Lawyers from Citibank and Bankers Trust were to meet the team at Skadden Arps with copies of the final loan documents. As they walked out, Bason handed Truesdell an NEC portable telephone.

Fifteen minutes later, with the four lawyers scribbling furiously in their seats, the car sagged in heavy traffic at Fourteenth Street. At Davis Polk, Bason crossed his fingers and kept his eyes glued to the clock. Goldstone, returning from Shearson, joined him, along with Johnson and Horrigan. Johnson, the only one relaxed, took in the scene and smiled. "At least we're going to have some fun with this."

Every five minutes Goldstone dialed Truesdell, who rode shotgun: "Where are you now? What block are you on?"

Worried looks broke out at Davis Polk as the cab nosed through heavy traffic in the Thirties and Forties. With fifteen minutes to go, the cab turned off the parkway onto First Avenue. Ten minutes later, it crawled to a stop at Fifty-fifth and First, where it froze in the grip of a Friday afternoon traffic jam.

Goldstone was on the verge of hysteria. Horrigan, too, was beside himself. "Why's this taking so long?" he demanded.

Panicking, Goldstone grabbed the phone. "Get out of the cab and run!" he barked at Truesdell. The four attorneys piled from the taxi and began sprinting the two long blocks to Skadden Arps. By then Johnson was laughing uncontrollably. "I hope your guy was a cross-country runner," he told Goldstone, "because there's no way he's going to make it by five o'clock."

Goldstone's eyes were glued to the clock. They weren't going to make it. Seconds later he had Bason call an Atkins aide, Mike Gizang. "We're faxing the bid letter," Bason said. "It's coming to you now."

As clerks began feeding the bid letter page by page into the fax machine, Goldstone listened to Truesdell's labored breathing over the portable phone.

"We're at Fifty-fifth and Second!"

34. Kohlberg Kravis Roberts & Co., circa 1985 (*clockwise from top left*): Henry Kravis, George Roberts, Jerome Kohlberg, Robert MacDonnell. The tiny firm had buying power greater than the gross national product of Pakistan.

35–37. Kravis and Roehm on the party circuit: His surprise attack was Johnson's worst nightmare, but a series of immediate setbacks and an avalanche of stinging publicity left him morose. (*Insets*): *Fortune*, the *Business Week* cover.

38. Dick Beattie: Caught between two old friends, Kravis's astute *consigliere* weathered insinuations he was a double agent.

39. Scott Stuart: Kravis was beset by last-minute doubts after his hard-working young associate, forced to decipher RJR Nabisco's values with little outside guidance, was off by $1 billion.

40. Jim Maher: After eight months of withering internal warfare, his First Boston group's desperation bid threw history's largest takeover battle into chaos.

41. Kim Fennebresque: Maher's impish chief lieutenant was eager to strike back at Bruce Wasserstein.

42. Brian Finn: His plan would have boosted the federal deficit by 2 percent.
"It's clear Washington would go apeshit."

43. Jay Pritzker: After nearly backing out at the last minute, the Chicago investor worried that his partners at First Boston weren't up to snuff.

44–45. Eric Gleacher and Steve Waters: The two Morgan Stanley bankers were links between Johnson and Kravis.

46. Ted Forstmann: His obsession with Kravis fed his desire for a final showdown at RJR Nabisco.

47. Bruce Wasserstein: Kravis so distrusted Wall Street's leading deal maker he excluded him from key meetings, saying, "We didn't want the guy anywhere near us."

48. Peter Atkins: As the
auction's principal referee,
the taciturn lawyer guided
the board through a mine-
field of legal and ethical
quandaries.

49. Matthew Rosen: Asked to make the board's
key decision, the young attorney fretted
about his possible conflict of interest.

50. John Greeniaus: After
being excluded from the
management group, Johnson's
would-be successor set
in motion a secret plan
for revenge.

51–53. Items from the anti-Johnson underground.

54· The caption for this underground cartoon read: "Happiness is when you wake up and see Ross's picture on the milk carton."

55. Johnson with Warren Burger and Ronald Reagan at the White House: "Ross," the president said, "I can't help but notice you're getting some publicity."

56. Johnson with Brian Mulroney and the Reagans.

57. Cohen and Kravis at the Literary Lions dinner: frozen in the headlights of nouvelle society.

58. The *Time* cover: the final nail in Johnson's coffin.

59. "Mt. Paymore": Beattie, Roberts, Kravis, and Paul Raether in a Kohlberg Kravis in-house send-up.

60–61. Dick Beattie directing the troops at the closing ceremonies.

62. Roberts and Kravis signing on the dotted line.

63. Moments after: Congratulations.

64. Jeff Beck and Dick Beattie at the closing ceremonies:
The Mad Dog freed from the doghouse.

65. A feast for Wall Street: RJR Nabisco products atop the cake at Kravis's closing dinner.

The minutes ticked by. Johnson fielded a call from a worried Charlie Hugel. "Where's your bid, Ross?" Hugel asked. "Where's your bid?"

Johnson, amused, tried to sound earnest. "We're still thinking about it, Charlie."

Horrigan was in a white fury. "Can you believe this! I can't believe this!" Andy Sage, who had also shown up, was dumbstruck by the spectacle. "This is the gang who couldn't shoot straight."

When Truesdell's breathless group reached Skadden Arps, their path was blocked by a throng of photographers and television cameras. The newsmen, spotting the portable phone, crowded around and began shouting questions. The lawyers plunged like fullbacks through the assembly and into the lobby.

Inside, there was no sign of the bank team. "Where are they?" the lawyers asked, craning their necks and turning round like tops. "Where are they?" Darrow, the only one who knew the bank lawyers by sight, scurried about the lobby like a child lost at the zoo.

Seconds later, Goldstone reached Truesdell.

"Richard, where are you!"

"In the elevator!"

On the thirty-fourth floor, a receptionist directed the four lawyers to an upper floor. "Wait, wait, wait!" Bason's reedy voice chirped over Truesdell's phone. Bason ordered a last-minute check on the preferred stock's dividend rate. Precious seconds ticked by as the number was double-checked.

As Truesdell and his three companions spilled from the elevator on the upper floor, their way was blocked by an enormous security guard. A minute later, Truesdell was escorted into the reception area, where, exhausted, he handed Peter Atkins the binder containing the group's bid. The bank letters wouldn't arrive for another forty-five minutes.

Darrow looked at his watch. It was 5:01. The largest takeover bid in corporate history was late. He prayed no one would notice.

The Kohlberg Kravis bid under one arm, Casey Cogut glided unnoticed past the photographers and into Skadden Arps's lobby at ten minutes before five. Upstairs, Cogut ducked past the security guard and called for Atkins with minutes to spare. When Atkins arrived, Cogut was sitting on the floor in a hallway, shuffling papers into his bid package to make a last-minute change.

Cogut watched the guard stop everyone entering the reception area. A Skadden Arps partner, caught in the net by mistake, was screaming at the guard. "I'm a goddamn partner! I'm a goddamn partner! Now let me in!"

Cogut handed Atkins the binder and left.

———

By seven o'clock, a full two hours after the deadline had passed, First Boston still had no bid. Maher had faxed copies of the letter to Jay Pritzker in Chicago. The investor and his attorneys were still ordering minor revisions. Some of the pressure had lapsed once the deadline passed, but Maher was running out of patience. This was amateurish, and he wanted the letter sent.

In Chicago, Pritzker himself was having doubts about First Boston's competence. By seven, he was wondering aloud to Jerry Seslowe whether to scrap the whole effort. "Do you feel First Boston is up to the task?" he asked.

Seslowe knew Pritzker was on the verge of backing out. All afternoon the investor had warned Seslowe he didn't want to be embarrassed by this bid. The passing of the deadline and the letter's ragged quality only fanned his concerns.

"Jay, look," Seslowe said. "It's clear they're not what they used to be. But they're still damn good. They have a good structure here."

"Do you think we ought to go through with this?" Pritzker asked. "Jerry, how embarrassing is it for us if we back out now? Should we? Why don't we just pack it up and go home."

"I still think they can pull it off," Seslowe said. "Let's just ride this thing out." Seslowe knew he was putting his own word on the line, a fact he wasn't entirely comfortable with.

By nine o'clock Maher had had enough. After suggesting to Pritzker that future snafus could be avoided if the investor's lawyers were in New York, he ordered the letter sent.

Attorneys were still suggesting changes as copies were being run off. They were shouted down. All pretense at diplomacy was dropped as shouts ricocheted through First Boston's emptying halls.

———

"Just get it out! Get it out! Forget about that! Go on! Go on! Get out of here!"

The television cameras and reporters were long gone when a pair of First Boston bankers, Brian Finn and Scott Lindsay, trudged the five blocks up to Skadden Arps at half past nine. It was cold, and the two men were miserable. Upstairs, no one waited to take their bid. The vast law firm's corridors were quiet as Finn and Lindsay made their way to Atkins's corner office.

The lawyer wasn't there. When Finn offered to wait, Atkins's secretary said he was in a meeting and couldn't be bothered. Finn handed the woman the letter. Leaving a phone number, the two men swiftly retreated.

CHAPTER
15

Ross Johnson and Henry Kravis weren't the only ones interested in owning RJR Nabisco. By Federal Express and fax machine the bids came that Friday: strange, unwanted letters, Wall Street's equivalent of crank calls. By the time RJR Nabisco's auction was over, Hugel's committee would see their share of joke bids, each, of course, checked out by Dillon Read or Lazard. A Maryland man faxed in a bid of $126 a share, or $28.4 billion. He was narrowly topped by a Winston-Salem stockbroker at $127 a share. "While I currently do not have a major investment bank retained for this purpose," the broker wrote, "I am confident that upon acceptance of this proposal the services of several will be available to me."

Hugel's favorite came from a Toronto banker. He laughed as he passed it around to the directors and investment bankers milling about a forty-seventh-floor conference room Friday evening. The fellow offered $123 a share, but with a twist. He proposed paying each member of the special committee $7 million for his vote, "to pay respect for their many years donated to the company." Other directors would get $5 million.

As the bids arrived, Peter Atkins held court in his corner office filled with its collection of carved wooden ducks and the usual Lucite tombstones. Shadowing Atkins was Mike Mitchell, a professorial trial lawyer who worked from a casual, cluttered office down the hall. Atkins was well aware the night's events might someday be replayed in a courtroom, and Mitchell was there to make sure they played by the rules.

Mitchell stood in a corner, smiling as the messengers, lawyers, bankers, and directors scurried in and out of Atkins's office. The scene reminded him of a Charlie Chaplin film. It took nearly an hour for the management group's bank documents to arrive. Every ten minutes or so Jim Maher called and assured them his letter would arrive any minute.

A feeling of relief swept the assembled lawyers when they finally peeked at the two bids.

It wasn't even close.

Kravis had bid $94 a share, or $21.62 billion.

Johnson had swamped him with a bid of $100 a share, or $23 billion.

This was going to be easy. By nine o'clock Atkins dismissed the investment bankers and told the directors that they, too, could go home. The committee would meet Sunday morning to formally declare Johnson the winner. In the meantime, representatives from both bidding groups would come in Saturday to explain the securities in their bids. Both included large amounts of PIK securities, and Atkins needed that "paper" valued for the presentation Sunday morning. It was a formality, but Atkins was determined to cover all the bases.

When First Boston's proposal was finally passed to him, Atkins read it closely. He hoped to brush it off as he had the other joke bids. Maher's proposal was only half-formed, he could see, really no more than an idea. It had no financing; it wasn't even clear Maher had talked with a bank. Yet First Boston was suggesting it could attain between $105 and $118 a share in a restructuring using Brian Finn's installment notes strategy.

The key to the proposal was taxes, and Atkins was no tax expert. At first glance, he knew he couldn't easily disprove its thesis. If Maher could do what he said—and Atkins had little reason to believe he could—First Boston's approach could be worth $3 billion more than the other proposals. This would be a matter for Skadden's tax counsel.

Until the plan could be checked, Atkins and a dozen colleagues gathered in a glass-enclosed conference room to eat dinner, and hash through Maher's strange idea. Cartons of Chinese food were arrayed on a large oak table. Between them were small round containers holding dozens of sharpened pencils. A ficus tree hung lazily over their deliberations. Out the window Manhattan's Upper East Side and, beyond it, Harlem were gearing up for the weekend. Copies of Maher's nine-page proposal were run off and passed around; the lawyers flipped through it while eating.

Around eleven o'clock they were joined by Matthew Rosen, the team's thirty-six-year-old tax counsel. Rosen was a lawyer from the "Thirtysomething" crowd: Italian suits, tassled loafers, an office crammed with modern art, the kind of early 1970s rabble-rouser embarrassed to tell his Swarthmore class reunion he now made millions sniffing out tax loopholes for corporate takeovers.

"How'd you like to be witness number one to the lawsuit?" Mitchell asked Rosen.

"What are you talking about?"

Mitchell handed Rosen the First Boston binder. "Read this," he said. "It's all tax."

Matt Rosen looked at the proposal for a minute, then retreated to a conference room to examine Maher's desperation bid more closely. At its core, he could see, the First Boston letter harbored a nasty knot of tax assumptions whose viability was far from certain. Rosen immediately realized that the fate of the proposal—and thus of the entire auction—rested on his judgment of how reliable those assumptions were. It was up to him to advise Atkins and Mitchell whether $4 billion in taxes could actually be deferred. The senior attorneys would almost certainly take his advice. If Maher's proposal could work, Rosen knew, a new wild card would emerge and the entire process would probably be thrown into chaos.

He tried to clear the enormity of his task from his mind and concentrate on the letter before him. But as he leafed through Maher's tax assumptions, Rosen's stomach began doing somersaults. As if the stakes weren't already high enough, Rosen now noticed something far more worrisome. As he worked through the First Boston proposal, he was confronted with a single, unavoidable fact: Several of its core conclusions, including a crucial assumption on the exact treatment of the tax deferrals, were *his*.

Rosen had been afraid this would happen. As December 31 approached, installment sales were all the rage on Wall Street. Every investment bank seemed to have a dozen in the hopper; Brian Finn was applying the same idea to at least four other major takeover situations for First Boston. And Finn's favorite tax lawyer was Matt Rosen.

The two young men were kindred spirits and over the years had become close friends. Many of Finn's Rube Goldberg restructuring ideas turned on esoteric tax strategies, and the two often discussed them for hours on end, especially after Finn acquired a car phone and took to badgering

Rosen during his hour-long evening commutes. Finn prized Rosen for his creative solutions to the thorniest tax problems; Rosen appreciated Finn's quick mind. The young tax lawyer was already working with First Boston on an installment sale for General Cinema, which wanted to buy some Pepsi bottling operations. Now, to Rosen's growing horror, he was being asked to pass judgment on ideas he himself had helped conjure.

Rosen and Finn hadn't specifically discussed RJR Nabisco; they didn't work that way. Finn talked in hypotheticals, tossing what-if scenarios to Rosen. In a kind of mental tennis game, Rosen swatted the ideas back to him, usually not knowing what companies he was discussing. But as he looked at the First Boston proposal, Rosen easily identified it as the fruit of the pair's recent conversations.

Conflict of interest: Rosen hated the thought. But he knew it might apply to him. Given the nasty nature of the RJR Nabisco fight, it would only be a matter of time before someone found out about his work with Finn. In his heart Rosen told himself he could be fair, that he wouldn't put his career on the line to help a friend. But in the litigious atmosphere of a major takeover, appearances of impropriety can prove as damaging as the real thing.

Rosen was pondering his plight forty-five minutes later when Atkins interrupted him. The senior lawyer couldn't stand waiting any longer for an opinion on the bid's viability.

"What do you think?" he asked.

Rosen took a deep breath. "Well, I've got some technical problems. A couple of things here, I think, are screwed up. You just can't tell—there's not enough here. If you're asking the question, Peter, whether or not this is a deal that could be done, with massaging and modification, I'd have to say yes, it could be done."

Rosen then explained his problem with Finn. He trusted Atkins, had invited him to his wedding six months earlier. "Peter, you know I'm very familiar with this thing. We've spent a lot of time working with First Boston on just this kind of proposal."

Atkins put Rosen's concerns aside for the moment.

"Talk to me about the proposal," he said. "What problems stand in the way of its working?"

Rosen ticked off several. For one thing, there was nothing about financing; billions of dollars would have to be raised. A real question existed as to whether First Boston could complete its work before the tax loophole expired at year end—now just forty-two days away. In such a short time, every day would count: The deal could be derailed if First Boston were forced to undergo a lengthy antitrust review by the Federal Trade Commission. Exactly who would own which of RJR's businesses was also unclear. These were details that would have to be worked out with First Boston, Rosen said.

"This is not off the wall, Peter. At its heart is a basic analysis that I'm comfortable with." Too comfortable, Rosen thought. "If the five or six questions I have are resolved favorably, as a legal matter do I think this works?"—Rosen paused—"Yeah. I think this works."

Peter Atkins trusted Rosen. He wasn't all that worried about the young lawyer's fear of a conflict of interest; as far as he was concerned, the matter would be their little secret. At least partly to blunt any suggestions of impropriety, though, Atkins suggested Rosen run his advice past one of the lawyers working with Lazard and Dillon. Rosen promised to do it first thing the next morning.

Into the wee hours Rosen endured the cross-examination of his partners, including Mitchell, the crack trial lawyer. Each probed Rosen's reasoning for defects, for an opening, for a reason to ignore the troublesome First Boston letter. But Rosen held his ground; he couldn't say flat-out the idea wouldn't work.

As Friday slid into Saturday, the weary lawyers left, one by one, for their homes in the suburbs. At four o'clock Skadden's offices were still. Outside the streets were quiet. In a conference room down the hall, cartons of Chinese food lay cold, half-eaten.

Atkins and Mitchell were the only ones left. They sat alone among the wooden ducks in Atkins's office. Rosen had left earlier, promising to talk the next day with Brian Finn. Unless Rosen changed his mind after talking to Finn, the two lawyers could tell where they were headed.

"I don't see what else we can do," Mitchell was saying. He stared at a copy of the First Boston letter on Atkins's desk. "How do you ignore something like that?"

Atkins nodded. He looked at Mitchell and sighed. "This is just the way it'll have to be."

There were a few seconds of silence. The two men were old friends, joined by their love of the law. Pending Rosen's talk with Finn, they had made their decision; all that was left was the special committee's approval Sunday morning. Mitchell sensed the importance of the moment.

"Boy," he said. "Whoever expected this to happen."

Friday evening Kravis grew excited when he heard his group had been invited to appear at Skadden Arps the next morning. It wasn't clear what the committee wanted, but word was that talks apparently weren't being held with Johnson's group. Suddenly the malaise that led to the $94 bid lifted. "God," Kravis said. "Maybe we're in good shape here."

There was a moment of panic when the Kravis troops realized that Drexel's Peter Ackerman, the point man on the bid's securities, had boarded a plane to return to Beverly Hills. Ackerman would have to be put on speaker phone for the session. A different dilemma arose with Bruce Wasserstein. After the newspaper leaks, Kravis didn't trust Wasserstein and didn't want him at the meeting. The problem, Ted Ammon explained to Dick Beattie, was getting Wasserstein's assistant, Mack Rossoff, who was needed to explain some securities in the package.

"You've got to call Rossoff and get him to the meeting without Bruce," Ammon said.

"Me? Why do I have to do it?"

"You've got to."

"Oh, no," Beattie said, laughing. "*You* do it. He's your investment banker. I want no part of this." In the end Wasserstein was told he wouldn't be needed.*

Saturday morning at seven, nearly two dozen investment bankers and lawyers gathered at Kohlberg Kravis's offices. Two hours later Kravis led the group to Skadden Arps. Once upstairs, they kept a sharp lookout for any sign of the management group. Kravis ran into Ira Harris in a hallway. As the two men exchanged small talk, Kravis searched Harris's face for any signal of their status, a telltale smile, a shrug of the shoulders, anything: Had the management group been called? Where do we stand? But Harris was a cipher.

The Kravis contingent was issued into a large conference room where it was met by a pair of investment bankers, Bob Lovejoy of Lazard and

---

* Wasserstein denies this, saying he saw no reason to be part of "the technical team" sent to Skadden Arps that morning.

John Mullin of Dillon Read. Wasserstein's aide, Mack Rossoff, had a sinking feeling as he saw the pair. Where was Felix Rohatyn? Where was Ira Harris? This, Rossoff could see, was the B team. A bad sign.

Kravis, too, noticed they hadn't drawn the first team. He was startled by the presence of a junior Skadden Arps attorney named Bill Frank. What did he know about their deal? And where was Atkins? For the first time Kravis realized that a meeting with the management group must be going on simultaneously. He grew nervous.

For more than an hour Kravis's bankers and lawyers explained in detail each component of their bid package, with particular emphasis on its securities. This was nuts-and-bolts Wall Street work. The meeting droned on and on, as representatives from each of Kravis's half-dozen investment and commercial banks proudly explained their specialties.

Then, as Scott Stuart was reciting a set of Kravis's projections, Bob Lovejoy stopped him. The data Stuart was reading didn't match the figures among the papers in Lovejoy's lap, the Lazard banker said. If the special committee had done its job, everyone should have been working from the same projections.

"Looks like you don't have the most up-to-date information," Lovejoy said, a worried look crossing his face.

Well, Stuart countered, what numbers was the special committee using? The two men compared numbers. Both appeared confused.

Across the room alarm bells clanged in Dick Beattie's head. He scrawled a note to Cliff Robbins, an associate sitting beside him. "Our numbers ARE bad," he wrote. "We've got to do something about this." Robbins nodded.

Afterward, there was pandemonium among the Kravis troops. As they rode down to the lobby, the elevator was filled with curses and shouts. "They're cooking the books!" people were yelling. "They're cooking the books!" Beattie was incensed. "This is outrageous. Goddamn it, they haven't given us accurate information. We've been screwed."

Pausing in the lobby, Kravis, Roberts, and Beattie pondered what to do. Earlier they had discussed their options in the event they found themselves trailing the management group. Their problem getting information, however bothersome, was their ace in the hole; it gave them grounds for a protest. If Kohlberg Kravis hadn't been given accurate information, the auction had been flawed. If so, they had to stop the process before it went too far.

Beattie returned to his office across from Grand Central Station, dictated a short letter, and sent it off immediately to Peter Atkins. It read, in part: "We learned from John Mullin and Bob Lovejoy that we may have received inaccurate information from the management of RJR with respect to certain financial aspects. . . . [If so] it may be that we will want to discuss our offer with you in light of any new or more accurate information we receive."

The pleasant words masked a sharp message. Not long after, an irritated Atkins phoned Beattie. A warning from Henry Kravis was not something he could ignore. He was equally irritated that Beattie's protest would be a black mark on the auction's otherwise spotless record. "I wish you had spoken to me and not written this down," Atkins told Beattie. "I take this very seriously."

For the moment, though, Atkins wasn't willing to pass any new information to Kohlberg Kravis. The investment bankers, Lovejoy and Mullin, replied to Beattie's letter with one of their own, suggesting—strangely, Beattie thought—that there was no problem with the information flow. Confused and angry, the Kravis troops could do little but await the board's decision.

Later that afternoon, Beattie took a second call from Atkins. "Dick," he said, "we won't need you tonight. You can let your troops go home."

Fear rose in Beattie's throat. "Are you giving the same message to the other side?"

"Yes, I am."

Beattie relaxed. A little.

Peter Cohen's troops had gone through a similar grilling that morning at Skadden Arps. A trio of committee advisers led by Ira Harris pelted his people with questions aimed at establishing the exact value of the group's securities. As the meeting wound down, Luis Rinaldini of Lazard asked Tom Hill for copies of the group's cash flow projections. The projections, Rinaldini suggested, could be invaluable in valuing the securities.

"No way," Hill said. The projections were the management group's secret weapon, the very heart of Johnson's value to them.

Why not? Rinaldini wondered.

"We regard our projections as proprietary," Hill said. "What's to prevent you from giving them to KKR?"

"Come on . . ." Rinaldini said.

Jim Maher woke Saturday with few illusions about his chances of success. There was virtually no possibility, he knew, that First Boston's proposal would be accepted as a winning bid. At best, Maher figured, he had a slim chance of interesting the board enough to force some kind of extension in the auction process.

All morning he paced his apartment, waiting for a call. Around eleven o'clock it came. "Jimmy, you're going to get a letter," Peter Atkins announced. "We have a number of questions about your proposal. We need to clarify some things."

As always, Atkins was hard to read. Maher hung up thinking the call was a good sign. *He's not calling for his health.* On the other hand, Maher reasoned, Atkins could be attempting to establish grounds to reject their offer.

A messenger delivered the letter five minutes later. The questions were basic, mechanical, tax oriented. Without due diligence, Maher could tell, he couldn't answer most of them. First Boston simply had to know more before it could guarantee the plan could work.

Atkins called several times that afternoon with further questions, all of which remained complicated and tax oriented, on issues that Maher felt should be subject to negotiation. "Peter, we can't be pinned down on some of this stuff," Maher repeated. "We've got to sit our people down with your people and work these things out."

At one point Maher called Brian Finn and read him the letter from Atkins. Finn didn't like what he heard.

"It sounds like they're just trying to generate a record to show why they wouldn't work with us," Finn said.

"I don't think so," Maher said. "From my conversations with Atkins, I don't think that's the case."

"I hope you're right," Finn said.

The two men discussed what they should do. Normally they would respond to Atkins's letter in writing, or have First Boston's tax counsel meet with Skadden's. Neither option looked appealing. Meetings took time, and time was of the essence.

Finn felt First Boston had a trump card in Matt Rosen. The tax lawyer's familiarity with Finn's idea, not to mention their personal relationship, had to be an advantage, he said. "Why don't I just call Rosen and go through their questions?" Finn asked Maher. A quick call, he felt, could cut through the red tape. Maher agreed.

Finn reached Rosen at Skadden around noon. The tax lawyer sounded tired. "I tell you what makes me nervous, Matt," Finn said, testing the waters. "It looks like you're setting up a record to show why we didn't get the job."

"Well," Rosen said. "I can't tell you what's going on. But that's not the case. That's not fair."

Finn allowed himself to feel relieved. He didn't think Rosen would lie to him. The tax lawyer had dozens of questions for Finn. To most Finn pleaded ignorance. "I can't definitely answer that question without due diligence," he repeated. "I just can't."

Finn hammered home the theme for more than an hour. "Come on, Matt, we know each other," Finn pleaded. "You know we're not here to make headlines with something that doesn't work. You've got to let us in the door. You've just got to. I can't make this better without going through the due diligence."

When he hung up, Finn was still nervous. He knew Rosen understood the beauty of their proposal. But would he stand up for it with $20 billion at stake?

Saturday was Jim Robinson's fifty-third birthday, and the Robinsons retreated to their thirty-five-acre Connecticut farm to await the bidding's outcome. Around three o'clock, Jim Robinson was surprised to see Ross and Laurie Johnson drive up.

It was good to see the Johnsons, even better for all of them to get away from the city for a while. Laurie joined the Robinsons in their weight room, which was adorned by a picture of a young, unsmiling Jim Robinson hoisting a barbell. Johnson piled up on a couch, read newspapers, and watched college football on television. All four found it impossible to think about anything except the committee's deliberations. All afternoon and into the evening they waited expectantly for a phone call that never came.

Dinner at the Robinson house that evening was Chinese food and telephone receivers. The Robinsons had five separate phone lines, and

Linda had three phones brought to the dinner table. All through their meal Johnson and the Robinsons worked their sources for information. Rumors were flying about the First Boston bid, although they couldn't tell what, if any, impact it had had.

It was Johnson who finally hit pay dirt. They had known in advance that both the special committee and the full board were to meet the following day; the committee would vote on a recommendation, and the board, in all probability, would rubber-stamp it. Johnson, hoping to learn more about the meetings, had called a source in RJR Nabisco flight operations, a loyal employee who had worked at his side for twenty-nine years. From the worker Johnson learned that the planes normally reserved for the directors' trips to New York had been grounded. Apparently the full board meeting had been canceled.

"That's funny," Johnson said. "Why the hell would they cancel it?"

Either the committee's recommendation was being delayed, Johnson reasoned, or it wasn't making one altogether. That meant one of two things: The bids were too close to call or there was no winner. Johnson and the Robinsons debated the factors that could have gummed up the works, including the strange First Boston bid and the remote chance the committee had thrown out all bids in favor of a restructuring.

"Something is very, very peculiar," Johnson said. But whatever the reason for the delay, he told the Robinsons, "this is bad news for us."

Linda Robinson passed on the news to Cohen, who was home alone at his Manhattan apartment while his wife visited friends in Florida. Despite Johnson's pessimism, the group at the Robinson farm remained optimistic. It was premature, they agreed, to draw ironclad conclusions from news of the board's flight schedules.

After dinner a beaming Linda Robinson brought out her husband's birthday cake, which she had designed herself. A carrot cake with white frosting, it was decked with Oreos; graham crackers; and honey, cinnamon, and chocolate Teddy Grahams, Nabisco's popular new cookie. But the *pièce de résistance* was the candles, or what at first glance appeared to be candles. On closer inspection one could see they were actually Winston and Salem cigarettes, each merrily lit atop the cake and wafting curls of smoke.

By the time Hugel brought the committee to order Sunday morning at a quarter past ten, everyone in the conference room knew what had to be done. Matt Rosen's tax opinion meant they couldn't ignore the First Boston proposal and its promise of a bid as high as $118 a share. In order to give Maher's troops time to firm it up, a second round of the auction would be declared. All bids, including the management group's winning $100 offer, would be thrown out.

Atkins and Mitchell had made the final decision Saturday afternoon after Rosen's conversation with Finn. Not everyone was happy about it: Fritz Hobbs of Dillon Read thought Maher's proposal was harebrained and said so. But as always, no one was willing to argue too strongly with the lawyers, not with lawsuits hanging over their heads. If Atkins needed any further convincing, Beattie's angry letter had given it to him. Several of his colleagues expressed quiet relief that, by forcing a second round, the First Boston proposal allowed them to evade a legal challenge from Kravis.

Charlie Hugel wasn't pleased with the idea of a second round, either. The First Boston proposal was iffy at best, and he remained convinced Johnson would team up with Kravis. "If we extend," Hugel said, "and First Boston drops out, these guys get together and then what have we got? We're back to ninety-three."

Hugel drew a sharp rebuttal from Marty Davis. It was in the board's best interest to draw this contest out, Davis argued: Make the bidders sweat, drive them into a competitive frenzy, buy time to work on the restructuring option.

The issue had already touched off one conflict between the two men. Davis was furious Thursday afternoon when he saw a statement from Hugel on the Reuters financial wire, to the effect that the Friday bidding deadline was firm and there would be no extensions. Davis immediately dialed Hugel. "What the hell is this about on Reuters?" he stormed, then read him the item. "That isn't our view; that isn't right."

"I didn't say that," Hugel maintained.

Davis didn't believe him. He thought Hugel was a babe in the woods or a pawn for Johnson. Maybe both. Marty Davis was, assuredly, neither. He was now a leading special-committee hawk, advocating whatever it took to get top dollar and cutting no slack for the management group. He had been prepared to argue that Beattie's letter alone was grounds to extend the auction.

The directors agreed without much debate: Extending the auction was a risk they would have to take. Rosen was trotted out to give an explanation of the tax factors. The matter of his friendship with Brian Finn wasn't mentioned.* Hugel and the other directors questioned Rosen thoroughly but, in the end, went along with his advice. No matter how much they wanted to get this over with, it looked as if they weren't yet finished. Before adjourning at one o'clock, Atkins left the room to see how much time Maher would need.

By Saturday evening Maher had relaxed. From the tone of Atkins's questions, he could tell First Boston had somehow gotten its foot in the door. He wasn't surprised when Atkins called again Sunday morning.

The board is prepared to give you a crack at this if you're ready, Atkins said. "Are you prepared to dedicate the resources here, Jim?" he asked. "And how much time would you need?"

Maher wanted two weeks but knew he couldn't get it. Atkins suggested extending the bidding deadline to a week from Monday, just eight days away. Maher, mindful that the upcoming Thanksgiving holiday might make it difficult to get funding commitments, suggested a ten-day extension, instead. Okay, Atkins said. Tuesday, November 29, at five o'clock it would be.

When he put down the receiver, Maher smiled and thought to himself: *I'll show you Mickey Mouse.*

On Sunday morning Jerry Seslowe was reading the Sunday papers at his Long Island home, trying to take his mind off the goings-on at Skadden Arps. A driving rainstorm outside made him glad to stay in.

The phone rang. It was Scott Lindsay, one of Maher's aides. "Peter Atkins wants you to come in and sign a confidentiality agreement. We've got our foot in the door!"

Exultant, Seslowe wasted no time in climbing into his BMW 325ii and plunging into the flooded streets. An hour later he met Brian Finn at Skadden Arps, where he found Atkins's mood matched the stormy weather.

The lawyer was downright hostile. Seslowe felt he was being blamed for having to extend the auction and complicating Atkins's mission. It was

---

* The Finn–Rosen link came up again the following week, when First Boston requested Rosen's services on a separate deal. According to Finn and Rosen, Atkins vetoed Rosen's hiring to avoid any appearance of impropriety.

evident Atkins was dead tired and wanted to go home. He must have been up seventy-two hours straight, Seslowe thought. In a corner, Atkins's assistant Mike Gizang looked like a rag doll.

"All right, you're in the deal now," Atkins lectured. "We're taking you seriously. Okay? What we don't want to see is another Forstmann Little. They made a lot of noise but never came to the table. We're counting on you, by letting you in, to be real."

Seslowe nodded. They would be real.

"Sign this." Atkins put a confidentiality agreement before Seslowe.

"I can't sign anything without a lawyer reviewing it first," the accountant said.

"Fine," Atkins said abruptly. "I'm leaving."

"I can't sign," Seslowe protested. "I can't."

"You have to sign."

Seslowe pleaded to be permitted to fax a copy of the agreement to Pritzker's lawyer, Hank Handelsman, in Chicago. Atkins made it clear he should hurry.

Soon Handelsman was on the phone, requesting changes in the document. Seslowe, eyeing a stern-faced Atkins, cut him off. "Hank, let's talk real world here," he said. "We either sign this right now, or we go home. . . . No, Hank, now. You've got three seconds. Peter Atkins is standing right here. We have to sign."

By noon a group had gathered at Kravis's offices. There was nothing to do but wait. Most of the bankers and lawyers assembled in a conference room and cheered on the New York Jets in a game against Buffalo. Someone made popcorn and passed it around. Peter Ackerman of Drexel, who had returned to New York shortly after landing in Los Angeles, stepped out and brought back an armload of books. Kravis spent the day pacing his office.

"When are we going to hear something?" he kept asking. "Goddamn it, when are we going to hear something?"

From time to time Paul Raether called Dick Beattie, who remained at home, trying to lose himself in a copy of Richard Rhodes's *The Making of the Atomic Bomb*.

"What's going on?" Raether asked.

"I don't know," Beattie said. "What do you want me to do, call over there?"

"No, don't call 'em," Raether said. The last thing they wanted to do was be pests.

At the Robinson farm Johnson's day of decision wore on. He was the only one of the four friends who didn't seem obsessed by the committee's deliberations. For much of the day he sat on a sofa reading newspapers. As the afternoon dragged along with no news, Johnson maintained his cheery facade, even as Linda Robinson nervously threw out calls seeking signs of the auction's outcome.

"Don't worry, Linda," he admonished his hostess. "Eventually they gotta tell us."

But to himself, Johnson was growing pessimistic. The board meeting's cancellation weighed heavy on his mind. On that news alone, it seemed likely there wouldn't be a clear resolution of the bidding, at least not today. He guessed the bidding must be in a dead heat; given all the publicity over the management agreement, that was bad news.

"If the bids are close," he predicted, "we're dead. The board won't vote for us."

Around four o'clock the two couples prepared to return to New York. Outside, a heavy rainstorm raged. The weather was so bad that the helicopter they were to take back to the city was grounded. As the rain continued, everyone piled into two cars, the Robinsons in front with a driver. John Martin had come up that day in his white Range Rover, and the Johnsons joined him for the drive back.

The tiny caravan made slow progress as the weather brought traffic to a crawl on the Hutchinson Parkway. In the lead car, Linda clutched a cellular phone to her ear, still plying her sources. As the cars crossed the New York state line, the phone bleated. It was a reporter with a copy of a press release about to be issued by the committee. Linda Robinson listened with growing incredulity as she was read the release. Minutes later she put the phone down and turned to her husband.

"You're never going to believe this . . ."

For fifteen minutes Linda Robinson tried in vain to call the phone in Martin's Range Rover. But the driving storm fouled communications. Finally, just past Mamaroneck, she got through.

Shouts of anguish erupted within the Range Rover.

"We've been robbed!" Martin yelled. "We've been robbed!"

In the blink of an eye Johnson saw all hope for victory evaporate. "That's it," he quietly told his wife. "Good-bye."

————

Linda Robinson passed the news on to a second newspaper reporter, who quickly relayed it to Dick Beattie at the lawyer's home. Beattie listened with surprise as he learned Kohlberg Kravis had finished third in what was supposed to be a two-horse race. "Son of a bitch!" he exclaimed.

As the reporter finished, Beattie heard the telltale click of another caller on his call waiting. Hanging up, he took the second line, and interrupted Peter Atkins before he could say a word. "Peter," he said. "Let me tell you what you you're about to tell me." He ticked off the three bids and the new deadline.

For the first time in a month, Beattie heard Atkins lose his composure. "Holy shit," Atkins said. "How did you get that?"

Beattie just laughed.

————

After dropping off their belongings, Johnson and the Robinsons joined the rest of the management group, which had gathered at Jack Nusbaum's law firm, Willkie Farr & Gallagher. There they found a crowd of furious Salomon investment bankers. The Sausages were raging at their former colleague Ira Harris, who they blamed for bringing in the First Boston–Pritzker group and snatching their victory. "That fat fucker!" people were saying. "He's out to fuck us! He's just trying to fuck us!"

Jim Robinson, his usual statesmanlike self, attempted to calm the heated rhetoric. Nusbaum tried to put an optimistic spin on events. "Well, obviously we're in a good position," the Shearson lawyer said. "The First Boston thing will fall through, and we'll still be in the lead."

"I don't believe it," Johnson said. "They now know our maximum bid. They know where we are." No, Johnson told the group, this indicated something far more sinister at work among the board members. "Under no circumstances is the management group going to get this bid," he predicted. "It's absolutely clear."

Johnson was ready to give up and go home. "We always have the option to just not bid again," he told the group. "Fuck 'em. We've done our part.

We played honest with these guys. Fuck it. We're getting pilloried, pissed on, and every other goddamn thing. Let's just leave. Let them explain that to the shareholders."

It was hyperbole. But as he listened to Johnson, Peter Cohen feared he was right. For the first time Cohen began to realize what a liability Johnson had become. Maybe the directors really wouldn't give the company to him.

"Ross," John Gutfreund asked, "do you think that that board is really against you?"

"Well, the relationship only goes so far," Johnson said. The threat of lawsuits tended to spoil even the best friendships. "They're not against me," he explained, "they're for themselves. It's a pretty big damn difference."

At Nine West, Kravis didn't know whether to kick himself or shout "Hallelujah!"—by all rights they should have lost. Johnson and Cohen had simply blown them away. Not in his wildest dreams had Kravis expected the management group to jump to $100 a share. His anger, however, quickly gave way to relief as the significance of First Boston's long-shot bid sank in. "God," Kravis said. "We just got another life."

That afternoon he and Roberts scrambled to learn more details of the First Boston offer. It was a shocker. "Where the hell did these guys come from?" Kravis wondered aloud. At first they couldn't understand what Maher was up to. Then, as details of the bid dribbled in, Kravis saw how flimsy it was. He couldn't believe the board had seen fit to give Maher a chance. In his judgment, there was no way First Boston could complete its plan by year end—no way. Still, it had happened, and for that, Kravis would be eternally grateful. He called Roehm and, in a voice filled with relief, told her, "At least we're alive."

Late that afternoon Kravis, Roberts, and Beattie gathered in Kravis's office to ponder their next move. On the face of it, they agreed, they were in a rotten position.

Hold on a minute, Roberts said. He had been giving their plight some thought and wasn't so sure third place was that bad. In fact, Roberts said, "We're exactly where we want to be."

His statement was met with questioning glances.

"Look," he said. "Let's just lay low. We'll put out the word we don't know what we're going to do. It's the truth. There's no reason to say we're really going after this deal. Let's let the world know we may not be there."

You're right, Kravis said, catching on. "The last thing we need to do is go out and beat the tom-toms, especially if we're not going to bid again." It made perfect sense: If they were coming back strong in the second round, why let on? And on the remote chance they backed out, why not save themselves some embarrassment?

Roberts smiled as the outlines of a plan formed in his mind. He had the perfect venue from which to launch their little misinformation campaign: Wasserstein and their leak-prone investment bankers. "I think," he said, "we ought to put on a real show for Bruce."

The first step was a press release. "We must carefully consider our alternatives," the firm announced Sunday evening, "in light of new information we will be receiving before reaching any judgment on what further steps, *if any,* we might take."

When Kravis arrived home, he appeared tired and depressed and talked about giving up the fight. Carolyne Roehm, a woman who believed in female intuition, searched her husband's face for signs of his true feelings. Did he mean it? Could he really be serious about letting the biggest prey of his life get away?

It just wasn't like Kravis to scuttle off with his tail between his legs. Underneath the weary words she sensed a new resolve in her husband. No, Roehm decided, there was no way he was letting this one get away twice. She gave it more thought and finally she was sure of it. Henry Kravis had a plan.

CHAPTER
16

An eerie stillness descended over Wall Street as the bidders began their postmortems Monday morning. The financial markets calmed. The investment bankers slowed. Behind closed doors, Wall Street's vast takeover machine had ground to a halt.

The reason was simple: The commercial banks, poised to commit nearly $15 billion or more to the eventual victor of the RJR Nabisco auction, had all but stopped work on every other takeover until their decks were cleared. Most deals were put on hold, as all eyes turned to RJR Nabisco. The information-starved arbitragers, flush against their trading limits, could do little but wait and watch. More than one trader was reminded of an old Western where townspeople cleared the streets so the outlaws could fight.

"Mickey Mouse," Jim Maher announced with a smile, "has just become Mighty Mouse!"

Wall Street may have been becalmed, but there was nothing calm about the goings-on at First Boston Monday morning. Maher's troops weren't simply enthused; they were *pumped*. They had succeeded where no one—not even themselves—had expected. And if they didn't win it, if they never did another deal, they would never forget how good breaking into this one felt.

By eight o'clock Maher's top aides had gathered in his glass-walled office to congratulate themselves and prepare for what promised to be a rigorous week ahead. "My friends," said Greg Malcolm, the junk-bond chief, "the dog has done caught the bus."

Laughter filled the office. Maher loved it. It was just the kind of esprit de corps the place needed. Especially to tackle this project. He wasn't sure they could do it. But they sure as hell were going to try.

When the laughter faded, Maher got down to business, parceling out assignments to each of his team leaders. They had just eight days to mount the largest, most complicated takeover bid in Wall Street history. Maher knew it would be the ultimate test of the department's viability, of whether they could reclaim the top without Bruce Wasserstein.

Kim Fennebresque, Maher's wisecracking sidekick, would head the team analyzing Nabisco to estimate how much First Boston could get selling Nabisco's businesses. Brian Finn would free-lance, advising all the groups. Greg Malcolm had the toughest job, leading the financing team. Not only were Malcolm's people to raise more than $15 billion to buy RJR's tobacco business at a time most banks were already neck-deep in LBO loans, but he was charged with finding a bank to breathe life into Finn's installment notes scheme. It was a dicey proposition at best: Nothing like it had ever been attempted. Malcolm had to convince a bank to lend First Boston up to $15 billion against the installment notes it would issue. Everyone in the room knew it was the single hardest task before them.

Afterward Maher strode up to the forty-fourth-floor boardroom, where he was to lunch with Jay Pritzker. Pritzker had flown in from Chicago that morning and seen Jerry Seslowe, his point man on the deal. Seslowe wasn't surprised to find Pritzker still bothered by the group's Keystone Kops performance Friday. "Are they just doing this as an exercise to reestablish themselves?" Pritzker asked.

In the boardroom, Seslowe took Fennebresque aside and put the question to him bluntly. "How much of this is being done because you feel you have to be in the game?" he asked. "I don't want to be embarrassed here, and neither does Jay. I'm out on a limb with you guys. Forget about all the nice words. Are you guys serious about this?" Fennebresque assured him they were. They weren't in this business to look stupid.

During lunch Maher updated Pritzker on their progress and discussed the values locked inside RJR Nabisco. Mel Klein, the Pritzker aide up from Corpus Christi, surprised Maher by saying he'd been in touch with his old friend Henry Kravis. "I'm not sure what we're going to do," Kravis had told Klein Sunday evening. "We're trying to make up our mind."

Everyone at the table wondered if Kravis would drop out of the bidding; his $94 bid was a joke. They theorized that Kravis was tiring of exposure to the gruesome combination of mudslinging, politics, and publicity. Whatever the case, Klein said, he wanted to meet with Kravis to feel him out about a possible partnership. "Listen," Pritzker told Maher, "we're not going to do anything you don't want us to do. We just think we ought to talk with him."

Maher agreed. He would be more than happy—thrilled, in fact—to split $25 billion of turf with Kravis. "Hey, we want to make an investment here," Maher told Pritzker. "I've got no problem with that. Don't worry about our position."

Pritzker had one other message. He wanted the Pritzker name kept out of the headlines. From here on out, he said, chopping the table with his hand for emphasis, the group must always be identified as "the First Boston group." No one could tell whether the request was made out of altruism or fear of humiliation.

Monday found Johnson in a foul mood. "We got the shaft, Charlie," he complained to Hugel that day. "It's obvious to everybody."

"I really feel badly about it, Ross," Hugel said. "But there was nothing we could do about it. It had to be done this way."

"I just think we got the shaft."

"That's what the lawyers told us to do," Hugel said. "We could not turn down an offer potentially worth one hundred and ten a share."

Nothing Hugel could say would soothe Johnson's simmering anger. The longer he stewed, the worse he felt. He had been cheated by his own board, people he considered his own friends. Steve Goldstone had been right. They weren't his friends anymore. He hadn't wanted to believe it then, and he didn't want to believe it now. But down deep Johnson knew it was true. He had lost his own board's support.

Macomber he could understand. He'd long had it in for Johnson. But Marty Davis? From what Johnson heard, Davis had turned the farthest against him. Bill Anderson? Albert Butler? Johnson had taken to calling them the "pseudoindependent" committee. They all had become captives of their Wall Street handlers, particularly Atkins, the taciturn lawyer Johnson had taken to calling "Laughing Boy." Of them all, Ira Harris's behavior hurt the worst. Johnson heard that Harris was badmouthing him on golf tees across the country. He had known Harris for fifteen years. It stung.

By Tuesday Johnson was ready to give up one minute and wring the board's collective neck the next. In one black moment, he told Laurie to begin cleaning out their company-owned apartment. Together they sorted through their belongings, earmarking some to be moved to Atlanta, some to the Colorado house, some to Florida.

There was little to be done to prepare for the second round. Johnson had been amazed by the $100 number and couldn't fathom going any higher. "Whatever we do the second time," he told Jim Robinson, "it certainly can't be much in excess of what we were looking at the first time around. You may want to mix it up a little bit"—change the cash component—"but in no case should we go much beyond where we are."

Tuesday afternoon the pendulum of Johnson's mood swung again. He summoned Goldstone to Nine West with an idea for dealing with the board. "Tell 'em if we don't get a definitive agreement, we're walking," Johnson said. "All the heat's been put on us, why don't we put some heat on them? We're not using the power we have, as a bidder. They're writing all the rules. Why don't we write some rules?"

Goldstone knew it was too late to play hardball. The auction was too public, the game had gone too far. He held off calling Atkins, and the next day managed to talk Johnson out of doing anything rash. Wednesday afternoon Johnson packed his bags and boarded his Gulfstream jet for a Florida Thanksgiving.

As the dust settled, the spies came out.

Monday morning Dick Beattie talked with Bob Millard, the Shearson trader. The two friends had kept up their back-channel dialogue for almost five weeks. Millard was as valuable an intelligence asset as Beattie had. The trader served as Beattie's—and thus Kravis's—best read on Peter Cohen.

That morning Beattie sounded as downbeat as Millard had ever heard him. "Congratulations," the lawyer said, "you guys sure had the best bid."

The conversation immediately turned to the First Boston "miracle" bid. "The First Boston thing is clearly a sham," Beattie said. "We thought about that transaction, and it doesn't work. It's a bunch of bullshit."

Millard wondered aloud what Kravis's next move might be. Beattie said he didn't know, and then volunteered to share insights on First Boston's tax strategy.

"We know a lot about that transaction," Beattie said. "If we can be helpful on that, we will."

Millard was struck by the offer and by Beattie's tone. He sounded beaten. It sounded as if Kravis was all but out of the bidding. Millard ventured a suggestion. "Why don't you call Peter and congratulate him," he said. "Just call him. I know he'd love to talk to you."

A conversation with Cohen, Millard figured, might be invaluable.

Cohen returned Beattie's call that afternoon from his limousine, which was speeding toward JFK International Airport. He was due in Brussels the next day for a board meeting of Carlo De Benedetti's Société Générale de Belgique.

"That bid was a winner, Peter," Beattie said. "I got to tell you, nice job. Terrific."

"Yeah, well. Thanks. What do you think of the First Boston thing?"

"It's crazy. It won't work. We've gone through the analysis ourselves. We're looking at it in another deal right now. They can't do it. Not by the end of the year. No way."

"That's what we think, too," Cohen said. "We really got screwed. What are you guys doing?"

"Oh, I don't know," Beattie said. "Everybody around here's pretty depressed. I don't know what we're going to do about this second-round thing. We may not do anything. We're all going to take off for the holiday, I think. George is going back to San Francisco. I think Henry's going skiing."

"Yeah," Cohen said. "I'm going to take a couple of days off, but probably not till next weekend. I think Karen and I are going to go out to East Hampton. I gotta get out of here. I'm really tired."

After hanging up, Beattie looked at the phone a minute. He hadn't lied. He hadn't intentionally misled Cohen. It was true: Kravis didn't know what he was going to do. On the other hand, he sensed no skepticism from

Cohen. If Cohen got the impression Kravis was out of the bidding, well, so be it.

Dick Beattie couldn't know it would be the last civil conversation he and Peter Cohen would have for a very long time.

To the public the bidding for RJR Nabisco seemed frenzied, the emergence of a third bidding group transforming it into a wide-open race. But in the subdued hallways and offices of Lazard Freres and Dillon Read, there was no such enthusiasm. To the board's advisers, the First Boston bid was hardly good news. Few among them had any confidence that Maher's troops would come back in eight days with a concrete proposal.

Far more worrisome was the poor showing by Kravis. His $94 bid left everyone scratching their heads. What could have gotten into them? Was Kravis *trying* to lose? Their Sunday evening press release, with its suggestion that no second bid might be forthcoming, seemed ominous.

From the beginning, the committee's mission had been to keep alive two viable bidders. When it got two, it aimed for three, and so on. It tried anything, in short, to produce the highest possible value for shareholders. If both First Boston and Kravis failed to surface with second bids, the committee was left with one alternative: Ross Johnson.

That made Felix Rohatyn, the dean of the committee's bankers, uneasy. Working with Dillon and Skadden in the days before Thanksgiving, Rohatyn marked out two paths of action. First, Kravis had to be saved. Whatever the cost, they needed him at the bidding table the following Tuesday. That meant plying him with data and advice that showed RJR Nabisco warranted a strong second-round bid. Second, the committee had to work hard to refine a recapitalization plan that, in the worst case, could be used as leverage in the event Johnson came to the bidding table alone. It would involve a big, one-time payout to shareholders financed by borrowings and asset sales.

The campaign to save Kravis began Monday. "What do you guys need to get back in the hunt?" Lazard's Bob Lovejoy asked Paul Raether in a conference call that afternoon.

Raether, presiding over a growing mountain of computer runs, said he needed more information—real information—if Kravis could entertain the idea of bidding again. "We want to meet the tobacco guys, for one thing," Raether said. "And we want Ed Horrigan there. We want to hear his game plans. If there are really no savings here, we want to hear it from him."

Raether had seen what John Greeniaus could do with Nabisco. He strongly suspected Horrigan and Johnson had an undisclosed plan for exacting similar savings from the tobacco business, and he said so. "Look," Lovejoy said, "if there's some master plan, we don't know about it. If there is, they're lying to us. They've sworn up and down they don't have one."

Monday night Lovejoy led a procession to Kohlberg Kravis's offices to meet with Raether and Scott Stuart. A Lazard team had combed through every piece of information received from RJR Nabisco and, using what little new data they received from Johnson's bid that weekend, compiled a revised, rosier set of projections for Kravis. Now the Lazard bankers bore in, making sure Kravis got the message that there was more inside Johnson's company than met the eye.

Josh Gotbaum, a thirtyish Lazard banker who sported a peace-sign ring, suggested to Raether that an additional $150 million in annual savings could be wrung from the tobacco business. It was a powerful statement. Spread over ten years, that was $8 or $9 a share, enough to boost Kravis well over $100 a share. Lovejoy could tell from their expressions the message was sinking in.

In fact, Raether wasn't totally convinced. He knew that the Lazard bankers had an interest in keeping Kravis at the table, so he took their advice with a grain of salt. On the other hand, he had to admit, their message made him feel better. At one point, a Lazard banker named Stephen Golub took Raether aside. Raether had known Golub for years and trusted him.

"I've never seen a company like this," Golub said. "I've never seen a company waste so much money. I was at GM"—notable for overspending—"and these guys make GM look like paupers. There's money lying on the floor for the taking here. Whatever you do, don't be too conservative. Don't be too cautious."

———

"Gentlemen, don't bother to get up," Horrigan said as he strode into the packed conference room. "We all know why we're here."

Horrigan was in full battle dress for his interrogation by Kravis Tuesday morning. More than a dozen bankers and lawyers from Kohlberg Kravis and the special committee were arrayed around the cherry table at RJR

Nabisco's New York offices. To a man it was clear that Horrigan was mad as hell, and it took less than a minute to find out why.

"I understand you fired me this morning," Horrigan announced, tossing a newspaper article onto the table. That morning the *Greensboro* (N.C.) *News & Record* was reporting that Horrigan and Johnson would be "terminated" if Kravis won the bidding contest. If that wasn't bad enough, the news had come during an interview with Paul Sticht, Horrigan's sworn enemy.

"We don't know anything about that," Kravis said calmly.

"I know Paul Sticht talked," Horrigan said. "I talked to the reporter."

"I know nothing about it," Kravis repeated. "That's irresponsible and totally incorrect."

Horrigan launched into a tirade against Paul Sticht: how he had ruined the tobacco company and how Horrigan's troops had single-handedly resurrected it. "I wish you a lot of luck if you think that geriatric old fool is going to come riding back into town on a horse," he said. "The horse had better know the way because the man is blind. You've made the wrong deal there."

"That's fine," Kravis said. "But we came to talk about the business."

Horrigan talked for a while about the tobacco industry and about Reynolds. When he was through, the Kravis contingent began peppering him with questions, but it was immediately apparent Horrigan wasn't going to help.

"What can you do to cut costs?" Cliff Robbins asked.

"Nothing."

"How will you and Ross run it?" Paul Raether asked. "What're your plans? There have to be some savings here."

"No," Horrigan said, "there aren't. We think we run a tight ship here, a very lean operation. We don't piss away money."

"Well," Robbins said, "what about all these people, these head counts?"

"Oh, no. In corporate headquarters, we've got nobody."

Horrigan was a stone wall. Kravis and others put the same questions to him four or five different ways, and each time Horrigan denied any cuts could be made.

"Well, let's talk about your numbers," Robbins continued, referring to the sketchy projections he had received. "Can you do any better with your numbers?"

"Oh, no."

"You can't do better?"

"No. We're doing the best we can."

"So your projections are your projections," Kravis said.

"Absolutely," Horrigan said. "There's nothing we can do. That's it. We won't do better, we won't do worse." Horrigan launched into a speech about the importance of Premier and other projects he had underway.

"Is there any other analysis you've given the Shearson people?" Robbins asked. "Have you given them anything you haven't given us?"

"No," Horrigan said. "Nothing."

When Robbins asked whether they could raise the price of the discount Doral brand, Horrigan snapped, "You do that, and the goddamn floor will drop right out of the bottom of it." He refused to take any more questions from the young associate.

"You know," Kravis said at one point, "this is really fascinating. You can't do any better at all. Boy, and you can't cut anything here. Well, if that's the case, I got to tell you, I think we overbid at ninety-four. If you can't cut anything out of here, if you can't cut anything at all—"

"Nope," Horrigan interjected. "I sure can't."

"Well, that's just great. We made our first offer too high then. I just don't see how we can offer any more."

Disgusted with Horrigan's performance, Kravis headed back downstairs for lunch. He was scheduled to dine with a group including Jay Pritzker, Mel Klein, and Jerry Seslowe. Kravis wasn't expecting much from the lunch. Klein had been pestering him for days to meet, saying how wonderful it would be for their two groups to get together. Fat chance, Kravis thought, although he wagered a meeting might be helpful to gauge how seriously to take Maher's strange effort.

Over spaghetti Mel Klein talked in glowing terms about RJR Nabisco and its cash flows. He talked for a while about First Boston's tax strategy and how they hoped it would work. The only way to improve their effort, Klein suggested, was if the Pritzkers could team up with Henry Kravis.

"What about First Boston?" Kravis asked.

"They'll be happy whatever happens," Klein said.

"Fine," Kravis said. "On what basis would you like to work?"

"We'll just be partners," Klein said. "Fifty-fifty."

Kravis shook his head. "That's never going to happen. If we even have an interest, which I don't think we do, it would be for you to have less than twenty-five percent. You guys could make an investment with us. But we're going to run the thing and be in control."

"No," Pritzker said. "That's never going to work. We just don't have any interest in that."

It was clear there was little room for compromise. From their interest in joining him, Kravis gleaned that the Pritzkers were less than confident in their chances of victory. After lunch Kravis called Dick Beattie, laughing as he related details of the meeting.

"Those guys," Kravis said, "are nowhere."

Tuesday afternoon the Kohlberg Kravis troops began to scatter for the holidays. Roberts boarded a plane for San Francisco. Ted Ammon headed for a resort in the Dominican Republic, while Scott Stuart opted for Barbados. Raether flew to Florida, where he planned to spend Thanksgiving with his family at Lost Tree. Kravis planned to fly with Roehm and his three children to Vail at two-thirty Wednesday afternoon.

As he prepared to leave, Kravis took a call from Linda Robinson, who was phoning from a limousine en route to Connecticut. Robinson insisted she wasn't calling about business. Having just bought a horse together, they had talked about buying a second, which had now become available.

"We've got to make a decision on this this week," she said. "Other people are waiting in line to buy him." She groaned. "Oh, this all is just terrible, isn't it? It just goes on and on."

"You mean RJR?"

"Yeah."

"I don't find it terrible at all."

"Why not? God, it's horrible."

Kravis didn't believe for a minute that Robinson was calling about horses. She wanted to know if he would bid again. For the first time, Kravis decided to lay it on thick. He wanted Linda Robinson to run back to her husband with news that he was out of the bidding.

"Nah, I don't find it bad at all, Linda. We're in great shape. We're in third place. It's a terrific position to be in." Kravis hoped the obvious sarcasm would have its intended effect.

"I'm just tired," he went on, turning on the sincerity. "I'm leaving this afternoon. I'm taking my children and Carolyne to Vail to spend Thanksgiving. I can't wait. I've told all my people they ought not to think about this deal, not even think about it, while they're away. I really don't know what we're going to do about next week. We probably won't even bid at all."

Months later Linda Robinson insisted she didn't believe for a minute that Kravis was bowing out. "I thought Henry was trying to snow me. He was trying too hard."

———

Wednesday afternoon John Martin's assistant, Bill Liss, took a troubling call from one of RJR Nabisco's media buyers. The company was one of *Time* magazine's largest advertisers, and the buyer said he had just heard from a contact at *Time* that the magazine planned a cover story titled "Greed on Wall Street," featuring none other than F. Ross Johnson on the cover. It was a courtesy of *Time*'s advertising department to alert a major advertiser to a negative piece so that it could pull its ads, if it chose.

Liss called John Martin, who relayed the news to Linda Robinson. All three were worried: A hard-hitting *Time* cover was all they needed with bids due in less than a week. It had to be stopped, and Robinson and Martin agreed their only leverage was Johnson. Every major news organization wanted an interview with him, and so far all had been declined. The two instructed Liss to use the prospect of an exclusive Johnson interview as a bargaining chip with *Time*. Maybe, just maybe, they could keep Johnson off the cover.

Liss was in a difficult position. Since the formation of the special committee, he had become its official spokesman with media around the world. But Liss was a Johnson loyalist, and when Martin gave him orders, he went fervently to bat for Johnson with *Time*.

At Robinson and Martin's direction, Liss called *Time*'s Atlanta bureau chief, Joe Kane, Wednesday night offering an exclusive interview with Johnson if the magazine would take him off its cover. Kane demurred, saying it wasn't his decision. Desperate, Liss offered to make Johnson available if *Time* would only put Johnson in a "gallery" of pictures. At least Johnson wouldn't stand out, they figured. Kane begged off, suggesting Liss call his bosses in New York.

In Florida, Johnson wasn't at all sure he wanted to give his first interview. Looking for advice, Johnson called his pal Jack Meyers, the former

Time publisher who had been at the Castle Pines shindig that August. "Jack," he asked, "do you think this is something that is, you know, worthwhile?"

Meyers found out that the story's writer was a veteran *Time* correspondent named Frederick Ungeheuer, and he suggested Johnson go ahead with the interview. "Ross, I guess I don't see any downside here," Meyers said. Johnson was already taking a beating. How could it be worse? Johnson agreed. "You know me," Johnson said. "I'll give 'em the straight story."

Ungeheuer was flown to Jupiter for an interview Friday morning. Martin and Linda Robinson coached Johnson at length beforehand: no flip remarks, stress shareholder value, expect tough questions on the management agreement. The night before, Robinson had relayed news of the interview to Peter Cohen, who was immediately alarmed. Cohen had returned from Brussels—he had slept all the way to Europe—and had spent Thanksgiving puttering in his garden. Like Steve Goldstone, he was worried what the unpredictable Johnson might say. But Robinson assured him Johnson had been well coached.

The next morning Johnson met Ungeheuer at the Jupiter Hilton, and the *Time* correspondent found RJR Nabisco's president his usual, breezy self. Afterward Ungeheuer dashed off to write his story—the magazine was due on newsstands the following Monday—and Linda Robinson called to ask Johnson how it went.

"Goddamn if I know," he said. "Journalists are journalists. They'll take out of it what they want to take out of it."

———

After spending the holiday with his family, Maher was back in his office at First Boston Friday morning. Most of his teams had stayed through Thanksgiving, their feasts consisting of pressed-turkey dinners in Styrofoam containers from a nearby delicatessen. The place looked like a fraternity house on Sunday morning. Pizza boxes and nearly empty cartons of Chinese food were strewn about. A dozen pencils jutted crazily from the ceiling, no doubt a product of some late-night brainstorming session.

The Nabisco team was making headway, thanks to the appearance three days earlier of John Greeniaus. Greeniaus, after guiding Kravis through the company, was now blazing the same trails for First Boston.

Kim Fennebresque had become the Nabisco chief's shadow. Fennebresque thought so much of Greeniaus he suggested hiring him to run the company if they won. Greeniaus demurred; they could cross that bridge later.

Tylee Wilson also joined the ragtag First Boston team. He and Smith Bagley had met with Fennebresque Tuesday morning. Bagley was mulling an offer to become an investor in the group (First Boston thought he might lend some name value), while Wilson was mulling an offer to be named CEO-in-waiting. Bagley declined; Wilson enlisted.

He attacked the mounds of RJR documents that had been delivered to First Boston. He interpreted numbers, cautioned on pitfalls, searched for an edge. Wilson was delighted to finally join the battle, although he had deep doubts about First Boston's chances. Fennebresque was delighted to get Tylee Wilson's credibility, although he had deep doubts about the man. "Wilson basically wanted to ride back into Winston-Salem in a blaze of glory," Fennebresque would later say. "What he wanted from us was a cure for retired CEO-itis."

Tylee Wilson did have his limitations. When it came to lobbying directors, he could only turn to two remaining friends on the board, John Medlin and John Clendenin. "Could you get word to Hugel that these people are for real?" Wilson asked. "They've got an interesting concept. I think it's remote that it will work, but it's a helluva lot more than is currently on the table." When First Boston was cleared to interview some tobacco executives, they asked Wilson to come along. "No way," he said. "If I walk through that door those people are going to clam right up. Do you think they could go back to Horrigan and say they'd told Tylee Wilson anything?"

Despite some progress, Maher was deeply worried. None of their preparation mattered if Greg Malcolm's bank team couldn't obtain the funding for Finn's monetization proposal, and Malcolm was clearly having trouble. So far every major bank had thumbed its nose at funding Finn's brainchild. With three major bidding groups, the banks were already spread pretty thin, and it was Thanksgiving, to boot. Citibank had the gall to demand $5 million just to look at their plans. Things didn't look good, not good at all.

Maher retreated to his office to think. Maybe this was too much to pull off. Some deals, he knew, became watersheds in a Wall Street firm's life. He thought back on the takeovers that had advanced Wasserstein and

Perella's careers, half-forgotten takeovers such as Carborundum and Pullman and Conoco. Getting those done had made First Boston what it was today, or at least what it was before everyone left. RJR Nabisco, he had hoped, would bring back that old glory, but now those hopes were fading fast.

Maybe we ought to fold the tent, Maher thought. *Cut your losses.*

The possibility of giving up made him wince; humiliating wasn't a strong enough word for what that would feel like. All day Maher silently fought his demons. Then, Friday afternoon, came a glimmer of hope.

Greg Malcolm called, sounding excited. Chase Manhattan had agreed to look at the monetization proposal, Malcolm said, "and from the tone of the guy's voice, we may really have a chance."

Maher crossed his fingers.

Friday afternoon Johnson squeezed in a round of golf and afterward suggested to Laurie that they invite John Greeniaus and his wife over for dinner. The Greeniauses were spending Thanksgiving at The Breakers in Palm Beach. Johnson sensed his protégé's concern about Nabisco's future and wanted to assure him that he would be taken care of. "It's been tough for the kid," Johnson told Laurie.

Greeniaus, who continued to talk daily with Fennebresque while in Florida, arrived at Johnson's condo at seven-thirty. He was petrified. The two men hadn't talked at any length for two weeks, and Greeniaus dreaded Johnson's questioning what he had been up to.

Once inside the condo, with its views of the Atlantic in front and the lush greenery of the Intracoastal Waterway out back, Greeniaus found Johnson his normal, bubbly self. He'd just been interviewed by *Time,* Johnson said, and it looked like he was going to make the cover. The cover! He was excited. Not everyone made the cover, you know. "I'm not as bad as Khomeini," Johnson joked, "but he made it."

Johnson, as usual, monopolized the conversation. Afterward he sat Greeniaus down and talked to him about the incredible opportunities he faced now that Nabisco was going to be sold.

"Listen, even if we take a little less, a little bit of a haircut, I want to make sure Nabisco gets in with the appropriate company," Johnson said. "It'll give you and your guys a chance to be top banana." Why, Johnson and the Standard Brands Mafia had done it twice already. What an opportunity!

Greeniaus nodded a lot.

"I'm convinced I can do something that makes a hell of a lot of sense for you," Johnson said. "For your people, John, you're far, far ahead, because there's many more paths of progress as part of a Kraft, a Philip Morris, a Nestlés, a Unilever, whoever it might be. Because they sure as hell don't have the skills you have at Nabisco."

Nabisco and Reynolds and Del Monte just didn't belong together, Johnson said. They had nothing in common. No synergy. No flow of ideas or people back and forth. It just made sense to break them up. "You understand, don't you, Johnny?"

Greeniaus nodded again, which Johnson took as agreement.

As the night wore on, Johnson talked to Greeniaus as if he were a member of the management team, confiding his innermost concerns about the upcoming bid. One hundred dollars a share was a hell of a bid, Johnson said: Don't know if we can boost it.

"I've really got my doubts, Johnny," he said. "I don't know if we can go this high. They want a lot of cash. My biggest problem will be to try and hold my investors to the one hundred number. A short-term trader like John Gutfreund, you know, his attitude is the other guy is at ninety-four, 'Why the hell should I come in at one hundred again, why shouldn't we come in at ninety-seven or ninety-eight?' "

Even so, Johnson made it clear he wasn't considering any bid much over $100 a share. From a financial point of view, it just didn't make any sense. "Hell, we coughed up our goddamn toenails the first time around," he said. "I haven't seen anything that's changed in the last ten days to enable us to bid any more."

When the time came to leave, long past midnight, Greeniaus was immensely relieved. Not once, in more than five hours of conversation, had Johnson asked Greeniaus how he had been spending his time.

Later, the only words Johnson could remember Greeniaus uttering all evening were these: "Ross, I just pray you get it."

On Friday Paul Raether, whose eagerness for the bidding was mounting daily, reached George Roberts at his home, hoping to gauge Roberts's own enthusiasm for the second round.

"Gee, I don't know," Roberts said. "I'm trying to clear my mind of all this. I'm sick of talking about it."

"Have you talked to Henry?"

"No, we're intentionally not talking to each other."

Roberts was a problem, Raether knew. He never had completely shared the rest of the firm's ardor for RJR Nabisco. He seemed to pride himself on being the governor on Kravis's engine. But in the battle for RJR Nabisco, Roberts had kept their speed so low they had finished last. Raether was worried whether Roberts would even make it to the starting line for the final round.

"I'm telling you, George, we can bid as high as the one-oh-five range and still get good returns," Raether said.

But Roberts was being cagey. Raether couldn't tell whether his message had any effect.

Kravis stretched his arms and took a deep breath of the cool Colorado air. It was good to be away from the rigors of wrestling with Ross Johnson. For two days Kravis had put RJR Nabisco out of his mind. He hadn't talked much to Raether or Roberts, and didn't mind a bit.

It was the Kravises' second Thanksgiving at their new Vail home. Few places were better suited for a retreat. Two years earlier Kravis, while on a skiing vacation, had called his wife in New York and suggested they look for a chalet here. They both loved to ski so much, it only made sense. Kravis's only condition was that he be able to ski in and out of the new house. Together they had tramped through home after home, never finding the perfect one. Finally they came on the right hillside, although the house atop it appeared to be a disaster—at least it looked that way from the outside. Kravis and Carolyne never actually went in, but simply bought it, tore it down, and had a new home designed in its place.

The result, a Tyrolean symphony of stone, wood, and glass, had been finished at Thanksgiving a year earlier. They named it Woodhaven. Kravis loved it. The house was surrounded by towering silver aspens, and the air smelled of pine. Inside, the living room was dominated by a massive seventeenth-century French hearth and twenty-four-foot arched windows overlooking the slopes. The library's intricate paneling was of Hawaiian koa wood, hand tooled and rubbed by an Austrian-born artisan who spent months on the task.

Kravis had stopped talking about the deal the minute they arrived. Only once did Roehm bring it up. "What do you think you're going to do?" she wondered.

"I don't know," Kravis replied.

Roehm again searched for clues in her husband's face, but found none. "He was playing the great poker hand," she said later. "He played it very close to the vest, even with me."

On Thanksgiving they celebrated their third wedding anniversary. Carolyne gave Kravis a two-week-old black Labrador retriever. Actually, she gave him a picture of herself with the puppy in her arms. Kravis already had a yellow Lab named Kristi, which Roehm had given him for Christmas two years earlier.

"What are you going to name the dog?" one of Kravis's children asked.

Kravis thought a moment. "If we end up bidding for RJR Nabisco, and if we win, his name's going to be Nabisco. If we don't get it, we'll have to figure out another name."

The kids weren't too hot on Nabisco. "Why don't we call him Oreo instead?" one suggested.

Kravis was on his way to the slopes Saturday morning when he returned a call from Paul Raether.

"Have you talked to George yet?" Raether wondered.

"No, have you?"

"Yeah, yesterday."

"Where is he?"

"He's not sure he wants to do this at all."

"Where are you?" Kravis asked.

"Jeez, you know where I am," Raether said. "I've always been more bullish on this than George."

They debated for a while about how intransigent Roberts would be, and agreed to meet first thing Monday to plan their strategy. "You know George won't want to leave till Monday morning," Kravis reminded him. Roberts hated New York so much he tended to hang on to every last minute of California time. "We really ought to get together Monday night then," Raether said.

By the weekend, the drumbeat that had begun so quietly in the days before Thanksgiving was growing louder and louder. All weekend Shearson and the management team heard the same message repeated from every corner:

Kravis won't be there.

Kravis won't be there.

Kravis won't be back.

Through every back channel, from every Kravis investment banker and lawyer, the rumor spread. Relaxing in Connecticut, Jim and Linda Robinson heard it and recalled Linda's strange conversation with Kravis. In the Hamptons, Peter Cohen heard it and thought of his talk with Dick Beattie. In his home on the north shore of Long Island, Tom Hill heard it and thought of his own discussions with Bruce Wasserstein. The rumor spread to each of the Salomon Sausages and through the ranks at Lazard and Dillon Read. In Florida, Johnson heard it from Linda Robinson. All of them heard the same thing. Kravis was bidding low if he was bidding at all.

The question was: Would they believe it?

Jim Maher's team worked feverishly through the weekend, inching toward the Tuesday deadline. Among the sundry investors roped into the bid was a British sugar company named S&W Berisford. Jay Pritzker held an 11 percent stake in Berisford, which also paid Jerry Seslowe for financial advice.

Seslowe had penciled in the British company for $100 million of the $1.2 billion in equity First Boston needed. Saturday the group's tax attorneys ruled that, of the $250 million in equity required for buying Nabisco itself, at least half must come from a third party unaffiliated with the Pritzkers or First Boston. Seslowe immediately thought of Berisford.

Two of the British company's senior executives were in New York, but no one could find them. Seslowe phoned Berisford's chief financial officer in London, who reminded the accountant why he couldn't locate the men. They were orthodox Jews. They couldn't work on the sabbath, or even answer the phone. Seslowe waited all day. Shortly after sunset, he took a call from Howard Zuckerman, head of Berisford's U.S. operations.

"Howard, we need a commitment within two days."

"If it's so important," Zuckerman replied, "how about meeting tonight?"

Wonderful, Seslowe said. Come on over.

Fennebresque greeted the two Berisford executives when they arrived at First Boston that evening. Ushering them into a conference room, he thought he heard a young First Boston associate softly whistling. Fennebresque turned and looked at Berisford's chairman, Ephraim Margulies, and immediately recognized the tune. It was the theme from Alfred Hitchcock's 1950s television show. Margulies was the spitting image of the renowned British director.

Fennebresque's food team made a forty-five-minute presentation. Afterward Maher's aide was pleased; he thought the odds good that the Berisford people could make their decision by Tuesday. Twenty minutes later, Howard Zuckerman took Fennebresque aside.

"We'll do it."

Fennebresque didn't understand. "You'll do what?"

"We'll take the $125 million."

Fennebresque watched in disbelief as Zuckerman picked up a discarded pizza box and, on its rear flap, scribbled out a wire authorizing Berisford's London office to make the investment. He had never seen anyone work so fast.

Brian Finn turned to Hank Handelsman and asked, smiling, "Do these people have any idea what they're doing?"

"No," Handelsman said. "Not really. Why?"

"Well, it's important, I would think. I mean, they're going to commit $125 million. Why should they do it?"

Handelsman stared at Finn as if it was the silliest question he'd ever heard.

"Jay asked them to."

Monday morning Felix Rohatyn convened a meeting of the board advisers in conference room 32C at Lazard. Inside the firm, 32C was known as the queen of conference rooms. It had paneling.

There was much to do in the final thirty-six hours before bids were due. Everyone had heard the worrisome rumors about Kravis. If that weren't bad enough, ominous noises were beginning to emanate from First Boston as well. No longer could they be certain that either group would bid tomorrow.

Now, more than ever, they had to examine the feasibility of a restructuring. Luis Rinaldini had worked long hours formulating the plan and was convinced it would work. Others, including Rohatyn, had their doubts. What happened to the company after that? And, most important, who would run it? "How do you run a recap without management?" Rohatyn asked rhetorically.

Johnson would have smiled had he known the only candidate to step forward and offer to assume that leadership. It was John Macomber—the same Macomber who as a special committee member now sat in judgment of Johnson and who, on at least two prior occasions, had been involved in aborted attempts to head RJR Nabisco. When the subject of a restructuring had come up weeks earlier, Macomber had approached Hugel and volunteered to run the company if Johnson was thrown out. It was no coincidence that Macomber was also the biggest supporter of the recap among the five committee members.*

The advisers decided to take a risk. If they were certain the recap could be valued at $100 a share, why not let the bidders know it? That way they could set a bidding floor, hinting pointedly that the board stood ready to reject anything less. It was a bluff, more or less. And while directed mainly at the management group, fairness dictated the same message be passed to all three. Therein lay the gamble: laying a $100 floor might be enough to scare off at least one of the other bidders.

First stop on the board's eleventh-hour drive was the management group. Monday at twelve-thirty a Shearson–Salomon contingent led by Tom Hill met with a squad of board advisers at Dillon Read.

To the board bankers, Hill seemed unbelievably cocky. He had fallen hook, line, and sinker for Kravis's disappearing act, and First Boston, he said, was a joke, "an air ball." In a sidebar conversation with his golfing buddy Rinaldini, Hill put his fists together and pumped them up and down, mimicking a bellows, as if to suggest the board had been pumping up another player to roll out against Kravis and Johnson. "Hill was his usual arrogant self," recalled one of the committee bankers. "Only worse."

Dillon and Lazard brought several messages for Hill's group. One, firm up your securities. Unlike the Kravis securities, Shearson's had no "reset" mechanisms that, in effect, guaranteed a security would trade at a certain

---

* Macomber denies nominating himself.

number over time. Shearson's junk bonds could float up or down at will, leaving the buyer open to the vagaries of the market. The board advisers also rolled out the $100 recap plan. Anything less, they suggested, would be rejected as inadequate.

Rather than thanking them, Hill fought every suggestion. There was nothing wrong with their securities, he said. And the recap? A bluff. That day Hill was a man who thought he held all the cards. The bankers wasted little time arguing: If Hill chose to ignore them, it was his funeral.

Monday afternoon Felix Rohatyn passed on similar messages to Jim Robinson and Henry Kravis, who had returned to New York Sunday evening. "I'm not sure what we're going to do," Kravis told Rohatyn. "I don't know if I'm going to bid at all. I've just had all this bad publicity . . ."

Rohatyn encouraged Kravis to bid. "Winning will only help your public posture, Henry. You've been hurt as much as you're going to be. I can't imagine your public posture would be any worse if you won than if you just dropped out."

Monday afternoon, with twenty-four hours to go, the Kravis troops remained scattered. Raether, having returned from Florida, had driven to New England to move his daughter into a new private school. That morning he was buying supplies in a hardware store in Manchester, Vermont; by noon he was pounding hooks into the walls of his daughter's dorm room. Roberts was in the air over the Midwest; both were due in by late afternoon.

That evening Kravis hosted a dinner for Roberts, Raether, and a dozen others from the firm. Gathered beneath the Marquis of Londonderry's stern gaze, they talked about what a victory would mean for the firm. For the most part eschewing financial details, they worried about the repercussions from Washington, life in the media spotlight, and the practical difficulties of swallowing a company the size of RJR Nabisco. The firm only had fifteen deal makers. Did it want to buy a company that would require the attention of eight or nine?

To Raether's consternation, Roberts remained downbeat.

"Let's just not bid," Roberts urged at one point.

"No, George, come on," Raether said. "We can't do that. If we don't want to bid, let's at least reaffirm our earlier position."

They talked for a time about what bothered each of them, but the issue of their bid remained unresolved. Tomorrow would tell.

On Monday First Boston's carefully wound ball of string began to unravel. The first to falter was Jerry Seslowe. Pritzker's aide had gathered from his investors informal commitments totaling more than $600 million—half again the $400 million he needed. Almost all, though, were contingent on meeting with First Boston and reviewing RJR Nabisco's financial data. Seslowe arranged to assemble his stable at First Boston Monday afternoon for a presentation, after which he planned to rake in formal pledges.

Skadden Arps, always edgy about the issue of preselling, okayed Seslowe's plan, but with a caveat. To attend the meeting Seslowe's people would have to sign a confidentiality agreement. No sooner had Seslowe faxed a copy of the agreement to each of the investors than objections came flying back.

Among its clauses was one limiting the sale of RJR stock. Nearly all Seslowe's backers were active stock players and had accumulated large RJR positions. Men like Martin Gruss, the New York investor, pointed out to Seslowe that signing the agreement would lock them into their positions, leaving them vulnerable to massive losses should the inflated stock somehow collapse. One by one, Seslowe's investors began backing out.

"No . . . no . . ." Seslowe moaned as the impact sank in. "This is complete bullshit! This is a catch-22. They won't invest until they meet with First Boston. This is a disaster!"

Skadden Arps refused to budge on the agreements. Seslowe did the only thing he could; he panicked. All Monday and into Tuesday, he scrambled for commitments: Not all his investors held stock. Maher and the Pritzkers looked on warily, hoping Seslowe could come up with the money by five o'clock.

At least the bank situation had firmed up. Against all odds, First Boston's bank team was nearing success. It hadn't been easy. Every major U.S. bank was committed to helping Kravis or the Shearson group. None was enthusiastic about fielding a third team to help First Boston's iffy bid. The Japanese banks had their own problems. "We'd love to work with you," one Tokyo banker told First Boston's Dave Batten, "but we're already working with two other groups, and we've run out of people who speak English."

Somehow Greg Malcolm had managed to gain multibillion-dollar pledges from Credit Suisse and a French bank for the tobacco half of their plan. All that remained was for Chase Manhattan to finish work on the monetization proposal.

Monday afternoon Malcolm took a call from David Maletta, First Boston's liaison to the banks on the monetization project. With any luck, Malcolm thought, Chase Manhattan had finally signed off.

"We've got a big fucking problem," Maletta said.

"What's the problem?"

"Chase won't do it."

Malcolm's heart sank. "You're kidding."

"No, I'm not."

"What happened?"

First Boston had crawled upward through layer after layer of bureaucracy, Maletta explained, only to be tomahawked by Chase Manhattan's senior credit officer. Malcolm was stunned. When Jim Maher heard the news, he closed his eyes. "We're in big trouble."

Time magazine hit the newsstands Monday, and it was even worse than Linda Robinson had feared. "A Game of Greed," the cover blared over a picture of a thoughtful Ross Johnson, hand on chin. "This man could pocket $100 million from the largest corporate takeover in history," it read. "Has the buyout craze gone too far?"

As bad as the cover was, the worst damage to Johnson was, as usual, self-inflicted. What about the outsize management agreement? "My job is to negotiate the best deal that I can for my people." Does a chief executive deserve that kind of reward? "It's kind of Monopoly money." Wouldn't lots of people lose their jobs? Sure, Johnson said, "But the people that I have, particularly the Atlanta people, have very portable types of professions: accountants, lawyers, secretaries. It isn't that I would be putting them on the breadline. We have excellent severance arrangements."

That wasn't quite true. The special committee wanted each bidder to include employee-protection guarantees in their draft merger agreements, a notion the management group was stoutly resisting. The point would take on significance, because a longtime employee was lobbying hard for the employee protections.

Ward Miller, the special committee's secretary, was a longtime top legal officer for Johnson. The former Vice President of Worry would now also turn on Johnson. Miller had joined Standard Brands fresh out of law school in 1961. Now he was fretting for all his many old colleagues who would be fired as Nabisco was broken up. In this lull between bidding rounds, he had a chance to do something about it.

To each of the directors, Miller insisted on several points: guaranteeing pay and benefits of RJR Nabisco employees for three years; giving remaining employees the right to quit with sweet severance packages if they were forced by RJR's new owners to move more than thirty-five miles; assuring that retirees' medical benefits would continue.

The Kohlberg Kravis lawyers didn't like Miller's ideas, but they negotiated them. The management group's lawyers wouldn't budge. Miller went back to the board members and peevishly let them know it. The only employee Johnson seemed interested in was John Martin. He was beginning to lobby directors for a fat pension for a man who'd joined the company in January.

Johnson talked to Hugel Monday afternoon. "I won't even ask you if this will be a fair bid," he said. "If you ask me, 'Do I trust the people on the special committee,' the answer is no."

Hugel assured Johnson the process would be fair. But when he started to pound the restructuring drums again, Johnson cut him off. "Oh come on, Charlie," he said, "that shit's getting pretty tiresome."

Tuesday morning Hugel was astounded to take a call in his hotel room from Johnson. He looked at the clock; it was six-ten. "What are you doing up?" Hugel asked. The only time Johnson was ever awake at six o'clock, he figured, was when he had stayed up all night.

"We're trying to figure out what's going to happen on the bids," he said. The Shearson camp was divided, Johnson went on. Most thought Kravis was bowing out; a few, like Johnson, feared he might come in with a blockbuster bid.

"I don't know what they're going to do," Johnson said.

"What the hell are you asking me for?" Hugel said. "I don't know either. Just go as high as you can."

On Tuesday morning First Boston's bid hung in limbo. For hours Seslowe had assured Maher he would assemble his share of the pot. As Seslowe scrambled, Mel Klein kept the Pritzkers updated. Jay was negotiating a cruise ship deal in Miami; Tom, who had suffered an ear injury in a scuba diving accident, couldn't fly and was marooned in a Los Angeles hotel. Both father and son worried that if Seslowe "cratered," First Boston would turn to them to make good on his pledge. And $400 million wasn't pocket change, not even to Jay Pritzker.

"Be ready to make a decision," Klein counseled that morning. "Today is the day."

That morning Maher and his aides were busy arm-twisting senior officials at Chase Manhattan on the monetization proposal. They got nowhere. Klein's partner Harry Gray got the bank's chairman on the line, but the executive was leaving for Russia in less than an hour and wasn't inclined to spend the time overruling his senior credit officer.

Maher was badly wounded. Without bank backing, Finn's idea was just that, an idea. Maher decided to lower his sights. If a bank wouldn't agree to fund the monetization proposal, First Boston had to get someone to vouch for the soundness of the idea. Maher needed something—anything —to give the board to convince them the project was workable.

Mel Klein tried Bankers Trust, but was told it had no extra people to spare. Then, at noon, Harry Gray tried Citibank once more and struck pay dirt. A team would be over to First Boston at two o'clock.

It was going to be close.

———

The unenviable task of compiling First Boston's scattered documents and data into a single, three-inch-thick binder fell to thirty-one-year-old Gordon Rich, a short, excitable banker with thinning brown hair.

By Monday afternoon Rich had no idea what form First Boston's bid would take: a merger, a recapitalization, or something else entirely. "Look, I'm running out of time here," he told a gathering in Maher's office. "I'm going back to my office and writing this deal now. If you guys don't tell me the deal, I'm submitting what I wrote, not what you agree on." Rich then stalked out.

By one o'clock Tuesday morning, when Rich convened a meeting of lawyers in the forty-fourth-floor boardroom, he still hadn't calmed down. Going around the table one by one, each lawyer had something to say about a document in Rich's package. The speeches droned on and on. At such times some men might count sheep. Gordon Rich counted lawyers. He got to thirty-eight before losing his temper.

"Look, if it's not vitally important, I don't want to hear it," Rich announced. "I don't care about every last little change. This will be done my way."

All Monday night and into Tuesday morning, Rich stalked First Boston's halls demanding the material he had to send to Atkins. "Shut the fuck up!" he yelled at attorneys. "This is how we're doing it. If you want to complain, go to Maher!"

By early Tuesday afternoon, Rich was beside himself. For four days he had pleaded with these people to deliver their work twenty-four hours ahead of time. Yet here it was, just hours to go, and he still didn't have half the documents he needed.

Like some fairy-tale troll, Rich began grabbing people as they walked by his office, demanding to know when their part of the package would be delivered. At the height of his frustration, he managed to snag Brian Finn. For some reason—Rich wouldn't remember why—speaking to Finn was vitally important. When a lawyer named Mike Rothfeld stuck his head into Rich's office and summoned Finn, Rich angrily objected.

"No. No. You can't have him," Rich shouted at Rothfeld. "Get out of here!"

When Finn rose to leave, Gordon Rich lost it. He grabbed his gray plastic phone, stretched the cord to its full length and hurled the receiver against its console with all his strength. Both the receiver and the console were demolished. Finn and Rothfeld beat a hasty retreat.

Afterward, Rich left his office and wandered through empty offices on the forty-first floor. He was so tired he thought about simply leaving the building. Figuring he'd probably be fired, Gordon Rich returned to his office to wait.

The team from Citibank arrived at First Boston at two o'clock. For some reason, the bankers had come down from an office in New York's northern suburbs.

With three hours to go, Fennebresque didn't have time to worry about itineraries and escorted the bankers upstairs to an unoccupied dining room. "Look, here's the situation," he explained to the bank team's leader. "In a few hours we've got to put a bid in. One of the banks crapped out on us at the last minute. There's no doubt this bid is eminently financeable. There's no doubt once the logjam breaks, there will be bank money here. We'd like you to give us the strongest letter you can."

For ninety minutes Fennebresque briefed the bankers on First Boston's strategy. In case they didn't understand, he handed them a draft letter he had written. Maybe something like that, he added. Suggestions never hurt.

All that day Brian Finn wandered from room to room, grazing on sandwiches and answering questions. His duties were long over. Everything now was a matter of dollars and cents. Around three o'clock Finn encountered Hank Handelsman in a hallway. Pritzker's lawyer was scowling.

"Finn, I've got a big problem."

"What's that?"

"We're short a quarter billion dollars."

"You're what?" Finn was aghast. "What you are talking about?"

"Seslowe didn't deliver."

The two men walked for a few minutes as the lawyer explained the depth of their predicament. They paused by an empty desk outside Maher's office. Inside, Finn could see a downcast Seslowe issuing what must been a series of mea culpas. The accountant walked out toward where Finn and Handelsman stood. He stopped, then turned away. Finn glanced at Handelsman. There was no mistaking the malice in the lawyer's glare.

Handelsman turned to Finn as Seslowe wandered off. "I could ask Jay for the money," the lawyer said, "but I'm not real excited about the prospect."

"I don't know about that," Finn said, "but we don't send that letter without the equity."

If the Pritzkers ponied up the money and won, both men knew they could syndicate most of it within days; banks and institutional investors would be clamoring for a piece of the action. But that didn't put money in their pockets now.

"You've really got no choice," Finn said. "You make the call to Jay, or we're out. Even with the equity, this thing's a long shot. Without it, we haven't got a snowball's chance in hell."

Maher, too, rejected any suggestion of delivering a bid without equity commitments. Lacking the monetization commitment was bad enough; lacking the downpayment bordered on black comedy.

Mel Klein now called around to a number of his fund's investors and managed to pick up $5 million here, $10 million there. It was pocket change. An hour before bids were due, they were still $200 million short. Everyone—Klein, Maher, Finn, and Handelsman—knew there was only one place that money could come from. If it came at all.

The clock beside Jim Maher's desk read four-fifteen when Mel Klein finally got the Pritzkers on the line.

Klein quickly explained the situation. "Guys, we've got to make the commitment now. No one else can write a check for this in five minutes."

There was silence on the other end of the line.

"Jay, Tom, we're here now," Klein said. "We're ready to go. We need a commitment for another $200 million."

Jay Pritzker spoke. "Mel, is there another choice?" Klein knew it was probably twice the largest commitment the Pritzker family had ever made.

Klein was looking out the window. "Jay, you're in Florida and Tom, you're in California. I don't know if either of you is looking at the sunset." Klein turned to Maher, who stood unsmiling by his desk. "I'm looking at Jim Maher. And there's only one thing he wants to hear to enable us to go forward with the First Boston offer. And that's, we need to hear you are behind the Resource Holdings equity."

Again there was silence on the line. "Mel, that's a lot of money," Tom Pritzker said.

"I know, fellas, that's why I'm talking to you. We need to know."

"Is there any other alternative?" Jay Pritzker asked again.

"No, not at this point."

"Are we morally obligated to First Boston for this?" Tom Pritzker asked.

Klein thought for a moment. He glanced at Maher. "Yes."

"Do you think First Boston thinks we should step forward with the equity?"

"Yes."

There was a long silence. Mel Klein held his breath.

"Dad . . ." Tom Pritzker began.

"I know," Jay Pritzker said. "That's it. We'll do it."

Klein exhaled. "Thanks, guys."

He hung up and turned to Maher, who stood by his desk like a cigar-store Indian. "That's it. The Pritzkers are committed for the whole thing."

For the first time that day, Maher had a reason to smile.

———

At eleven o'clock Tuesday morning Kravis and Roberts met with their investment bankers, telling them in uncertain tones they hadn't decided whether they would bid that afternoon. Both men had their own ideas, but the last people they were telling them to were their investment bankers. With any luck, someone would unknowingly pass the misinformation within earshot of Peter Cohen.

No one was concerned about First Boston. From his bank contacts Kravis knew of Maher's mounting problems. Mel Klein had kept calling, and now it sounded as if First Boston might have some interest in a minority share of the Kohlberg Kravis deal; Kravis knew a sign of weakness when he saw one. Through a clever ruse, they had also learned of a consensus forming among Atkins and the board attorneys that First Boston's monetization scheme was almost certainly unworkable. Dick Beattie had simply had his tax attorneys call up and ask about trying the same thing. Don't try it, they were told, it'll never work.

Afterward Kravis and Roberts convened the informal roundtable in Kravis's corner office. The associates were so tired of these talks they dubbed them "the circle jerks." Starting with Scott Stuart, they went around the room, each man offering his viewpoint one final time: Should we do it? Stuart and Cliff Robbins gave qualified thumbs-ups. Ted Ammon was on the fence. Bob MacDonnell, the general partner from San Francisco, pushed hard, extolling at length the values of brand names like Oreo, Nabisco, and Ritz. Paul Raether was ready to bid.

So was Henry Kravis. After a week of keeping his own counsel, Kravis was prepared to lead the final charge. No one in the room was surprised. Those who knew Kravis best never believed he could let go a deal this size. And if we bid, Kravis emphasized, we bid to win.

Finally George Roberts spoke. "I think we should all ask ourselves, 'Is this really worth all the headaches? Do we really want to do this to ourselves?' We're going to take a lot of heat from Washington, a lot of heat from our partners." Roberts looked at each man in the room as he spoke. "The one thing I don't want to see happen is for this company to get in trouble. It could end the whole thing, the whole industry. I'm just not comfortable with the idea we have to do this deal."

Roberts's speech left them at an impasse. It wasn't often that Kravis and Roberts openly disagreed. Several in the room exchanged anxious looks. What now?

"Look," Kravis said, "we founded this firm on the basis that George and I are going to agree on everything or we're not going to do it at all." He turned to Roberts. "Maybe we ought to go off and talk about this ourselves for a while." Roberts nodded.

For a moment the deal teetered there. Then Jamie Greene spoke. Greene, an associate in San Francisco, was in charge of assembling the billions in bank money Kohlberg Kravis would need if it bought RJR Nabisco. Among the Kravis troops, that gave Greene's opinions added weight.

"Wait a minute, just wait a minute," Greene said. "George, I just really think we ought to do this deal. Sure, it's going to be tough to do. But I think this is a wonderful deal."

It was the single, gung ho statement Roberts had been looking for for days, and it changed the whole mood. Within minutes they moved from discussing if they would bid, to how much they would bid.

"Okay," Roberts said, "if we're going to do this, it's got to be safe. It's got to be a lot less cash than we've been talking about. At the end of the day, the board's not going to be too concerned with three or four more dollars in cash. They're going to look at the higher value. . . .

"And if it's close," Roberts continued, "we'll win."

For hours they worked on refining a financial structure, opting for safety by boosting the share of PIK securities and reducing the actual cash paid to shareholders. Several times an anxious Dick Beattie stuck his head into the room. "Damn it, give me the bid," he said. "Time is running out here."

"Go away, Dick," Roberts said, smiling. "All you have to do is change a few numbers. We'll let you know."

Peter Cohen convened the management group that afternoon at Shearson. Everyone had an idea where the bid should be: Johnson's aides, Benevento and Sage, were throwing around numbers in the vicinity of

$110 a share but, as usual, no one listened to them. Cohen and John Gutfreund had the only opinions that mattered.

Cohen later said he favored a bid of $102, maybe $103. Gutfreund, wary to the end about "deal heat," actually wanted to reduce the bid, maybe $97, $98. In the end they split the difference. One hundred dollars a share—simply repeating their earlier bid—was felt to be a slap in the board's face. The group believed some kind of raise was in order, if only to allow directors to save face for having extended the auction deadline. It wouldn't do to further alienate the board, no doubt already incensed at Johnson's *Time* debacle. In the end, Cohen and Gutfreund settled on $101, a $1 bump.

Later the strategy behind the bid would be hotly debated. Did Cohen and the others genuinely believe Kravis was bowing out of the bidding? "There is no question we were fooled," recalled Jack Nusbaum, Cohen's attorney and confidant. "No question. How could anyone say anything else?" According to Nusbaum, the key was Dick Beattie's call to Cohen. "That's what bagged us," he said. "Beattie's clear indication was that they were through. When he said it, Peter believed it. . . . We figured Kravis wouldn't be there. We figured our only competition was First Boston."

Chaz Phillips, the Salomon banker, recalled that "Hill felt the strongest that KKR wasn't there." Hill reluctantly concurs. "With Henry going to Vail," he said, "there was a good sense that Henry [was] not hot on the case. That, in fact, was an excellent head fake." As for Cohen, Hill says, "Peter firmly believed that KKR was not there. In his roots, he really did believe it." According to Hill, when Cohen returned to New York from Brussels, "he said, he had reason to believe from Dick Beattie that KKR was out of it."

Despite the recollections of Hill, Nusbaum, and others, Cohen insists he never believed Kravis had given up. "I always thought he was there," Cohen said. "Hill was very cocky and sure he wasn't going to be there. I told him, 'We're not going to make that assumption.' I believed Henry was going to be there. . . . He goes to Vail for Thanksgiving every year. [Actually, it was only Kravis's second Vail Thanksgiving.] All you had to have was a fax machine and you were in business."

Debate aside, the truest indication of the management group's belief was its final bid. Any competitor seeking RJR Nabisco would naturally seek to top the $100 bid already on the table. Cohen's $101 was a tacit confirmation that, just as they had in the weeks before their initial announcement, the management group once again expected no competition. "It was," said Nusbaum, "our fatal error."

At First Boston, Fennebresque hovered over the Citibank team all afternoon. All he needed was a letter saying Finn's idea was doable. He felt like an expectant father outside the delivery room. Every ten minutes, it seemed, the phone outside the dining room rang. *"Where's the letter! Where's the goddamn letter?"*

"Hold on, just hold on," Fennebresque repeated, "we're trying to get it. . . ."

It was after four-thirty when the Citibank team leader emerged from the dining room. Fennebresque was pacing nervously outside. "Thanks," Fennebresque said, taking the letter and shaking the banker's hand. "Thanks a lot."

The letter was quickly inserted into the bid packet, which was then messengered over to Skadden. In its wake, Jim Maher was philosophical. The packet was nowhere near what he expected to produce. The monetization letter was, well, less than he had hoped. He told himself it had been a valiant effort. Their chances of success seemed minuscule but, Maher reasoned, he had beaten long odds before—just nine days earlier.

"Shit," he said, "maybe it'll happen again."

George Roberts's head was bowed as he entered the Kohlberg Kravis boardroom a few minutes before five o'clock.

Arrayed before him, a dozen of Wall Street's highest paid investment bankers waited anxiously for news of Kohlberg Kravis's bid. Each of the bankers wondered the same thing: Would Roberts and Kravis throw up another dead duck? Or did they want to win? As much as each would later brag of having Kravis's ear, the truth was that few had a clue what the two would do. The answer meant tens of millions of dollars in fees to every banker in the room.

Roberts, with Kravis at his side, was the picture of dejection, head slowly shaking, eyes downcast, hands deep in his pockets. He addressed the group in funereal tones.

"We're sorry," he said. "We decided to forget it. It was just too much."

He paused a time or two to let the message sink in. "We just couldn't get there."

The room fell utterly silent—the sound of $100 million in fees slowly evaporating.

Roberts sighed. "What did we bid, Henry? I think it was one-oh-six. Is that right?"

Kravis nodded. "I think that's right."

Standing to one side, Dick Beattie would never forget the bankers' reaction when the charade was unveiled. "You could see the dollar signs light up in their eyes," he would recall. "It was like 'Whooo! We're back in the ballgame! Yeah!' "

Invigorated, they all sat back to wait.

CHAPTER

17

Spirits were high in the Shearson camp.

Despite the *Time* cover, despite the avalanche of bad publicity, despite the obvious ill will among board members, Cohen and Hill were convinced they were on the verge of victory. No one gave Kravis much thought. Everything now depended on First Boston. If the board bought Jim Maher's bizarre scheme, First Boston would win. Few believed that would happen, but if it did, so be it. No one could compete with the returns Maher was promising. "There was a real good feeling," Jack Nusbaum recalled. "We'd either be blown away [by First Boston] or we'd win."

An hour after submitting its bid Tuesday afternoon, the management group scattered. Cohen, thinking they might hear news by eight o'clock, ducked out to dinner to celebrate his twentieth wedding anniversary with his wife and children. He was back at Willkie Farr by eight. John Gutfreund led a group of Salomon bankers to dinner at Christ Cella, a midtown steakhouse, where they ran into Citibank's chairman, John Reed. They too were at Willkie Farr by eight o'clock.

By six o'clock there had been no call.

By seven there had been no call.

By eight there was still no call.

No one at Willkie Farr was particularly worried. Gutfreund and Jim Stern started a poker game. Some of the Salomon bankers sat in a corner reading the latest *Car & Driver* and *Road and Track*.

By nine Cohen and Nusbaum were on the phone to Goldstone, who remained at his downtown office, well away from the Salomon contingent. All three were growing nervous: If Kravis was out and First Boston was really an air ball, they should have heard something by now. Gutfreund, too, was growing impatient, despite his mounting poker winnings—he had managed to shake nearly $400 out of Stern and Bob O'Brien of Bankers Trust. As always Gutfreund hated being kept in the dark. "How come we never know what's going on?" he groused.

Jim and Linda Robinson dashed out to a black-tie dinner that evening at the Marriot Marquis in midtown Manhattan. Texaco chief James Kinnear, a client and good friend of Linda's, was being honored at another Boys Club ceremony.

Among those at the Robinsons' table was Eric Gleacher of Morgan Stanley, who also worked with Texaco. Gleacher noticed the aerial of a portable phone protruding from Jim Robinson's tuxedo pocket and grinned.

Before dinner Linda Robinson attempted to ease the suspense with small talk.

"So," she asked Gleacher, "what did you guys bid?"

Gleacher demurred. He had guessed Linda might want to play this game. She probably thought he would actually tell her what Henry Kravis had offered.

"Oh, come on, it's over," she pressed. "You can tell me."

Gleacher shrugged. If she wanted to play games, he would play along. "Ninety-four," he said with a straight face. "They didn't raise the bid."

He paused. "What did you guys bid?"

"What do you think?"

"Kind of where you were before."

"Yeah," Linda Robinson said. "That's pretty close."

For those gathered at Kohlberg Kravis, the waiting was agony.

The halls were filled with pacing investment bankers. There was nothing to do but wait. After a couple of hours, pizza was ordered.

Then, a few minutes before nine o'clock, Dick Beattie took a call from Peter Atkins. "We'd like you and some of your team to come over," Atkins said.

Beattie fought the urge to grow excited. "Are we the only one getting called?" he asked. "Is the other side being invited over as well?"

"I can't answer questions like that."

The two lawyers talked for several minutes about who would be needed at Skadden. Only lawyers and associates—the detail squadron—would be needed for the moment. Beattie, eyeing the pizzas, had one last concern.

"You guys got food over there?"

"Yeah," Atkins said.

Beattie relayed news of the call to Kravis. Kravis, too, held his excitement; they had been through this drill before. Told they wouldn't be needed at Skadden, Kravis and the four general partners headed out to dinner at an East Side Italian restaurant, Campagnola.

As they did, Beattie hastily assembled a small squad of lawyers, investment bankers, and associates for the trip to Skadden Arps. The group left in pairs, so as not to arouse suspicion if the management group had lookouts posted in the lobby. Once downstairs, Cliff Robbins detoured briefly to have a private word with a security guard. Robbins wanted to make sure that, if Johnson also left the building, Kravis knew about it quickly.

Kravis had just ordered dinner when he was called from his table to the phone. It was Beattie.

"They're going to want you to come over here in about forty-five minutes."

"Well, we're eating. We'll be there."

"We're in good shape," Beattie said. "Things look good. Felix is waiting for you here."

For the first time Kravis allowed himself to sense victory. He returned to the table and excitedly passed on the news. "Things are looking good," he said, smiling. Everyone felt a victory was within their grasp.

Kravis was halfway through dinner when he was pulled away to take another call. It was Beattie again.

"Goddamn it, where are you guys?"

"We thought we'd eat dinner," Kravis said.

"Felix is getting impatient."

"We're coming, we're coming."

"Come on, Henry. They want to get this thing done and get out of here."

"Okay, okay. We'll be there in a minute."

Mildly irritated, Kravis returned to the table. "They really want us to go down there now," he said. "I guess Felix wants to go home early tonight."

After hurriedly finishing dinner, the five general partners piled into Kravis's blue Mercedes 500. They were at Skadden within minutes. Upstairs, Kravis, Roberts, and Raether were escorted into a conference room, where they were met by Felix Rohatyn, Ira Harris, and Peter Atkins.

Kravis looked for signs of the management group, but saw none. Rohatyn began reeling through a list of open issues. Lazard and Dillon, he said, wanted to learn more about the securities Kravis proposed to include in his offer. There were some other points, all minor. Then Rohatyn asked, "Is this your best offer?"

"Yes," Kravis said.

"Well, if we can work out the securities and get comfortable with regard to the financing, we are prepared to recommend your bid to the special committee."

Kravis and Roberts broke into smiles.

A winner.

After six weeks, Kravis and Roberts were on the brink of victory. All that remained were two sets of final negotiations. A Kravis lawyer, Robert Spatt, headed to an upstairs conference room to negotiate the merger agreement. The investment bankers were issued into another room to explain the bid's securities. There Lazard and Dillon hailed them with questions, including, one final time, what Kravis would do in the event Drexel were indicted.

With any luck, Kravis figured, both sets of talks could be wrapped up in a few hours. The committee was scheduled to meet the next morning to make its recommendation. With nothing else to do, Kravis and Roberts sat back to wait.

Once the meetings were underway, Atkins headed upstairs to his office.

A stack of phone messages awaited him there. The first call he returned was to Jim Maher. For all the Sturm und Drang, First Boston's final bid had been quickly dismissed. Practically all the key questions about the initial proposal, such as the timing of antitrust approvals, remained unresolved. The fatal flaw was the monetization letter; First Boston had nothing resembling a solid bank commitment to back it. What Maher sent, in fact, prompted peals of laughter among the committee's investment bankers. The Citibank letter Fennebresque had worked so hard to procure had only a typed letterhead, and that from a Citibank office on Mamaroneck Avenue in Harrison, New York. It had been signed by a vice president. It was hardly what the committee had been looking for.

Maher, at home in his West Side apartment, hadn't been able to stand the waiting any longer. "Peter," he said when Atkins called, "I'm sitting here, you know, this is killing me. Should I sit up waiting? Or can I go to bed?"

"Nah," Atkins said "I think you can go to sleep."

Maher knew the truth then. He had fallen one miracle short.

"Well," he said. "That's too bad."

Maher hung up and called one of his aides, Gordon Rich. "I think we're done, Gordo. I think we're done."

Where was the call? Where was Atkins?

As the evening wore on, Steve Goldstone paced his office nervously. No news, he told himself, was bad news. Something has gone wrong. Maybe they're taking First Boston seriously, he thought. God forbid, maybe Kravis bid.

Where were they?

As he paced, Goldstone indulged a nervous habit that never failed to irk his colleagues. At times of high stress, he took to squeezing the erasers off the ends of number-two pencils. Sometimes he pressed so hard the tiny pink dots popped across the room and bounced off people's foreheads. That night Goldstone's office floor was littered with severed eraser heads.

By half past nine Goldstone could stand the suspense no longer. First he phoned his partner Dennis Hersch at home; Goldstone put Hersch on a speaker phone to listen as he called Atkins. The Skadden lawyer, just finishing his conversation with Jim Maher, returned the call minutes later.

"Peter, I've got a pile of people waiting around," Goldstone said. "Are you guys going to make a decision tonight? Do we need to be waiting around?"

"I'd say there's no reason for your people to hang around tonight," Atkins said. "We'll be in touch with you tomorrow."

The words were a splash of ice water in Goldstone's face.

"What are you saying? What does that mean?" Anxiety crept into Goldstone's voice. "Are we out of it?"

Atkins was a blank wall. "Look, I can't say any more."

Goldstone persisted. "Are we out of it?"

"Look," Atkins said, "all I can tell you is, we don't need you tonight. You can tell your people to go home."

Goldstone's call sent electric shocks through the gathering at Willkie Farr. The poker game was forgotten; the car magazines were tossed in a corner. Worried looks broke out as questions swept the group loitering at Nusbaum's office.

What does that mean?

What's going on?

Minutes later the group suffered a second, greater shock. Nusbaum took a call from a reporter, who passed along the information that Kravis had just been summoned to Skadden Arps. Had Shearson?

"No," Nusbaum stammered, "we haven't."

Nusbaum was thunderstruck.

Kravis?

He couldn't believe it. Peter Cohen couldn't believe it, either. All at once he knew something had gone terribly, terribly wrong.

Chaos broke out among the advisers at Willkie Farr. Everyone had an idea what had happened, what to do. Gutfreund, having pocketed his poker winnings, angrily demanded that someone—*anyone*—get over to Skadden right away.

"This is bullshit!" Gutfreund railed. "Get in there. Just get somebody in there. Here we are standing around playing with ourselves. Let's get someone in there. . . ."

Nusbaum thought quickly. Something had to be done fast. A letter: that was the answer. As many lawyers do when nursing a grievance, Nusbaum knew it was important to get their anger down into writing. As

Cohen and the investment bankers shouted and cursed around him, he began dictating.

Bob Hope had almost finished the evening's program at the Boys Club dinner when Linda Robinson was called from the table for an urgent telephone call. Excusing herself, she hustled into the Marriott's kitchen to take it.

When she returned, Eric Gleacher could tell she was fuming. *She knows where we are,* he thought. Gleacher couldn't help but smile. The moment the program ended, the Robinsons were up and away from the table.

Linda Robinson had one parting line for the Morgan Stanley banker. "Gleacher," she said, "you're a fucking liar." There was the wisp of a smile on her lips.

Gleacher looked Jim Robinson's wife square in the eyes.

"Linda, you just don't get it, do you? There's just no way this board is going to give this company to Ross Johnson."

Johnson, Horrigan, and the rest of the RJR Nabisco executives were passing the time over drinks at Nine West when they heard the news. Bit by bit reports dribbled in, and they were all bad. Atkins had told Goldstone he could go home, and Kravis was invited to Skadden. If that weren't bad enough, Bill Liss—still supposedly representing the special committee—called and said he had been asked to ready a public announcement the next morning. The signs of defeat were unmistakable.

"That's it. Lights out," Johnson said. "As far as I'm concerned, it's sayonara."

When Goldstone heard Kravis was at Skadden Arps, he immediately redialed Atkins. Twenty billion dollars and more than a few careers, maybe even his own, were on the line. Atkins put him on the squawk box. Soon the lawyer's office was filled with the anguished tones of Goldstone's voice.

The management group had been cheated, Goldstone insisted. They had been placed in an untenable position, indeed robbed of victory, by that lunatic First Boston bid. As the first round's high bidder, they had no incentive to boost their offer. In essence, Goldstone argued, they were forced to bid against themselves. To be fair, he insisted, there had to be another, final round of bidding.

"We're not done!" Goldstone insisted, pacing amid the eraser heads littering his office floor. "Peter, we're willing to bid more. We'll bid more! What is this nonsense about starting an auction and shutting it down an hour later? There are no rules governing these procedures. We put in a bid saying we'll bid more, and we will. How can you do this? It's not fair!"

Atkins tried to calm the feverish lawyer but got nowhere.

"Peter, you've got to keep the bidding open. You've got to keep the bidding open as long as people are willing to bid."

For forty-five minutes Goldstone pounded at the same theme, and Atkins, emotionless, assured Goldstone his arguments would be taken into account. But there was nothing he, Atkins, could do until the committee met the next morning. Privately, Atkins and the Skadden litigator, Mike Mitchell, found Goldstone's argument no more persuasive than others he had made over the past six weeks. The crux of Goldstone's case seemed to be that management was entitled to two out of three falls.

A few minutes before eleven o'clock, as his impassioned soliloquy stretched on, Goldstone mentioned to Atkins that he would be receiving a letter of protest from Jack Nusbaum. The letter "has been tempered somewhat," Goldstone allowed. "But Peter, you've got to understand. People are bouncing off the walls over here. They're really upset."

At eleven o'clock the letter was delivered to Atkins's office. "I've got it now," he told Goldstone, glad for the excuse to end the lawyer's pleas. "We'll get back to you later."

Atkins hung up and looked at Nusbaum's letter. It was on the stationery of the lawyer's firm, Willkie Farr & Gallagher.

Gentlemen:

. . . During the last several hours we have been receiving regular reports from the press advising us of the precise nature of the bid submitted today on behalf of the management group, as well as periodic reports that you or your representatives have met earlier this evening with representatives of another bidding group whose bid, if the reports we are receiving are accurate, has seemed to improve as the evening has progressed.

We believe that the Management Group has been disadvantaged

throughout the entire process and we must now insist that if you are talking to other bidders you must talk to us as well so that we have an opportunity to consider our response to any bid which may exceed ours, just as other bidding groups had an opportunity to bid against our winning bid which you published on November 18th.

Our letter to you today indicated a willingness to discuss all aspects of our proposal. We reiterate that willingness and look forward to the opportunity to continue the bidding process, if that is appropriate, in the full light of day with details of all the present bids being known to all parties.

The members of the Management Group are at the offices of the undersigned and would appreciate a prompt telephonic response to this letter.

Sincerely,

Jack Nusbaum

Atkins set down the letter and frowned. It was going to be another long night.

With their protest issued the group at Willkie Farr cooled down and awaited a response. Clusters of tired men stood talking in the halls. In Nusbaum's conference room Gutfreund sat in one corner, reading the latest copy of *Manhattan, inc.* A few people dozed off. George Sheinberg of Shearson showed up and passed around a handful of cigars. For an hour there was peace.

At Nine West, the Robinsons joined the group in Horrigan's corner office. The couple's formal attire prompted a round of jokes from Johnson. "A bottle of white and a bottle of red," he requested of the tuxedoed Robinson. There was little to do but wait. From time to time Johnson tried to reach Charlie Hugel at his hotel room. Maybe, he thought, Hugel could make some sense of all this.

Having missed dinner, Hugel was starved. Shortly after eleven o'clock he left Skadden for his suite at the Regency, where he prowled the lobby looking for a restaurant. Finding none open, he went up to his room and, stomach growling, prepared for bed. Minutes later his phone rang. "Mr. Johnson would like to speak with you," a secretary's voice said.

Hugel sat on hold, waiting for Johnson to pick up. As he did, the telephone's second line glowed red. Putting Johnson's secretary on hold, he punched the button to take the incoming line. It was Peter Atkins, who quickly briefed Hugel on Goldstone's angry call. He warned him that the management group was on the warpath and might contact him. "They're really pissed," Atkins said.

So that's what Johnson wants, Hugel thought. He noticed the red light showing Johnson's call had gone off. Hugel hung up and dialed back Nine West.

When Johnson came on the line, Hugel could tell he was upset. But the first thing out of Johnson's mouth had nothing to do with losing the largest takeover in history.

"We've heard they're going to cancel the golden parachutes," Johnson said. "Is that true?"*

Hugel was surprised. Could he have heard Johnson right? Golden parachutes? With the fate of his company hanging in the balance, Johnson was fretting about his severance benefits? Hugel suspected Ed Horrigan had put him up to it. It sounded like vintage Horrigan.

"That's ridiculous," Hugel said. "What would make you think we're doing that? Anyway, Ross, I'm not exactly worried about that right now, you know. We're all a little more concerned about the future of the company."

"Well," Johnson asked, instinctively avoiding controversy. "What's going on? I understand our people have been told to go home. Would you like to embellish that a little?"

Hugel chuckled. "Well, remember our phone conversation this morning?"

"Yeah."

"Well, they bid."

"You mean a blockbuster bid?"

"Yes."

"Well, how much of a blockbuster?"

"I really can't tell you." Just talking to Johnson, they both knew, amounted to a breach of the auction process.

"Are we talking in the neighborhood of five dollars?" Johnson asked.

"Yes."

"You mean one-oh-six?"

"You hit it."

There was a snort of disbelief from Johnson.

* Johnson denies asking Hugel about severance benefits.

"Well, okay. We're out of it," he said. "That's the end. God bless 'em."

Johnson, alone in Horrigan's office with Jim Robinson, put down the phone. There was a moment of silence as he digested the news. Finally, he said, "It's over."

Together the two men walked into Horrigan's anteroom, where Horrigan, Linda Robinson, and the others were waiting impatiently.

"Well, what's the news?" someone asked. "What did he say?"

"Look, it's over," Johnson said quietly. "Let's just say this is where it ended."

A cacophony of voices assaulted Johnson. *What do you mean? What do you mean? What did he say? How much did they bid?*

In no time Horrigan was raging at the board, at Kravis, at everything. Everyone in the room wanted to know what Hugel had said, what had happened.

"Listen, I can't tell you," Johnson said. "I gotta respect Charlie's confidence. But," he added, "the spread is substantial."

A few minutes later Johnson called Peter Cohen and the group at Willkie Farr. Jack Nusbaum put him on a speaker phone in his conference room.

"It's all over," Johnson said. "KKR won."

An uproar engulfed the conference room as Johnson was again assaulted by angry questioners in a virtual replay of the Horrigan group's reaction.

"What do you mean they won?" Cohen asked. "What are the terms? Do we know what they bid? What happened?"

"I can't tell you," Johnson said. "But I know the price is substantially above ours."

Outraged, Cohen and the others pressed Johnson for more information. "I can't tell you much," Johnson said, finally. "But I believe there's a four- or five-dollar spread. I can tell you, you're not going to beat a five-dollar difference. They really brought in the heavy artillery."

———

At Johnson's direction, Linda Robinson began calling reporters at half past twelve. "It's over," she told one. "We're out of it. There will be no more bids."

Peter Atkins got back to Goldstone at twelve-thirty.

"Look, Steve, I've discussed your views with our group," Atkins said. "All I can tell you is, your views of fairness in this auction process are misplaced. The fact that your clients were high in the first round doesn't remove their obligation to bid high now. There is no question of fairness." And, Atkins made clear, no question of reopening the auction.

"I can't say this strongly enough," Goldstone replied calmly. "You have a legal obligation to hear our second bid. The directors are obligated to do it. They simply can't turn their backs on us now. We want to bid again."

Goldstone was right, in one regard. There were no rules governing the bidding process. What exists is a constantly changing body of law developed during a series of takeover battles in the mid-1980s. The cases, most decided by the Delaware Chancery Court, say volumes about the obligations of directors to run fair auctions. What they don't say is how to end one. During the late 1980s board after board unsuccessfully grappled with the question. The $6 billion auction of Federated Department Stores in early 1988 stretched on for weeks, despite determined attempts to conclude it. In the end, most auctions closed when bidding got too high for all but one party.

Atkins and Goldstone talked for nearly an hour, batting the same, tired arguments back and forth like tennis balls. The irony, of course, was that Goldstone had no idea whether Shearson and Salomon were willing to bid again. Johnson certainly wasn't. Even so, Goldstone knew they wouldn't have the opportunity if he couldn't succeed in reopening the auction.

Peter Cohen had too much on the line to give up now, no matter what Johnson said.

Minutes after Johnson's call he hit the phones, calling reporters and anyone else he could think of that might have information about Kravis's bid. He wanted to fight, but first he had to know what he was up against. Immediately he picked up rumors about the composition of Kravis's bid. Apparently Kravis had boosted his number by offering more securities than Shearson and less cash.

At first Cohen couldn't understand it. All along, Johnson, quoting Hugel, had repeated the same theme: "Cash is king." If Kravis had crammed his bid with securities, Cohen figured, then somehow the rules had changed. *Again!*

The idea of increasing the "paper" portion of a bid struck him. If Kravis could do it, why couldn't Shearson? Cohen got on the phone with his aide, Andrea Farace, and ordered up a new set of computer runs, boosting the paper and lowering the cash. It was too early to seriously consider a new bid. That would come later, if at all. But to Cohen it was clear they had to look at every option.

Another thing was clear: Their decision to withdraw was premature. Cohen called Johnson and asked to hold off on any press release.

"It's too late," Johnson said. "It's already out."

"Look, it's kind of like an election night thing," Cohen said. "We don't know enough to concede yet. We probably did lose, but let's wait until we know more about it."

"Shit, Peter, the goddamn deal is done," Johnson said, the irritation clear in his voice. "Why the hell do you want to put out a new release?"

"Well, no," Cohen said. "It looks like we could bid again."

"How the hell can you bid again?"

"Listen, we can bid as long as we want."

"Well, what do you want to bid?"

Cohen had no idea; he simply wanted to keep his options open. Johnson was flummoxed. He couldn't understand how Shearson could possibly jump start the bidding at this late hour. He certainly had no desire to.

Johnson called Goldstone, who returned to his timeworn theme. "Ross, it's their money," the lawyer said. "If they want to bid, you have to let them. . . . At this stage, unless you think you don't want to run the company, you have to let them bid."

"But it's over . . ."

"Ross, you can't say that. You've got to hold on. They've got to bid something tonight. There is no tomorrow."

Johnson thought the whole thing was ludicrous. It had the same dream-like quality so much of the last six weeks had had. Reluctantly, he gave the okay to issue a new press release. At one-thirty an annoyed Linda Robinson began redialing reporters to rescind their early release. Some were already asleep. Only a handful of papers, including *The New York Times*, were able to shoehorn the news into their latest editions.

As Johnson pondered this latest twist, Frank Benevento came hustling in, waving a new computer run. Benevento was excited. If the group cut the cash component of its bid, he said, it could drastically increase the securities portion. It could, in effect, increase the face value of its bid without increasing its risk.

Johnson was skeptical. Replacing cash with securities of questionable value made no sense to him. "Frank, how the hell can you evaluate it like that?"

"You can't," Benevento said. "But obviously, they are."

"That's horseshit," Johnson said. "That makes no sense at all. All along Charlie's been telling us cash is king. Who in their right mind would see the world that way?"

Around three o'clock Johnson left for his apartment, wanting nothing more to do with a buyout he half-wished he'd never thought of. As he walked out he gave little thought to the Cohens and Beneventos who wanted to resurrect the bidding. It was just the kind of talk you would expect from tired, frustrated men running on too much energy and too little sleep.

As far as Johnson was concerned, the snake was dead. Only its tail was still flipping around.

———

Alone in his office, Goldstone wasn't inclined to give up so easily. Never mind what Johnson wanted. If they wanted to win, they had to bid. And they had to bid right now.

Put on the speaker phone at Willkie Farr, Goldstone pressed his case. Atkins wasn't willing to reopen the auction, he said. "Decide your best bid and put it in now. Wait for them to invite you in, and it'll be over. . . . Guys, actions speak louder than words. Forget about sending letters. Just bid!"

"Wait a minute," John Gutfreund said. "We don't know what's going on. We don't want to bid against ourselves."

Gutfreund, like Cohen, wanted to win as badly as anyone, and worse than most. But with billions of dollars at stake, the two CEOs weren't willing to boost their offer while they were flying blind: For all they knew, Kravis was only a dollar ahead. Johnson had been wrong before. If they raised their bid five dollars a share—more than $1 billion—on a hazy tip from Johnson, they risked wasting it. They would look like fools and would leave themselves open to criticism from their own boards, not to mention lawsuits. "Look, we're not going to bid until we know what we're bidding against," Gutfreund repeated.

Gutfreund didn't believe for a moment that Kravis had come in at $105 or $106. It was too high. The Salomon chairman, frustrated for six weeks by Goldstone's inability to discern the committee's needs, also suspected that Johnson knew more than he was letting on.

"I am very concerned that Davis Polk is conspiring with Ross Johnson to withhold information from us," Gutfreund told Goldstone. "Ross knows what the bid is. And I'd like to know it. Now ask him."

"No, he doesn't," Goldstone responded. He wasn't lying; Johnson hadn't told him full details of his conversation with Hugel. "Listen, you've just got to bid."

"Steve," Tom Hill interjected, "we have to know what Henry bid."

"It's unlikely we'll ever find that out," Goldstone countered. "And while we're trying, KKR is going to spend all night negotiating a merger agreement. We have to move now."

As the arguments dragged on, Goldstone realized the only way he could push Shearson and Salomon into bidding was to find out what Kravis bid. He called Atkins. This time he was practically shouting into the phone.

"This is outrageous! You have to tell us what the other side bid!" Goldstone insisted. "The bids are so close, we have to know before we can bid again."

"Look," Atkins said, "why don't you talk to Ross Johnson. I'm not going to tell you anything. Talk to Johnson. He's talked to Hugel."

Goldstone hung up, confused. Why was Atkins suggesting he call Johnson? Johnson didn't know anything. Or did he?

Goldstone reached Johnson before he left Nine West. "Ross, what happened when you talked to Hugel?" he asked. "What's going on here?"

Johnson, still protecting Hugel, ducked the question. He repeated what he had said earlier about "a four- or five-dollar spread."

"Steve, it's over," he said.

Hanging up, Goldstone dreaded calling the group at Willkie Farr. He could hear the edge in Gutfreund's voice; the Salomon executives' contempt for him was evident. Nevertheless, he called one last time. "Look, you don't need to know the exact number," Goldstone said. "Just bid."

In the end, he got nowhere. When he put down the phone for the last time, Goldstone realized Dennis Hersch was still on the speaker phone. Hersch had been sitting in his pajamas, drinking coffee and listening to

Goldstone's rantings all night. "Jeez, you're not in the Supreme Court, Steven," he said. "But nice try."

By three o'clock the group at Willkie Farr was exhausted. Drawn faces had replaced their fighting spirit. By sunrise, they knew, Kravis would probably have a merger agreement. Maybe, they said, shaking their heads, it really was over. Slowly, people began to leave.

Gutfreund approached Cohen. "Peter, it was a great partnership we had here," he said. "We worked well together. We enjoyed it, and we learned a lot. Let's get the next one."

"We'll get the next one," Cohen said.

Four blocks away, negotiations at Skadden Arps crept on through the early morning hours. Kravis, Roberts, and Raether sat in a conference room, idly passing the time while their lawyers and investment bankers handled the final details. Kravis was thrilled. They had the company. The deal was all but over.

As the hours wore on, they grew restless. What was taking so long? Then, shortly after midnight, Bruce Wasserstein jumped up to take a call from his partner, Joe Perella, who was in Tokyo. "That global bank, Wasserstein Perella, has a bulletin for us," joked Roberts.

The joking stopped when Wasserstein got off the phone. Perella had just seen a wire story carrying details of Kohlberg Kravis's bid. Wasserstein passed the phone to Kravis, who listened, stone faced, as Perella read the story. Within minutes he was faxed a copy.

The story, an early version of what would appear in the next morning's *Wall Street Journal,* had the management group's bid pinned at $101 a share and speculated the Kravis bid was at $103 a share or higher. It suggested Johnson might bid again.

"What do you mean, they're going to bid again?" Kravis said. "The bids are closed!"

Roberts hit the roof. Someone, probably on the special committee, was leaking details of their bid, no doubt in an effort to spur a higher bid from the management group. The auction was supposed to be over. Neither Kravis nor Roberts would tolerate being trifled with.

The Kravis contingent stalked into the conference room where the board's bankers were still working out kinks in the bid's securities. "Goddamn it," Roberts said, passing around the story. "We're being jerked around, and I don't like it."

The bankers from Lazard and Dillon threw up their hands. Dick Beattie grabbed Casey Cogut and went in search of Atkins. This was a serious breach of security: If Perella had seen the story in Tokyo, so, too, in all probability, had Shearson and Salomon. If the management group wanted to come back fighting, Beattie worried, they now had an idea what price they had to beat.

Beattie and Cogut were followed upstairs by a pair of the committee's bankers, Bob Lovejoy of Lazard and Fritz Hobbs of Dillon Read, who were also irritated at the leak. For nearly half an hour the four men waited outside Atkins's office. A Skadden lawyer, Mike Gizang, was guarding the door and refused them entrance.

Finally Lovejoy and Hobbs barged past Gizang and into Atkins's office. Inside, nearly a dozen Skadden lawyers stood around the room in the thick of a debate. Atkins sat behind his cluttered desk. Quickly the two bankers were briefed on Goldstone's increasingly rancorous protests.

Lovejoy, an ex-lawyer himself, was well acquainted with the lawyers' propensity for fingernail biting. He was far more concerned with the angry George Roberts he had left behind. "What the fuck are you talking to the management group for? We're not supposed to be communicating with them. We're supposed to be doing a deal with KKR. These threats seem silly. Why are you taking them so seriously?"

Atkins didn't say much in response. He rose to go downstairs and deal with Kravis and Roberts.

Outside Atkins's door, Beattie and Cogut watched Mike Mitchell and other attorneys scurrying in and out with worried frowns. The two attorneys exchanged puzzled looks.

What's going on?

Beattie thought he knew.

"The other side giving you a hard time?" he probed Mike Gizang. From Gizang's expression Beattie knew Shearson must be counterattacking. When Atkins walked out a few minutes later, Beattie confronted him.

"We have a few problems," Atkins said, motioning back to his office. "We have some people a little crazed."

Atkins followed the Kravis lawyers downstairs to the conference room where Kravis, Roberts, and the others waited. Kohlberg Kravis simply wouldn't tolerate leaks that might encourage Shearson, Beattie said. "Our bid is not supposed to be shopped. It's outrageous, and we won't stand for it any more."

While upstairs Beattie had overheard the board's secretary, Ward Miller, calling directors and alerting them to be at either a seven-thirty special committee meeting or the eleven o'clock meeting of the full board.

"Look," Raether now said, "fuck this seven-thirty stuff. Get 'em up, and get 'em on over here. Let's sign this thing up. This is just crazy."

"We can't do that," Atkins said firmly. "These guys are asleep."

Kravis was furious. "We played by the rules. Now goddamn it, somebody has taken our bid, and we're being used."

"You're not being used," Atkins said. "You're absolutely not being used."

"But we are!" Kravis said, brandishing a copy of the story. "I mean, look at this. How can this be?"

Unsatisfied, Kravis and Roberts retreated to a conference room to ponder their next move. As they did, Wasserstein ambled up as if to enter the room. Casey Cogut, knowing Kravis no longer trusted Wasserstein, closed the door in front of the famed strategist. "Sorry, Bruce, this is privileged," Cogut said in earnest. Raether cracked up in laughter.*

The danger of a Shearson counterattack was real, the Kravis group decided. It was, after all, what they themselves would do. It was impossible to stop Cohen from bidding, Kravis and Roberts realized, but they could hope to hurry the board by placing a deadline on their bid. They settled on one P.M., just two hours after the board meeting the next morning. It gave the management group an eight-hour window in which to attack. With any luck, Kravis bet, they had already given up.

They hadn't.

When Cohen woke that morning, every bone in his body screamed to rejoin the fight for RJR Nabisco. He called Andrea Farace, who confirmed what Cohen already suspected: By adding "paper" and cutting cash, they could boost the face value of their bid without boosting the actual money

---

* Kravis said of Wasserstein: "We didn't want the guy anywhere near us. [I feared] the same problem we had from the beginning of the deal, when Beck and Wasserstein got on the phone and started leaking."

they would pay out. Cohen touched base with Tom Strauss and found the Salomon executives ready to fight.

Next he dialed Nusbaum at the lawyer's home. "What's to stop us from making another bid?" Cohen asked.

"Nothing."

"This is what I want to do . . ."

CHAPTER

18

"It is important," Peter Atkins began, "that today be as clear and thought-ful as any day ever spent in a boardroom."

It was a quarter to eight, Wednesday morning, November 30. As the directors trickled into Skadden Arps, Atkins gathered them in a window-less conference room on the thirty-fifth floor. Nondescript modern art adorned the white walls at both ends of the room. Charlie Hugel took a seat at the head of a long, horseshoe-shaped, oak conference table dotted with buckets of sharpened pencils. He seemed to be in a good mood; he had picked up an apple from a street cart to calm his growling stomach.

To Hugel's right sat Marty Davis, to his left Atkins, Bill Anderson, Albert Butler, and John Macomber. Four other outside directors were also present: Bob Schaeberle, Juanita Kreps, Vernon Jordan, and John Medlin. At the far end of the table the bankers from Dillon Read and Lazard found seats. Beyond the bankers a buffet table was piled high with crois-sants, bagels and cream cheese, pitchers of orange juice, and pots of coffee.

"We must try," Atkins was saying, "to reach a decision in the best interests of shareholders. There will be charges about the process. There will be litigation, including perhaps from the bidders." Atkins went on, underscoring what he called "one fundamental caution: 'No comment' is the only proper response to any inquiry" about what was about to happen. "Secrecy must be maintained at all costs."

Atkins then began updating the directors on the previous night's events: Jack Nusbaum's letter was read aloud, and details of Goldstone's frantic calls were aired. The quick demise of the First Boston bid was recounted. Negotiations on Kravis's securities were also detailed, as were his complaints about a leak after the Dow Jones story surfaced in Tokyo.

"They've given us an ultimatum," Atkins said. "If their bid is not acted on by one o'clock, they will withdraw it."

Felix Rohatyn could see on the directors' faces their relief at being able to select Kravis the winner. Everyone could hear the murmurings among directors as they gathered for the meeting and compared horrified reactions to the *Time* cover. . . . *Looks awful. How could they have been so stupid. . . . Had to know he might say just anything. . . . Why didn't they send him to Patagonia . . .*

Ross Johnson had become a national symbol of greed. No one in this room wanted to hand this company to him. If he had come in as the far-and-away high bidder, they would have no choice but to declare him the winner. But many were secretly glad their choice was clear.

For three hours the board and its advisers reviewed the events of the last ten days. Lazard and Dillon went over the bids in detail, focusing especially on the esoteric characteristics of both sides' securities. Ron Grierson, on the speaker phone from London, asked dozens of nit-picking questions, all fueled, everyone knew, by his fear of lawsuits. As the meeting wound down a few minutes before eleven, Hugel alerted his fellow directors to a few bits of news. After a short break, he said, Henry Kravis and George Roberts would be invited in to address the board.

Oh, and one more thing, Hugel said.

"Ross Johnson is here."

Johnson awoke that morning feeling as if a great weight had been lifted from his chest. In a way, it felt good to have the whole fight over with. Now, at least, everyone could get on with their lives. "I think what we'll do," he told Laurie, "is attend the board meeting today and then fly back to Atlanta tomorrow."

Around nine o'clock Johnson walked across the plaza to his office. He hadn't been there long before Cohen called, sounding excited. "We're going to make another bid. What do you think about going higher?" he said, mentioning a figure based on low cash, high PIK. "All the numbers work. . . . Would you go along?"

Johnson had long since lost his capacity for disbelief. Nothing coming from the mouth of a Wall Street executive would ever surprise him again. "Are you telling me those numbers will work the same as ninety, six, and four?" he asked, referring to the components of their earlier bid.

"Absolutely," Cohen said. "From your perspective running the company, you'll actually be better off because we'll be using less cash."

Johnson thought for a second. "What the hell," he said. "If you want to go in there and raise hell, go in there and raise hell." His only caveat, Johnson added, was that he could no longer guarantee his team could make the budget cuts necessary to make the deal profitable at these levels.

"Don't expect miracles," Johnson told Cohen. "Because we are now in the land of miracles." Johnson hung up feeling like a mourner at his own funeral. This was Shearson's game now.

Johnson arrived at Skadden for the board meeting a few minutes before eleven o'clock, with the new Merry Men—Horrigan, Harold Henderson, Jim Welch and Bob Carbonell—in tow. Even though he was sure they had lost, Johnson was enjoying himself. He looked forward to watching the fireworks when Cohen lobbed in his grenade. After a month of being pilloried as a symbol of corporate greed, Johnson welcomed the opportunity to watch his directors sweat. "It'll be fun to see them pin the tail on the donkey on some other donkey for a while," he chuckled on the drive over. "Let's watch 'em squirm."

Cohen's team was ready, too. Jack Nusbaum was to meet Johnson a few minutes before eleven in the lobby at Skadden Arps. He had brought a second threatening letter—they hadn't received an answer from the one the night before—demanding that the auction be reopened. Together, Nusbaum and Johnson would march into the board meeting and attempt to pry open the auction.

But when Nusbaum arrived, Johnson was nowhere to be found. He waited ten minutes before heading upstairs. There he found Johnson's group cooling their heels in a thirty-second-floor conference room, three floors below where the board was assembled.

Johnson was upbeat, laughing and cracking jokes as he waited to be admitted into the boardroom. "Isn't this crazy?" he asked Nusbaum. Johnson didn't know what to expect, but he promised Nusbaum one thing. "We're going to get our pound of flesh back."

Nusbaum was in no mood for joking. As they waited, he paced nervously. He looked at his watch. It was eleven-fifteen, and if the board began on schedule, it might already be voting on a deal with Kravis. He couldn't afford to wait any longer. Time was running out.

He called Atkins's office. His message was simple: If the directors wouldn't let Johnson into his own board meeting, they would send the letter in without him. Nusbaum hung up and waited another fifteen minutes. Atkins didn't return the call.

Nusbaum dialed Cohen at Shearson. His voice was uncharacteristically tense.

"Look, Peter, we're being stonewalled. Ross isn't being allowed in. The meeting's going on without us. If we're going to go with a higher bid, we'd better damn well do it now."

Cohen listened. "I'll call you back."

At twelve minutes past eleven, Kravis and Roberts walked into the boardroom, accompanied by Raether and Beattie.

The four had arrived at Skadden that morning at 9:45, expecting to sign a merger agreement and buy RJR Nabisco. Instead, they had been shown to seats in a reception area. By and by the team's investment bankers began arriving. Wasserstein was there. Gleacher came in, angry that he hadn't been invited the night before. Jeff Beck, back from his exile, was also there. After a while, Casey Cogut went in search of an empty office where Roberts, Kravis, and Raether could consult out of earshot of their talkative bankers.

All three men were getting nervous. That morning the papers reported that Johnson's group hadn't backed out of the bidding. So far there was no sign of them. As they waited, they wondered anxiously what had become of the board. Finally Hugel came in and asked them to address the directors.

Now, as they entered the boardroom, Kravis and Roberts were all business. This was not the occasion to complain about Johnson or anything else. If ever they were to win over the board, this was the time. Davis, Hugel, Macomber, all of them—each had to be convinced the Kohlberg Kravis bid was safe, secure, and in the best interests of employees and shareholders.

As the directors fell silent, Roberts outlined their strategy. Kohlberg Kravis wasn't here to bust up RJR Nabisco, he said. If successful, they intended to keep the company as intact as possible. Roughly 20 percent of the company's assets would be sold. Shareholders would be able to share in their profits through a 25 percent equity stake to be distributed in the form of warrants. Roberts emphasized that he wanted this to be a safe deal. The largest buyout in Wall Street history was no time to gamble with thin coverage ratios. They would take special care of employees. Kohlberg Kravis companies employed more than 300,000 workers, Roberts said, and the firm knew the value of keeping them happy.

It was a solid presentation, tailored to soothe. For another fifteen minutes Roberts and Kravis took questions. What would Paul Sticht's role be? Purely an interim chief, Roberts said.

"How firm is one o'clock?" a director asked.

"Very firm," Roberts said.

"Let's stick as close to one as possible," Kravis said.

Afterward Hugel and Atkins followed the Kravis contingent into another room. Hugel was adamant that before a final vote was taken, a number of issues be negotiated. They were so-called Schedule Two items, dealing with employee benefits, such as moving expenses. For twenty minutes they plodded through an intricate negotiation dealing with items as esoteric as how far an employee had to move before becoming eligible for reimbursement—what an amazed Raether described as "incredibly chickenshit stuff." To one side, Roberts looked to Kravis and rolled his eyes.

One hour to deadline.

Weighty matters like moving expenses put away, Beattie deposited Kravis and Roberts in an empty office to await the board's final vote. The office they chose was strategically well situated, around a corner barely twenty feet from the boardroom. By standing at the corner itself, one could easily see all traffic passing through the boardroom doors. After a few minutes Beattie emerged from the small office, walked past a seven-foot Kenthia palm in a large white pot, and took a post at the strategic corner.

For half an hour he watched a steady stream of lawyers and bankers file in and out of the board meeting. A friend to many of them, Beattie managed to collar a lawyer here, an investment banker there. A few minutes before noon he noticed a surge of activity. Lawyers with anxious expressions shuttled in and out like ants. As they passed, Beattie grabbed one by the arm. "What's going on?" he asked.

"Ross and Nusbaum are here," the lawyer said, scurrying on.

Beattie cursed. He was angry but unsurprised. Atkins and the committee had been dragging their heels for more than twelve hours now. It was only a matter of time before Johnson put in another bid. Beattie trotted back into the small office where Kravis and Roberts waited restlessly.

Roberts didn't take the news well. "Goddamn, what's going on here!" he seethed. "We've been here since nine-thirty last night, and we're getting jerked around. We're being used!"

At Shearson, Cohen's office was a hive of activity. Tom Hill and a dozen others shuttled in and out. Cohen stood by his desk, puffing a cigar, studying a series of new computer runs. He was ready with a bid number when Nusbaum called. He checked with Gutfreund and Strauss at Salomon, who had closeted themselves in Gutfreund's art-deco office. All that was needed was Johnson's approval and, not incidentally, his pledge to further cut the management agreement if the group should triumph.

Cohen passed on both requests to Steve Goldstone at Davis Polk, who relayed them to Johnson at Skadden. When Johnson heard the bid Cohen had in mind, he began laughing. "You can't be serious," he said. Thoroughly detached from the action, Johnson approved any amendment of the management agreement that might be needed.

Ten minutes later Cohen got back to Nusbaum.

"Put in this bid," he said. He reeled off a set of numbers, cash and stock.

Nusbaum nearly choked. "Okay," he said.

The bid was $108 a share. Twenty-five billion dollars.

Nusbaum's mind raced. Wanting to bid was one thing; getting the board to take it was another. They had been at Skadden Arps for an hour now and were being ignored. Somehow they had to apply pressure to reopen the bidding. Nusbaum looked at his watch. It was past noon. "They don't want us here, Peter," Nusbaum said. "This thing is beginning to smell like a cover-up."

"If they won't take a bid," Cohen said, "we'll just put something out ourselves." The board couldn't ignore a public announcement. A press release had to be drawn up.

Minutes later, Nusbaum dialed Atkins's office a second time.

"Tell Mr. Atkins," he told the secretary, "we have a new bid to put in and we're announcing it publicly."

Nusbaum thought: Maybe that'll get their attention.

It did.

Minutes after Nusbaum's call, Atkins was handed the message in the boardroom. He grabbed Mike Mitchell, and the two men walked briskly out past the waiting area brimming with Kravis's idle investment bankers and down Skadden's internal stairway. When they reached the thirty-second floor, they turned right and headed down a hallway. They found Nusbaum standing alone in an office containing nothing but a desk and a phone. There was no chair, no art on the walls, nothing but a nice view of the Queensboro bridge, just two blocks away.

Atkins could tell Nusbaum was nervous.

"Look, I've got this letter here, which my litigators have drawn up," Nusbaum said. "I'll give it to you, but please disregard it. What I'm really here to say is, here is our bid."

No one had a pad to write it down. Mitchell fished a scrap of paper from his wallet and jotted down what Nusbaum told him: $84 a share in cash, $20 a share in PIK preferred stock, and $4 a share in convertible debentures. Twenty-five billion dollars.

"I want to emphasize," Nusbaum concluded, "that everything is negotiable."

Atkins nodded. As he and Mitchell left the office, they shared a private smile.

"This is going to be a very interesting day," Mitchell said.

Nusbaum phoned in an after-action report. "I don't know what's going to happen," he told Cohen. "But I think we've wedged ourselves back in."

Outside the boardroom, Beattie was roaming the hallways looking for information. So far there had been no sighting of Johnson or his people, only unconfirmed reports that they were in the building. Beattie collared Atkins as the lawyer returned from talking to Nusbaum.

What are Johnson and Nusbaum up to? Beattie asked.

"Well," Atkins responded, "we're going to have to deal with what they've given us."

"What have they given you?"

"I can't tell you."

"Come on, Peter, my guys have been here all night. They're tired of being used. Our best bid is on the table. I'm telling you, they're going to leave if this thing goes on. And if they do, you know as well as I the other side is free to do whatever they want."

"I hear you," Atkins said, disappearing into the boardroom.

That morning Mel Klein and three other Pritzker aides were at La Guardia preparing to board an American Airlines flight to Chicago. When the airline couldn't seat the four exhausted men together, they decided to take the next flight. Klein walked down to the Admiral's Club and, with nothing else to do, called Jim Maher.

Maher passed on the news that the bidding wasn't yet over. Kravis was offering something like $106 a share and looked like he might win. The Pritzker team began to get excited.

Is there an opening? Klein wondered. Can we reach Jay and Tom? Could we up the cash part of our offer?

In minutes they realized they were kidding one another.

"Sorry, Mel," Maher said, "it's over."

It was twenty minutes before one when Atkins returned to the small office where Kravis and Roberts waited. The atmosphere inside was chilly as Atkins spoke. "We have received something, and we can't live with your one o'clock deadline," the lawyer said. "We need an extension."

"Absolutely not," Kravis said.

Roberts's reply was equally sharp. "We're not going to do that." When Roberts was mad his lips became small and tight, slits on an angry face. "This is outrageous," he said, barely holding his temper.

"Peter, we're not going to be diddled around," Kravis said. "Last night you tell us you're going to recommend us to the board and we've got a deal and everything's fine. Now it turns out our bid's being shopped. We're not giving you any more time."

Beattie intervened. "Hold it, hold it," he said. The lawyer turned to Atkins. "Peter, can you give us a couple minutes?"

Atkins left. When the door closed, Beattie spoke to Kravis and Roberts

481

in a tone he would never use in a larger group.

"George, Henry, just settle down," Beattie said. "They're under a lot of pressure. They want to make sure things are done right. And we're not helping them any here . . ."

At 12:50 a headline crawled across the Dow Jones News Service. In boardrooms and trading floors across the country, brokers and investors looked up in amazement.

"RJR MANAGEMENT GROUP BOOSTS BID TO $108 A SHR . . ."

A minute later, Beattie interrupted his speech to Kravis and Roberts to take an urgent phone call. On the line was a Kohlberg Kravis associate.

"They just bid again," the associate said.

"Who?"

"The management group."

"What?"

"The management team just went across the tape with a new bid. They're at one-oh-eight."

"I don't believe it. You've got to be kidding me."

"It's true."

Beattie hung up and turned to Kravis and Roberts.

"You're not going to believe this. But the tape says they just bid one-oh-eight."

Kravis had to sit down. It was the realization of his worst fears, although he had to admit, it didn't entirely surprise him. Johnson had all night and all morning to assemble a new bid.

Now, twenty minutes from victory, everything had changed.

The auction wasn't over. The company wasn't theirs. The world wasn't fair.

And suddenly they were behind: $108 to $106.

Curses filled the room. "They're not going to sign us up!" Raether said, one eye on the clock. "Jesus, what are we going to do now?"

Then, as abruptly as their anger flourished, it cooled. It dawned on both Kravis and Roberts what Cohen had done. For the first time in twelve hours, they knew where the management group was. Maybe, they reasoned, they could make this work to their advantage. It would require finesse. No longer could they simply threaten to walk out. They debated their next move for another twenty-five minutes, then called for Atkins at one-fifteen.

We're prepared to extend our deadline, Kravis said, on one condition: Pay our expenses to date, and we'll stay another hour. It made sense. Kravis believed he was in a position of strength; he knew the management group's securities hadn't been negotiated, as his had. He saw no reason to panic and boost the bid; they would have the opportunity to do that later, if needed. This way they kept pressure on the board, at the same time making sure that, no matter what happened, they came out with something.

How much are your expenses? Atkins asked. Raether had done the arithmetic. Their total expenses approached $400 million, but Raether, careful not to push too hard, asked for only $45 million.

"I think I can sell that to the special committee," said Hugel, who had stepped into the room. He returned minutes later with the board's approval. The agreement was scribbled on a yellow legal pad. Beattie smiled. No matter what happened, he was getting paid.

Forty-five million dollars to wait sixty minutes. Incredibly, Atkins and Company thought it was a good deal.

Jack Nusbaum waited in the empty office overlooking the Queensboro bridge for forty-five minutes, speaking from time to time with Cohen and fielding technical questions from the committee's investment bankers.

Then, a few minutes past one, he took a call from Atkins.

In lobbing in the $108 bid, Nusbaum had emphasized that all its components were negotiable. Now, Atkins said, it's time to end this thing, once and for all. "We want your highest and best bid," the lawyer said. "We'd like it in fifteen minutes if you can."

"It might take a little longer."

"Well, do the best you can."

In seconds Nusbaum was on the line with Cohen. "The bidding's reopened," he said. "We're back in. They want our best bid."

"How long do we have?"

"Fifteen minutes."

"That's not very much time."

"I know."

Down the hall, Johnson applauded the invitation for another bid. He had long since stopped worrying about the bidding levels. To Nusbaum he said, "Let her rip."

Now it was Cohen's turn to take a deep breath.

For the second time that day, he was entering uncharted waters. He still had no idea where Kravis's bid was. Quickly he conferred with Hill and the others in his office, then called Gutfreund at Salomon. He was surprised when Gutfreund demanded a more aggressive bid. Cohen had to think fast. Whatever level they went to, they would need more money from the management agreement. A concession from Johnson was a must.

He called Goldstone. "We could go as high as one-fifteen," Cohen told the lawyer. "I really think that's what we ought to do. I want to be preemptive. It's time to end this thing."

Goldstone wanted to pinch himself.

One-fifteen? Just six weeks ago Shearson was telling Johnson this company was worth seventy-five.

What Shearson needed in order to proceed, Cohen explained, was for Johnson to chop two more points off the management agreement, to 4 percent, almost half what he was to have received. "Now," Cohen said, "I want to know if Ross will accept that."

Goldstone thought the number and the request were absurd. But he relayed them to Johnson who, when he heard what Cohen had in mind, was reduced to helpless giggles.

"My God, that's crazy!" he exclaimed. "How could this be a good investment? I don't think he ought to do it, do you?"

Goldstone thought it was time for some Merger 101.

"Listen, Ross, they have their reasons for doing this other than just buying the company," he explained. He mentioned the $200 million in upfront fees Shearson would reap from a successful deal. He talked about the unmatched franchise benefits it would reap from having completed history's largest LBO. Johnson's problem was that he insisted on thinking in terms of the real world, real money, real investments. In effect, Goldstone said, this wasn't the real world. This was Wall Street.

"Well, to me, that's crazy," Johnson protested.

There's something else, Goldstone said. "If you're prepared to agree," he went on, "they're going to want significant new adjustments in your compensation. Will you do it?"

This is the moment of truth, Goldstone thought.

"Sure, why not?" Johnson said with an ironic laugh. He had given everything else away. The management group's cut had started at 8.5 percent with an eye on 20 percent. Now it was down to 4 percent. "But if we go any further," Johnson said, "we're going to be owing them money." He chuckled. "And Steve . . ."

"Yes?"

"Remember. We can't go below zero."

Goldstone hung up and dialed Cohen. "You got it. Go."

Cohen rifled through the numbers one last time before relaying the group's new bid to Nusbaum at Skadden Arps.

Jack Nusbaum, Wharton Business School, Columbia Law, senior partner of one of New York's largest law firms, had a succinct reaction to Peter Cohen's new bid.

"Ho-ly shit."

He hung up and relayed the news to Atkins: Ross Johnson, Shearson Lehman, and Salomon Brothers were boosting their bid to $112 a share. He didn't have time to do the math. On its face, the bid was $25.76 billion. At 1:24 Atkins delivered the news to the board.

Shearson's new bid seriously complicated Atkins's life. On one hand, he had Kravis at $106 a share. Because Kravis's securities had been negotiated, the advisers were comfortable the bid's values were close to what Kravis said they were. It was good. It was solid. It was also second.

On the other hand, he had the management group at $112 a share. Not only weren't Cohen's securities firmed up to the point of Kravis's, the management group seemed to have paid little attention to the advice they had received from Dillon and Lazard just the day before. Their securities remained "soft," that is, they included no "reset" mechanism that would guarantee they would trade where Shearson said they would. Cohen valued his bid at $112 but, for all Atkins knew, it was worth $105. To determine its precise value would take time. And, with thirty minutes until Kravis's two o'clock deadline, time was a luxury Atkins didn't have.

Sure, Atkins told himself, Kravis could be bluffing. But with $25 billion at stake, could he really afford to take that chance? Somehow, he knew, they had to push the Kravis deadline back again.

From his perch outside the boardroom door, Dick Beattie's soft blue eyes took in the scene as Atkins and the other board advisers hustled into a corner office across the way. *Something's going on,* he thought, resisting the urge to edge across the open space toward the door.

Inside, the advisers were locked in debate. "You've got to give KKR some goodies," argued Dennis Block, a lawyer working with the board's investment bankers. "You have to protect what is already on the table. We don't want to be left without any bidder."

They had to find a way to keep Kravis at the table while they negotiated the management group's securities. Already they had given Kravis $45 million in expenses. What more did they have to offer?

Ira Harris came up with the idea: Give Kravis a merger agreement. Make him extend his deadline one week. Give him all his expenses— nearly $400 million—plus $1 a share, or another $230 million, in a so-called breakup fee, payable if Johnson's group managed to top the Kravis bid during the one-week extension. At that point, Kravis would still have the right to bid once more.

"Yeah," Block said. "That way we keep KKR on the reservation."

Mike Mitchell, the Skadden litigator, wasn't so sure. "Look, one-oh-eight is already on the tape. KKR will know it. They'll think we're just using them to get a higher bid out of Shearson."

Mitchell's worry aside, it seemed the only solution. For Kravis, it seemed like a no-lose situation. He got a merger agreement and expenses, and gave away nothing. But the best reason of all was apparent on every man's wrist: They were running out of time.

A few minutes before two o'clock, Atkins led a small procession into the office where Kravis and Roberts waited. Atkins thought the two cousins looked as if they'd been carved from blocks of ice. Their jaws were tightly clenched, their expressions grim.

Mitchell explained the proposal. Would they take it?

"Absolutely not," Kravis said. "What the fuck are you talking about? We're here to buy this company. We want a deal. If we leave this office, we're gone. You can kiss us good-bye."

As always, Beattie was the voice of reason. "Where's the other side?" he asked. "Are you proposing something like this to them?"

No answer. Beattie should have known better.

"We saw on the tape management has gone to one-oh-eight," Beattie asked. "Is that right?"

Atkins knew his answer had better be precise. In no way could he let on that Cohen had charged ahead to $112.

"You shouldn't assume anything," he said.

Beattie indicated they would need a few minutes to think about the proposal, and Atkins & Co. departed.

Kravis thought Atkins was bluffing. Of course Cohen was still at $108. Why on earth would he have boosted again? Atkins was engaging in brinkmanship, Kravis decided, trying once more to squeeze the last penny out of him. If they matched the management bid of $108, Kravis felt they would win.

"We're going to win in a tie," Kravis said. "We've got better paper. And you know we've got better credibility than Johnson. You know the board is pissed at him after this *Time* thing. A tie will win."

If they pressed hard now, Kravis was willing to bet, the board would be forced to capitulate. Their bid was the bird in hand, and the board couldn't risk losing it.

Raether and Ted Ammon came up with the extra $2 a share—an extra dollar in PIK paper and an extension in the redemption period of their debentures. It was financial hocus-pocus, they knew, but the board didn't have time to argue. If Kravis said it was worth $2, the board would believe him. At five minutes past two Atkins was summoned.

"Peter," Kravis said, "we're not going to accept your offer."

The lawyer wore his Buddha's face: no reaction there. "Do you want to do anything with your bid?" Atkins asked.

Kravis explained how they proposed to boost the bid to $108 from $106. When Atkins left, Kravis and Roberts expected a decision from the board within minutes.

Atkins and the board advisers were stunned; they had been convinced that Kravis would jump at their offer.

Now what?

At ten minutes past two, Hugel brought the board meeting back to order. "KKR just came in with its latest proposal," Atkins announced: eighty dollars a share in cash, eighteen a share in preferred stock, and ten a share in debentures securities.

Dennis Block noticed something.

"Any time restrictions?" he asked.

Atkins thought for a moment. "No . . ."

It was a stroke of luck. Kravis and Roberts had forgotten to lay down a new deadline. Lazard and Dillon would need several hours to evaluate the securities in the management group bid. Thanks to Kravis's oversight, they now had them.

But first there was the question of the merger agreement. If the management group was to be taken seriously, the board needed assurances Cohen would consent to the same agreement, including the so-called Schedule Two items, that Kravis had. A letter of agreement was drafted for Nusbaum to sign. "If they don't sign the letter," Hugel said, "we go with KKR. If they do sign, we have to get advice about what to do."

Mike Gizang carried the message down to Nusbaum on the thirty-second floor. It was scrawled in twenty-one lines on a yellow legal pad. Nusbaum read it, then called Cohen, who arranged a conference call with Gutfreund and Strauss at Salomon Brothers. The agreement was quickly agreed to, and after making a few minor changes, Nusbaum handed it back to Gizang.

Not only was Kravis's perch well suited for monitoring traffic into the boardroom, it lay astride the shortest route to the men's room. Throughout the day, whenever a director would walk past, Kravis would dispatch an associate to stand beside him at the urinals and strike up a conversation. The "urinal patrol" finally paid off when Roberts cut off Hugel and Vernon Jordan en route to the facilities.

It was past three o'clock and Kravis and Roberts had been waiting for nearly an hour. "What the hell is going on?" Roberts asked.

The board hasn't begun deliberating on your bid, Hugel said.

"What do you mean?" Roberts was stunned.

Roberts was so angry he followed the two board members into the bathroom and, as Hugel and Jordan attended to matters at hand, continued to badger them. "If the board hasn't been meeting, what the hell have you been doing in there?" he asked.

Hugel was vague, mumbling something about legal delays. Moments later he and Jordan emerged, Roberts a step behind. Kravis was waiting for them.

"What the hell is going on?" he demanded.

Double-teamed, Hugel paused. "Come on, guys," he said, "just give us some more time."

"This has gone on long enough," Kravis said.

"We'll get it resolved," Hugel said. "It's going to be done."

"How long is this going to be?" Kravis asked.

"I need two hours. Just give me two hours. We'll get it done."

Hugel smiled, and motioned at Jordan, who at well over six feet towered over the diminutive financiers. "I got a big guy here in case Ross gets out of hand," Hugel said, smiling.

———

Down on the thirty-second floor, Johnson and the remaining members of the management group spent the afternoon cracking jokes and trying to keep abreast of the events hurtling past them. As the hours passed, they found themselves marveling at the ways of Wall Street which had led their great adventure so far astray.

Of particular interest to Johnson were the many uses the bidders had found for the strain of junk bonds known as pay-in-kind securities, or PIK. The management group's decision to "pile on the PIK" in place of cash still boggled his mind.

"Hey," Johnson said, "why don't we start a new company and it'll be all PIK? I wonder if I could pay all the advertisers, or buy space in *Time*. Think we could do it in PIK?

"I mean," Johnson went on, "we have found something that's better than the U.S. printing press. And they've got it all down here on Wall Street. And nobody knows it's going on. I wonder if the World Bank knows about it. You could solve the third world debt crisis with this stuff. It's a brand new currency . . ."

Johnson was in hysterics by now. He mimicked a printing press. *"Chuck-oon, chuck-oon, chuck-oon.* Just print it and let her fly."

They could devise a charter for their new company, Johnson said. Call it PIK Associates. And it would include what Johnson dubbed the three rules of Wall Street: "Never play by the rules. Never pay in cash. And never tell the truth."

———

In the boardroom Hugel and the directors now pondered the question of valuing the management group's securities. No one looked forward to lengthy negotiations. Dennis Block had a suggestion. Cohen had already agreed to duplicate Kohlberg Kravis's merger agreement. Why not see if they would agree to duplicate its securities, as well? Block wrote a letter on a yellow note pad and Bob Lovejoy of Lazard ran it down to Nusbaum. After a few minutes, Lovejoy reentered the boardroom.

No deal.

The board was in a quandary. Three hours earlier it had been on the verge of giving RJR Nabisco to Kravis and Roberts. Even with Johnson at $112, it was clear that every director in the room still wanted to go with Kravis. The only problem was the scoreboard: Johnson 112, Kravis 108.

"If they say it's worth one-twelve, until you test it you can't take the one-oh-eight," Mike Mitchell insisted. "You simply can't take one-oh-eight in the middle of the afternoon, even if everyone wants to. We have to go back to the management group and find out if it's really worth one-twelve."

The pressure was intense, and it affected each director differently. Charlie Hugel's gout flared up, causing him to limp about like a cripple. He'd forgotten to take his gout pills. Albert Butler, who hadn't had a cigarette since heart surgery eight years before, reached for the pack John Medlin was smoking. "For God's sake, give me one of those," Butler growled. The two North Carolinians soon finished off the pack and began bumming smokes from others.

In the end, they had no choice but to negotiate with Cohen's people. At ten minutes to four, Luis Rinaldini of Lazard reluctantly led a team of investment bankers downstairs to begin discussing the management group's securities.

Restless, Kravis and Roberts went for a walk. Together they left the building, strode south down Park Avenue, then turned right and headed back to Nine West. As they strolled, Roberts tried to see what cigarette brands passersby were smoking. A few were puffing Winstons or Salems, but twice as many seemed to prefer Marlboros. "Well, one out of three isn't bad," he quipped.

Returning to his forty-second-floor office, Kravis returned some phone calls, including one from Jim Maher at First Boston.

"I had called to congratulate you," Maher said when he came onto the line.

"I came back to the office because I couldn't deal with it any longer over there," Kravis said.

Kravis was tired but gracious. "Listen," he said, "without you guys, we wouldn't be in there. Thank you very much."

"Just remember that," Maher said.

Kravis and Roberts returned to Skadden Arps around five o'clock. Dick Beattie, his lower back aching from an old football injury, was sprawled out on the floor, asleep. Paul Raether had tried to read *The Wall Street Journal*, but was forced to move to another room to escape Beattie's snoring.

"Have you seen anybody, heard anything?" Kravis asked.

"Not a thing," Raether said.

Roberts rousted Beattie and sent him on another scouting mission. "Goddamn it, Dick, go find Peter Atkins," he said. "This is ridiculous."

Minutes later, Beattie managed to collar Atkins in a hallway.

"Peter, these guys are going to leave," he said. "I'm not kidding you. They'll walk out of the bidding. They will."

"Dick," Atkins said, "tell them to remain patient."

Beattie resumed his post outside the boardroom. A steady stream of investment bankers was hustling between its double doors and the nearby staircase. It dawned on Beattie that the board must be negotiating with Cohen and Johnson. When Kravis and Roberts heard that, they came to see for themselves.

Just as they did, the board broke. A number of directors emerged and headed for the men's room. Bob Lovejoy, the Lazard banker, meandered over to speak with Roberts and Raether. "I know it's going slow," he said, "but we're getting there."

George Roberts had had enough. With every bit of anger he could muster, he tore into Lovejoy. "What the fuck is going on! You're screwing us. We know what you're doing! You're down there negotiating with Johnson! I won't stand for it!"

Stunned by the unexpected onslaught, Lovejoy tried to calm Roberts. "George, you're wrong. You have my word. We're negotiating in good faith with you. You're not being placed at a disadvantage. You're actually in pretty good shape."

"It sure doesn't look like that to me," Roberts said. "Put yourself in my shoes. We've been here since nine-thirty last night!"

Moments later, Lovejoy beat a swift retreat. "Jesus Christ," Raether heard him mumble, "I'm sorry I came over here . . ."

Five minutes later, Lovejoy sought out Kravis and Roberts in an empty office. He had Felix Rohatyn in tow. Clearly Roberts's speech had had an effect.

"We're not negotiating with Johnson," Rohatyn assured Roberts calmly. "We're just trying to understand where he is. We're just getting clarification."

Fuming, Kravis and Roberts sat back to wait. Again.

———

Three floors below, Johnson, growing restless, also took a walk around the block, his now not-so-Merry Men in tow. As he left, he saw the worried faces of Nusbaum and the others involved in negotiating securities with the board: By now the lawyer had been reinforced by Steve Goldstone, Shearson's Jim Stern, and Chaz Phillips of Salomon. Johnson didn't intervene. "I wouldn't know a reset," he cracked, "if it shook hands with me."

By seven o'clock Johnson had had enough. He asked Goldstone whether he was needed. When the lawyer said no, Johnson's group prepared to go to dinner at one of Horrigan's favorite restaurants, Scarlatti, on East Fifty-second. Before leaving, Johnson called John Martin, who remained behind at Nine West.

What are our chances? Martin wondered.

"They're not going to give it to us," Johnson said.

Minutes later, Johnson emerged from the building's lobby into a gaggle of television cameras.

"Who won?" reporters shouted. "Who won?"

"The shareholders," Ross Johnson said, not missing a beat.

———

To those inside the boardroom, it seemed as if the Kravis contingent had been slowly creeping toward their door all day. To leave the room meant running a gauntlet of Kravis people. Going to the bathroom, Albert Butler observed, was like facing a receiving line. Most directors stayed put rather than venture outside. Finally, Hugel could stand it no longer and made a break for the men's room.

At a urinal, he found himself standing side by side with the young Kravis associate, Scott Stuart.

"So how's it going in there?" Stuart asked.

Hugel's first impulse was to throw up his hands—Who knows?—but to do so might have caused an embarrassing accident.

"Don't worry," Hugel said, "it'll be over soon."

The board reconvened at ten past six. Luis Rinaldini ran down their progress with the management group. In general they agreed to what the board sought, with one major exception. Cohen and Gutfreund refused to put a reset on their bid's securities, fretting that it would lock them into guarantees that could cost them tens of millions of dollars. They insisted instead that Shearson and Salomon would use their "best efforts" to guarantee the securities traded at their stated values.

Felix Rohatyn summed up the situation for the board. "We have one-ten-plus with a problem on the reset versus one-oh-eight. But without that reset, one-ten starts to erode. I'm not sure that either firm [Lazard or Dillon] is ready to give you an opinion that the management offer is ahead."

The directors discussed going back to the management group on the question of a reset one final time. Rinaldini called Jim Stern. One last time: Would the management group consider installing a reset? Stern refused.

———

Finally, it was time to deal with Kravis.

Even before hearing Shearson's answer, Atkins & Co. had resolved to give Kravis the same chance to make a final bid they had given Nusbaum six hours earlier. Around the table, the drawn and gaunt directors hoped Kravis would make this easier for them. As Atkins led a procession out of the room, John Medlin had a final word for him. "Tell them," he said, "we need another dollar of cash to tilt it in their direction."

As Atkins and his group entered the corner office, Kravis sat on a rattan sofa, tired, poker faced, right hand propping up his head. Roberts sat beside him, lips stretched tight across his face. Above the cousins' heads hung a giant blue Marlin, the trophy of some lawyer's summer vacation. Raether and three Kohlberg Kravis associates, flanked by Beattie and Cogut, lined the walls. An aquarium filled with multicolored fish burbled to one side.

The board, Atkins said, was willing to give Kohlberg Kravis one final opportunity to bid. "If you haven't already done so, this is the time to put in your best bid."

Silence.

Kravis and Roberts were too startled to speak. Beattie and Cogut exchanged a glance of amazement. *One final bid? Hadn't they been through this five hours ago?*

Felix Rohatyn's voice filled the void.

"This is a serious offer. You should do your best to respond to it." Then, looking Kravis square in the eye, Rohatyn said: "We want your highest and last offer."

"This is the craziest thing we've ever seen," Kravis said. "We gave it to you five hours ago!"

A half hour later, Beattie and Cogut emerged from the aquarium room and sought out Atkins. They found him leaning against a wall outside the boardroom.

Kohlberg Kravis has two conditions before it will place its final bid on the table, Beattie said. First: A merger agreement must be drawn up and submitted to directors as part of the offer. "Because we want this to end," Beattie explained. Second, and most important, Kravis and Roberts wanted the board's promise that, if they bid, neither Johnson nor any member of management would be allowed into the final board meeting.

"We're not going to give you another offer if it's going to be reviewed by a board that includes Johnson or anyone in management," Beattie said.

"Why not?" Atkins asked.

"Peter, for obvious reasons. Ross'll just stand up and bid again." Cogut chimed in: "If we say X, he'll just say X plus one. He's always got the last bid."

Atkins had to admit they had a point. This was something he hadn't thought of. Assuring the two lawyers he would get back to them, Atkins walked off to find some help.

Five minutes later, Atkins closeted himself in an empty office with Mike Mitchell and Dennis Block. The trio was among the most experienced on Wall Street. But this one had them stumped: How do you uninvite a chief executive to his own board meeting?

"It's clear to me you can't just exclude him," Block said. "What do we do?"

Law books were pulled down from shelves and thumbed through, but an answer evaded them. Johnson seemed to have every right to attend the meeting. Holding the meeting without him invited a lawsuit. "There's no way we can keep 'em out," Mitchell said.

The minutes ticked by.

Could he be fired? Too messy, they decided.

Atkins was growing desperate. The fate of the entire $25 billion deal hung in the balance.

Then, suddenly, Mitchell asked the obvious question: "Why don't we ask them if they plan to attend?"

It was so simple. Maybe Johnson wouldn't want to come. Atkins found Goldstone in a hallway. Giving no hint of why he was asking, the Skadden lawyer explained that the board was set to meet and choose a victor.

"Will your people be there?" he asked in an offhand manner.

"Wait a second," Goldstone said. "We'll check."

Goldstone returned minutes later with a question. "Will KKR be at the meeting?" he asked.

"No."

"Well then, no, we don't plan to be there unless KKR will be."

Atkins heaved an inner sigh of relief. Unwittingly, Goldstone had just laid the groundwork for Kravis to boost his bid one final time.

No one bothered to ask Johnson whether he wanted to attend his final board meeting. By then Johnson and his aides were into their first round of drinks several blocks away.

————

Dick Beattie and Felix Rohatyn, both active in New York political circles, leaned against a wall outside the boardroom and discussed ways to improve city schools as they waited for Atkins. Finally Atkins returned and stated: "We can assure you management will not be in the meeting." Beattie pushed off from the wall and headed for the aquarium room, where Kravis waited.

————

Kravis went around the room one last time: What should we bid?

This time the debate was tense. Every man in the room knew the fate of the deal—and possibly their entire industry—was on the line. Fifty cents a share too much or too little could be the difference. Already the bidding had reached heights all but the foolhardy were uncomfortable

————

495

with. More than once that day Kravis and Roberts had talked about walking away from this deal. One wrong move could be fatal.

Scott Stuart sat on the couch beside Roberts, thumbing through a sheaf of computer runs, answering questions as Kravis went around the room. "Let's just go home," Stuart said. "We're being jacked around here."

Paul Raether wanted to stay, but could see no reason to raise their bid. "This is just bullshit," he said. "I think we ought to tell 'em that's all there is."

Around and around the room they went, and when they stopped no one was surprised to find they were boosting their bid again. The verdict seemed unanimous. They would throw in one last raise, just fifty cents a share in cash, roughly $115 million.

"Is everybody comfortable with that?" Roberts asked.

All around, heads bobbed.

Then: "No, I'm not."

The voice was Jamie Greene's. For the second time in two days the young San Francisco associate would be responsible for initiating a shift in strategy. "I don't know if we should do it at all," Greene said. "But if we do, let's do it with a dollar in cash. We've come this far. We want to win this deal."

"I think he's right," Roberts said. "That's exactly what we should do. We've gone this far. We've made up our minds we want to own this company. Let's not get shortsighted now."

Kravis agreed. Greene's last raise was swiftly approved.

The last issue was a deadline. Once before Kravis's group had forgotten it, allowing the process to drag on another six hours. They wouldn't forget it this time. Someone suggested a half hour. Roberts voted for fifteen minutes.

"Nah, George," Beattie said, "you can't do anything in fifteen minutes." Thirty minutes it was.

Beattie summoned Atkins and Rohatyn to hear the final bid. Kravis, sitting on the couch, spoke first. "You'll now hear our final bid, and Cliff will read it to you." He motioned to Robbins, who sat in a chair beside the aquarium. The young associate read out the new bid. Then he handed Atkins a merger agreement signed by both Roberts and Kravis. If the bid was accepted, Atkins was to return the agreement with Hugel's signature.

"We want it back signed in thirty minutes," Roberts said.

Kravis nodded. "We're leaving in a half hour."

His face blank, Atkins retreated, followed by Rohatyn. It was 8:15. The fuse had been lit.

————————

Three floors below, Steve Goldstone was famished. He hadn't eaten all day. He decided to wait out the committee at a Chinese restaurant just across Lexington Avenue.

As he left, Goldstone turned to Jack Nusbaum.

"What do you think?" he said. "KKR?"

Nusbaum nodded.

————————

The last bid in hand, Rohatyn and the investment bankers huddled in a corner of the boardroom. To the untrained eye, Johnson's group was the clear winner: $112 versus $109. But things are rarely that simple on Wall Street. Cohen and Gutfreund's refusal to include a reset mechanism meant their bid had to be discounted.

Minutes later Rohatyn addressed the board. "Both bids," he announced, "are between one-oh-eight and one-oh-nine. When you get that close, and when you're dealing with securities in amounts that have never been dealt with before, in my business judgment these offers are essentially equivalent. They are both fair from a financial point of view. They are close enough that we can't tell you one is clearly superior to the other."

A dead heat.

It was the last thing the directors wanted to hear. Now they would have to make a decision. In their hearts every person in the room knew how the board felt. The problem was finding a legally defensible reason to feel that way.

To help the board make its decision, Rohatyn pointed out a half-dozen differences between the two bids. As the directors had long requested, Kravis had promised to leave 25 percent of the stock in shareholders' hands; Shearson, despite repeated emphasis by the board's bankers, opted for just 15 percent.* Kravis promised to sell only a portion of Nabisco;

* Later, Tom Hill and others would claim the special committee never emphasized the need to leave stock in shareholders' hands. The evidence suggests otherwise. According to several people, Lazard and Dillon had done exactly that in their meeting with Hill on Monday. Chaz Phillips of

Shearson would sell it all. Shearson's failure to guarantee its securities via a reset was mentioned. So, too, was the management group's inflexibility on guaranteeing employee benefits such as relocation expenses; Cohen wanted these matters to be negotiable with the ultimate buyers of RJR Nabisco businesses.

Like some financial smorgasbord, each board member now seized on one of the differences to justify his selection. John Medlin chose the reset. "Shearson's 'best efforts' promise isn't good enough," Medlin said. "You don't do that in a twenty-five-billion-dollar deal. We've got to know where those securities will trade."

Nods all around. Al Butler thought of his friends holding stock in Winston-Salem and seized on the stock disparity. Juanita Kreps cited Kravis's promises to treat employees more fairly. Bill Anderson liked that one, too. "Can I assume that KKR will look after employees better?" he asked.

More nods.

———

Security guards had finally released Kravis's clamoring investment bankers from the reception area where they had been held all day. The cream of Wall Street's merger society, including Gleacher, Wasserstein, and Beck, had passed the time cracking jokes and passing rumors. Now, let through the dike, the bankers clustered around the entrance to the corner room where the Kohlberg Kravis contingent waited. Casey Cogut once more closed the door in their faces.

As they waited for the board's verdict, Kravis and Roberts decided to blunt the crackling tension with a prank. Everyone inside the room picked up his coat and computer runs and, without saying a word, got up and walked out the door, past the bankers, and down the hall, as if to leave.

The bankers didn't believe it for a second.

No one was crazy enough to leave now.

———

The half hour was nearly up. Felix Rohatyn left the boardroom and hustled down to where Kravis and Roberts waited.

Salomon, who attended the session, recalled the bankers' admonition, but admits his group was overconfident and refused to listen. "We basically ignored it," he says.

"We need another ten minutes," he said.

"Ah, come on," Roberts said. "We're not going to do this."

"Just bear with us," Rohatyn said. "At this point, it's clearly in your best interest to stay around."

"Is this really ten minutes?" Kravis asked.

"Yes."

"Fine," Kravis said, "you've got it." He wasn't going to lose a $25 billion deal over ten minutes.

Five minutes later discussion inside the boardroom ebbed.

"Time is running out," Hugel said. "Call for a motion."

Marty Davis spoke first. "I move we award to KKR."

"Second," said John Macomber.

"All in favor," Hugel said.

Hands filled the air.

"All opposed?"

No hands.

"The vote," Hugel said, "is unanimous."

Atkins led a cluster of board advisers to the Kravis contingent. In his hands was a copy of the merger agreement. His face betraying no emotion, Atkins opened the agreement and pointed out a tiny clause that needed approval. "Dick, what is this?" Kravis said, unsure what Atkins was up to.

Beattie leaned over and inspected the change. It had to do with severance provisions for RJR Nabisco executives. "Yeah," he said. "We'll agree to that."

Atkins closed the contract and handed it to Kravis. "Here's your signed contract," the lawyer intoned. "Congratulations. It's yours."

Kravis went numb. He had been fighting for this so long. He had lost eight pounds in the last six weeks. He took the agreement from Atkins and said, "Great." Roberts said little: All he could think of was how much work was ahead.

There were congratulations all around. After a minute, Kravis turned to Cliff Robbins. "Get all the bankers into a conference room and stay with 'em," he said. "And don't let any of them use the phones. Especially Wasserstein."

Atkins next led his procession three flights down to the Shearson group. When they reached the conference room where Nusbaum, Stern, and the others waited, only Atkins went in. Steve Goldstone was called at the Chinese restaurant and put on a speaker phone. Goldstone's stomach was in knots as he took the phone.

Atkins's tone was funereal.

"Steve, this is Peter."

"Hi."

"I'm sorry to report the board has signed a merger agreement with KKR. The bids were dead even. But the board decided to sign with KKR for other reasons."

Goldstone went numb.

"What were those other reasons, if you can tell me?" he asked, mechanically.

Atkins explained that all the facts would be contained in an SEC filing in the next few days. Then he shrugged his shoulders and walked out.

At Scarlatti, Johnson took Goldstone's call at the maître d's station. "Hey, Ross," the lawyer said. "Guess what." The tone of his voice told Johnson everything.

"Surprise," Johnson said. His bemusement was gone. He was very tired.

"KKR got the bid."

"Fine," Johnson said after a moment. "Let's get together at Nine West and see the guys."

Johnson returned to the table a moment later and broke the news. "I don't much feel like eating," he said. "Let's go back and see the troops."

Amid the backslapping and congratulations Charlie Hugel collared Kravis and guided him into an empty office. "Congratulations, it's a great company you're buying," he said. "You know, you only made one mistake."

"What was that?" Kravis asked.

"Paul Sticht. Just be careful about that. That got a lot of people on the board upset. You've got to understand there's a history there."

Kravis nodded.

"Go slow now," Hugel said. "You've got good people down there. I'll help you in any way I can during the transition."

Afterward, Hugel, his gouted foot throbbing, limped down to the lobby, where a security guard tried to sneak him out a back door to avoid the television cameras milling about outside. Hugel barely made it to his car when the crowd spotted him and ran up. Seeing their approach, the security guard slammed shut the car door—right on Hugel's foot. It hurt so bad he wanted to scream. A fitting conclusion, he would acknowledge, to a painful process.

When the camera crews chased after Hugel, Kravis and Roberts slipped unnoticed out the front door and spent the evening celebrating at Il Nido, a nearby Italian restaurant.

Carolyne Roehm sat by the phone at their Park Avenue apartment all night, waiting for the word. At 10:36—she would never forgot the minute—it finally rang.

"We got it," Kravis said.

Roehm let out a whoop of joy. "YEA!!"

Johnson was gracious in defeat. Arriving at Nine West, the first thing he did was open the bar. Then, scotch in hand, he took time to talk with each of his executives, clapping them on the back and congratulating them for fighting the good fight.

"We're now going to go the high road," Johnson told Jim Robinson, who showed up with his wife and Steve Goldstone. "These people have got new owners. We don't want a lot of acrimony being created. The game is over. We've played it into overtime. Whether they gave you an elbow in the eye or crack-blocked your butt end, it doesn't matter. That's the score. Let's get on with our lives."

Not everyone took defeat as well. As the evening wore on, Ed Horrigan grew bitter and morose. Unlike Johnson, who had bounced from job to job in a long career, Horrigan was a longtime Reynolds man. He was used to being the big wheel in Winston-Salem. Despite Johnson's warnings, he had never really believed they could lose.

"We got the goddamn shaft," he complained to Johnson.

"Ed, you know we've been getting it for a long time," Johnson said. "Shit, I've been the lightning rod. But we've got to get on. We've got to get back, get the businesses in shape." He went on. "You watch, there'll be a big social change. It'll be fine for a while. Then people will be surging over to the new owners. You know, the King is dead, long live the King."

Horrigan only grew angrier. At one point, Johnson was forced to intervene in a nasty confrontation between Horrigan and John Martin in a hallway. Searching for scapegoats, Horrigan was railing about Martin's handling of the press. "You're the most ineffective, immature, son of a bitch that ever walked the face of the earth!" Horrigan shouted.

"Ed," Martin responded, "you come to your conclusions, and I'll come to mine."

Johnson, fearing the two men might come to blows, swiftly broke them up. "Gentlemen, this is no time for this. We've been a great team. We've done a good job. If anything went wrong, it was me."

Horrigan and Martin were glaring at each other. "Come on, now," Johnson said, "shake hands."

"I'm not going to shake his fucking hand," Horrigan sputtered.

Well after midnight, everyone had left except Goldstone, the Robinsons, and Ross and Laurie Johnson. The five of them sat around the table in the fishbowl conference room. Linda was helping Johnson with a press release to be issued the next morning.

Goldstone could tell Johnson was starting to wind down. "You remember that time we talked about the price of doing something like this?" Johnson asked the attorney.

Goldstone smiled. He thought about that day on the porch, long ago, it seemed, watching the red Florida sun sink.

Johnson laughed. "It surely was painful. Just like you said. But I'll tell you the same thing I told you then. I don't know what else I would've done. It was the best thing for shareholders. It was the right thing to do."

Johnson's driver, Frank Mancini, was up on the floor, waiting for the group to break up. Johnson rose from the table and said, "Let's go home."

EPILOGUE

On the morning after, Ross Johnson boarded a plane for Atlanta. Before leaving he dictated a press release that, among other things, noted "the best bid" had won. When Linda Robinson ran a copy by Peter Cohen, Cohen grew incensed. He fired off a call to Steve Goldstone. "If this goes out, we're dead," Cohen said. "This release will kill us."

For an instant Goldstone was confused. He thought they *were* dead. The bidding was over. Goldstone hung up and called Johnson aboard the plane racing south. Johnson was irked. For the first time in six weeks he decided to put his foot down. In minutes he was on the phone to Cohen. "It's over, Peter," Johnson said. "I've had it. What point are we serving now? We're not serving the company or the shareholders. . . . It's over."

Still, Cohen, Hill, and the other Shearson deal makers spent days thrashing out ways to get back at Kravis. A lawsuit was considered. In the end, of course, they did nothing. Five days after Kravis was crowned the winner, Shearson Lehman Hutton issued a press statement officially closing the battle for RJR Nabisco.

Wednesday night Jim Maher was thinking about heading home early when Kim Fennebresque came bounding into his office. "John Greeniaus is in town," Fennebresque said, "and he wants to talk to us." The Nabisco executive was in a downstairs conference room, the banker said. Maher canceled a meeting and walked downstairs with Fennebresque, who led his boss into the room.

"Surprise!"

Maher was speechless. He had almost forgotten Wednesday was his birthday. The room was filled with balloons and cake and champagne and friends. Fennebresque gave a toast. "I never pass up the opportunity to toast the boss in December," he said, alluding to Wall Street's January bonuses. "On behalf of everyone who worked so hard in the last two weeks, we very much appreciate your inspirational leadership."

Its RJR Nabisco experience proved a boon for Maher's troops. Despite the doomsayers, First Boston completed more mergers than any other Wall Street firm during the first six months of 1989. Its work with Jay Pritzker paid off in a number of Pritzker-related assignments, culminating in the joint First Boston–Pritzker purchase of American Medical International for $1.6 billion in 1989. In September 1990, Maher was named vice chairman of First Boston.

The morning after winning the greatest victory of his career, Kravis flew to Florida for his mother's eightieth birthday. The next day he hopped north to Atlanta to inspect his new prize. Johnson, upright in defeat, was waiting for him at the airport.

"Well," Johnson said, "congratulations to you, pal. You've got a hell of a company here."

Johnson drove them in his Mercedes to the Galleria, where he gave a tour of the headquarters and offered to turn over his office to Kravis on the spot. "I'm here for you to do anything you want," Johnson said. "The planes are yours, it's your company."

"Ross, Ross, go slow," Kravis said, reminding him the company wouldn't change hands for months yet. "You just keep running the company as you have in the past."

That afternoon Kravis flew to Winston-Salem and met with Ed Horrigan. Horrigan was every bit as gracious as Johnson, although, it was soon clear, for different reasons. Kravis, like Johnson before him, needed Horrigan's tobacco expertise and so, with Kravis's encouragement, Horrigan agreed to become a tentative member of the Kohlberg Kravis team.

A week later, Kravis took a call from Horrigan in New York. "I just want to tell you, I'm not going to be number two anymore," Horrigan said. "I have worked for three guys who are now history: Paul Sticht, Tylee

Wilson, and Ross Johnson. I either want to be CEO or I leave."

Thus began an intricate pas de deux. As each major presentation to bank lenders approached, Horrigan would say he didn't feel right about appearing if he wasn't going to be CEO. He didn't want to mislead the bankers if he wasn't going to be with the company. Kravis would adroitly side-step, promising to make clear that Horrigan's future was undecided. By the third round, Kravis had had enough. "I don't think you should speak," he said. "Why don't you just quit?"

In mid-February, Horrigan did. His resignation came with: a sumptuous office in Winston-Salem, with secretary; an option to buy his company apartment in New York and house outside Palm Beach, promptly exercised; and a golden parachute worth $45.7 million. Later, he used some of the proceeds to buy a candy company in Atlanta.

At 8 A.M. on February 9, 1989, Kravis opened the floodgates for a torrent of money. That morning, Drexel Burnham Lambert delivered $5 billion worth of checks—the bridge loan it had promised. Kohlberg Kravis transferred $2 billion from its own bank account to RJR Nabisco's. Manufacturers Hanover Trust Co. gathered $11.9 billion from banks throughout the world and deposited the loaned money into an escrow account for Kohlberg Kravis.

It totaled $18.9 billion, the amount needed to pay the cash portion of the buyout. It was the biggest river of money ever to course through the U.S. financial system. The Federal Reserve Bank couldn't wire money in amounts over $1 billion, so the banks moved it around in increments of $800 million to $950 million. The flow was so big it made U.S. money-supply statistics temporarily bulge as it roared through the system.

A thirtieth-floor conference room at Dick Beattie's firm, Simpson Thacher & Bartlett, was packed with 200 lawyers and bankers, acting as a financial Corps of Engineers. They carefully monitored the river, seeing that tributaries entered and locks opened at the right times. By 10:45 A.M. it was over. The money had all changed hands, and so had the ownership of RJR Nabisco.

Johnson officially resigned that day, pulling the chord on his $53 million golden parachute.* His fanciest Gulfstream jet yet, ordered before the LBO battle, flew him to Jupiter on its maiden voyage. Johnson

*Total value calculated by *Business Week*.

released a final statement before leaving: "The process we commenced last October has benefitted the company's shareholders and has proven the financial strength of our varied businesses."

Yet in the world's greatest concentration of RJR shareholders—Winston-Salem, North Carolina—they weren't thanking Johnson even as the money gushed into town. No sooner had Kravis won than signs began popping up: "Good-bye Ross, Hello KKR." Nearly $2 billion of checks arrived there in the late-February mail. Now, more than ever, Winston-Salem was "the city of reluctant millionaires." The river of money had washed away the last of RJR's stock. Local brokers and bankers who managed people's money got calls from distraught clients. "I won't sell my stock," more than one sobbed. "Daddy said don't *ever* sell the RJR stock." They were patiently told they had to. They were told the world had changed.

No sooner had the checks arrived than out-of-town "financial consultants" descended on Winston-Salem to advise its residents on how best to spend their new riches. In leaflets tucked under windshields in the Reynolds parking lot, in pesky phone calls, in seminars at the Holiday Inn, stockbrokers offered to help people reinvest their windfall in the market. The frequent, incredulous response: "You want me to buy *stock?*"

"You have to understand," said Nabby Armfield, Jr., a retired stockbroker, "Reynolds wasn't a stock. It was a religion." Mr. Armfield even recorded a song to express the community's frustrations that became an underground hit. Sung to the tune of "Frosty the Snowman," the chorus went:

> F. Rossie the snowman had a triple comma dream,
> You can have the skim milk and I'll make do with cream.
> Hey all you bucolics, here's a deal that's really sweet.
> You take title to the chaff and I'll haul off the wheat.

In December Johnson sent each director a dozen roses with a note: "Congratulations on a great job. The shareholders won." He had one more dinner with them before his last board meeting in December, where everyone made polite conversation but made no amends. John Macomber was in an avenging spirit, advancing the idea of scrapping the management team's 1988 bonuses. Bob Schaeberle was practically in tears as he talked about the breakup of Nabisco. Marty Davis squelched the idea of paying each special committee member a $250,000 fee.

The Winston-Salem directors took the brunt of public criticism there. A high-society matron was seen elaborately crossing the names of John Medlin and Albert Butler from her Christmas party list. A tobacco employee walked up to Medlin one day and declared: "I wish I had a million dollars in your bank so I could take it out and really hurt you."

For the other directors, life went on, rather more pleasantly. *USA Today* named Charlie Hugel one of its business heroes of 1988. His Combustion Engineering Co. was bought by a Swedish company the following year, and Hugel accepted a familiar title under the new ownership: non-executive chairman. John Macomber was named chairman of the U.S. Export-Import Bank. Vernon Jordan went on RJR's reconstituted board, joining Medlin as a holdover.

Paul Sticht swung into his third term as chairman of RJR, and wasted no time causing a commotion by announcing (incorrectly) that headquarters would return to Winston-Salem. Once again he flew around the country in his beloved corporate jets and settled into his old office in the Glass Menagerie. He was pleased to see the end of Ross Johnson—but, he admitted, the price was horrible. "I feel bad," he told a visitor a few days after his return. "I wish it had never happened."

Sticht, of course, was a figurehead as RJR's interim chief executive. Kravis surrounded him with an "operating committee" of partners and trusted RJR executives, to keep him from any mischief. Kravis also stepped up his search for a permanent chief executive.

At the same time, on Thursday evening, March 9, Jim Robinson got a call at his apartment from his longtime number two, Louis Gerstner, a dynamic executive whose signature adorned the American Express travelers check. "I have to see you in the morning," Gerstner said. Robinson pleaded that his schedule was crowded; Gerstner said it was urgent. They agreed to meet at the Robinsons' apartment soon after dawn the next day. There Gerstner dropped a bomb: he was to be the next chief executive of RJR Nabisco.

Later that morning, a startled Robinson was riding in his limousine when he took a call from Kravis. The buyout king apologized for luring away Gerstner and said he hoped it wouldn't cause American Express too much trouble. Jim Robinson was nothing if not diplomatic. "Henry, I want to compliment you on your judgment," he said. "You only made one mistake. You didn't offer it to me first." Both men laughed, but the sting was undeniable.

Wall Street is a small place, and in the interests of harmony Kravis wasted no time healing wounds inflicted during the fight. He made peace with Peter Cohen at a summit in February and actually hired Tom Hill to investigate the possible takeover of Northwest Airlines. Relations between Kravis and Tom Strauss remained strained. Shortly after the deal closed, the Strausses moved into a new Park Avenue apartment directly below the Kravises. When the Salomon executive had some remodeling done, a crack appeared in the wall of Kravis's apartment.

Kravis also moved to smooth relations with Linda Robinson. Soon after the Gerstner episode, Linda took a message that Kravis had called. She ignored it. Within days she received a small ceramic doghouse with a cute note from Kravis, suggesting he was in the Robinsons' doghouse. Linda Robinson waited a few days, then sent Kravis a twenty-pound bag of dog food. All was forgiven. She and Kravis still own "Trillion."

Fees, of course, went infinitely further toward soothing Wall Street's wounds. In the coming months, it rained money at the firms lucky enough to be on the winning side in the RJR Nabisco fight. Drexel Burnham reaped $227 million in fees from a $3.5 billion bridge loan. It got even more from selling junk bonds. Merrill Lynch got $109 million for its role in the bridge financing. A syndicate of 200 banks collected $325 million for committing $14.5 billion of loans. Kohlberg Kravis itself collected $75 million in fees from its investors. Morgan Stanley and Wasserstein, Perella got $25 million apiece. Kravis even spread the largesse to those whose feelings he might have bruised. Geoff Boisi's Goldman Sachs got the job of auctioning Del Monte, while Felix Rohatyn's Lazard Freres did the same for the company's stake in ESPN.

The closing dinner Kravis threw to commemorate the deal will long be remembered. Held in the Pierre Hotel's grand ballroom, four hundred investment bankers, lawyers, and other friends of the firm feasted on lobster, followed by veal with morel sauce and a three-foot-high cake decorated with edible replicas of Nabisco products, all washed down with Dom Perignon.

"It's wonderful to see all these friends of KKR here tonight," Dick Beattie opened the evening. "To think it only took a billion dollars in fees to get us all together."

Beattie was in rare form, roasting enemy and friend alike. "I see Jeff

Beck over there," the lawyer noted. "Jeff, I want to remind you that this dinner is off the record." Amid gales of laughter, Beck's voice echoed through the hall. "Talk to Wasserstein! Talk to Wasserstein!"

RJR Nabisco may have been the Mad Dog's last hurrah. In January 1990 *The Wall Street Journal* printed a lengthy article suggesting that much of Beck's colorful background was fictitious. For years, stories of the investment banker's days as a decorated Vietnam jungle fighter and heir to a billion-dollar fortune had been repeated as fact. Some of these anecdotes made it as far as early, unpublished versions of this book. But during the fact-checking process, Beck's tales couldn't be corroborated and so were dropped from the finished manuscript. That discovery led to the *Journal* article. After its publication Mr. Beck resigned from Drexel.

In the months after his victory, Kravis shone. At parties, nouvelle society's adoring courtiers cheered, "Make way for King Henry!" In May, he and Roehm and a group of friends toured India, dining with Prime Minister Rajiv Gandhi and the Maharaja of Jaipur. Kravis and Roehm wore thick leis of jasmine, tuberose, and roses and were honored guests at an elephant festival, where the beasts paraded in gold and multihued costumes. They slipped down a river by barge, were serenaded with sitars and ate feasts cooked over open fires. At the Maharaja's, fans blew cold air off blocks of ice topped by jasmine. "My goodness," said Oscar de la Renta, "if this is not refinement, what is?" Life, as they say, was good.

But Kravis's victory tour proved shortlived. In August, his simmering dispute with Jerry Kohlberg burst into the open when Kohlberg sued Kohlberg Kravis, claiming he had been cheated out of the proceeds from several LBO investments. The suit was settled in early 1990; terms weren't disclosed. Soon after Kohlberg's suit, Kravis encountered his first publicized problems when he was forced to reschedule or miss debt payments on three LBOs, including Owens-Illinois. "Cracks in House That Debt Built," read *The New York Times* headline.

Kravis insisted it was much ado about nothing and began focusing his attention on European targets. Yet a year after the fight for RJR broke out, Kravis had yet to initiate a new LBO. Competition remained stiff and, after his brush with publicity during RJR, Kravis was reluctant to enter heavily publicized fights like the Northwest Airlines fray. For the first time, newspapers and competitors began openly speculating if Kravis had lost his touch.

At RJR, Lou Gerstner wasted no time whittling down Johnson's empire. With Dick Beattie at his side, Gerstner sold seven out of eight corporate jets, plus more than a dozen corporate apartments and homes. Only Johnson's prized hangar proved unsalable. "It's just too grandiose," Beattie fretted in September 1989. "We can't give the thing away."

McKinsey & Co. consultants swarmed the Atlanta headquarters, evaluating everything and alienating many. Employees felt as though they were in an occupied land. For many, it was the final straw. When Kravis announced in April that headquarters would be moved to New York, only 10 percent of the managers offered jobs there agreed to go. "I don't feel like I work for a company anymore," said one refusenik, "I feel like I work for an investment."

Just how good an investment it would prove remained unclear. The company reported a $1.15 billion net loss in 1989, after paying its $3.34 billion debt tab. It ran up a $330 million deficit in the first half of 1990. But its all-important cash flow was robust and its divestitures of some food businesses reaped nearly $5 billion. (The Del Monte canned-foods operation was sold to a group which included Bob Carbonell. He became the new company's chairman.)

John Greeniaus proved true to his word, improving Nabisco's operating profit by half and tripling its cash flow in 1989. The Dinah Shore LPGA budget was halved, PGA sponsorships were scuttled, and much of Team RJR Nabisco was given its unconditional release. And while Nabisco's gains proved hard to sustain, Greeniaus became a Kravis favorite. He was named to RJR Nabisco's board.

Reynolds Tobacco, however, was embattled. In March 1989, RJR killed Premier. In the next few months, it trimmed the payroll by 2,300 employees. In the course of the year, Philip Morris widened its lead ever further over RJR, taking advantage of the disarray. Attacks by health advocates grew fiercer. RJR had to scrap a new black-oriented cigarette, called Uptown, after Health and Human Services Secretary Louis W. Sullivan blasted the brand. Even Winston-Salem's neighboring city, Greensboro, joined the trend toward antismoking ordinances.

Yet the business still generated prodigious cash under its new chief executive, a forty-three-year-old New York banker named Jim Johnston. A onetime marketing whiz at Reynolds Tobacco, Johnston was fired in 1984 for opposing cigarette loading. He ended the practice upon his return, forcing $340 million in write-offs but boosting factory and distribution efficiency. That change, together with deep cost-cutting, produced a 46 percent gain in operating profit for tobacco in the first half of 1990.

1990 brought the first serious challenge to RJR Nabisco's health, and ironically it came from Wall Street. That all-important "reset" provision, forged in the final desperate hours of bidding, called for more than $4 billion of bonds to be restored to their original face value by April 1991. And as the date approached, the bonds were trading at a deep discount: the cost of a true "reset" could run into the billions, more than enough to break the company. Grasping for levity at a particularly black moment, George Roberts quipped that, without some form of immediate rescue, the sequel to *Barbarians at the Gate* might be called *Huns on the Run.*

To its credit, Kohlberg Kravis wriggled out of its fix. In July 1990, it announced a $6.9 billion refinancing package, enabling it to buy back the junk bonds and substitute less onerous forms of debt. The costly maneuver probably assured that, as a buyout, RJR would neither be a free-fall disaster nor a windfall profit for Kohlberg Kravis. Whatever the case, it assured big paydays for the bankers and lawyers who reconfigured the original deal: another $250 million in fees.

For Kravis ultimate success, it was clear, was years away. To make matters worse, Philip Morris, sensing RJR's vulnerability, moved in for the kill, pummeling the company in a number of key markets. It expanded its sales force, undercut Reynolds on pricing, and attacked its strong discount brand, Doral, with two new off-price brands of its own. Analysts predicted RJR's cigarette volume could fall 7 percent to 8 percent in 1989, while Philip Morris gained volume.

"Philip Morris is eating our lunch," Cliff Robbins of Kohlberg Kravis acknowledged in October 1989. "Marlboro is an unstoppable machine. We have a lot to do."

By 1990, Wall Street's party was over, the memories of massive takeovers and buyouts receding more each day. In the wake of RJR Nabisco, LBO activity had dropped sharply, and by the fall of 1989, neither Kohlberg Kravis nor Forstmann Little had initiated a single major buyout. The prospect of anti-LBO legislation, raised during RJR, delayed many deals. What came to be known as the "Ross Johnson" factor nixed others: Few chief executives, after all, were willing to go through the public pillorying Johnson had endured.

But what brought Wall Street to a grinding halt were tremors in the junk-bond market. The first eight months of 1989 saw $4 billion worth of junk-bond defaults and debt moratoriums, the most spectacular being the troubles of Canadian entrepreneur Robert Campeau's U.S. retail empire. In October, the unraveling of a $6.79 billion buyout of United Airlines caused a panic on Wall Street, sending the Dow Jones Industrial Average down nearly 200 points and prompting fears of a new market crash.

As Ted Forstmann had pointed out, junk bonds could be a useful tool, if used correctly. The problem, of course, was that they had been abused and overused. In the months to come, the junk-bond slump deepened, cutting off the fuel to Wall Street's takeover engine. When its banks put the squeeze on Drexel Burnham—already staggering from having paid $650 million in fines to settle its portion of the Milken case—the firm that symbolized the junk-bond era filed for bankruptcy protection and announced its intention to liquidate.

With Drexel's demise, and the guilty pleas of financial titans Ivan Boesky and Michael Milken in the insider-trading scandals, popular opinion turned strongly against Wall Street and the unfettered greed of the 1980s. That backlash, combined with deteriorating financial fundamentals, effectively spelled the end to an era unlike any Wall Street has ever seen.

A new wind was blowing. As the new decade dawned, the hottest specialty for young MBAs became financial restructuring, i.e., fixing the broken takeovers of the eighties. Thousands of Wall Streeters, including a goodly number of under-thirty millionaires, lost their jobs as finance skidded into what promised to be a years-long slump. The memoirs of a young Salomon Brothers bond salesman, *Liar's Poker*, which lampooned Wall Street's decade of excess, hit the bestseller list and stayed there for nearly a year. Everywhere, investment bankers and their merger brethren were attacked as something akin to low-grade war criminals. As a concept, takeovers were openly derided, even, sometimes, by those who made their fortunes on them.

For the most part, The Group's members emerged from the wreckage in good shape. In September 1990, Tom Hill was named co-chief executive of Shearson Lehman's investment banking unit. Eric Gleacher left Morgan Stanley to start his own boutique, Gleacher & Co., and quickly struck pay dirt, putting together ConAgra's $1.34 billion acquisition of

Beatrice from Henry Kravis. Steve Waters was among two investment bankers to take the reins at Morgan after Gleacher's departure. Bruce Wasserstein suffered a barrage of media criticism for his roles in a number of disappointing deals.

Among those who didn't survive the era's end was Peter Cohen, who agreed to resign as Shearson's chairman under pressure in January 1990. Relations between Cohen and Jim Robinson, already tense after the RJR Nabisco fight, deteriorated rapidly in 1989 as Shearson floundered through a number of setbacks, including a widely unpopular restructuring that led to the resignation of its president, Jeff Lane. On publication of this book, Cohen was surprised to learn details of Linda Robinson's secret role negotiating with Henry Kravis. The disclosure came at a sensitive moment for Cohen, who felt it undermined his authority, and led to the final breach with the Robinsons. Afterward, he told a number of people that this book portrayed him unfairly and that Jim Robinson was party to every decision he made in the Nabisco deal, including negotiation of Ross Johnson's benefits package.

Ted Forstmann, of course, felt thoroughly vindicated by the collapse of the junk-bond era. He was the hero of a series of laudatory press clippings, the lonely voice in the dark who had triumphed over greed. His advisers told Forstmann to cool it, and to an extent he did. But the pull of righteousness was often too much, and Forstmann lapped up the attention, which, of course, he deserved. The final irony came in early 1990 when, as Henry Kravis scraped to keep RJR Nabisco together, Forstmann began doing deals again. Not many—just a deal here, a deal there—but it was more than anyone else in the LBO business managed. With junk bonds out of fashion, Forstmann's "real money" returned to the fore. For the first time in years, Ted Forstmann was the toast of the town.

In Atlanta, Johnson took perverse pride in the slowdown. "I scared them all back into the closet," he said, giggling, in May 1989. "Eighty or ninety percent of companies had LBO studies. Now I have people telling me, 'Jesus, Ross, we burned every file we had.'"

Unlike others, Johnson neither brooded nor looked back. Jobless, he moved into offices in another building at the Galleria, where he shared a floor with a country music radio station. His new enterprise, a partnership with John Martin, was called RJM Associates. The two pals were always hard-pressed to say exactly what RJM Associates did, though it seemed to involve giving ad hoc advice to their friends for a dollar-a-year fee. (With an $18.2 million golden parachute of his own, Martin no more needed the income than Johnson.)

Johnson did invest with some old pals in a venture that bought Nabisco's Far East operations. But mostly he enjoyed himself. Between golf and ski vacations, Johnson puttered around with the seven corporate boards he was on. He went to movies with Laurie and continued the vigil for son Bruce, who emerged from his coma but remained in a trauma clinic, unable to speak. He has begun to communicate through spelling. "We're quite encouraged," Johnson said in the summer of 1990.

Though Johnson professed to be delighted with the semiretired life, friends doubted he would stay that way. For one thing, it wasn't in his nature to fly commercial. It might take a rehabilitation period for his reputation, friends said, but Ross Johnson would be back. In words that could be his epitaph, he didn't deny it. "I'm always available," he said, "for change."

For all the upheaval, few in Winston-Salem blamed Kravis. Instead it was Johnson they continued to villify. Only a few took a broader view. "If Ross Johnson hadn't existed," said Gene Hoots, RJR's former pension manager, "it would have been necessary for Wall Street to invent him."

In a sense it had. Johnson was a product of his times, as surely as R. J. Reynolds was of his. The Roaring Eighties were a new gilded age, where winning was celebrated at all costs. "The casino society" Felix Rohatyn once dubbed it. The investment bankers were part croupiers, part alchemists. They conjured up wild schemes, pounded out new and more outlandish computer runs to justify them, then twirled their temptations before executives in a "devil dance." That, at any rate, is what Johnson took to calling it. Depending on one's viewpoint, the "dance" Johnson initiated at RJR will go down as either the high point or the low point of an era.

It wasn't an accident that RJR Nabisco should provide that moment. In its final decade Reynolds had become less a great company than a great dream machine. Its torrent of tobacco money allowed egos to run wild and fantasies to become true. Paul Sticht could walk with kings. Ed Horrigan could live like kings. Directors could be treated like kings.

Hoisted onto the auction block, the company became a vast prism through which scores of Wall Streeters beheld their reflected glories. Jim Maher could restore First Boston's greatness. Ted Forstmann could pursue his final jihad. Peter Cohen could go from administrator to merchant-banking prince. Henry Kravis could have an empire's crowning touch. John Gutfreund could get the left side of the ultimate tombstone.

The founders of both RJR and Nabisco would have utterly failed to understand what was going on here. It is not so hard, in the mind's eye, to see R. J. Reynolds and Adolphus Green wandering through the carnage of the LBO war. They would turn to one another, occasionally, to ask puzzled questions. Why did these people care so much about what came out of their computers and so little about what came out of their factories? Why were they so intent on breaking up instead of building up? And last: What did this all have to do with doing business?

INDEX